D0150911

SECOND EDITION

PROGRAMMING LANGUAGES
Concepts and Constructs

RAVI SETHI
Bell Labs, Lucent Technologies
Murray Hill, New Jersey

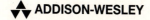 **ADDISON-WESLEY**

An imprint of Addison Wesley Longman, Inc.

Reading, Massachusetts • Harlow, England • Menlo Park, California • Berkeley, California
Don Mills, Ontario • Sydney • Bonn • Amsterdam • Tokyo • Mexico City

Senior Acquisitions Editor *Tom Stone*
Associate Editor *Deborah Lafferty*

Senior Production Supervisor *Helen Wythe*
Cover Supervisor *Barbara Atkinson*
Manufacturing Coordinator *Judy Sullivan*
Copy Editor *Stephanie Magean*
Text Designer *Sandra Rigney*

Many of the designations used by the manufacturers and sellers to
distinguish their products are claimed as trademarks. Where those
designations appear in this book, and Addison-Wesley was aware of
a trademark claim, the designations have been printed in initial cap
or all caps.

Library of Congress Cataloging-in-Publication Data

Sethi, Ravi.
  Programming languages : concepts & constructs / Ravi Sethi. -- 2nd
ed.
  p. cm.
  Includes bibliographical references and index.
  ISBN 0-201-59065-4
  1. Programming languages (Electronic computers) I. Title.
QA76.7.S48 1996
005. 13--dc20   95-40528
                                                          CIP

Reprinted with corrections, April 1997.

 AT&T
Copyright © 1996 AT&T. All rights reserved.

Reproduced by Addison-Wesley from camera-ready copy supplied
by the author.

All rights reserved. No part of this publication may be reproduced,
stored in a retrieval system, or transmitted, in any form or by any
means, electronic, mechanical, photocopying, recording, or otherwise,
without the prior written permission of the publisher. Printed in
the United States of America.

    6 7 8 9 10-MA-98

For Dianne

who taught me yet another language

Preface

This book is designed for junior/senior level courses on programming languages. A minimal pre-requisite is an introductory programming course. With supplementary readings, the book can also be used for graduate courses.

What's New in this Edition?

Changes on the language scene and feedback from the use of the book have prompted a thorough revision. Instructors liked the emphasis on concepts, but asked that the concepts be illustrated using fewer languages. Meanwhile, Modula-2 has faded, and C++ has taken off as a language for production programming. Candidates for functional languages now include Standard ML, Haskell, and Miranda.

The new edition has 15 chapters, three more than the first edition. The role of the three new chapters is as follows:

- Data types like arrays, records, and pointers have a new chapter.
- Functional programming is introduced using ML in a new chapter.
- Language summaries appear in a final chapter.

Language description and syntax are now treated early, in Chapter 2.

Organization of this Book

The emphasis is on concepts and how they work together, rather than on language features. Related concepts are therefore covered together, to allow meaningful examples and programming exercises along the way. Just enough of a language is introduced, as needed, for the examples and exercises. Language summaries appear in Chapter 15.

Part I: Introduction

Chapter 1 traces the role and development of programming languages. It introduces the programming paradigms in this book. They include imperative, object-oriented, functional, and logic programming.

Syntax description is treated in Chapter 2, so it can be applied in the rest of the book. The examples in the chapter deal with expressions, since methods for describing the syntax of expressions carry over to the rest of a language.

Part II: Imperative Programming

The imperative family is treated in Chapters 3–5. The term "imperative" comes from command or action; the computation model is that of a sequence of actions on an underlying machine.

Chapter 3 deals with control flow. Structured constructs like **while** statements organize the flow of control so that the unit of programming is a structured statement, instead of an individual assignment. Students in a course that emphasizes imperative programming are usually familiar with Pascal, so this chapter goes beyond assignments and structured statements to consider programming with invariants. The examples deal with basic values, like integers, and arrays.

Chapter 4 deals with data in imperative languages. Data representation facilities such as arrays, records, and pointers, have been stable since Pascal and C appeared. The treatment of these facilities anticipates their use to represent objects in Chapters 6 and 7.

Chapter 5 rounds out the discussion of the core of imperative languages, embodied in a language like Pascal or C. Among the topics are the distinction between the source text of a procedure and its activations, parameter passing, scope rules, and storage allocation.

This book illustrates imperative programming using Pascal, where possible. Pascal suffices as a vehicle for Chapters 3–5. C is an alternative.

Part III: Object-Oriented Programming

As programs get larger, the natural unit of programming is a grouping of data and operations. The progression of concepts for such groupings can be described in terms of modules, user-defined types (for example, stacks), and classes (as in object-oriented programming).

Chapter 6 begins with of programming with procedures, modules, and classes. These constructs serve distinct needs and can be used in combination with each other: procedures are needed to implement operations in a module or class; modules can be used to statically partition the source text of a program with classes. Some versions of Pascal support modules; they can be used for the first half of Chapter 6 as well. C++, an extension of C, is introduced in Chapter 6.

The model of computation in Chapter 7 is that of independent objects. The objects interact by sending messages to each other. The first third of the chapter introduces object-oriented programming in general, using a running example that has similar implementations in C++ and Smalltalk. The rest of the chapter has independent coverage of C++ and Smalltalk, so either one can be used to explore object-oriented programming. Based on feedback from instructors, this edition covers C++ before Smalltalk, inverting the order in the previous edition. Object-oriented programming is illustrated using both C++ and Smalltalk, since the two represent different approaches.

All of the concepts in Chapters 3–7 can be illustrated using C++. Students can be introduced directly to C++, without going through C.

Part IV: Functional Programming

Functional programming is worth studying as a programming style in its own right; as a setting for studying concepts such as types; and as a technique for language description. The emphasis in Chapter 8 is on concepts, in Chapters 9 and 10 on programming style, and in Chapter 13 on language description. The computational model is based on an expression interpreter; an expression consists of a function applied to subexpressions.

The emphasis in Chapter 8 is on concepts. The simplicity of functional languages makes them convenient for introducing concepts such as values, types, names, and functions. The simplicity results from the emphasis on expressions and values, independent of the underlying machine. The chapter treads ground common to functional languages, using ML as the working language.

The fundamental difference between ML and Lisp is that ML is typed; the influence of types permeates the language. Chapter 9 uses ML to illustrate the use of functions and datatypes. As first-class citizens, functions have the same status as any other values in functional programming. This first-class status permits the creation of powerful operations on collections of data.

Functional programming originated with Lisp. Programs and data are both represented by lists in Lisp; the name is a contraction of "List Processor." The uniform use of lists makes Lisp eminently extensible. Chapter 10 explores the use of lists, using the Scheme dialect of Lisp.

See also Chapter 13, which contains an interpreter for a small subset of Scheme, and Chapter 14, which covers the lambda calculus.

Part V: Other Paradigms

Logic programming goes hand in hand with Prolog, in Chapter 11. Logic programming deals with relations rather than functions. Where it fits, programs are concise, consisting of facts and rules. The languages uses the facts and rules to deduce responses to queries.

Concurrent programming is illustrated using Ada, in Chapter 12. An alternative approach would have been to cover concurrent programming after object-oriented programming. Processes can be formed by giving each object its own thread of computation. The present organization puts functional programming before concurrent programming.

Part VI: Language Description

The methods for language description in Chapter 13 are aimed at specialists. The methods range from attributes used for language translation, to logical rules for used type inference, to interpreters used for clarifying subtle language questions.

A language can be described by writing a definitional interpreter for it, so called because its purpose is to define the interpreted language; efficiency is not a concern. McCarthy's & original definitional interpreter for Lisp in Lisp remains important for language description, so language description is illustrated using the Scheme dialect of Lisp. Chapter 13 develops an interpreter for a small subset of Scheme.

The lambda calculus is the intellectual ancestor of functional languages. The small syntax of the lambda calculus has also led to its use as a vehicle for studying languages. Variants of the lambda calculus are introduced in Chapter 14. The chapter progresses from the pure untyped lambda calculus to typed lambda calculi.

Chapter 15 contains brief summaries of the languages in this book.

Acknowledgments From the First Edition

A graduate seminar at Rutgers University gave me both the opportunity and the incentive to collect material on programming languages. I'd like to thank Alex Borgida, Martin Carroll, Fritz Henglein, Naftaly Minsky, Bob Paige, and Barbara Ryder for keeping the seminar lively.

An undergraduate course at Harvard University used an early draft of this book. Written comments by the students in the course were very helpful.

The organization of this book has benefited greatly from the comments and especially the criticism of the then anonymous reviewers contacted by Addison-Wesley. They are Tom Cheatham, Harvard University, John Crenshaw, Western Kentucky University, Paul Hilfinger, University of California, Berkeley, Barry Kurtz, New Mexico State University, Robert Noonan, College of William and Mary, Ron Olsson, University of California, Davis, William Pervin, University of Texas at Dallas, Paul Reynolds, University of Virginia, David Schmidt, Kansas State University, and Laurie Werth, University of Texas at Austin.

For all their technical help, I am grateful to Al Aho, Jon Bentley, Gerard Berry, Eric Cooper, Bruce Duba, Tom Duncan, Rich Drechsler, Peggy Ellis, Charlie Fischer, Dan Friedman, Georges Gonthier, Bob Harper, Mike Harrison, Bruce Hillyer, Brian Kernighan, Kim King, Chandra Kintala, Dave MacQueen, Dianne Maki, Doug McIlroy, John Mitchell, Mike O'Donnell, Dennis Ritchie, Bjarne Stroustrup, Chris Van Wyk, and Carl Woolf.

This book on programming languages was produced with the help of a number of little languages. The diagrams were drawn using Brian Kernighan's Pic language; the grey-tones in the diagrams rely on the work of

Rich Drechsler. The tables were laid out using Mike Lesk's Tbl program. Eqn, Lorinda Cherry and Brian Kernighan's language for typesetting mathematics, handled the pseudo-code as well. The Troff program was originally written by the late Joe Ossanna and is kept vital by Brian Kernighan. Page layout would have suffered without a new Troff macro package and post-processor by Brian Kernighan and Chris Van Wyk. The indexing programs were supplied by Jon Bentley and Brian Kernighan. Cross references were managed using scripts written with the help of Al Aho for managing the text of the "dragon" book.

Finally, I'd like to thank Bell Labs for its support. I have learnt more from my colleagues here than they might suspect. Whenever a question occurred, someone in the building always seemed to have the answer.

Acknowledgments

I really appreciate the comments I have received on the first edition. The experience of instructors and the frank opinions of reviewers have guided the revision.

Debbie Lafferty of Addison-Wesley has been the voice on the phone through the months, coordinating reviews and credits, and generally keeping the project on track. I now know that the reviewers include Bill Appelbe, Michael Barnett, Manuel E. Bermudez, Ray Ford, Aditya P. Mathur, L. A. Oldroyd, and Hamilton Richards — thanks.

For technical help and discussions, I am grateful to Jon Bentley, Lorinda Cherry, Brian Kernighan, Dave MacQueen, Jon Riecke, Bjarne Stroustrup, and Rich Wolf. My colleagues at Bell Labs have been greatly supportive.

A lot has happened while I have been immersed in the Book, including a death, a birth, a move, a fire. Dianne Maki has helped me navigate through it all.

RS

Contents

I   INTRODUCTION   1

1   The Role of Programming Languages   3

    1.1 Toward Higher-Level Languages   4
    1.2 Problems of Scale   8
    1.3 Programming Paradigms   11
    1.4 Language Implementation: Bridging the Gap   18
        EXERCISES   21
        BIBLIOGRAPHIC NOTES   23

2   Language Description: Syntactic Structure   25

    2.1 Expression Notations   28
    2.2 Abstract Syntax Trees   31
    2.3 Lexical Syntax   33
    2.4 Context-Free Grammars   35
    2.5 Grammars for Expressions   41
    2.6 Variants of Grammars   46
        EXERCISES   49
        BIBLIOGRAPHIC NOTES   52

II   IMPERATIVE PROGRAMMING   55

3   Statements: Structured Programming   59

    3.1 The Need for Structured Programming   59
    3.2 Syntax-Directed Control Flow   63
    3.3 Design Considerations: Syntax   72
    3.4 Handling Special Cases in Loops   77
    3.5 Programming with Invariants   80

3.6   Proof Rules for Partial Correctness   86
3.7   Control flow in C   90
       EXERCISES   94
       BIBLIOGRAPHIC NOTES   99

4   **Types: Data Representation**   **101**

4.1   The Role of Types   102
4.2   Basic Types   107
4.3   Arrays: Sequences of Elements   111
4.4   Records: Named Fields   117
4.5   Unions and Variant Records   120
4.6   Sets   123
4.7   Pointers: Efficiency and Dynamic Allocation   125
4.8   Two String Tables   133
4.9   Types and Error Checking   136
       EXERCISES   143
       BIBLIOGRAPHIC NOTES   146

5   **Procedure Activations**   **147**

5.1   Introduction to Procedures   148
5.2   Parameter-Passing Methods   155
5.3   Scope Rules for Names   160
5.4   Nested Scopes in the Source Text   166
5.5   Activation Records   172
5.6   Lexical Scope: Procedures as in C   181
5.7   Lexical Scope: Nested Procedures and Pascal   190
       EXERCISES   198
       BIBLIOGRAPHIC NOTES   202

III   **OBJECT-ORIENTED PROGRAMMING**   **205**

6   **Groupings of Data and Operations**   **209**

6.1   Constructs for Program Structuring   210
6.2   Information Hiding   217
6.3   Program Design with Modules   220
6.4   Modules and Defined Types   229
6.5   Class Declarations in C++   232
6.6   Dynamic Allocation in C++   238

6.7 Templates: Parameterized Types 244
6.8 Implementation of Objects in C++ 245
EXERCISES 248
BIBLIOGRAPHIC NOTES 251

7 Object-Oriented Programming **253**

7.1 What is an Object? 253
7.2 Object-Oriented Thinking 256
7.3 Inheritance 260
7.4 Object-Oriented Programming in C++ 267
7.5 An Extended C++ Example 274
7.6 Derived Classes and Information Hiding 281
7.7 Objects in Smalltalk 285
7.8 Smalltalk Objects have a Self 291
EXERCISES 294
BIBLIOGRAPHIC NOTES 299

IV FUNCTIONAL PROGRAMMING **301**

8 Elements of Functional Programming **305**

8.1 A Little Language of Expressions 306
8.2 Types: Values and Operations 313
8.3 Function Declarations 318
8.4 Approaches to Expression Evaluation 321
8.5 Lexical Scope 327
8.6 Type Checking 331
EXERCISES 335
BIBLIOGRAPHIC NOTES 339

9 Functional Programming in a Typed Language **341**

9.1 Exploring a List 342
9.2 Function Declaration by Cases 346
9.3 Functions as First-Class Values 351
9.4 ML: Implicit Types 357
9.5 Data Types 360
9.6 Exception Handling in ML 367

9.7   Little Quilt in Standard ML   369
        EXERCISES   380
        BIBLIOGRAPHIC NOTES   383

10 Functional Programming with Lists   385

10.1 Scheme, a Dialect of Lisp   386
10.2 The Structure of Lists   392
10.3 List Manipulation   396
10.4 A Motivating Example: Differentiation   404
10.5 Simplification of Expressions   409
10.6 Storage Allocation for Lists   413
        EXERCISES   417
        BIBLIOGRAPHIC NOTES   421

V   OTHER PARADIGMS   423

11 Logic Programming   425

11.1 Computing with Relations   426
11.2 Introduction to Prolog   430
11.3 Data Structures in Prolog   438
11.4 Programming Techniques   442
11.5 Control in Prolog   450
11.6 Cuts   461
        EXERCISES   470
        BIBLIOGRAPHIC NOTES   472

12 An Introduction to Concurrent Programming   475

12.1 Parallelism in Hardware   476
12.2 Streams: Implicit Synchronization   478
12.3 Concurrency as Interleaving   482
12.4 Liveness Properties   485
12.5 Safe Access to Shared Data   489
12.6 Concurrency in Ada   491
12.7 Synchronized Access to Shared Variables   498
        EXERCISES   507
        BIBLIOGRAPHIC NOTES   510

VI LANGUAGE DESCRIPTION   513

13 Semantic Methods   515

13.1 Synthesized Attributes   517
13.2 Attribute Grammars   520
13.3 Natural Semantics   523
13.4 Denotational Semantics   529
13.5 A Calculator in Scheme   530
13.6 Lexically Scoped Lambda Expressions   532
13.7 An Interpreter   535
13.8 An Extension: Recursive Functions   542
      EXERCISES   545
      BIBLIOGRAPHIC NOTES   546

14 Static Types and the Lambda Calculus   547

14.1 Equality of Pure Lambda Terms   549
14.2 Substitution Revisited   554
14.3 Computation with Pure Lambda Terms   556
14.4 Programming Constructs as Lambda-Terms   561
14.5 The Typed Lambda Calculus   566
14.6 Polymorphic Types   569
      EXERCISES   576
      BIBLIOGRAPHIC NOTES   577

15 A Look at Some Languages   579

15.1 Pascal: A Teaching Language   579
15.2 C: Systems Programming   583
15.3 C++: A Range of Programming Styles   591
15.4 Smalltalk, the Language   594
15.5 Standard ML   598
15.6 Scheme, a Dialect of Lisp   602
15.7 Prolog   607

Bibliography   613

Credits   627

Index   629

I

INTRODUCTION

The widespread use of programming languages began with the arrival of Fortran in 1957. It allowed scientists and engineers to write formulas using traditional symbols from mathematics — the use of + for addition dates back to the fifteenth century and the use of * for multiplication dates back to the seventeenth century. Such notations were therefore a natural starting point for the design of programming languages.

The formula $b^2 - 4ac$ was written in Fortran as the expression

```
B**2 - 4.0*A*C
```

Fortran takes its name from *For*mula *Trans*lation; readable formulas were translated into machine instructions for the IBM 704. Besides describing a result, a formula or expression $x + y * z$ can be treated as an algorithm for computing the result. The algorithm is to multiply y with z and add the result to x. An expression can therefore be translated into machine instructions for evaluating the expression.

Hundreds of programming languages have since been designed and implemented. Related programming languages are grouped into *families*; members of a family differ in taste more than substance. Having learned one member, it is easier to learn another, since concepts from one member carry over to other members of a family.

Chapter 1 begins with the need for programming languages and goes on to introduce four approaches to programming: imperative, functional, object-oriented, and logic programming. These approaches are explored in the rest of this book.

Chapter 2 deals with language description. It introduces grammars, which are a notation for describing the syntax of programming languages.

1

The Role of
Programming Languages

Is a programming language a tool for instructing machines? A means
for communicating between programmers? A vehicle for expressing
high-level designs? A notation for algorithms? A way of expressing
relationships between concepts? A tool for experimentation? A
means for controlling computerized devices? My conclusion is that a
general-purpose programming language must be all of those to serve
its diverse set of users. The only thing a language cannot be—and
survive—is be a mere collection of "neat" features.

> – Stroustrup [1994], commenting on the apparent lack of "agreement on what a language really is and what its main purpose is supposed to be."

Programming languages are notations. They are used for specifying, organizing, and reasoning about computations. Just as English compositions range
from notes to sonnets, programs range from prototypes that are used once and
forgotten to production tools that are shared and supported. This range of
needs has motivated the creation of hundreds of programming languages.

Language designers balance

- making computing convenient for people with
- making efficient use of computing machines.

Convenience comes first. Without it, efficiency is irrelevant.

Chapter Overview

Programming languages have evolved far beyond their origins in machines.
As we see in Section 1.1, machine language is unintelligible. Languages can
help not only by improving the readability of individual program fragments,
but by providing ways of organizing and managing large programs. People

make mistakes. Section 1.2 contains an example of a program gone wrong, of a spectacular failure caused by a simple error.

Section 1.3 introduces four approaches to programming that are studied in Parts II–V of this book. These are imperative programming, in languages like Pascal and C; functional programming, which motivated the design of Lisp and its successors; object-oriented programming in languages like C++ and Smalltalk; and logic programming in a language like Prolog. Also covered in Part V is concurrent programming.

A readable program in any programming language cannot be run directly on a machine. Section 1.4 outlines two approaches to running or implementing a program: It can be run by compiling it or by interpreting it.

1.1   TOWARD HIGHER-LEVEL LANGUAGES

*machine language
is unsuitable for
programming*

Programming languages were invented to make machines easier to use. They thrive because they make problems easier to solve.

The informal term *level* is useful for gross distinctions between languages. Levels of readability for programs are analogous to levels of readability for English text. Consider English text. Are the individual words readable? Do the sentences make sense? What are the main ideas? Words, sentences, paragraphs, sections, chapters are levels of structure in English.

Machine computations are low level, full of details that have more to do with the inner workings of the machine than with what the computation is for. A typical machine-level operation might add numbers or compare characters.

Machine language is the native language of a computer; it is the notation to which the computer responds directly. The term *code* originally referred to machine language, although code is now used more broadly to refer to any program text.

Programming languages are designed to be both higher level and general purpose. A language is *higher level* if it is independent of the underlying machine. A language is *general purpose* if it can be applied to a wide range of problems. For example, Fortran was initially created for numerical computing, Lisp for artificial intelligence, Simula for simulation, Prolog for natural language processing. Yet, these languages are general enough to have been applied to wide range of problems.

Machine Language Is Unintelligible

Programs in machine language are usually unintelligible at the lowest level, the most detailed level, since they consist only of 0s and 1s.

Example 1.1   Here is a code fragment for the original so-called von Neumann machine, designed in 1946; modern computers resemble the original sufficiently that they are said to have a von Neumann architecture. The fragment is

```
00000010101111001010
00000010111111001000
00000011001110101000
```

This fragment adds the numbers in locations 10 and 11 and stores the result in location 12. Goldstine [1972] writes, "While this enumeration is virtually unintelligible to a human, it is exactly what the machine *understands*."

Machine language is unintelligible and English is verbose without being very informative. "We therefore adopted another language for writing out our programs. This was a symbolic or mnemonic one," Goldstine continues. Although the symbolic notation was hand-translated into machine code, the movement away from machine language had begun. □

Assembly Language Is Low Level

readability is a property of programs, not instructions

Assembly language is a variant of machine language in which names and symbols take the place of the actual codes for machine operations, values, and storage locations, making individual instructions more readable.

Individual instructions in assembly language are readable, but limitations of the underlying machine can lead to convoluted programs.

Example 1.2 The model computer in this example illustrates programming at the assembly level. As we shall see, the individual instructions inside the machine in Fig. 1.1 are quite readable. Nevertheless, it is far from obvious that the program in Fig. 1.1 reads a sequence of integers like

```
1 1 2 2 2 3 1 4 4
```

and writes out the sequence with adjacent duplicates removed, as in

```
1 2 3 1 4
```

A readable relative of this program is developed in Section 3.1.

A *random-access machine* (RAM) has four main components:

- A memory
- A program
- An input file
- An output file

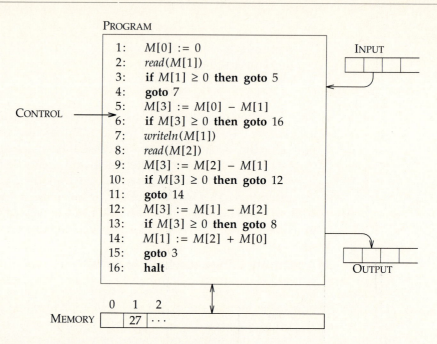

Figure 1.1   A random-access machine (RAM).

The memory consists of a sequence of locations $0, 1, \cdots$, each capable of holding a single integer value at a time. A *machine address* is the number of a location in memory. The integer held in a location will be referred to as the *contents* of the location.

A *program* consists of a sequence of *instructions*. The instruction set in Fig. 1.2 has instructions for assignment, input/output, and control flow. The assignment

$$M[l] := M[j] + M[k]$$

puts into location l the sum of the values in locations j and k. Thus, an assignment changes a value stored in the machine's memory.

An *input file* consists of a sequence of values consumed one at a time by read instructions. An *output file* consists of the sequence of values produced one at a time by write instructions.

Execution of a program begins with the first instruction. Control normally flows from one instruction to the next, except that an instruction

$M[l] := n$	Put integer n into location l.
$M[l] := M[j] + M[k]$	Put the sum of the values in locations j and k into location l.
$M[l] := M[j] - M[k]$	Put the difference of the values in j and k into location l.
$M[l] := M[M[j]]$	Let k be the value in location j. In effect, $M[l] := M[k]$.
$M[M[j]] := M[k]$	Let l be the value in location j. In effect, $M[l] := M[k]$.
$read(M[l])$	Get the next input value and put it into location l.
$writeln(M[j])$	Produce the value in location j as the next output value.
goto i	Next, execute the instruction in location i.
if $M[j] \geq 0$ **then goto** i	Next, execute the instruction in location i if $M[j] \geq 0$.
halt	Stop execution.

Figure 1.2   The instruction set for a random-access machine.

    goto i

sends control to instruction i. The conditional goto

    if $M[j] \geq 0$ **then goto** i

sends control to instruction i if the value in location j is greater than or equal to 0. Here, $M[j] \geq 0$ is called the test or the condition in the instruction. The program stops upon executing a halt instruction.   □

Benefits of Higher-Level Languages

higher-level languages replaced assembly language

Higher-level languages have replaced machine and assembly language in virtually all areas of programming, because they provide benefits like the following:

- Readable familiar notations
- Machine independence
- Availability of program libraries
- Consistency checks during implementation that can detect errors

Portability is another term for machine independence; a language is *portable* if programs in the language can be run on different machines with little or no change.

Such benefits led to Fortran's immediate acceptance as the language of choice for scientific programming. The next example illustrates the benefits of programming languages for building programming systems.

Example 1.3 Originally written in assembly language, the UNIX operating system kernel was rewritten in the programming language C in 1973. Ritchie [1978] recounts the resulting benefits:

- *New users and programs*. The use of a higher-level language led to software packages "that would never have been written at all if their authors had had to write assembly code; many of our most inventive contributors do not know, and do not wish to learn, the instruction set of the machine."

- *Readability*. "The C versions of programs that were rewritten after C became available are much more easily understood, repaired, and extended than the assembler versions. This applies especially to the operating system itself. The original system was very difficult to modify, especially to add new devices, but also to make even minor changes."

- *Portability*. "An extremely valuable, though originally unplanned, benefit of writing in C is the portability of the system. . . . It appears to be possible to produce an operating system and set of software that runs on several machines and whose expression in source code is, except for a few modules, identical on each machine."

Ritchie concludes, "Although [a comprehensive study of the space and time inflation due to the use of C] might be interesting, it would be somewhat irrelevant, in that no matter what the results turned out to be, they would not cause us to start writing assembly language."   □

1.2 PROBLEMS OF SCALE

a minute detail can crash a program

The lesson of the story in this section is that the problems of programming are ones of scale. Any one change to a program is easy to make. Any isolated program fragment can be understood and checked in its entirety. With large programs, the effect of a change can ripple through the program, perhaps introducing errors or *bugs* into some forgotten corner.

Programming languages can help in two ways. First, readable and compact notations reduce the likelihood of errors. Small programs are easier to get right than large ones. With large programs, programming languages can help by providing ways of organizing computations so that they can be understood one piece at a time.

The Human Error Factor

Due to a programming error, the rocket carrying Mariner I, an unmanned probe to the planet Venus, had to be destroyed 290 seconds after launch on July 22, 1962. The program in the ground computer was supposed to behave as follows:

> **if not** in radar contact with the rocket **then**
>   do not correct its flight path

But, in error, the initial **not** was missing. As a result, the ground computer continued to blindly guide the rocket even after radar contact was lost. The rocket wobbled astray and was destroyed before it could endanger human lives. The program had previously been used without fault in four lunar launches.

During an investigation into the loss, NASA scientists attempted to explain the error to a lay audience; an excerpt from the committee hearing appears in Fig. 1.3. The committee members had difficulty understanding why such a simple error — a missing **not** — was not caught earlier. For example,

> *Question.* Does NASA check to see that the computers are correctly programmed?
>
> *Answer.* This is a minute detail of the program . . .

Implicit in the committee's questions in Fig. 1.3 are helpful suggestions for how to detect errors:

> *Code inspection.* [*Doesn't any outside inspector check that the computers are correctly programmed*?] During code inspection, one or more people read someone else's program, line by line.
>
> *Program testing.* [*300 test runs did not uncover the error.*] Program testing consists of running the program on sample input data.

Both techniques are standard practice in software engineering. They can be used with any programming language. Both techniques are incomplete; they rely on the imagination and foresight of the inspectors and testers, and are subject to human limitations. Inspectors must imagine what the program they are reading will do when it runs. Testers must foresee all possible uses of the program. In the Mariner example, the testers did not have the foresight to test for the loss of radar contact.

Dijkstra [1972] writes, ''Program testing can be used to show the presence of bugs, but never to show their absence!''

CHAIRMAN: Who was responsible for leaving this [**not**] out? . . .

Mr. WYATT: It was a human error. . . .

Mr. FULTON: Does NASA check to see that the computers are correctly [programmed]? Doesn't any outside inspector check, or is it just up to the [programmer] and if he does not do it nobody else knows about it?

Dr. MORRISON: This is a minute detail of the [program], which I agree should be checked. However, in good management practices, if we followed every detail to this point, we would have a tremendous staff.

Mr. FULTON: . . . the loss up to $18 or $20 million, plus the time, plus the loss of prestige . . . would seem to me to require a system of checking to see that the contractor programmed correctly . . .

Dr. MORRISON: This is true. I would like to point out there were 300 runs made of this [program; the error was not uncovered] . . .

Mr. FULTON: My point is that we know of one [error], but we do not know if there were others . . .

Mr. WAGGONNER: . . . I share your concern there. I would have to be reluctant to say we hire enough personnel to check every [programmer]. That would mean . . . two people doing every job—a man checking every man. . . .

CHAIRMAN: . . . I feel that I have a vague knowledge of what you are talking about, but we certainly should be able to devise some system for checks that will not allow this type of error to creep in.

Figure 1.3 Excerpts from a hearing before the Committee on Science and Astronautics, U.S. House of Representatives, July 31, 1962, George P. Miller (chairman). Mr. Wyatt and Dr. Morrison represented NASA, the National Aeronautics and Space Agency. The others were members of Congress.

A Role for Programming Languages

A more complete statement of Dijkstra's position is that it is hopeless to establish the correctness of a program by testing, unless the internal structure of the program is taken into account. Our only hope is to carefully design a program so that its correctness can be understood in terms of its structure. In his words,

- "the art of programming is the art of organising complexity," and
- "we must organise the computations in such a way that our limited powers are sufficient to guarantee that the computation will establish the desired effect."

Dijkstra took this position in the context of structured programming, considered in Chapter 3. Nevertheless, the following conclusion applies in general: A role for programming languages is to provide ways of organizing computations.

1.3 PROGRAMMING PARADIGMS

New languages are not introduced lightly. A language takes on a life of its own as people invest in it by learning it and building up collections of programs in it. The effort needed to introduce a new language is substantial, not only in designing it and implementing it, but in teaching it and supporting it.

Some of the selected languages in Fig. 1.4 introduced new programming paradigms, new ways of thinking about programming. Fortran, Lisp, Simula, and Prolog are examples. Other languages in Fig. 1.4 are evolutionary successors of earlier languages. For example, C++, an evolutionary successor of C, was introduced to bring the benefits of Simula to C. The arrows in the figure illustrate primary influences between languages. There is a dotted arrow if a language borrows a specific idea or construct from another.

The languages in boldface in Fig. 1.4 were selected because they are representative, influential, and available. Related languages were then added to the figure to provide the context in which the selected languages were developed.

Imperative Programming

Pascal and C embody key ideas of imperative programming

Imperative languages are action oriented; that is, a computation is viewed as a sequence of actions. The imperative family in Fig. 1.5 begins with Fortran; Pascal and C are general-purpose imperative languages.

Backus et al. [1957] anticipated the two key ingredients of Fortran's success: familiar notations and efficiency. Efficiency was emphasized because it was widely believed in the 1950s that translation would be inefficient. That is, hand-crafted machine language programs would be shorter and would run faster than the results of translation.

Fortran was convenient enough and efficient enough that it quickly became the language of choice for scientific programming. The reliance on a mathematical notation led to a language that was largely machine independent, despite the fact that Fortran was initially designed for a specific computer, the IBM 704. Its designers had no idea that it would be used for any other IBM computer, much less any computer from another manufacturer.

Others followed. The proliferation of essentially similar languages stimulated efforts toward a common language that would allow programs to be shared. The designers of Algol retained the goal of using the language for "the description of numerical processes in publications." (Perlis and Samelson [1958])

Algol 60 dominated the programming language scene through the 1960s, to the extent that the imperative family of languages was referred to as the

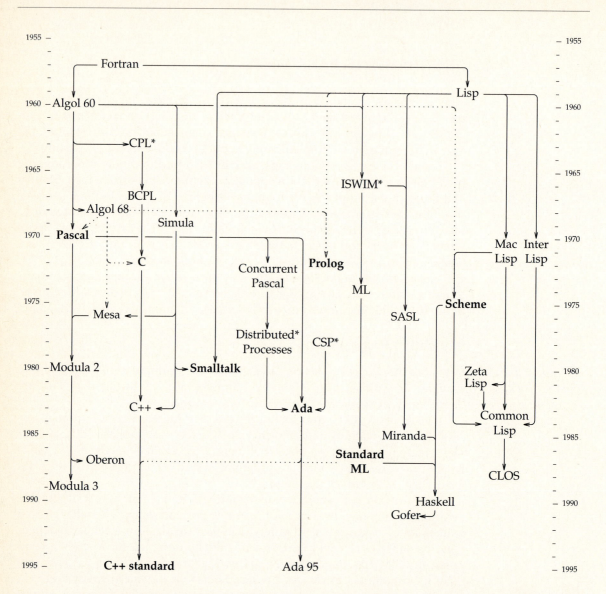

Figure 1.4   The languages in boldface are discussed in this book. The other languages in the diagram were selected because they either influenced or were influenced by the languages in boldface. Dates marking the availability of a language are subject to discussion, since several years might have elapsed between initial design and the actual use of a language. An asterisk (*) next to a language indicates that it was never fully implemented.

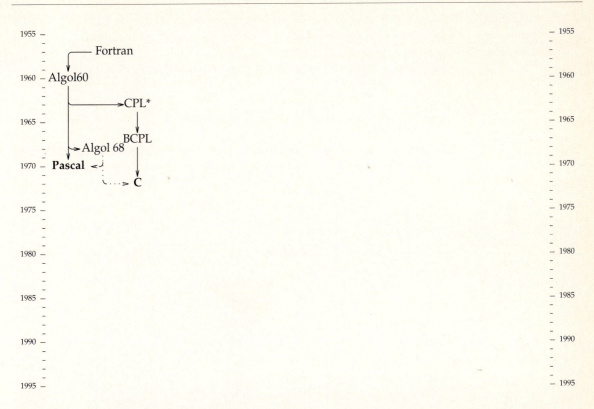

Figure 1.5 Selected members of the imperative family of languages, starting with Fortran. Algol 60 dominated the scene in the 1960s. CPL was never fully implemented. Concepts from Algol 68 were picked up by other languages. Pascal and C continue to be popular.

Algol family. Nevertheless, Algol was admired more widely than it was adopted.

Pascal was designed as a teaching language. Although there were some syntactic differences, Algol 60 remained enough of a subset that Wirth [1971] hoped "conversion of Algol 60 programs to Pascal can be considered as a negligible effort of transcription."

C was created in 1972 by Dennis Ritchie as an implementation language for software associated with the UNIX operating system. In 1973, the UNIX system itself was rewritten in C. C provides a rich set of operators, a terse syntax, and efficient access to the machine. It is a general-purpose programming language that is available on a wide range of machines.

Functional Programming

functional programming transcends Lisp

The basic concepts of functional languages originated with Lisp, a language designed in 1958 for applications in artificial intelligence. Selected functional languages appear in Fig. 1.6.

The name Lisp is an acronym derived from *List* Processor. An example of a list is

```
(shakespeare wrote (the tempest))
```

Parentheses enclose list elements. This list thus has three elements: shakespeare, wrote, and the sublist (the tempest), representing a title.

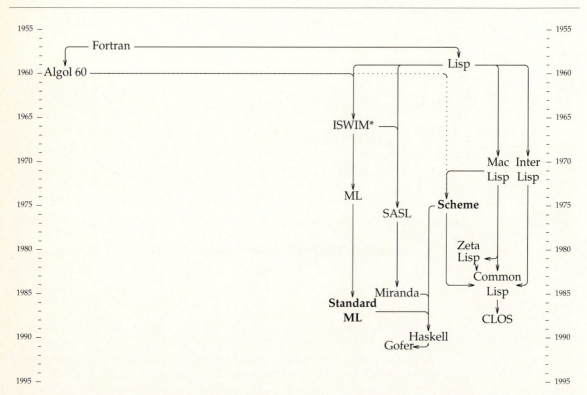

Figure 1.6 The functional family of languages begins with Lisp. Lisp has spawned numerous dialects; a few of them appear in the diagram. Lisp's primitives for manipulating lists were inspired by those of an extension of Fortran called FLPL, for Fortran List Processing Language. Lisp was designed in part because FLPL did not have recursion and conditionals within expressions. Mathematical elegance came later. The asterisk next to ISWIM indicates that it was never fully implemented.

McCarthy et al. [1965] explained Lisp as follows:

> The LISP language is designed primarily for symbolic data processing. It has been used for symbolic calculations in differential and integral calculus, electrical circuit theory, mathematical logic, game playing, and other fields of artificial intelligence.

Functional programming transcends Lisp. ISWIM was Landin's [1966] attempt to deliver functional programming from Lisp's parentheses-laden syntax and commitment to lists. Although ISWIM was a theoretical exercise and was never implemented, it was used as a starting point for exploring programming concepts and language designs.

ML, like many functional languages, is a vehicle for studying languages

The introduction to functional programming in Chapter 8 treads a middle ground common to ML, Miranda, and the Gofer subset of Haskell. The examples in Chapter 8 are clothed in Standard ML, the primary functional language in this book. As Milner [1984], the originator of ML wrote of a proposal leading up to Standard ML,

> The proposed ML is not meant to be *the* functional language. There are too many degrees of freedom for such a thing to exist.

Language description motivated the introduction of Scheme, a spare version of Lisp, popular for research and teaching because of its clean design. Scheme was developed in 1975 by Steele and Sussman [1975].

One of the classics of functional programming is McCarthy's description of Lisp in Lisp itself. This description led to the initial implementation of Lisp and ultimately to numerous dialects. The MacLisp/InterLisp era occurred during the late 1960s into the 1980s. MacLisp emphasized performance and production quality, in contrast to the slow Lisp of the early 1960s. InterLisp introduced the notion of a programming environment with a structured editor tied to the syntax. The proliferation of Lisps prompted the creation of Common Lisp by 1984. CLOS is an object-oriented extension; the full name is Common Lisp Object System.

Object-Oriented Programming

C++ and Smalltalk are popular for object-oriented programming.

Object-oriented programming owes much to Simula's origins in simulation. The language was designed as both a description language and a programming language by Kristen Nygaard and Ole-Johan Dahl between 1961 and 1967. Simula changed the way people think about programming.

The key concept from Simula is that of a class of objects. A traffic simulation can have many cars and many trucks, all of which share certain properties. In modern terminology we would say that the simulation has objects of the class of cars and objects of the class of trucks. Furthermore, cars and trucks are all vehicles. The classification of objects into classes and subclasses is central to object-oriented programming.

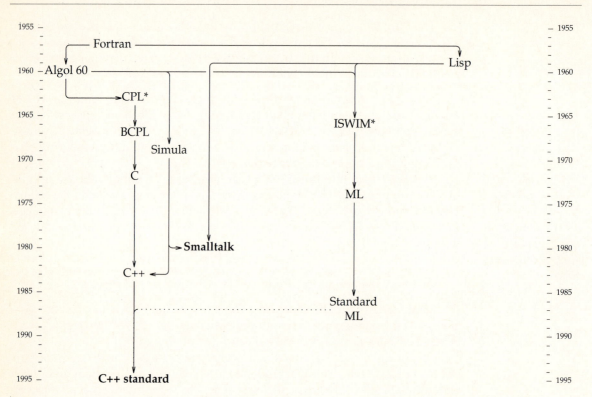

Figure 1.7   Object-oriented programming owes much to Simula. C++ and Smalltalk are popular languages for object-oriented programming.

C++ and Smalltalk are popular languages for object-oriented programming. Although both got the notion of objects and classes from Simula, the two languages grew out of different programming traditions (see Fig. 1.7).

C++ was designed to bring the benefits of objects to imperative programming in C. C++ retains the efficiency of C. Smalltalk was designed as part of a personal computing environment. It is more than a language; it is an interactive system with a graphical user interface. The design of Smalltalk was influenced by Lisp.

Logic Programming

Prolog comes from programmation en logique

Prolog was developed in 1972 for natural language processing in French by Alain Colmerauer and Philippe Roussel. The first large Prolog program was for human-machine interactions like the following:

```
Every psychiatrist is a person.
Every person he analyzes is sick.
Jacques is a psychiatrist in Marseille.
Is Jacques a person?
Where is Jacques?
Is Jacques sick?
```

Prolog uses a specialized form of logical reasoning to answer such queries.

Prolog has since been used for a range of applications from databases to expert systems. Prolog programs have the brevity and expressiveness of logic.

Choice of Language

The choice of programming language depends in part on the programming to be done, and in part on external factors, such as availability, support, and training.

For example, the initial prototype of the UNIX system spelling checker, outlined in the next example, was written in an afternoon, by combining existing utility programs (tools) in the UNIX environment. Several years later, once the spelling checker became sufficiently popular, an improved version was implemented in C to speed up checking. Differing goals led to the two versions being implemented in different languages.

Example 1.4 The UNIX system spelling checker began as a prototype, based on the following idea:

Create a list of words in the document.

Sort the list.

Remove duplicate words.

For each word, report if it is not in a dictionary.

Each line corresponds to an operation supported by an existing UNIX tool. The data objects are documents, words, and lists of words. The "create a list" operation is applied to a document; it produces a list of words as a result. The operations on the next three lines are applied to lists of words and produce lists of words as results. When applied to

```
deu to a programing error
```

the prototype produces the following list as a result:

```
deu, programing                                      □
```

Since prototypes could quickly be created, new ideas could easily be tried out. For example, names like Pascal do not appear in most dictionaries, so they are reported along with genuine spelling errors. Experiments with the initial prototype confirmed that better results are obtained by ignoring technical terms that are not in a dictionary.

Several years later, much care and effort went into a C program that squeezed a "dictionary" into the memory of the machine.

1.4 LANGUAGE IMPLEMENTATION: BRIDGING THE GAP

The two basic approaches to implementing a program in a higher-level language are illustrated in Fig. 1.8.

In one approach, the language is brought down to the level of the machine, using a translator called a *compiler*. In the other, the machine is brought up to the level of the language, by building a higher-level machine called an *interpreter*. These approaches have a subtle influence on language design, so it is worth knowing about them at the outset.

Compilation

a compiler translates a program into code that runs

The input and output languages of a translator are identified by referring to them as its *source* and languages, respectively. The target language in Fig. 1.8(a) is assumed to be machine code.

The translation of a source program into target code is said to occur at *translation time*, shown above the dotted line in Fig. 1.9. In the figure, "source program" refers to a program in the source language that the compiler trans-

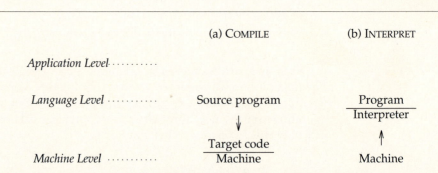

Figure 1.8   A language can be implemented by (a) translating it down to the level of the machine, or (b) by building a higher-level machine called an interpreter that can run the language directly.

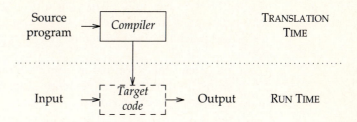

Figure 1.9   A source program is translated into a target program, which is run.

lates into an equivalent program in the target language. Once translation is complete, the target code is run at a later time, called *run time*.

Example 1.5   Suppose that a target language has instructions of the form

$$a := b + c$$

This instruction adds b and c and assigns the result to a. In other words, the sum of b and c becomes the value of a.

The Fortran expression

$$B**2 - 4.0*A*C$$

translates into a sequence of assembly instructions:

```
R1  := B
R1  := R1 * R1
R2  := 4.0
R3  := A
R2  := R2 * R3
R3  := C
R2  := R2 * R3
R1  := R1 - R2
```

When run, these instructions assign R1 the value of the Fortran expression.

What runs is the target code, consisting of the sequence of target instructions, not the source program text, consisting of the Fortran expression.   □

Interpretation

an interpreter runs
programs directly

The alternative in Fig. 1.8(b) is to view a programming language as being the native language of an interpreter. An interpreter behaves as if it were a new higher-level machine, one that can directly run programs in the programming language.

An interpreter takes a program and its input at the same time, as in Fig. 1.10. It scans the program, implementing operations as it encounters them, and doing input/output as needed.

Example 1.6   The following is an outline of an expression evaluator in a functional language:

> **function** *eval*(E) =
>   **if** E is the constant i **then** i
>   **else if** E is the sum of E_1 and E_2 **then** *eval*(E_1)+*eval*(E_2)
>   **else if** E is the product of E_1 and E_2 **then** *eval*(E_1)*eval*(E_2)

This interpreter computes the value of an expression by examining its structure. The value of the expression 3 is 3. The value of 4*5 is computed by extracting subexpressions 4 and 5, computing their values, and multiplying them. Similarly, 3+4*5 is the sum of 3 and 4*5, so the interpreter computes its value by adding the values of 3 and 4*5.

Sums and products are so familiar that the expression interpreter may seem like a toy. The approach of evaluating an expression by examining its structure, however, generalizes nicely.   □

Compilation and Interpretation: A Comparison

A *static* property of a program is a property that is evident from the program text. A *dynamic* property is evident only upon running the program. Compiled languages have a bias toward static properties, since all compiling decisions are made using the source text at translation time. Interpreted languages can deal with dynamic properties.

Compilation and interpretation can be compared as follows:

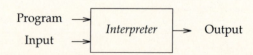

Figure 1.10   An interpreter takes both a program and its input, and produces output.

- *Compilation can be more efficient than interpretation.* Both compilation and interpretation impose some performance penalties, compared to carefully tailored machine code, written by hand. Compilation can, however, be an order of magnitude faster than interpretation for the same programming language. The performance penalties due to compilation take two forms:

    1. Machine time is needed to compile a source program into target code.

    2. The target code created by a compiler typically takes longer to run and occupies more space than carefully written machine code.

    Unlike a compiler, which translates the source program once and for all, an interpreter examines the program repeatedly. Every time 3+4*5 is reached in Example 1.6, the interpreter reexamines its structure. This repeated examination is a source of inefficiency.

- *Interpretation can be more flexible than compilation.* The repeated examination of the source program by an interpreter allows interpretation to be more flexible than compilation. An interpreter directly runs the source program, so it can allow programs to be changed "on the fly" to add features or correct errors. Furthermore, an interpreter works with the source text, so it can pinpoint an error in the source text and report it accurately.

    With a compiler, on the other hand, all translation is completed before the target program is run, which prevents the target program from being readily adapted as it runs.

The above description compares pure compilation with pure interpretation. In practice, a language could be implemented using a combination of the two techniques.

Exercises

1.1 In words, describe a program to read a sequence of integers and to write the integers that appear one or more times in the input sequence. For example, if the input sequence is 617, 201, 415, 201, then 201 must appear just once in the output.

1.2 Describe a program that produces the output sequence of Exercise 1.1 incrementally. That is, an integer that is seen for the first time in the input is written before any more integers are read.

1.3 Describe solutions to the following variants of Exercise 1.1:
   a. Output one copy of only the duplicates in a list of elements.
   b. Count the number of times an element appears in a list.

    c. Count the ten most frequently occurring words in a sample of English text.

1.4 In the language of your choice, write programs to read two integers m and n and produce the desired result without using multiplication and division. Use repeated additions and subtractions instead.
    a. $m * n$ (the result of multiplication).
    b. m **div** n (the result of integer division).
    c. m **mod** n (the remainder after integer division).

1.5 How would you test the programs in Exercise 1.4?

1.6 Describe how addition and multiplication of complex numbers can be implemented in terms of operations on real numbers.

1.7 Implement floating point addition in terms of integer arithmetic operations. Represent floating point numbers as pairs of integers (m, n), where m is a four-digit integer; that is, either $1000 \leq m \leq 9999$, or $-9999 \leq m \leq -1000$. The pair (m, n) represents $m * 10^{n-4}$. For example, $(3142, 1)$ represents $3142 * 10^{1-4} = 3.142$.

1.8 The Rambler language is an extension of the RAM instruction set in Fig. 1.2. It allows names to be used instead of memory locations. Thus, a name x can be used instead of $M[j]$, so $read(x)$ and $x := y + z$ are allowed. Further, in addition to $\geq$, the relations $<, \leq, =, \neq,$ and $>$ are allowed in conditionals. Do Exercise 1.4 using Rambler.

1.9 Under what conditions does the following RAM program terminate?

    1:   $read(M[1])$
    2:   $read(M[2])$
    3:   $M[1] := M[1] - M[2]$
    4:   **if** $M[1] \geq 0$ **then goto** 3
    5:   $M[1] := M[1] + M[2]$
    6:   $writeln(M[1])$
    7:   **halt**

1.10 Individual RAM instructions may be readable, but the limitations of the instruction set lead to convoluted programs. RAMs support conditionals of the form

    if $M[j] \geq 0$ **then goto** i

but not of either of the forms:

    if $M[j] = 0$ **then goto** i
    if $M[j] = M[k]$ **then goto** i

```
1:   M[0] := 0
2:   read(M[1])
3:   if M[1] = 0 then goto 9
4:   writeln(M[1])
5:   read(M[2])
6:   if M[2] = M[1] then goto 5
7:   M[1] := M[2] + M[0]
8:   goto 3
9:   halt
```

Figure 1.11   The conditionals in this program extend the RAM instruction set.

The program in Fig. 1.11 relies on these extensions to the RAM instruction set. Explain why this program is equivalent to the program within the RAM on page 6.

Bibliographic Notes

Programming predates computers. Around 1801, Joseph Marie Jacquard invented a programmable loom; a loom is a device for weaving thread into fabric. Intricate patterns like flowers and leaves could be woven by controlling which threads went over and which threads went under others. The Jacquard loom was controlled by punched cards; a different pattern could be woven by changing the cards. Morrison and Morrison [1961] mention "a remarkable woven silk portrait ... showing the inventor Jacquard surrounded by machines of his trade. This work was woven with about 1,000 threads to the inch and resembled a line engraving in fineness of detail. A total of 24,000 cards, each one capable of receiving 1,050 punch-holes, was used to weave its five square feet."

Glimmerings of modern computers appear in the 1864 description by Babbage of a proposed "Analytical Engine" consisting of two parts:

1. The store in which all the variables to be operated upon, as well as all those quantities which have arisen from the results of other operations, are placed.

2. The mill into which the quantities about to be operated upon are always brought. (Morrison and Morrison [1961])

For the early history of computers, see Goldstine [1972] and Metropolis, Howlett, and Rota [1980].

The Electronic Numerical Integrator and Computer (ENIAC), arguably the first general-purpose electronic digital computer, was programmed by moving cables and wires. Its program trays were heavy metal objects, 8 feet long. Wires plugged through holes in program trays controlled the machine. The motivating application was wartime calculation of firing tables; the design of the machine began in 1943, during World War II. ENIAC was created by a group led by John Presper Eckert, Jr., and John William Mauchly at the Moore School of Electrical Engineering at the University of Pennsylvania.

Even before the ENIAC was completed in 1945, it was understood that machines could be controlled by instructions stored inside the machine itself. John von Neumann participated in the design of a stored-program successor, called the EDVAC, at the Moore School. Subsequently, the so-called von Neumann machine was designed in 1946 at the Institute for Advanced Study in Princeton.

The early history of programming languages, up to the arrival of Fortran, is traced by Knuth and Trabb Pardo [1977]. Reflections on 13 major languages, including Fortran, appear in a collection of papers (Wexelblat [1981]) by participants in the creation of the languages. A second collection of historical papers appear in *ACM SIGPLAN Notices*, March 1993. Wegner [1976] traces milestones along the development of languages.

Dijkstra's [1972] ''Notes on structured programming'' stressed the role of structure in programming and gave rise to the term ''structured programming,'' explored in Chapter 3.

Writing on language design, Hoare [1973] observes, ''there are so many important but conflicting criteria, that their reconciliation and satisfaction is a major engineering task, demanding of the language designer a deep understanding of all aspects of the art of programming, a familiarity with a wide range of computer architecture on which his language may be implemented, and a knowledge of the wide range of applications to which his language will be put.'' Hoare's criteria for good language design are: ''simplicity, security, fast translation, efficient [target] code, and readability.''

Shepherdson and Sturgis [1963] introduced random-access machines as a more convenient alternative than Turing machines for theoretical studies of computation; the instruction set in Section 1.1 is from Cook and Reckhow [1972].

Steve Johnson wrote the prototype of the UNIX system spelling checker, described in Example 1.4. McIlroy [1980] developed the production version, written in C.

2

Language Description: Syntactic Structure

The author had hoped to complete a formal description of the set of legal [Algol 58] programs and of their meanings in time to present it here. Only the description of legal programs has been completed however. Therefore the formal treatment of the semantics of legal programs will be included in a subsequent paper.

  — Backus [1960], introducing grammars, which are widely accepted for specifying the syntax of programming languages. Several approaches to formal semantics have been developed, but none come close to grammars in popularity.

All this indicated a crying need for integrating the formulation of a precise and complete language description into the actual language development process. I was led to the conviction that the formulation of a clear and complete description was more important than any particular characteristic of the language.

  — Naur [1981], recalling being disappointed at two things: the lack of agreement on Algol 58 revealed by Backus's grammar, and the subtle semantic questions left unresolved by the grammar. Naur embraced grammars and used them to draft a report on Algol 60, with examples and semantics (in English) attached to the grammar rules — he soon became the editor of the Algol 60 report.

the state of the art: formal syntax, informal semantics — Clear and complete descriptions of a language are needed by programmers, implementers, and even language designers. This chapter deals with the easy part, the description of syntax. The hard part, semantics, is deferred until Chapter 13. The state of the art can be summarized by saying that a language is described by a combination of formal syntax and informal semantics.

The *syntax* of a language specifies how programs in the language are built up. The *semantics* of the language specifies what programs mean.

Suppose that dates are built up from digits represented by D and the symbol /, as follows:

$$D\ D\ /\ D\ D\ /\ D\ D\ D\ D$$

According to this syntax,

```
01/02/2001
```

is a date. The day this date refers to is not identified by the syntax. In the United States, this date refers to January 2, 2001, but elsewhere 01 is interpreted as the day and 02 as the month, so the date refers to February 1, 2001. The same syntax therefore has different semantics in different parts of the world.

Organization of Language Descriptions

Grammars are convenient enough for syntax that they are used by all communities: programmers, implementers, designers.

Semantic descriptions, however, are seldom both readable enough to be suitable for a beginner and precise enough to specify a language fully. Several distinct styles of language description have arisen to meet the conflicting needs of readability and precision.

- *Tutorials*. A tutorial introduction is a guided tour of a language. It provides impressions of what the main constructs of the language are and how they are meant to be used. Examples typically drive the organization of a tutorial. The syntax and semantics are introduced gradually, as needed. Complete, working, and useful examples allow a reader to learn by imitating and adapting.
- *Reference Manuals*. A reference manual describing the syntax and semantics of a language is traditionally organized around the syntax of the language. This tradition began with the Algol 60 report, which attached English explanations and examples to the syntactic rules of the language; the report was remarkably free of ambiguities.
- *Formal Definitions*. A formal definition is a precise description of the syntax and semantics of a language; it is aimed at specialists. English descriptions leave room for conflicting interpretations, so precise formal notations have been developed. The training and effort needed to learn such notations are balanced by their promise for clarifying particularly subtle points. The benefits of a formal notation are truly realized when it can be mechanically checked and processed.

Methods for formal semantics include operational semantics, denotational semantics, axiomatic semantics or proof rules, and attribute grammars. Overviews of these methods appear in Chapter 13, except for proof rules, which will be considered along with statements in Chapter 3. Proof rules or axiomatic semantics work well on statements in an imperative language; they are harder to apply to data structures and procedures.

Chapter Overview

The informal description of expressions in Section 2.1 serves two purposes. First, it introduces notations for expressions, the starting point for languages. Second, it provides examples for the syntax description methods in later sections. Methods for describing the syntax of expressions carry over readily to the rest of a language. Although expressions like $a + b*c$ may be more familiar than, say, functions, expressions present more of a challenge for description than the rest of the language. Constructs that are marked by keywords like **begin** and **end** are easier to describe than expressions.

Section 2.2 deals with abstract syntax, which captures intent, independent of notation. The intent in each of the following is to apply the operator + to the operands a and b:

```
a+b
(+ a b)
ADD a TO b
```

The written representation is different in each of these cases, but the abstract syntax is the same. It helps to have a clear sense of abstract syntax before the syntax of a language is described formally.

The formal syntax of a language usually consists of two layers, a lexical layer and a grammar layer. Lexical syntax corresponds to the spelling of words; for example, the symbol ≠ is written as <> in Pascal. The Pascal operators <>, <=, and < are treated as units and have different meanings, although all of their spellings begin with the character <. Lexical syntax is described informally in Section 2.3, since informal descriptions suffice in this book. Treatments of regular expressions, a convenient notation for lexical syntax, can be found in books on compilers for programming languages.

Section 2.4 introduces grammars, the key formalism for describing syntax; BNF is a notation for writing grammars. Grammars arose out of an international effort to create a universal programming language, which came to be called Algol 60. A draft, Algol 58, had enough ambiguities and omissions that a need was felt for precise descriptions of the syntax and semantics of languages. Grammars describe syntax alone, but the combination of grammars for syntax and English for semantics is the de facto standard for organizing reference manuals.

The design of grammars for expressions is explored in Section 2.5.

Alternative notations for writing grammars appear in Section 2.6: Extended BNF is a variant of BNF; syntax charts are a graphical notation.

2.1 EXPRESSION NOTATIONS

Expressions such as $a + b * c$ have been in use for centuries and were a starting point for the design of programming languages. Fortran allowed a scientist familiar with mathematical formulas such as

$$(-b + \sqrt{b^2 - 4*a*c} \,) \,/\, (2*a)$$

to write an expression such as

$$(-b + sqrt(b*b - 4.0*a*c)) \,/\, (2.0*a)$$

programming languages use a mix of infix, prefix, and postfix notations

Programming languages use a mix of notations, with most operators written between their operands, but some written before and some written after their operands. For example, $+, -, *$ and $/$ are written between their operands in this Fortran expression, but $-$ is also written before b in $-b$ and *sqrt* is written before the expression it is applied to.

A *binary* operator is applied to two operands. In *infix* notation, a binary operator is written between its operands, as in the expression $a + b$. Other alternatives are *prefix* notation, in which the operator is written first, as in $+\, a\, b$, and *postfix* notation, in which the operator is written last, as in $a\, b\, +$.

An expression can be enclosed within parentheses without affecting its value. Expression E has the same value as (E), as a rule.[1]

Prefix and postfix notations are sometimes called *parenthesis-free* because, as we shall see, the operands of each operator can be found unambiguously, without the need for parentheses.

Prefix Notation

An expression in prefix notation is written as follows:

- The prefix notation for a constant or a variable is the constant or variable itself.
- The application of an operator **op** to subexpressions E_1 and E_2 is written in prefix notation as **op** $E_1\, E_2$.

An advantage of prefix notation is that it is easy to decode during a left-to-right scan of an expression. If a prefix expression begins with operator $+$,

---

[1] Lisp, discussed in Chapter 10, is a rare exception to this rule. In Lisp, parentheses enclose elements of a list, so (E) is a list containing one element, E.

the next expression after + must be the first operand of + and the expression after that must be the second operand of +.

Example 2.1   The sum of x and y is written in prefix notation as $+ \ x \ y$. The product of $+ \ x \ y$ and z is written as $* + x \ y \ z$. Thus, $+ \ 20 \ 30$ equals 50 and

$$* + 20 \ 30 \ 60 \ = \ * \ 50 \ 60 \ = \ 3000$$

Similarly,

$$* \ 20 + 30 \ 60 \ = \ * \ 20 \ 90 \ = \ 1800 \qquad \square$$

The decoding of prefix notation extends to operators with a fixed number $k \geq 0$ of operands. The number of operands of an operator is called its *arity*. The application of an operator $\mathbf{op}^k$ of arity $k \geq 0$ to $E_1, E_2, \ldots, E_k$, is written in prefix notation as $\mathbf{op}^k \ E_1 \ E_2 \cdots E_k$. During a left-to-right scan, the ith expression to the right of $\mathbf{op}^k$ is the ith operand of $\mathbf{op}^k$, for $1 \leq i \leq k$.

The expressions $read(x)$ and $max(x, y)$ are in a variant of prefix notation, in which the operator is written to the left and the operands are enclosed within parentheses and separated by commas. This notation allows operators to take a variable number of arguments; for example, the operator *write* has one operand in $write(root)$ and four operands in $write(root, a, b, c)$.

A further variant of prefix notation is used in Lisp: parentheses enclose the operator and its operands, as in $(read \ x)$ and $(max \ x \ y)$.

Postfix Notation

An expression in postfix notation is written as follows:

- The postfix notation for a constant or a variable is the constant or variable itself.
- The application of an operator **op** to subexpressions E_1 and E_2 is written in postfix notation as $E_1 \ E_2 \ \mathbf{op}$.

An advantage of postfix expressions is that they can be mechanically evaluated with the help of a stack data structure; see Exercise 2.8 at the end of this chapter.

Example 2.2   The sum of x and y is written in postfix notation as $x \ y \ +$. The product of $x \ y \ +$ and z is written as $x \ y \ + \ z \ *$. Thus, $20 \ 30 \ +$ equals 50 and

$$20 \ 30 + 60 \ * \ = \ 50 \ 60 \ * \ = \ 3000$$

Similarly,

$$20 \ 30 \ 60 + * \ = \ 20 \ 90 \ * \ = \ 1800 \qquad \square$$

Infix Notation: Precedence and Associativity

In infix notation, operators appear between their operands; + appears between a and b in the sum $a+b$. An advantage of infix notation is that it is familiar and hence easy to read.

infix notation comes with rules for precedence and associativity

But, how is an expression like $a+b*c$ to be decoded? Is it the sum of a and $b*c$, or is it the product of $a+b$ and c? Such questions are answered in this section by introducing the concepts of precedence and associativity of operators. A grammar for infix expressions appears in Section 2.5.

The operator $*$ usually takes its operands before + does. Thus, the operands of $*$ in $a+b*c$ are b and c, and the operands of + are a and $b*c$.

An operator at a higher *precedence level* takes its operands before an operator at a lower precedence level. A traditional convention for grouping infix arithmetic expressions is that multiplication and division have higher precedence than addition and subtraction. The operators $*$ and / are usually together at the same precedence level, with the operators + and − together at a lower precedence level.[2]

Using parentheses to show the structure of infix expressions, $a+b*c$ is equivalent to $a+(b*c)$ and $d*e+f$ is equivalent to $(d*e)+f$. Without rules for specifying the relative precedence of operators, parentheses would be needed in expressions to make explicit the operands of an infix operator.

Operators with the same precedence are typically grouped from left to right. The expression $4-2-1$ is grouped as $(4-2)-1$, which evaluates to 1:

$$4 - 2 - 1 \;=\; (4 - 2) - 1 \;=\; 2 - 1 \;=\; 1$$

An incorrect result 3 is obtained if $4-2-1$ is evaluated as if it were written $4-(2-1)$.

An operator is said to be *left associative* if subexpressions containing multiple occurrences of the operator are grouped from left to right. The subtraction operator is left associative because the subtraction to the left is done first in $4-2-1$. The arithmetic operators +, −, $*$, and / are all left associative. Expression $b*b - 4*a*c$ is therefore equivalent to

$$(b * b) - ((4 * a) * c)$$

An operator is said to be *right associative* if subexpressions containing multiple occurrences of the operator are grouped from right to left. For example, exponentiation is right associative:

$$2^{3^4} = 2^{(3^4)} = 2^{81}$$

---

[2] Among the languages in this book, the Smalltalk-80 programming language in Chapter 7 is an exception to this rule. All arithmetic operators in Smalltalk have the same precedence, and expressions are read from left to right, so $a + b * c$ is equivalent to $(a + b) * c$, the product of $a+b$ and c.

Mixfix Notation

Operations specified by a combination of symbols do not fit neatly into the prefix, infix, postfix classification. For example the keywords **if**, **then**, and **else** are used together in the expression

$$\textbf{if } a > b \textbf{ then } a \textbf{ else } b$$

The meaningful components of this expression are the condition $a > b$ and the expressions a and b. If $a > b$ evaluates to true, then the value of the expression is a, otherwise, it is b.

When symbols or keywords appear interspersed with the components of an expression, the operation will be said to be in *mixfix* notation.

2.2 ABSTRACT SYNTAX TREES

The *abstract syntax* of a language identifies the meaningful components of each construct in the language. The prefix expression $+ab$, the infix expression $a + b$, and the postfix expression $ab +$ all have the same meaningful components: the operator $+$ and the subexpressions a and b. A corresponding tree representation is

A better grammar can be designed if the abstract syntax of a language is known before the grammar is specified.

Tree Representation of Expressions

A *tree* consists of a *node* with $k \geq 0$ trees as its children. When $k = 0$, a tree consists of just a node, with no children. A node with no children is called a *leaf*. The *root* of a tree is a node with no parent; that is, it is not a child of any node.

an operator and its operands are represented by a node and its children

If an expression is formed by applying an operator **op** to operands $E_1, E_2, \ldots, E_k$, for $k \geq 0$, then its tree has a node for **op** with k children, the trees for the subexpressions. A diagram for the tree is

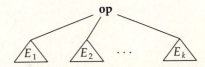

If an expression is a constant or a variable, then its tree consists of a leaf.

Example 2.3   A tree for the expression $b*b - 4*a*c$ appears in Fig. 2.1. This expression has the form $E_1 - E_2$, where E_1 is $b*b$ and E_2 is $4*a*c$. Its tree in Fig. 2.1 therefore has a node for the $-$ operator; the two children of the node are the subtrees for $b*b$ and $4*a*c$.

The subexpression $4*a*c$ has the form $E_1 * E_2$, where E_1 is $4*a$ and E_2 is c. The corresponding subtree

has a node for $*$ with the subtrees for $4*a$ and c as its children.

The subtree for the constant 4 is a leaf, a node with no or zero children.   □

Trees showing the operator/operand structure of an expression are called *abstract syntax trees*, because they show the syntactic structure of an expression independent of the notation in which the expression was originally written. The tree in Fig. 2.1 is the abstract syntax for each of the following:

PREFIX: $-\; *\; b\; b\; *\; *\; 4\; a\; c$
INFIX: $b\; *\; b\; -\; 4\; *\; a\; *\; c$
POSTFIX: $b\; b\; *\; 4\; a\; *\; c\; *\; -$

Abstract syntax trees can be extended to other constructs by making up suitable operators for the constructs. An abstract syntax tree can be built for

if $a > b$ **then** a **else** b

by creating an operator **if-then-else**:

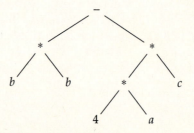

Figure 2.1   An abstract syntax tree for $b*b - 4*a*c$.

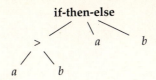

2.3 LEXICAL SYNTAX

grammars deal with units called tokens

Keywords like **if** and symbols like <= are treated as units in a programming language, just as words are treated as units in English. The meaning of the word `dote` bears no relation to the meaning of `dot`, despite the similarity of their written representations.

The two-character symbol <= is treated as a unit in Pascal; it is distinct from the one-character symbols < and =, which have different meanings of their own. See Fig. 2.2 for the written representations of common operators in Pascal and C.

Tokens and Spellings

The syntax of a programming language is specified in terms of units called *tokens* or *terminals*.

A *lexical syntax* for a language specifies the correspondence between the written representation of the language and the tokens or terminals in a grammar for the language.

Alphabetic character sequences that are treated as units in a language are called *keywords*. For example, `if` and `while` are keywords in both Pascal and C. Keywords are *reserved words* if they cannot be used as names.

The actual character sequence used to write down an occurrence of a token is called the *spelling* of that occurrence. Tokens will be written using a bold font and spellings will be written using a typewriter-like font; so the keyword **while** has spelling `while`.

Subscripts can be used to distinguish between occurrences of a token; the subscript might be the spelling for a token representing a name, or the value for a token representing a number. Using token **name** for names and token **number** for integers, the character sequence

```
b * b - 4 * a * c
```

is represented by the token sequence

$$\textbf{name}_b \ast \textbf{name}_b - \textbf{number}_4 \ast \textbf{name}_a \ast \textbf{name}_c$$

White space in the form of blank, tab, and newline characters can typically be inserted between tokens without changing the meaning of a program. Sim-

binary operation	symbol	Pascal	C
less than	<	<	<
less than or equal	≤	<=	<=
equal	=	=	==
not equal	≠	<>	!=
greater than	>	>	>
greater than or equal	≥	>=	>=
add	+	+	+
subtract	−	−	−
multiply	*	*	*
divide, reals	/	/	/
divide, integers	**div**	div	/
remainder, integer	**mod**	mod	%

Figure 2.2   The mathematical symbols for some common operations and their representations in Pascal and C. For example, $x \neq y$ is true if x is not equal to y; it is false otherwise. This expression is written in Pascal as x<>y and in C as x!=y.

ilarly, *comments* between tokens are ignored. In Pascal, comments appear between (* and *); in C, comments appear between /* and */.

Informal descriptions usually suffice for white space, comments, and the correspondence between tokens and their spellings, so lexical syntax will not be formalized in this book. Real numbers are a possible exception. The most complex rules in a lexical syntax are typically the ones describing the syntax of real numbers, because parts of the syntax are optional. The following are some of the ways of writing the same number:

```
314.E-2     3.14      0.314E+1      0.314E1
```

The leading 0 can sometimes be dropped, making .314E1 an additional possibility.

2.4 CONTEXT-FREE GRAMMARS

The *concrete syntax* of a language describes its written representation, including lexical details such as the placement of keywords and punctuation marks.

Context-free grammars, or simply grammars, are a notation for specifying concrete syntax. BNF, from Backus-Naur Form, is a way of writing grammars. Other ways of writing grammars are considered in Section 2.6.

Introduction to Grammars

context-free syntax is hierarchical

A grammar for a language imposes a hierarchical structure, called a *parse tree* on programs in the language. The following is a parse tree for the string 3.14 in a language of real numbers:

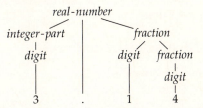

The leaves at the bottom of a parse tree are labeled with terminals or tokens like 3; tokens represent themselves. By contrast, the other nodes of a parse tree are labeled with *nonterminals* like *real-number* and *digit*; nonterminals represent language constructs. Each node in the parse tree is based on a *production*, a rule that defines a nonterminal in terms of a sequence of terminals and nonterminals. The root of the parse tree for 3.14 is based on the following informally stated production:

A real number consists of an integer part, a point, and a fraction part.

Together, the tokens, the nonterminals, the productions, and a distinguished nonterminal, called the *starting nonterminal*, constitute a grammar for a language. The starting nonterminal may represent a portion of a complete program when fragments of a programming language are studied.

Both tokens and nonterminals are referred to as *grammar symbols*, or simply *symbols*.

Definition of Context-Free Grammars

Given a set of symbols, a *string* over the set is a finite sequence of zero or more symbols from the set. The number of symbols in the sequence is said to be the *length* of the string. The length of the string `teddy` is 5. An *empty* string is a string of length zero.

A *context-free grammar*, or simply *grammar*, has four parts:

1. A set of tokens or terminals; these are the atomic symbols in the language.
2. A set of nonterminals; these are the variables representing constructs in the language.
3. A set of rules called productions for identifying the components of a construct. Each production has a nonterminal as its left side, the symbol ::=, and a string over the sets of terminals and nonterminals as its right side.
4. A nonterminal chosen as the starting nonterminal; it represents the main construct of the language.

Unless otherwise stated, the productions for the starting nonterminal appear first.

BNF: Backus-Naur Form

The concept of a context-free grammar, consisting of terminals, nonterminals, productions, and a starting nonterminal, is independent of the notation used to write grammars. Backus-Naur Form (BNF) is one such notation, made popular by its use to organize the report on the Algol 60 programming language.

A BNF grammar for real numbers appears in Fig. 2.3.

Terminals and Nonterminals

In BNF, nonterminals are enclosed between the special symbols ⟨ and ⟩, and the empty string is written as ⟨*empty*⟩. Terminals consisting of symbols like + and * usually appear as is, but they can be quoted for emphasis.

The nonterminals of the grammar are written as ⟨*real-number*⟩, ⟨*integer-part*⟩, ⟨*fraction*⟩, and ⟨*digit*⟩. The tokens are the digits 0, 1, . . . , 9 and the decimal point.

Productions

Read the symbol ::= as "can be" and read the symbol | as "or." Then,

---

$$
\begin{array}{rcl}
\langle real\text{-}number\rangle & ::= & \langle integer\text{-}part\rangle \; . \; \langle fraction\rangle \\
\langle integer\text{-}part\rangle & ::= & \langle digit\rangle \mid \langle integer\text{-}part\rangle \; \langle digit\rangle \\
\langle fraction\rangle & ::= & \langle digit\rangle \mid \langle digit\rangle \; \langle fraction\rangle \\
\langle digit\rangle & ::= & 0 \mid 1 \mid 2 \mid 3 \mid 4 \mid 5 \mid 6 \mid 7 \mid 8 \mid 9
\end{array}
$$

Figure 2.3 BNF rules for real numbers.

$$\langle \mathit{fraction} \rangle \ ::= \ \langle \mathit{digit} \rangle \mid \langle \mathit{digit} \rangle \langle \mathit{fraction} \rangle$$

can be read aloud as, "A fraction part can be a digit, or it can be a digit followed by a fraction part." For example, a fraction part can be a single digit 2 or it can be a digit followed by another fraction part, as in 142, where digit 1 is followed by 42.

Each alternative separated by $\mid$ is a distinct rule, so this notation can be rewritten equivalently as

$$\langle \mathit{fraction} \rangle \ ::= \ \langle \mathit{digit} \rangle$$
$$\langle \mathit{fraction} \rangle \ ::= \ \langle \mathit{digit} \rangle \langle \mathit{fraction} \rangle$$

It is sometimes convenient to use subscripts on the right side, as in

$$\langle \mathit{fraction} \rangle \ ::= \ \langle \mathit{digit} \rangle \langle \mathit{fraction}_1 \rangle$$

to distinguish between occurrences of a construct. If nonterminal *fraction* represents 789, then *digit* represents 7 and $\mathit{fraction}_1$ represents 89.

The variable $\langle \mathit{empty} \rangle$ represents an empty string of length 0. It is useful for specifying optional constructs.

For example, suppose that the 0 in 0.5 is optional. This syntax is specified by the rules

$$\langle \mathit{real} \rangle \ ::= \ \langle \mathit{integer\text{-}part} \rangle \ . \ \langle \mathit{fractional\text{-}part} \rangle$$
$$\langle \mathit{integer\text{-}part} \rangle \ ::= \ \langle \mathit{empty} \rangle \mid \langle \mathit{digit\text{-}sequence} \rangle$$
$$\langle \mathit{fractional\text{-}part} \rangle \ ::= \ \langle \mathit{digit\text{-}sequence} \rangle$$

In words, a real number has an integer part, a decimal point, and a fractional part. The integer part is an optional digit sequence; the fractional part is a digit sequence. It follows from the rule

$$\langle \mathit{integer\text{-}part} \rangle \ ::= \ \langle \mathit{empty} \rangle$$

that the integer part can be empty, as in ".5", where the one-digit sequence 5 is the fractional part.

Parse Trees Depict Concrete Syntax

The productions in a grammar are rules for building strings of tokens. A parse tree shows how a string can be built.

A parse tree with respect to a grammar is a tree satisfying the following:

- Each leaf is labeled with a terminal or $\langle \mathit{empty} \rangle$, representing the empty string.

- Each nonleaf node is labeled with a nonterminal.
- The label of a nonleaf node is the left side of some production and the labels of the children of the node, from left to right, form the right side of that production.
- The root is labeled with the starting nonterminal.

A parse tree *generates* the string formed by reading the terminals at its leaves from left to right. A string is in a language if and only if it is generated by some parse tree. The construction of a parse tree is called *parsing*.

Example 2.4   A nonleaf node labeled *real-number* with three children *integer-part*, "." and *fraction*,

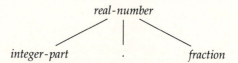

can appear in a parse tree with respect to the grammar in Fig. 2.3.

The nonterminals *integer-part* and *fraction* impose different hierarchical structures on strings of digits. In the parse tree for the real number 123.789 in Fig. 2.4, note how the portion of the tree that generates 123 grows down to the left, whereas the portion of the tree that generates 789 grows down to the right. Semantic considerations influence the choice of hierarchical structure, and hence the choice of productions for a nonterminal.[3]   □

Parse trees for realistic programs are large enough that *parsing*, the job of constructing parse trees, is best done by a computer.

Syntactic Ambiguity

A grammar for a language is *syntactically ambiguous*, or simply *ambiguous*, if some string in its language has more than one parse tree. Programming languages can usually be described by unambiguous grammars. If ambiguities exist, they are *resolved* by establishing conventions that rule out all but one parse tree for each string.

The following grammar is ambiguous, since the string $1-0-1$ has two parse trees, corresponding to the parenthesizations $(1-0)-1$ and $1-(0-1)$:

$$E ::= E - E \mid 0 \mid 1$$

---

[3] The choice of productions for the integer part and the fraction part is influenced by the rules for determining the values of these parts. The grouping to the left in the integer part allows the value 123 to be constructed from 12 and 3; it is $12*10+3$. The grouping to the right in the fraction part allows the value 0.789 to be constructed from 0.7 and 0.89; it is $0.7 + 0.89/10$.

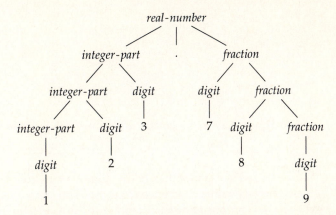

Figure 2.4   A parse tree with respect to the expression grammar in Fig. 2.3. It generates 123.789.

The two possible parse trees for $1 - 0 - 1$ are

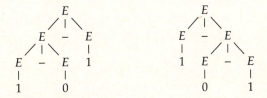

Dangling-Else Ambiguity

A well-known example of syntactic ambiguity is the *dangling-else* ambiguity, which arises if a grammar has the two productions

    S ::= **if** E **then** S
    S ::= **if** E **then** S **else** S

where S represents statements and E represents expressions. Neither production by itself leads to an ambiguity. Together, however, they permit constructions like the following, where it is not clear to which **if** an **else** belongs:

    if E_1 **then if** E_2 **then** S_1 **else** S_2

This construction motivates the example in Fig. 2.5, which shows only the relevant parts of two parse trees. Subtrees below some of the nodes are omit-

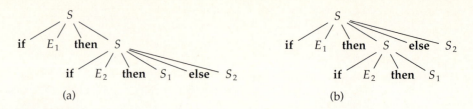

Figure 2.5   In (a) the **else** is matched with the nearest unmatched **if**.

ted. The subscripts in the figure on symbols S and E simply distinguish between the occurrences of these symbols.

The dangling-else ambiguity is typically resolved by matching an **else** with the nearest unmatched **if**. Thus, the alternative in Fig. 2.5(a) is chosen.

Derivations

A *top-down* parser works from the root (top) of a parse tree toward the leaves. A *bottom-up* parser works from the leaves (bottom) of a parse tree toward the root.

The following sequence of partial parse trees illustrates the beginning of a top-down parse for the token stream 21.89 (the symbol $\Rightarrow$ separates trees in the sequence):

$$
\textit{real-number} \quad \Rightarrow \quad
\begin{array}{c}
\textit{real-number}\\
\diagup\ |\ \diagdown\\
\textit{integer-part}\ .\ \textit{fraction}
\end{array}
\quad \Rightarrow \quad
\begin{array}{c}
\textit{real-number}\\
\diagup\quad\diagdown\\
\textit{integer-part}\qquad\\
\diagup\ \diagdown\qquad\\
\textit{integer-part}\ \textit{digit}\ .\ \textit{fraction}
\end{array}
$$

The trees are drawn so their leaves line up; nonterminals at the leaves represent uncompleted subtrees. If we look only at the leaves in the snapshots, and ignore the rest of the tree, we get a sequence called a derivation:

$$\textit{real-number} \Rightarrow \textit{integer-part . fraction} \Rightarrow \textit{integer-part digit . fraction} \Rightarrow$$

A *derivation* consists of a sequence of strings, beginning with the starting nonterminal. Each successive string is obtained by replacing a nonterminal by the right side of one of its productions. A derivation ends with a string consisting entirely of terminals.

The following derivation begins with the starting nonterminal *real-number* and ends with the string of terminals 21.89. In each snapshot, the leftmost nonterminal is replaced by the right side of one of its productions:

$$real\text{-}number \Rightarrow integer\text{-}part \, . \, fraction$$

$$\Rightarrow integer\text{-}part \; digit \, . \, fraction$$

$$\Rightarrow digit \; digit \, . \, fraction$$

$$\Rightarrow 2 \; digit \, . \, fraction$$

$$\Rightarrow 2 \; 1 \, . \, fraction$$

$$\Rightarrow 2 \; 1 \, . \, digit \; fraction$$

$$\Rightarrow 2 \; 1 \, . \, 8 \; fraction$$

$$\Rightarrow 2 \; 1 \, . \, 8 \; digit$$

$$\Rightarrow 2 \; 1 \, . \, 8 \; 9$$

2.5 GRAMMARS FOR EXPRESSIONS

A well-designed grammar can make it easy to pick out the meaningful components of a construct. In other words, with a well-designed grammar, parse trees are similar enough to abstract syntax trees that the grammar can be used to organize a language description or a program that exploits the syntax. An example of a program that exploits syntax is an expression evaluator that analyzes and evaluates expressions.

after expressions, the remaining syntax is often easy

The grammars for expressions in this section take associativity and precedence into account. Once expressions are specified, the rest of the syntax of a language often falls into place; this is especially true for bracketed constructs that begin and end with keywords or other punctuation marks. The syntax of statements is considered in Chapter 3.

This section begins with a grammar for arithmetic expressions. We then consider the influence of associativity and precedence on the design of grammars for expressions.

Lists in Infix Expressions

An expression $a+b+c+d$ can be treated as a list of elements separated by + symbols; the elements are called *terms*. Since $*$ has higher precedence than +, the expression $a*b+c*d+e$ can be viewed as a list of terms $a*b, c*d$ and e, separated by + symbols.

The idea of lists carries over to terms. A term $4*a*c$ can itself be treated as a list of elements separated by $*$ symbols; the elements are called *factors*.

This list-oriented approach motivates the grammar in Fig. 2.6. Nonterminals E, T, and F represent expressions, terms, and factors, respectively.

The partial parse trees

$$E \ ::= \ E + T \ | \ E - T \ | \ T$$
$$T \ ::= \ T * F \ | \ T / F \ | \ F$$
$$F \ ::= \ \textbf{number} \ | \ \textbf{name} \ | \ (\ E \ )$$

Figure 2.6 A grammar for arithmetic expressions.

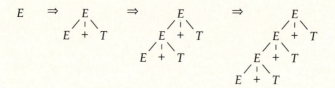

illustrate the use of the productions to generate a list of terms. Each time one of the productions

$$E ::= E + T$$
$$| \ E - T$$

is applied, another term is added at the beginning of the list. The list stops growing when the production

$$E ::= T$$

is applied. These productions allow a list of terms to be separated by either + or − symbols.

The productions for T are similar to those for E.

The complete parse tree in Fig. 2.7 generates the string

$$\textbf{number}_7 * \textbf{number}_7 - \textbf{number}_4 * \textbf{number}_2 * \textbf{number}_3$$

From Abstract to Concrete Syntax

A grammar for a language is usually designed to reflect the abstract syntax; that is, the productions are chosen so that parse trees are as close as possible to abstract syntax trees. The abstract syntax

$$E_1 \quad \overset{\textbf{op}}{\diagup \diagdown} \quad E_2$$

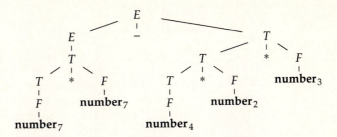

Figure 2.7 A parse tree with respect to the expression grammar in Fig. 2.6.

describes an expression built up by applying a binary operator **op** to two subexpressions E_1 and E_2. If **op** is +, then the value of E is the sum of the values of E_1 and E_2. Otherwise, if **op** is ∗, then the value of E is the product of the values of E_1 and E_2, and so on.

When expressions are written in infix notation, we need a grammar that makes it easy to identify the subexpressions of an expression.

Handling Associativity

Consider infix expressions formed by applying the addition and subtraction operators to numbers. Some examples are

    4 − 2 − 1
    9 + 7 − 5 − 3

Since + and − are left associative, their abstract syntax trees grow down to the left:

The following is a suitable grammar for left associative operators + and − applied to sequences of numbers:

$$L ::= L + \textbf{number}$$
$$| \quad L - \textbf{number}$$
$$| \quad \textbf{number}$$

A less desirable grammar is

$$R ::= \textbf{number} + R$$
$$| \ \textbf{number} - R$$
$$| \ \textbf{number}$$

Parse trees for $4 - 2 - 1$ with respect to these two grammars appear in Fig. 2.8. Although both grammars are unambiguous, the grammar with starting nonterminal L is more suitable for left associative operators because its parse trees grow down and to the left, so they are closer to the abstract syntax of expressions. (Similarly, the grammar with starting nonterminal R is more suitable for right associative operators.)

Since $-$ is left associative, the subexpressions of

$$4 - 2 - 1$$

are $4-2$ and 1. These subexpressions are easier to identify when $4 - 2 - 1$ is generated by the production $L ::= L_1 - \textbf{number}$ than the production $R ::= \textbf{number} - R$. At the root of the parse tree in Fig. 2.8, L generates $4-2-1$, L_1 generates $4-2$, and **number** generates 1.

Handling Associativity and Precedence

The syntax of expressions in a language can be characterized by a table giving the associativity and precedence of operators. For example, a fairly complete table of binary operators in C appears in Fig. 2.9. All operators on the same line have the same associativity and precedence. The assignment operator = in C is right associative; the remaining operators in Fig. 2.9 are left associative.

use one nonterminal per precedence level, and one for factors

A grammar for expressions can be designed by choosing a nonterminal for each precedence level or line in a table such as Fig. 2.9. An additional nonterminal is needed for the "factors" or smallest subexpressions. For example, consider the following table with three precedence levels (in order of increasing precedence):

Figure 2.8 Parse trees with respect to two grammars.

assignment	=
logical or	||
logical and	&&
inclusive or	|
exclusive or	^
and	&
equality	== !=
relational	< <= >= >
shift	<< >>
additive	+ -
multiplicative	* / %

Figure 2.9   A partial table of binary operators in C, in order of increasing precedence; that is, the assignment operator = has the lowest precedence and the multiplicative operators *, /, and % have the highest precedence. All operators on the same line have the same precedence and associativity. The assignment operator is right associative; all the other operators are left associative.

$:=$ right associative

$+$ $-$ left associative

$*$ $/$ left associative

Let the nonterminals for the three levels be A, E, and T, and let F be the nonterminal for the factors. Since the assignment operator $:=$ is right associative, the productions for A correspond to those for nonterminal R in the parse tree in Fig. 2.8. The productions for E and T correspond to those for nonterminal L. The grammar is

$$A \ ::= \ E := A \ | \ \ E$$
$$E \ ::= \ E + T \ | E - T \ | T$$
$$T \ ::= \ T * F \ | \ T / F \ | F$$
$$F \ ::= \ (E) \ | \ \textbf{name} \ | \ \textbf{number}$$

2.6 VARIANTS OF GRAMMARS

the variants,
EBNF and syntax
charts, are for
convenience

The running example of this section is a grammar for arithmetic expressions like $b*b+4*a*c$. The grammar, written in BNF in Fig. 2.10, will be rewritten in two other notations called EBNF and syntax charts.

EBNF is an extension of BNF that allows lists and optional elements to be specified. Lists or sequences of elements appear frequently in the syntax of programming languages. The appeal of EBNF is convenience, not additional capability, since anything that can be specified with EBNF can also be specified using BNF.

Syntax charts are a graphical notation for grammars. They have visual appeal; again, anything that can be specified using syntax charts can also be specified using BNF.

Extended BNF

Lists or sequences of elements, be they of statements, declarations, or parameters, can be classified by asking the following questions:

- Can the sequence be empty? That is, can it have zero elements?
- Does a delimiter, if any, separate elements or terminate them? A delimiter *separates* elements if it appears between them. A delimiter *terminates* elements if it appears after each element.

EBNF has
shortcuts for lists

In a representative extension of BNF, braces { and }, represent zero or more repetitions of the enclosed string. Thus,

   { ⟨*statement*⟩ ; }

$$
\begin{aligned}
\langle expression \rangle \ ::= \ & \langle expression \rangle + \langle term \rangle \\
 | \ & \langle expression \rangle - \langle term \rangle \\
 | \ & \langle term \rangle \\[4pt]
\langle term \rangle \ ::= \ & \langle term \rangle * \langle factor \rangle \\
 | \ & \langle term \rangle / \langle factor \rangle \\
 | \ & \langle factor \rangle \\[4pt]
\langle factor \rangle \ ::= \ & \textbf{number} \\
 | \ & \textbf{name} \\
 | \ & (\ \langle expression \rangle \ )
\end{aligned}
$$

Figure 2.10   BNF syntactic rules for arithmetic expressions.

---

represents zero or more statements terminated by semicolons. The production

$$\langle statement\text{-}list \rangle \ ::= \ \{ \ \langle statement \rangle \ ; \ \}$$

is equivalent to the pair of BNF productions

$$\langle statement\text{-}list \rangle \ ::= \ \langle empty \rangle$$
$$| \ \langle statement \rangle \ ; \ \langle statement\text{-}list \rangle$$

Such extensions to BNF are shortcuts; they may reduce the number of productions and nonterminals, but they do not change what can be specified.

Another common extension is the use of [and] to enclose an optional construct. For example, an optional integer part in a real number can be specified by the following:

$$\langle real\text{-}number \rangle \ ::= \ [\langle integer\text{-}part \rangle] \ . \ \langle fraction \rangle$$

The production is equivalent to the pair of BNF productions

$$\langle real\text{-}number \rangle \ ::= \ \langle integer\text{-}part \rangle \ . \ \langle fraction \rangle$$
$$| \ . \ \langle fraction \rangle$$

The term EBNF simply means an extension of BNF. Here is a representative definition:

- Braces, { and }, represent zero or more repetitions.
- Brackets, [and], represent an optional construct.
- A vertical bar, | represents a choice.
- Parentheses, (and), are used for grouping.

Symbols such as { and }, which have a special status in a language description, are called *metasymbols*.

EBNF has many more metasymbols than BNF. Furthermore, these same symbols can also appear in the syntax of a language—the index i in $A[i]$ is not optional—so care is needed to distinguish tokens from metasymbols. Confusion between tokens and metasymbols will be avoided by enclosing tokens within single quotes if needed, as in '('.

An EBNF version of the grammar in Fig. 2.6 is

$$\langle expression \rangle \ ::= \ \langle term \rangle \ \{ \ (+|-) \ \langle term \rangle \ \}$$
$$\langle term \rangle \ ::= \ \langle factor \rangle \ \{ \ (*|/) \ \langle factor \rangle \ \}$$
$$\langle factor \rangle \ ::= \ \text{'('} \ \langle expression \rangle \ \text{')'} \ | \ \textbf{name} \ | \ \textbf{number}$$

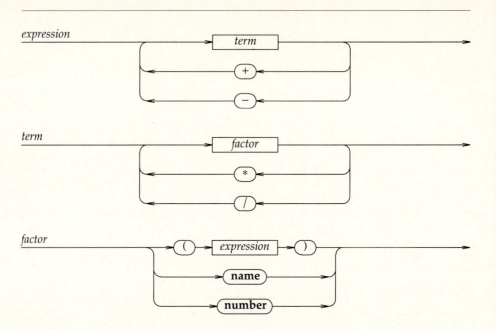

Figure 2.11   A syntax chart corresponding to the BNF grammar in Fig. 2.6. Note that the paths through the subcharts for *expression* and *term* have loops, but the subchart for *factor* does not.

Here ⟨*term*⟩ { (+|−) ⟨*term*⟩ } represents a sequence of one or more terms separated by either + or − symbols. The parentheses around +|− ensure that the vertical bar represents a choice between + and −. In the right side for ⟨*factor*⟩, parentheses are quoted because they are tokens.

Syntax Charts

paths in syntax charts are like productions

A *syntax chart*, syntax graph, or syntax diagram, is another way of writing a grammar. There is a subchart for each nonterminal, as in Fig. 2.11. Each path through a subchart corresponds to a production for the nonterminal. Along the path are the terminals and nonterminals on the right side of the production; the terminals are enclosed in rounded boxes and the nonterminals in rectangular boxes.

Besides their visual appeal, an advantage of syntax charts is that all of the nonterminals in a chart are meaningful. With BNF, it is sometimes necessary to make up auxiliary nonterminals to achieve the effect of alternative paths and loops in a syntax chart.

Exercises

2.1 Rewrite the following expressions in prefix notation. Treat *sqrt* as an operator with one argument.

a. $a * b + c$

b. $a * (b + c)$

c. $a * b + c * d$

d. $a * (b + c) * d$

e. $(b/2 + sqrt((b/2) * (b/2) - a*c))/a$

2.2 Rewrite the expressions of Exercise 2.1 in postfix notation.

2.3 Draw abstract syntax trees for the expressions in Exercise 2.1.

2.4 Give context-free grammars describing the syntax of each of the following:

a. Strings of length one or more over the set of terminals {**blank**, **tab**, **newline**}.

b. Sequences of letters or digits, starting with a letter.

c. Real numbers in which either the integer part or the fractional part can be empty, but not both. Thus, the grammar must allow 31., 3.1, and .13, but not a decimal point by itself.

2.5 Consider the grammar for real numbers in Fig. 2.3.

a. Give a leftmost derivation of the string 2.89.

b. Draw tree snapshots corresponding to the derivation in (a).

2.6 For each of the following strings, draw a parse tree with respect to the grammar for arithmetic expressions in Fig. 2.6:

a. $2 + 3$

b. $(2 + 3)$

c. $2 + 3 * 5$

d. $(2 + 3) * 5$

e. $2 + (3 * 5)$

2.7 Draw abstract syntax trees for the expressions in Exercise 2.6.

2.8 Postfix expressions can be evaluated with the help of the stack data structure, as follows:

1. Scan the postfix notation from left to right.

    a. On seeing a constant, push it onto the stack.

    b. On seeing a binary operator, pop two values from the top of the stack, apply the operator to the values, and push the result back onto the stack.

2. After the entire postfix notation is scanned, the value of the expression is on top of the stack.

Illustrate the use of a stack to evaluate the expression 7 7 * 4 2 * 3 * −.

2.9 The BNF rules in each of the following cases describe a construct that consists of a list of elements. Describe the list. How many elements does it have? Does anything appear between or after the elements?

a. ⟨*name-list*⟩   ::= ⟨*name*⟩
             | ⟨*name*⟩ , ⟨*name-list*⟩

b. ⟨*field-list*⟩   ::= ⟨*field*⟩ ;
             | ⟨*field*⟩ ; ⟨*field-list*⟩

c. ⟨*statement-list*⟩   ::= ⟨*empty*⟩
             | ⟨*statement*⟩ ; ⟨*statement-list*⟩

d. ⟨*term*⟩   ::= ⟨*term*⟩ * ⟨*factor*⟩
             | ⟨*factor*⟩

e. ⟨*variables*⟩   ::= ⟨*empty*⟩
             | **var** ⟨*var-decls*⟩
  ⟨*var-decls*⟩   ::= ⟨*name-list*⟩ : ⟨*type*⟩ ;
             | ⟨*name-list*⟩ : ⟨*type*⟩ ; ⟨*var-decls*⟩

f. ⟨*constants*⟩   ::= ⟨*empty*⟩
             | ⟨*const-decls*⟩
  ⟨*const-decls*⟩   ::= **const** ⟨*name*⟩ = ⟨*constant*⟩ ;
             | ⟨*const-decls*⟩ ⟨*name*⟩ = ⟨*constant*⟩ ;

2.10 The operators of Pascal are as follows:

```
< <= = <> >= > in      in tests set membership
+ - or
* / div mod and
not
```

All of these operators are left associative. All operators on the same line have the same precedence. The lines are in order of increasing precedence.
a. Write an expression grammar for Pascal.
b. Extend your grammar to handle expressions with a leading minus sign, to allow −1 and − (a−b), but not 2 + − 3.

2.11 For each of the following expressions, draw parse trees with respect to your grammar for Exercise 2.10.
a. i >= 0
b. (i >= 0) and not p
c. i >= 0 and not p
d. (i >= 0) and (x <> y)

2.12 Write an expression grammar using the table of C operators in Fig. 2.9.

2.13 For each of the following expressions, draw parse trees with respect to your grammar for Exercise 2.12.
a. i >= 0
b. (i >= 0) && ! p
c. i >= 0 && ! p
d. i >= 0 && x != y

2.14 The following grammar is based on the syntax of statements in Pascal:

$$
\begin{array}{lll}
S & ::= & \textbf{id} := \textbf{expr} \\
  & | & \textbf{if expr then } S \\
  & | & \textbf{if expr then } S \textbf{ else } S \\
  & | & \textbf{while expr do } S \\
  & | & \textbf{begin } SL \textbf{ end} \\
SL & ::= & S \text{ ;} \\
   & | & S \text{ ; } SL
\end{array}
$$

Draw parse trees for each of the following:
a. while expr do id := **expr**
b. begin id := **expr end**
c. if expr then if expr then *S* **else** *S*

2.15 The following grammar is motivated by declarations in C:

$$
\begin{array}{lll}
\textit{Declaration} & ::= & \textit{Type Declarator } ; \\
\textit{Type} & ::= & \textbf{int} \\
 & | & \textbf{char} \\
\textit{Declarator} & ::= & * \textit{ Declarator} \\
 & | & \textit{Declarator } '[' \textbf{ number } ']' \\
 & | & \textit{Declarator } '(' \textit{ Type } ')' \\
 & | & '(' \textit{ Declarator } ')' \\
 & | & \textbf{name}
\end{array}
$$

a. Prove the syntactic ambiguity of this grammar by finding a string that has more than one parse tree. Draw the parse trees.
b. The constructs '[' **number** ']' and '(' *Type* ')' can be thought of as being postfix operators with a declarator as an operand. Suppose that * has lower precedence than these operators. Write an unambiguous grammar that generates the same strings as this grammar and makes it easy to identify the components of a declarator.
c. Suppose that the first production for *Declarator* is changed to make * a postfix operator. Why is the resulting grammar unambiguous?

2.16 The following EBNF grammar is based on the syntax of statements in the Modula-2 programming language:

$$
\begin{aligned}
S \;\; ::= \;\; & [\,] \\
| \;\; & \textbf{id} := \textbf{expr} \\
| \;\; & \textbf{if expr then } SL \;\{ \textbf{ elsif expr then } SL \;\} \; [\textbf{ else } SL \;] \textbf{ end} \\
| \;\; & \textbf{loop } SL \textbf{ end} \\
| \;\; & \textbf{while expr do } SL \textbf{ end} \\
SL \;\; ::= \;\; & S \;\{ \; ; \; S \;\}
\end{aligned}
$$

Token **id** represents a variable and token **expr** represents an expression. Note that [ ] stands for the empty string.

a. Write a BNF version of this grammar.

b. Write a syntax chart for this grammar.

2.17 Describe how you would construct an EBNF grammar from a syntax chart.

2.18 Describe how you would construct a BNF grammar from an EBNF grammar.

2.19 The dangling-else ambiguity arises if a grammar has the following two productions

$$
\begin{aligned}
S \;\; ::= \;\; & \textbf{if } E \textbf{ then } S \\
S \;\; ::= \;\; & \textbf{if } E \textbf{ then } S \textbf{ else } S
\end{aligned}
$$

Write an unambiguous grammar that generates the same conditionals and matches an **else** with the nearest unmatched **if** (see Abrahams [1966]).

2.20 In a table of operators, such as that in Fig. 2.9, why do all operators at the same precedence level have the same associativity (either all left associative or all right associative)?

2.21 The following grammar generates numbers in binary notation:

$$
\begin{aligned}
C \;\; ::= \;\; & C \; 0 \;\;|\;\; A \; 1 \;\;|\;\; 0 \\
A \;\; ::= \;\; & B \; 0 \;\;|\;\; C \; 1 \;\;|\;\; 1 \\
B \;\; ::= \;\; & A \; 0 \;\;|\;\; B \; 1
\end{aligned}
$$

a. Show that the generated numbers are all multiples of 3.

b. Show that all such numbers are generated by the grammar.

Bibliographic Notes

Grammars were introduced independently by Chomsky [1956] and Backus [1960]. Backus's notation was immediately adopted for describing Algol 60, and has come to be called Backus-Naur Form (BNF); Naur [1963a] edited the Algol 60 report. It was later learned that a notation similar to BNF was used by Panini between 400 B.C. and 200 B.C. to describe the complex rules of Sanskrit grammar (Ingerman [1967]).

McCarthy [1963] introduced a specific form of abstract syntax with predicates to recognize a construct and functions to extract its components. He argued that an abstract syntax was all that was needed to translate a language or define its semantics. "That is why we do not care whether sums are represented by $a + b$, or $+ab$, or (PLUS A B), or even by Gödel numbers $7^a 11^b$."

Syntax has been studied extensively; more information can be found in books on compilers, such as Aho, Sethi, and Ullman [1986].

Gannon and Horning [1975] suggest that semicolons are less likely to be misplaced if statements are terminated rather than separated by semicolons. Exercise 2.15 is based on Sethi [1981].

Taylor, Turner, and Waychoff [1961] is an early reference for syntax charts.

II

IMPERATIVE PROGRAMMING

Part II, consisting of Chapters 3 through 5, contains the core concepts of imperative programming, embodied in languages like Pascal and C. Both were designed around 1970, Pascal as a teaching language, and C as an implementation language, together with the UNIX operating system. The facilities provided by Pascal and C are developed enough that later languages have simply borrowed them, and built on them.

The progression in Part II is as follows: statements, data structures, procedures. Statements are constructs for directing the flow of control through a program. Fortran was a big improvement over machine and assembly languages because it improved the readability of programs at the expression level. But, Fortran continued to rely on **goto** statements, making it hard to grasp the flow of control through Fortran-like programs. Better statement constructs came with Algol 60, although it took nearly a decade for a disciplined or structured approach to programming to take hold.

Chapter 3 deals with structured programming at the statement level, with program fragments that are small enough to be grasped in their entirety by one person. Typical constructs are **while**-**do** for looping and **begin**-**end** for statement grouping.

Basic values like integers, which can be held in machine locations, are first-class citizens in imperative languages. The designation "first class" means that basic values can be used freely; for example, in Pascal, integer values can be compared for inequality as in $x \neq 0$, read using *read*, and assigned as in $i := 1$. Data objects that are not built into an imperative language have to be programmed explicitly: They have to be laid out or represented using the data structuring facilities of the language; and, operations on them have to be specified using procedures.

Chapter 4 deals with data structures, including arrays, records, and pointers. For example, entries for the index to a book consist of an index term and a page number. An index term can be represented as a sequence of characters; a page number can be represented as an integer. These representations can be manipulated using procedures.

Chapter 5 deals with procedures, especially the use of names within procedures. Names like *x* can be used in different senses in different procedures — the scope rules of a language determine which sense applies to an occurrence of *x*. Variable names in imperative languages denote storage locations for holding values, so the emphasis in Chapter 5 is on the storage allocation for names in procedures.

The discussion in Part II applies broadly to imperative languages. This material must not, however, simply be a recitation of features from various languages. The experience of using a language depends on how its features work together; for example, although Pascal and C both provide arrays, records, and pointers, the style and feel of the languages is different.

The discussion is clothed primarily in Pascal, since Pascal is widely used as a teaching language. A few times, Pascal is compared with Modula-2, an evolutionary successor that might easily have been named Pascal-2; the same person, Niklaus Wirth, designed them both. At other times, Pascal is compared with C.

Fig. II.1 is intended as a roadmap to be consulted from time to time while reading Part II. Here, we mention some differences between

```
     read(x);
  2: if x = 0 then goto 8;
     writeln(x);
  4: read(next);
     if next = x then goto 4;
     x := next;
     goto 2;
  8: ;
```

(a) Using goto statements

```
  read(x);
  while x ≠ 0 do begin
      writeln(x);
      repeat
          read(next);
      until next ≠ x;
      x := next;
  end;
```

(b) Using structured
    statements

```
  readentry(e);
  while not endmarker(e) do begin
      writeentry(e);
      repeat
          readentry(f)
      until not equalentry(e, f);
      copyentry(e, f);
  end;
```

(c) Using procedures

Figure II.1   Three program fragments for illustrating imperative programming, using the syntax of Pascal. The problem they address, introduced in Section 3.1, is to remove adjacent duplicates from a list of entries. Fragment (a) uses **goto** statements the way Fortran programs do. In Fragment (b), the flow of control follows the syntactic structure. Fragment (c) uses procedures to manipulate list entries; it can thus be used not only for integer entries but for entries of any type.
Fragment (b) is from Section 3.2 and Fragment (c) is from Section 4.7.

the program fragments in the figure; the fragments themselves will be discussed in the sections they are taken from.

The fragment in Fig. II.1(a) corresponds roughly to programming with **goto** statements in Fortran. It is more readable than the machine-level program within the RAM in Fig. 1.1 on page 6, but we can do better.

The fragment in Fig. II.1(b) is taken from page 68. The benefit of constructs like **while-do** for looping and **begin-end** for statement grouping is that control flows in a disciplined way through these constructs.

The fragment in Fig. II.1(b) deals with integer values; it is almost a complete program, since basic values like integers and characters are built into imperative languages. The fragment in Fig. II.1(c) manipulates entries for the index to a book; entries have to be represented using the data structuring facilities and manipulated using procedures, so there is a fair amount of code that is not shown.

3

Statements:
Structured Programming

Eventually, one of our aims is to make such well-structured programs that the intellectual effort (measured in some loose sense) needed to understand them is proportional to program length (measured in some equally loose sense).

— Dijkstra [1972] proposing that statements be designed so that "progress through the computation" can be understood in terms of "progress through the text."

In imperative programming,

- the values of variables can change as a program runs, and
- programs — what we write — are not the same as computations — the actions that occur when a program runs.

These motivate the two key concepts in this chapter: structured statements and invariants.

3.1 THE NEED FOR STRUCTURED PROGRAMMING

values of variables can change The basic units of imperative programming are *actions*, which can change the values of variables. A typical action is an assignment. The following assignment changes the value of variable x:

$$x := 2+3$$

The assignment symbol := appears between the variable x and the expression $2+3$. This assignment computes the value 5 of the expression $2+3$ and associates it with x; the old value of x is forgotten.

The array is the only data structure in this chapter. An array supports random access to a sequence of elements of the same type. Random access means that elements can be selected by their position in the sequence. An assignment

$$x := A[i]$$

assigns to x the value of the ith element of array A. The assignment

$$A[i] := x$$

changes the value of $A[i]$ to that of x.

The actions in this chapter include procedure calls. We will use them primarily for input/output, as in

$$read(x)$$
$$writeln(x)$$

Here, $read$ and $writeln$ are names of procedures, and x is a parameter. A procedure call can change the values of variables; $read(x)$ changes the value of x. Predefined procedures will be used without explaining how they are implemented; see Chapter 5 for more on procedures.

Static Programs, Dynamic Computations

programs specify computations

A *sequential computation* consists of a sequence of actions, such as

$$writeln(1, 1*1)$$
$$writeln(2, 2*2)$$
$$writeln(3, 3*3)$$

A program is a succinct representation of the computation that occurs when the program runs. A few lines in a program can be executed over and over again, possibly leading to a long computation. For example, the above sequence of three actions can be specified succinctly by the following program in pseudocode:

for i from 1 to 3 **do** $writeln(i, i*i)$

The program text specifies that $writeln(i, i*i)$ is to be executed three times, with i taking on the values 1, 2, and 3.

The computation set up by the following program is repetitive; however, the number of repetitions is not known in advance:

> **while** there is input **do** something

The program text specifies the something that is to be done and the condition for doing it.

Thus, the static text of a program is distinct from the dynamic computations that occur when the program runs. Problems occur if a reader of a program cannot readily understand the actions that occur when the program runs. These problems have motivated the design of language constructs that are easy to understand.

Design Principles for Imperative Languages

structure and efficiency

The control-flow constructs in Section 3.2 are designed with the following principle in mind:

> *Structured programming.* The structure of the program text should help us understand what the program does.

The emphasis on structure and correctness is independent of efficiency. Carefully designed structured programs can be just as efficient as unstructured ones. In fact, the readability of structured programs can make them easier to modify and tune for efficiency.

In reality, efficient use of the underlying machine has always been a primary design goal for imperative languages. Language designers have achieved efficiency by staying true to the machine, using the following design principle:

> *Efficiency.* A language must allow an underlying assignment-oriented machine to be used directly and efficiently.

Efficiency is likely to remain a driving influence.

A Running Example

careful program design pays

Language constructs will be illustrated by considering the following problem: Remove adjacent duplicates from a list of elements. For example, the removal of adjacent duplicates from

> 1 1 2 2 2 3 1 4 4

yields the list

> 1 2 3 1 4

The remaining occurrences of 1 are not adjacent.

This problem can be solved by treating the input not as a list of elements, but as a list of runs, where a *run* consists of one or more copies of the same element. Runs are boxed in the following diagram:

$$\boxed{1\ 1}\quad\boxed{2\ 2\ 2}\quad\boxed{3}\quad\boxed{1}\quad\boxed{4\ 4}$$

The approach is to repeatedly

> read element x;
> write x;
> skip past the duplicates of x;

Even with this simple problem, careful program design pays off, because of the following: How do we tell when the duplicates of x have indeed been skipped? Answer: When we read too far, since an element must be read before any decisions are made about it.

Invariants: Program Design

invariants relate programs and computations

Programming language design must deal at some level with program design; after all, the purpose of programming languages is to make programming easier. Invariants are a key concept for designing imperative programs. The following discussion of invariants is a preview of Section 3.5.

An *invariant* at some point in a program is an assertion that holds whenever that point is reached at run time—that is, whenever control reaches that point. An *assertion* is a true/false condition about the state of a computation. An example is the condition $x > y$, which relates the values of x and y.

Some of the difficulty in writing correct code is that correctness is a property not of the static source text we write but of its dynamic computations— when the program is run it must do such and such. Invariants can help us relate the two. Invariants are attached to a program point and tell us about a property of its computations; so they are a bridge between the static program text and the dynamic progress of a computation.

Technically, we work with assertions, yet we talk about invariants, since the intent is to work with properties that hold every time control reaches a program point.

Rather than writing a program and then retrofitting invariants, it is best to start with invariants and use them to design the program. A program to remove adjacent duplicates can be designed by starting with the invariant:

> { here, x is the first element of a run }

Invariants will be enclosed within braces { and } so they can be readily identified.

read(x);
while x is not the end marker **do begin**
    { here, x is the first element of a run }
    writeln(x);
    repeat *read*(*next*) **until** *next* ≠ x;
    x := *next*;
end

Figure 3.1 A program fragment for removing adjacent duplicates. For simplicity, suppose that the starting list is presented as input elements that are read one by one. The list ends with an end marker that is not part of the list.

The following pseudocode writes x and then repeatedly reads elements to skip past duplicates of x. It reads elements into the variable *next* until *next* is not equal to x:

    { here, x is the first element of a run }

    writeln(x);

    repeat *read*(*next*) until *next* is not equal to x

    { here, we have read one element too many }

Having read too far, the variable *next* either holds the first element of the next run or we have reached the end of the input. A completed program fragment appears in Fig. 3.1.

3.2 SYNTAX-DIRECTED CONTROL FLOW

structured statements are by definition single-entry and single-exit

The constructs in this section are motivated by the following variant of the structured programming principle from Section 3.1:

Structured Control Flow. A program is *structured* if the flow of control through the program is evident from the syntactic structure of the program text.

This definition deals with the specific notion of flow of control through a program instead of the general notion, "the program text should help us understand what the program does." It deals with the specific notion of syntactic structure instead of "structure" in general.

When is control flow "evident" from the program text? In this section, "evident" is defined as *single-entry/single-exit*; control flows in through a single entry point and flows out through a single exit point (see Fig. 3.2).

Constructs called *statements* specify actions and the flow of control around actions. All of the statement constructs of Pascal, except gotos, are single-entry/single-exit. The BNF rules in Fig. 3.3 specify the syntax of statements in this section.

Composition of Statements

Control flows sequentially through a sequence of statements like

$temp := x; \ x := y; \ y := temp$

Such a sequence can be grouped into a compound statement by enclosing it between the keywords **begin** and **end**. The compound statement can then appear wherever a statement is expected. For example, a compound statement for the above sequence is

begin $temp := x; \ x := y; \ y := temp$ **end**

The statement sequence can be empty, as in

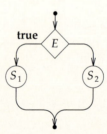

Figure 3.2   Control flow through a conditional **if** E **then** S_1 **else** S_2. The flow of control is represented by arrows in this flow diagram. E represents an expression and S_1 and S_2 represent statements.

Control enters through an imaginary entry point at the top, marked by •, and flows to the diamond marked E. If expression E evaluates to **true**, control flows to S_1; otherwise control flows to S_2. The only way to reach S_1 or S_2 is by following the appropriate arrow in the diagram. After either S_1 or S_2 is executed, control flows to the imaginary exit point at the bottom, also marked by •.

⟨*statement*⟩   ::= ⟨*expression*⟩ := ⟨*expression*⟩

| ⟨*name*⟩ (⟨*expression-list*⟩)

| **begin** ⟨*statement-list*⟩ **end**

| **if** ⟨*expression*⟩ **then** ⟨*statement*⟩

| **if** ⟨*expression*⟩ **then** ⟨*statement*⟩ **else** ⟨*statement*⟩

| **while** ⟨*expression*⟩ **do** ⟨*statement*⟩

| **repeat** ⟨*statement-list*⟩ **until** ⟨*expression*⟩

| **for** ⟨*name*⟩ := ⟨*expression*⟩ **to** ⟨*expression*⟩ **do** ⟨*statement*⟩

| **for** ⟨*name*⟩ := ⟨*expression*⟩ **downto** ⟨*expression*⟩ **do** ⟨*statement*⟩

| **case** ⟨*expression*⟩ **of** ⟨*cases*⟩ **end**

⟨*statement-list*⟩ ::= ⟨*empty*⟩

| ⟨*statement*⟩ ; ⟨*statement-list*⟩

⟨*cases*⟩   ::= ⟨*constant*⟩ : ⟨*statement*⟩

| ⟨*constant*⟩ : ⟨*statement*⟩ ; ⟨*cases*⟩

Figure 3.3   BNF rules for statements, using the syntax of Pascal.

> **begin   end**

with nothing between **begin** and **end**.

By design, semicolons separate statements in Pascal—that is, semicolons appear between the statements in a sequence. The preferred alternative design is for semicolons to terminate statements—that is, for a semicolon to appear after each statement. The placement of semicolons is discussed in Section 3.3.

Selection: Conditional Statements

A *conditional* statement selects one of two alternative substatements for execution. A conditional statement has the form

> **if** ⟨*expression*⟩ **then** ⟨*statement$_1$*⟩ **else** ⟨*statement$_2$*⟩

If *expression* is true, then control flows through *statement$_1$*; otherwise, control flows through *statement$_2$*.

This description of control flow through a conditional is in terms of the syntax of the construct; it is purely in terms of the components of this construct and can be understood independently of the rest of a program. A variant of this statement is

if ⟨*expression*⟩ **then** ⟨*statement*⟩

with no **else** part. Here *statement* is executed only if *expression* is true.

style:
avoid nesting in
then *parts*

When conditionals are nested, the following style guideline improves readability: use the general form

if	···	then ···
else if	···	then ···
else if	···	then ···
else	···	

which avoids nesting in the **then** parts.

Example 3.1   The following conditional statement assigns **true** to variable *leap* if the value of variable *year* corresponds to a leap year. The rules for determining leap years are based on a decree by Pope Gregory XIII, which was eventually adopted in Great Britain and its colonies for years following 1752. The rules can be summarized as follows:

> Every fourth year is a leap year, so 1756, 1760, ··· are leap years. But 1800, 1900, ··· — years divisible by 100 — are not leap years. Finally, years divisible by 400 are leap years, so 2000, 2400, ··· are leap years.

A corresponding conditional is

> **if** (*year* **mod** 400) = 0 **then true**
> **else if** (*year* **mod** 100) = 0 **then false**
> **else if** (*year* **mod** 4) = 0 **then true**
> **else false**   □

Looping Constructs: While and Repeat

Looping constructs can be divided roughly into two groups, depending on whether or not we can predict the number of times the loop will be executed.

A *definite* iteration is executed a predetermined number of times. By contrast, the number of executions of an *indefinite* iteration is not known when control reaches the loop; the number is determined by the course of the computation.

The quintessential construct for indefinite iteration is

while ⟨*expression*⟩ **do** ⟨*statement*⟩

while: *test upon loop entry*

The ⟨*statement*⟩ after **do** is called the *body* of the while construct. The expression and the body are evaluated alternately as long as the expression is true. As soon as the expression evaluates to false, control leaves the construct. The body is skipped if the expression is false the very first time it is evaluated.

For example, if *x* is 0 when control reaches the statement,

while $x \neq 0$ **do begin** $\cdots$ **end**

then the statements between **begin** and **end** are skipped. Otherwise, they are executed and the condition $x \neq 0$ is retested. Clearly, the statements must be capable of changing the value of *x*, or the value of *x* will remain 0 and control will never leave the while statement.

A variant of this construct allows statements to be executed repeatedly until a condition becomes true:

repeat ⟨*statement-list*⟩ **until** ⟨*expression*⟩

repeat: *test after each pass*

The statements in *statement-list* are executed before the condition represented by *expression* is evaluated. Control leaves the repeat construct if the condition is true; otherwise, the statements in *statement-list* are repeated.

For example, the following statement reads a value into variable *next*, checks whether $next \neq x$, and repeats if the condition is not yet true:

repeat *read*(*next*); **until** $next \neq x$

Thus, the effect of **repeat** *S* **until** *E* is: do *S*, test *E*, do *S*, test *E*, and so on, until *E* evaluates to true, whereupon control leaves the statement. Alternatively, the meaning of **repeat** *S* **until** *E* is given by

S; **while not** *E* **do** *S*

Similarly, the meaning of **while** *E* **do** *S* can be given using a conditional and a repeat-until statement, as follows:

if *E* **then repeat** *S* **until not** *E*

Example 3.2 The complete Pascal program in Fig. 3.4 illustrates the use of actions, composition of statements, while statements, and repeat statements.

The program reads a sequence of numbers ending in 0 and removes adjacent duplicates. As in Section 3.1, the input is treated as a sequence of runs,

```
program uniq(input, output);
var x, next : integer;
begin
    read(x);
    while x <> 0 do begin
        writeln(x);
        repeat read(next); until next <> x;
        x := next;
    end;
end.
```

Figure 3.4   A Pascal program to remove adjacent duplicates. A typewriter-like font shows the program as it was presented to a Pascal compiler. Keywords and other names appear in the same font. Some symbols are written as two-character combinations; for example, the symbol $\neq$ is written as <>.

where a run consists of one or more copies of the same number. Runs are boxed in the following diagram:

$$\boxed{1\ 1}\quad \boxed{2\ 2\ 2}\quad \boxed{3}\quad \boxed{1}\quad \boxed{4\ 4}$$

The copies of an element x are skipped using the statement

repeat $read(next)$; **until** $next \neq x$

which reads elements into variable $next$ until the value of $next$ is not equal to that of x — that is, the statement reads elements as long as they are duplicates of x.

The statement is part of a sequence

begin
      $writeln(x)$; **repeat** $read(next)$; **until** $next \neq x$; $x := next$;
end

that writes the first element of a run, skips duplicates, and assigns x the next element that is not a duplicate.

The **while** statement

while $x \neq 0$ **do begin**
      $writeln(x)$; **repeat** $read(next)$; **until** $next \neq x$; $x := next$;
end

ensures that this activity occurs while x denotes a nonzero integer — that is, while there are elements to be read.   □

Definite Iteration: For Each Element Do

for: design
depends on index,
step, and limit

The **for** statement of Pascal is a simplification of earlier designs. One form of the **for** statement in Pascal is

> **for** ⟨*name*⟩ := ⟨*expression*⟩ **to** ⟨*expression*⟩ **do** ⟨*statement*⟩

For example,

> **for** i := 1 **to** *limit* **do** $A[i]$:= 0

The assignment $A[i]$:= x is executed with i taking on the values $1, 2, \ldots,$ *limit* on successive executions; that is, i is incremented by 1 for the next execution.

The alternative form of the **for** statement in Pascal is:

> **for** ⟨*name*⟩ := ⟨*expression*⟩ **downto** ⟨*expression*⟩ **do** ⟨*statement*⟩

The variable is decremented for the next execution of the statement.

The design of **for** statements in a language depends on the treatment of

- the *index* variable, which controls the flow through the loop;
- the *step*, which determines the value added to the index variable each time through the loop;
- the *limit*, which determines when control leaves the loop.

The treatment of the index variable, step, and limit depends on answers to questions like the following:

- Are the step and the limit computed once, just before loop entry, or are they recomputed each time control flows through the loop?
- Is the limit tested at the beginning or at the end of each pass through the loop?
- Can the value of the index variable be changed, say by an assignment, within the loop?
- Is the index variable defined upon loop exit?

The answers for Pascal are as follows. The step and limit are evaluated once only. The limit is tested at the beginning of each pass, and if the test fails, the statements within the loop are skipped without being executed. The index variable must not be changed within the loop. The value of the index variable is not defined upon loop exit.

Selection: Case Statements

case:
substatements
selected by
constants

A case statement uses the value of an expression to select one of several substatements for execution. Thus, a case statement is made up of an expression and a sequence of cases, where each case consists of a constant and a substatement:

> **case** ⟨*expression*⟩ **of**
> ⟨*constant*$_1$⟩ : ⟨*statement*$_1$⟩;
> ⟨*constant*$_2$⟩ : ⟨*statement*$_2$⟩;
> $\cdots$
> ⟨*constant*$_n$⟩ : ⟨*statement*$_n$⟩
> **end**

Execution begins with the evaluation of *expression*. If its value equals that of one of the constants, say *constant*$_i$, then control flows to the corresponding *statement*$_i$. After execution of the selected substatement, control leaves the case statement.

Case statements vary from language to language, but they tend to agree on the following points:

- Case constants can appear in any order.
- Case constants need not be consecutive. It is legal to have cases for 1 and 3 without a case for 2.
- Several case constants can select the same substatement.
- Case constants must be distinct. Otherwise, if *constant*$_i$ and *constant*$_j$ above are equal, should control go to *statement*$_i$ or to *statement*$_j$? This ambiguity is avoided if no two constants are equal.

The detailed treatment of case statements can affect programming style in a language. Modula-2 improves upon Pascal in two ways:

1. Modula-2 allows a default case, to be selected if none of the case constants are selected. For example, the default case might be used to emit a message that none of the cases were selected. An error occurs in Pascal, if none of the cases are selected.

2. Modula-2 is one of the few languages to allow ranges like '0'..'9' to appear as case constants. The alternative of writing out '0'..'9' in full,

> '0', '1', '2', '3', '4', '5', '5', '7', '8', '9' : *lookvalue* := 0;

is error-prone (look at the list again, carefully). Fifty-two constants, for the lowercase and uppercase letters, would be needed if '*a*' .. '*z*', '*A*' .. '*Z*' were written out in full.

Implementation of Case Statements

statements have efficient implementations

Except for case statements, the statement constructs in imperative languages can be used without thinking about how they are implemented, since they translate directly and efficiently into machine code. For example, the translation of while-loops in Fig. 3.5 evaluates the expression E, and if it is false, jumps out of the loop; otherwise, the statements in the body are executed, and a jump takes control back to reevaluate the expression.

The implementation of case statements can affect their usage. Some implementations recommend that a case statement be used only when the case constants are essentially adjacent. Where the case constants are not adjacent, as in Fig. 3.6(a), conditionals can be used instead, as in Fig. 3.6(b). Furthermore, an else part can be added to the nested conditional to achieve the effect of a default case.

Other implementations, encourage the use of case statements. The code generated by good compilers depends on the distribution of case constants:

1. A small number of cases (say less than seven) is implemented using conditionals. The code therefore looks like that in Fig. 3.6(b): If the first condition is true, then do the first substatement; if the second condition is true, then do the second substatement, and so on.

2. For a larger number of cases, the range in which the constants appear is checked to see if an array constituting a "jump table" can be used. Entry i in the jump table is a machine instruction that sends control to the code for case i. The value of the expression becomes an index into the jump table, so selection of each case occurs efficiently by indexing

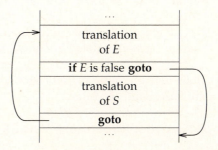

Figure 3.5 Conditional and looping constructs translate into efficient machine code. This diagram illustrates the translation of **while** E **do** S into target code. Besides the instructions for evaluating E and the loop body S, the translation has a conditional goto through which control leaves the loop and a goto at the bottom to send control back to the beginning of the loop.

$$
\begin{array}{l}
\textbf{case } E \textbf{ of} \\
\quad 1 : \quad S_1; \\
\quad 11 : \quad S_2; \\
\quad 121 : \quad S_3 \\
\textbf{end}
\end{array}
\qquad
\begin{array}{l}
n := E; \\
\textbf{if } n = 1 \textbf{ then } S_1 \\
\textbf{else if } n = 11 \textbf{ then } S_2 \\
\textbf{else if } n = 121 \textbf{ then } S_3
\end{array}
$$

(a)   (b)

Figure 3.6   The choice between the equivalent fragments in (a) and (b) depends on the implementation. With implementations that recommend that case constants be essentially adjacent, the approach using conditionals in (b) is preferred.

into the table and then jumping to the code for the case. If the smallest constant is *min* and the largest is *max*, then the jump table has $max - min + 1$ entries. Of course, only the entries for the case constants that actually appear are used. The compiler in question uses a jump table if at least half the entries will be used.

3. Finally, if the number of cases is large enough, and if too many entries in a jump table would remain unused, the compiler uses a hash table to find the code for the selected substatement.

3.3   DESIGN CONSIDERATIONS: SYNTAX

syntax affects usability

Although details such as the placement of operators, keywords, and semicolons have nothing to do with the meaning of a program, they do affect the usability of a language. Ritchie [1993] makes the observation about C, "An accident of syntax contributed to the perceived complexity of the language." The reference is to the prefix operator * for indirection through pointers. (Pointers and other data structures are discussed in Chapter 4.)

This section deals with two syntactic concerns: the placement of semicolons and the dangling-else ambiguity in conditionals. The examples compare Pascal and Modula-2.

Sequences: Separators Versus Terminators

better for semicolons to terminate statements

Sequences — of statements, declarations, parameters — can be classified by asking the following questions:

- Can the sequence be empty? That is, can it have zero elements?
- If there is a delimiter, does it separate elements or terminate them? A delimiter *separates* elements if it appears between them; it *terminates* elements if it appears after each element.

Fewer programming errors are believed to occur if semicolons terminate statements than if they separate statements.

Pascal: Semicolons and Empty Statements

Pascal uses semicolons primarily to separate statements, as in

$$\textbf{begin} \quad \textbf{stmt}_1 \; ; \; \textbf{stmt}_2 \; ; \; \textbf{stmt}_3 \quad \textbf{end}$$

A parse tree for this string appears in Fig. 3.7. The grammar itself, shown in Fig. 3.8, has productions for a fragment of Pascal. The grammar is kept small by using the token **expr** to represent an expression and the token **stmt** to represent the remaining statement constructs.

At first glance, empty statements allow semicolons as terminators as well as separators. Think of there being an empty statement between the semicolon and **end** in

$$\textbf{begin} \quad \textbf{stmt}_1 \; ; \; \textbf{stmt}_2 \; ; \; \textbf{stmt}_3 \; ; \quad \textbf{end}$$

A parse tree for this string appears in Fig. 3.9. By allowing occurrences of S to "disappear," the production

$$S \; ::= \; \langle empty \rangle$$

allows semicolons to be inserted before or after statements, as in

$$\textbf{begin} \; ; \; \textbf{stmt} \; ; \; ; \; \textbf{stmt} \; ; \; ; \; ; \; \textbf{end}$$

But empty statements make the placement of semicolons significant; insertion of a semicolon can change the meaning of a program in Pascal. Insertion

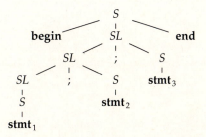

Figure 3.7 A parse tree for **begin stmt ; stmt ; stmt end**.

$$S \quad ::= \quad \langle \textit{empty} \rangle$$

$$\quad | \quad \textbf{stmt}$$

$$\quad | \quad \textbf{begin } SL \textbf{ end}$$

$$\quad | \quad \textbf{if expr then } S$$

$$\quad | \quad \textbf{if expr then } S \textbf{ else } S$$

$$\quad | \quad \textbf{while expr do } S$$

$$SL \quad ::= \quad SL \; ; \; S$$

$$\quad | \quad S$$

Figure 3.8   A grammar for a fragment of Pascal.

of a semicolon after the keyword **then** has the presumably unintended effect of inserting an empty statement after **then**. Thus,

> **if expr then ; stmt**

is a sequence of two statements, semantically equivalent to

> **if expr then begin end ; stmt**

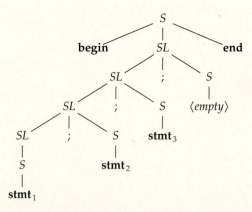

Figure 3.9   An empty statement is used to get a semicolon after **stmt**$_3$.

Here, **begin end** makes it explicit that no action is taken if **expr** represents **true**.

Why does insertion of a semicolon after S_1 in

$$\textbf{if expr then } S_1 \textbf{ else } S_2$$

lead to a syntactic error?

Modula-2: Closing Keywords

a closing **end** *helps with statement sequences and avoids dangling elses*
Modula-2 avoids confusion due to misplaced semicolons by attaching a closing keyword **end**. The grammar in Fig. 3.10 has the production

$$S \ ::= \ \textbf{if expr then } SL \textbf{ end}$$

instead of

$$S \ ::= \ \textbf{if expr then } S$$

in Fig. 3.8. This change allows a statement list to appear between **then** and **end**, so extraneous semicolons between these keywords are harmless.

Avoiding Dangling Elses

As discussed in Section 2.4, the dangling-else ambiguity arises in Pascal because its grammar has productions corresponding to

$$S \ ::= \ \textbf{if expr then } S$$
$$S \ ::= \ \textbf{if expr then } S \textbf{ else } S$$

$$
\begin{aligned}
S \ &::= \ \langle empty \rangle \\
&\mid \ \textbf{stmt} \\
&\mid \ \textbf{if expr then } SL \textbf{ end} \\
&\mid \ \textbf{if expr then } SL \textbf{ else } SL \textbf{ end} \\
&\mid \ \textbf{while expr do } SL \textbf{ end} \\
SL \ &::= \ SL \ ; \ S \\
&\mid \ S
\end{aligned}
$$

Figure 3.10   A grammar for a fragment of Modula-2.

An example of a dangling else is the **else** in

> **if expr then if expr then** *S* **else** *S*

Which **if** does the **else** belong to? Most languages, including Pascal, resolve this ambiguity by matching an **else** with the nearest unmatched **if**, the second **if** in this example.

Modula-2: Additional Keywords

but with closing **end** *come more keywords*

Modula-2 avoids the dangling-else ambiguity because conditionals have a closing keyword **end**. The troublesome Pascal example is forced to be rewritten unambiguously as either of the following:

> **if expr then** ⌐**if expr then** *SL* **else** *SL* **end**⌐ **end**

> **if expr then** ⌐**if expr then** *SL* **end**⌐ **else** *SL* **end**

Closing delimiters can lead to a proliferation of keywords. If the Pascal-like string

> **if expr$_1$ then stmt$_1$**
> **else if expr$_2$ then stmt$_2$**
> **else if expr$_3$ then stmt$_3$**
> **else**
>   **stmt$_4$**

is rewritten with closing keywords, we get

> **if expr$_1$ then stmt$_1$**
> **else**   **if expr$_2$ then stmt$_2$**
>   **else**   **if expr$_3$ then stmt$_3$**
>   **else**
>   **stmt$_4$**
>   **end**
>   **end**
> **end**

Modula-2 avoids a proliferation of **end** keywords in nested conditionals by allowing optional **elsif** parts, as in

> **if expr$_1$ then stmt$_1$**
> **elsif expr$_2$ then stmt$_2$**
> **elsif expr$_3$ then stmt$_3$**
> **else**
>   **stmt$_4$**
> **end**

The general form is as follows, in EBNF notation:

if expr then *SL* { **elsif expr then** *SL* } [**else** *SL*] **end**

The braces { and } enclose the part that can be repeated zero or more times, and the brackets [and] enclose the optional part.

3.4   HANDLING SPECIAL CASES IN LOOPS

The statement constructs in this section lead to readable programs and mesh well with invariants, although they are not single-entry/single-exit in the sense of if and while statements. Loops remain single-entry/single-exit in this section.

The use of invariants for program design is illustrated in Section 3.5.

Break and Continue Statements in Loops

Break and continue statements facilitate the handling of special cases in loops:

- A *break* statement sends control out of the enclosing loop to the statement following the loop. It can be used to jump out of a loop after establishing the conditions upon exit from the loop.

- A *continue* statement repeats the enclosing loop by sending control to the beginning of the loop. It can be used to restart the loop after reestablishing the loop invariant, the condition that holds upon loop entry.

The names break and continue are from C; the exit statement in Modula-2 is related to the break statement in C.

break *after handling special case*

One use of break statements is to break out of a loop after handling a special case, as in the pseudocode

```
while condition do
    if special case then
        take care of the special case;
        break;
    end if;
    handle the normal cases;
end while
```

This organization is convenient if the code for the special case is short. Attention can then be focused on the code for the normal case with the assurance that the special case cannot occur.

continue after handling normal case

A corresponding fragment for continue statements is the pseudocode

    while condition **do**
        if normal case **then**
            handle the normal case;
            continue;
        end if;
        take care of the special cases;
    end while

The continue statement in this outline ensures that control flows back to the beginning of the loop immediately after taking care of the normal case.

A more mundane reason for using break and continue statements is to reduce indentation of the source text — that is, to reduce blank space at the beginning of a line. The preceding fragment can be rewritten without a continue statement as

    while condition **do**
        if normal case **then**
            handle the normal case;
        else
            take care of the special cases;
        end if;
    end while

The code for taking care of the special case now appears indented within an else clause. Nested conditionals in this code can lead to further indentation to the point where the code crowds the right margin of a page.

Example 3.3 This example illustrates the effect of break and continue statements on the flow of control in and out of a loop. Since break and continue statements are used frequently in C programs, we use a C-like pseudocode.

C dispenses with keywords like **begin**, **do**, **then**, and **end**; a sequence of statements is grouped by enclosing it within braces, { and }. The following table gives the correspondence between the syntax of conditional and while statements in C and Pascal:

C	*Pascal*
`if ( `E` ) `S	**if** E **then** S
`if ( `E` ) `S_1` else `S_2	**if** E **then** S_1 **else** S_2
`while ( `E` ) `S	**while** E **do** S

The following C-like pseudocode uses a break statement:

```
while ( E₁ ) {
    if ( E₂ ) {
        S₁
        break;
    }
    S₂
}
```

This while loop is single-entry/single-exit, but the conditional inside it has two exits. Depending on the value of E_2, control either flows out of

```
if ( E₂ ) { S₁ break; }
```

to S_2, the next statement in sequence, or it flows out of the while loop.

Flow diagrams are unwieldy for most programming purposes, but they are good for making explicit the flow of control. The diagram in Fig. 3.11 illustrates the flow of control within the while loop of this example. The diagram has a single entry at the top and a single exit toward the bottom right. Control can reach the loop exit in two ways: either from the test E_1 or after the statement S_1 (due to the break statement). ◻

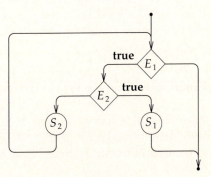

Figure 3.11   A flow diagram for a while loop. The loop has a single exit; however, control can reach the exit in two ways. Note that, for ease of drawing, the **true** label for E_1 appears on the edge to its left, but the **true** label for E_2 appears on the edge to its right.

Return Statements

Execution of a statement

   return ⟨*expression*⟩

sends control back from a procedure to a caller, carrying the value of ⟨*expression*⟩. If the return statement is not in a procedure, then the program halts.

Both return and break statements send control out of an enclosing construct; a return out of an enclosing procedure, and a break out of an enclosing loop. Return statements allow linear search to be implemented as follows:

   for $i = n$ **downto** 1 **do**
      if $x = A[i]$ **then return** i;
   return 0;

Goto Statements

A statement **goto** L interrupts the normal flow of control from one statement to the next in sequence; control flows instead to the statement labeled L somewhere in the program. Label L is typically attached to a statement by writing

   L: ⟨*statement*⟩

By itself, **goto** L gives no indication of where label L is to be found. Similarly, by itself, the labeled statement L: ⟨*statement*⟩ does not indicate from where control might come to it.

Although **goto** statements can be misused to write unreadable programs, there is still a need for them. An algorithm for generating subprograms may introduce goto statements that a person might not. Programs are not always written by people.

3.5 PROGRAMMING WITH INVARIANTS

an invariant holds every time control reaches a program point

With the single-entry/single-exit constructs of Section 3.2, the flow of control is evident from the program text—in fact, single-entry/single-exit was taken as the definition of "evident" control flow. How does that help with program design?

With single-entry/single-exit constructs, the behavior of a statement S can be characterized purely by conditions at the entry and exit to the statement. Such conditions are called preconditions and postconditions, respectively.

This section illustrates the informal use of invariants, which are properties that hold every time control reaches a program point. Proof rules, a theoretical basis for invariants, appear in Section 3.6.

A systematic approach to program design, using invariants, owes much to Dijkstra's [1972] influential "Notes on Structured Programming." The approach is motivated by examples like the following.

Example 3.4   Bentley [1986] asked more than a hundred professional programmers to convert the following brief description of binary search "into a program in the language of their choice; a high-level pseudocode was fine." He reports, "I was amazed: given ample time, only about 10 percent of professional programmers were able to get this small program right."

> We are to determine whether the sorted array $X[1 .. N]$ contains the element T. Binary search solves the problem by keeping track of the range within the array in which T must be if it is anywhere in the array. Initially, the range is the entire array. The range is shrunk by comparing its middle element to T and discarding half the range. The process continues until T is discovered in the array or until the range in which it must lie is known to be empty.

Bentley offers this advice: "Most programmers think that with the above description in hand, writing the code is easy; they're wrong. The only way you'll believe this is by putting down this column right now, and writing the code yourself. Try it."   □

Preconditions and Postconditions

try invariants just before and just within a loop

A *precondition* is attached just before and a *postcondition* is attached just after a statement; both are assertions. Invariant assertions can play the following roles with while loops:

- A precondition just before the loop can capture the conditions for executing the loop.
- An invariant just within the loop body can capture the conditions for staying within the loop.
- A postcondition just after the loop can capture the conditions upon leaving the loop.

The rule relating these assertions appears in Section 3.6. Meanwhile, consider the while statement

while $x \geq y$ **do**
  $x := x - y$

Every time control reaches the assignment $x := x - y$, it must be true that $x \geq y$. Not just the first time, not just the fifth time, but every time control reaches $x := x - y$, no matter what the rest of the program does, no matter what state the machine is in, it must be true that $x \geq y$.

We follow the convention of enclosing assertions between braces, { and }. Thus, the invariant assertion $x \geq y$ can be written within the program fragment, as follows:

> **while** $x \geq y$ **do**
>   { $x \geq y$ *if we get here* }
> $x := x - y$

The first time control reaches the loop, suppose that the invariant

> { $x \geq 0$ **and** $y > 0$ }

is true. The test expression $x \geq y$ between **while** and **do** further ensures that $x \geq y$ just before the assignment $x := x - y$.

> { $x \geq 0$ **and** $y > 0$ }
> **while** $x \geq y$ **do**
>   { $y > 0$ **and** $x \geq y$ }
> $x := x - y$

After the assignment, the changed value of x must satisfy $x \geq 0$:[1]

> { $x \geq 0$ **and** $y > 0$ }
> **while** $x \geq y$ **do**
>   { $y > 0$ **and** $x \geq y$ }
> $x := x - y$
>   { $x \geq 0$ **and** $y > 0$ }

Control flows from the body of the while back to the test; so after the assignment, the invariant will hold for the next iteration.

Example: Linear Search

The time to think about invariants is at the beginning, before a program is written. Then, the invariants can be used to guide program development. Invariants will be used now to develop a small program fragment for linear or sequential search through a table of elements. The approach is long and detailed, considering the size of the resulting program, but the approach is usually implicitly applied without the gory details. Rigorous mathematical proofs are long and detailed too, yet the concept of a proof is useful.

---

[1] Suppose that a is the old value of x. From $y > 0$ and $a \geq y$, it follows that $a - y \geq 0$. Since the changed value of x is $a - y$, after the assignment, we get $x \geq 0$.

A Table Organized Around an Invariant

invariants can describe data structures

A table, organized as in Fig. 3.12, supports two operations, *insert*(x) and *find*(x). Initially, there are no elements in the table, and $n = 0$. Elements are inserted from left to right, starting at position 1, so the inserted elements are $A[1]$, $A[2]$, ..., $A[n]$, for $n \geq 0$. (There will soon be a role for position 0.)

The intent of the table organization in Fig. 3.12 is captured by an invariant about the used table elements and the variables n and *limit*. The notation $A[m..n]$, where $m \leq n$, refers to the subarray consisting of the elements $A[m]$, $A[m+1]$, ..., $A[n]$. When $m > n$, the subarray $A[m..n]$ is empty; for example, the subarray $A[1..0]$ has no elements.

The table will be maintained so that

the elements of the table are in the subarray $A[1..n]$, for $0 \leq n$, and $0 \leq n \leq limit$

Consider the problem of implementing *find*(x). Operation *find*(x) returns 0 if x is not in the table; otherwise, it returns the position in the table at which x was inserted most recently.

Linear search proceeds by examining all the elements until either x is found or no elements remain to be examined. This is not a difficult problem, and perhaps the approach in Fig. 3.13 has already come to mind. The program fragment in this figure qualifies as being well structured, although it is not single-entry/single-exit, due to the **return** within the **then** part. Control can leave the conditional, either by returning or by flowing through the else part to the program point immediately after the conditional.

This fragment uses two tests: one in the while statement to check whether elements remain to be examined and another in the conditional to check whether the current element is found to be x. An unsuccessful search stops when no elements remain to be examined and x is not found.

Linear Search with a Sentinel

Now, consider a more efficient but more subtle approach.

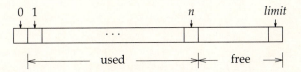

Figure 3.12 Table organization for linear search with a sentinel.

start with the last inserted element
while elements remain to be examined **do begin**
    if this element is x **then**
        return its position
    else
        consider the element to its left
end
not found, so return 0

Figure 3.13   An approach to implementing linear search.

Linear search with a *sentinel* uses a single test to look for x and stop the search. An initial assignment $A[0] := x$ puts x in the otherwise unused position 0 of the array. A search for x therefore ends successfully with x found at some position i within the table, or it ends unsuccessfully with x found at position 0.

Let us see how invariants can help to develop the code. For ease of comparison, Fig. 3.14 collects the code fragments with which this example deals.

The initial code sketch in Fig. 3.14(a) allows for initialization, the search, and a conditional to return a result. The postcondition for the search is given by:

do the search;
{ (x *is not in the table*) **or** (*the most recent* x *is* $A[i]$ **and** $0 < i \le n$) }

A diagram for this condition is

    Case: x *is not in the table*   **Case**: *most recent* x *is* $A[i], 0 < i \le n$

In both cases, we have

$$x = A[i] \quad \textbf{and} \quad x \text{ is not in } A[i+1..n]$$

The key difference between the two cases is in the value of i. If x is not in the table, then the search ends with $i = 0$; otherwise, it ends with $0 < i \le n$. In both cases, the value to be returned is the value of i, either $i = 0$ to signal that x is not in the table, or $i > 0$ to signal that the most recent x is $A[i]$.

Initial Code Sketch

> initialization;
> do the search;
> { (*x is not in the table*) **or** (*the most recent x is* $A[i]$ **and** $0 < i \leq n$) }
> **if** x is not in the table **then**
>   **return** 0;
> **else**
>   **return** i;   (a)

Simplified Computation of the Result

> initialization;
> do the search;
> { $x = A[i]$ **and** *x is not in* $A[i+1..n]$ **and** $0 \leq i \leq n$ }
> **return** i;   (b)

Making the Sentinel Explicit

> $A[0] := x$;
> further initialization;
> { $x = A[0]$ **and** *x is not in* $A[i+1..n]$ **and** $0 \leq i \leq n$ }
> **while** not yet time to stop and x not found at i **do**
> $i := i - 1$;
> { $x = A[i]$ **and** *x is not in* $A[i+1..n]$ **and** $0 \leq i \leq n$ }
> **return** i;   (c)

Final Developed Program Fragment

> $A[0] := x$;
> $i := n$;
> **while** $x \neq A[i]$ **do**
> $i := i - 1$;
> **return** i;   (d)

Figure 3.14 Development of a program for linear search with a sentinel.

These cases can therefore be combined. The postcondition after the search

do the search;
{ (*x is not in the table*) **or** (*the most recent x is A*[i] **and** $0 < i \le n$) }

can equivalently be rewritten as

{ $x = A[i]$ **and** *x is not in* $A[i+1..n]$ **and** $0 \le i \le n$ }

The program fragment in Fig. 3.14(b) uses this rewritten condition and a single **return** *i* statement.

The program fragment in 3.14(c) incorporates two changes:

- The sentinel is made explicit by the assignment $A[0] := x$ during initialization.

- The backward search from the last element to the first is written as a while-loop.

The search stops if *x* is found or if we run out of elements — that is, if $x = A[i]$ or if $i = 0$. From the postcondition, these both boil down to $x = A[i]$. Thus, the condition for staying within the while-loop is $x \neq A[i]$, and the completed program fragment is as shown in Fig. 3.14(d).

3.6   PROOF RULES FOR PARTIAL CORRECTNESS

Subtle code remains subtle, no matter how clearly the flow of control through it is expressed. Nor is size an indicator of subtlety. Proof rules, the theory behind invariants, are good training for dealing with subtle code, even if they are applied informally.

We now review the theoretical basis for invariants. Invariants were not formalized to begin with, for two reasons. First, formal application of the rules can be long and tedious even for short programs. Second, the rules are syntax-directed and geared to simple constructs like if and while statements. They are hard to formulate for constructs like break statements in Section 3.4, which send control out of an enclosing loop. Rules for procedures and data structures present additional challenges.

This section contains rules called proof rules for associating preconditions and postconditions with assignments, conditionals, while statements, and sequences of statements. We assume that expressions do not have side effects; that is, the evaluation of an expression does not change the state of the underlying machine.

Assertions and Formulas

partial correctness means the program is correct if it terminates

Rules for manipulating invariants deal with formulas of the form

$$\{ \langle precondition \rangle \} \ \langle statement \rangle \ \{ \langle postcondition \rangle \}$$

For example,

$$\{j - 1 = 0\} \ j := j - 1 \ \{j = 0\}$$

The intuitive idea is as follows: If the precondition is true before the statement begins, and if execution of the statement terminates, then the postcondition holds after the statement is executed. Statement termination must be proved separately.

Since termination is not guaranteed, proofs based on the formulas are called *partial correctness* proofs. *Total correctness* consists of establishing both partial correctness and termination.

Letters P, Q, and R, possibly with subscripts, will be used for preconditions and postconditions, and letter S will be used for statements. Thus, a typical formula is

$$\{P\} \ S \ \{Q\}$$

We write $P \wedge Q$ for "P and Q," $P \vee Q$ for "P or Q," and $\neg P$ for "not P."

Preconditions and postconditions are also called *assertions* or *predicates*.[2]

Rule for Statement Composition

For a sequence of statements $S_1 \ ; \ S_2$, we might expect that

given $\qquad \{P\} \ S_1 \ \{Q\}$ and $\{Q\} \ S_2 \ \{R\}$

it follows that $\qquad \{P\} \ S_1; S_2 \ \{R\}$

Here, from formulas for statements S_1 and S_2, we get a formula for the combined statement $S_1; S_2$. This reasoning is written as a proof rule by writing the given formulas above the line and the conclusion below the line:

$$\frac{\{P\} \ S_1 \ \{Q\}, \quad \{Q\} \ S_2 \ \{R\}}{\{P\} \ S_1; S_2 \ \{R\}} \qquad \text{(Composition Rule)}$$

---

[2] Formally, P and Q are assertions of a first-order language with equality. Simply stated, any boolean expression is an assertion, and if P and Q are assertions, then so are $P \wedge Q$ (P and Q), $P \vee Q$ (P or Q), $\neg P$ (not P), $\forall x. \ P$ (for all x, P), and $\exists x. \ P$ (for some x, P).

Rule for Conditionals

The rule for the conditional **if** E **then** S_1 **else** S_2 takes expression E into account, because control flows to S_1 if E is true and it flows to S_2 if E is false. Suppose precondition P holds before the conditional. Since we have assumed that evaluation of E does not have side effects, the condition P continues to hold after E is tested. Control then reaches S_1 with condition $P \wedge E$, because both P and E hold. Otherwise, control reaches S_2 with condition $P \wedge \neg E$, because P holds but E is false. The rule is

$$\frac{\{P \wedge E\} \ S_1 \ \{Q\}, \quad \{P \wedge \neg E\} \ S_2 \ \{Q\}}{\{P\} \ \textbf{if } E \textbf{ then } S_1 \textbf{ else } S_2 \ \{Q\}} \qquad \text{(Conditional Rule)}$$

Again, the reasoning proceeds from the components of the statement to the overall statement. The rule is therefore syntax-directed; from the components in the syntax of a construct, we conclude something about the construct.

Rule for While Statements

The rule for **while** E **do** S is

$$\frac{\{P \wedge E\} \ S \ \{P\}}{\{P\} \ \textbf{while } E \textbf{ do } S \ \{P \wedge \neg E\}} \qquad \textbf{(while Rule)}$$

Below the line, if the precondition for a while loop is the invariant P, then the postcondition must be $P \wedge \neg E$. The reason is that control leaves the loop only when the expression E is false. Since side effects have been ruled out, evaluation of expression E leaves invariant P unchanged. Hence the postcondition $P \wedge \neg E$.

The formula above the line in the while rule means that both invariant P and expression E are true when control reaches the loop body S and that execution of S reestablishes the invariant P:

Rule for Assignments

Since the assignment $x := E$ is an atomic statement, its proof rule has no formulas above the line. Such rules are called *axioms*. Proof rules for a language have therefore been referred to as an "axiomatic semantics" for a language.

whatever holds for x after x:=E must hold for E before the assignment

What do we know about an assignment of $x := E$? The value of E before the assignment becomes the value of x after the assignment. The order is significant, since the value of x changes during the assignment, and x can appear within E, as in $j := j-1$.

The assignment axiom is illustrated in Fig. 3.15. Any assertion involving the postassignment value of x must hold for the preassignment value of E,

Figure 3.15 A schematic diagram for the assignment axiom.

since x gets that value of E. This relationship is expressed formally as the axiom

$$\{Q\,[E/x]\}\;\; x := E\;\; \{Q\} \qquad\qquad \text{(Assignment Axiom)}$$

The postcondition Q holds with the postassignment value of x. The notation $Q[E/x]$ represents the result of replacing all occurrences of x in Q by E. Each of the following formulas is an application of this axiom:

$$\{i > 0\} \qquad j := i \qquad \{j > 0\}$$
$$\{i-1 > 0\} \qquad j := i-1 \quad \{j > 0\}$$
$$\{j-1 > 0\} \qquad j := j-1 \quad \{j > 0\}$$

In each case the precondition is obtained by substituting the right side of the assignment for j in the postcondition $j > 0$.

The assignment axiom only appears to be backward. The intuition behind the first formula is that if $i > 0$ holds before the assignment $j := i$, then $j > 0$ holds after the assignment. In the second formula, given the precondition $i-1 > 0$, the assignment $j := i-1$, leads to $j > 0$. Similar remarks apply to the third formula, even though j appears on both the left and right side of the assignment. The old value of j is used in the precondition and the new value is used in the postcondition.

Rule for Simplification

Finally, the simplification of a predicate like $i-1 > 0$ into $i > 1$ is permitted by the following rule:

$$\frac{P \text{ implies } P',\quad \{P'\}\; S\; \{Q'\},\quad Q' \text{ implies } Q}{\{P\}\; S\; \{Q\}} \qquad \text{(Rule of Consequence)}$$

Statements in Pascal

Pascal was designed to allow proof rules

Statements in Pascal were designed so proof rules could be written easily, which may explain why control flow in Pascal is purely syntax-directed; that is, the flow of control through a construct can be described purely in terms of the components of the construct. Control flow through **if** E **then** S can be described purely in terms of the value of E and control flow through S. These remarks apply to all statements except goto statements.

3.7 CONTROL FLOW IN C

The following correspondence between conditional and while statements in C and Pascal is from Section 3.4:

C	Pascal
if (E) S	if E then S
if (E) S_1 else S_2	if E then S_1 else S_2
while (E) S	while E do S

Virtually all the statement constructs in this chapter have counterparts in C. Statements in C were not introduced earlier to minimize the amount of syntax in earlier sections. This section uses a sequence of small examples to illustrate statements in C (see Fig. 3.16 for their syntax).

Assignment Operators

= is for assignment, == tests equality

The assignment operator in C is =, the equality-test operator is ==, and the inequality test operator is !=. The C counterpart of

> **while** $x \neq A[i]$ **do** $i := i-1$

is

```
while( x != A[i] ) i = i-1;
```

Test expressions in while-loops and conditionals must be enclosed within parentheses. C dispenses with keywords such as **begin**, **do**, **then**, and **end**; a sequence of statements is grouped by enclosing it within braces, { and }. Thus, the while loop can be rewritten equivalently as

```
while( x != A[i] ) { i = i-1; }
```

```
S   ::=   ;
      |   E ;
      |   { Slist }
      |   if ( E ) S
      |   if ( E ) S else S
      |   while ( E ) S
      |   do S while ( E ) ;
      |   for ( Eopt ; Eopt ; Eopt ) S
      |   switch ( E ) S
      |   case Constant : S
      |   default : S
      |   break ;
      |   continue ;
      |   return ;
      |   return E ;
      |   goto L ;
      |   L : S
Slist  ::=  ⟨empty⟩
       |    Slist S
Eopt   ::=  ⟨empty⟩
       |    E
```

Figure 3.16   Syntax of statements in C.

A special increment operator, ++, and a special decrement operator, --. change the value of an integer variable by 1. Thus, the above while-loop can be written as

```
while( x != A[i] ) --i;
```

The test expression in a do-while-loop is evaluated after the statement is executed. The statement

```
do ++i; while( A[i] > v );
```

increments i and then tests whether A[i] > v. If so, control returns for another iteration of the do-while-loop.

Assignments Within Expressions

a nonzero value is treated as true

C allows assignments to appear within expressions. An expression $E_1 = E_2$ is evaluated by placing the value of E_2 into the location of E_1. The value of $E_1 = E_2$ is the value assigned to the left side E_1.

Example 3.5 The expression

```
c = getchar()
```

assigns to c the input character read by the standard procedure getchar(). The value assigned to c also becomes the value of c=getchar(), so it can appear as a subexpression within a larger expression:

```
(c = getchar()) != EOF
```

Constant EOF, from "end of file," signifies the end of the input; this expression thus reads a value using getchar, saves the value by assigning it to c, and then tests if the value equals the constant EOF.

Such expressions are sometimes used as tests in while loops. The following statement reads and writes characters until the end of file is reached.

```
while( (c = getchar()) != EOF )
    putchar(c);
```

The standard procedure putchar writes a character. Alternatively, the effect of this statement can be achieved by:

```
while( 1 ) {
    c = getchar();
    if( c == EOF ) break;
    putchar(c);
}
```

Control can leave this while loop only through the break statement, since the test expression 1 in the while loop is treated as true. □

For Loops in C: Indefinite Iteration

for statements are for indefinite iterations

The for statement has the form

```
for( E₁; E₂; E₃ ) S
```

E_1 is evaluated just before loop entry, E_2 is the condition for staying within the loop, and E_3 is evaluated just before every next iteration of the loop. Both E_1 and E_3 can have assignments within them; E_1 can thus be used for initialization and E_3 can be used to prepare for the next iteration.

The while loop

```
while( x != A[i] )
    i = i-1;
```

can be rewritten as

```
for( ; x!=A[i]; i=i-1)
    ;
```

This for-loop has no initialization; the condition for staying in the loop is `x!=A[i]`, and the assignment `i=i-1` is executed before the next iteration. The loop body is empty.

The expressions $E_1, E_2,$ and E_3 are optional in

```
for( E₁; E₂; E₃ ) S
```

A missing E_2 is taken to be true; `for(;;)` can thus be read as "forever" because it sets up an infinite loop.

Break and Continue Statements in Loops

As discussed in Section 3.4, a break statement sends control out of the enclosing loop, and a continue statement sends control to the beginning of the loop.

Execution of a continue statement within the loop body S in

```
for( E₁ ; E₂ ; E₃ ) S
```

is equivalent to reaching the end of the statement S. In either case, expression E_3 is executed to set up the next iteration.

Example 3.6 This example illustrates the use of break and continue statements within for-loops. The program fragment in Fig. 3.17 skips over consecutive blank, tab, and newline characters, and keeps track of line numbers by incrementing variable `lineno` every time a newline character appears in the input. The symbol `'\t'` represents a tab character and `'\n'` represents a newline character.

An empty test expressions is assumed to be true; control thus stays within this loop until the break statement sends it out. If c equals a blank or a tab, the `continue` statement restarts the loop after executing `c = getchar()`. If c

```
for( ; ; c = getchar() ) {
    if( c==' ' || c=='\t' )
        continue;
    if( c != '\n' )
        break;
    ++lineno;
}
```

Figure 3.17   A program fragment that uses break and continue statements.

does not equal a newline character, then control leaves the loop through the break statement. Otherwise, lineno is incremented and the loop restarts after the call c = getchar().   □

Exercises

3.1 Rewrite the following conditionals as sequential choices so that no **if** statement is nested within the **then** part of another **if**. Use the **else if** form instead. Feel free to replace any boolean expressions by an equivalent one and to use null or empty statements.

    a. **if** $c \leq$ 'I' **then**
              if $c <$ 'I' **then** S_1
        else S_2

    b. **if** $count < max$ **then**
              if $count > min$ **then** S_1
              else S_2
              end
        end

    c. **if** $n \geq 60$ **then**
              if $n < 80$ **then**
                    if $n \geq 70$ **then** $seventy(n)$
                    else $sixty(n)$
                  end
              else $eighty(n)$
              end
        else $twenty(n)$
        end

3.2 Draw flow diagrams for the following program fragments:

  a. **if** E_1 **then** S_1
    elsif E_2 **then** S_2
    else S_3
    end

  b. **repeat** S **until** E

  c. **loop**
      S_1;
      if E **then exit end**;
      S_2
    end

  d. **repeat**
      S_1;
      if E **then**
          done := **true**
      else
          S_2
    until *done*

3.3 The C operators && and || are "short-circuit" versions of the boolean **and** and **or** operators, respectively. That is, they evaluate their second argument only if it is necessary. Draw flow diagrams for the following C program fragments:

  a. `if ( E && F ) S`
    `else` T

  b. `if ( E || F ) S`
    `else` T

  c. `if ( d[1] < '0' || d[1] > '7' )`
        S
    `else if ( d[2] >= '0' && d[2] <= '7'`
        `&& d[3] >= '0' && d[3] <= '7' )`
        T
    `else`
        `error();`

3.4 The program fragment in Fig. 3.18 has four **if** statements, beginning on lines 1–4, but only two **else** parts, on lines 5 and 11.
  a. Mark each **else** keyword with the line number of the **if** it belongs to.
  b. Draw a flow diagram for the program fragment, consistently drawing the **true** exit of each test to the left and the **false** exit to the right.
  c. Rewrite the fragment, following the instructions for Exercise 3.1.

```
(1)  if  character is printable  then
(2)       if  p ≤ bound  then
(3)            if  font ≠ normal  then
(4)                 if  font is unknown  then  print ' * '
(5)                 else  print name of font;
(6)                 end;
(7)                 print ' ';
(8)            end;
(9)            print the character;
(10)       end
(11) else  print a message;
(12) end
```

Figure 3.18   Pseudocode for a conditional from a typesetting program.

---

    d. Draw a flow diagram for your answer to (c), again drawing the **true** exit of each test to the left.

3.5 Rewrite the construct **for** $i := E_1$ **to** E_2 **do** SL **end**, making sure that i does not take on values larger than the initial value of E_2. Assume that all values are integers.

    a. Use conditionals and goto statements to do only as much work as is necessary.

    b. Use only assignments, conditionals, while, and repeat statements, as needed. Feel free to use extra variables; see for example the use of the boolean variable *done* in Exercise 3.2(d).

3.6 Develop a program for binary search from the description in Example 3.4, on page 81.

3.7 Develop a program to find the kth occurrence of x, from left to right, $k \geq 0$, in a subarray $A[i..n]$.

3.8 Rewrite the Pascal program for removing adjacent duplicates in Fig. 3.4, page 68, in C, using the following as the only looping construct:

```
for ( ⟨initialize⟩ ; ⟨test⟩ ; ⟨step⟩ ) ⟨statement⟩
```

This statement is equivalent to the program fragment

```
⟨initialize⟩ ;
while ( ⟨test⟩ ) {
    ⟨statement⟩
```

```
    ⟨step⟩ ;
}
```

(except for the treatment of continue statements within ⟨statement⟩; see Exercise 3.9). Typically, ⟨initialize⟩ and ⟨step⟩ are assignments that initialize a variable and prepare the variable for the next iteration, respectively, although any expression can appear in their place.

3.9 Since the normal activity is to evaluate ⟨step⟩ at the end of each iteration, a continue within ⟨statement⟩ evaluates ⟨step⟩ before sending control back to the beginning of the loop. Rewrite each of the following program fragments, using goto statements to explicitly show the flow of control through a loop.

a.
```
for (i = n; i > 0; i = i+1)
    if ( x != A[i] )
        break;
```

b.
```
for (c = getchar(); c != EOF; c = getchar()) {
    if ( c == ' ' )
        continue;
    if ( c == '\n' )
        lineno = lineno + 1;
    else
        break;
}
```

3.10 In the imperative language of your choice, write a program to implement the pseudocode

> **loop**
>   copy characters up to '(*';
>   throw away characters until '*)' is seen;
> **end**;

This exercise explores the use of break and continue statements; goto statements may be used to simulate break and continue by sending control to null statements just after and just before a loop, respectively. The implementation must consist of statements without calls to user-defined procedures, and must handle the end of file gracefully.

3.11 The heart of quicksort, an elegant and efficient sorting algorithm, is a procedure called *partition*, which uses a value v to rearrange the elements of a subarray $A[m..n]$. Informally, the subarray is partitioned into two "halves," consisting of elements smaller and larger than v:

$\leq v$	$\geq v$

Develop a program based on the following invariant:

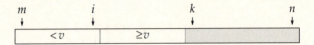

The subarray $A[m..i]$ consists of elements that are now known to be less than v. The middle subarray $A[i+1..k-1]$ consists of elements that are greater than or equal to v, and the gray area $A[k..n]$ consists of the elements that remain to be partitioned. The idea is to shrink the gray area from the left by incrementing k and then reestablishing the invariant if $A[k] < v$. When $A[k] < v$, the invariant can be reestablished by exchanging $A[k]$ and $A[i+1]$.

3.12 Develop an implementation of the procedure *partition* in Exercise 3.11, based on the diagram in Fig. 3.19. The diagram leads to an efficient implementation that shrinks the gray area alternately from the left and from the right.

The loop invariant appears in Fig. 3.19(a). The gray part of the array, $A[i+1..j-1]$, consists of elements that have not yet been looked at. The elements $A[m..i]$ are known to be less than or equal to v, and the elements $A[j..n]$ are known to be greater than or equal to v. Initially, $A[m] \leq v$ and $A[n] \geq v$, so $i = m$ and $j = n$ are suitable initial values for i and j. Starting with $A[i+1]$, let $A[i']$ be the first element from the left that is greater than or equal to v, and starting with $A[j-1]$, let $A[j']$ be the first element from the right that is less than or equal to v. The relative positions of i' and j' are shown in Fig. 3.19(b).

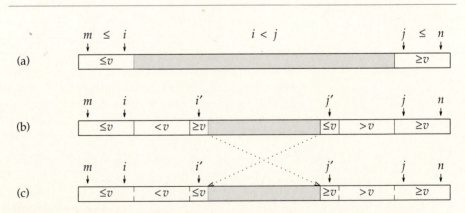

Figure 3.19   Partitioning an array into elements smaller than and larger than v.

If $i' \geq j'$, then the gray region is empty and partitioning is complete. Otherwise, the loop invariant can be restored by exchanging $A[i']$ and $A[j']$, as in the transition from Fig. 3.19(b) to (c).

3.13 Break statements do add expressive power to a language. Prove that the following program fragment cannot be implemented using **if and **while** statements as the only control constructs, even if S and T can be duplicated any finite number of times.

> **while** E **do**
> S;
>   **if** F **then break end**;
> T
> **end**

3.14 Show that every flow diagram can be implemented using conditional and while statements if auxiliary boolean-valued variables can be added. The auxiliary variables can be assigned **true** and **false** and can appear as test expressions in conditional and while statements.

Bibliographic Notes

Fortran, which became available in 1957, was based on the concepts of assignments, arrays, and DO statements, which are a precursor of **for** statements. Backus [1981] traces the history of Fortran.

Although Algol 60 provided structured control flow constructs, the examples in the Algol 60 report do contain goto statements. Knuth [1974] traces the historical background of the avoidance of goto statements; he credits Naur [1963b] with the first published remarks on the harmful nature of goto statements and Dijkstra [1968a] with making "the most waves" with a famous letter entitled "Go to statement considered harmful." The letter notes, "The go to statement as it stands is just too primitive; it is too much an invitation to make a mess of one's program."

With respect to structured statement constructs, experiments by Gannon and Horning [1975] suggest that fewer programming errors occur if statements are terminated rather than separated by semicolons. The case statement is the language design proposal that Hoare [1981] is "still most proud of."

Zuse's Plankalkül had both break and continue statements (Knuth and Trabb Pardo [1977]). Since the Plankalkül lay forgotten until it was rediscovered in the 1970s, these constructs must have been reinvented several times.

Floyd [1967] used invariant assertions to prove properties of individual programs; he attached invariants to points in the flow diagram for a program. The proof rules in Section 3.6 are from Hoare [1969]. Apt [1981] surveys the extensive literature on proof rules.

Dijkstra [1976] advocates the systematic development of programs from assertions. He gives numerous small examples, using statement constructs that differ from the ones in this chapter because they allow nondeterminism (see the bibilographic notes for Chapter 12). Additional examples of program development are given by Gries [1981]. Bentley [1986] makes informal use of invariants to develop a program for binary search. Kernighan and Plauger [1978] give rules for good programming style and then apply the rules to rewrite fragments taken from published programs.

Sentinels, discussed in Section 3.5, are an old idea, going back to "tags" in Wilkes, Wheeler, and Gill [1951].

The pseudocode in Exercise 3.4 is adapted from the description of string handling in TEX in Knuth [1986].

Quicksort by Hoare [1962] has been studied extensively. Exercise 3.12 leads to a program fragment close to one studied by Sedgewick [1978].

Exercise 3.13 is based on Kosaraju [1974]; see also Baker and Kosaraju [1979]. Böhm and Jacopini [1966] show that every flow diagram can be implemented using conditionals and while-loops if auxiliary boolean variables can be added; see also Cooper [1967] and Bruno and Steiglitz [1972].

4

Types:
Data Representation

It was interesting to me to test the efficiency and general scope of the Plankalkül by applying it to chess problems. I learned to play chess especially for this purpose. This field seemed to me to be suited for the formulation of rather sophisticated data structures, nested conditions, and general calculations.

[Data structures in the Plankalkül were built up hierarchically, with bits at the lowest level:] Any arbitrary structure may be described in terms of bit strings; and by introducing the idea of levels we can have a systematic code for any structure, however complicated, and can identify any of its components.

– Zuse [1980], looking back on a programming language he designed in 1945 as a theoretical investigation; it was never implemented.

This chapter deals with data in imperative languages. The reasons for considering imperative languages separately from, say, functional languages, include the following:

- The emphasis in imperative languages is on data structures with assignable components; that is, components that can hold individual values.
- The size and layout of data structures tends to be fixed at compile time in imperative languages, before a program is run. Data structures that grow and shrink are typically implemented using fixed-size cells and pointers.
- Storage in imperative languages must typically be allocated and deallocated explicitly.

By contrast, in functional languages, the emphasis is on values, independent of how they are stored; operations of values implicitly grow and shrink the underlying data structures; and, storage is recycled automatically, using garbage collection. The treatment of functional languages begins in Chapter 8.

Proponents of imperative languages like the ability to manipulate the representation of data; proponents of functional languages like the ability to work with values independent of how they are stored.

4.1 THE ROLE OF TYPES

objects have representations

The term *object* or *data object* refers to something meaningful to an application; the term *representation* or *data representation* refers to the organization of values in a program. Thus, objects in an application have corresponding representations in a program.

Example 4.1 The objects in this example are days like May 6 and their representations are integers like 126.

A parking-lot company counts the number of cars that enter the lot each day. A day of the year is a data object in this parking-lot application. In a program, a day can be represented by an integer between 1 and 366. January 1 is represented by 1, January 31 by 31, February 1 by 32, and so on.

The correspondence between application and program is as follows:

	application	*program*
data	January 31	31
data	May 6	126
variable	*d*	*n*
operation	*tomorrow*(*d*)	*n* + 1

Once days are represented as integers, the integers can be manipulated using arithmetic operations like = and + on integers. For example, if *d* is a day and *n* is its integer representation, then the next day, *tomorrow*(*d*), is represented by $n+1$. □

Confusion between objects and their representations can lead to errors. It makes sense to multiply two integers, but it does not make sense to multiply two days. Furthermore, the representation may not be unique; the day May 6 is represented by the integer 126—or is it 127? The answer depends on whether the month of February has 28 or 29 days that year.

Values and Their Types

Data representations in imperative languages are built up from values that can be manipulated directly by the underlying machine.

basic values typically fit in machine locations

Values held in machine locations can be classified into basic types, such as integers, characters, reals, and booleans. Integers and other basic values are first-class citizens. As a first-class citizen, an integer can be denoted by a name, an integer can be the value of an expression, an integer can appear on the right side of an assignment, and so on. Operations on basic values are built into the languages.

constructed types are built up from simpler ones

In addition to basic types, languages support constructed or structured types that are built up from simpler types and are laid out using sequences of locations in the machine. The structured types considered in this chapter include arrays, records, and pointers.

Type Expressions

types classify representations

A *type expression* describes how a data representation is built up. The term "type expression" will be abbreviated to *type* to avoid confusion between a type expression like

array [0..99] **of char**

and an arithmetic expression like

$a + b * c$

Types are also used to lay out values in the underlying machine and to check that operators are applied properly within expressions.

It is the use that determines the role of a type. Multiple uses can be achieved by treating types as just a classification mechanism for values, as if they were colors painted on values; integers are blue, characters are green, and so on. By itself, a color (type) does not mean much; however, as long as a color scheme (type classification) exists, it can be used to guide the use of types to declare variables or lay out values or check that operators are applied properly.

In summary, types can be used to

- represent data objects,
- lay out values in the underlying machine,
- check that operators are applied properly within expressions.

Types in this Chapter

The types in this chapter are representative of those provided by imperative languages. Basic types, arrays, and records are so useful for examples that we introduce them together in this section before discussing them individually in Sections 4.2–4.4.

For convenience, we use the syntax of Pascal. From the rules in Fig. 4.1, a simple type can be a type name like **integer** or it can be an enumeration or a subrange. A constructed type can be an array, a record, a set, or a pointer type. Array, record, and set types begin with keywords; pointer types begin with the symbol ↑. The rules in Fig. 4.1 can be applied in any order to build up hierarchically structured data representations. For example, we can build arrays of arrays or pointers to records containing arrays, as desired.

C and C++ make extensive use of pointers. Differences between C and Pascal will be explored by considering how some well-known programs deal with character strings; see Section 4.8. The chapter concludes with Section 4.9 on type checking.

Static Layout Decisions

A value of a basic type occupies a fixed amount of space in the machine; for example, characters might fit in a byte, integers in a machine word.

The layout of constructed types in the underlying machine is illustrated in Fig. 4.2. Array elements are laid out in consecutive machine locations. All elements have the same type, so each occupies the same amount of space. Each field of a record has its own type with its own layout. A pointer usually fits in a machine word, independent of the size of the data it points to. Sets are implemented with a bit for each potential element; the bit for an element has value 1 if the element is in the set.

$\langle simple \rangle$ $::=$ $\langle name \rangle$

                  $|$ $\langle enumeration \rangle$

                  $|$ $\langle subrange \rangle$

$\langle type \rangle$ $::=$ $\langle simple \rangle$

                  $|$ **array** [$\langle simple \rangle$] **of** $\langle type \rangle$

                  $|$ **record** $\langle field\text{-}list \rangle$ **end**

                  $|$ **set of** $\langle simple \rangle$

                  $|$ ↑ $\langle name \rangle$

$\langle enumeration \rangle$ $::=$ ($\langle name\text{-}list \rangle$)

$\langle subrange \rangle$ $::=$ $\langle constant \rangle$ . . $\langle constant \rangle$

$\langle field \rangle$ $::=$ $\langle name\text{-}list \rangle$: $\langle type \rangle$

Figure 4.1   Types, using the syntax of Pascal.

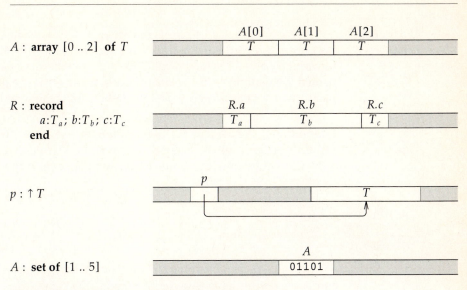

Figure 4.2 Layout of arrays, records, and pointers.

A Preview of Type Names, Arrays, and Records

type names The following are some names of basic types:

> **boolean, char, integer, real**

In addition, a type can be named, in a declaration of the form:

> **type** ⟨*name*⟩ = ⟨*type*⟩ ;

Such type declarations are often used to name record types. Synonyms for types can also be used to simplify and clarify code, and to improve type checking.

an array is a
sequence of
elements

An *array* consists of a sequence of elements of the same type. An array supports random access to its elements. $A[i]$ is the syntax for the ith element of array A, and i is called the *index* of the ith element. Random access means that the time to access $A[i]$ is independent of the value of i.

The following type denotes an array of 100 character elements:

> **array** [0..99] **of char**;

A variable A can be declared to have this type by writing

var *A* : **array** [0..99] **of char**;

a record has
named fields
A *record* consists of a set of components, each with its own type. The components of a record have names and are called *fields*. Field names are referred to variously as *selectors*, field identifiers, or member names. A record supports named access to its fields. Named access means that if expression *E* denotes a record with a field named *f*, then the field itself is denoted by *E.f*.

Example 4.2 Entries for the index to a book can be represented using a combination of basic types, arrays, and records. An entry consists of an index term and a page number. Some terms and pages from this book are

```
Backus, John            11
Babbage, Charles        23
Backus, John            25
```

General purpose languages like Pascal and C know nothing about index entries, so entries have to be represented using types. Here is one approach:

A page number is represented as an integer.

An index term is represented as a character string.

An entry is represented as a record, consisting of
the representations for an index term and a page number.

This last statement can be programmed using *entryrep* and *typerep* as type names. In words, type *entryrep* is a record consisting of a *termrep* named *term* and an integer named *page*, denoting a page number:

type *entryrep* = **record**
        term : *termrep*;
        page : **integer**;
     end

Turning to type *termrep* for index terms, suppose that a character string is stored as in Fig. 4.3. That is, characters are held in an array, starting with the first element, and an integer *length* gives the index of the last character. This data structure can be represented by the following record type:

type *termrep* = **record**
        spell : **array** [0 .. 99] **of char**;
        length : **integer**;
     end;   □

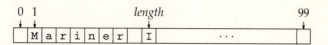

Figure 4.3   A string stored as a sequence of characters, in array elements 1 through *length*.

4.2   BASIC TYPES

Values associated with basic types can be used freely and efficiently in imperative languages. They can be compared for equality, they can appear on the right sides of assignments, and they can be passed as parameters. Operations on basic values often correspond to single machine instructions or short sequences of machine instructions, so the operations are implemented efficiently.

Enumerations

An *enumeration* is a finite sequence of names written between parentheses. The declaration

> **type** *day* = (*Mon*, *Tue*, *Wed*, *Thu*, *Fri*, *Sat*, *Sun*);

makes *day* an enumeration with seven elements.

enumerated names
are constants
Names like *Mon* are treated as constants. From an occurrence of a constant *Fri* in a program, we need to be able to determine that it belongs to type *day*. Pascal and C insist that a name appear in at most one enumeration.

The basic type boolean is treated as the predeclared enumeration

> **type boolean** = (**true**, **false**);

Similarly, **char** is treated as an enumeration determined by the instruction set of the machine. The widely used ASCII (American Standard Code for Information Interchange) character set has 128 elements.

A character constant is enclosed between single quotes, as in `'&'`. Single quotes are denoted by `''`, so the character constant for a single quote is `''''`.

The elements of an enumeration are ordered; that is,

> *Mon* < *Tue* < ⋯ < *Sun*

*operations deal
with the order of
enumerated names*

The following Pascal operations apply not only to enumerations but to integers as well:

- *Ordinal*. Function $ord(x)$ maps name x to its integer position in the enumeration. Thus, $ord(Sun)$ equals 7.
- *Successor*. Function $succ(x)$ maps name x to the next name in the enumeration; an error occurs if x is the last name.
- *Predecessor*. Function $pred(x)$ maps name x to the previous name in the enumeration; an error occurs if x is the first name.

For example, a function $tomorrow(x)$ on days can be implemented as follows:

> **if** $x = Sun$ **then** *result* := *Mon* **else** *result* := $succ(x)$

Integers and Reals

*integers and reals
get machine
support*

The values associated with the basic types **integer** and **real** are determined by the underlying machine, with the largest and smallest numbers determined primarily by the number of bits in a machine word. The supported integer values are between $-MaxInt$ and $MaxInt$, where $MaxInt$ is a predefined constant for an implementation.

The operators of Pascal are

```
<  <= = <> >= > in     in tests set membership
+ - or
* / div mod and
not
```

The inequality relation is typed as `<>`. The `in` operation is shown only for its precedence; it tests set membership. The operator `div` is for integer division; the operator `mod` returns the remainder after integer division. Thus,

```
5 div 3 = 1
5 mod 3 = 2
```

All binary operators associate to the left, operators on the same line have equal precedence, and operators on a line have lower precedence than those on successive lines. Thus, + has higher precedence than <, and + has lower precedence than `and`. The parentheses in

```
(i >= 0) and (x <> A[i])
```

are therefore necessary.

C has a richer set of operators and precedence levels. A partial list is as follows:

| | | logical or, short circuit
&& | logical and, short circuit
== != | equality test, inequality test
< > <= >= |
+ - |
* / % | % returns remainder after integer division
! | logical negation

Short-Circuit Evaluation of Boolean Expressions

C uses *short-circuit evaluation* for the boolean operators || and &&; that is, the second operand is evaluated only if necessary. Pascal's successor, Modula-2, uses short-circuit evaluation for **or** and **and**.

Short-circuit evaluation is useful in the following C program fragment because control reaches the text x!=A[i] only if the expression i>=0 is true:

```
while( i >= 0 && x != A[i] ) i = i-1;
```

Such a test can be used to ensure that subscript i is within the range expected for the array.

With short-circuit evaluation, if E_1 is true, then the whole expression E_1 **or** E_2 is true; E_2 is not evaluated. Similarly, if E_1 is false, then E_1 **and** E_2 is false; E_2 is not evaluated.

Subranges

subranges specify bounds

Subranges are a special case of basic types because they restrict the range of values of an existing type. An example is the subrange 0 .. 99, which restricts attention to the integer values 0 through 99. The values of the underlying type must be integers or they must be of some enumerated type; subranges of reals are not permitted.

The syntax of a *subrange* in Pascal is

$$\langle constant_1 \rangle \; .. \; \langle constant_2 \rangle$$

where $\langle constant_1 \rangle$ and $\langle constant_2 \rangle$ are of the same type, and $\langle constant_1 \rangle$ is less than or equal to $\langle constant_2 \rangle$. The values in the subrange denoted by

$$low \; .. \; high$$

are low, $low+1, \ldots, high$, if low and $high$ are integers.

Subranges are typically used for array bounds.

The operations on subranges are the same as those on the underlying type — that is, on the type from which the subrange is drawn.

Layout of Basic Types

Basic types are laid out by using the machine representation of the values, where possible. On most machines, characters fit in a byte, integers in a word, and real numbers in two contiguous words. Where the machine provides options, knowledge of the range of values of a type can help a language implementation choose between the options.

Programming Style: Characters and Type Conversion

The programming style that develops around a language is influenced by details like coercions between characters and integers and the efficiency with which case statements are implemented.

C coerces characters to integers

A *coercion* is an automatic conversion between types. In C, characters are implicitly coerced to integers. The typical use is for character input. The function getchar returns an integer. Such an integer either corresponds to a character or it is a special integer constant EOF that cannot be confused with any character (see Fig. 4.4).

The following is a complete program from Chapter 1 of Kernighan and Ritchie [1988], a definitive book on C. Although the program reads characters from its input, and writes them to its output, the only declaration says that c denotes integers, not characters. Why?

```
#include <stdio.h>
main() {
    int c;
    c = getchar();
    while( c != EOF ) {
```

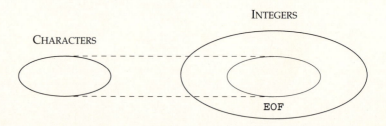

Figure 4.4   The coercion of characters into integers in C.

```
                    putchar(c);
                    c = getchar();
            }
    }
```

The first line allows the program to use the standard input/output library, which defines the integer constant EOF. The value of EOF is different from the value of any character. Function getchar returns EOF if there are no more characters to be read — that is, when the end of the input file is reached. Declaring c to be an integer allows it to take on the integer value of EOF. In fact, an assignment c=getchar() results in a coercion because the character on the right side is coerced to an integer when the assignment occurs.

Conversion between characters and integers must be done explicitly in Pascal. Function $ord(c)$ maps a character c to an integer i. The inverse operation $chr(i)$ maps an integer to a character. Thus

$$c = chr(ord(c))$$
$$i = ord(chr(i))$$

4.3 ARRAYS: SEQUENCES OF ELEMENTS

issues: efficient access and storage allocation

An array is a data structure that holds a sequence of elements of the same type. The fundamental property of arrays is that $A[i]$, the ith element of array A, can be accessed quickly, for any value of i at run time. The index i is often an integer, but it does not need to be. A language designer can allow the index to be any type or value, so long as $A[i]$ can be accessed efficiently. This section contains an example of an array indexed by characters.

When are array bounds computed? When is storage for an array allocated? These questions are intertwined because the array bounds determine the amount of storage needed for an array. Conversely, the bounds are not needed until storage is allocated. Storage allocation will be discussed briefly in this section; it is treated more fully in Chapter 5.

Array Types

array types are often indexed by integers, and they can be indexed by enumerations

An array type specifies the index of the first and last elements of the array and the type of all the elements. The index of the first element is called the *lower bound* and the index of the last element is called the *upper bound* of the array.

An array type has the form

array [⟨*simple*⟩] **of** ⟨*type*⟩

where ⟨*type*⟩ gives the type of the array elements and [⟨*simple*⟩] specifies the lower and upper bounds.

Pascal allows the array index type to be an enumeration or a subrange. The following are some examples of array types:

> **array** [1996..2000] **of real**
>
> **array** [(*Mon, Tue, Wed, Thu, Fri*)] **of integer**
>
> **array** [**char**] **of** *token*

The last declaration is used in the following example.

Example 4.3 A lexical analyzer uses an array to map characters to tokens. It reads the input characters in expressions like

> ```
> (512-487)*2;
> ```

and groups them into tokens for the arithmetic operators, parentheses, semicolon, and numbers. Since numbers are made up digits — 512 is made up of three digits — not all tokens correspond to characters.

The following enumeration introduces names for tokens:[1]

> **type** *token* = (*plus, minus, times, divide, number, lparen, rparen, semi*);

An array *tok* to map characters to their corresponding tokens can be declared as follows:

> **var** *tok* : **array** [**char**] **of** *token*;

The array needs to be initialized by assignments of the form:

> *tok*['+'] := *plus*;
> *tok*['−'] := *minus*;
> . . .

Finally, here is a program fragment that uses array *tok*. This fragment is reached with variable *ch* holding the next input character. If the character is an arithmetic operator, a parenthesis, or a semicolon, the corresponding token *tok*[*ch*] is assigned to variable *lookahead*:

---

[1] The use of an enumerated type for tokens is motivated by the parser in Wirth [1981]. Since C coerces characters to integers, the Yacc parser generator (Johnson [1975]) follows the convention of treating tokens as integers. Tokens for numbers and keywords are encoded as integers that cannot be confused with the integer representation of a character.

```
case ch of
'+', '−', '*', '/', '(', ')', ';': begin
    lookahead := tok[ch];
    ch := ' '
  end;
'0', '1', '2', '3', '4', '5', '6', '7', '8', '9': begin
    . . .
    lookahead := number
  end
end
```

This fragment will be revisited once sets are introduced.   □

Do Array Types Include Array Bounds?

Pascal initially included the bounds in an array type. The problem with this approach is that an array of 10 integers then has a different type from an array of a 100 integers. The problem shows up when procedures are considered. A Pascal procedure expects arguments of a specific type, so a program would need different procedures for sorting arrays of 10 elements and arrays of 100 elements.

Such problems can be solved by using parameterized types, where the array bounds are passed as parameters.

Array Layout

distinguish layout from allocation

The *layout* of an array determines the machine address of an element $A[i]$ relative to the address of the first element. Layout can occur separately from *allocation*, which reserves the actual machine addresses for the array elements.

We begin with layout. Allocation will be discussed next.

Relative Addresses

After the variable declaration

   var A : **array** [*low .. high*] **of** T

the elements of array A appear in consecutive locations in the underlying machine. Let w be the *width* of each array element — that is, each element of type T occupies w locations. Then, if $A[low]$ begins at location *base*, $A[low+1]$ begins at $base+w$, $A[low+2]$ at $base+2*w$, and so on.

Efficient Address Computation

The address of an array element can be computed in two parts: a part that can be precomputed as soon as the array is declared and a part that has to be computed at run time because it depends on the value of an array subscript.

Although the layout of array elements may be known in advance, the actual element $A[i]$ is not, since the value of i can change at run time. The formula for computing the address of $A[i]$ therefore depends on the value of i. A formula for the address of $A[i]$ is best expressed as

$$i*w + (base - low*w) \qquad (4.1)$$

where $i*w$ has to be computed at run time, but where $(base - low*w)$ can be precomputed. In C, the first element of an array is the zeroth element; so $low = 0$, and the formula simplifies to $i*w + base$.

The number of instructions needed to compute the formula (4.1) is independent of the value of i. Each element can therefore be accessed in constant time, providing random access to array elements.

precompute the   The subexpression $(base - low*w)$ can be precomputed and stored, say as
constant part c. The address of $A[i]$ can then be computed as

$$i*w + c \qquad (4.2)$$

Layout of Arrays of Arrays

Arrays of arrays can be defined as well:

var M : **array** $[1 .. 3]$ **of** $[1 .. 2]$ **of integer**

Now $M[1]$, $M[2]$, and $M[3]$ are subarrays; each subarray is indexed by values in the subrange $[1 .. 2]$. If we write $M[i][j]$ as m_{ij}, then $M[1]$, $M[2]$, and $M[3]$ can be viewed as the rows of the following matrix:

$$\begin{bmatrix} m_{11} & m_{12} \\ m_{21} & m_{22} \\ m_{31} & m_{32} \end{bmatrix}$$

$M[i][j]$ implies   The layout in Fig. 4.5 is called *row-major layout* because the "rows" $M[1]$,
row-major layout $M[2]$, and $M[3]$ appear side by side. In other words, in row-major layout, the elements $M[i][j]$ are laid out with the last subscript j varying faster than the first subscript i.

A formula for the address of $A[i_1][i_2]$ is

$$i_1*w_1 + i_2*w_2 + (base - low_1*w_1 - low_2*w_2) \qquad (4.3)$$

where w_1 is the width of the row $A[i_1]$, w_2 is the width of the element $A[i_1][i_2]$, and low_1 and low_2 are the lower bounds for a row and an element of a row, respectively. Incidentally, w_1, the width of a row, is $n_2 * w_2$, where n_2 is the number of elements in a row — that is, $n_2 = high_2 - low_2 + 1$.

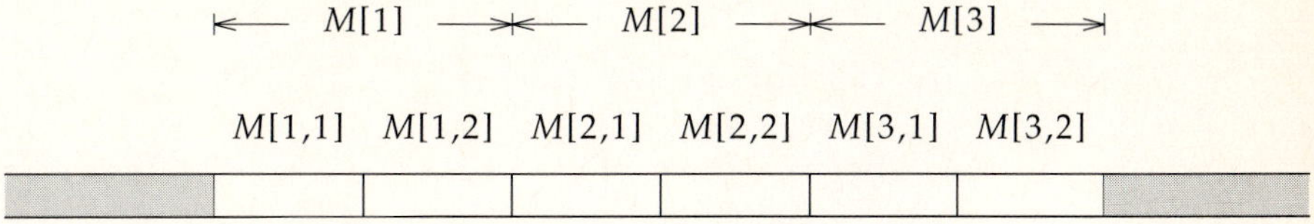

$$M[1] \quad M[2] \quad M[3]$$

$$M[1,1] \quad M[1,2] \quad M[2,1] \quad M[2,2] \quad M[3,1] \quad M[3,2]$$

Figure 4.5   Row-major array layout.

Again, precomputation of $(base - low_1 * w_1 - low_2 * w_2) = d$ reduces the run-time address computation of (4.3) to

$$i_1 * w_1 + i_2 * w_2 + d \tag{4.4}$$

In *column-major layout*, the first subscript of the two subscripts in $M[i,j]$ varies fastest:

$$M[1,1], M[2,1], M[3,1], M[1,2], M[2,2], M[3,2]$$

Both row-major and column-major layout generalize to more than two levels of subscripts.

Array Bounds and Storage Allocation

Algol 60 allowed array bounds to be specified by expressions. The following declaration is from the Algol report, rephrased in a Pascal-like syntax:

var A : **array** [(**if** $c < 0$ **then** 2 **else** 1) .. 20] **of integer**;

This example is contrived, but it makes the point that the bounds of array A depend on the value of c. If the value of c is known at compile time, then the bounds can be computed at compile time. If the value will not be known until run time, then array layout and allocation are deferred to run time and done dynamically.

The timing of array layout and allocation interacts with procedure calls in imperative languages. Storage for all values and variables, not just arrays, is closely tied to procedures, the subject of Chapter 5. This preview of procedures allows array layout and allocation to be discussed together with other properties of arrays.

Storage allocation for the values and variables in a procedure or function is done when the function is called — that is when control reaches or enters the procedure. For example, the function *getnum* declares a variable *value*, and storage for *value* is allocated afresh each time the function is called:

```
function getnum: integer;
   var value : integer;
begin
   value := 0;
   repeat
      value := value*10 + ord(ch) − ord('0');
      getch
   until (ch < '0') or (ch > '9');
   getnum := value
end;
```

Separating Layout from Allocation

Array layout in C is done statically at compile time. Storage allocation is usually done upon procedure entry. It is done statically, however, if the keyword `static` appears before a variable declaration.

An array is called *static* if both layout and allocation are done statically. The elements of a static array retain their values from one procedure call to the next.

The following C procedure `produce` declares two arrays, `buffer` and `temp`:

```
int produce() {
static char buffer[128];
       char temp[128];
   ...

}
```

The keyword `static` identifies `buffer` as a static array, so its storage is allocated at compile time and its elements retain their values across calls of `produce`.

Storage for array `temp` is allocated afresh each time control enters procedure `produce`. The elements of array `temp` lose their values between procedure calls because they can have different locations in different calls.

Pascal does not allow static arrays.

Static and Dynamic Array Bounds

Now, suppose that when array bounds are computed, layout and allocation are done at the same time. The following are some of the options for computing array bounds:

Static evaluation. Array bounds are computed at compile time. Pascal allows bounds like [*xmin* .. *xmax*] where *xmin* and *xmax* are constants. C allows constant expressions, which can be evaluated at compile time.

Evaluation upon procedure entry. In Algol 60, array bounds were computed when control entered a procedure.

Dynamic evaluation. In C++, an expression of the form **new char**[*size*] can be evaluated at any time. It uses the current value of *size* at run time to allocate an array of *size* elements, with lower bound 0 and upper bound *size* − 1.

See Chapter 5 for more on storage allocation and procedures.

Array Values and Initialization

The emphasis in this section has been on the values of individual array elements, rather than on the value of an array as a whole. Does it make sense to talk about pure array values? Is there an array counterpart of an integer value like 2?

Imperative languages favor values that can be held in machine locations, so whole array values appear in specialized contexts. An example is array initialization in C. An array initializer is a sequence of values for array elements. Initializers can be used only in declarations to initialize an array variable.

The following declaration specifies that `coin` is an array whose elements are initialized with the values on the right side of the = sign :

```
int coin[] = { 1, 5, 10, 25, 50, 100 };
```

Since the array bounds are not specified, the size of the array `coin` is taken from the number of elements on the right side. That is, the array has six elements, `coin[0]` through `coin[5]`.

C blurs the distinction between arrays and pointers, and it treats an array value as a pointer to the first element. The properties of pointers are discussed in Section 4.7, and the relationship between arrays and pointers in C is discussed in Section 4.8.

4.4 RECORDS: NAMED FIELDS

The representation of an object may involve variables of different types. A simple example is an index term represented as sequence of characters together with the length of the sequence.

Records allow variables relevant to an object to be grouped together and treated as a unit.

A Record Type Specifies Fields

A record type with k fields can have the following form:

> **record**
> $\langle name_1 \rangle : \langle type_1 \rangle$;
> $\langle name_2 \rangle : \langle type_2 \rangle$;
>   . . .
> $\langle name_k \rangle : \langle type_k \rangle$;
> **end**

Here, $\langle name_i \rangle$ is the name of field i and $\langle type_i \rangle$ is the type of field i. Each field within a record has its own distinct name.

a record type is a template

The type *complex* in the following declaration is a record type with two fields, *re* and *im*:

> **type** *complex* = **record**
>   *re* : **real**;
>   *im* : **real**;
>   **end**;

Declarations of fields with the same type can be combined, as in the following, where the fields *re* and *im* are declared together to have type **real**:

> **type** *complex* = **record**
>   *re*, *im* : **real**;
>   **end**;

A change in the order of the fields of a record should have no effect on the meaning of a program because the fields are accessed by name, not by relative position, as in an array.

A Variable Declaration Allocates Storage

The record type *complex* is simply a template for two fields called *re* and *im*. Storage is allocated when the template is applied in a variable declaration, not when the template is described.

Once a record type is declared, it can be used in a variable declaration, as in

> **var** x, y, z : *complex*;

The variables x, y, and z, have storage associated with them; the layout of this storage is determined by the type *complex*.

Operations on Records

If expression E denotes a record with a field named f, then the field itself is denoted by $E.f$. Expression $E.f$ has both a location and a value. In

$$z.re := x.re + y.re$$

the sum of the values of fields $x.re$ and $y.re$ is placed in the location of $z.re$.

Pascal allows record assignment; that is, all of the fields in a record can be assigned component-wise, as in

$$x := y$$

This assignment sets $x.re$ to $y.re$ and $x.im$ to $y.im$.

A Comparison of Arrays and Records

The array element selected by $A[i]$ can change at run time, depending on the value of i, but the record field $E.f$ is fixed at compile time; thus, there is more flexibility in selecting array elements than in record fields. On the other hand, the fields of a record can have different types, but all array elements must have the same type; thus, there is more flexibility in choosing field types than array element types.

The rest of this section explores the comparison summarized in Fig. 4.6.

Component Types

An array is a homogeneous collection of elements; that is, all elements have the same type. So, the type of $A[i]$ is known at compile time, even though the actual element denoted by $A[i]$ depends on the value of i at run time.

A record is a heterogeneous collection of elements; that is, each element can have a different type. Record components are selected by names that are known at compile time, so the type of the selected component is also known at compile time. The name f in an expression $E.f$ uniquely determines a field, so the type of $E.f$ is the type of the field named f.

	arrays	*records*
component types	homogeneous	heterogeneous
component selectors	expressions evaluated at run time	names known at compile time

Figure 4.6　A comparison between arrays and records.

Layout and Component Selection

The layout of both arrays and records is determined at compile time. The difference between them is that actual array elements are selected at run time, while record elements are selected at compile time.

An array is a homogeneous collection, so each element occupies the same amount of space. If each element occupies w locations, then the storage for $A[2]$ begins w locations after that for $A[1]$, the space for $A[3]$ begins $2*w$ locations after that for $A[1]$, and so on. Formulas for using the value of i at run time to compute the location of $A[i]$ appear in Section 4.3.

A record is a heterogeneous collection, so each field can have a different type and can occupy a different amount of space. Field selection is known at compile time, so the space for a field can be anywhere; it need not be next to the space for other fields in the same record. Allocation and deallocation is easier if space for the fields is contiguous.

4.5 UNIONS AND VARIANT RECORDS

variant records have a common part and a variant part

As a programming technique, unions and variant records have been eclipsed by objects (see Chapter 7); they are included because they illustrate a possible implementation for objects.

Records (the usual ones, without variants) are for representing objects with common properties; all records of the same type have the same fields in common. Variant records are for representing objects that have some but not all properties in common.

A *union* is a special case of a variant record, with an empty common part.

Variant records have a part common to all records of that type, and a variant part, specific to some subset of the records. Specifically, suppose that objects in a set can be classified into n disjoint subsets, where $n > 1$. Such objects can be represented by records with n variant parts, one per subset, and a part common to all subsets.

Before introducing syntax for variant records, we consider an example.

Example 4.4   Consider the nodes in the following expression tree:

```
        and
       /   \
      ≥     not
     / \     |
    x   0    p
```

Such nodes can be classified into those for variables, constants, binary operators, and unary operators. All nodes have some common properties; however, they can have different numbers of children. Nodes for variables and con-

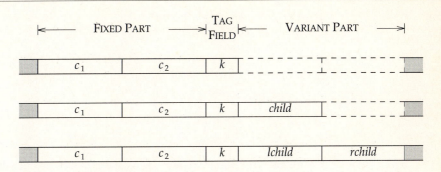

Figure 4.7 A layout for a variant record for nodes with zero, one, or two children.

stants have no children, nodes for binary operators have two children, and nodes for unary operators have one child.

Variant records for nodes with zero, one, or two children can be laid as in Fig. 4.7. There is a common fixed part, shown here as consisting of two fields, c_1 and c_2. An optional tag field k is used to distinguish between variants. The variant part corresponds to nodes with zero, one, or two children. □

Layout of Variant Records

We use the following simplified syntax to explore the layout of variant parts within a record:

> **case** ⟨*tag-name*⟩ : ⟨*type-name*⟩ **of**
>   ⟨*constant₁*⟩ :   (⟨*fields₁*⟩) ;
>   ⟨*constant₂*⟩ :   (⟨*fields₂*⟩) ;
>   · · ·
>   ⟨*constantᵥ*⟩ :   (⟨*fieldsᵥ*⟩) ;

In Pascal, a variant part appears after the fixed part of a record.

The constants in the syntax

$$\langle constant_1 \rangle, \langle constant_2 \rangle, \ldots, \langle constant_v \rangle$$

correspond to distinct states of the variant part; each state has its own field layout. The state depends on the constant stored in a special field, called a *tag field*, with name ⟨*tag-name*⟩ and type given by ⟨*type-name*⟩.

The record type *node* in Fig. 4.8 has three states corresponding to the layouts in Fig. 4.7. Fields c_1 and c_2 are in the common fixed part of the type *node*. On the borderline between the fixed and variant parts is the tag field k, of type

---

type *kind* = (*leaf*, *unary*, *binary*);
    node = **record**
            $c_1 : T_1$;
            $c_2 : T_2$;
            case $k : kind$ **of**
               leaf : ( );
               unary : (*child* : T_3);
               binary : (*lchild*, *rchild* : T_4);
        end;

Figure 4.8   The variant part of the record type *node* begins with **case**.

---

kind, an enumeration with three elements, corresponding to the three kinds of nodes. It is present in all variants and thus behaves like the fixed fields, yet it exists only because of the variant part.

The space reserved for a variant part is just enough to hold the fields in the largest variant. In Fig. 4.7 the variant part of *node* has distinct field layouts corresponding to the constants *leaf*, *unary*, and *binary*. The choice between these three variant layouts depends on the value of the tag name *k*. If *k* has value *leaf*, then the variant part is empty; it has no fields. If *k* has value *unary*, then the variant part has just one field named *child*. If *k* has value *binary*, then the variant part has two fields named *lchild* and *rchild*.

Variant Records Compromise Type Safety

Variant records introduce weaknesses into the type system for a language. Compilers do not usually check that the value in the tag field is consistent with the state of the record. Furthermore, tag fields are optional.

Example 4.5   The tag name can be dropped, as in the following declaration of type *t*:

    type *kind* = 1 .. 2;
        t = **record**
            case *kind* **of**
               1 : (*i* : **integer**);
               2 : (*r* : **real**)
            end;
    var   *x* : *t*;

Record type *t* consists of only a variant part. The type name *kind* after **case** provides for the variant part to be in one of two states, given by constants

1 and 2 associated with *kind*. Since a tag name does not appear between **case** and the type name *kind*, there is no tag field; the state of the variant part therefore cannot be stored within the record. The only possible fields for variable *x* are *x.i* and *x.r*, only one of which exists at any given time.

Since the state is not stored within the record, an implementation cannot check whether *x* is in state 1 when *x.i* is selected and whether *x* is in state 2 when *x.r* is selected. Unsafe program fragments like

> *x.r* := 1.0;
> *writeln*(*x.i*)

therefore go undetected. An execution of such a program fragment produced the machine-dependent output

> 16512   □

The states of a variant record correspond to classes, which will be introduced in Chapter 6.

4.6 SETS

set operations turn into bit operations

Sets can be implemented efficiently using bits in the underlying machine. Operations of sets turn into bit operations. Pascal allows sets to be used as values. It also provides a type constructor **set of** for building set types from enumerations and subranges.

Set Values

A set is written in Pascal by writing its elements between the set brackets, [and]. The following are examples of sets:

> [ ]
> ['0'..'9']
> ['a'..'z','A'..'Z']
> [*Mon..Sun*]
> ['+', '−', '*', '/', '(', ')', ';']

The elements of a set can be written individually or as subranges. The empty set is [ ], the set with no elements.

All set elements must be of the same simple type—specifically, integer, an enumeration, or a subrange of these types.

Set Types

The type

set of S

represents subsets of S. For example, consider variable A declared by

var A : **set of** $[1 .. 3]$

A can denote one of the following sets:

[ ], [1], [2], [3], [1, 2], [1, 3], [2, 3], [1, 2, 3]

Since these are all the subsets of [1, 2, 3], the type **set of** S in Pascal should perhaps be called "subset of S."

Implementation of Sets

These sets can all be represented using three bits. Element 1 is represented by the first bit, element 2 by the second bit, and element 3 by the third bit. The set [1, 3] can then be encoded by the bit vector

```
101
```

A set of n elements is implemented as a bit vector of length n. Since the bit vector must typically fit in a word, an implementation is allowed to impose a limit on the maximum number of elements in a set, thereby restricting the usefulness of sets. The purpose of the limit is to allow sets to be represented by one or more machine words.

Operations on Sets

The basic operation on sets is a membership test. The operation **in** tests if an element x belongs to a set A.

Bit vectors allow the following operations on sets to be implemented efficiently, by using bit-wise operations:

$A + B$	set union $A \cup B$	
$-$	set difference $A - B = \{x \mid x \in A$ **and** $x \notin B \}$	
*	set intersection $A \cap B$	
/	symmetric difference $(A - B) \cup (B - A)$	

Sets can be compared using the relational operators $\leq$, $=$, $\neq$, $\geq$, where $\leq$ is interpreted as subset and $\geq$ is interpreted as superset. Note, however, that the operations $<$ and $>$ are not allowed.

Example 4.6   The following program fragment from Example 4.3 will be rewritten using sets:

> **case** *ch* **of**
> ′+′, ′−′, ′∗′, ′/′, ′(′, ′)′, ′;′: **begin**
>   *lookahead* := *tok*[*ch*];
>   *ch* := ′ ′
>   **end**;
> ′0′, ′1′, ′2′, ′3′, ′4′, ′5′, ′6′, ′7′, ′8′, ′9′: **begin**
>   · · ·
>   *lookahead* := *number*
>   **end**
> **end**

If the labels that select a statement are grouped into a set, then a membership test can be used to select the statement, as in

> **if** *ch* **in** [′+′, ′−′, ′∗′, ′/′, ′(′, ′)′, ′;′] **then begin**
>   *lookahead* := *tok*[*ch*];
>   *ch* := ′ ′
> **end**
> **else if** *ch* **in** [′0′ .. ′9′] **then begin**
>   · · ·
>   *lookahead* := *number*
> **end**   □

4.7   POINTERS: EFFICIENCY AND DYNAMIC ALLOCATION

A *pointer* type is a value that provides indirect access to elements of a known type. Pointers are motivated by indirect addresses in machine language, the main difference being that a pointer *p* points only to objects of a specific type *T*.

Pointers are used as follows:

- *Efficiency*. Rather than move or copy a large data structure in memory, it is more efficient to move or copy a pointer to the data structure.
- *Dynamic data*. Data structures that grow and shrink during execution can be implemented using records and pointers.

Pointers are first-class citizens; that is, they can be used as freely as any other values, including integers. Type checking prevents pointers of one type from masquerading as integers or even as pointers of another type.[2]

---

[2] "Because it descended from typeless languages, C [had] traditionally been rather permissive in allowing dubious mixtures of various types; the most flagrant violations of good practice involved

Pointers have a fixed size, independent of what they point to. They typically fit into a single machine location.

Pointer Types

A pointer type in Pascal has the form

$$\uparrow \langle type\text{-}name \rangle$$

The restriction to type names in ↑⟨*type-name*⟩ instead of ↑⟨*type*⟩ can be programmed around, since a type declaration can be used to give a name to any desired type.

In the following declaration, type *link* is a pointer to a *cell*:

type *link* = ↑ *cell*;

Except in pointer types like ↑*cell*, types must be declared before they are used. Thus, *link* can be declared before *cell*, and then used within the declaration of *cell*, as we shall see. All pointer types ↑*T* have the same layout, independent of the pointed-to type *T*; the pointer layout is thus known even if type *T* has yet to be declared.

Operations on Pointers

dereferencing provides indirect access

The basic operation on pointers is *dereferencing*, written in Pascal as a postfix ↑. The symbol ↑ does double duty in Pascal: as a prefix operator in pointer types and as a postfix dereferencing operator in expressions. The type ↑*T* denotes "pointer to *T*." The expression *p*↑ denotes the object pointed to by *p*.

Data structures of type *T* can be created by executing the Pascal statement **new**(*p*), where *p* is of type pointer to *T*. Storage for the new structure is taken from a special area of memory called a *heap*. The storage exists until it is explicitly deallocated by executing **dispose**(*p*).

The special pointer value **nil** corresponds to a pointer that does not point to anything. It can be assigned to a variable of any pointer type.

Here is a summary of the operations on pointers in Pascal (in each case, *p* is a pointer to type *T*):

Dynamic allocation on the heap. Execution of **new**(*p*) leaves *p* pointing to a newly allocated data structure of type *T* on the heap.

Dereferencing. Expression *p*↑ denotes the data structure pointed to by *p*.

the confusion between pointers and integers.'' (Johnson and Ritchie [1978]) A project to move UNIX from one machine to another revealed widespread type-checking violations in programs that worked on one machine but not on the other. The type system was extended in 1977 to improve the portability of C programs. C++ and ANSI C now strictly check the use of pointers.

Assignment. Assignments are permitted between pointers of the same type.

Equality testing. The equality relation = tests if two pointers of the same type point to the same data structure. An inequality test ≠ is allowed as well.

Deallocation. A dynamic data structure exists until it is explicitly released by execution of a statement **dispose**(*p*).

Data Structures that Grow and Shrink

pointers serve as links between cells

The ability to grow data structures is desirable in programs like compilers, which must handle source text ranging from a few lines to several thousand lines. The compiler's internal data structures can then start out at a size adequate for typical source text, growing only if a large program comes along.

Data structures that grow and shrink during execution are implemented using records and pointers because of the following language-design principle:

Static layout principle. The size and layout of the storage for each type are known statically, before a program runs.

Since layout is done at compile time, data structures that grow and shrink at run time are implemented using fixed-size cells. The data structure grows when a cell is allocated and linked in and it shrinks when a cell is removed.

Cells and links are also used to implement data structures such as lists and trees. A cell in a singly linked list appears in Fig. 4.9. Its type can be declared as follows:

```
type link = ↑ cell;
     cell = record
              info : integer;
              next : link;
            end;
```

Type *link* is a pointer to a *cell*, and a *cell* is a record with an information field and a link to the next cell. Note *link* is defined before *cell* and is used in the record denoted by *cell*.

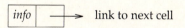

link to next cell

Figure 4.9   A cell in a linked-list data structure.

Example 4.7 Suppose p and *front* have type *link*. The linked lists in Fig. 4.10 can be created by repeatedly executing a sequence of statements such as the following:

new(p);	leaves p pointing to a newly allocated cell
$p\uparrow.info := i$;	set *info* field of the cell
$p\uparrow.next := front$;	set *next* field
front $:= p$;	move *front*, as in Fig. 4.10

The statement **new**(p) leaves p pointing to a newly created cell. An assignment $p\uparrow.info$ puts i in the *info* field of the cell pointed to by p. A similar assignment puts *front* in the next field.

The list on the left in Fig. 4.10 can be built by starting with *front* = **nil**. Successive executions of this program fragment with $i = 1, 2, 3$ build the list on the left. For the transformation in Fig. 4.10, i is 4.   □

The conceptual or logical organization of a linked data structure is separate from its physical position in memory. The links between cells determine the logical organization. The connected cells need not be physically adjacent to each other; they can be anywhere in memory. As long as links between them are maintained, cells can even be moved without disturbing the data structure.

Dangling Pointers and Memory Leaks

pointer operations affect access to storage

A *dangling pointer* is a pointer to storage that is being used for another purpose; typically, the storage has been deallocated. Operation **dispose**(p) leaves p dangling. See also page 186 for another form of dangling pointers.

Storage that is allocated but is inaccessible is called *garbage*. Programs that create garbage are said to have *memory leaks*. Assignments to pointers can lead to memory leaks.

Suppose p and q are pointers to cells, as in Fig. 4.11(a). The pointer assignment

$$p := q$$

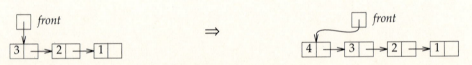

Figure 4.10 Inserting a cell at the front of a linked list.

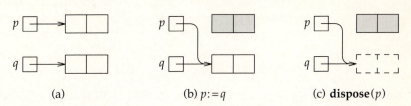

(a)   (b) $p := q$ (c) **dispose**(p)

Figure 4.11   Pointer assignment can result in memory leaks and **dispose** can result in dangling pointers.

leaves p and q pointing to the same cell, the cell that q was pointing to, as shown in Fig. 4.11(b). The cell that p pointed to is still in memory, but it is inaccessible, so we have a memory leak.

Now,

dispose(p)

deallocates the cell that p points to. Not only does that leave p dangling, it leaves q dangling, since they were both pointing to the same cell.

Design of Pointer Operations in Pascal

Pascal restricts pointer operations, C stresses flexibility

Dangling pointers are unsafe because the result of dereferencing a dangling pointer is unpredictable. Pascal therefore restricts operations on pointers so that dangling pointers are created only through **dispose**. If an implementation disallows **dispose** or simply ignores it by doing nothing in response to **dispose**(p), then there can be no dangling pointers. (Memory leaks occur if nothing happens in response to **dispose**(p), since the object p used to point presumably turns into garbage. Over time, memory leaks can degrade the performance of a running program, but they do not compromise safety.)

Pascal prevents dangling pointers except through **dispose** by using the following approach:

Confine pointers to the heap. Pointers cannot be used to access storage for variables. In other words, a pointer cannot access any value or any component of a data structure denoted by a variable.

The operations on pointers are designed to maintain the separation between pointers and variables. Execution of **new**(p) leaves p pointing to a newly created data structure on the heap. An assignment $p := q$ between pointers leaves p pointing within the heap. Furthermore, the only way of dynamically allocating storage on the heap is through **new**. Thus, pointers are confined to the heap.

The operations on pointers in Pascal stress safety over flexibility. C stresses flexibility, trusting the programmer to use it safely. The trade-offs between the two approaches will be illustrated in Section 4.8 by comparing string layouts in representative Pascal and C programs.

Pointers as Proxies

pointers can be rearranged inexpensively

Since pointers can be used freely and efficiently, large data structures are often manipulated indirectly through pointers. This use of pointers will be illustrated by considering an example from Section 4.1. The program fragment in Fig. 4.12 repeats the representation of index entries from Section 4.1.

As data structures go, index entries represented by type *entryrep* are not very large. Nevertheless, it is more efficient to work with pointers to entries than with entries directly. The layout of a value of type *entryrep* must allow enough space for a field *term* of type *termrep* and a field *page* of type integer; the layout of a record of type *termrep* must allow space for 100 characters, corresponding to the array *spell*, and an integer field *length*. Thus, the layout of an entry takes significantly more space than a pointer to an entry.

The following declaration introduces *entry* as a pointer to the actual representation of an entry:

    type *entry* = ↑ *entryrep*;

The variable declaration

    var *e, f* : *entry*;

```
program index(input, output);
   type termrep  =  record
                        spell : array [0 .. 99] of char;
                        length : integer;
                    end;
        entryrep =  record
                        term : termrep;
                        page : integer;
                    end;
        entry    =  ↑ entryrep;
   var  e, f : entry;
```

Figure 4.12 An excerpt from a Pascal program. The declarations in this excerpt specify a representation for index entries.

---

in Fig. 4.12 declares e and f to be of type *entry*. This variable declaration allocates storage for e and f, so when the program begins, e and f denote locations capable of holding a pointer. However, no entries have yet been allocated for them to point to.

Let storage for records of type *entryrep* be allocated by executing **new**(e) and **new**(f). Suppose that we read an index entry

```
Backus, John            11
```

into the data structure pointed to by e. The resulting data layout must be something like

$$e \longrightarrow \boxed{\text{B}\,|\,\text{a}\,|\,\text{c}\,|\quad \cdots \quad|\,12\,|\,11\,}$$

Inside the data structure pointed to by e are the following: a sequence of locations for the spelling of an index term; a location for the length of the term; and a location for the page number. The length of the term in this snapshot is 12, and the page number is 11.

Into the data structure pointed to by f, suppose we read the entry

```
Babbage, Charles        23
```

At this point, the Before snapshot in Fig. 4.13(a) applies.

Rearranging Pointers

Pointers can be rearranged inexpensively, leaving the pointed-to objects undisturbed in place. It takes less work to rearrange pointers e and f, as in Fig. 4.13, than it does to exchange the entries that they point to.

The pointers can be rearranged by the assignments:

```
temp := e;
e := f;
f := temp
```

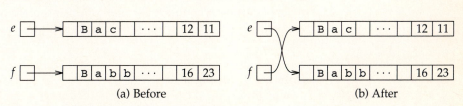

(a) Before   (b) After

Figure 4.13   The effect of swapping pointers e and f.

Code involving pointers can be tricky because a pointer assignment

$$e := f$$

is very different from the indirect assignment

$$e\uparrow := f\uparrow$$

With e and f as in Fig. 4.13(a), the pointer assignment $e := f$ would leave e and f pointing to the same data structure:

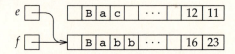

The assignment $e\uparrow := f\uparrow$, on the other hand, means that to the data structure pointed to by e, assign the data structure pointed to by f.

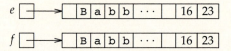

Such an assignment is a complex assignment because each element of the data structure pointed to by f is assigned to the corresponding element of the data structure pointed to by e. Among the components of type *entry* is an array of 100 elements, which means that $e\uparrow:=f\uparrow$ would result in at least 100 element-by-element assignments. The larger the object, the more the assignments to corresponding elements.

Operations on Entries

The illusion that variables of type *entry* are proxies for index entries can be heightened by hiding all pointer manipulations in suitable procedures and functions.

For example, suppose we are interested in removing adjacent duplicates from a list of entries. The integer variant of this problem was solved in Section 3.1 by developing the following program fragment (it assumes the list ends with 0):

```
while x ≠ 0 do begin
    writeln(x);
    repeat read(next) until next ≠ x;
    x := next;
end
```
(4.5)

This fragment reads and writes integers, it compares integers for equality, and it uses the names *x* and *next* to refer to integers.

The corresponding operations are as follows:

procedure	*readentry(e)*	Read an entry *e*.
function	*endmarker(e)*	Is *e* the end marker?
procedure	*writeentry(e)*	Write an entry *e*.
function	*equalentry(e, f)*	Are *e* and *f* equal?
procedure	*copyentry(e, f)*	Update *e* from *f*.

Here is the result of substituting the procedures for the phrases in pseudocode (4.5):

```
readentry(e);
while not endmarker(e) do begin
    writeentry(e);
    repeat readentry(f) until not equalentry(e, f);
    copyentry(e, f);
end;
```

This fragment manipulates entries only through procedures, which hide the representation of entries. All pointer manipulations are now hidden in the procedures.

4.8 TWO STRING TABLES

From a distance, types in Pascal and C are very similar; both have arrays, records, and pointers. Differences in the treatment of pointers, however, lead to differences in style between the two languages, as this section illustrates. We consider representations of variable-length strings from two well-known programs. The Pascal representation is adapted from the published code of the TEX typesetting program by Knuth [1986]. The C representation is adapted from the code for the Yacc parser generator by Johnson [1975]. The Yacc code was not written for publication, but its treatment of strings is representative of C style.

Both programs maintain a table of variable-length strings; lexical analyzers use such tables to hold keywords and names.

A Representation in Pascal

indirect access through an array   The TEX typesetting program uses two arrays, say *pool* and *start*, to hold character strings like

```
TeX
troff
Word
```

The individual characters in a string are kept in array *pool*, as in Fig. 4.14. Elements of the other array, *start*, point to the first character of each string.

The actual array names in the code for TeX are *str_start* and *str_pool*.

Element *start*[*s*] is the index of the first character of string *s*. In Fig. 4.14, *start*[0] = 0 is the index of T, the first character of TeX, *start*[1] = 3 is the index of t, the first character of troff, and so on. That is,

$$pool[start[0]] = \text{'T'}$$
$$pool[start[1]] = \text{'t'}$$
$$pool[start[2]] = \text{'W'}$$

The length of string *s* is given by

$$start[s+1] - start[s]$$

Integers as Pointers

The disadvantage of storing integer index values in array *start*, rather than explicit pointers, is that the compiler cannot check that index values are used only to point to characters.

A Representation in C

indirect access through pointers

The layout of strings in Fig. 4.15 is adapted from Yacc.

By convention, the end of a string in C is marked by the constant EOS, defined to be '\0'. Elements of array pool hold the individual characters in the strings. A pointer to the first character in string s is held in start[s]. We see next that operations on pointers in C allow successive characters in a string to be accessed; the lack of such operations in Pascal must be one of the reasons why array *start* in Fig. 4.14 holds integer index values rather than pointers.[3]

Instead of *pool*, the actual array name in the code for Yacc is cnames. The counterpart of *start* is an array of structures, as records are called in C, with a field for a pointer and a field for a value. Only the pointer is shown in Fig. 4.15.

---

[3] Another trade-off between the layouts in Figs. 4.14 and 4.15 is in the space required for the array *start*. For example, index values might be declared to be short integers, which fit into half a machine word, whereas a pointer might occupy a full machine word. The difference between using a half word or a full word is likely to be irrelevant for most programs.

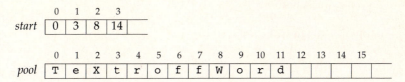

Figure 4.14 String layout from a Pascal program.

Arrays and Pointers in C

an array name in
C is a pointer to
the zeroth element

Arrays and pointers are intimately related in C. For all arrays A, if p points to A[i], then p+1 is a pointer to A[i+1]. In fact, an array name A is simply a pointer to the zeroth element A[0]. Thus, A+1 points to A[1]; more generally, A+i points to A[i].

The pointer dereferencing operator in C is *, and the operator & yields a pointer to its operand. The assignment

```
p = &x;
```

makes p a pointer to x, so

```
*p = *p + 1;
```

has the same effect as

```
x = x + 1;
```

The string layout in Fig. 4.15 cannot be used if the only operations on pointers are dereferencing and comparing two pointers for equality or inequality. Given a pointer to the first character of s, dereferencing and equality testing cannot extract the second and successive characters of s. Note that

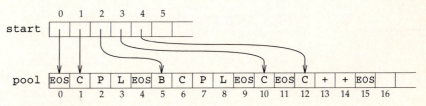

Figure 4.15 String layout in a C program.

the individual characters in a string s must be accessed by an operation that compares s with a string in a buffer.

In C, the code for copying a string from a buffer into the pool can be written as follows:

```
p = start[next];
q = buffer;
for(;;) {
    *p = *q;
    if( *p == EOS ) break;
    p++;
    q++;
}
```

Suppose start[next] points to the next available element of array pool and array buffer holds the string to be copied. After the first two lines, p points to where the first character will be copied and q points to the first element of array buffer.

Read for(;;) as "forever." The statements between braces are repeated until the break statement is reached. The assignment

```
*p = *q;
```

is equivalent to $p\uparrow:=q\uparrow$ in Pascal; it copies a character. If the character is EOS, the end of a string, then control leaves the loop through the break. Otherwise, the postfix ++ operator is applied to increment p and q so they point to the next available pool element and the next character to be copied, respectively.

Discussion

The comparison between the array of pointers in Fig. 4.15 and the array of integer index values in Fig. 4.14 shows how C is often used; type checking can catch some errors of indirection through array start.

4.9   TYPES AND ERROR CHECKING

Since types apply to values and expressions, they are usually studied using expression-oriented or functional languages. As the concepts have been refined, they have been applied to imperative languages as well. This section on types in imperative languages overlaps Section 8.6 on type checking in a functional language. The overlap allows this chapter to be read independently of Chapter 8.

Type distinctions between values carry over to expressions. Values have fixed types. The constant 3.14 is a real number, the constant **true** is a boolean, and real number and boolean are different types.

types extend from values to expressions

This section extends the notion of types from values to variables, and from variables to expressions. If x denotes 3.14, then it denotes a real number. Alternatively, if x denotes **true**, then it denotes a boolean value. The type of an expression $x+y$ can be inferred from the types of x and y. Since 2 and 2 are integers and the sum of two integers is an integer, $2+2$ must also denote an integer.

The rules in this section for inferring the type of an expression deal with basic types like integer and real. Similar rules can be formulated for structured types like arrays and records.

Variable Bindings: The Type of a Variable

The language design determines whether a variable has a fixed type. In Pascal and C, the type of a variable is fixed; if i is declared to have type integer, then it must denote an integer, although the integer it denotes can change at run time. The assignment $i:=i+1$ changes the value denoted by i, but the new value is again an integer.

Lisp and Smalltalk do not restrict the types of the values a variable can denote at run time.

interpreted languages can have dynamic type bindings

This distinction between Pascal and Lisp can be explained in terms of binding times. A *variable binding* associates a property with a variable. Thus, an assignment $x:=3.14$ is a binding that associates the value 3.14 with x. A binding is static if it occurs before a program runs; it is dynamic if it occurs at run time. Static bindings are sometimes referred to as *early bindings*, and dynamic bindings are referred to as *late bindings*. Thus, Pascal has static binding of types and dynamic bindings of values to variables, whereas Lisp has dynamic binding of both values and types.

Type Systems: The Type of an Expression

A widely followed principle of language design is that every expression must have a type that is known and fixed at compile time. The expression $2+3$ must denote an integer because 2 and 3 are integers and the sum of two integers is an integer. Using such rules, the type of an expression can be inferred at compile time.

A *type system* for a language is a set of rules for associating a type with expressions in the language. A type system *rejects* an expression if it does not associate a type with the expression.

The rules of a type system specify the proper usage of each operator in the language.

Example 4.8 This example illustrates a type system for arithmetic expressions, based on the original Fortran manual. An expression is either a variable or a constant, or it is formed by applying one of the operators +, −, *, or / to two subexpressions. The type of an expression is either **int** or **real**.

*expression types
are inferred*

An expression gets a type if and only if one of the following rules applies to the expression:

- Variable names starting with the letters I through N have type **int**. All other names have type **real**. By this implicit rule, COUNT has type **real**.

- A number has type **real** if it contains a decimal point; otherwise it has type **int**. Thus, 0.5, .5, 5., and 5.0 all have type **real**.

- The classification of variables and constants into **int** and **real** carries over to expressions. If expressions E and F have the same type, then

$$E + F$$
$$E - F$$
$$E * F$$
$$E / F$$

are expressions of that same type.

Thus, I+J has type **int** and X+Y has type **real**. But what about X+I? The type system in this example rejects X+I because X and I have different types. Since none of the rules apply to X+I, it does not have a type and is rejected.   □

The Basic Rule of Type Checking

Rules in a type system are based on the following property of functions:

> When a function from a set A to a set B is applied to an element of set A, the result is an element of set B.

Arithmetic Operators

Arithmetic operators are functions. Associated with each operator **op** is a rule that specifies the type of an expression E **op** F in terms of the types E and F. An example is

> If E and F have type **int**, then
> $E + F$ also has type **int**

Overloading: Multiple Meanings

Familiar operator symbols like + and * are *overloaded*; that is, these symbols have different meanings in different contexts. In Example 4.8, + is used for both integer and real addition, so it has two possible types. The treatment of + in Example 4.8 can therefore be restated using the following pair of rules:

If E has type **int** and F has type **int**, then
$E + F$ also has type **int**

If E has type **real** and F has type **real**, then
$E + F$ also has type **real**

Coercion: Implicit Type Conversion

The original Fortran type system rejected expressions like X+I and 2*3.142, since one operand is an integer and the other is a real. This restriction was lifted in later versions of Fortran. Most programming languages treat the expression 2*3.142 as if it were 2.0*3.142, the product of two reals.

A coercion is a conversion from one type to another, inserted automatically by a programming language. In 2*3.142, the integer 2 is coerced to a real before the multiplication is done.

Coercion between characters and integers was considered in Section 4.2.

Polymorphism

A *polymorphic* function has a parameterized type, also called a *generic* type. Data structures like stacks and queues can be defined to hold values of any type. Thus, we can define stacks of integers, stacks of grammar symbols, and so on. When code for such data structures is put into a library, a library designer cannot possibly anticipate all future uses of the data structure. Polymorphic types allow such a data structure to be defined once and then applied later to any desired type.

In imperative languages like Pascal and C, the only polymorphic functions are operations on built-in types. C++ supports parameterized types, using a construct called templates (see Section 6.5).

Functional languages have long supported polymorphic types (see Section 8.6 for an introduction to polymorphic types in ML).

Type Names and Type Equivalence

What does it mean for two types to be equal? The question of type equivalence arises during type checking.

Example 4.9   Are the following two types equal?

  array [0 .. 9] **of integer**
  array [0 .. 9] **of integer**

In a larger context, if variables x, y, and z are declared as follows, are their types equal?

x, y : **array** [0 .. 9] **of integer**
z : **array** [0 .. 9] **of integer**

In Pascal, x and y have the same type, because they are declared together, but z does not.

In the corresponding C fragments, x, y, and z all have the same type.   ☐

This example motivates a close look at type equivalence.

Structural Equivalence

Two type expressions are *structurally equivalent* if and only if they are equivalent under the following three rules:

SE1. A type name is structurally equivalent to itself.

SE2. Two types are structurally equivalent if they are formed by applying the same type constructor to structurally equivalent types.

SE3. After a type declaration, **type** $n = T$, the type name n is structurally equivalent to T.

By these rules, the types **char** and **char** are structurally equivalent, and so are the type names S and T:

type S = **array** [0..99] **of char**;
type T = **array** [0..99] **of char**;

Forms of Name Equivalence

More limited notions of type equivalence are obtained if we restrict rules SE1–SE3. Some possibilities follow:

- *Pure name equivalence.* A type name is equivalent to itself, but no constructed type is equal to any other constructed type.

- *Transitive name equivalence.* A type name is equivalent to itself and can be declared equivalent to other type names. Then, the following types S, T, and U are equivalent to each other and to **integer** because **integer** is a type name also:

    type S = **integer**;
          T = S;
          U = **integer**;

- *Type expression equivalence.* A type name is equivalent only to itself. Two type expressions are equivalent if they are formed by applying the same constructor to equivalent expressions. In other words, the expressions have to be identical.

Type Equivalence in Pascal/Modula-2

Type equivalence was left ambiguous in Pascal. Its successor, Modula-2, avoided ambiguity by defining two types to be *compatible* if

C1. they are the same name, or

C2. they are *s* and *t*, and *s* = *t* is a type declaration, or

C3. one is a subrange of the other, or

C4. both are subranges of the same basic type.

Type Equivalence in C/C++

C uses structural equivalence for all types except records, which are called structures in C. Structure types are named in C and C++ and the name is treated as a type, equivalent only to itself. This constraint saves C from having to deal with circular types, which can arise when structures and pointers are used to implement linked data structures.

Circular Types

Linked data structures give rise to recursive or circular types. Type *link* is defined in terms of type *cell*:

$$\textbf{type} \quad link \, = \, \uparrow cell;$$

Furthermore, type *cell* is defined in terms of *link* because a cell is a record with a field holding a link:

$$\textbf{type} \quad cell \, = \, \textbf{record}$$
$$info : \textbf{integer};$$
$$next : link;$$
$$\textbf{end};$$

Thus *link* and *cell* are defined circularly, in terms of each other.

The circular dependency between *link* and *cell* can be seen from the types of the following expressions (assume that *p* is declared to have type *link*):

Expression	Type
p :	$link$
$p\uparrow$:	$cell$
$p\uparrow.next$:	$link$
$p\uparrow.next\uparrow$:	$cell$
$p\uparrow.next\uparrow.next$:	$link$
$p\uparrow.next\uparrow.next\uparrow$:	$cell$

$$\cdots$$

This progression continues indefinitely.

Circular dependencies between types occur only through pointer types in Pascal and C. In the declarations of *link* and *cell*, the first occurrence of *cell* is on the right side of

type *link* = ↑ *cell*;

At this point, *link* depends on *cell*, but *cell* has yet to be declared. Subsequently, type *cell* is defined in terms of *link*, thereby setting up a circular dependency.

Static and Dynamic Checking

a type error occurs if an operation is improperly applied

Type checking ensures that the operations in a program are applied properly.

The purpose of type checking is to prevent errors. During execution, an error occurs if an operation is applied incorrectly — for example, if an integer is mistakenly treated as something else. More precisely, a *type error* occurs if a function *f* expects an argument of type *S*, but *f* is applied to some *a* that does not have type *S*. A program that executes without type errors is said to be *type safe*.

As far as possible, programs are checked statically, once and for all, by examining the program text, usually during translation. Using the rules of a type system, a compiler can infer from the source text that a function *f* will be applied to an operand *a* of the right type, each time the expression $f(a)$ is evaluated.

Dynamic checking is done during program execution. In effect, dynamic checking is done by inserting extra code into the program to detect impending errors. Extra code for dynamic checking takes up both time and space, so it is less efficient at run time than static checking. A more serious failing of dynamic checking is that errors can lurk in a program until they are reached during execution. Large programs tend to have portions that are rarely executed, so a program could be in use for a long time before dynamic checking detects a type error. Static checking is effective enough and dynamic checking is expensive enough that language implementations often check only those properties that can be checked statically from the source text. Properties that depend on values computed at run time are rarely checked. For example, imperative languages rarely check that an array index is within bounds.

strong typing ensures freedom from type errors

The terms strong and weak refer to the effectiveness with which a type system prevents errors. A type system is *strong* if it accepts only safe expressions. In other words, expressions that are accepted by a strong type system are guaranteed to evaluate without a type error. A type system is *weak* if it is not strong.

By themselves, the terms strong and weak convey little information. As in Fig. 4.16, a strong type system accepts some subset of safe programs; however, we have no information about the size of this subset. If a type system carries a

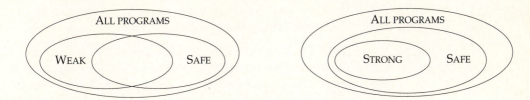

Figure 4.16   Weak type checking allows some unsafe programs to slip through.

"better safe than sorry" philosophy too far, it will reject too many programs. A pathological example is a type system that rejects all programs. Such a system is strong but useless.

To summarize this discussion, the following are some questions to be asked about type checking in a language:

- Is the checking done statically or dynamically?
- How expressive is the type system; that is, among safe programs, how many does it accept?
- Is the type system strong or weak?

Exercises

4.1   Using the string layout in Fig. 4.3, create a program fragment to compare two strings s and t for equality. That is, assume s and t are variables of type *termrep*, as in Section 4.1.

4.2   *Bucket sorting* is a technique that relies on random access to array elements. Suppose that the elements to be sorted have values in the range *low . . high*. The idea is to use an array with lower bound *low* and upper bound *high* as a sequence of "buckets." Bucket i holds a count of the number of elements with value i. Write a program that bucket sorts a sequence of input values i, where $1 \le i \le 99$. A 0 input value marks the end of the input.

4.3   Write a program to read test scores in the range 0..100.
    a. Summarize them by writing the number of scores in the ranges [0 .. 9], [10 .. 19], . . . , [100 .. 109].
    b. Modify the program to take the number values in a subrange as a parameter. For example, with parameter 5, the ranges are [0 .. 4], [5 .. 9], . . . , [100 .. 104].

4.4   The following subproblem arose when the political districts in a state were redrawn. The state consists of precincts numbered between 1 and 27,000. Write a program that takes as input a sequence of precinct numbers and prints them out in increasing order.

4.5   A *text file* X in Pascal consists of a sequence of zero or more lines, where each line consists of zero or more characters followed by an end-of-line marker. The end of the file is marked by an end-of-file marker. Each text file has a *cursor* positioned just before a character or marker; the cursor is said to be *at* the character or marker. If the cursor is at a character, then *read*(X, c) reads the character into c and moves the cursor past the character. Similarly, *readln*(X) moves the cursor past an end-of-line marker. Some operations on text files appear in Fig. 4.17. The following program reads the input file and writes it to the output file:

```
program echo(input,output);
var c: char;
begin
   while not eof(input) do begin
      while not eoln do begin
         read(input, c);
         write(output, c);
      end;
      readln(input);
      writeln(output);
   end;
end.
```

a. Modify the program to count and output the number of characters and end-of-line markers in an input file.

b. Modify the program to count the number of lines in an input file.

4.6   Write a program that magnifies input lines by doubling each character and writing the doubled line twice. Assume that each input line has at most 35 characters, and that two consecutive empty lines mark the end of the input. For example, the input lines

```
///~~~///~~~///~~~///~~~
/    */   */    */    *
```

result in the output

```
//////~~~~~~//////~~~~~~//////~~~~~~//////~~~~~~
//////~~~~~~//////~~~~~~//////~~~~~~//////~~~~~~
//            **//            **//            **//            **
//            **//            **//            **//            **
```

read(X, c)	Read the next character from file X into c.
readln(X)	Read an end-of-line marker from file X.
write(Y, c)	Write c as the next character of file Y.
writeln(Y)	Write an end-of-line marker to file Y.
reset(X)	Set the cursor at the beginning of file X.
eof(X)	Is the cursor at the end-of-file marker?
eoln(X)	Is the cursor at an end-of-line marker?

Figure 4.17 Operations on text files in Pascal. Here, c is declared to be of type **char**. The text file X can be omitted if it is the standard input file *input*, and the text file Y can be omitted if it is the standard output file *output*. Thus, *read*(c) can be written instead of *read*(*input*, c).

4.7 With the string layout in Fig. 4.14, array *pool* holds the individual characters, and elements of array *start* point to the first character of each string. Element *start*[s] is the first character of string s. How would you do the following:
  a. Compute the length of string s?
  b. Output string s?
  c. Determine whether strings s and t are equal?

4.8 With cells and linked lists as in Section 4.7, give a program fragment that removes an element from the front of one list and inserts it at the front of another list.

4.9 A binary search tree is a data structure for maintaining sets of values like integers, which can be compared using a $\leq$ relation. A binary search tree is either empty, or it consists of a node with two binary search trees as subtrees. Each node holds an integer element. Binary search trees satisfy the following invariant: The elements held in the left subtree of a node are smaller than the element n at the node, and the elements held in the right subtree of the node are larger than n.
  a. Describe an implementation of binary search trees in terms of records and pointers.
  b. Write a function *member* to determine if an integer is held at some node in a binary search tree.
  c. Write a function *insert* to add an integer to a binary search tree.
  d. Write a function *print* that prints the elements within a binary search tree in increasing order.

*4.10   Arrays that can be indexed by character strings are a powerful facility in languages like Awk and Perl. The set of index strings can change dynamically; it is not known in advance.

   a. Design a language facility that allows arrays to be indexed by character strings.

   b. Describe an efficient implementation.

Bibliographic Notes

The data structuring facilities in this chapter can be found in languages like Pascal and C. These facilities began with arrays in Fortran and Algol 60, which were designed primarily for scientific computing. Cobol, designed for business data processing, provided a form of records. Records and pointers were incorporated into Algol W, a precursor of Pascal (Wirth and Hoare [1966]). Pascal and C were also influenced by Algol 68.

The hierarchical construction of types, starting with basic types, dates back to Zuse's Plankalkül (Bauer and Wössner [1972]).

5

Procedure
Activations

We really did not understand the implications of recursion, or its value, at the ALGOL 60 meeting in Paris. McCarthy did, but the rest of us didn't.

*—Perlis [1978], on the introduction, almost as an afterthought, of recursive procedures into Algol 60. There was some confusion about whether the committee narrowly voted against recursive procedures or whether it voted against allowing the keyword **recursive** before a procedure declaration.*

For the European group, Samelson, Rutishauser, and I—we had a clear plan for such a compiler, including block structure, including storage allocation even for recursive situations.

—Bauer [1981], on attention to implementation during the Paris meeting.

Before there were programming languages, there were procedures. Hopper [1981] recalls, "as early as 1944 we started putting together things which would make it easier to write more accurate programs and get them written faster." Their approach was to build programs by copying "pieces of coding" out of each others' notebooks.

Procedures are a construct for giving a name to a piece of coding; the piece is referred to as the procedure *body*. When the name is called, the body is executed. Each execution of the body is called an *activation* of the body.

This chapter explores what happens when a procedure body is activated; specifically, it explores the treatment of names in procedure activations.

Names in procedures require care, because a sequence of language-design decisions determines how we get from a name to its value. Fig. 5.1 applies to variable names in an imperative language, where the mapping from a name in

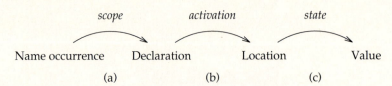

scope   *activation*   *state*

Name occurrence   Declaration   Location   Value

(a)   (b)   (c)

Figure 5.1   (a) An occurrence of a name in a program is within the scope of a declaration. (b) A variable declaration can be bound to a different location each
time a procedure is called or activated. (c) A location can hold different
values as the state of the computation evolves.

the source text to its value at run time depends on answers to questions like
the following:

a. *From names to their declarations.* The same name x can be used in different senses in different parts of a program. A drawing procedure might
use x to specify the position of a point in x-y coordinates; a parsing procedure might use x for a grammar symbol. When the same name x is
used in different senses, which sense or declaration applies to a given
occurrence of x?

b. *From declarations to storage locations.* Each time a procedure is executed
or activated, the variables in the procedure are bound to locations.
Which location does a name in a declaration denote?

c. *From locations to values.* A variable x in an imperative program can
denote both a location and the value in that location. Does an occurrence of a variable name x refer to its value or to its location? (For the
distinction between values and locations, consider an assignment
$x := x + 1$, which changes the value but not the location of x.)

Such questions will be addressed in this chapter by progressing from the
static source text of a program to the dynamic computations that occur when
the program runs. Section 5.4 relates occurrences of names with their declarations in the source text. Section 5.5 relates declarations to the procedure activations that occur dynamically at run time. Sections 5.6 and 5.7 describe the
implementation of procedure activations in C and Pascal, respectively.

5.1 INTRODUCTION TO PROCEDURES

Procedures take two forms: (1) *function procedures*, which extend the built-in
operators of a language, and (2) *proper procedures*, which extend the built-in

actions or statements. We usually abbreviate "function procedure" to *function* and "proper procedure" to *procedure*.

Procedure Calls

a procedure call is a use of a procedure

The use of a procedure is referred to as a *call* of the procedure. Functions are called from within expressions, as in the call of *sin* with parameter *angle* within the expression

$$r * sin(angle)$$

Proper procedures are treated as atomic statements; an example is a call

$$read(ch);$$

which is executed for its effect on the variable *ch*; it reads a value and assigns it to *ch*.

Prefix notation is the rule for procedure calls:

⟨*procedure-name*⟩ (⟨*parameters*⟩)

actuals or arguments are parameters in a call

The parameters in a call are referred to as *actual parameters*, or simply, *actuals*. Thus, *angle* is the actual parameter in the call *sin(angle)* and *ch* is the actual in the call *read(ch)*.

The parentheses around parameters are a syntactic cue to a procedure call. Some languages therefore require parentheses even when there are no parameters. In C and Modula-2, a parameterless procedure *getch* is called by writing *getch( )*. Pascal drops the parentheses if there are no parameters. The statement

begin while *eoln* **do** *readln*; *read(ch)* **end**

contains three calls: (1) *eoln*, a parameterless function call that checks for the end of a line in the input; (2) *readln*, a parameterless procedure call that moves past the end of a line in the input; and (3) *read(ch)*, a procedure call with variable *ch* as a parameter.

Elements of a Procedure

Despite their distinct roles as operators and actions, functions and procedures are very similar. The only difference between them is that function procedures return a result and proper procedures do not. No wonder one language (C) calls them both "functions" and another (Modula-2) calls them both "procedures."

a procedure has a name, a body, formals, and a result type

A procedure declaration makes explicit the elements or parts of a procedure:

- a name for the declared procedure,
- a body consisting of local declarations and a statement,
- the formal parameters, which are placeholders for actuals, and
- an optional result type.

The elements of a procedure can be illustrated by considering a function *square*, such that

$$square(2) = 2*2 = 4$$
$$square(3) = 3*3 = 9$$

Using name x as a placeholder for actual parameters like 2 and 3, function *square* is such that

$$square(x) = x*x$$

Placeholders like x are known as formal parameters, or simply, *formals*.

The elements of function procedure *square* are as follows:

PROCEDURE NAME: *square*
FORMAL PARAMETER: x of type **integer**
RESULT TYPE: **integer**
PROCEDURE BODY: Return the value of $x*x$.

The next two examples illustrate the syntax of procedures and functions in Pascal.

Example 5.1   A procedure declaration begins with keyword **procedure** in Pascal:

```
procedure getch;
   begin
      while eoln do readln;
      read(ch)
   end;
```

The name of this procedure is *getch*. When the name *getch* is called, the statement

begin while *eoln* **do** *readln*; *read*(*ch*) **end**

is executed.   □

In most languages, including Pascal's successor Modula-2, the result of a function procedure is returned explicitly by a return statement in the procedure body, like

return $x*x$;

Pascal itself has unusual syntax for returning a result, as we see in the next example.

Example 5.2   The declaration of a function procedure begins with keyword **function** in Pascal. Figure 5.2 contains an annotated declaration of *square*. The formal parameter x and its result type **integer** appear within parentheses after the procedure name. The result type, also **integer**, appears after the formal parameter. The procedure body is enclosed between the keywords **begin** and **end**.

The value returned from *square* is determined by the assignment

$square := x*x$

within the function body.

Pascal follows the unfortunate practice of indicating a return value by assigning to the function name. On the left side of an assignment, the function name is treated as a variable. When control leaves the function body, the value associated with the function name is returned as a result.   □

Realistic programming examples involve collections of procedures and data; such collections are considered in Chapter 6. Meanwhile, here is a complete program containing procedures.

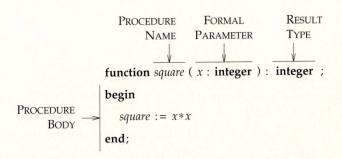

Figure 5.2   The elements of a function procedure *square*, in Pascal.

Example 5.3   The area under a curve can be approximated by using straight lines as in Fig. 5.3. The four-sided shaded shape in the figure, called a trapezoid, approximates the area under the curve *f* between *a* and *b*.

The complete Pascal program in Fig. 5.4 uses a variable *result* and two function procedures, *square* and *area*. Function *square* corresponds to the curve *f* in Fig. 5.3. Function *area* approximates the area under a curve; it takes three parameters, *a*, *b*, and a function *f*. Thus, *area* is called as follows

area(2, 5, *square*)

to approximate the area under the curve *square* between 2 and 5.

Function *area* corresponds to an abstraction, "area under a curve *f* from *a* to *b*." The specific approximation, using a straight-line segment along the curve, as in Fig. 5.3, is one possible implementation. Since the approximation is isolated in function *area*, it can be improved by changing only the body of function *area*, without affecting the rest of the program. For example, a better approximation is obtained if instead of one straight-line segment, the curve is approximated by two or more straight-line segments.   □

Recursion: Multiple Activations of a Procedure

a recursive procedure can activate itself
Each execution of a procedure body is referred to as an *activation* of the procedure. A procedure is *recursive* if it can be activated from within its own procedure body, either directly by calling itself, or indirectly through calls to other procedures. A recursive procedure can have multiple activations in progress at the same time.

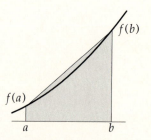

Figure 5.3   The area under the curve is approximated by the shaded area, bounded by straight lines. The approximate area is obtained by multiplying the horizontal length $b-a$ by the average of the two vertical lengths $f(a)$ and $f(b)$. The result is $(b-a)*(f(a)+f(b))/2$.

```
program trap(input, output);
   var result: real;

   function square(x: real): real;
   begin
      square := x * x;
   end;

   function area(a, b : real; function f(x: real): real): real;
   begin
      area := (b − a) * (f(a) + f(b))/2
   end;

begin
   result := area(2, 5, square);
   writeln(2, 5, result)
end.
```

Figure 5.4   A complete Pascal program with two functions, *square* and *area*. Execution begins in the body of the program, which is the statement

> **begin**   *result* := *area*(2, 5, *square*); *writeln*(2, 5, *result*)   **end**

on the last four lines.

Example 5.4   The factorial function is a short common example of recursion:

```
function f(n: integer): integer;
begin
   if n = 0 then f := 1 else f := n*f(n−1);
end;
```

Function f is recursive because $f(n)$ is computed in terms of $f(n-1)$, $f(n-1)$ in terms of $f(n-2)$ and so on, until $f(0)=1$ is computed. The sequence of activations that are set up during the evaluation of the call $f(3)$ are illustrated in Fig. 5.5.

In response to the call $f(3)$, the function body is executed with $n=3$:

if $3 = 0$ **then** $\cdots$ **else** $\cdots$

Since $3=0$ is false, control reaches the expression $3*f(3-1)$. This expression simplifies to $3*f(2)$.

Now, the value of $f(2)$ is needed for the multiplication, so f is called recursively to evaluate $f(2)$. Similarly, $f(1)$ is called during the activation for $f(2)$, and $f(0)$ is called during the activation of $f(1)$. ☐

$$f(3) = 3 * f(2)$$
$$f(2) = 2 * f(1)$$
$$f(1) = 1 * f(0)$$
$$f(0) = 1$$
$$f(1) = 1$$
$$f(2) = 2$$
$$f(3) = 6$$

Figure 5.5 Multiple activations of a factorial function.

Benefits of Procedures

procedures are one way of organizing programs

The user of a procedure needs to know what a procedure does, not how the procedure works. This separation of "what" from "how" or of behavior from implementation allows a program to be partitioned into pieces that can be understood in isolation.

The benefits of procedures include the following:

- *Procedure abstraction*. Descriptive procedure names like *sort* allow us to abstract away from implementation details and think in terms of operations that are relevant to the problem being solved. The name *sort* conveys the intent of the procedure; it conveys what the procedure is supposed to do.

- *Implementation hiding*. Algorithms isolated within procedures can later be modified by changing only the procedure, not the rest of the program. For example, suppose a procedure *getch* reads an input character, skipping over the ends of lines. Since input is isolated in procedure *getch*, only *getch* needs to be changed if the program is modified — say, to handle errors due to the unexpected end of the input, or to use a more efficient implementation.

- *Modular programs*. Procedures can be used to partition programs into smaller pieces that can be understood in isolation. Procedures therefore allow us to manage larger programs than we otherwise could.

- *Libraries*. Standard collections of useful procedures are a way of extending a language. Operators like + and * are usually provided within the language, but mathematical functions like *sin* and *log* are provided by a library, as are input/output procedures.

5.2 PARAMETER-PASSING METHODS

The formal parameters in a procedure declaration are placeholders for the actual parameters supplied in a procedure call. Consider formal x in the following declaration of *square*:

> **function** *square*(x: **integer**): **integer**
> **begin**
>   *square* := $x*x$
> **end**;

The call *square*(2) computes 4 by evaluating $x*x$ with 2 in place of x; the call *square*(3) computes 9 by evaluating the same expression $x*x$ with 3 in place of x.

Parameter passing refers to the matching of actuals with formals when a procedure call occurs. Differing interpretations of what a parameter stands for lead to different parameter-passing methods. Does an actual parameter $A[j]$ in a procedure call $P(A[j])$ represent its value, its location, or the program text $A[j]$ itself? Some possible interpretations are as follows:

- *Call-by-value*. Pass the value of $A[j]$.
- *Call-by-reference*. Pass the location of $A[j]$.
- *Call-by-name*. Pass the text $A[j]$ itself, avoiding "name clashes."

This section deals with call-by-value, call-by-reference, and a variant, call-by-value-result. With call-by-name, we need to be careful with different uses of the same name; it will therefore be examined in Section 5.3 along with scope rules, which give meaning to names.

We say *value parameter* for a parameter that is passed by value, *reference parameter* for a parameter that is passed by reference, and so on for other methods.

A parameter in Pascal is normally passed by value. It is passed by reference, however, if the keyword **var** appears before the declaration of the formal parameter. C uses call-by-value; C++ uses call-by-value and call-by-reference.

Call-by-Value

a formal value parameter takes on the value of an actual

Under call-by-value, a formal parameter corresponds to the value of an actual parameter. That is, the formal x of a procedure P takes on the value of the actual parameter. The idea is to evaluate a call $P(E)$ as follows:

> $x := E$;   { pass the value of E to x }
> execute the body of procedure P
> if P is a function, return a result

Example 5.5 Under call-by-value, the result 4 of the call $square(2)$ is computed by evaluating the body $x*x$ with actual 2 in place of formal x. In the call $square(2+3)$, the actual $2+3$ is evaluated, and its value 5 becomes the value of x. The result of the call is 25.

Alternatively, the effect of a call $square(E)$ is as follows:

```
x := E;          { pass the value of E by assigning to x }
square := x*x    { execute body of function square }
return square    { return a result }
```

Call-by-value works most of the time — in fact, often enough that it is the primary parameter-passing method in C and Pascal. Examples like the following, however, motivate consideration of additional methods.

Example 5.6 Procedure *nget* in this example is a variant of *getch* in Example 5.1. The new procedure *nget* attempts to read into a formal c:

```
procedure nget(c : char);
   begin
       while eoln do readln;
       read(c)
   end;
```

Under call-by-value, $nget(ch)$ has no effect on ch. The call begins with formal c being assigned the value of actual ch; however, when a character is read into the formal c, variable ch is left unchanged.

A standard example for illustrating parameter-passing methods is a procedure $swap(x, y)$, which exchanges the values of x and y.

Example 5.7 An abortive attempt at *swap* in Pascal is

```
procedure muchAdo(x, y: T);
var z: T;
begin
   z := x; x := y; y := z;
end
```

A call $muchAdo(a, b)$ does nothing to a and b. To see why, consider the effect of this call, under call-by-value:

$$
\begin{array}{ll}
x := a; & \{\text{ pass the value of } a \text{ to } x \} \\
y := b; & \{\text{ pass the value of } b \text{ to } y \} \\
z := x; \; x := y; \; y := z; & \{\; a \text{ and } b \text{ are unchanged } \}
\end{array}
$$

This program fragment does not change a and b, although the values of x and y are indeed exchanged. □

Call-by-Reference

a formal reference parameter denotes the location of an actual

Under call-by-reference, a formal parameter becomes a synonym for the location of an actual parameter. Keyword **var** makes y a reference parameter in the following Pascal declaration:

> **procedure** $P(\; x : T_x; \;$ **var** $y : T_y \;); \; \cdots$ **end**;

By default, x is a value parameter. The call $P(a+b, c)$ has the following effect:

> $x := a+b$;
> make the location of reference parameter y the same as that of c;
> execute the body of procedure P;

An actual value parameter can be an expression, but an actual reference parameter must have a location; that is, it must be either a variable name or an assignable component of a data structure.[1]

The location of an actual parameter is computed and passed-by-reference just before the procedure body is executed. In the following example, one of the actual parameters is $A[i]$, and the value of i changes during the procedure call. The location that is passed is the location denoted by $A[i]$ at the beginning of the procedure call.

Example 5.8 Here is a Pascal version of $swap(x, y)$:

> **procedure** $swap(\;$ **var** $x :$ **integer**;   **var** $y :$ **integer** $\;)$;
> **var** $z :$ **integer**;
> **begin**
> $z := x; \; x := y; \; y := z$;
> **end**;

---

[1] Early versions of Fortran did not check whether actual reference parameters were assignable. Consequently, a call $swap(1, 2)$ might have swapped the constants 1 and 2, affecting subsequent computations using these constants. Since each constant is held in some location in the machine and $swap$ interchanges the values of its parameters, it would interchange the constants as well. Some languages avoid such problems by using call-by-value for actuals that are constants or expressions that are not assignable.

Both x and y are reference parameters, so a call $swap(i, A[i])$ does the following:

make the location of x the same as that of i;
make the location of y the same as that of $A[i]$;
$z := x;\ \ x := y;\ \ y := z$

If i is 2 and $A[2]$ is 99, the effect of these statements is

$z := 2;\ \ i := 99;\ \ A[2] := z$

Thus, these assignments exchange the values in i and $A[2]$.   □

pointers can simulate reference parameters even with call-by-value

The only parameter-passing method in C is call-by-value; however, the effect of call-by-reference can be achieved using pointers. The address-of operator & in C constructs a pointer to a variable. The actual parameters in the call

$swapc(\&a,\ \&b);$

are the address of a and the address of b. The body of procedure $swapc$ can then exchange the values of a and b, using indirect addressing.

In more detail, procedure $swapc$ can be implemented as follows (the = sign is the assignment operator in C):

```
void swapc(int * px, int * py) {
    int z;
    z = *px; *px = *py; *py = z;
}
```

A prefix "*" is the pointer dereferencing operator in C. If pa is a pointer to a, then $*pa$ can appear in place of a; that is, on the right side of an assignment $*pa$ denotes the value of a, and on the left side, $*pa$ denotes the location of a.

Now, pointers $\&a$ to a and $\&b$ to b can be used to exchange the values of a and b:

$px\ =\ \&a;$	{ pass the address of a to px }
$py\ =\ \&b;$	{ pass the address of b to py }
$z\ =\ *px;$	{ assign z the initial value of a }
$*px\ =\ *py;$	{ assign a the value of b }
$*py\ =\ z;$	{ assign b the initial value of a, saved in z }

Call-by-Value-Result

value-result parameters are copied in on entry and copied out on exit

Call-by-value-result is also known as *copy-in/copy-out* because the actuals are initially copied into the formals and the formals are eventually copied back out to the actuals. Actuals such as $2+3$ that do not have locations are passed by value.

Actuals with locations are treated as follows:

1. *Copy-in phase*. Both the values and the locations of the actual parameters are computed. The values are assigned to the corresponding formals, as in call-by-value, and the locations are saved for the copy-out phase.
2. *Copy-out phase*. After the procedure body is executed, the final values of the formals are copied back out to the locations computed in the copy-in phase.

Legal Ada programs are expected to have the same effect under call-by-reference and copy-in/copy-out, so an implementation can choose to use either one. Ada supports three kinds of parameters:

- **in** parameters, corresponding to value parameters,
- **out** parameters, corresponding to just the copy-out phase of call-by-value-result, and
- **in out** parameters, corresponding to either reference parameters or value-result parameters, at the discretion of the implementation.

A call $swap(i, A[i])$ does indeed exchange the values of i and $A[i]$ under call-by-value-result. Suppose, again, that i is initially 2 and that $A[2]$ is initially 99. Since the locations of the actuals i and $A[i]$ are computed at the start, the copy-out phase affects $A[2]$ even though the final value of i is 99.

Programs that produce different results under call-by-reference and copy-in/copy-out can be contrived with the help of aliases — two expressions denoting the same location are said to be *aliases* for each other. By definition, Ada programs that use aliases are viewed as being erroneous, although an implementation cannot always check the use of aliases.

Example 5.9 Procedure *foo* in this example has two ways of changing the value of a variable i: (1) directly through an assignment to i and (2) indirectly through the copy-out of a formal x. The indirect change will undo the effect of the direct assignment.

A contrived program fragment is

program
        . . .
        procedure $foo(x, y)$; **begin** $i := y$ **end**;
        . . .

```
begin
    i := 2;  j := 3;
    foo(i, j);
end.
```

The body of procedure *foo* is the assignment $i := y$, which mentions i explicitly. Since i is also passed as an actual in the call $foo(i, j)$, x becomes an alias for i. The call $foo(i, j)$ leaves both i and j unchanged because the copy-out phase restores their values:

$px := \&i;$	{ save the location of actual i }
$py := \&j;$	{ save the location of actual j }
$x := i;$	{ copy-in value of actual i into formal x }
$y := j;$	{ copy-in value of actual j into formal y }
$i := y;$	{ change value of i }
$*px := x;$	{ copy out x, thereby restoring i }
$*py := y;$	

Here $*px$ and $*py$ are indirect addresses. Since px is assigned the address of i, an assignment to $*px$ has the same effect as an assignment to i. Similarly, an assignment $*py$ has the same effect as an assignment to j. Thus, the last two assignments restore the values of i and j to those at copy-in time.

Call-by-reference, on the other hand, will change the value of i.   □

5.3 SCOPE RULES FOR NAMES

scope rules
determine which
declaration applies
to a name

Names in programming languages can denote anything, including procedures, types, constants, and variables. A declaration of a name introduces a new sense in which a name is used. The declaration of name z

var $z : T;$

introduces z as a variable.

The treatment of names in procedures requires an association or binding between each use of a name and a declaration. The *scope rules* of a language determine which declaration of a name x applies to an occurrence of x in a program, illustrated by the following diagram:

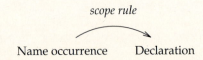

scope rule

Name occurrence   Declaration

Intuitively appealing treatments of names can result in unexpected behavior; so before jumping into the proper implementation of procedures and names, this section uses examples to distinguish between two kinds of scope rules, called lexical and dynamic scope rules. The rest of this chapter is devoted largely to the implementation of lexical scope.

Most languages use lexical scope. The idea of procedures as pieces of code motivates *copy rules*, which implement or explain procedures by copying a procedure body at the point of a call. One of the simplest copy rules, macro expansion, is considered in this section. Naive copying results in dynamic scope. If lexical scope is desired, then some renaming may be needed during copying, as in the original explanation of the call-by-name parameter-passing method in the Algol 60 report. Call-by-name, mentioned in Section 5.2, is explained in this section.

Lexical and Dynamic Scope

most languages use lexical scope

Under *lexical scope rules*, the binding of name occurrences to declarations can be done statically, at compile time, for all programs in a language. Lexical scope rules are also known as *static scope rules*.

Under *dynamic scope rules*, the binding of name occurrences to declarations is done dynamically, at run time. In the following example, an occurrence of a name n is bound to two different declarations during program execution.

Example 5.10   Program L in Fig. 5.6 produces different output under lexical and dynamic scope rules. The program contains a procedure W that writes out the value of a variable n that is declared elsewhere:

procedure W; **begin** *writeln*(n) **end**;

Variable n is not declared within W; it is declared in program L, and again in procedure D.

The body of the program is the statement

begin $n := 'L'$; W; D **end**

made up of an assignment and two procedure calls. Procedure D also calls W, so W is called twice at run time. Each call of W writes out the value of "n."

Under lexical scope, the occurrence of n in procedure W must be bound to a declaration in terms of the source text at compile time. Using the rules of Pascal or C, the occurrence of n in W refers to the n declared in program L. Thus, the two calls of W, from within the main program L and from within procedure D, write out the value of n in L. The program therefore produces the output:

```
program L;
    var n : char;           { n declared in L }

    procedure W;
    begin
       writeln(n)           { occurrence of n in W }
    end;

    procedure D;
        var n : char;       { n redeclared in D }
    begin
       n := 'D';
       W                    { W called within D }
    end;

begin { L }
    n := 'L';
    W;                      { W called from the main program L }
    D
end.
```

Figure 5.6 The output of this program is different under lexical and dynamic scope.

```
L
L
```

Under dynamic scope, the occurrence of *n* in procedure *W* is bound to a declaration at run time. Lisp traditionally used dynamic scope, although modern Lisps tend to use lexical scope. Using traditional Lisp rules, the two calls of *W* bind *n* to different declarations. When the program runs, the first call of *W* is from within the program body; it uses the declaration of *n* in program *L*. The second call is from within procedure *D*; it uses the declaration of *n* in procedure *D*. The program therefore produces the output:

```
L
D                                                                          □
```

Lexical Scope and the Renaming of Locals

if local variables can be renamed, the result is lexical scope

When the initial implementation of Lisp was found to use dynamic scope, its designer, McCarthy [1981], "regarded this difficulty as just a bug." Consider the effect of renaming the variable in procedure *D* in Fig. 5.6. Rename it to *r*:

```
procedure D;
    var r: char;
begin
```

$r := \,'D';$
W
end;

Now, there is only one declaration of n in the program, which means every time procedure W is called, it writes out the value of n declared in program L. The output of the program is now

```
L
L
```

under both lexical and dynamic scope.

Lexical scope is deeply related to renaming of variables. It should not matter whether a program uses r or n as the name of a local variable. Let us state this supposition as a principle:

> *Renaming of local variables.* Consistent renaming of local names in the source text has no effect on the computation set up by a program.

The renaming principle motivates lexical scope because a language that obeys the renaming principle uses lexical scope. The reason is that the renaming principle can be applied to rename local variables until each name has only one declaration in the entire program. This one declaration is the one obtained under lexical scope.

Macro Expansion and Dynamic Scope

a formal macro parameter is replaced by an actual's text

If a procedure body is simply copied or substituted at the point of call, we get dynamic scope. A *macro processor* does the following:

1. Actual parameters are textually substituted for the formals.
2. The resulting procedure body is textually substituted for the call.

Textual substitution means that a string is literally substituted, as is.

C uses a macro preprocessor to support language extensions such as named constants and file inclusion. Preprocessor lines begin with a #. The line

```
#define MAXBUF 4
```

defines MAXBUF to be the string 4. Every occurrence of MAXBUF is replaced by 4 before the program is compiled.

Naming Conflicts

Textual substitution of a procedure body for a call can lead to dynamic scope due to conflicts between different uses of the same name in the calling and called procedures.

Example 5.11   This example deals with a "what if" scenario: what if macro expansion were used for the program in Fig. 5.6? The fragments in Fig. 5.7 illustrate the effect of macro expanding the call of procedure W:

> **procedure** W;
>   **begin**; $writeln(n)$ **end**;

Note that n is not declared in procedure W.

   If the body of procedure W is substituted for the call in procedure D, the variable n is "captured" by the declaration of n in procedure D. The output of the macro-expanded program is the same as that under dynamic scope.   □

Parameter Passing: Textual Substitution

Macro expansion uses textual substitution for parameter passing, which can produce results that differ from any of the parameter-passing methods in Section 5.2.

Example 5.12   Unfortunately, $swap(i, A[i])$ does not simply exchange the values of i and $A[i]$ under macro expansion. Textual substitution of the actuals into the procedure body yields

> $z := i; \ i := A[i]; \ A[i] := z$

If i is initially 2 and $A[2]$ is initially 99, this sequence is equivalent to

---

```
procedure D;                          procedure D;
    var n : char;                         var n : char;
begin                                 begin
    n := 'D';                             n := 'D';
    W                                     begin writeln(n) end
end                                   end
```

    (a) Call of W (b) After macro expansion

Figure 5.7   If the call W in (a) is macro expanded, then the code in (b) is obtained. These procedures are taken from the program in Fig. 5.6.

$$z := 2; \ i := 99; \ A[i] := 2$$

The final assignment uses the modified value of i, so $A[99]$ and not $A[2]$ is set to the initial value of i. $\qquad\qquad\qquad\qquad\qquad\qquad\qquad\qquad\qquad\qquad$ □

Call-by-Name and Lexical Scope

call-by-name avoids name conflicts by renaming locals

Call-by-name, which is now primarily of historical interest, and call-by-value were the two parameter-passing mechanisms in Algol 60. The rules for call-by-name were carefully specified to get lexical scope. The rules avoid naming conflicts like the one in Fig. 5.7, where the calling procedure D has a local variable n that conflicts with a nonlocal variable n in the called procedure W. The naming conflict disappears if the procedure D uses a fresh name r as its local variable instead of n. The rules for call-by-name resolve naming conflicts by renaming locals.

The Algol 60 report describes call-by-name as follows (the examples are in the syntax of Algol 60):

1. Actual parameters are textually substituted for the formals. Possible conflicts between names in the actuals and local names in the procedure body are avoided by renaming the locals in the body. Suppose that name i appears in a procedure call $P(A[i])$, and that the body of P contains a local i:

   procedure $P(x)$;
       begin integer i; $\cdots i := i+n$; $x := x+n$; $\cdots$ **end**;

   Then the local i in the body of P would be renamed. Using j instead, the body after substitution of actual $A[i]$ is

   begin integer j; $\cdots j := j+n$; $A[i] := A[i]+n$; $\cdots$ **end**;

2. The resulting procedure body is substituted for the call. Possible conflicts between nonlocals in the procedure body and locals at the point of call are avoided by renaming the locals at the point of call. Above, n appears as a nonlocal in the procedure body; suppose now that at the point of call, n is local:

   begin integer n; $\cdots n := n-1$; $P(A[i])$; $\cdots$ **end**;

   Then, the local n at the point of call would be renamed. Using m instead, the calling program fragment becomes

   begin integer m;
      $\cdots$
     $m := m-1$;
      begin integer j; $\cdots j := j+n$; $A[i] := A[i]+n$; $\cdots$ **end**;
      $\cdots$
   end;

5.4   NESTED SCOPES IN THE SOURCE TEXT

This is the first of a sequence of sections on lexical scope rules. It deals with the binding of names to declarations in the source text. Scope rules will be illustrated by considering variable declarations in C and procedure declarations in Pascal. In both cases, the declarations appear in constructs that can be nested, one inside the other.

Pseudocode Based on C

Several of the examples in this chapter use pseudocode based on C, to contrast the treatment of names in Pascal and C. In C, a type name appears before the variable name in a declaration. Variable i is declared to have type integer in

> **int** i;

Braces { and } group statements; they correspond to **begin** and **end** in Pascal. The assignment symbol is =. Thus, the Pascal program fragment

> **while** $x \neq A[i]$ **do begin**
> $i := i-1$
> **end**

has a C counterpart

> **while**($x \neq A[i]$) {
> $i = i-1$;
> }

Parentheses must appear around the condition in a while loop or an if statement in C.[2]

The Scope of a Declaration

Care is needed not only in dealing with names in programming languages, but even with the term ''name'' itself. It is common practice to say ''name x'' when the discussion is really about a specific declaration of x. Similarly, the term ''declaration'' has a specific meaning in each programming language.

When the need for precision arises, the technical terms binding occurrence and bound occurrence are helpful. A *binding occurrence* of a name introduces a new sense in which a name is used; all other occurrences of a name are said

---

[2] C programs are traditionally published in a typewriter-like font. Such a font will be used when actual C code is presented. For the moment, the emphasis is on general concepts of imperative languages, with examples from Pascal and C, so the publication style is that of imperative programs, with keywords such as **while** in bold.

to be *bound occurrences*. The term "binding occurrence of a name" covers constructs like formal parameters in addition to covering variable, procedure, and other declarations.

Example 5.13 The following Pascal procedure has binding occurrences of a procedure name, formal parameters, and a local variable:

> **procedure** *swap*(**var** *x*, *y*: *T*);
>   **var** *z* : *T*;
> **begin**
>   *z* := *x*; *x* := *y*; *y* := *z*
> **end**

The occurrence of *z* within the declaration on the second line is a binding occurrence. The two occurrences of *z* within the procedure body are bound occurrences.

The occurrences of *swap*, *x*, and *y* on the line

> **procedure** *swap*(**var** *x*, *y*: *T*);

are all binding occurrences. The two occurrences each of *x* and *y* in the procedure body are bound occurrences. □

The scope rules of a language determine which binding occurrence of a name *n* applies to a bound occurrence of *n*. Each bound occurrence is said to be within the *scope* of its binding occurrence.

Example 5.14 Pascal uses lexical scope, so the relation between binding and bound occurrences can be illustrated in terms of the source text. The dashed lines in the following diagram go from a binding occurrence to bound occurrences within its scope.

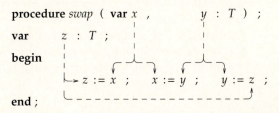

This procedure declaration contains binding occurrences of the procedure name *swap*, the formal parameter names *x* and *y*, and the variable name *z* in the body. The scopes of the formal parameters *x* and *y* and the scope of variable *z* in procedure *swap* consist of the procedure body. Only the procedure name can be used outside the procedure. □

The usage of terms like "declaration" and "name" can now be explained in terms of binding and bound occurrences. A declaration of x is a binding occurrence of x. It is common practice to say "name x" when the discussion is really about a declaration of x. Thus, the statement

the scope of formal parameter x is contained within procedure *swap*

has a precise counterpart

the scope of the declaration of x as a formal parameter is contained within procedure *swap*.

A declaration of a name n is *visible* at a point in a program if an occurrence of n at that point would be within the scope of this declaration. When a specific declaration d is clear from the context, we defer to common practice and say "name n is visible," for "declaration d of name n is visible." In this spirit, a name is *local to* or *bound within* a program fragment if it is visible only within that program fragment.

In C, a nonlocal name is said to be *global* because it is then visible in all procedures. We use *locals* as an abbreviation for local variables, *globals* as an abbreviation for global variables, and so on.

Nested Scopes: Variable Declarations in C

the most-closely-nested declaration applies to an occurrence of a name

As an example of lexical scope rules, we consider the rules that apply to names within compound statements in C. Variable declarations can appear within any grouping of statements in C. Compound statements are grouped within braces { and }, and optional declarations can appear just after the opening brace, as in

{ ⟨*declaration-list*⟩ ⟨*statement-list*⟩ }

Such a grouping of declarations and statements will be called a *block*. Specifically, C does not allow a procedure to be declared inside another, so the optional declarations in a block cannot contain procedure declarations.[3]

Declarations within statements allow names to be declared where they are needed. In the following block, variable i is declared close to where it is used to control the number of executions of a loop body:

```
{
    int i;
    i = 0;
    while( i ≤ limit ) {
```

---

[3] The term "block" has been used in the literature for constructs ranging from sequences of statements grouped between **begin** and **end** to nested procedures. A language that allows a procedure to be declared nested inside another is sometimes called *block-structured*.

$$\cdots$$
$$i = i+1;$$
$$\}$$
$$\}$$

If blocks are not permitted, then all declarations must appear at the beginning of the procedure body, even if they are needed only in a small fragment of the procedure.

Since each compound statement begins with an opening brace, {, and ends with a closing brace, }, compound statements are nested one inside the other. The compound statements in Fig. 5.8(a) are boxed to emphasize their nesting. Statement nesting is usually shown by indentation in the source text. A more deeply nested statement is indented more than a less deeply nested one.

Just as statements nest one inside the other, scopes nest one inside the other. The scope of a declaration of x in a statement is that statement, including any nested statements, provided x is not redeclared in the nested statements.

a redeclaration creates a hole in the scope of enclosing declarations

A redeclaration of x creates a *hole* in the scope of any outer bindings of x. The shaded portion of Fig. 5.8(b) shows the scope of the binding of i_1. The subscripts on the occurrences of i in Fig. 5.8(b) are not part of the program text; they simply allow us to talk about the three occurrences. The declarations of i_2 and i_3 create holes in the scope of i_1. By contrast, there are no holes in the scope of c, since c is not redeclared.

Another way of relating to the scope of a binding of a name x is from the viewpoint of an occurrence of x in its scope. This viewpoint leads to the *most-closely-nested rule*: an occurrence of a name is in the scope of the innermost enclosing declaration of the name. That is, a bound occurrence of x is in the scope of the binding of x in the innermost enclosing block that contains a binding of x.

Nested Scopes: Procedure Declarations in Pascal

most-closely-nested rules also apply to nested procedures

Most-closely-nested scope rules are a form of lexical scope rule because they specify the scope of a binding occurrence in terms of nesting in the source text. They apply not only to compound statements in C but also to constructs with the following properties:

- The constructs nest one inside the other.
- The construct can contain declarations and the scope of a declaration is contained within that construct. (Often, the scope extends from the point of declaration to the end of the construct.)
- The redeclaration of a name in a nested construct creates a hole in the scope of any enclosing declarations of the name.

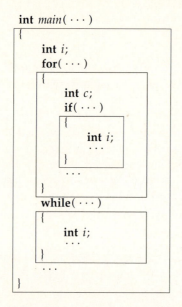

(a) Nested compound statements.   (b) Scope of i_1.

Figure 5.8 Nesting of statements and scopes. The pseudocode corresponds to a C program consisting of a single function named *main*. Execution of a C program begins in *main*.

For example, Pascal allows procedure declarations to be nested; that is, a procedure can be declared inside another. Procedures can contain declarations, and the scope of a contained declaration from the point of declaration to the end of the procedure. Finally, redeclaration of a name in a nested procedure creates a hole in the scope of any enclosing declaration.

Figure 5.9 contains the declarations in a Pascal program, with boxes to show nesting. Nested within the outer box for the whole program are boxes for the procedures declared within the program. The scope of a declaration of x in a box is that box and any enclosed boxes, provided x is not redeclared in the enclosed box.

The declarations in the outermost box, for the whole program, are for *token, lookahead, lookvalue, ch, tok, scan, scaninit,* and *expr*. Nested within procedure *scan* are the declarations of *getch* and *getnum*. An occurrence of variable *ch* in the body of *getch* is within the scope of the declaration of *ch* in the outermost box.

```
program Evaluator;
    type  token = ··· ;
    var   lookahead : token;
          lookvalue : integer;
          ch : char;
          tok : array [ char ] of token;
    ┌──────────────────────────────────────────────┐
    │ procedure scan;                              │
    │   ┌────────────────────────────────────┐     │
    │   │ procedure getch;                   │     │
    │   │   ···                              │     │
    │   │ end                                │     │
    │   └────────────────────────────────────┘     │
    │   ┌────────────────────────────────────┐     │
    │   │ function getnum : integer          │     │
    │   │   ···                              │     │
    │   │ end                                │     │
    │   └────────────────────────────────────┘     │
    │ begin                                        │
    │     ···  (∗  statements in scan  ∗)          │
    │ end;                                         │
    └──────────────────────────────────────────────┘
    ┌──────────────────────────────────────────────┐
    │ procedure scaninit;                          │
    │   ···                                        │
    │ end;                                         │
    └──────────────────────────────────────────────┘
    ┌──────────────────────────────────────────────┐
    │ function expr : integer                      │
    │     var val : integer                        │
    │   ┌────────────────────────────────────┐     │
    │   │ function term : integer            │     │
    │   │     var val : integer              │     │
    │   │   ┌──────────────────────────┐     │     │
    │   │   │ function factor : integer│     │     │
    │   │   │     var val : integer    │     │     │
    │   │   │ begin                    │     │     │
    │   │   │   ···                    │     │     │
    │   │   │ end;                     │     │     │
    │   │   └──────────────────────────┘     │     │
    │   │ begin                              │     │
    │   │   ···  (∗  statements in term  ∗)  │     │
    │   │ end;                               │     │
    │   └────────────────────────────────────┘     │
    │ begin                                        │
    │     ···  (∗  statements in expr  ∗)          │
    │ end;                                         │
    └──────────────────────────────────────────────┘
begin
    ···  (∗  execution begins here  ∗)
end.
```

Figure 5.9 Each procedure declaration is enclosed in a box, as is the whole program.

Nested within function *expr* is the declaration of function *term*; nested within that is function *factor*. The name *val* is redeclared within *factor*, so occurrences of *val* in the body of *factor* are within the scope of the declaration within *factor*.

5.5   ACTIVATION RECORDS

at activation time,
each declaration is
bound to a location

Recursion has significant implications for language implementation, especially the treatment of names in procedures. A recursive procedure can have multiple activations or executions of its procedure body at the same time. The factorial of n is defined in terms of the factorial of $n-1$, so a factorial function can have multiple simultaneous activations. Each activation needs its own storage for local variables. A local variable x in a recursive procedure will denote a different location in each simultaneous activation.

Associated with each activation of a procedure is storage for the variables declared in the procedure. The storage associated with an activation is called an *activation record*.

This section deals with activations and the storage within an activation record for a variable. It deals with the second mapping in Fig. 5.10, from declarations to locations in an activation.

In a lexically scoped language, the three mappings or bindings in Fig. 5.10 are done at three different times:

1. *Compile time*. The binding of name occurrences to declarations is defined in terms of the source text; alternatively it is defined in terms of the lexical context, so it is done at compile time, as in Section 5.4.

2. *Activation time*. The binding of declarations to locations is done at *activation time*, when an activation is set up, as discussed in this section. Even if a program has no name conflicts in the source text because all of the declared names are distinct, the binding of declarations to locations can change from activation to activation.

3. *Run time*. The binding of locations to values is done dynamically at run time and can be changed by assignments.

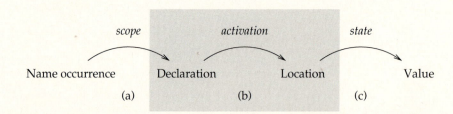

Figure 5.10   This repeats the diagram in Fig. 5.1 at the beginning of this chapter. The second mapping, from variable declarations to locations, is specific to an activation. A local variable in a recursive procedure denotes a different location in each simultaneous activation of the procedure.

Control Flow Between Activations

procedures execute completely before returning control

In a sequential language, control can be in at most one procedure at a time — specifically, in one activation of a procedure at a time. When P calls Q, execution of P is put on hold when control flows to Q; execution of P resumes when control returns from Q.

We concentrate on procedures, which execute completely before returning control to their callers. That is, control flows between procedure activations in a last-in/first-out manner. If

P calls Q, and Q calls R,

control returns

from R back to Q, and from Q back to P.

Similarly, with activations of a recursive procedure P, if

activation P_1 sets up P_2, and P_2 sets up P_3,

then control returns

from P_3 back to P_2, and from P_2 back to P_1.

An alternative to procedures are *coroutines*, which can suspend execution, return control back to the caller, and then resume execution later from the point of suspension. One of the earliest illustrations of coroutines is a producer-consumer pair, where the producer produces a sequence of data objects and the consumer consumes this sequence of data objects. With coroutines, control can flow back and forth between the producer and consumer, as needed. Simula 67 had an explicit **resume**(X) statement to resume execution of coroutine X.

This chapter concentrates on procedures.

Example 5.15 Control flow between activations can be illustrated by inserting write statements into procedure bodies. In the following version of the factorial function, control reaches a write statement just after it enters and another just before it leaves the function body:

```
function f(n: integer): integer;
begin
    writeln('→f(', n, ')');
    if n = 0 then f := 1 else f := n*f(n−1);
    writeln('←f(', n, ')');
end;
```

Such write statements trace the flow of control between activations.

The trace in Fig. 5.11 uses indenting to illustrate nested activations. Read the symbol → as "entering an activation" and the symbol → as "leaving an activation." The trace illustrates the effect of a call $f(3)$.

Note that the → and ← symbols are properly nested in the trace, corresponding to last-in/first-out flow of control between activations. Execution of activation $f(3)$ is on hold while control is within the activations $f(2)$, $f(1)$, and $f(0)$. □

Activation Trees

The flow of control between activations can be depicted by a tree called an *activation tree*. The nodes in the tree represent activations. When activation P calls activation Q, the node for P has the node for Q as a child. If P calls Q before it calls R, then the node for Q appears to the left of the node for R:

$$P$$
$$Q \diagup \quad \diagdown R$$

Example 5.16 Consider a variant of the factorial function, which computes $n-1$ by calling a function $pred(n)$, as in the following program:

```
program activations;
    function pred(m: integer): integer;
    begin
      pred := m − 1
    end;

    function f(n: integer): integer;
    begin
      if n = 0 then f := 1 else f := n * f(pred(n))
    end;
```

→ $f(3)$
  → $f(2)$
    → $f(1)$
      → $f(0)$
      ← $f(0)$ = 1
    ← $f(1)$ = 1
  ← $f(2)$ = 2
← $f(3)$ = 6

Figure 5.11   Recursive evaluation of the call $f(3)$, where f is the factorial function.

> **begin**
> $f(3)$
> **end**.

The activation tree in Fig. 5.12 illustrates the activations that occur during an execution of this program. For clarity, the actual parameters in function calls appear between parentheses in the figure. (Parameters are passed by value in this example. The idea of activation trees is independent of the parameter-passing method.)

The program begins with the activation $f(3)$. Since $3 = 0$ is false, control flows to the assignment with right side

$$n * f(pred(n))$$

With $n = 3$, this expression is evaluated by calling $pred(3)$. Once control returns from $pred(3)$ with result 2, the call $f(2)$ occurs. Similarly, the call $f(2)$ results in the calls $pred(2)$ and $f(1)$, and so on.   □

Elements of an Activation Record

storage for local data is in the activation record

Data needed for an activation of a procedure is collected in a record called an *activation record* or *frame*. The record contains storage for local variables, formal parameters, and any additional information needed for the activation. These elements of an activation record are illustrated in Fig. 5.13.

The detailed layout of activation records varies from language to language; a layout for C appears in Section 5.6 and a layout for Pascal appears in Section 5.7.

Example 5.17 The storage needed for an activation of function *readentry*

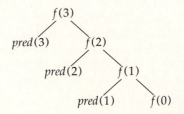

Figure 5.12 An activation tree for the program in Example 5.16.

| Control link |
| Access link |
| Saved state |
| Parameters |
| Function result |
| Local variables |

Figure 5.13   The elements of an activation record.

function *readentry*(*u*: *link*) : **boolean**;
var *i*: **integer**;
     c: **char**;
begin
    . . .
end;

includes storage for the formal parameter *u*, the boolean result, the variables *i* and *c*, any temporary storage needed for evaluating expressions within the function body, and the storage needed to manage activations.   □

An Activation and Its Local Data

each recursive activation needs its own activation record

In a language with recursive procedures, each activation has its own activation record. The following example motivates the use of fresh locations for declarations in each activation.

Example 5.18   Each activation of the functions *f* and *pred* in Fig. 5.12 needs storage for its formal parameter; the functions are from Example 5.16. Formal parameter *n* is local to *f*. The recursive activations $f(3)$, $f(2)$, and $f(1)$ each need storage for the formal parameter *n* of *f*. Furthermore, since activation $f(2)$ occurs during the activation $f(3)$, the storage for formal *n* in $f(2)$ must be distinct from the storage for formal *n* in $f(3)$.

Thus, each activation of a recursive procedure needs distinct storage for its formal parameters. Similarly, each activation needs distinct storage for local variables.   □

Declarations in a procedure result in storage being allocated within the activation records for the procedure. All the records for a procedure have the same layout. The layout of storage for variables depends on the types of the variables, as discussed in Chapter 4. Thus, a single location is reserved for basic types like integers. A sequence of locations is reserved for arrays.

Control and Access Links

Activation records can be managed by maintaining two kinds of links between them:

1. A *control link*, also called a *dynamic link*, points to the activation record of the run-time caller.

2. An *access link*, also called a *static link*, is used to implement lexically scoped languages.

A control link points to its caller. If P calls Q, then the control link in an activation of Q will point to an activation of the caller P.

The next example illustrates the need for access links.

access links are used to implement lexical scope

Example 5.19   Program L in Fig. 5.14 produces different output under lexical and dynamic scope.

Under lexical scope, nonlocal n in procedure W is within the scope of the outermost declaration of n in program L. Under dynamic scope, the first call of W, from within L, binds n to the outermost declaration, but the second call of W, from within D, binds n to the declaration of n in D. For a fuller explanation, see Example 5.10 on page 161.

The activation tree in Fig. 5.15 illustrates the computation of the program in Fig. 5.14. The subscripts in W_1 and W_2 distinguish between the activations of procedure W. The main program L calls W_1 directly. Then it calls D, which calls W_2.

Also shown in the figure are activation records corresponding to the activation tree. These activation records exist at some point during the computation. (In Pascal and C, the activation record for W_1 will be deallocated before the activation record for D is created; we shall get to deallocation shortly.)

The arrows between activation records represent control links.

Since n is nonlocal to W, the storage for n must be found in some other activation record. Under dynamic scope, the storage for n can be found by following control links to find the nearest binding of n. From the activation record for W_1, the nearest binding of n is in the activation record for L; but, from the record for W_2 the nearest binding is in the record for D.

Under lexical scope, the techniques of Sections 5.6–5.7 are needed to find the binding of nonlocal n in W. The Pascal implementation in Section 5.7 uses an explicit access link. The access link points from an activation record of W to that of L, since procedure W appears within L in the source text.   □

```
program L;
    var n : char;          { n declared in L }

    procedure W;
    begin
        writeln(n)         { occurrence of n in W }
    end;

    procedure D;
        var n : char;      { n redeclared in D }
    begin
        n := 'D';
        W                  { W called within D }
    end;

begin { L }
    n := 'L';
    W;                     { W called from the main program L }
    D
end.
```

Figure 5.14   This program repeats Fig. 5.6. Its output is different under lexical and dynamic scope.

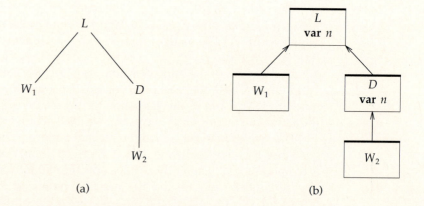

(a)   (b)

Figure 5.15   (a) Activation tree and (b) activation records for a computation of the program in Fig. 5.14. The arrows between activation records represent control links.

Heap Allocation and Deallocation

heap allocation is being considered for imperative languages

A general technique for managing activation records is to allocate storage for them in an area called the *heap*; the records stay on the heap as long as they are needed. A technique called *garbage collection* is used to automatically reclaim storage that is no longer needed.

The *lifetime* of an activation record begins when the activation record is allocated and ends when the locations in the activation record can no longer be accessed from the program.

With heap allocation, the lifetimes of activation records need not be tied to the last-in/first-out flow of control between activation. Even after control returns from P, an activation record for P can stay on the heap as long as needed.

Pascal and C follow the Algol tradition of using stack allocation, which is considered next. Some successors of Pascal, such as Oberon and Modula-3 have abandoned stack allocation in favor of heap allocation.

Stack Allocation and Deallocation

imperative languages traditionally use stack allocation

Pascal and C were designed so that activation records can be held in a stack. The technique of using a stack for storage allocation was introduced to handle recursion in Algol 60. It has become a language design principle for most, but not all, imperative languages. A language that permits stacklike allocation is said to obey a *stack discipline*.

The stack discipline allows storage to be reused efficiently. Storage for local variables is allocated when an activation begins and it is released when the activation ends. When P calls Q and Q calls R, storage is therefore used in a last-in/first-out or stacklike manner. The stack in Fig. 5.16 grows downward, as activations are set up for P, Q, and R. Then the stack shrinks as control returns from R to Q to P. Each box in the figure represents an activation record.

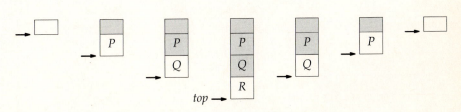

Figure 5.16 Stacklike storage allocation for activations.

Limitations of the Stack Discipline

the stack discipline influences language design

A stack can be used if storage for locals is not needed once an activation ends; the storage can then be deallocated. This deallocation imposes restrictions on programs — and even on language design.

In Chapter 4, the heap was used for dynamic allocation and deallocation of data. The stack discipline motivates restrictions in imperative languages on the treatment of procedures as parameters and results. Imperative languages require all procedures to be declared in the source text; they do not allow procedures to be defined dynamically at run time. Functional languages, on the other hand, treat functions as first-class citizens. The term "first-class" means that functions can be created dynamically, can be passed as parameters, and can be returned as results, just like integers. The implications for storage allocation will become evident in Chapter 13, where "closures" will be constructed; so a function can carry with it its bindings from names to values. Storage allocation for closures cannot be purely stacklike.

Allocating Static Variables at Compile Time

the lifetime of a static variable is the entire computation

Static variables within a procedure retain their values between activations; they are shared by all activations of the procedure. Local variables are bound to distinct storage in each activation, except if they are declared to be static. Storage for them is allocated statically at compile time. In a language without recursive procedures, such as Fortran, all variables can be treated as static.

The lifetime of a static variable is the entire computation; it retains its value from activation to activation. In C, the keyword `static` can be used to specify that a variable in a declaration is static. The declaration

```
static int count = 0;
```

declares `count` to be a static variable of type integer, with initial value 0.

Example 5.20   The following function in C contains the declarations of a static variable `count` and a local variable `result`:

```
int f(int n) {
static int count = 0;
      int result;
      count = count + 1;
      if(n == 0 )
          result = 1;
      else
          result = n*f(n-1);
```

```
        return result;
    }
```

Again, the = symbol is the assignment symbol in C, and the == symbol is used to test equality.

The static variable `count` is incremented each time the function is activated; it therefore counts the number of activations of `f`.

Execution of a C program begins in a function `main`. Suppose that the body of `main` consists of the call

```
    f(3);
```

The trace in Fig. 5.17 corresponds to an execution of this program. It represents output that would be produced if appropriate write statements were inserted into the function body. Again, read "entering f" for ->f and "leaving f" for <-f.

Access to static data is determined at compile time, since storage for it is allocated at that time.

5.6 LEXICAL SCOPE: PROCEDURES AS IN C

Compilers for imperative languages often use a stack to organize storage for local variables. Last-in/first-out flow of control between activations is not enough to allow the use of a stack for storage; we also need the following language design principle:

> *Lifetimes of locals*. Storage for a variable declared within a procedure is local to a procedure activation.

Storage for the locals of an activation is allocated when the activation is set up and is deallocated when the activation ends. This principle couples alloca-

```
->f: n = 3; count = 0
->f: n = 2; count = 1
->f: n = 1; count = 2
->f: n = 0; count = 3
<-f: n = 0; count = 4; result = 1
<-f: n = 1; count = 4; result = 1
<-f: n = 2; count = 4; result = 2
<-f: n = 3; count = 4; result = 6
```

Figure 5.17 A trace showing the values of variables.

tion of activation records with the last-in/first-out or stacklike flow of control between activations.

When activation records are held on a stack, they are sometimes called stack frames. This section considers stack frames for procedures in C.

a variable in C is either local to a procedure or global to all procedures

C was designed so it can be implemented with just a control link. Access links are not needed since C does not allow procedure bodies to be nested, one inside the other. Hence, there are only two places to look for a declaration of a name in a procedure P: either within the same procedure P, or outside all procedures. Storage management for Pascal, considered in Section 5.7, requires access links and represents the general case of storage management for imperative languages that obey the stack discipline.

Memory Layout for C Programs

A C program consists of a sequence of global declarations of procedures, types, and variables. Types and variables can also be declared local to a procedure; however, a procedure cannot be declared local to another.

The scope of a declaration in C is either contained within some procedure or it is global to all procedures that are compiled together. Storage for global data can be allocated at compile time, before any procedures are called, so storage for globals is known at compile time. Thus, the emphasis in storage management for C is on storage management for variables in individual procedures.

The elements of a running C program are illustrated in the memory layout in Fig. 5.18. A machine register called a *program counter* keeps track of the flow of control through the code for the program. The code does not change during execution. Global data is held in statically allocated memory locations. Local data is held on a stack that grows and shrinks as activations start and end. At the other end of memory is a heap, which holds dynamic data that is allocated and deallocated through library procedures.

Storage for Local Variables

A block in C is a grouping of declarations and statements, except that a block cannot contain procedure declarations. Variables declared within a block are local to an execution of the block. Variable c is local to the following block:

    { int c; ··· }

Conceptually, c is bound to a location when control enters the block, and there is no further use for the location when control leaves the block.

The last-in/first-out flow of control through blocks implies that blocks could be implemented by setting up a stack frame for each block: the frame is allocated upon block entry and the frame is deallocated upon block entry.

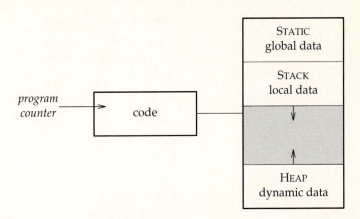

Figure 5.18   Memory layout for C programs.

C compilers, however, tend to treat procedure activations as the unit for storage allocation. That is, blocks can be implemented by reserving storage for their local variables in the stack frame of the procedure in which they appear.

Variables in disjoint blocks within a procedure can share storage because they are not needed simultaneously. The declarations of i and j in the following pseudocode can share storage, since their scopes do not overlap:

```
{ int c;
    { int i; · · ·
    }
    · · ·
    { int j; · · ·
    }
}
```

Procedure Call and Return in C

control links are needed since frame sizes vary

The basic frame layout in Fig. 5.19 is from Johnson and Ritchie [1981]; it has been adapted to implement C on several machine architectures. The field for saved state information includes a control link that points to the caller's activation record. Control links are needed with stack allocation since the sizes of activation records vary from procedure to procedure. All activation records for a procedure P have the same size; however, the size of activation records of another procedure Q depends on the code for Q and will in general be different from that of records for P.

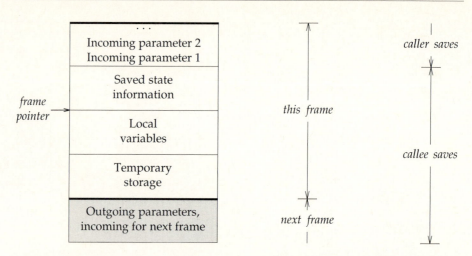

Figure 5.19   Layout of activation records for C. The frame pointer points within the top frame, the frame that is presently at the top of the stack. The shaded box at the bottom will become part of the next frame to appear at the top of the stack. The work of setting up a frame is split between a calling and called procedure. A caller saves parameters that become incoming parameters for its callee.

The caller and callee split the work of allocating and filling in the fields in the callee's frame. The owner of the frame, the callee, determines the sizes of the fields, except perhaps for the field for incoming parameters. If the callee accepts a variable number of arguments, then the incoming-parameter field will vary in size from call to call.

The C compiler ensures that the following actions occur when a procedure is called:

caller saves

1. C uses call-by-value, so the caller evaluates the actual parameters for the call and places their values in the activation record for the callee. In the call $f(n-1)$, n is local to the caller, so it is the caller's responsibility to evaluate the actual parameter $n-1$.

2. Information needed to restart execution of the caller is saved. This information includes the address to which control must return on completion of the procedure call.

callee saves

3. The callee allocates space for its local variables. Temporary storage for partial results during expression evaluation is also reserved. An expression $(a+b)*c$ is implemented by a sequence of instructions of the form

$$t_1 := a+b; \quad t_2 := t_1 * c;$$

where t_1 and t_2 are compiler-generated names. The values of compiler-generated names are held in temporary storage.

4. The body of the callee is executed. Additional activations may occur during this execution. The shaded field at the bottom of Fig. 5.19 is for outgoing parameters, for a call that might occur during this activation. These outgoing parameters become the incoming parameters of the next callee. The size of the field for outgoing parameters can vary from call to call; the size for a call $P(x,y)$ can be different from the size for a call $Q()$.

5. Control returns to the caller. A return value, if there is any, is placed where the caller can find it, and the machine registers are restored, as needed, to their status when the call began. Control then goes to the saved return address. The stack is popped so that subsequent activations will be properly positioned in the stack.

Variable Access at Run Time

The layout of an activation record is known at run time, although its position in memory is not. Once a frame is put on the stack, the storage within it can be accessed relative to the frame pointer. Thus, the values of variables in an activation can be accessed using addresses of the form:

frame-pointer + displacement

where *displacement* is computed at compile time.

The layout in Fig. 5.19 actually allows for procedures such as *printf* (the Pascal counterpart is *writeln*), whose parameters can vary from call to call. Such procedures can be handled by using the first incoming parameter, the one closest to the frame pointer, to describe the remaining parameters. Thus, the first parameter is found in a known place, next to the saved state information, and other parameters can be accessed using the description in the first parameter.

Procedures as Parameters

Some examples of the use of procedures as parameters in C programs are as follows:

- A program to sort lines of text takes a comparison function as a parameter. With one comparison function, it treats the lines as strings to be sorted into dictionary order; with another, it treats the lines as numbers to be sorted in numeric order.

- An interactive program responds to commands selected from a menu. Associated with each menu item is a procedure that the menu manager takes as a parameter and calls when the item is selected.

The passing of procedures as parameters in C is facilitated by the two-level classification of names into those that are global and those that are local to some procedure. Globals are taken from the lexical environment of a procedure. Their locations are known at compile time, so the code for a procedure body knows where to find them.

Dangling Pointers

A *dangling pointer* is a pointer that refers to storage that is being used for another purpose.

There is no problem with function f, which declares x, initializes it to 1, and returns its value.

```
int f(void) {
    int x = 1;
    return x;
}
```

Once control returns from f, there is no further need for the storage for x, and no way of accessing x.

Function g, however, returns a dangling pointer since it returns the address or location of local x:

```
int g(void) {
    int x = 1;
    return &x;
}
```

The operator & returns the address of its argument. Once control returns from g, the storage for local x is deallocated, turning the returned address into a dangling pointer. Any attempt to use the dangling pointer produces unpredictable erroneous results.

Tail-Recursion Elimination

Storage allocation for procedures will be illustrated by first considering a recursive procedure `search` and then modifying `search` to eliminate the recursion.

tail recursion can be implemented efficiently

When the last statement executed in the body of a procedure P is a recursive call, the call is said to be *tail recursive*. A procedure as a whole is *tail recursive* if all its recursive calls are tail recursive. Tail-recursive calls can be eliminated and replaced by control flow within the procedure, thereby avoiding the overhead of a call.

Example 5.21   The binary search procedure `search` in Fig. 5.20 is tail recursive. It looks for `T` in a sorted array `X[lo..hi]` by comparing `T` with the middle element of the range. If the range is empty because `lo>hi`, it returns `no`. If the middle element is `T`, it returns `yes`. Otherwise, it discards half the range and calls itself recursively on the smaller range. As soon as either of the two recursive calls `search(lo,k-1)` or `search(k+1,hi)` is completed, control flows back to the caller of `search(lo,hi)`. For more on binary search, see Example 3.4, page 81.

In more detail, `main` uses the library function `scanf` to read an integer into the *l*-value of `T`. It then calls `search(1,N)`, which returns either `yes` or `no`.

The snapshots in Fig. 5.21 show how a search for 55 proceeds. The initial call `search(1,7)` results in the creation of an activation record with

$$lo_1 = 1; \ hi_1 = 7; \ k_1 = 4;$$

```c
#include <stdio.h>
int yes = 1, no = 0;
#define N 7
int X[] = { 0, 11, 22, 33, 44, 55, 66, 77 };
int T;
int search(int lo, int hi) {
    int k;
    if( lo > hi ) return no;
    k = (lo + hi) /2;
    if( T == X[k] ) return yes;
    else if( T < X[k] ) return search(lo, k-1);
    else if( T > X[k] ) return search(k+1, hi);
}
int main(void) {
    scanf("%d", &T);
    if( search(1,N) )
        printf("found\n");
    else
        printf("notfound\n");
    return 0;
}
```

Figure 5.20   A tail-recursive binary search procedure.

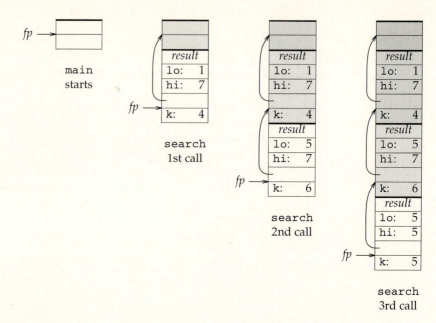

Figure 5.21   An execution of the recursive binary search program in Fig. 5.20.

Subscripts are used here to distinguish among the locals in the first, second, and third activations of search. Since 55 is greater than X[k], a recursive activation is set up with

$$lo_2 = 5; \quad hi_2 = 7; \quad k_2 = 6;$$

Now 55 is less than X[k], so a third and final activation occurs with

$$lo_3 = 5; \quad hi_3 = 5; \quad k_3 = 5;$$

Since 55 equals X[k], the result yes is copied back up to main as the recursion unwinds.   □

A tail-recursive call P(a,b) of a procedure P with formals x and y can be replaced by

```
x = a; y = b;
goto the first executable statement in P;
```

Suppose label `L` is attached to the first executable statement in procedure `search` in Fig. 5.20. Then, the call `search(lo,k-1)` can be replaced by

```
lo = lo; hi = k-1;
goto L;
```

Redundant assignments like `lo=lo` are omitted from the nonrecursive binary search procedure in Fig. 5.22, obtained from Fig. 5.20 by eliminating tail recursion and rearranging the goto statements.

Each activation of `search` executes the same code. The first activation finds parameter lo_1 at the same position relative to its frame pointer fp_1 as the second activation finds lo_2 with respect to fp_2, and so on. Once a tail-recursive call occurs, the locals in the calling activation just sit there, waiting to be deallocated when the recursion unwinds.

```c
#include <stdio.h>
int yes = 1, no = 0;
#define N 7
int X[] = { 0, 11, 22, 33, 44, 55, 66, 77 };
int T;
int search(int lo, int hi) {
    int k;
L:  if( lo > hi ) return no;
    k = (lo + hi) /2;
    if( T == X[k] ) return yes;
    else if( T < X[k] ) hi = k-1;
    else if( T > X[k] ) lo = k+1;
    goto L;
}
int main(void) {
    scanf("%d", &T);
    if( search(1,N) )
        printf("found\n");
    else
        printf("notfound\n");
    return 0;
}
```

Figure 5.22   The program obtained after eliminating tail recursion from the procedure `search` in Fig. 5.20.

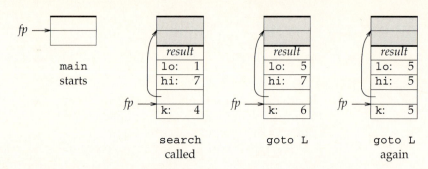

Figure 5.23   An execution of the program in Fig. 5.22. After tail recursion is eliminated, there is only one call of procedure search.

The snapshots in Fig. 5.23 show a nonrecursive search for 55. Instead of
setting up tail-recursive activations, the new program overwrites the affected
fields in place, in the same activation record.

5.7 LEXICAL SCOPE: NESTED PROCEDURES AND PASCAL

Pascal also uses the stack discipline for organizing storage for local variables.
The flow of control through a program can be represented by an activation
tree, as in Section 5.5, where each node in the tree represents an activation of a
procedure. The stack corresponds to the last-in/first-out flow of control
between activations; the stack holds activation records for the live activations.

The differences between storage management for Pascal and storage management for C are due primarily to block structure in Pascal, with nested procedures. Procedure Q is nested inside procedure P if it is declared inside P. A
procedure nested inside P is hidden from all other procedures outside P. The
emphasis in this section is on the implications for storage allocation of procedure nesting. The role of procedures and modules as programming constructs
are considered in Chapter 6.

The term block in this section refers to a construct that can contain declarations, including procedure declarations. With this terminology, a Pascal
program as a whole is a block, as is any procedure in the program.

Visibility Rules

The visibility rules for nested procedures are similar to those for blocks consisting of compound statements with declarations. As in Section 5.4, the scope

of a declaration in a procedure is that procedure and any nested procedures, except for holes due to redeclarations of the name.

Thus, in a program with the following procedures

> **program** U;
> > **procedure** V;
> > > **procedure** W;
> >
> > **procedure** A;
> > > **procedure** B;

a variable declared in program U is visible in all of U, V, W, A, and B. A variable declared in V is visible in V and W. A variable declared in W is visible only in W.

These visibility rules apply to procedure names as well.[4] The procedure name V is visible in procedures V, W, A, and B, but W is not visible in either A or B.

Access to Nonlocals: Control and Access Links

Suppose that memory is divided into areas for the code, static data, a run-time stack, and a heap, as in Section 5.6. Each procedure has an activation record with fields for parameters, saved state information, local variables, and compiler generated temporaries.

The frame layout in Fig. 5.24 is based on the Pascal P-compiler, a part of the portable "P-kit" that was a key to Pascal's spread to many computers (Nori et al. [1981]).

The layout in Fig. 5.24 has fields for two kinds of links:

1. A control link, also called a dynamic link, points to the activation record of the run-time caller. The control link corresponds to *mark* at the beginning of the layout in Fig. 5.24.

2. An access link, also called a static link, points to the most recent activation of the lexically enclosing block. Specifically, chains of access links are easier to follow if the access link in an activation record points to the access link field in the record for the lexically enclosing block.

---

[4] Technically, a procedure name must be declared before it can be used; however, a **forward** declaration allows a procedure body to appear later in the program. A **forward** declaration introduces the procedure name, parameter declarations, and result type (if the procedure is a function), as in

> **procedure** $P(x : $ **integer**$)$; **forward**;

Other procedures can then be declared before the body appears, as in

> **procedure** P; **begin** $\cdots$ **end**;

The parameters and result type are not repeated.

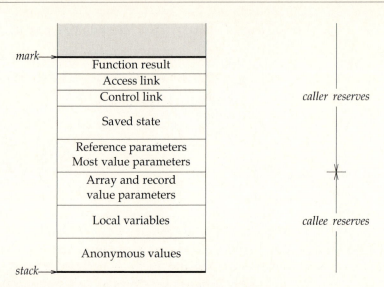

Figure 5.24   A layout of activation records for Pascal.

Access to nonlocals will be illustrated by considering the program outline in Fig. 5.25. A real program, however, is unlikely to use its variables in the way the outline uses x, y, and z.

In the program text, the bindings of nonlocals y in Q and z in R appear in the enclosing procedure P. Thus, at run time, the locations of y and z appear in an activation record for P.

The snapshots of the run-time stack in Fig. 5.26 correspond to an execution of the program in Fig. 5.25. Subscripts distinguish between activations of a procedure. After

M calls P, P calls Q, and Q calls R,

the stack is as in Fig. 5.26(a). In each of these calls, the callee is lexically nested within the caller, so both the control and the access links point from the callee to its caller. The control link points to the beginning, to the *mark*, in the caller's activation record. The access link points to the access link in the caller's activation record.

access links are   In (b), R has just called P. That is, activation R_1 has made a recursive call
needed since the   to P_2. The control link from P_2 points to its caller R_1; the access link points to
number of M, the most recent activation of the lexically enclosing block.
intervening stack   Are access links needed? Yes. Consider, procedure P declared within M
frames varies   in Fig. 5.25. In Fig. 5.26(b), there are two simultaneous activations of P. Since

```
program M;
      procedure P;
            var x, y, z;
            procedure Q;
                  procedure R;
                  begin (* R *)
                        ··· z := P; ···
                  end R;
            begin (* Q *)
                  ··· y := R; ···
            end Q;
      begin (* P *)
            ··· x := Q; ···
      end P;
begin (* M *)
      ··· P; ···
end M;
```

Figure 5.25   An illustration of nonlocal access within nested procedures.

P can be called recursively, the number of simultaneous activations cannot be predicted at compile time. Therefore, the relative positions of the frames for M and for the activations of P cannot be predicted at compile time. Access links from activations like P_1 and P_2 are needed at run time to find the frame for M.

Variable Access

find the frame by following a known number of access links

Let us examine how access links are used before considering how they are maintained. Each activation of P in Fig. 5.26 gets its own locals x, y, and z. Thus, in activation Q_1 nonlocal y refers to a location in P_1, and in activation Q_2 nonlocal y refers to a location in P_2. Similarly, z in R_1 refers to a location two access links away in P_1, and z in R_2 refers to a location two access links away in P_2.

find the location using a relative address within the frame

The number of links to be followed to access a nonlocal can be computed at compile time, from the *nesting depth* of a block. Let the nesting depth of the block for the program be 1. The nesting depth of an enclosed block is 1 greater

---

[5] Nesting depth carries over from programs to modules: the nesting depth of a module is 1, and the nesting depth of an enclosed block is 1 greater than the nesting depth of its enclosing block.

This definition does not apply to local modules, as in Modula-2; a local module can be declared inside another module. Wirth [1988] notes, "Experience with Modula over the last eight years has shown that *local modules* were rarely used. Considering the additional complexity of the compiler required to handle them, and the additional complications in the visibility rules of the language definition, the elimination of local modules [from Oberon] appears justified."

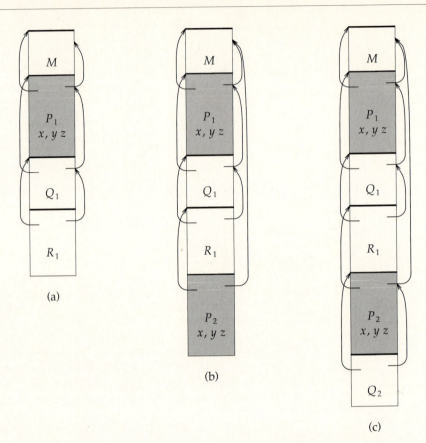

(a)

(b)

(c)

Figure 5.26 Stack snapshots during an execution of the program in Fig. 5.25. Control links are to the left and access links are to the right. Activations of procedure P are shaded.

than the nesting depth of its enclosing block.[5] The *distance* between two blocks is the absolute value of the difference between their nesting depths.

In general, the address for a nonlocal occurrence of a name x has two parts:

1. *The number of access links to be traversed*. This number is the distance between the block with the nonlocal occurrence of x and the block containing the most-closely nested declaration of x.
2. *The relative address of x within the activation record reached*. With respect to Fig. 5.24, one approach would be to compute relative addresses as displacements from the position of the access link.

Each nonlocal variable can then be accessed by following a known number of access links, and then using a known displacement off the address reached. Here, "known" means "known at compile time."

Local variables are found at a known position within the current activation record.

Setting Up Access Links

The distance between blocks is also needed to set up access links when a non-local procedure is called. For example, 3 is the distance between the block for R containing a call to nonlocal P and the block for M where P is declared. Also, 3 is the number of access links that take us from R_1 to the activation record for M. In more detail, when R_1 calls P_2, we do the following:

1. Follow 3 access links from R_1 to find the activation record for M.
2. Set the access link in P_2 to point to M.

Procedure Call and Return

The following actions occur when a procedure is called using the activation record layout in Fig. 5.24:

caller saves

1. The caller allocates fields for a function result, the access and control links, and the saved state information needed to resume execution of the caller.

2. The control link in the callee points to the beginning of the caller's frame.

3. If the callee is declared within the caller, then the access link points to the access link in the caller's frame. Otherwise, the access link in the callee is determined by using the nesting depths of the caller and callee. If the difference between their nesting depths is d, then the callee's access link will point to a frame found by following d access links from the callee's frame.

4. Information needed to restart execution of the caller is saved. This information includes the address to which control must return on completion of the procedure call.

5. The caller allocates a field for all reference parameters, address information about arrays and records passed by value, and all value parameters. The caller must fill in this field, since names in the actual parameter list use the access link in the caller.

callee saves

6. Control flows to the callee. The callee allocates a field for arrays and records passed by value. It copies values into this field. This work could have been done by the caller. The use of two fields for parameters and the division of the work of setting up these fields is particular to this implementation.

7. The callee reserves space for local variables and temporary storage for partial results during expression evaluation.

8. The body of the callee is executed. Further activations may occur during the execution of the body.

9. Control returns to the caller. A return value, if any, is placed in the field for the function result. Control then goes to the saved return address. The stack is popped so that subsequent activations will be properly positioned in the stack.

Procedures as Parameters

A procedure that is passed as a parameter carries its lexical environment along with it. That is, when a procedure X is passed as a parameter, an access link a goes with it. Later, when X is called, a is used as the access link for its activation record.

The issues that arise with procedure parameters are similar to those that arise in functional languages, where functions can be passed freely. For more information, see the discussion of "closures" in Section 13.6.

Displays for Faster Access

a display is an array of access links

Displays are an optimization technique for obtaining faster access to nonlocals. A *display* is a global array d of pointers to activation records, indexed by lexical nesting depth. Array element $d[i]$ is maintained so that it points to the most recent activation of the block at nesting depth i. In effect, the elements of the display are the access links that would be reached by following the chain of access links from the current activation record back up to the record for the main program. The number of display elements is known at compile time from lexical nesting within the source text.

The display in Fig. 5.27(a) is an array $d[1 .. 4]$ with $d[1]$ pointing to the activation record M, $d[2]$ pointing to P_1, and so on. In (b) only the display elements $d[1]$ and $d[2]$ are shown, since P_2 can refer only to names declared in enclosing blocks. On return from P_2 to R_1, the display must be restored to its status in Fig. 5.27(a).

With a display, a nonlocal x can be found as follows:

1. Use one array access to find the activation record containing x. If the most-closely nested declaration of x is at nesting depth i, then $d[i]$ points to the activation record containing the location for x.

2. Use the relative address within the activation record to find the location for x. Display element $d[i]$ points to a predetermined position in the activation record—say the beginning of the activation record. At compile time, the location of x can be expressed as a displacement from the predetermined position.

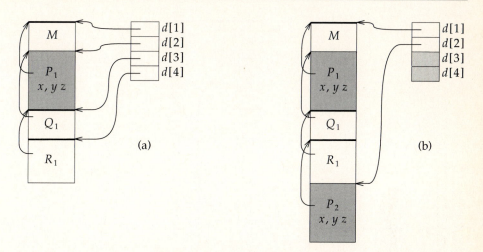

Figure 5.27   Display elements, indexed by nesting depth, point to visible blocks.

Display Maintenance

When a procedure P is called, the global display must be set up so an activation of P can use it. A general technique for maintaining a display is for the caller to save the entire array within its own activation record. The callee can then use the global array for its own display. The size of the array is the maximum nesting depth in the program, which is usually small. For the running example of this section the maximum nesting depth is 4. When control returns to the caller, the caller restores the global display from the stored array in its activation record.

This technique handles procedures that are passed as parameters, but it increases the overhead of a procedure call because the entire display has to be stored.

Displays in the Absence of Procedures as Parameters

An alternative technique, illustrated in Fig. 5.28, works well when procedures are not passed as parameters and can be made to work when they are. The idea is to save only $d[i]$ when an activation at nesting depth i occurs. The old value of $d[i]$ is saved within the activation record of the callee.

The complication with procedures as parameters is that the parameter needs the entire display to set up its lexical environment.

In Fig. 5.28, R_1 has called P_2. Since P_2 is at nesting depth 2, display element $d[2]$ points to P_2. The old value of $d[2]$ is saved within the activation record for P_2; it is shown by a heavy line. Display elements $d[3]$ and $d[4]$ are

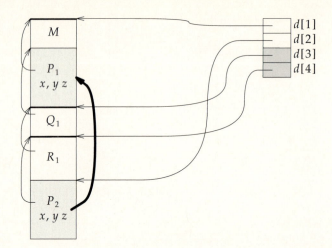

Figure 5.28   Display maintenance in the absence of procedures as parameters.

inaccessible. They remain in place, however, for use upon return from P_2 to R_1.

In summary, the part of the calling sequence for maintaining the display is as follows:

1. Save $d[i]$ in the activation record of the callee at nesting depth i.
2. Make $d[i]$ point to the callee.

Display maintenance in the return sequence from callee to caller is done simply by restoring $d[i]$ from the saved value in the callee.

Exercises

5.1   Give a single program fragment that produces different results under each of the following parameter-passing methods:
   a. Call-by-value
   b. Call-by-reference
   c. Call-by-value-result
   d. Call-by-name.

5.2   Suppose that procedure *swap2* is declared as follows:

```
procedure swap2(x, y : integer);
    procedure f() : integer;
        var z : integer;
    begin (* f *)
```

$$z := x; \quad x := y; \quad \textbf{return } z$$
$\textbf{end } f;$
$\textbf{begin } (* \; swap2 \; *)$
$\quad y := f()$
$\textbf{end } swap2;$

Describe the effect of the procedure call $swap2(i, A[i])$ under each of the following parameter-passing methods:

a. Call-by-value

b. Call-by-reference

c. Call-by-value-result

d. Macro expansion.

5.3 Suppose that the call-by-name method is used to pass parameters to the procedure $swap2$ in Exercise 5.2. Suppose also that an assignment $E_1 := E_2$ is implemented as follows:

> compute the location of E_1;
> compute the value of E_2;
> place the value of E_2 into the location of E_1

a. Explain why $swap2(i, A[i])$ exchanges the values of i and $A[i]$.

b. Under what conditions will the call $swap2(i, A[p()])$ fail to simply exchange the values of i and the array element $A[p()]$, where function p is declared by

> $\textbf{procedure } p() : \textbf{integer};$
> $\textbf{begin}$
> $\quad i := i + 1; \quad \textbf{return } i$
> $\textbf{end } p$

5.4 Procedure `parens` in Fig. 5.29 is from a C program that reads strings such as

```
[]
<[]<[]>>
()()
```

The program checks whether an input string is balanced; that is, if each opening parenthesis has a matching closing parenthesis. For the purposes of this exercise, brackets, [and], and the symbols < and > will also be referred to as parentheses. Any enclosed substrings must themselves be balanced. Complete the program by giving an implementation for procedure M and supplying an appropriate procedure `main`. The program must produce as output the string `balanced` if the input string consists of balanced parentheses.

5.5 Suppose that a C program consists of three procedures, called `main`, `M`, and procedure `parens` in Fig. 5.29. Characterize the activation trees

```
void parens(void) {
    for(;;) {
        switch(lookahead) {
        case '(':
            M('('); parens(); M(')'); continue;
        case '<':
            M('<'); parens(); M('>'); continue;
        case '[':
            M('['); parens(); M(']'); continue;
        default:
            return;
        }
    }
}
```

Figure 5.29   A C procedure to parse balanced parentheses.

that correspond to the possible executions of the program. Assume that `main` calls `parens`, and that M returns without calling any procedures. The program checks whether its input consists of balanced parentheses, as described in Exercise 5.4.

5.6 The dynamic scope rule specifies that nonlocals must be evaluated in the calling environment. Explain why macro expansion of procedure calls produces the same result as would be obtained under the dynamic scope rule.

5.7 Quicksort is an algorithm for sorting the elements of a subarray $A[m .. n]$ in place. It works as follows (see Fig. 5.30):
1. If the subarray has at most one element, do nothing. The remaining steps assume that the subarray has at least two elements.
2. Choose some element of the subarray, and call it a *pivot*. In Fig. 5.30, the pivot is 31, enclosed within dashed lines.
3. Rearrange the elements of the subarray so that elements less than or equal to the pivot appear to its left, and elements greater than or equal to the pivot appear to its right (use the algorithm from either Exercise 3.11 or 3.12).
4. Apply quicksort to recursively sort the smaller and larger elements in place.

Implement quicksort in the language of your choice. Insert print statements on entry and exit to each procedure to show the activations that

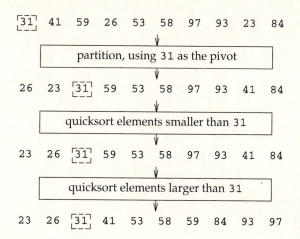

Figure 5.30 An illustration of quicksort.

occur when quicksort is applied to the initial subarray in Fig. 5.30.

5.8　The procedure call and return sequence for C must be capable of handling the standard function `printf`, which presents the following problem: the number and type of its arguments can vary from call to call. The first argument of `printf` specifies the output format for the remaining arguments. The `%d` within the first argument string in the call

```
printf("found %d ", n);
```

tells us that there must be a second argument of type integer, whose value must be printed in decimal notation. Adapt the procedure call and return sequence in Section 5.6 to handle `printf`. Note that the caller of `printf` knows the arguments at compile time, but that the callee needs to examine the first argument of a call to determine the number and types of the remaining arguments of that call.

5.9　The snapshots of the stack of activation records in Fig. 5.22 and 5.23 illustrate recursive and nonrecursive binary searches for 55. Draw corresponding snapshots to illustrate searches for 40, which is not in the table.

5.10　The lower and upper bounds of a *dynamic array* are computed on procedure entry. Thus, if dynamic array *A* is declared in procedure *P*, then the lower and upper bounds of *A* can be given by expressions whose values are recomputed for every activation of *P*.

    a. Adapt the layout of activation records in Section 5.6 to include space for dynamic arrays. Indicate any changes to the procedure call and return sequence.

    b. Assuming row-major layout, give a formula for computing the address of $A[i_1][i_2] \cdots [i_k]$, where $k \geq 1$. Precompute expressions where possible to reduce run-time address computation.

    c. Assuming column-major layout, give a formula as in (b).

5.11 The pseudocode in Fig. 5.25 contains nested procedures with nonlocal variables. For each assignment in the pseudocode, describe the actions that occur every time the assignment is executed. Be explicit about the procedure call and return sequences and the use and maintenance of the control and access links.

5.12 Redo Exercise 5.11 to use a display instead of access links.

Bibliographic Notes

Naur [1981] notes, "Recursive procedures were becoming known just barely at the time [when Algol 60 was defined], and mostly through McCarthy's work on LISP." The treatment of activation records in this chapter is suitable for a language in the Algol family but not for a language like Lisp; scope rules for nonlocals in functional languages are examined in Section 13.6. Exception handling, another topic that is related to the material in this chapter, is discussed in Section 9.6.

Recursion was added almost as an afterthought to Algol 60, by the addition of a clarifying sentence, "Any occurrence of the procedure identifier within the body of the procedure other than in a left part in an assignment statement denotes activation of the procedure (Naur [1963a])." An immediate consequence of recursion is that more than one activation of a procedure can be alive at the same time, ruling out the possibility of static or compile-time allocation of storage for variables. The techniques in Section 5.7 for handling block structure were developed soon thereafter. Dijkstra [1960] discusses the use of displays for accessing nonlocals in a lexically scoped block-structured language. Randell and Russell [1964] describe a compiler for Algol 60, complete with stack allocation, displays, and dynamic arrays (see Exercise 5.10). For more information, see textbooks on compilers, such as Aho, Sethi, and Ullman [1986].

The benefits of block structure and procedure nesting have been questioned from time to time; see Wulf and Shaw [1973], Clarke, Wileden, and Wolf [1980], and Hanson [1981].

Exercises 5.2 and 5.3 are motivated by Fleck [1976], who discusses the difficulties of implementing a *swap* procedure using call-by-name.

Johnson and Ritchie [1981] discuss the nuances of procedure call and return sequences for C, including the handling of the standard function `printf` (Exercise 5.8).

III

OBJECT-ORIENTED PROGRAMMING

Part III considers ways of organizing and structuring programs, starting with procedures and leading up to object-oriented programming. Chapter 6 deals with procedures, modules, and defined types. Chapter 7 deals with object-oriented programming.

Decomposition of a Task into Subtasks

Careful program organization is as important for one programmer as it is for a large project with several hundred programmers.

Large projects are partitioned into smaller pieces that are implemented by one or more people. The pieces must fit together, so the interactions between the pieces are specified. The cleaner the partitioning, the easier the overall system is to understand. That is, if the smaller pieces are relatively independent, then the overall system can be understood in terms of how the pieces fit together and interact.

Individual programmers also benefit from task partitioning because of inherent human limitations. Miller [1967] has observed that people can keep track of about seven things, be they bits, words, colors, tones, or tastes. Is this why there are seven wonders of the world, seven ages of man, seven deadly sins, and so on? More seriously, he continues, "Tentatively, therefore, we are justified in assuming that our memories are limited by the number of units or symbols we must master, and not by the amount of information that these symbols represent. Thus it is helpful to organize material intelligently before we try to memorize it. The process of organization enables us to package the same amount of information into far fewer symbols, and so eases the task of remembering."

Abstraction: Procedure, Module, Data, Object

The flip side of decomposition is abstraction. An *abstraction* consists of just those properties essential to a purpose; details that can safely be ignored are hidden. Among the forms of abstraction are procedures, modules, user-defined types, and objects.

Procedure abstraction was the first to be applied to programming. The earliest book on programming is a collection of procedures or *subroutines* by Wilkes, Wheeler, and Gill [1951]. As Wheeler [1952] noted, "When a programme has been made from a set of sub-routines the breakdown of the code is more complete than it would otherwise be. This allows the coder to concentrate on one section of a programme at a time without the overall detailed programme continually intruding."

Modular abstraction was practiced long before modules appeared as a programming construct. A module is defined in Chapter 6 to be a collection of related declarations. Typically, a module collects related variables (data) and procedures (operations), and related constants and types. The original Fortran translator consisted of six "sections" corresponding to modules; the implementation effort was 18 staff-years over a 36-month period.

A key insight into program organization is that data and the operations on the data belong together. This insight underlies criteria for module design; for example, it is better to design modules around the data than around the actions in a program. This insight underlies the concept of data abstraction.

A data abstraction is a user-defined type. Stacks and search trees are examples of data abstractions. We use "defined types" as an abbreviation for user-defined data types. A defined type, *Stack*, can be used to create as many stacks as needed in a program.

The discussion of types in Chapter 4 dealt with values and operations on built-in types like integers and arrays. Chapter 6 considers language facilities for defined types, where data and operations are specified explicitly in terms of variables and procedures. The data and operations abstract away from the representation and implementation of the data type.

Object-oriented programming (or object abstraction, to be consistent with other forms of abstraction) treats an overall system as a collection of interacting objects. The objects interact by sending messages to each other.

Language Support: Information Hiding

Language support for program structuring typically relies on the following idea:

> Information hiding can make programs easier to read and maintain.

The word "support" in "language support" is crucial. A programming language *supports* a programming style if the style can be expressed, if conformance with the style can be checked, and if the style is implemented efficiently. A language merely *permits* the style if with sufficient care and inventiveness the style can be practiced in the language.

Information hiding is a technique for supporting the various forms of abstraction. It is usually practiced by controlling the visibility of names. If a name is hidden within one part of a program, then it cannot be accessed from other parts of the program. Thus, visibility control is a way of achieving access control.

The idea behind information hiding can be summarized briefly:

> Access control can make programs easier to read and maintain.

6

Groupings of
Data and Operations

We propose instead that one begins with a list of difficult design decisions or design decisions which are likely to change. Each module is then designed to hide such a decision from the others. Since, in most cases, design decisions transcend time of execution, modules will not correspond to steps in the processing.

– Parnas [1972], on criteria for decomposing systems into modules.

The idea that data and operations go together was independently discovered in several contexts in the early 1960s. It is the basis for modules. It was also one of the early lessons of the Simula project; Nygaard and Dahl [1981] recall seeing many useful applications in which collections of variables and procedures served as "natural units of programming." When programming with procedures in Pascal or C, the "natural units" are in the mind of the programmer.

With modules, the groupings of variables and procedures are explicit in the source text. Pascal, extended with a form of modules called *units*, will be used to illustrate modules. Commercial versions of Pascal support units, although Standard Pascal does not. Units are not as complete a solution as modules in Modula-2, but we stay primarily with Pascal since it is a familiar language, and since the benefits Modula-2 would provide are incremental.

User-defined data types will be illustrated using classes in C++. C++ is a compatible extension of C, designed by grafting the class construct of Simula 67 onto C.[1]

C++ supports a range of programming styles:

[1] Kernighan and Ritchie [1988] "used Bjarne Stroustrup's C++ translator extensively for local testing" of the ANSI C programs in their book, before final approval of the C standard.

- C++ can be used for imperative programming with procedures, just like C, since C programs are accepted essentially as is by C++.

- C++ provides the same support for defined types that it does for built-in types. Once defined, stacks or complex numbers can be used as readily as records.

- C++ is widely used for object-oriented programming, the subject of Chapter 7.

Support for a range of styles makes C++ a relatively large language. This book introduces just enough of the language, as needed, to illustrate concepts.

6.1   CONSTRUCTS FOR PROGRAM STRUCTURING

This section is an overview of programming with procedures, modules, and classes.

The treatment of procedures in Chapter 5 dealt more with their implementation than with their use. Realistic examples of their use involve collections of procedures (and variables); hence, this chapter is a natural place to illustrate procedures and then point out how modules and classes can help manage collections of procedures.

In general, the *behavior* of a construct is what is observable from outside the construct—that is, through the effect of executing the construct. The effect may be observed through parameters and results, through input/output, through changes in the values of variables.

The *implementation* of a construct is the part that is accessible only from within the construct.

Procedures: Raising the Level of a Computation

design procedures corresponding to actions and operators

Procedures have been in use since the earliest days of programming. Once a procedure is defined, its implementation can be abstracted away. Function procedures can be thought of as extending the built-in operators of a language, and proper procedures can be thought of as extending the built-in actions.

Program Design with Procedures

Program design with procedures can proceed as follows:

1. *Behavior*. Define procedures corresponding to what an algorithm does; for example, if an algorithm sorts numbers, then define a procedure to sort numbers. If a complex operation partitions into simpler ones, then the simpler ones may be candidates for procedures.

2. *Implementation*. Hide the details of an algorithm in the procedure body, so the algorithm can be changed without affecting the rest of the program. Further candidates for procedures may surface during implementation. Duplicated or similar code fragments are candidates for procedures.

The abstraction process of defining procedures will be illustrated by considering an example of an expression parser and evaluator. The evaluation of an expression

```
(512-487)*2;
```

can be partitioned into scanning and parsing, as in Fig. 6.1. Scanning or lexical analysis groups individual characters into tokens. Parsing or syntax analysis then uses the syntactic structure of the expression to determine its value.

The design of the evaluator begins with two procedures:

procedure *scan*   form the next token

function *expr*   parse and evaluate an expression

Further procedures will be defined as this design is developed in Section 6.3.

Procedures help, but modules help more, because procedures *scan* and *expr* also work with data.

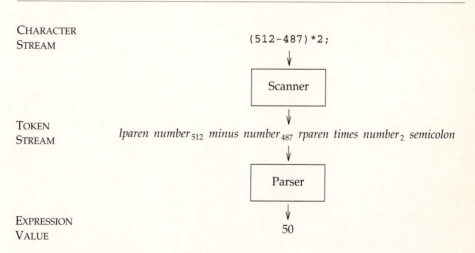

CHARACTER
STREAM

`(512-487)*2;`

Scanner

TOKEN
STREAM

lparen number$_{512}$ *minus number*$_{487}$ *rparen times number*$_{2}$ *semicolon*

Parser

EXPRESSION
VALUE

50

Figure 6.1   An expression evaluator, partitioned into a scanner for lexical analysis and a parser for syntax analysis.

Modules Partition the Static Program Text

*design modules
around the data in
a program*

A *module* is a collection of declarations, typically including both variables and procedures. We cannot create new modules or copies of existing modules dynamically as a program runs.

A module serves as a black box with which the rest of the program interacts through an interface. The *interface* of a module is a subset of the declarations in the module. An interface can contain types, variables, procedures, and so on. An implementation of the module consists of everything else about the module, including the code for the procedures and for initialization. Interfaces and implementations are also referred to as the *public* and *private* views, respectively, of the module.

The partitioning of the expression evaluator in Fig. 6.1 corresponds naturally to the modules *Scanner* and *Parser* in Fig. 6.2. The private views of the modules are shaded. The interface of module *Scanner* contains not only procedure *scan* but also a type *token* and two variables *lookahead* and *lookvalue*. The interface of module *Parser* consists of the function procedure *expr*. These modules are discussed in Section 6.3.

Program Design with Modules

Program design with modules can proceed as follows:

1. *Role*. Modules are usually organized around data. If an operation affects some data, then the operation and the data may belong together

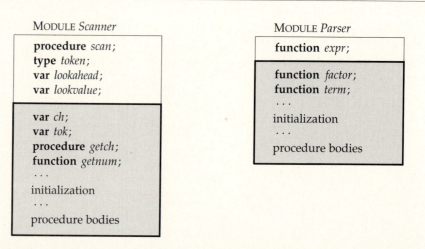

Figure 6.2 Public and private views of two modules; see Fig. 6.1 for the roles of these modules.

in a module. Describe the roles of the modules in general terms, not in terms of specific procedures or variables.

2. *Interface*. Once the roles are clear, design the module interfaces. The procedures in the interface determine the behavior of the module, as observed from the rest of the program.

3. *Implementation*. Hide design decisions in the private part of a module. The private part includes procedures and variables that are of no interest to the rest of the program.

Using Modules to Simulate Defined Types

The stack data structure is a canonical example for illustrating constructs that group data and operations. Operation *push*(*a*) adds *a* to the stack. Operation *pop* removes the most-recently added element. Stacks are also called last-in/first-out data structures.

Instead of a single stack, suppose we want two or more stacks. The module *StackManager* in Fig. 6.3 permits the creation of multiple stacks. Procedures *push* and *pop* take stacks as explicit arguments:

pop(*s*)   remove and return top element from stack *s*

push(*a*, *s*)   add element *a* to stack *s*

The module's interface contains a type name *stack*, which is used to declare variables of type *stack*.

One limitation of module *StackManager* is that function *newstack* has to be called explicitly to create a new stack, as in the following program fragment, which declares variables *s* and *t* and then assigns new stacks to them:

MODULE *StackManager*

type *stack*;
function *pop*(*s* : *stack*) : **integer**;
procedure *push*(*a* : **integer**; *s* : *stack*);
function *newstack* : *stack*;

representation of stacks
· · ·
initialization
· · ·
procedure bodies

Figure 6.3   The function procedure *newstack* creates a new stack *s*. The procedures *pop* and *push* take a stack as an explicit argument.

```
    var s, t : stack;
    begin
        s := newstack;
        t := newstack;
        push(10, s);
        . . .
    end.
```

Further discussion of this example appears in Section 6.4. The type name *stack* will be implemented as a pointer to a record that holds the data for a specific stack.

User-Defined Data Types

design types corresponding to what the program manipulates

A class corresponds to a type. The term *class* is an abbreviation of "class of objects," as in class of stacks, class of trees, or class of circles. For the moment, an *object* is a run-time entity with data on which operations can be performed. For example, a stack is an object with data corresponding to the stack contents. Objects can be created and deleted at run time.

Classes as Type Names

Section 6.5 treats classes as user-defined data types. The following pseudocode declares a class *Stack*:

```
    class Stack {
    public:
                    Stack();
            void  push(int a);
            int   pop();
    private:
            . . .
    };
```

Procedures *push* and *pop* operate on private data (not shown). The procedure *Stack*, with the same name as the class, is a *constructor*, using C++ terminology. The constructor is called automatically when an object of the class is created, so initialization code can be put in the constructor. A class can also have a *destructor* procedure, which is called automatically just before the object disappears. If class *Stack* had a destructor, it would be called ~*Stack*. Code for cleanup or "last-rites" can be put in the destructor.

A class is just like a record type with fields for the data in the class. Thus, the class name *Stack* can be used as a type name to declare variables *s* and *t*:

Stack s, t;
s.push(7);
t.push(8);

The objects denoted by *s* and *t* are initialized automatically by calling the constructor, so that *s* and *t* can be used immediately.

The limitation of defined types is that the types cannot be customized, as they can in object-oriented programming.

Comparison of the Approaches

The comparison in this subsection provides perspective on procedures, modules, and classes, so that the right construct can be chosen, depending on the need. These constructs serve distinct needs and can be used in combination with each other: procedures are needed to implement operations in a module or class; modules can be used to statically partition the source text of a program with classes.

The comparison of programming with procedures, modules, and classes will be done by applying them to a specific problem. Stacks and complex numbers are common examples of defined types — perhaps too common, so the comparison uses the problem of removing adjacent duplicates from a list of entries. In each case, the amount of code is about the same; the same data representation is used, and essentially the same procedures have to be written. The differences between the approaches are in the support for organizing the code and for having that organization be evident to a reader.

Background

The following pseudocode works with a list of integer entries (the list is assumed to end with 0):

```
read x;
while x ≠ 0 do begin
    write x;
    do read x while next = x;
    x := next;
end
```

This fragment is a variant of a Pascal fragment developed in Section 3.1. It reads and writes integers, it compares integers for equality, and it uses the names *x* and *next* to refer to integers.

Comparison

If list entries do not correspond to a built-in type, then the representation of entries and operations on entries have to be programmed explicitly.

- *Procedures*. The representation of entries and all details about the procedures are accessible throughout the program. Define procedures for reading, writing, comparing entries for equality, and so on. Say, an entry is represented as a pointer to a record containing the data for an entry (for example, see page 133). This representation is known throughout the program.

- *Modules*. Hide the representation of entries in an entry-manager module, which provides public operations for creating, reading, writing entries, and so on. The advantage over procedures is that the representation is hidden and access is checked. The hiding and checking contribute to the feel of entries as objects rather than pointers.

- *Defined Types*. Define a class *Entry*, so entries can be manipulated readily. Pseudocode for such a class appears in Fig. 6.4. As with modules, the representation is hidden, access is checked. In addition, objects are initialized upon creation. With procedures and modules, the suffix *-entry* was used to distinguish procedure *readentry* from procedures for reading other objects. With classes, such a suffix is not needed.

With type *Entry* as in Fig. 6.4, adjacent duplicates can be removed as follows:

Entry e, f;
e.read();
while not *e.endmarker()* **do begin**
    e.write();
    do *f.read();* **while** *e.equal(f);*

CLASS *Entry*

---

procedure	*read();*
procedure	*write();*
function	*endmarker()* : **boolean**;
function	*equal(Entry)* : **boolean**;
function	*copy(Entry)* : **boolean**;
constructor	*Entry;*
destructor	*~Entry;*

---

representation of entries
. . .
procedure bodies

Figure 6.4 Pseudocode for a defined type *Entry*.

$$e.copy(f);$$
end

Since variable e has type *Entry*, the procedure call $e.read()$ refers to the *read* in the class definition.

6.2 INFORMATION HIDING

hide implementations so they can be changed

This section is a language-independent discussion of support for information hiding. For convenience, we talk of objects; the discussion also applies to modules. Information hiding prevents the rest of the program from accessing the private part of an object.

Motivation: Distinguishing Behavior from Implementation

An *abstract specification* tells us the behavior of an object independent of its implementation; that is, an abstract specification tells us what an object does independent of how it works. A *concrete representation* tells us how an object is implemented, how its data is laid out inside a machine, and how this data is manipulated by its operations.

For example, the abstract notion of the sequence of primes from 7 through 47 can be written concretely as

$$7, \ 11, \ 13, \ 17, \ 19, \ 23, \ 29, \ 31, \ 37, \ 41, \ 43, \ 47$$

or it can be laid out in consecutive array elements, or it can be held in cells in a linked list. The array and linked-list layouts are concrete implementations.

The creation of truly abstract specifications, or *data abstraction*, is an ideal that is rarely attained. Instead, as terms like *implementation hiding*, *encapsulation*, and *representation independence* suggest, objects are packaged so that details of a concrete representation, such as data layouts, are not visible from the outside. We state this as an informal principle:

Implementation hiding. Design a program so that the implementation of an object can be changed without affecting the rest of the program.

Scope rules, which control the visibility of names, are the primary tool for achieving implementation hiding. The idea is to specify which names are visible in the rest of the program, and which names remain private to the object. Private names can be changed without affecting the rest of the program.

Example 6.1 The buffer in this example is motivated by communication protocols that limit the number of outstanding messages that have been sent but not yet received.

A bounded buffer behaves as a queue; elements leave it in the order that they enter. The buffer's interface consists of the following messages:

- *put*(*x*). Enter element *x* into the buffer.
- *get*( ). Extract an element from the buffer, in a first-in/first-out order.

This public interface says nothing about the implementation of the buffer.[2]

A sequence of snapshots of the public and private views of the buffer appears in Fig. 6.5. From the outside, the buffer behaves as a first-in/first-out queue. After *put*(*a*), the buffer holds just one element *a*, and after *put*(*b*), the buffer has two elements *a b*. Now, *get* returns *a*.

The private view of the buffer includes the data structures needed to hold elements inside the buffer. This private view is that of an underlying array with variables *front* and *rear* to mark the front and rear, respectively. The value of *front* is shown in Fig. 6.5 by the arrow from above the array, the value of *rear* by the arrow from below the array. In the implementation, the buffer contents wrap around the right end of the array. In the snapshot with contents *c d*, element *d* is held in the leftmost array element. □

Data Invariants

design objects around data invariants

A grouping of data and operations has a local state, consisting of the values of its variables.

A *data invariant* for an object is a property of its local state that holds whenever control is not in the object. The following are data invariants for the bounded buffer, implemented using an array in Example 6.1:

The buffer is empty if array index *front* equals index *rear*.
The buffer is full if the next element after *rear* is *front*.
The elements between *front* and *rear* are in the order they entered.

A counterpart of the structured programming principle is

Data. Design an object around a data invariant.

Initialization of Private Data

Since the private data of an object is inaccessible from the outside, initialization of the data belongs with the code for the object. Initialization is needed to

---

[2] What happens when an attempt is made to put an element into a full buffer and when an attempt is made to get an element from an empty buffer? For buffers to be usable in all contexts, their abstract specification must specify what happens when such attempts occur. One approach would be for *put* and *get* to return special values; another would be to use a language construct called exceptions. Even if the preconditions guarantee that *put* will not be called on a full buffer and *get* will not be called on an empty buffer, defensive programming still encourages specifications for responses to such unexpected calls.

operation	PUBLIC VIEW *buffer contents*	PRIVATE VIEW *implementation*
put(a)	a	
put(b)	a b	
get()	b	
put(c)	b c	
get()	c	
put(d)	c d	

Figure 6.5   Public and private views of a bounded buffer.

set up data invariants when the object is created. An implementation of a queue must set up front and rear pointers before any elements are entered into the queue. These remarks are independent of whether we work with classes or modules.

It is most convenient if initialization is done automatically, by executing programmer-supplied initialization code. If a language does not help with initialization, then errors can occur if private data is inadvertently used before the expected data invariants are established.

Visibility of Data

Assignments to public variables can change the local state of an object. It is up to the user to ensure that such assignments do not disturb the desired data invariants.

For example, consider a desk-calculator program with the two modules *Scanner* and *Parser*. Each time its operation *scan* is called, the *Scanner* reads enough input characters to isolate the next token in the input. This token is then held in a variable *lookahead*, and the value of the token is held in a variable *lookvalue*. If *lookahead* and *lookvalue* are public, then the other module *Parser* can change their values, disturbing the invariant that *lookahead* represents the next token.

If variables are hidden, then the value of a variable v can be accessed through two procedures, one for returning the value of v, and the other for assigning a value to v:

$$getv() \quad \text{returns the value of } v$$
$$setv(a) \quad \text{equivalent to } v := a$$

Note that $getv()$, by itself, provides read-only access to the value of v.

Data is usually private. If outside code does need read and write access to data, then the trade-off is between providing procedures like $getv$ and $setv$ and putting a variable v in the public interface.

Implementation Hiding and Program Development

Techniques like information hiding preserve the integrity of a design; they are not a substitute for clean design. In fact, they make clean design more critical. Classes and modules formalize the structure of a program and allow a language to prevent attempts to compromise the structure. If the structure is inappropriate, then information hiding stands in the way.

Unfortunately, the hardest task of program design is discovering the right objects, the right modules, the right viewpoint from which to design a computation. Program development is therefore likely to involve periodic adjustments to the structure of the program.

Compromises in program design and structure are often made in the name of program optimization — of running time or storage. The expectation that the structure of a program is likely to change during development reinforces Jackson's [1975] two fundamental rules for program optimization:

> *Rule* 1: Don't do it.
> *Rule* 2: Don't do it yet.

6.3 PROGRAM DESIGN WITH MODULES

The informal equation

$$\text{modules } = \text{ visibility} + \text{initialization}$$

summarizes the role of modules to partition the text of a program statically.

If initialization is not supported, then modules simply control visibility and have no effect on the run-time computations set up by a program.

design proceeds from role to implementation to interface

Programming with modules is illustrated in this section by considering the structure of an expression evaluator, a modest-sized program containing several short procedures. Expression evaluators are interesting in their own right, since they are a starting point for studying interpreters and compilers.

Modules are useful during program design, even if the programming language does not support them. After designing the modules in the evaluator, we contrast three possible implementations, using procedures, nested procedures, and modules.

Design of the Expression Evaluator

An expression evaluator deals with two distinct representations of expressions: an external one made up of characters and an internal one made up of tokens. Manipulation of the character representation will be done in a module called the scanner, and manipulation of the token representation will be done in a module called the parser. The design of these modules proceeds from their role to their interfaces to their implementation.

Role of the Scanner and the Parser

The program repeatedly evaluates expressions like

```
(512-487)*2;
```

Conceptually, evaluation proceeds as follows:

1. *Scanner*: A lexical analyzer reads input characters and groups them into tokens.
2. *Parser*: A syntax analyzer parses the token stream and evaluates expressions.

The parser is in charge of expression evaluation. It gets tokens from the scanner as needed. Tokens correspond to operators like + and *, parentheses, and numbers. Names like *plus* and *number* for tokens can be introduced by declaring an enumeration type *token*:

type *token* = (*plus, minus, times, divide, number, lparen, rparen, semi*);

With input

```
(512-487)*2;
```

the scanner first produces the token *lparen* corresponding to a left parenthesis. It must then produce token *number*. Numbers like 512 and 487 are denoted by token *number*; their value is passed along with the token to the parser.

Scanner Interface

Question: How is a token and its value passed between the scanner and the parser?

Answer: It is common practice in compiling to use two variables, one for the token and the other for its associated value. Since the values of these variables are set by the scanner, they can be part of the scanner's interface. Let variable *lookahead* hold the token and let *lookvalue* hold its value. The name *lookahead* is motivated by the way the parser uses the token to analyze the syntax of expressions.

This discussion motivates the following design of the public interfaces of the scanner and the parser:

MODULE *Scanner*

> **type** *token* = (*plus, minus, times, divide, number, lparen, rparen, semi*);
>
> **procedure** *scan*   put next token in *lookahead*, its value in *lookvalue*
>
> **var** *lookahead*: *token*;
>   *lookvalue*: **integer**;

MODULE *Parser*

> **function** *expr*   parse and evaluate an expression

Implementation: Informal

Both modules have additional private variables and procedures.

In the scanner, procedure *scan* uses a procedure *getch* to read characters and a function *getnum* to collect the digits in a number. A private variable *ch* holds characters as they are read. Array *tok* maps a character like + to its corresponding token *plus*. Finally, procedure *scaninit* initializes the variables *ch* and *tok* before the first call to *scan*. The private part of the scanner is

> **var** *ch*: **char**;
>   *tok*: **array**[**char**] **of** *token*;

> **procedure** *getch* · · ·   read next character into variable *ch*
> **function** *getnum* · · ·   read a number, return its value
> **procedure** *scaninit* · · ·   initialize *lookahead, lookvalue, ch, tok*

In the parser, function *expr* evaluates an expression. The functions *expr*, *term*, and *factor* are abstractions corresponding to the nonterminals in the EBNF syntax:

> ⟨*expr*⟩   ::= ⟨*term*⟩ { *plus* ⟨*term*⟩ }
>
> ⟨*term*⟩   ::= ⟨*factor*⟩ { *times* ⟨*factor*⟩ }
>
> ⟨*factor*⟩ ::= *number* | *lparen* ⟨*expr*⟩ *rparen*

As in BNF, a vertical bar "|" on the right side of a production is read as "or;" it appears between two alternatives. Braces, "{" and "}", denote zero or more repetitions of the enclosed string.

The private part of the parser is

> **function** *factor* · · ·   corresponds to ⟨*factor*⟩
> **function** *term* · · ·   corresponds to ⟨*term*⟩

Program Organization

Outlines of three Pascal implementations follow. The third uses units, a form of modules. The progression is as follows:

- *Procedures at the same level*. The program consists of a sequence of useful procedures at the same level; that is, they can call each other. Unfortunately, the partitioning of the evaluator into a scanner and a parser is lost if we program using procedures.

- *Nested procedures*. Procedure nesting is an attempt to manage programs with many procedures. Procedure Q is nested inside procedure P if it is declared inside P. A procedure nested inside P is hidden from all other procedures outside P. Independent of its merits as a programming technique, nesting is worth examining because it affects the implementation of all procedures in a language like Pascal. C and C++ do not allow procedure nesting.

- *Modules*. The conceptual leap from procedures to modules can be summarized as follows: a procedure represents an action, whereas a module represents a collection of data and related actions; it has an invariant associated with it.

A Sequence of Procedures

example of procedures operating on global data

A Standard Pascal program must be read as a whole, since all declarations of the same kind are collected together—the declarations of all labels are followed by all constants, by all types, by all variables, and finally, by all procedures. A program has the form:

> **program** ⟨*name*⟩ ;
>   ⟨*label-declarations*⟩
>   ⟨*constant-declarations*⟩
>   ⟨*type-declarations*⟩
>   ⟨*variable-declarations*⟩
>   ⟨*procedure-declarations*⟩
> **begin**
>   ⟨*statement-list*⟩
> **end** .

The outline in Fig. 6.6 has sections for types, variables, and procedures. For ease of comparison with alternative ways of organizing programs, each procedure declaration is enclosed in a box, as is the whole program.

Type *token* introduces names like *plus* and *times* for tokens. Keyword **var** marks the beginning of the variable declarations. All nonlocal variables are declared together:

```
program Evaluator;
    type  token = ··· ;
    var   lookahead : token;
          lookvalue : integer;
          ch : char;
          tok : array [ char ] of token;

        ┌─────────────────────────────────────────┐
        │ procedure getch;                         │
        │     ···                                  │
        │ end                                      │
        └─────────────────────────────────────────┘
        ┌─────────────────────────────────────────┐
        │ function getnum : integer                │
        │     ···                                  │
        │ end                                      │
        └─────────────────────────────────────────┘
        ┌─────────────────────────────────────────┐
        │ procedure scan;                          │
        │     ···                                  │
        │ end;                                     │
        └─────────────────────────────────────────┘
        ┌─────────────────────────────────────────┐
        │ procedure scaninit;                      │
        │     ···                                  │
        │ end;                                     │
        └─────────────────────────────────────────┘

        ┌─────────────────────────────────────────┐
        │ function factor : integer                │
        │     ···                                  │
        │ end;                                     │
        └─────────────────────────────────────────┘
        ┌─────────────────────────────────────────┐
        │ function term : integer                  │
        │     ···                                  │
        │ end;                                     │
        └─────────────────────────────────────────┘
        ┌─────────────────────────────────────────┐
        │ function expr : integer                  │
        │     ···                                  │
        │ end;                                     │
        └─────────────────────────────────────────┘
    begin
        ···  (*  execution begins here  *)
    end.
```

Figure 6.6 A program for an expression evaluator, with procedure declarations enclosed in boxes.

```
var lookahead : token;
    lookvalue : integer;
    ch : char;
    tok : array[char] of token;
```

A drawback of the program outline in Fig. 6.6, is that the design of the program in terms of a scanner and a parser is left in the mind of the designer. It is not explicit in the program; hence it cannot be checked and enforced. For example, variables *ch* and *tok*, which are shared only by procedures in the scanner, are now visible in all procedures. Subsequent changes to the program, perhaps by someone else, can violate the intended partitioning without any warnings from the compiler.

Nested Procedures

nesting is for hiding procedures

Procedure nesting is used to group and hide procedures; the idea is to declare a procedure inside another. In functional languages it is routine and convenient to declare nested functions close to where they are used.

The outline in Fig. 6.7 is the result of nesting some of the procedures in Fig. 6.6. Again, each procedure declaration is enclosed in a box. The outermost box for the program encloses the boxes for *scan*, *scaninit*, and *expr*. Procedures *getch* and *getnum* are now declared within *scan*. Procedure *term* is declared within *expr*, and *factor* is declared within *term*.

Procedure nesting allows procedures to be hidden, but, at least in Pascal, it can interfere with readability. In Pascal, the statements in a procedure body appear after all the declarations of nested procedures, which means that the statements could appear several pages after the procedure name and parameters. In Fig. 6.7, the nested procedures *term* and *factor* separate the procedure name *expr* from its statements. Furthermore, from Section 5.7, there can be some overhead associated with variables accessed from a nested procedure.

With procedures, the emphasis in program design is on the actions and operations of a program. A lesson from experience is that actions and operations need to be considered together with the data they work with.

Modules

with modules, the design is explicit in the source text

A module is a grouping of declarations, which can include types, variables, and procedures. The program outlined in Fig. 6.8 is written in an extension of Pascal with explicit support for modules. A module has the form

> **unit** ⟨*name*⟩ ;
> **interface** ⟨*declarations*⟩
> **implementation** ⟨*declarations*⟩
> **end** .

Execution of a program begins in a special program module:

> **program** ⟨*name*⟩ ;
> ⟨*declarations*⟩
> **begin**
> ⟨*statement-list*⟩
> **end** .

```
program Evaluator;
     type  token = · · · ;
     var   lookahead : token;
           lookvalue : integer;
           ch : char;
           tok : array [ char ] of token;
     procedure scan;
           procedure getch;
               · · ·
           end

           function getnum : integer
               · · ·
           end
     begin
        · · ·  (∗  statements in scan  ∗)
     end;

     procedure scaninit;
        · · ·
     end;

     function expr : integer
           var val : integer

           function term : integer
                 var val : integer

                 function factor : integer
                       var val : integer
                 begin
                     · · ·
                 end;
           begin
              · · ·  (∗  statements in term  ∗)
           end;
     begin
        · · ·  (∗  statements in expr  ∗)
     end;
begin
   · · ·  (∗  execution begins here  ∗)
end.
```

Figure 6.7 The use of procedure nesting. Each procedure declaration is enclosed in a box, as is the whole program. The boxes for nested procedures are shaded.

```
unit Scanner;
interface
    type token = ··· ;
    var   lookahead : token;
          lookvalue : integer;
    procedure scan;
    procedure scaninit;
implementation
    var   ch : char;
          tok : array [ char ] of token;
    procedure getch;
        ···
    end;
    function getnum : integer;
        ···
    end;
    procedure scan;
        ···
    end;
    procedure scaninit;
        ···
    end;
end.
```

```
unit Parser;
interface
    uses Scanner;
    function expr: integer;
implementation
    function factor : integer;
        ···
    end;
    function term : integer;
        ···
    end;
    function expr : integer;
        ···
    end;
end.
```

```
program Controller;
    uses Scanner, Parser;
begin
    ···   (* execution begins here *)
end.
```

Figure 6.8 Program organization using units. Units are enclosed within boxes, and the implementation part of a unit is shaded.

The program in Fig. 6.8 consists of three units: *Scanner*, *Parser*, and *Controller*, where *Controller* is the program module. This organization makes modules explicit, so a compiler can check that modules interact only through interfaces.

Procedure names can appear in the interface, but procedure bodies are moved into the private implementation part. Any private declarations are hidden from the rest of the program, so private variables can be accessed only from the procedure bodies in the implementation part. Thus, variables *ch* and *tok* in the implementation part of *Scanner* can be accessed only from the procedure bodies for *getch*, *getnum*, *scan*, and *scaninit*. Procedures *getch* and *getnum* are also private to the *Scanner*.

Unfortunately, initialization of units is not supported, so procedure *scaninit* has to be called explicitly from the program module.

The declaration

uses *Scanner*;

in the interface to *Parser* allows the parser to access the scanner's interface. That is, the **uses** declaration allows the code in the implementation part of *Parser* to use the declarations in the interface of unit *Scanner*. Thus, the code can call procedure *scan*; however, it cannot call procedures *getch* and *getnum*, because they are not in the interface.

Discussion: Program Organization

The design of the program in this section began with a general description of the roles of the scanner and the parser. The key interface is that of the scanner. It consists of procedure *scan*, type *token*, and the variables *lookahead* and *lookvalue*.

The implementation of procedure *scan* involves procedures and variables that help *scan* but are of no interest to the rest of the program. For example, the implementation of *scan* uses procedure *getch* to read characters and procedure *getnum* to read numbers. It also uses an array *tok* to determine the token that corresponds to a character. Array *tok* has to be initialized before *scan* is called for the first time, and a procedure *scaninit* is used for this purpose.[3]

The evaluator organized using units in Fig. 6.8 has the same procedures and variables as the evaluator organized using procedures in Fig. 6.6. At run time, the same procedures carry out the same computation. (The outline using nested procedures in Fig. 6.7 has its own counterpart using units because any

---

[3] A benefit of Modula-2 is that code for initializing the variables in a module can appear hidden within the module itself; it is called automatically when execution begins. In the absence of support for automatic initialization of units, any initialization code must be called explicitly. Procedure *scaninit* is in the interface of unit *Scanner* because it is called explicitly from the controller to initialize the scanner's variables.

Pascal procedure, including one with nested procedures, can appear in the implementation part of a unit.)

6.4 MODULES AND DEFINED TYPES

This section is a bridge between modules and user-defined data types or defined types. Modules permit defined types, classes support them. That is, with some care, defined types can be implemented in a language with modules. Specifically, defined types can be imitated by putting a type and related operations in a module's interface.

Exported and Imported Names

A name is said to be *exported* from a construct if it is explicitly identified as a name that can be used outside the construct. A name exported by one construct can be *imported* by another; that is, another construct can choose to include an exported name among its own names. Imported names are treated as if they were declared at the point of import.

In the program in Fig. 6.8, unit *Parser* contains a **uses** clause that imports all the names exported by unit *Scanner*:

> **unit** *Parser*;
> **interface**
>   **uses** *Scanner*; · · ·

Modula-2 allows names to be imported selectively, using an **import** clause. For example, the following pseudocode imports *ReadInt* and *WriteInt* from a module *InOut*, but not any of the many other names exported by *InOut*:

> **from** *InOut* **import** *ReadInt*, *WriteInt*;

Exported Types

export a type and associated operations

Types exported from a module can imitate defined types. Module *StackManager* in Fig. 6.9 exports type *stack*.

In Modula-2, *opaque export* of a type occurs when the type is exported by mentioning only its name in the interface, as in

> **type** *stack*;

An importer of *stack* knows nothing about the structure of *stack*, although it is implicit that an opaque type is a pointer type.

Module *StackManager*

```
type stack;
function pop(s : stack) : integer;
procedure push(a : integer; s : stack);
function newstack : stack;
```

```
type stack = ↑ rep;
      rep = record
                  elements : array [0..100] of integer;
                  top : integer
             end
function newstack : stack;
    var s : stack;
begin
    new(s);  s↑.top := 0;  newstack := s
end;
...
procedure bodies for pop and push
```

Figure 6.9   Type *stack*, in the public interface of module *StackManager* is implemented as a pointer to a record containing the data for a stack.

Once a type name, say *stack*, is imported, it can be used to declare variables, as in

var *s, t* : *stack*;

The language supports assignment of opaque types and tests for equality and inequality. All other operations on an opaque type have to be exported along with the type. Module *StackManager* exports *newstack* for creating a stack, and *pop(s)* and *push(a,s)* for manipulating a stack passed as an explicit argument, as in

var *s t* : *stack*;
s := *newstack*;
t := *newstack*;
push(10, *s*);
push(20, *t*);

This approach permits a careful programmer to use modules to obtain some of the benefits of defined types.

Limitations of Exported (Pointer) Types

There are two main limitations of opaque types in Modula-2:

- Variables have to be initialized explicitly.
- Equality and assignment obey the rules for pointers.

In a program fragment

```
var s, t : stack;
   ...
   s := newstack;
```

variables and s and t are uninitialized until the function *newstack* is called to explicitly initialize them. Until then, s and t are dangling references.

If the exported type is a pointer, as it is in Fig. 6.9, then equality and assignment obey the rules for pointers. For example, if s and t are stacks, what is the meaning of the equality test

```
s = t
```

With opaque types in Modula-2, s = t is true when s and t point to the same object. Thus, s = t can be false if s and t point to different stacks with the same elements.

Furthermore, an assignment

```
s := t;
```

leaves s and t pointing to the same object, as in Fig. 6.10. The assignment in Fig. 6.10 creates garbage because the data structure previously pointed to by s becomes unreachable.

Such limitations are overcome by classes, which are designed to be used as defined types.

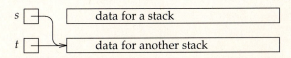

Figure 6.10 The result of the assignment s:=t, where s and t are of a pointer type.

Implementation of Exported Types

In the private shaded part of module *StackManager* in Fig. 6.9, type *stack* denotes a pointer to a record that holds the data for a stack:

> **type** *stack* = ↑ *rep*;
>   *rep* = **record**
>   *elements* : **array** [0..100] **of integer**;
>   *top* : **integer**;
>   **end**;

Now, using the operations on records and pointers from Chapter 4, we can implement the operations *newstack*, *push*, and *pop*. The following code is from Fig. 6.9:

> **function** *newstack* : *stack*;
>   **var** *s* : *stack*;
> **begin**
>   **new**(*s*); *s*↑.*top* := 0; *newstack* := *s*
> **end**;

This procedure declares a local variable *s* of type *stack*. It calls **new** to allocate storage for a stack, and initializes the stack by assigning 0 to field *top* in the record. It then returns a pointer to the initialized storage.

6.5   CLASS DECLARATIONS IN C++

C++ was designed to provide the same support for user-defined types that built-in types enjoy. This section considers the basic facilities for defining and using classes. See Section 6.6 for dynamic allocation of objects and Section 6.8 for implementation considerations.

This section begins with the grouping of data and operations in class declarations. Classes will then be used like types to declare variables. Finally, public and private access to class members will be introduced.

Data and Operations in a Class Declaration

functions and variables can be members of a class

Classes in C++ are a generalization of records, called *structures* in C and C++. A structure is traditionally a grouping of data; C++ allows both data and functions to be structure members. Like record types, classes can be used to declare variables and create objects.

Structures: Classes with Public Members

Structures and classes are closely related in C++. The only difference is that, by default, all members of a structure are public, whereas, by default, all members of a class are private. Accessibility rules for members will be considered shortly; until then, the discussion is in terms of structures.

A structure declaration begins with the keyword `struct` and consists of a sequence of declarations enclosed within braces `{}`. The declarations within braces are said to be those of *members* of the structure.

For example, all of the data and functions relevant to stacks of characters can be collected in a structure declaration:

```
struct Stack {
    int   top;
    char elements[101];
    char pop();
    void push(char);
        Stack();
};
```
(6.1)

This structure has two variables and three functions as members. Since a structure is a special case of a class, structure `Stack` is at the same time class `Stack`.

Class `Stack` is from the complete C++ program in Fig. 6.11. The program is designed to illustrate language constructs, not the stack data structure. A more complete example of a stack would include additional functions `isempty` for testing whether it is empty, and `isfull` for testing whether it is full, and related checks in the implementations of `push` and `pop`.

The program consists largely of the declaration of class `Stack` and its member functions; these declarations appear above the line

```
#include <stdio.h>
```

which provides access to an input/output library. Below this line is the function `main`, where `Stack` is used as a type to declare variable `s`.

The data members of class `Stack` are `elements` and `top`. An object of this class holds characters in array `elements`. The integer member `top` gives the index of the top element.

The function members are identified by parentheses after the type name; the parentheses enclose the types of the parameters. The return type appears before the function name. Thus, the line

```
char pop();
```

means that function `pop` is a member of the structure. Function `pop` takes no parameters and returns a character. Function `push(c)` adds element `c` to the stack and returns nothing, denoted by `void`.

```
struct Stack {
    int    top;
    char elements[101];

    char pop();
    void push(char);
        Stack()    { top = 0; }
};
char Stack::pop() {
    top = top - 1;
    return elements[top+1];
}

void Stack::push(char c) {
    top = top + 1;
    elements[top] = c;
}
#include <stdio.h>
main() {
    Stack s;
    s.push('!'); s.push('@'); s.push('#');
    printf("%c %c %c\n", s.pop(), s.pop(), s.pop());
}
```

Figure 6.11 A complete C++ program. The program begins with the declarations of class `Stack`, and member functions `pop` and `push` of class `Stack`. The line starting with `#include` provides access to an input/output library. Execution of the program begins in the function `main`.

Special Members: Constructors and Destructors

constructors are for initialization, destructors are for cleanup

A special member function called a constructor has the same name as the class in which it appears. The constructor for class `Stack` is a parameterless function:

```
Stack();
```

A constructor is called automatically when an object is created, so it can be used to initialize the variables in a class.

A class can also have a destructor function, with the name of the class preceded by ~, as in ~`Stack`. A destructor is called automatically to clean up just before the lifetime of an object ends A variant of the stack example in Section 6.6 includes a destructor function.

Full Member Names

The full name of a member is written as

⟨*class-name*⟩ : : ⟨*member-name*⟩

When the class name is known from the context, the ⟨*member-name*⟩ can be used by itself. The operator : : is called the *name-resolution* operator.

Thus, the full name of member function `pop` of class `Stack` is `Stack::pop`. This full member name will be used shortly when member functions are discussed.

Code for Member Functions

For convenience, short function bodies can be included in a class declaration. The following redeclaration of `Stack` includes a function body for the constructor:

```
struct Stack {
    int  top;
    char elements[101];
    char pop();
    void push(char);
        Stack()      { top = 0; }
};
```
(6.2)

The function body of constructor `Stack` consists of the assignment `top=0;`. With this declaration, the bodies of the function members `pop` and `push` have to be declared separately.

The full member name must be used when the body of a member function appears outside a class declaration, as in the following pseudocode:

```
char Stack::pop()        { /* body of pop */ }
void Stack::push(char c) { /* body of push */ }
```

The full member names `Stack::pop` and `Stack::push` are needed to make explicit that these member functions belong to class `Stack`.

Using Class Names as Defined Types

After a class is declared, its name can be used as a type name to declare variables, as in

```
Stack s;
```

which declares variable s to be of type `Stack`. The lifetime of the object denoted by s is determined by the scope and lifetime rules of the language. In C and C++, a local variable exists during a procedure activation; see Section 5.6.

Dot notation is used to refer to members of an object, so function `pop` of s is denoted by `s.pop()`, as in

```
··· c = s.pop(); ···
```

A syntactic difference between C and C++ is that C requires the keyword `struct` when a structure name is used as a type name, but C++ does not. After `Complex` is declared to be a structure, it can be used in C to declare a variable x as follows:

```
struct Complex x;
```

The keyword `struct` can be dropped in the corresponding C++ declaration:

```
Complex x;
```

Initialization with Parameters

constructors can be parameterized

Proper initialization of an object may require the passing of parameters to a constructor. Constructor `Complex` in the following declaration takes two parameters, r and i:

```
struct Complex {
    float re;
    float im;
        Complex(float r, i) { re = r; im = i; }
};
```

The following variable declaration declares and initializes a complex number x:

```
Complex x(1,2);
```

Actual parameters for the constructor appear in parentheses to the right of a declared variable. This declaration creates an object, calls the constructor with arguments 1 and 2, and leaves x as the name of the complex number. The integer parameters are coerced to floating point values.

Overloaded Function Names

constructors can be
overloaded

The same name can be given to more than one function in a class, provided we can tell the overloaded functions apart by looking at the number and types of their parameters.

Constructors are functions, so they too can be overloaded. Class `Complex` has two constructors:

```
struct Complex {
   float re;
   float im;
         Complex(float r)    { re = r; im = 0; }
         Complex(float r, i) { re = r; im = i; }
};
```

The constructor with a single parameter is called in a declaration like

```
Complex y(1);
```

Public, Private, and Protected Members

access is controlled
through keywords
in a class
declaration

Privacy and access control in C++ are class based. That is, access to members is restricted through keywords in a class declaration. The restrictions apply to code that is outside the class. Member functions in a class have full access to the data in all objects of the class.

The public members of a class specify the public view of objects of the class; that is, they specify the interface to objects of the class. The remaining members are inaccessible to the rest of the program, except as discussed in Chapter 7. The examples in this chapter use only public and private members; protected members are introduced here for completeness.

C++ has three keywords—`public`, `private`, and `protected`—for controlling the accessibility of member names in a class declaration:

- *Public members* are accessible to outside code.
- *Private members* are accessible to the member functions in this class declaration. They are accessible to all objects of this class.
- *Protected members* behave like private members except for derived classes, which are discussed in Chapter 7. Protected members are visible through inheritance to derived classes but not to other code.

A structure declaration

```
struct X { ⟨member-declarations⟩ };
```

is just shorthand for

```
class X { public: ⟨member-declarations⟩ };
```

Conversely, a class declaration

```
class X { ⟨member-declarations⟩ };
```

is just shorthand for

```
struct X { private: ⟨member-declarations⟩ };
```

The following declaration of class `Stack` hides the member variables in the structure declaration (6.1):

```
class Stack {
public:
        Stack();
    char pop();
    void push(char);
private:
    int  top;
    char elements[101];
};                                                      (6.3)
```

6.6 DYNAMIC ALLOCATION IN C++

objects created by new exist until they are explicitly deleted

C++ objects can be created in three ways: (1) through variable declarations as in Section 6.5; (2) dynamically through `new` as discussed in this section; and (3) as static objects whose lifetime is the entire life of the program.

Objects created by `new` exist until they are destroyed by `delete`. For any type `T`, built-in or user-defined, execution of the expression

```
new T
```

creates an object of type `T` and returns a pointer to the newly created object. Conversely, execution of

```
delete p
```

destroys the object that `p` points to.

Pointers to Objects

As in C, the pointer-dereferencing operator is a prefix `*`. Read the declaration

```
Cell * p;
```

as "p is a pointer to `Cell`."

Pointers to structures and class objects are used so frequently that there is special syntax for accessing members. C++ borrows the C syntax `p->info` for referring to member `info` of the structure pointed to by p. The notation `p->info` is an abbreviation of `(*p).info`, which explicitly uses `*` to dereference p and then uses dot notation to select member `info`.

A null pointer, pointing to no object, is written as `0` — zero being heavily overloaded in C and C++.

Within the code for an object, the special name `this` denotes a pointer to the object itself. This special name will be used in this section to create a circularly linked list.

A summary of these notations is as follows:

notation for pointers to objects

`p->info`	member `info` of object pointed to by p
`0`	null pointer, pointing to no object
`this`	used within member functions to point to this object itself

Dynamic Allocation Using Constructors and Destructors

The size of an object can be determined at run time by passing a parameter to its constructor. The constructor can then dynamically allocate storage off the heap, using the `new` function.

By confining allocation and deallocation within constructors and destructors, the rest of the program can be insulated from storage management.

Example 6.2 The declaration (6.3) of class `Stack` in Section 6.5 used a fixed-size array to hold elements. This example modifies the class to make the size of the array a parameter. The constructor `Stack` uses the parameter to allocate an array of that size.

Dynamically allocated storage is taken off the heap, so it has to be explicitly deallocated. The destructor `~Stack` in the following class releases the storage allocated in the constructor:

```
class Stack {
    char * elements;
    int    top;
    int    size;
public:
    void   push(char);
    char   pop();
           Stack(int);
```

```
            ~Stack();
    };
```
(6.4)

For completeness, the code for the constructor is as follows:

```
Stack::Stack(int n) {
    size = n;                          // set member size
    elements = new char[size];         // allocate an array
    top = 0;                           // initialize top
}
```

After the array is allocated, the elements of the array can be referred to as usual as

```
elements[0], elements[1],..., elements[size-1]
```

The destructor simply deletes the array pointed to by `elements`:

```
Stack::~Stack() { delete elements; }
```                                   □

Cells in a Linked List

The rest of this section consists of an example that applies several of the concepts in Sections 6.5 and 6.6: public and private members, dynamic allocation, the use of `this` to refer to this object itself, and overloaded constructors.

The example involves two classes, `List` and `Cell`. Class `List` supports typical list operations that check whether a list is empty and add or remove elements from the ends of the list. These operations present an interface that is independent of the implementation.

Class `Cell` is part of the implementation of lists. It is not meant to be used directly. Cells will be linked to form circular lists, as in Fig. 6.12, to choose one from among several possible implementations. Another possibility is a linear list with pointers to the first and last cells.

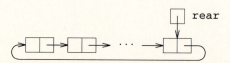

Figure 6.12   A circularly linked list.

Friends Have Access to Private Members

a class can declare
its friends

Since class `Cell` is part of the implementation of class `List`, access to members of `Cell` will be restricted to members of `List`. The use of `Cell` as a type to declare variables and create objects can be prevented by making the constructors of `Cell` inaccessible.

The members of a class are private unless they are explicitly declared to be public. Since the keyword `public` does not appear in the following declaration, all members are private, by default:

```
(1) class Cell {
(2)     int    info;
(3)     Cell * next;
(4)           Cell(int i) { info = i; next = this; }
(5)           Cell(int i, Cell * n) { info = i; next = n; }
(6) friend class List;
(7) };
```

The line numbers in parentheses on the left are not part of the code; they show how the program fragments in this section fit together to form a C++ program.

A cell has an integer member `info` and a pointer `next` to another cell. The member functions are the two constructors on lines (4–5).

A *friend* declaration within a class gives nonmember functions access to the private members of the class. Line (6) declares `List` to be a friend, so the functions of class `List` can access the private members of `Cell`. Since `public` does not appear in the declaration of class `Cell`, its members are hidden from all other code.

Cell Constructors

a use of `this`

An empty list is implemented by a cell that points to itself:

Such a cell is constructed by executing the expression

```
new Cell c(0)
```

This expression creates an object of class `Cell` and calls the first constructor with parameter 0.

The special name `this` denotes an object itself, so execution of

```
next = this;
```

in the constructor results in a cell that points to itself.

The other constructor, with two parameters i and n, will be called to link a new cell in front of the cell that n points to.

Linked Lists

Class List has one variable rear, as in Fig. 6.12:

```
(8) class List {
(9)      Cell * rear;
(10) public:
(11)      void    put(int);
(12)      void    push(int);
(13)      int     pop();
(14)      int     empty() { return rear == rear->next; }
(15)              List()   { rear = new Cell(0); }
(16)              ~List() { while( !empty() ) pop(); }
(17) };
```

This declaration uses the constructors of class Cell. Permission to use these private constructors comes from the friend declaration in class Cell; specifically, Cell gets to name its friends.

Constructor List initializes a list by executing

```
rear = new Cell(0);
```

which creates a cell, circularly linked to itself, and assigns rear a pointer to the new cell. This list corresponds to an empty list. Since this cell points to itself, it satisfies

```
rear == rear->next
```

which happens to be what member empty returns.

Member push adds a cell to the front of the list (in a circularly linked list, rear->next points to the front cell):

```
(18) void List::push(int x) {
(19)      rear->next = new Cell(x, rear->next);
(20) }
```

The statements

```
List s;
s.push(1);
s.push(2);
```

create the following list:

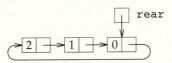

Member put adds a cell at the back of the list. Thus, put allows a list to be used as a queue. The code for put is presented without further explanation:

```
(21) void List::put(int x) {
(22)     rear->info = x;
(23)     rear = rear->next = new Cell(0, rear->next);
(24) }
```

Member function pop returns the value of the cell at the front of the list and deletes the cell:

```
(25) int List::pop() {
(26)     if( empty() ) return 0;
(27)     Cell * front = rear->next;
(28)     rear->next = front->next;
(29)     int x = front->info;
(30)     delete front;
(31)     return x;
(32) }
```

The behavior of pop on an empty list is somewhat unsatisfactory, because it simply returns 0.

Otherwise, it uses a local variable front to keep track of the front cell and a local variable x to hold the value to be returned. The front cell is removed from the list by first routing the linked list around the front cell by executing

```
rear->next = front->next;
```

and then executing

```
delete front;
```

6.7   TEMPLATES: PARAMETERIZED TYPES

class and function declarations can be parameterized

Data structures such as stacks are called containers because they hold objects. The *push* and *pop* operations on stacks do not examine the objects held in the stack, so these operations can be defined for any type. Thus, we can have stacks of integers, stacks of grammar symbols in a parser, and so on.

Parameterized or polymorphic types have long been a key feature of functional programming languages. They will be examined in some detail when static type checking in ML is considered. Meanwhile here is an example of how parameterized types can be used in C++.

A type parameter T can be introduced by writing

```
template<class T>
```

before a class or function declaration. In the following declaration of class Stack the type parameter T denotes the type of the elements held in a stack:

```
template<class T> class Stack {
   int  top;
   int  size;
   T *  elements;
public:
        Stack(int n){size=n; elements=new T[size]; top=0;}
        ~Stack()    { delete elements; }
   void push(T a)   { top++; elements[top] = a; }
   T    pop()       { top--; return elements[top+1]; }
};
```

The variable element will now point to the first of an array of elements of type T. In the constructor, the operator new is applied to T[size] to allocate an array of Ts, where the number of elements is given by size. The function push takes an argument of type T, and the function pop returns a value of type T.

For completeness, skeletal implementations of push and pop are included. The body of push needs to check that top will remain within the array bounds before it executes top++ to increment top. Similarly, the body of push needs to check that top will remain within the array bounds before it executes top-- to decrement top.

When stack is used as a type name, it must be supplied a type as an explicit parameter. After the following declarations,

```
Stack<int>  s(99);
Stack<char> t(80);
```

s is declared to be a stack of integers of size 99 and t is declared to be a stack of characters of size 80.

If the body of a member function appears outside a class declaration, then a type parameter has to be introduced afresh, as in

```
template<class X> void Stack<X>::push(X a) {
    top++;
    elements[top] = a;
}
```

A type parameter is a local bound variable, so another name X can be used instead of T.

6.8 IMPLEMENTATION OF OBJECTS IN C++

Efficiency was a primary concern during the design of C++. Objects in C++ are laid out like records in Section 4.4. One of the criticisms of C++ is that the private members of a class appear in the class declaration; this design was influenced by implementation considerations. Finally, in this section, we consider in-line expansion, which makes function calls efficient.

A Simple Implementation

objects are laid out like records

The layout of a class can be just like the layout of a structure containing the data members.

The corresponding C++ and C programs in Fig. 6.13 illustrate how objects in a C++ program can be implemented. The layout of class Stack in Fig. 6.13(a) is given by the structure in Fig. 6.13(b)

```
struct Stacklay {
    int  top;
    char elements[101];
};
```

The member functions pop, push, and Stack in the C++ program have corresponding functions Stackpop, Stackpush, and StackStack in the C program. The C functions take as an explicit argument a pointer to the data for a stack — that is, a pointer to a structure Stacklay. This approach is similar to that in Section 6.4, where module *StackManager* had a public function *pop(s)*, with *s* as an explicit argument (*s* was a pointer to the data for a stack.)

In more detail, the constructor Stack::Stack has a corresponding C function

```
struct Stack {                          struct Stacklay {
    int   top;                              int    top;
    char elements[101];                     char elements[101];
                                        };
    char pop();
    void push(char);                    void StackStack(struct Stacklay * p) {
          Stack() { top = 0; }              p->top = 0;
};                                      }

char Stack::pop() {                     char Stackpop(struct Stacklay * p) {
    char c;                                 char c;
    c = elements[top];                      c = p->elements[p->top];
    top = top - 1;                          p->top = p->top - 1;
    return c;                               return c;
}                                       }

void Stack::push(char c) {              void Stackpush(struct Stacklay * p, char c) {
    top = top + 1;                          p->top = p->top + 1;
    elements[top] = c;                      p->elements[p->top] = c;
}                                       }

#include <stdio.h>                      #include <stdio.h>
main() {                                main() {
    Stack s;                                struct Stacklay s;
                                            StackStack(&s);
    s.push('!');                            Stackpush(&s, '!');
    s.push('@');                            Stackpush(&s, '@');
    s.push('#');                            Stackpush(&s, '#');
    printf("%c %c %c\n",                    printf("%c %c %c\n", Stackpop(&s),
        s.pop(), s.pop(), s.pop());             Stackpop(&s), Stackpop(&s));
}                                       }
```

          (a) C++ program   (b) C program

Figure 6.13 Stack objects in the C++ program in (a) are implemented efficiently using a structure in the C program in (b) to hold the data for a stack object.

```
void StackStack(struct Stacklay * p) {
    p->top = 0;
}
```

The formal parameter p in this C function serves the same purpose as the special name this in C++, which points to an object itself. The formal parameter is passed a pointer to the data for this object, so the C function can access the member `top` indirectly as `p->top`.

In-line Expansion of Function Bodies

in-line expansion eliminates function-call overhead

Implementation hiding can result in lots of little functions that manipulate the data in an object. C++ implements such functions efficiently by using in-line expansion, which replaces a call by the function body, taking care to preserve the semantics of the language (see Section 5.7). Thus, in-line expansion in C++ preserves the semantics of call-by-value parameter passing.

Suppose we were to add a public function `isempty` to class `Stack`:

```
int isempty() { return top == 0; }
```

This function returns a result computed from private data. If `s` is a stack object, then `isempty` can be used in a test of the form:

```
if( s.isempty() ) ···
```

In-line expansion implements this test as if it were written

```
if( (s.top == 0) ) ···
```

Since the expanded expression refers directly to the member `s.top`, it can be executed more efficiently than the original expression.

In-line expansion eliminates the overhead of function calls at run time, so it encourages free use of functions, even small functions. It also encourages data hiding, because private data can be accessed efficiently through in-line public functions.

Functions declared within a class declaration are expanded in-line, at the discretion of the compiler. For functions declared outside the class declaration, the keyword `inline` is a hint to the compiler to expand the function in-line.

Private Members in the Class Declaration

access restrictions are checked at compile time

All of the variables and functions relevant to a class appear in the class declaration, even if they are private and inaccessible from code outside the class.

In the declaration of class `Stack`, we can tell from the declarations of the private variables `elements` and `top` that the stack is represented as an array of characters. Changes to this representation will result in changes to the class declaration.

A class declaration would be more "abstract" if the representation appeared separately. With the present language design, inheritance, introduced in Chapter 7, can be used to separate the representation, if desired.

The C++ design was motivated in part by separate compilation. With separate compilation, portions of a program — say, the function bodies — can be put in a file and compiled separately. The separately compiled pieces are eventually linked together when the program runs.

The inclusion of the representation in the class declaration allowed the initial C++ implementation to figure out the layout. For example, suppose class name `Stack` is used to declare a variable *s* in a separately compiled file:

```
Stack s;
```

The declaration of class `Stack`, is needed before `Stack` can be used as a type name, although the bodies of the member functions of the class can appear in a separately compiled file.

From the declaration, the compiler can readily tell whether member `isempty` is to be expanded in-line. If it is, then

```
s.isempty()
```

can be expanded in-line.

Exercises

6.1 Design a program that uses an auxiliary stack to evaluate postfix expressions.

6.2 Section 6.2 ends with pseudocode for a class *Entry* in Fig. 6.4 and a program fragment for removing adjacent duplicates. Implement this pseudocode in C++.

6.3 Implement a table with two operations: *insert*(*x*) enters *x* into the table; *find*(*x*) returns **true** if *x* was previously inserted and returns **false** otherwise. Use your table to do the following:
   a. Count the number of times an integer is seen in an input sequence.
   b. Output one copy of integers that are seen more than once in an input sequence.

6.4 Example 6.1 describes a bounded buffer; see also Fig. 6.5.
   a. Design a corresponding module *Buffer*.
   b. Design a corresponding class *Buffer*.

6.5 Design an array implementation of a first-in/first-out buffer, based on the following invariants:

The buffer is empty when *holds* = 0.

The buffer is full when *holds* = *size*.

The first-in element is in *buf*[*front*].

The last-in element is in *buf*[*rear*].

The elements wrap around the right end of the array.

6.6 Using the representation of index entries in Example 4.2, write a C++ program to remove duplicates from a sequence of index entries.

6.7 Use exported types as in Section 6.4 to implement complex numbers.

6.8 Implement a noncircular variant of class `List` in Section 6.6.

6.9 In the language of your choice implement the expression evaluator discussed in Section 6.3. Expressions with the EBNF syntax

$$
\begin{aligned}
E &::= T \{ '+' T \mid '-' T \} \\
T &::= F \{ '*' F \mid '/' F \} \\
F &::= '(' E ')' \mid \textbf{number}
\end{aligned}
$$

can be evaluated by setting up procedures corresponding to the nonterminals *E*, *T*, and *F*. The body of the procedure for a nonterminal is constructed from the right side of the production as follows:

- The braces { and } correspond to loops.
- Alternatives separated by |lead to a case statement. An alternative is selected if the leading token in the alternative equals the lookahead token.
- A token in the right side matches the lookahead token in the input.
- A nonterminal results in a call to its procedure. A version of the procedure for *E* appears in Fig. 6.14. It combines evaluation with matching. The procedures for *E*, *T*, and *F* return an integer representing the value of the subexpression matched by an activation of the procedure. An activation of procedure `E` in Fig. 6.14 matches a sequence of terms separated by + or - signs, and returns the value of this sequence.

6.10 Design a lexical analyzer—a lexical analyzer groups characters into tokens—for expressions. Expressions are made up of tokens corresponding to names, integers, parentheses, and the operators +, -, *, `DIV`, and `MOD`. A name begins with a letter and consists of a sequence of letters and digits. Every time the lexical analyzer sees a new name, it assigns a sequence number to the name.

a. Design a client that asks for and displays tokens. Integers, parentheses, and operators must be displayed as is. Display names by writing `NAME[s]`, where *s* is the sequence number for the name. Thus, `b*b-4*a*c` must be displayed as

```
int E() {
    int value;
    value = T();
    for(;;)
        switch(lookahead) {
        case '+':
            scan(); value = value + T(); continue;
        case '-':
            scan(); value = value - T(); continue;
        default:
            return value;
        }
}
```

Figure 6.14   Procedure in C for evaluating a sequence of terms separated by + or − signs.

$$NAME[1] * NAME[1] - 4 * NAME[2] * NAME[3]$$

b. Modify the lexical analyzer to maintain a window on the input, consisting of the up to *windowsize* most recently read characters. The lexical analyzer must support an operation to display the window. Such windows are sometimes used to show the context in which an error is detected.

6.11 A *directed graph* consists of a set of *nodes* and a set of *edges* of the form $x \rightarrow y$, where x and y are nodes (see Fig. 6.15). Edge $x \rightarrow y$ is said to be *from x to y*. The set of all nodes reachable by zero or more edges from a starting node *start* can be computed using a data structure called a *closure-set*, which supports the following operations:

- *create()*. Creates and initializes a closure-set with no nodes in it.
- *insert(x : Node)*. Enters x as an unmarked node into the closure-set.

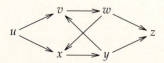

Figure 6.15   A directed graph.

- *find*(*x* : *Node*) : **boolean**.   Returns **true** if node *x* was previously inserted; otherwise, returns **false**.
- *worktodo*() : **boolean**.   Returns **true** if a previously inserted node has not yet been marked.
- *marknext*() : *Node*.   Returns and marks a previously inserted and as yet unmarked node.

Nodes reachable from *start* can now be computed by the pseudocode

```
create();
insert(start);
while worktodo() do
    x := marknext();
    for  each edge x → y  do
        if  not find(y)  then
            insert(y)
        end if
    end for
end while
(∗ the closure-set now contains the reachable nodes ∗)
```

a. Design a program that reads in a start node and a set of edges and prints out the nodes reachable from the start node. Use node numbers for input/output, so a node can be read by reading an integer and an edge can be read by reading a pair of integers.

b. Implement your design in C++.

6.12 A *keyword-in-context* (*KWIC*) *index*, or *permuted index*, consists of a sequence of lines, sorted by keywords appearing within the lines; the lines are circularly shifted so that the keywords line up. For each keyword in a line, the index contains a copy of the line. The lines

```
Ask not what your country can do.
Ask what you can do.
```

lead to the index entries in Fig. 6.16.

a. Design a program to produce a permuted index.

b. How would your design change if a sorting program were available?

Bibliographic Notes

The concepts of modules and objects are natural ones and were clearly developed independently in several contexts, including assembly language. The AED project exploited the idea of grouping operations with data (Ross and Rodriguez [1963]). Parnas [1972] begins with, "The major advancement in the area of modular programming has been the development of coding techniques

```
country can do.           Ask not what your
do.                       Ask what you can
   what your country      can do.           Ask not
      Ask what you        can do.
   Ask not what your      country can do.
      your country can    do.           Ask not what
      Ask what you can    do.
can do.            Ask    not what your country
                   Ask    what you can do.
can do.        Ask not    what your country
           Ask what       you can do.
do.        Ask not what   your country can
```

Figure 6.16   A permuted index.

and assemblers which (1) allow one module to be written with little knowledge of the code in another module, and (2) allow modules to be reassembled
and replaced without reassembly of the whole system." Parnas's thrust is to
present criteria for decomposing a system into modules, using permuted-
index programs as running examples; see also the permuted-index programs
in Kernighan and Plauger [1981], Morris, Schmidt, and Wadler [1980], and
Aho, Kernighan, and Weinberger [1988].

In the 1970s, constructs in the spirit of modules and classes were designed
into a number of languages, such as Mesa (Geschke, Morris, and Satterthwaite
[1977]) and CLU (see Liskov and Guttag [1986]). Mesa influenced the module
facility of Modula-2.

Wirth [1979] discusses the design decisions behind modules in Modula-2,
and notes, "A module is effectively a bracket around a group of (type, variable, procedure, etc.) declarations establishing a scope of identifiers." At the
time it seemed as if nested modules would be more useful than the ability to
define classes of objects. For perspective on the design decisions, see Wirth
[1988].

Stroustrup [1991], the primary reference for C++, contains the historical
note, "C is retained as a subset, and so is C's emphasis on facilities that are
low-level enough to cope with the most demanding systems programming
tasks. . . . The other main source of inspiration was Simula 67; the class concept (with derived classes and virtual functions) was borrowed from it."
Stroustrup [1994] is an account of the design and evolution of C++.

For an algebraic approach to data abstraction, see Goguen, Thatcher, and
Wagner [1978]; Liskov and Zilles [1974] is an early reference.

7

Object-Oriented Programming

> We needed a set of concepts and an associated language in terms of which one could understand and describe the complexity of the systems one had to deal with. . . . Our main reference frame was a set of examples of systems in the world around us: job shops, airports, epidemics, harbors, etc.
>
> *– Nygaard and Dahl [1981], on the motivation for developing the basic concepts of object-oriented programming and the Simula programming language.*

Object-oriented programming holds the promise of making complex systems easier to structure and manage. This promise can be realized by starting afresh from the problem to be solved and thinking at the application level, in terms of objects and interactions needed to describe the application. For example, if the application is a window system, then the relevant objects might be windows, scroll bars, buttons, and dialog boxes.

7.1 WHAT IS AN OBJECT?

an object-oriented program is a simulation

In effect, an object-oriented program is a description or simulation of an application. The objects in the program are the entities in the simulation.

Example 7.1 The concepts of object-oriented programming can be traced to Simula, a language designed both for describing and for programming simulations. An ''airport departure system'' was one of the key examples during the early work on Simula — and it is a variant of the system that this example deals with.

The scene is an airport. Passengers wait in line to check in for a flight. During check-in, a ticket agent examines each passenger's ticket.

253

The problem is to study the queue of waiting passengers: How does the queue build up before a flight? How long does a passenger wait in it? How much does it shrink if an extra ticket agent is put to work? We are given the rate at which passengers arrive and the time it takes a ticket agent to check in a passenger.

The problem can be studied by writing a program that simulates the airport scene. Passengers and ticket agents are simulated by objects in the program, as are additional concepts, such as queues.

Objects were introduced as a unifying concept after trying active and passive components in an early (1963) version of Simula. The airport departure system had dual descriptions: it could have active ticket agents serving passive passengers; or, it could have active passengers grabbing service from passive ticket agents. The distinction between active and passive components was dropped and objects were introduced.   □

External and Internal Views of Objects

An object can represent any entity in the solution of a problem: a passenger, a ticket agent, a queue, a ticket. This is an external or problem-oriented view of objects. A program designer dreams up the objects in a program. In a drawing program, the objects might be shapes such as boxes, ellipses, and lines.

objects respond to messages

Objects interact by sending messages to each other. A computation is characterized by the messages sent and received by the objects in a program. Thus, a computation is characterized in terms of the observable behavior of objects, not in terms of the details of how that behavior is implemented.

Alternatively, each object is like a separate computer with its own code and its own private memory to hold values. This is an internal or implementation-oriented view of objects. A message from one object to another is like a procedure call; the receiving object executes some code in response. As part of the response to a message, the receiving object may change values in its own private memory, it may send messages to other objects, and it may return a value.

Properties of Shapes

Diagrams built out of shapes, as in Fig. 7.1, are a rich setting for discussing objects. We discuss the setting informally, before getting into the specifics of objects.

Grouping Shapes into Classes

A shape can be classified, based on its properties: a shape can be a box (or rectangle), an ellipse, a line, or a text string. The diagram in Fig. 7.1 consists of the following:

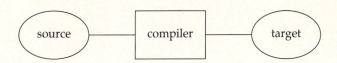

Figure 7.1   A diagram built out of shapes.

an ellipse
a text string, "source"
a line
a box
a text string, "compiler"
a line
an ellipse
a text string, "target"

Some properties are shared only by specific shapes, say, ellipses. All of the ellipses in the following diagram have the same geometry, although their widths and heights are different:

Given the width and height of an ellipse, we can determine the points on its boundary, relative to its center.

Some properties are shared by all shapes, be they boxes, ellipses, lines, or text. Each of the following shapes has a width and a height, although the values for the widths and heights may differ:

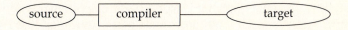

Each Shape Draws Itself

In the examples so far, a diagram consists of a list of shapes, and the shapes on the list align themselves next to each other from left to right. More diagrams can be drawn if shapes can align themselves in other directions, besides left to right. In the following diagram, the shapes align themselves in either an up-down or left-right direction:

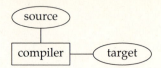

In general, a shape aligns itself at some angle to the previous shape:

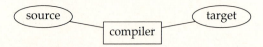

The richness of object-oriented programming shows up in how shapes are drawn. A diagram is drawn by drawing each shape in its list, one by one. Specifically, when a diagram receives a *draw* message it responds by asking each shape on its list to draw itself, next to the previous one. That is, it sends a *draw* message to each shape on its list. All of the code specific to drawing a box is known only to boxes, all of the code specific to drawing ellipses is known only to ellipses, and so on.

7.2 OBJECT-ORIENTED THINKING

Object-oriented programming is based on a small number of concepts, cloaked in unusual terminology. The vocabulary of object-oriented programming begins with the following:

object   A collection of data and operations.
class   A description of a set of objects.
subclass   A subset of a class, with additional properties.
instance   A technical term for an object of a class.
method   A procedure body implementing an operation.
message   A procedure call; request to execute a method.

The terms object, class, subclass, and instance come from Simula. The terms message and method were introduced to distinguish object-oriented programming in Smalltalk from procedural programming. They are popular enough that it is worth becoming familiar with them.

This section introduces object-oriented programming in language-independent terms. The shape example in this chapter has been implemented in both C++ and Smalltalk.

Grouping Objects into Class Hierarchies

In a program to draw diagrams, shapes will be represented by objects. Thus, each ellipse visible in Fig. 7.1 has a corresponding object, each line has an object, and so on.

Grouping Similar Objects into a Class

a class describes a set of similar objects

Similar objects, objects with common properties, are grouped into a *class*. A class can be thought of as the type of an object. The term class is an abbreviation of "class of objects," as in class of shape objects, class of ellipse objects, class of circle objects. For concreteness, suppose a box is an object of class *Box*, an ellipse is an object of class *Ellipse*, a line is an object of class *Line*, and a text string is an object of class *Text*.[1]

A Class Hierarchy

a set can have subsets; a class can have subclasses

Shapes are classified in Fig. 7.2. The nesting in Fig. 7.2 emphasizes that each object of a nested class, say *Box*, is also an object of the enclosing class *Shape*. Thus, all boxes are shapes, but not all shapes are boxes. The set of all boxes is a subset of the set of all shapes. This terminology carries over to classes.

A nested class is said to be a *subclass*; the converse of subclass is *superclass*. Thus, *Box* is a subclass of *Shape*, and *Shape* is a superclass of *Box*.

The nested classification in Fig. 7.2 leads to the class hierarchy in Fig. 7.3. A subclass *S* of a class *C* is depicted as a child of *C* in the hierarchy. Class *Shape* has four subclasses, *Box*, *Ellipse*, *Line*, and *Text*. Class *Ellipse* has one subclass, *Circle*.

This chapter concentrates on *single inheritance*, where a subclass has just one superclass. With *multiple inheritance*, a subclass can have more than one superclass. For example, a text string has a position within a diagram, a property it shares with shapes, and a font, a property it might share with another class of objects.

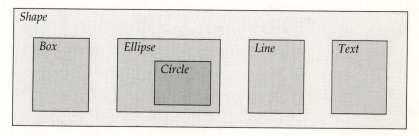

Figure 7.2   Classification of shape objects.

[1] Technically, an ellipse is a geometric concept and an ellipse object is the corresponding object in a program. It is convenient, however, to abbreviate "ellipse object" to "ellipse." Thus, instead of repeating the term "object," we sometimes use the same term for both a concept and an object that represents it.

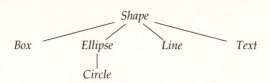

Figure 7.3   A class hierarchy corresponding to the nested classification of objects in Fig. 7.2.

Objects Respond to Messages, Objects Have State

an object responds to a message by executing a method

A *message* to an object corresponds to a procedure call; messages can carry parameters. In response to a message, the object executes a *method*, which corresponds to a procedure body; it returns an optional result. The result, if any, will itself be an object of some class.

A class specifies the properties of its objects. The class definition contains the methods that are executed when the object receives a message. The class definition also contains the variables for its objects. When storage is allocated for these variables, we say that an *instance* of the class is created. Technically, the term *object* of a class means an instance of that class.

an object has variables, with their own values

Methods and variables will now be illustrated by considering diagrams made up of a list of shapes. We begin with class *Diagram* because it is all by itself in its class hierarchy, with no subclasses. Class *Shape* and its subclasses will be considered later.

The definition of class *Diagram* is outlined in Fig. 7.4. Only the names of the methods and variables appear in the outline. A diagram object, or an instance of class *Diagram*, responds to four messages

initialize, add, setangle, draw

---

class *Diagram*
methods
    initialize, add, setangle, draw
variables
    shapelist, angle

Figure 7.4   Methods and variables for instances of class *Diagram*.

and has two variables

   shapelist, *angle*

Each diagram object binds the variables to distinct locations, so each diagram holds its own list of shapes.

Example 7.2   For concreteness, this example outlines how diagrams work. Each diagram has a list of shapes, held in variable *shapelist*.

A shape added to *shapelist* aligns itself at some angle to the previous shape, as illustrated in Fig. 7.5. When the angle is 0°, the default value, a new shape appears to the right of the previous one. Variable *angle* holds the default angle.

Method *setangle* assigns a new value to *angle*. Its pseudocode contains a single assignment:

   <u>**class** *Diagram*:   **method** *setangle*(*a*);</u>
       angle := *a*;

Class instances are usually initialized automatically, by executing some code supplied with the class. For instances of class *Diagram*, the variables *shapelist* and *angle* need initialization.

   <u>**class** *Diagram*:   **method** *initialize*;</u>
       shapelist := a new empty list of shapes;
       angle := 0;

Here *shapelist* and *angle* are local variables in an object (instance) of class *Diagram*.

Method *add* extends the list of shapes:

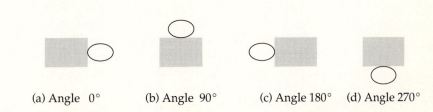

(a) Angle 0°   (b) Angle 90°   (c) Angle 180°   (d) Angle 270°

Figure 7.5   A newly added ellipse aligns itself at some angle to the previous shape, shown as a shaded box. When the angle is 0°, the ellipse appears to the right; when the angle is 90°, the ellipse appears above; and so on.

> **class** *Diagram*:   **method** *add*(shape *s*);
>   send message *setalign*(*angle*) to *s*;
>   add *s* to the end of *shapelist*;

In words, an object of class *Diagram* responds to a message *add*(*s*) by doing two things. First, it sends a message *setalign*(*angle*) to *s*, which includes the diagram object's local variable *angle* as a parameter. Second, it adds *s* to the end of its list of shapes.

Finally, the pseudocode for method *draw* simply asks each shape on *shapelist* to draw itself next to the previous one.

> **class** *Diagram*:   **method** *draw*;
>   *previous* := a new shape;
>   **for** each shape *s* on *shapelist* **do**
>   *previous* := the result of sending *draw*(*previous*) to *s*;

Variable *previous* holds the previously drawn shape; it is initialized to a new dummy shape to get the drawing process started. How shapes draw themselves will be considered when class *Shape* and its subclasses are considered. □

7.3   INHERITANCE

methods and variables are inherited

The basic idea of inheritance is that the children in a class hierarchy inherit the methods and variables of their ancestors. The term *inherit* means that all the methods and variables from the ancestor classes become methods and variables of the child class. This section deals with the basic idea of inheritance; the specific inheritance rules for C++ and Smalltalk and their treatment of variables will be discussed in later sections.

Figure 7.6 outlines the definitions of classes in a hierarchy with class *Shape* at the top. Class *Text* is a child of class *Shape* in the hierarchy, so class *Text* inherits the methods and variables of class *Shape*.

a subclass or derived class is an extension of a class

Any fresh methods or variables at a child in the hierarchy are simply added to the inherited methods and variables. Any methods redefined at a child in the hierarchy override the inherited methods in both C++ and Smalltalk. Otherwise, the inheritance rules for the two languages differ subtly and are discussed in the sections on these languages.

Thus, a text object has methods

initialize, *draw*, *offset*, *setwidth*, *setheight*, *setalign*

where *initialize* and *draw* are the methods redefined in class *Text*, and the remaining methods are as defined in class *Shape*.

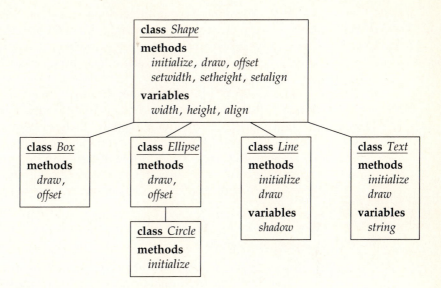

Figure 7.6   Class *Shape* and its subclasses or derived classes.

From the outline in Fig. 7.6, class *Text* defines variable *string*, so this variable is added to the three inherited from *Shape*:

width, height, align, string

In a class hierarchy, the terms subclass for child and superclass for parent are from Simula and Smalltalk. The terms subclass and superclass are natural when we classify objects. All boxes are shapes, so the set of boxes must be a subset of the set of shapes. Hence, class *Box* is a subclass of class *Shape*.

Alternatively, the relationship between text objects and shapes can be approached from the properties of text and shapes. Since all text objects are shapes, text objects have all the properties of shapes. The methods and variables in the definition of class *Text* are therefore extensions to the methods and variables in the definition of class *Shape*.

In a class hierarchy, the terms *derived class* for child and *base class* for parent are from C++. The terms derived class and base class are natural when we consider the properties of objects. The derived class inherits from or extends the base class.

The Receiver Determines the Meaning of a Message

a method in a subclass overrides an inherited method of the same name

An object determines how it implements a message. A shape determines what it does in response to a *draw* message. All of the classes in the hierarchy in Fig. 7.6 have their own methods to be executed in response to a *draw* message. Thus, a box, an ellipse, a line, and a text string can each respond in their own way to a *draw* message.

This ability of objects to respond in their own way is powerful. It allows design decisions and implementations to be localized and isolated so that they can be changed. Furthermore, certain changes become easy — a new shape can be added without touching the code for the existing shapes.

Generalizing from the example of boxes and ellipses responding to *draw*, an object of a subclass can implement a message in its own way by supplying its own method or code to be executed in response to the message.

Example 7.3 An object of subclass *Text* draws itself by centering its string on the previous shape:

> **class** *Text*: **method** *draw*(*previous*) **returns** *Shape*;
>   center *string* on *previous*;
>   **return** *previous*;

An ellipse draws itself differently. It needs to compute its center, relative to the previous shape, as in Fig. 7.5. The pseudocode is as follows:

> **class** *Ellipse*: **method** *draw*(*previous*) **returns** *Shape*;
>   *center* := center of this ellipse relative to *previous*;
>   lay out an ellipse centered at *center*;
>   **return** this ellipse object;

The ellipse object returns itself, so it can become the previous shape for the next shape to be drawn.

A new subclass *Arc* of *Shape* can be added without touching the code for the other objects. Furthermore, since arcs are shapes, they can immediately receive messages sent to shapes, even from objects defined before arcs were added. Specifically, the same "pre-arc" code for drawing diagrams will handle arcs as well, because a diagram continues to ask each shape on its list to draw itself.   □

Example 7.4 By way of contrast, a procedure-oriented approach to managing diagrams is to structure a program around the operations on shapes. A procedure to draw a diagram might look like the following pseudocode:

```
procedure draw(diagram d);
begin
    for each shape s in diagram d do begin
        case s of
        BOX:        code to draw a box;
        ELLIPSE: code to draw an ellipse;
    . . .
```

For each shape *s* in diagram *d*, this procedure classifies *s* and then executes code that is appropriate to drawing that kind of shape.

A problem with this approach is that the code for manipulating shapes is spread across various procedures. If a new shape is added, then code for handling the new shape has to be added to each procedure. For example, suppose that a new shape arc is added.

Procedure *draw* can be modified to draw arcs by adding a case of the form

```
    ARC:        code to draw an arc;
```

Even if the amount of new code is small, it is spread across procedures, each of which must be studied before the new code is added. □

Information Hiding for Extensibility

Information hiding facilitates two kinds of changes:

- *Implementation changes*. If all interactions with an object are through its interface, then the algorithms and data structures hidden behind the interface can be changed, as in Section 6.2.
- *Inheritance changes*. If all interactions are through the interface to a superclass, then the program can be extended by adding subclasses.

Suppose that the shaded box and the ellipse in Fig. 7.7(a) are represented by two objects in a program. If the ellipse interacts with a shaded shape, rather than a shaded box, then the same code can later be used to interact with another shape, say a shaded circle, as in Fig. 7.7(b).

The ellipse object wishes to align itself next to the box, at some angle *align* (in Fig. 7.7, *align* is 15°). Specifically, the problem is to compute the center *E* of the ellipse, relative to the center *B* of the box, given that line *BE* is at an angle *align* to the horizontal.

Part of the line *BE*, shown dashed, lies within the box. Since information about the box is hidden from the ellipse, it sends a message *offset*(*align*) to the box, asking for the point *P* on the border of the box at which the ellipse will attach itself. Once the box returns point *P*, the segment *PE* from *P* to *E*, lies within the ellipse, so the ellipse can use information about itself to compute the position of *E*.

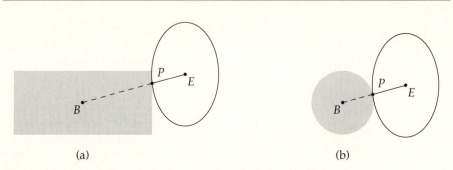

(a)   (b)

Figure 7.7   Each object computes the line segment within its own borders.

As in Example 7.3, the pseudocode within the ellipse object is as follows:

P := result of sending *offset*(*align*) to the box;
the ellipse computes E from P and other ellipse information;

Since the message *offset*(*align*) is the only interaction between the ellipse and the box, the ellipse does not even need to know that it is interacting with a box. In Fig. 7.7(b), the message *offset*(*align*) from the ellipse is received by a circle.

If the program is extended to add a new shape, the same code for ellipse not only will continue to work, it will work with the new objects as well.

Adding a Subclass

Object-oriented programming is often done by adapting or extending an existing program. In the next example a modest change, the addition of a subclass, extends a program significantly.

Example 7.5   This example adds a new subclass of *Shape* to allow diagrams like the one in Fig. 7.8. Note that this diagram is treelike; it is not simply a linear list of boxes, ellipses, lines, and text strings.

The solution is to add a new subclass *Brace* of *Shape* that allows a diagram to appear as a shape. Then, the treelike diagram in Fig. 7.8 can be built up from the following list of shapes:

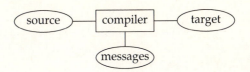

Figure 7.8 A treelike diagram that cannot be represented as a linear list of shapes.

Embedded in this list is the following brace object:

The class hierarchy in Fig. 7.9 is formed by adding subclass *Brace* to the hierarchy in Fig. 7.6. Variable *adiagram* in class *Brace* holds a diagram object. For example, *adiagram* might hold the up-down diagram consisting of a line, an ellipse, and a text string "messages".

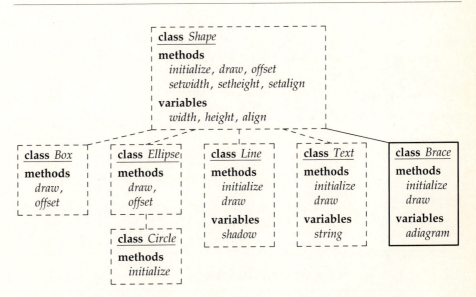

Figure 7.9 The result of adding subclass *Brace* to the class hierarchy in Fig. 7.6. The dashed classes are repeated from Fig. 7.6.

A brace responds to a *draw* message by simply forwarding the message to *adiagram*:

> <u>**class** *Brace*</u>:   **method** *draw*(*previous*) **returns** *Shape*;
>   send *draw*(*previous*) to *adiagram*;
>   **return** *previous*;

We are almost done. When programming with objects, the code for each individual operation is often small and seems to simply "pass the buck" by invoking operations in other objects.

The remaining change is to allow method *draw* of class *Diagram* to take a shape as a parameter. The only difference between the following version and the original on page 260 is in the initialization of variable *previous*. This version uses the parameter to initialize *previous*:

> <u>**class** *Diagram*</u>:   **method** *draw*(*init*);
>   *previous* := *init*;
>   **for** each shape *s* on *shapelist* **do**
>   *previous* := the result of sending *draw*(*previous*) to *s*;

The parameterless version needs an initial shape to start positioning the shapes on its list. The code for class *Shape* (not shown) is such that a new object has default values for the variables and draws itself at a default position. The parameterless version of *draw* in class *Diagram* therefore creates a new shape and uses it as a parameter for the version of *draw* with one parameter:

> <u>**class** *Diagram*</u>:   **method** *draw*;
>   send *draw*(a new shape) to this diagram object;

Method *draw* in class *Diagram* is now overloaded; that is, it has two versions, one with a parameter and one without. Such overloading does not present any problems.

With these modest changes — the addition of subclass *Brace* and the overloading of method *draw* in class *Diagram* — we can handle the treelike diagram in Fig. 7.8.   □

Objects and Classes

The key points in Sections 7.2 and 7.3 are as follows:

- An object responds to a message by executing a method. A message corresponds to a procedure call, a method to a procedure body.

- An object has its own internal state. That is, an object has variables, with their own values.

- A class specifies the properties of its objects. It specifies the methods and variables for objects of the class.

- A subclass or derived class is an extension of a class. The converse of subclass is superclass or base class. Thus, a derived class extends a base class; alternatively, a subclass extends a superclass. Fresh methods and variables in the derived class are added to those in the base class.

- An object of a subclass uses its own method to implement a message. That is, where possible, the method in the subclass is used.

7.4 OBJECT-ORIENTED PROGRAMMING IN C++

C++ supports multiple programming styles

C++ provides a transition path from C to object-oriented programming; compatibility with C helped C++ spread rapidly as a language for systems programming. Hence, by design, C++ supports multiple programming styles, including imperative programming in the C subset and object-oriented programming.

This section considers the use of C++ for object-oriented programming. As in Section 7.2, if boxes and ellipses are shapes, then a box or an ellipse can appear where a shape is expected.

C++ does strict compile-time type checking. Thus, the types of all variables and functions must be fully declared at compile time. Smalltalk by contrast checks dynamically whether the receiver of an object has a corresponding method.

Review of C++

C++ was introduced in Section 6.5 as a language for programming with user-defined data types. The following class declaration reviews some of its features:

```
class Cell {
    Cell * next;
public:
    int    info;
           Cell(int);
           ~Cell();
    Cell * step() { return next; }
    Cell * add(int, Cell *);
};
```

A class is a grouping of members, where members can be variables or functions. The variables in class `Cell` are `info`, an integer, and `next`, a pointer to an object of class `Cell`.

A constructor is a member function with the same name as the class; it is called automatically when the lifetime of an object of the class begins. Initialization code for variables in the class belongs in the constructor. The name of the destructor `~Cell` is made up of a prefix `~` and the class name; the destructor is called automatically just before the lifetime of an object ends.

The member functions `add` and `step` return pointers to cells. The body of a member function can appear within the class declaration, or it can appear separately. The body of parameterless function `step` appears within the class declaration. The body of `add` must be given separately.

C++ has three keywords, `public`, `private`, and `protected`, for controlling the visibility of members names. Public members are visible to outside code, and private members are not. Protected members are visible through inheritance but not to other code.

Base and Derived Classes

a derived class
adds members

In C++ terminology, the extension of a base class is called a *derived class*. Class `Box` can be derived from class `Shape` as follows:

```
class Box : public Shape {
    ⟨ added members ⟩
}
```

Class `Box` inherits all members of class `Shape`.

As an abstract example, class `D` adds a function to class `B`:

```
class B {                    // declaration of class B
public:
    int  x;                  // the full name is B::x
    char f();                // public member function
         B();
};
class D : public B {         // D derived from B
    int  x;                  // D::x is added, B::x is inherited
    int  g();                // added member function
};
```

Objects of the derived class `D` have four members: `x` and `f`, inherited from the base class `B`, and `x` and `g`, added in the declaration of `D`.

A member added by a derived class `D` can have the same name as a member of its base class `B`. If the same member name `m` appears in both, then the full name B::m can be used to refer to the member m of B. Similarly, D::m is the full name of member m of D.

Public Base Classes

members of a public base class remain visible

A distinguishing feature of object-oriented programming in any language is that an object of a derived class can appear where an object of a base class is expected. That is, a derived object can behave like a base object. Behavior in C++ is determined by members. If a base object is expected to have a member *m*, then a derived object must have one too.

These remarks motivate *public base classes* in C++, identified by the keyword `public` in the following syntax for class derivation:

```
class ⟨derived⟩ : public ⟨base⟩ {
    ⟨member-declarations⟩
};
```

Members of a public base class retain their visibility in the derived class. That is, a public member of the base class is a public member of the derived class, and similarly for protected and private members.

Object-oriented programming in C++ relies on the following property (note the use of "public base class"):

> An object of a derived class can appear wherever an object of a public base class is expected.

All of the base classes in this section are public base classes.

Virtual Functions

derived classes can supply bodies for virtual functions

In the shape example in Sections 7.2 and 7.3, a shape determined how it drew itself. In terms of messages, the receiving object determined the meaning of a message.

Virtual functions in C++ allow a derived class to supply the function body. Suppose base class `Shape` has a virtual function `draw`. If derived class `Ellipse` also has a function `draw`, then the body in the derived class is used, overriding the body in the base class.

The only difference between functions `f` and `g` in the following pseudocode is that keyword `virtual` appears before the declaration of `f`:

```
class B {
public:
virtual char  f()      { return 'B'; }
        char  g()      { return 'B'; }
        char  testF()  { return f(); }
```

```
          char  testG()  { return g(); }
};
```

The distinction between f and g will be tested using the following derived class, which redeclares f and g:

```
class D : public B {
public:
        char  f()        { return 'D'; }
        char  g()        { return 'D'; }
};
```

`B::f` and `B::g` return character 'B', and `D::f` and `D::g` return character 'D'.

The main function is

```
main() {
        D d;
        print d.testF(), d.testG();
}
```

What are the values of the expressions `d.testF()` and `d.testG()`? Functions `testF` and `testG` are declared in the base class B and remain public in the derived class D. The expressions `d.testF()` and `d.testG()` call f and g, respectively.

Virtual functions are taken from the derived class where possible, so the body of `B::testF` calls `D::f` and returns 'D'. On the other hand, g is not a virtual function, so the body of `B::testG` calls `B::g` and returns 'B'.

A virtual function `draw` appears in every class in Fig. 7.10. The classes are from a C++ implementation of the shape example of Section 7.2. For the moment, we consider only the role of `draw`. The next subsection gives details of the context in which these classes fit.

Since `draw` is virtual in each class in Fig. 7.10, the function body from the derived class will be used, where possible.

Suppose, variable s, a pointer to `Shape`, actually points to an object of derived class `Ellipse`:

```
Shape * s;
s = new Ellipse;
```

A call `s->draw(p)`, with a suitable parameter p, will call the member of class `Ellipse`:

```
class Shape {
protected:
        float   width;
        float   height;
public:
        float   align;
                Shape();
                Shape(float, float);
virtual Point * offset(float);
virtual Shape * draw(Shape *) { return this; }
};
```

```
class Ellipse : public Shape {
public:
                Ellipse();
                Ellipse(float, float);
virtual Point * offset(float);
virtual Shape * draw(Shape *);
};
```

```
class Text : public Shape {
                char *  str;
public:
                Text(char *);
virtual Shape * draw(Shape *);
};
```

```
class Circle : public Ellipse {
public:
                Circle() { width = height; };
                Circle(float rad)  : Ellipse(rad, rad) {}
virtual Shape * draw(Shape *);
};
```

Figure 7.10 Class hierarchy from a C++ implementation of the shape example in Sections 7.2 and 7.3.

```
Shape * p =  · · ·
s->draw(p);            // equivalent to s->Ellipse::draw(p);
```

Function draw is virtual in each class in the hierarchy, Shape, Ellipse, Circle. Hence, Circle::draw is called if s points to a circle:

```
s = new Circle;       // s has type Shape *
s->draw(p);           // equivalent to s->Circle::draw(p);
```

Had draw not been a member of Circle, then Ellipse::draw, the closest in the hierarchy between Circle and Shape would have been called.

Details of the Shape Example in C++

review of shapes   The classes in Fig. 7.10 are from a program that created the following diagram:

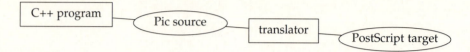

The diagram slopes down to the right. The objects in the diagram align themselves at a −4 degree angle to each other. The output from the C++ program
was translated into PostScript by some text-processing code. PostScript is the
page description language that was used to print this book. The C++ program
could have generated PostScript directly.

code to create a list   For concreteness, a diagram consisting of a list of shapes can be created as
of shapes   follows:

```
main() {
        Diagram * d;                    // declare d
        d = new Diagram;                // assign it a new diagram
        d->angle(-4);                   // default angle for shapes

        Box * b;                        // declare b
        b = new Box(1.00, 0.25);        // assign it a new box

        d->add(b);                      // add box to diagram
```

Execution of a C++ program begins in a function `main`; every program
must have one. Declarations and statements can be intermixed. A variable
can be declared the first time it appears in a function by specifying its type. In
fact, the actual code begins as follows:

```
main() {
    Diagram * d = new Diagram;

    d->angle(-4);
    d->add(new Box(1.00, 0.25));
    d->add(new Text("C++ program"));
```

each shape draws   A sequence of such calls leaves d pointing to a list of shapes. The diagram
itself   is drawn by executing

```
    d->draw();
```

which, in turn calls the `draw` function for each shape on its list.

In more detail, each shape aligns itself at some angle to a previous shape.
Variable `prev` holds the previous shape. In the following code, the call

```
s->draw(prev)
```

passes the previous shape as a parameter:

```
void Diagram::draw() {
    Shape * prev = new Shape;        // initialize prev
    Shape * s;
    ...
    for( each shape  s  in the list ) {
        ...
        prev = s->draw(prev);
    }
}
```

Note that variable s is a pointer to Shape, although it points to objects of classes derived from Shape.

There are differences of detail in how shapes draw themselves. For example, a text object draws itself at the center of prev and does not disturb the value of prev. In other words, the call s->draw(prev) returns prev if s points to a text object. The draw functions for the other objects return the object itself, denoted by the special name this.

The list is maintained as a linked list. The code for the list is short but unsurprising, so it is omitted.

Initialization and Inheritance

a base-class constructor is called before a derived-class constructor

Code for initialization belongs in the constructor for a class, since a constructor function is called automatically when an object is created. The constructor of a base class is called before that for the derived class.

With the class hierarchy in Fig. 7.10, suppose a circle object is created by executing

```
new Circle;
```

Here, there are no parameters after Circle, so the parameterless constructors are called in the following order:

```
Shape(); Ellipse(); Circle();
```

Now, consider constructors with parameters, as in the call

```
new Circle(0.5);
```

The constructor is declared as follows in Fig. 7.10:

```
      Circle(float rad) : Ellipse(rad, rad) {}
```

The body of the function is empty. All the work is done in the construct

```
      : Ellipse(rad, rad)
```

which passes parameters to the base class constructor. The body of constructor `Ellipse` (not shown in Fig. 7.10) also simply passes parameters to its base class:

```
    Ellipse::Ellipse(float w, float h) : Shape(w,h) {}
```

The constructors are therefore called in the following order:

```
    Shape(rad,rad); Ellipse(rad,rad); Circle(rad);
```

With destructors, the order is reversed. The destructor in the derived class is called before the destructor in the base class.

7.5   AN EXTENDED C++ EXAMPLE

This section illustrates inheritance in C++ by developing a program to find prime numbers. A prime number is divisible only by itself and 1; alternatively, n is a prime if its only factors are 1 and n itself. The prime numbers smaller than 50 are

2 3 5 7 11 13 17 19 23 29 31 37 41 43 47

The program in this section can be transliterated directly into Smalltalk.

A Prime Number Sieve

The Greek philosopher Eratosthenes is credited with the *sieve method* for computing primes. The underlying idea is that n is a prime if n is not a multiple of any prime p smaller than n. Thus, 3 is a prime because it is not a multiple of 2. The number 5 is a prime because it is a multiple neither of 2 nor of 3.

A variant of the sieve method begins with the sequence of integers, starting with 2 (see the top of Fig. 7.11). Primes and their multiples are repeatedly removed from the sequence. First, 2 is a prime, so 2 is output, and all multiples of 2 are removed from the sequence. Then, 3 is a prime, so 3 is output, and all multiples of 3 are removed from the sequence. In general, if a number is output, then it must be a prime.

	2	3	4	5	6	7	8	9	10	11	12	13	14	15	$\cdots$
2 is a prime	~~2~~	3	~~4~~	5	~~6~~	7	~~8~~	9	~~10~~	11	~~12~~	13	~~14~~	15	$\cdots$

	3	5	7	9	11	13	15	17	19	21	23	25	27	29	$\cdots$
3 is a prime	~~3~~	5	7	~~9~~	11	13	~~15~~	17	19	~~21~~	23	25	~~27~~	29	$\cdots$

	5	7	11	13	17	19	23	25	29	31	35	37	41	43	$\cdots$
5 is a prime	~~5~~	7	11	13	17	19	23	~~25~~	29	31	~~35~~	37	41	43	$\cdots$

Figure 7.11   At each step, the leftmost surviving number is a prime.

The program in this section is motivated by McIlroy [1968]. The approach of Fig. 7.11 will be implemented by assembling a network out of two kinds of objects: *counters* and *filters*. A counter emits integers, starting from some initial value; *counter*(2) in Fig. 7.12 starts from 2, and emits 2, 3, 4, $\cdots$. A filter *filter*(*n*) removes multiples of *n* from its input. Thus *filter*(2) allows only odd numbers to get through and *filter*(3) allows only numbers that are not divisible by 3 to get through. Sample inputs and outputs for these filters appear in Fig. 7.12.

Counters and filters will be put together dynamically, as in Fig. 7.13. On demand, *counter*(2) emits the integers 2, 3, 4, 5, $\cdots$, starting with the prime 2. On seeing 2, the *sieve* outputs it and immediately spawns a filter to remove subsequent multiples of 2. In general, if an integer *n* survives to reach the *sieve*, then it must be a prime. For each new prime *n*, the *sieve* spawns *filter*(*n*) to remove multiples of *n*.

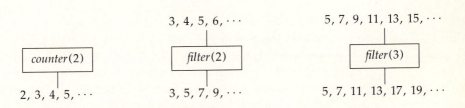

Figure 7.12   Components for computing primes.

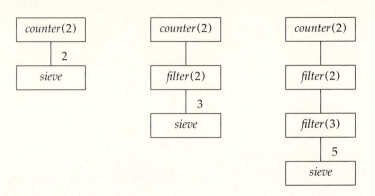

Figure 7.13   Each prime n reaching *sieve* spawns a filter that removes multiples of n.

A Base Class

The rest of this section consists of a C++ program, interspersed with commentary. Line numbers in parentheses show how the pieces of the program fit together; the numbers are not part of the program.

Counters, filters, and the sieve in Fig. 7.13 will be derived from class `Item`, declared on lines 2–7:

```
(1) #include     <stdio.h>
(2) class Item {
(3) public:
(4)          Item *source;
(5)              Item(Item *src) { source = src; }
(6) virtual int   out()                { return 0; }
(7) };
```

Each item has a member `source`, pointing to the source of its input. In Fig. 7.13, *filter*(2) gets its input from *counter*(2), and *filter*(3) gets its input from *filter*(2). The source for *sieve* changes every time a new filter is spawned. The only component without a source is *counter*(2). The absence of a source can be implemented by assigning the null pointer 0 to `source`.

The keyword `virtual` on line 6 makes member `out` a placeholder for functions of the same name to be provided later in derived classes. Each class in this section has a member `out`.

Derived Classes

Class `Counter` has `Item` as its public base class. We now examine the declaration

```
(8) class Counter : public Item {
(9)       int   value;
(10) public:
(11)      int   out()                    { return value++; }
(12)            Counter(int v) : Item(0) { value = v; }
(13) };
```

Class `Counter` uses a member, `value`, to keep track of the next value to be produced by the counter. Member `out` returns this value and then uses the ++ operator to increment variable `value` by 1. Since `value` will be initialized to 2, successive calls of member `out` return 2, 3, 4, $\cdots$, as desired (see again Fig. 7.12).

Initialization of Derived and Base Classes

Before considering the constructor declaration on line 12, let us examine the members inherited by class `Counter`. The class has the following members:

source	Pointer to an item, inherited from the base class
value	Integer counter value, added
Counter::out	Output function for the derived class, added
Item::out	Inherited virtual output function
Counter	Constructor for the derived class

The constructor declaration on line 12

```
Counter(int v) : Item(0) { value = v; }
```

has three parts:

1. `Counter(int v)` says that constructor `Counter` takes an integer argument.
2. `: Item(0)` passes the null pointer 0 as an argument to the constructor, `Item`, of the base class. C++ ensures that the base-class constructor is executed before the constructor of the derived class.
3. `{ value = v; }` is the body of the constructor in the derived class.

In other words, initialization information for the base class appears between the colon and the body of the derived constructor.

Class `Sieve` also has `Item` as its public base class:

```
(14) class Sieve : public Item {
(15) public:
(16)          int      out();
(17)                   Sieve(Item *src)  : Item(src)  {}
(18) };
```

The body of added member function out appears separately.
The constructor on line 17

```
Sieve(item *src): Item(src)  {};
```

results in the following initialization:

> call constructor Item of the base class with argument src;
> execute the empty body {} of constructor Sieve of the derived class;

Class Filter is declared by

```
(19) class Filter : public Item {
(20)     int factor;
(21) public:
(22)     int out();
(23)          Filter(Item *src, int f) : Item(src) { factor = f; }
(24) };
```

Subtypes and Supertypes

> All counters are items.
> c is a counter.
> Hence, c is an item.

Alternatively, an object of derived class Counter (a subtype) can appear where an object of public base class Item (its supertype) is expected.

The notion of subtypes is needed to explain the declarations on lines 26 and 27 in the main function:

```
(25) main() {
(26)          Counter c(2);
(27)          Sieve   s(&c);
(28)          int     next;
(29)          do {
(30)              next = s.out();
(31)              printf("%d ", next);
```

```
(32)          } while (next < 61);
(33)          printf("\n");
(34) }
```

For readability, we repeat the declarations of the constructors `Counter`, `Sieve`, and `Item`:

```
Counter(int v) : Item(0) { value = v; }
Sieve(Item *src) : Item(src) {}
Filter(Item *src, int f) : Item(src) { factor = f; }
```

The declaration on line 26,

```
Counter c(2);
```

creates a counter. The base class constructor `Item` is called with the null pointer 0, so the inherited member `source` is initialized to the null pointer. The constructor `Counter` uses the argument 2 to initialize `value`.

The declaration on line 27

```
Sieve s(&c);
```

creates a sieve. The argument `&c`, a pointer to the counter `c`, is passed to the base class constructor, so inherited member `source` is initialized to point to `c`. In more detail, the constructor `Sieve` expects its argument to be a pointer to an item. Instead, it is passed a subtype: pointer to counter. A pointer to a counter can appear where a pointer to an item is expected.[2]

Virtual Functions

The keyword `virtual` on line 6 before the declaration of `out` in class `item` is crucial. Without it, the output of the program in this section changes from

```
2 3 5 7 11 13 17 19 23 29 31 37 41 43 47 53 59 61
```

to

```
0 0 0 0 0 ···
```

---

[2] The converse, however, is not permitted in C++; that is, an object of a base class cannot appear in place of an object of a derived class. At compile time, the compiler has no way of knowing whether a particular item is a counter or a sieve. A dynamically checked implementation could check whether an item is a counter or a sieve.

A blow-by-blow description of the `out` functions of classes `Sieve` and `Counter` shows the use of virtual functions. The algorithm illustrated in Fig. 7.13 requires the sieve to spawn a filter as a side effect, each time a prime reaches it:

```
(35)  int Sieve::out() {
(36)        int n = source->out();
(37)        source = new Filter(source, n);
(38)        return n;
(39)  }
```

On line 36, function `Sieve::out` gets a prime from its source by calling `source->out()`. A filter is spawned on line 37.

How does the call `source->out()` get a number?

The declarations on lines 26 and 27

```
Counter c(2);
Sieve   s(&c);
```

initialize `s.source` to `&c`. The function call `s.source->out` therefore calls one of the two out functions belonging to c; that is, either the inherited function `Item::out` or the added function `Counter::out`. The keyword virtual, on line 6 in the base class `Item` says that given a choice between `Item::out` and `Counter::out`, the function to be used is `counter::out`.[3]

Spawning Filters

The rest of the story is anticlimactic.

The first filter is spawned when the prime 2 reaches the sieve directly from the counter. This prime arrives when control returns from the call `source->out()` on line 36. The assignment on line 37 that spawns a filter can be rewritten as follows to show the current values of the variables:

```
s.source = new Filter(&c, 2);
```

Informally, the right side creates a new filter with counter c as its source and 2 as its factor. The left side `s.source` is assigned a pointer to the newly created filter.

The Remaining Program

Here is how filters work:

[3] Although `s.source` points to c, the type of `s.source` is "pointer to `Item`." Had out not been virtual in the base class, the C++ compiler would take `s.source->out()` to be a call of `c.Item::out`. Virtual functions eliminate such ambiguities.

```
(40) int Filter::out() {
(41)        while(1) {
(42)            int n = source->out();
(43)            if (n % factor)
(44)                return n;
(45)        }
(46) }
```

Control can flow out of the while-loop on lines 41–45 only through the return on line 44. Each execution of the loop gets a number n from its source and returns it only if n mod `factor` is nonzero; that is, if n is not a multiple of `factor`.

7.6 DERIVED CLASSES AND INFORMATION HIDING

information hiding can interfere with the is-a *relation*

What if a derived class wants to hide some inherited members? Such hiding can interfere with a fundamental property, the ability of a derived object to appear wherever a base object is expected. Another way to think about inheritance is in terms of an *is-a* relation on objects. Using the shape example of Section 7.1, all boxes are shapes; in a box has an *is-a* relation with shapes. If a derived class hides some inherited members, such hiding may disable the *is-a* relation between derived and base objects.

The running example in this section is a class `List`, which allows elements to be added and removed from either end of the list. A stack, however, allows elements to be added and removed from just one end of a list of elements. The ability to restrict access to inherited members would allow a stack to be implemented by hiding some members of class `List`. But, then stacks would not have an *is-a* relation with lists, since a stack cannot respond to all the messages that a list can. The difficulty with hiding inherited members is that a derived object can no longer respond to all messages that a base object can.

C++ allows a derived class to restrict access to members; Smalltalk does not. This section considers the visibility and access rules of C++.

As mentioned earlier, C++ has three keywords—`public`, `protected`, and `private`—to control access to members. Public members are accessible from outside code, protected members are accessible from derived classes, and private members are accessible only to member functions of that class.

Public and Private Base Classes

Public base classes were used for object-oriented programming in Section 7.4. C++ also supports private base classes.

The keywords `public` and `private` before the name of the base class specify whether it is a public or a private base class.

From Section 7.4, the syntax for a public base class is as follows:

```
class ⟨derived⟩ : public ⟨base⟩ {
    ⟨member-declarations⟩
};
```

Members of a public base class retain their accessibility in the derived class. Thus, an object of a derived class has an *is-a* relation with objects of its public base class.

private base classes are for implementation sharing

The purpose of a private base class is quite different from that of a public base class. A derived class simply shares the code of the private base class. Such code sharing is sometimes called *implementation inheritance*.

The syntax for a *private base class* is as follows:

```
class ⟨derived⟩ : private ⟨base⟩ {
    ⟨member-declarations⟩
};
```

Keyword `private` means that, by default, all members inherited by ⟨derived⟩ from ⟨base⟩ become private members of ⟨derived⟩. Nonprivate inherited members can be made visible by writing their full names in the derived class, using the notation

⟨class-name⟩ :: ⟨member-name⟩

Class `List` in Fig. 7.14 is a public base class for `Queue` and a private base class for `Stack`. Private member `rear` of `List` is inaccessible to the member functions in the derived classes.

Privacy Principle

private means private from derived classes too

Functions in a derived class cannot access the private members of its base class. This restriction may seem surprising at first, but to do otherwise would violate the following principle:

Privacy principle. The private members of a class are accessible only to member functions of the class.

For perspective on this principle, consider class `Queue` from Fig. 7.14:

```
class Queue : public List {
public:
        Queue()      {}
```

```
                        class List {
                            cell * rear;
                        public:
                                    List();
                            int     empty();
                        protected:
                            void    add(int);
                            void    push(int);
                            int     get();
                        };
```

```
class Queue : public List {
public:
        Queue() {}
    int  get() { return List::get(); }
    void put(int x) { add(x); }
};
```

```
class Stack : private List {
public:
        Stack() {}
    int  pop() { return get(); }
    void push(int x) { List::push(x); }
        List::empty;
};
```

Figure 7.14 Class List is a public base class for Queue and a private base class for Stack.

```
    int  get()        { return List::get(); }
    void put(int x) { add(x); }
};
```

The base class members List::get and List::add are protected. Yet Queue makes them indirectly accessible by declaring new functions Queue::get and Queue::put, which simply call the underlying protected functions.

   If a derived class could access private members, then the same approach could be used to make private members accessible, in violation of the privacy principle.

Accessibility of Inherited Members

The accessiblity of the member of class Queue is summarized in Fig. 7.15.

The added members, Queue, get, and put are public by declaration. Note that the added function Queue::get is distinct from the inherited protected function List::get.

The inherited members retain their accessibility, since List is a public base class. Constructors are not inherited, so the only public inherited member is empty. Variable rear, the only private member of List is inaccessible to the functions added in the derived class. Function members of the base class List can access it.

Now consider class Stack, which has List as a private base class. The private member List::rear is inaccessible in Stack. The public and protected members are inherited as private members of Stack, by default. The explicit mention of

```
List::empty;
```

in the public part of Stack makes it public. Such explicit mention cannot increase the accessibility of a member; for example, Stack cannot simply declare List::push to be public. To do so would increase its accessibility from protected to public, which is not permitted. The derived class therefore explicitly declares a member push, full name Stack::push, which is different from List::push.

Public Functions

Queue	added constructor function
get	added
put	added
List::empty	inherited

Protected Functions

add	inherited
push	inherited
List::get	inherited

Private Variables (accessible to functions added by Queue)

Private Variables (accessible only to inherited functions)

rear	inherited

Figure 7.15   A complete listing of the members of class queue.

7.7 OBJECTS IN SMALLTALK

Smalltalk is built on the concepts of objects and messages. As in Section 7.2, objects interact by sending messages to each other. In response to a message, the receiving object executes some code called a method. Messages correspond to procedure calls and methods correspond to procedure bodies.

This section deals with how Smalltalk objects are defined and how they interact, in light of the following design principles:

- *Everything is an object*. All components are objects, even classes.
- *Data is private to an object*. An object's variables are not visible to any other object, even to other objects of the same class.
- *An object has a notion of self*. For example, when an object executes some code in response to a message, the name `self` refers to the object itself, even in inherited code.

This chapter deals only with the basic concepts of Smalltalk. System classes and Smalltalk's unusual syntax will be introduced only as needed.

Smalltalk, the language, is just one part of the Smalltalk system. The system has a sophisticated user interface, through which programs are written, viewed, and edited. Tools called "browsers" selectively display portions of the program text, a method or procedure at a time.

System Classes

all classes are part of the Smalltalk class hierarchy

Facilities like numbers, data structures, and input/output, which are built into other languages, are provided in Smalltalk by built-in system classes. A particular application can use system classes to define suitable objects, or the application can define new classes, through inheritance, from the system classes.

A new class B, defined by inheritance from a previous class A is called a subclass of A; conversely, A is called a superclass of B.

Inheritance is central to programming in Smalltalk. All classes in the Smalltalk system, including user-defined classes, are part of the subclass/superclass hierarchy. A portion of the hierarchy appears in Fig. 7.16; Goldberg and Robson [1983] devote several chapters to system classes. The three subclasses of the root class `Object` in Fig. 7.16 are `Magnitude`, `Collection`, and `BitBlt`. The details of system classes can vary between Smalltalk implementations.

Smalltalk tradition encourages the use of unabbreviated descriptive names. When two or more words are put together to form a name, the first letter of an embedded word is capitalized, as in `OrderedCollection`.

Example 7.6 A stack data structure can be implemented by using an object of the system class `OrderedCollection`.

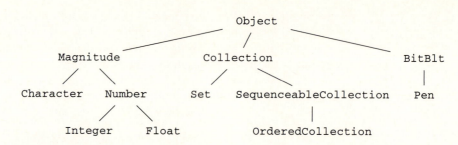

Figure 7.16   A portion of the Smalltalk class hierarchy, from Goldberg and Robson [1983].

An ordered collection holds a sequence of elements. The following messages are useful for implementing stacks:

`addLast: anObject`	Add `anObject` as the last element.
`removeLast`	Remove and return the last element.

These are just two of the many messages that ordered collections support. Other messages allow the first element of a sequence to be added and removed, so ordered collections can be used to implement queues as well.   □

Elements of a Class Definition

A class definition contains information about the data and operations relevant to a class and its objects. Variables hold data. Methods implement operations or messages. Instance is a technical term for an object of a class.

Just as individual objects have variables and methods, classes in Smalltalk can have variables and methods too:

- Class methods are used primarily to create instances.
- Class variables are used to share information between instances.

We informally consider the properties of classes and instances before examining the syntax of Smalltalk. For the moment, observe that the class definition in Fig. 7.17 has sections for instance variables, class methods, and instance methods.[4]

---

[4] The representation in Fig. 7.17 collects all of the elements of the class definition. The representation is not specified by Smalltalk. All code is entered and displayed through a programming environment provided by the system. These elements in Fig. 7.17 would be displayed selectively, say, a method at a time.

---

class `Stack`   **superclass** `Object`

instance variables
    `contents`

class methods
    `new`
       `^ super new initialize`

instance methods
    `push: anElement`
       `contents addLast: anElement`
    `pop`
       `^ contents removeLast`
    `initialize`
       `contents := OrderedCollection new`

Figure 7.17   A view of class `Stack` in Smalltalk.

Class Methods

classes respond to new by creating an instance

Most classes respond to the message new, as in

    `Stack new`

by creating an instance of the class. Here, new is a class method because it belongs to class `Stack`.

The principle that everything is an object applies to classes as well. Classes are objects. For example, a variable can be assigned a class as a value. The assignment

    `aShapeClass := Ellipse`

leaves variable `aShapeClass` with `Ellipse` as its value. Later in the computation, the expression

    `aShapeClass new`

can be evaluated to create an object of the class denoted by `aShapeClass`.

Instance Variables and Privacy

only the object can access its variables

An instance variable belongs to an instance. Its value can be changed only by operations belonging to the instance. It exists as long as the instance does.

A class method that creates a stack object cannot access the private variables of the object. How then are the private variables initialized? By sending a message to the object and asking the object to initialize itself.

An object of class `Stack` in Fig. 7.17 has one instance variable `contents`, which has to be initialized to hold an ordered collection. After class method `new` creates a stack, it sends a message `initialize` to the new stack object, so that the object can initialize itself. (The details of the implementation will be given after the syntax of messages and the role of the special name `super` are explained.)

Class variables are shared by all instances of a class. In Smalltalk V, class `Date` has a class variable `MonthNames`, which holds a dictionary to map names to numbers. The dictionary maps `January` to 1, `February` to 2 , and so on. By making `MonthNames` a class variable, all date objects in the program share this dictionary.

By convention, private variables begin with lowercase letters, as in `contents`, and shared variables begin with uppercase letters, as in `MonthNames`.

Global variables are shared by all instances of all classes.

Syntax of Messages

A message is written to the right of its recipient. A message without arguments, called a *unary message*, consists simply of a name, as in message `size` sent to `contents`

```
contents size
```

Messages that carry arguments are built of names that end in a colon; such names are called *keywords*. The expression

```
aStack push: 54
```

sends message `push:` with argument 54 to `aStack`.

Since an object's variables are private, Smalltalk programs often have short methods to set the value of a private variable. For example, method `width:` with formal parameter `aNumber` assigns the parameter to `width`, a private variable:

```
width: aNumber
    width := aNumber
```

The first line contains the method name and the formal parameter name. The second line contains the assignment to variable `width`.

The presence of the colon makes `width:` different from `width`. With the colon, `width:` is a keyword message. Without the colon, `width` is a variable name in this example.

The general form of a message in Smalltalk, called a *keyword message*, consists of a sequence of keyword-argument pairs. The expression

```
months at: 6 put: 'June'
```

sends `months` a message consisting of two keywords: keyword `at:` with argument 6 and keyword `put:` with the string `'June'` as its argument,

We talk of a message by concatenating its keywords together. In the preceding expression, an `at:put:` message is sent to object `months`.

Smalltalk uses the object/message paradigm uniformly, even for arithmetic. The value of an expression `2+3` is computed by sending the message `+` with argument 3 to object 2. Operators like `+`, written using one or two non-alphanumeric characters are called *binary* messages, in analogy with binary operators. Binary messages do not need to end with colons.

Expression Evaluation

all arithmetic operators have the same precedence

Within an expression, evaluation proceeds from left to right. Unary messages have the highest precedence. Then come binary messages corresponding to arithmetic operators like `+` and `<=`, all with the same precedence. Keyword messages have the lowest precedence.

Thus, the expression

```
contents size = 0
```

is equivalent to

```
(contents size) = 0
```

The parentheses in

```
((w*w) + (h*h)) sqrt
```

are necessary. Since `+` and `*` have the same precedence,

```
w*w + h*h
```

is equivalent to `((w*w)+h)*h`, since all arithmetic operators have the same precedence.

The assignment symbol is either ← or `:=`, depending on the Smalltalk implementation. The left side of an assignment must be a variable.

A sequence of expressions is separated by dots or periods. An example is as follows:

```
w := width/2.
h := height/2.
r := ((w*w) + (h*h)) sqrt
```

Returning Values

In response to a message, a receiver returns a value. That is, the receiver responds to a message by executing a method, and each method returns a value.

An explicit return value is preceded by ^; the default is to return the object itself, if no explicit return appears in the method.

For illustration, suppose that a method `isEmpty` is added to class `Stack` in Fig. 7.17:

```
isEmpty
    ^ contents size = 0
```

An instance of class `Stack` will then respond to message `isEmpty` by evaluating the expression

```
^ contents size = 0
```

The return value operator ^ has lower precedence than other messages, so this expression is equivalent to

```
^ ( (contents size) = 0 )
```

That is, variable `contents` is sent message `size` to determine the number of elements in the stack. This number is then compared to `0` and the boolean result of the comparison is returned as a value from method `isEmpty`.

The following method from Fig. 7.17 does not explicitly return a value, so the receiver of the message returns itself as a value:

```
push: anElement
    contents addLast: anElement
```

Conditionals and Blocks

blocks are objects   A message can carry code as an argument. An expression sequence enclosed within square brackets, [and], is called a *block*. The two blocks in the following consist of a single assignment each:

```
x > y ifTrue: [max := x] ifFalse: [max := y]
```

The test `x>y` returns one of the boolean values `true` and `false`. If `true` is returned, then the expression in the block following `ifTrue:` is evaluated; otherwise, `false` is returned, and the expression in the block following `ifFalse:` is evaluated.

The seemingly conventional behavior of blocks hides an unusual aspect of blocks. Blocks are objects. They can be assigned to variables and passed as arguments.

In more detail, the expression

```
x > y ifTrue: [max := x] ifFalse: [max := y]
```

is evaluated as follows. The subexpression `x>y` evaluates to a boolean value. This boolean object is then sent an `ifTrue:ifFalse:` message. Keyword `ifTrue:` carries the block

```
[max := x]
```

as an argument; keyword `ifFalse:` carries the other block. The boolean object then executes a method to evaluate the appropriate block.[5]

7.8 SMALLTALK OBJECTS HAVE A SELF

An object retains its variables and methods no matter what context it appears in. When a circle object x in Fig. 7.18 is treated as an ellipse or as a shape, it retains its variables and methods and it continues to exist as a circle.

subclasses can redefine methods but not variables

The inheritance rules of Smalltalk help to ensure that an object retains its variables in any context. Specifically, the rules allow a subclass to add variables but not to redefine any variables. If class A has an instance variable a, then a subclass B of A can add an instance variable b but it cannot redefine a. Thus, there can be no naming conflicts between variables that are inherited and variables that are defined.

The inheritance rules are as follows:

- Single inheritance sets up a hierarchy as in Fig. 7.16. Single inheritance means that each class has at most one superclass, although it can have several subclasses. At the root of the hierarchy is class `Object`. All classes except `Object` have exactly one superclass.

- A subclass inherits variables and methods from its superclass. Thus, instance variables of the superclass automatically become instance vari-

---

[5] Class `Boolean` has two subclasses, `False` and `True`; a boolean object is thus either a "false" object or a "true" object. The subclasses implement the `ifTrue:ifFalse:` message as desired, by evaluating one of the blocks.

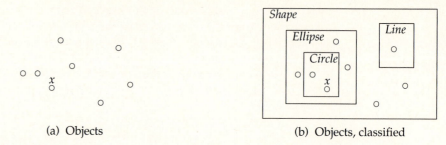

(a) Objects   (b) Objects, classified

Figure 7.18 Object x in (a) can be classified in (b) as a circle, an ellipse, or a shape.

ables of the subclass, instance methods are inherited as instance methods, class methods are inherited as class methods, and so on.

- In addition to the inherited variables, a subclass can declare fresh variable names, different from the inherited variables.

- Methods in the subclass override inherited methods. We noted earlier that a method is an implementation of an operation. Suppose that for some message, both the superclass and subclass provide methods. In this case, the method provided by the subclass is used.

- Rules for the special names `self` and `super` will be given separately.

The rules for methods ensure that an object of a subclass can respond to all the messages that an object of a superclass can. If an ellipse responds to a *draw* message, then a circle, an object of a subclass, will also respond to *draw*. The circle may draw itself differently by executing a different method, but it will respond to *draw*.

Messages to `self`

even in inherited methods, `self` *refers to an object itself*

Classes and objects can invoke one of their own methods by sending a message to the special name `self`. Thus, `self` within a class method refers to the class itself and `self` within an instance method refers to the instance itself.

A stack object can use

```
self isEmpty
```

to check if it has any elements. Method `pop` in Fig. 7.17 could be reimplemented to issue a warning if `pop` is sent to an empty stack. A possible reimplementation is

```
pop
    self isEmpty
        ifTrue: [self error: 'stack empty']
        ifFalse: [^ contents removeLast]
```

Suppose that the subexpression `self isEmpty` is true. Then, the block

```
[self error: 'stack empty']
```

is evaluated. When the stack sends itself the message `error:`, there is no corresponding method in class `Stack`. Message `error:` is handled by executing a method inherited from class `Object`.

Even within an inherited method, `self` refers to the object itself. The inherited method is treated as if it were defined in the subclass.

Example 7.7   Subclass B in Fig. 7.19 has the following two instance methods:

```
meShow      inherited from A
show        overrides show in A
```

The occurrence of `self` in

```
meShow
    ^ self show
```

refers to the object that uses `meShow`. Expression b `meShow`, following, therefore evaluates to `'2B'` and expression a `meShow` evaluates to `'1A'`:

```
class    A
instance methods
    show
        ^ '1A'
    meShow
        ^ self show

class    B    superclass    A
instance methods
    show
        ^ '2B'
```

Figure 7.19   Method `meShow` sending a message to `self`.

```
a := A new.      assign a an instance of A
b := B new.      assign b an instance of B
a show.          result '1A'
b show.          result '2B'
a meShow.        self refers to a; result '1A'
b meShow.        self refers to b; result '2B'              □
```

Messages to `super`

When a subclass overrides an inherited method, the special name `super` allows the overridden method to be used. Within the subclass, a message to `super` invokes the method that the superclass would use for that message.

The following class method is from class `Stack` in Fig. 7.17:

```
new
  ^ super new initialize
```

The subexpression

```
super new
```

uses method `new` from the superclass `Object` to create a stack object, which gets the `initialize` message.

Example 7.8   The only difference between Fig. 7.20 and Fig. 7.19 is the addition to B of method `bypass`.

```
bypass
  ^ super show
```

The discussion in Example 7.7 carries over to the modified classes in Fig. 7.20. In addition, we have

```
b := B new.      assign b an instance of B
b bypass.        result '1A'
```

Instance method `bypass` in subclass B uses `super show` to refer to method `show` in the superclass, which returns `'1A'`.   □

Exercises

7.1   An address book contains cards with names, addresses, and telephone numbers.
   a. Design classes corresponding to the address book and cards.

```
class   A
instance methods
    show
        ^  '1A'
    meShow
        ^ self show


class   B    superclass   A
instance methods
    show
        ^  '2B'
    bypass
        ^ super show
```

Figure 7.20 Method bypass sending a message to super.

b. Extend your design to attach notes to cards — for example, to keep track of birthdays or preferences. Allow each card to have multiple notes attached to it.

7.2 Design classes corresponding to bibliographic entries, including articles, books, reports, and manuscripts. Each entry has a title, one or more authors, and a date. Other attributes are specific to an entry. Entries for articles must include a journal or magazine, a date, and a volume number. Entries for books must give a publisher with a city. Entries for reports also provide a publisher and a city; however, entries for books and reports are presented differently.

a. How would you format or print bibliographic entries?

b. How would you determine the order of entries in a bibliography?

7.3 Represent binary trees, using a class for trees and a class for nodes. A binary tree is either empty or it consists of a root node with a left subtree and a right subtree, both of which are binary trees. At each node n in the tree, an *in-order* traversal visits the nodes in the left subtree of n, then visits n and the nodes in the right subtree of n.

a. How would you compute the number of nodes in a tree?

b. How would you compute the *height* of a tree, where the height of an empty tree is 0 and the height of any other tree is 1 plus the maximum of the heights of the left and right subtrees of the root node?

7.4 With nodes and trees as in Exercise 7.3, use subclasses to attach a string to each node in a binary tree.

a. Design a way of creating nodes, initialized with strings.

   b. How would you form or write the concatenation of the strings at
   the leaves of the tree, from left to right?

   c. How would you create a set consisting of the strings at the nodes in
   the tree?

7.5 Implement your binary tree representation from Exercise 7.3 in C++.

7.6 Implement your binary tree representation from Exercise 7.3 in
Smalltalk. Start with the partial description in Fig. 7.21.

7.7 Implement the shape example of Sections 7.1–7.3 in C++. A portion of
the class hierarchy from such an implementation appears in Fig. 7.10.

7.8 Implement the shape example of Sections 7.1–7.3 in Smalltalk.

7.9 Describe a class of queues, using the description of the Smalltalk class
`Stack` in Fig. 7.17, page 287, as a guide.

7.10 Function calls and function bodies in C++ correspond to messages and
methods, respectively, in Smalltalk. Compare the rules in C++
(Smalltalk) for determining the function body (method) to be executed
in response to a function call (message). Illustrate your answer by giv-

---

```
class Node superclass Object
instance variables
    leftNode                        The root of the left subtree.
    rightNode                       The root of the right subtree.
class methods
    left: lNode right: rNode        Return an initialized node.
instance methods
    isLeaf                          Are both leftNode and rightNode nil?
    left                            Return the value of leftNode.
    right                           Return the value of rightNode.
    do: aBlock                      Evaluate aBlock at each node during
                                       an in-order traversal.


class MyTree superclass Object
instance variables
    root                            The root of this tree.
instance methods
    isEmpty                         Is the root nil?
    do: aBlock                      Evaluate aBlock at each node during
                                       an in-order traversal.
```

Figure 7.21   Partial description of classes for implementing binary trees.

---

ing the following:

a. C++ counterparts of the Smalltalk classes in Fig. 7.20, page 295, which use `self` and `super` to influence the search for a method.

b. Smalltalk counterparts of the C++ classes B and D on page 270, which use virtual functions to influence the function body to be used in response to a function call.

7.11 The expression tree shown below has three kinds of nodes: (1) leaves with an integer value, (2) unary nodes with an operator and a single subtree, and (3) binary nodes with an operator and two subtrees.

The goal is to construct and print expression trees in parenthesized prefix notation, where parentheses enclose an operator and its operands. For example, the above tree must be printed as

```
(*  (-  5)  (+  3  4))
```

Develop the fragment in Fig. 7.22 into a C++ program. Note that a tree prints itself by asking its root node to print itself. Function `print` in class `Node` is virtual, so a derived class can supply a function body to be executed when `print` is called.

7.12 Redo Exercise 7.11 using variant records. Treat nodes as records with three variants, corresponding to leaves, unary nodes and binary nodes.

7.13 Suppose that we need to manipulate an array, A, whose elements are pointers to objects of either class D or class E. For simplicity, suppose that each object has two members: `id`, an identifying integer, and `print`, a function that prints the name of the class the object belongs to.

a. Derive D and E as subtypes of a base class B, and declare the array elements to be pointers to B. Check your work by evaluating `A[i]->print()` for each array element `A[i]`.

b. Let `dp` be a pointer to D—the type of `dp` is a subtype of the type of `A[i]`. C++ allows the assignment `A[i] = dp` but not `dp = A[i]` because, at compile time, we cannot tell whether `A[i]` points to an object of class D. Modify your solution to part (a) to simulate variant records by adding a tag to each object; the value of the tag specifies the class of the object. Check your work by evaluating `A[i]->print()` only if the run-time value of `A[i]` denotes a pointer to class D.

```
#include <stdio.h>
class Node {
public:
virtual void  print() {}
};
    ...
class Tree {
        Node *root;
public:
                Tree(int);
                Tree(char *op, Tree *p);
                Tree(char *op, Tree *1, Tree *r);
        void  print() { root->print(); }
};
main() {
    Tree t1("-", new Tree(5));
    Tree t2("+", new Tree(3), new Tree(4));
    Tree t("*", &t1, &t2);
    t.print();
    printf("\n");
}
```

Figure 7.22   Program for constructing and printing expression trees.

c. Suppose that instead of two classes D and E, we want to allow for additional subtypes F, G, H, ···. Add a virtual function isa to class B from (a), which takes a class name as an argument and returns true if the object belongs to that class. Note that a subtype of B must be independent of all other subtypes of B. Check your work by executing the following program fragment, where A[i]->print() must be executed only if A[i] denotes an object of class D:

```
for(i = 0; i < MAX; i++)
    if( A[i]->isa('D') )
        A[i]->print();
```

For simplicity, class names are taken to be single characters in this fragment. Extend the solution to allow strings to be class names — the library function strcmp can be used to compare strings.

Bibliographic Notes

Inheritance and data encapsulation allow programming to be done by building on existing code. They are a response to Hamming's [1969] complaint: "whereas Newton could say, 'If I have seen a little farther than others it is because I have stood on the shoulders of giants,' I am forced to say, 'Today we stand on each other's feet.' Perhaps the central problem we face in all of computer science is how we are to get to the situation where we build on the work of others rather than redoing so much of it in a trivially different way."

Nygaard and Dahl [1981] trace the parallel development of the concepts of object-oriented programming and of the Simula programming language.

Stroustrup [1991] is a primary reference for C++. Stroustrup [1994] is an account of the design and evolution of C++. Exercise 7.11 is from Koenig [1988].

A significant fraction of the book by Goldberg and Robson [1983] describes the class hierarchy that comes with the Smalltalk-80 system. They note, "The Smalltalk-80 system is based on ideas gleaned from the Simula language and from the visions of Alan Kay, who first encouraged us to try to create a uniformly object-oriented system." Exercise 7.6 is motivated by examples in their book. Deutsch [1984] presents techniques for the efficient implementation of Smalltalk. Borning and Ingalls [1982] extend Smalltalk to allow multiple inheritance — that is, to allow a class to have multiple superclasses. Ingalls [1978] describes Smalltalk-76, an earlier version of the system.

IV

FUNCTIONAL PROGRAMMING

Functional programming is considered in this book as

- a convenient setting for introducing concepts such as functions, values, and types (Chapter 8);
- a programming style in its own right (Chapters 9 and 10);
- a technique for language description (Chapter 13).

Part IV, consisting of Chapters 8–10, deals with the functional programming as a setting for concepts and as a programming style. Language description is the subject of Part VI.

Pure Functional Programming

This book deals with *pure functional programming*, which begins with the following principle:

The value of an expression depends only on the values of its subexpressions, if any.

The value of an expression like $a + b$ is simply the sum of the values of a and b. This principle rules out assignments, which can change the value of a variable. Pure functional programming is thus sometimes described as programming without assignments. Changes to the value of a variable during expression evaluation are called *side effects*.

Charmingly Simple, Surprisingly Powerful

Functional programming as a style is explored in Chapters 9 and 10. Functional programs can be charmingly simple and surprisingly powerful. The simplicity comes from the emphasis on values, independent of an underlying machine with its assignments and storage allocation. The power comes from recursion and the status of functions as "first-class" values, usable as readily as integers.

The simplicity of functional programming is due in part to implicit storage allocation. Users do not have to worry about managing storage for data:

> *Implicit storage management*. Storage is allocated as neccesary by built-in operations on data. Storage that becomes inaccessible is automatically deallocated.

The absence of explicit code for deallocation makes programs simpler and shorter. A consequence of this approach is that the language implementation must perform "garbage collection" to reclaim storage that has become inaccessible.

The power of functional programming is due in part to first-class functions:

> *Functions are first-class values*. Functions have the same status as any other values. A function can be the value of an expression, it can be passed as an argument, and it can be put in a data structure.

The treatment of functions as first-class values permits the creation of powerful operations on collections of data.

Languages for Functional Programming

These remarks about simplicity and power apply to both Standard ML, the working language of Chapters 8 and 9, and Scheme, a Lisp variant that is the working language of Chapters 10 and 13. Alternatives to these languages include Haskell and Miranda.

Some of the key ideas of functional programming came with Lisp, designed by John McCarthy in 1958. A classic program in both functional programming and language description is a short interpreter for Lisp, written in Lisp. Its convenience as a vehicle for language experimentation helped spawn numerous dialects of Lisp.

Lisp, like many languages for functional programming including ML, is impure because it does provide assignments. Nevertheless, programming style in these languages is dominated by the pure part of the language.

The fundamental difference between them is that ML is typed and the Lisp family is not. The readily apparent difference is that ML uses familiar syntax for expressions and the Lisp family has a unique syntax, with lots of parentheses. Lisp syntax is an acquired taste, but it is uniform and easy to parse; hence, programs can readily be treated as data.

8

Elements of Functional Programming

Functional programming as a minority discipline in the field of programming languages bears a certain resemblance to socialism in its relation to conventional, capitalist economic doctrine. Their proponents are often brilliant intellectuals perceived to be radical and rather unrealistic by the mainstream, but little-by-little changes are made in conventional languages and economies to incorporate features of the radical proposals.

— *Morris [1982], in a paper entitled, "Real programming in functional languages."*

Functional programming began as computing with expressions. The following are examples:

2	An integer constant
x	A variable
log n	Function *log* applied to *n*
2+3	Function + applied to 2 and 3

Expressions can also include conditionals and function definitions. The value of the following conditional expression is the maximum of *x* and *y*:

if $x \geq y$ **then** x **else** y

This chapter deals with concepts needed to explain expressions in any language, including values, types, names, and functions. Although the working language is Standard ML, the emphasis is on concepts. Thus, the discussion of expression evaluation includes "outermost evaluation," which is an alternative approach to the one taken in ML. Chapter 9 introduces higher-order functions, pattern matching, and additional features of functional languages.

305

For concreteness, specific ML examples will be written in a typewriter-like font; for example,

```
2+2;
```

A semicolon marks the end of an expression to be evaluated by the ML interpreter. Responses from the interpreter will be shown indented and in italics, as in the following example:

```
2+2;
    val it = 4 : int
```

Computing with expressions will be introduced by designing a little language of expressions from scratch in Section 8.1. The little language manipulates just one type of value: geometric objects called quilts. Expressions are formed by giving names to values and to operations on them. The constructs of the little language are borrowed from ML.

8.1 A LITTLE LANGUAGE OF EXPRESSIONS

The little language in this section is small enough to permit a short description, different enough to require description, yet representative enough of programming languages to make description worthwhile. The constructs in the language are expressions denoting geometric objects called quilts, such as those shown in Fig. 8.1. The language itself is called *Little Quilt*.

What Does Little Quilt Manipulate?

*values can be
anything, even
quilts*

Little Quilt manipulates geometric objects with a height, a width, and a texture. These objects can be visualized and discussed independently of the constructs in the language; with suitable display hardware, they can be manipu-

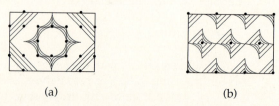

       (a)   (b)

Figure 8.1 Quilts made up of simpler pieces.

lated interactively by pointing, without using a language at all. The earliest programming languages began with integers, reals, and arrays of integers and reals; these too can be visualized and discussed independently of a particular language.

Basic Values and Operations

The two primitive objects in the language are the square pieces:

Quilts can be turned and can be sewn together, as in Fig. 8.2. Each quilt has a fixed direction or orientation, a height, a width, and a texture; turning therefore yields a different quilt. A lot of turning and sewing goes into making either quilt in Fig. 8.1 from copies of the primitive pieces; the dot in the north-east corner of each piece makes it a little easier to see how the quilts in Fig. 8.1 were put together.

Quilts and the operations on them in Fig. 8.2 are specified by the following rules:

1. A quilt is one of the primitive pieces, or
2. it is formed by turning a quilt clockwise 90°, or
3. it is formed by sewing a quilt to the right of another quilt of equal height.
4. Nothing else is a quilt.

Constants: Names for Basic Values and Operations

like words in English, constants are the start of language

The first step in constructing a language to specify quilts is to give names to the primitive pieces and to the operations on quilts. Let the pieces

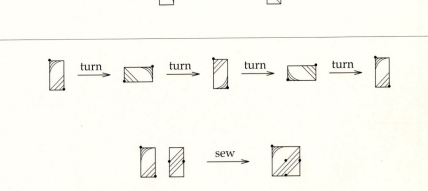

Figure 8.2   Operations on quilts.

be called *a* and *b*, respectively (for the arcs and bands in their textures). Let the operations in Fig. 8.2 be called *turn* and *sew*.

Expressions

expressions allow us to specify any quilt

Having chosen names for the built-in objects and operations, expressions are formed as follows. For the moment, the syntax of expressions mirrors the definition of quilts; complex expressions are built up from simpler ones, with the simplest ones being the names *a* and *b*. A BNF version of this syntax is

$$\langle expression \rangle ::= a$$
$$| \quad b$$
$$| \quad turn \; (\; \langle expression \rangle \;)$$
$$| \quad sew \; (\; \langle expression \rangle \; , \langle expression \rangle \;)$$

The semantics of expressions specifies the quilt denoted by an expression. What quilt does

$$sew(turn(turn(b)), a)$$

denote? The answer is built up in Fig. 8.3(a) from the quilts denoted by its subexpressions. The quilts denoted by the names *a* and *b* are the basic square pieces with arcs and bands on them, respectively. The quilts denoted by expressions of the form $turn(E_1)$ and $sew(E_1, E_2)$ are built up by applying the operations in Fig. 8.2 to the quilts denoted by E_1 and E_2.

The information in the table in Fig. 8.3(a) about expressions and the quilts they denote can be organized hierarchically, using a tree, as in Fig. 8.3(b). The numbers 1, 2, 3, 4, 5 in the figure relate entries in the table to corresponding nodes in the tree.

number	expression	quilt
1	*b*	
2	*turn(b)*	
3	*turn(turn(b))*	
4	*a*	
5	*sew(turn(turn(b)), a)*	

(a)

(b)

Figure 8.3   Subexpressions and the quilts they denote.

Convenient Extensions

Expressions will now be extended by allowing functions from quilts to quilts and by allowing names for quilts. These extensions allow quilts to be specified more conveniently.

User-Defined Functions

once defined, functions like unturn and pile can used as if they were built in

Frequent operations, like "unturning" a quilt counterclockwise, or attaching one quilt above another of the same width (see Fig. 8.4), are not provided directly by Little Quilt. These operations can be programmed — three turns make an "unturn," and a quilt can be "piled" above another using a combination of turning and sewing — but it would be convenient to give names to the operations. The operations can then be used without having to think about how, say, piling is implemented in terms of turning and sewing. It does not take too much turning and sewing to get an expression that is hard to understand.

The functions *unturn* and *pile* in Fig. 8.4 can be declared as follows:

fun $unturn(x) = turn(turn(turn(x)))$
fun $pile(x, y) = unturn(sew(turn(y), turn(x)))$

After these declarations, $unturn(E)$, for any expression E, is equivalent to

$$turn(turn(turn(E)))$$

Once declared, a function can be used to declare others; *pile* uses the previously declared function *unturn*.

Local Declarations

Let-expressions or *let-bindings* allow declarations to appear within expressions. They have the form

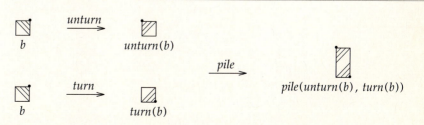

Figure 8.4   Using the derived operations *unturn* and *pile* to construct a quilt.

> **let** ⟨*declarations*⟩ **in** ⟨*expression*⟩ **end**

Let-expressions illustrate the use of names in programming languages and are found in functional languages, including dialects of Lisp.

For example, the following let-expression denotes the quilt built in Fig. 8.4:

> **let fun** *unturn(x) = turn(turn(turn(x)))*
> **fun** *pile(x, y) = unturn(sew(turn(y), turn(x)))*
> **in**
> *pile(unturn(b), turn(b))*
> **end**

User-Defined Names for Values

The final extension is convenient for writing large expressions in terms of simpler ones.

A *value* declaration

> **val** ⟨*name*⟩ = ⟨*expression*⟩

gives a name to a value. Value declarations are used together with let-bindings. An expression of the form

> **let val** $x = E_1$ **in** E_2 **end**

means: Occurrences of name x in E_2 represent the value of E_1. Any other name can be used instead of x without changing the meaning of the expression.

Let us rewrite the subexpression

> *pile(unturn(b), turn(b))*

in Fig. 8.4 using suggestive names. Use name *bnw* for *unturn(b)* because the dot moves to the northwest corner when b is "unturned." Similarly use *bse* for *turn(b)*. Then the quilt is formed by piling *bnw* above *bse*; that is, the subexpression can be rewritten as

> **let val** *bnw = unturn(b)* **in** *pile(bnw, turn(b))* **end**

or as

```
let   val bnw = unturn(b)
      val bse = turn(b)
in
      pile(bnw, bse)
end
```

The larger example in Fig. 8.5 shows how a slice of the quilt in Fig. 8.1(b) can be put together. Name *bb* refers to the subquilt studied in Fig. 8.4, formed by piling *unturn*(*b*) above *turn*(*b*). Name *aa* refers to a subquilt formed by piling a basic piece *a* above the result of turning *a* twice. The specification consists of a let-expression based on the schematic construction in the top half of the figure.

A summary of Little Quilt appears in Fig. 8.6.

Review: Design of Little Quilt

The language Little Quilt in this section was defined by starting with values and operations. The values are quilts, built up from two square pieces; the operations are for turning and sewing quilts. The language began with the names *a* and *b* for the square pieces and the names *turn* and *sew* for the operations.

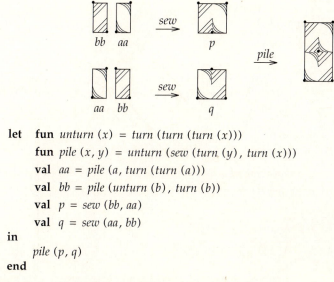

```
let   fun unturn (x) = turn (turn (turn (x)))
      fun pile (x, y) = unturn (sew (turn (y), turn (x)))
      val aa = pile (a, turn (turn (a)))
      val bb = pile (unturn (b), turn (b))
      val p = sew (bb, aa)
      val q = sew (aa, bb)
in
      pile (p, q)
end
```

Figure 8.5   Specification of a quilt.

⟨*expression*⟩ ::= *a* | *b*

Constant *a* = ▢ and *b* = ◩.

⟨*expression*⟩ ::= *turn*(⟨*expression*⟩) | *sew*(⟨*expression*⟩ , ⟨*expression*⟩)

The built-in functions *turn* and *sew* are illustrated in Fig. 8.2.

⟨*expression*⟩ ::= **let** ⟨*declarations*⟩ **in** ⟨*expression*⟩ **end**
⟨*declarations*⟩ ::= ⟨*declaration*⟩ | ⟨*declaration*⟩ ⟨*declarations*⟩

A let-expression localizes the effect of ⟨*declarations*⟩ to ⟨*expression*⟩. That is, the functions and variable names declared within ⟨*declarations*⟩ are available for use only within ⟨*expression*⟩. Optional semicolons are allowed after declarations.

⟨*declaration*⟩ ::= **fun** ⟨*name*⟩ (⟨*formals*⟩) = ⟨*expression*⟩
⟨*formals*⟩ ::= ⟨*name*⟩ | ⟨*name*⟩ , ⟨*formals*⟩

This construct is a function declaration. When the function is applied (see below) the body ⟨*expression*⟩ is evaluated after argument values are substituted for the formals.

⟨*expression*⟩ ::= ⟨*name*⟩ (⟨*actuals*⟩)
⟨*actuals*⟩ ::= ⟨*expression*⟩ | ⟨*expression*⟩ , ⟨*actuals*⟩

Here, ⟨*name*⟩ denotes a function to be applied to the actual argument expressions in parentheses. The evaluation order is: Evaluate the arguments, substitute their values for the corresponding formals in the function body, and return the value of the body.

⟨*declaration*⟩ ::= **val** ⟨*name*⟩ = ⟨*expression*⟩

This construct is a value declaration. It associates the value of ⟨*expression*⟩ with ⟨*name*⟩.

⟨*expression*⟩ ::= ⟨*name*⟩

A value declaration in an enclosing let-binding determines the value of ⟨*name*⟩.

Figure 8.6   A summary of Little Quilt.

The remaining constructs in this section are borrowed from ML. The borrowed constructs include expressions, which allows us to write

$$sew(turn(turn(b)), a)$$

Also borrowed are **fun** and **val** declarations, and **let**. Thus, Quilt-ML might be a more appropriate name for Little Quilt. Similarly, we can define Quilt-Haskell or Quilt-Scheme by starting with the names *a*, *b*, *turn*, *sew* and borrowing the syntax of expressions and declarations from the relevant language.

Quilt-ML will be implemented in Section 9.7 by telling ML how to interpret *a*, *b*, *sew*, and *turn*. ML already knows about expressions, **fun**, **val**, and **let**.

The rest of this chapter goes more deeply into the nature of values, functions, expressions, and names.

8.2 TYPES: VALUES AND OPERATIONS

A *type* consists of a set of elements called *values* together with a set of functions called *operations*. We say, "value *x* of type *T*," instead of the longer, "*x* is a member of the set of values associated with type *T*."

This section considers methods for defining structured values such as products, lists, and functions. The sets of values defined by these methods have corresponding types in ML. Types are denoted by *type expressions*; see Fig. 8.7 for the syntax of type expressions in this section.

Structured values such as lists can be used as freely in functional languages as basic values like integers and strings. Structured values are useful for tailoring the notion of value to a specific application. For example, each of the following applications has its own notion of values: proving theorems in geometry, determining whether chess moves are legal, differentiating algebraic expressions.

⟨*type-expression*⟩ ::= ⟨*type-name*⟩

    | ⟨*type-expression*⟩ → ⟨*type-expression*⟩

    | ⟨*type-expression*⟩ * ⟨*type-expression*⟩

    | ⟨*type-expression*⟩ **list**

Figure 8.7 In words, a type expression can be a type name, or it can denote a list, product, or function type. The operators →, *, **list** are in order of decreasing precedence.

Values in a functional language take advantage of the underlying machine, but are not tied to it. Integers are basic values and have direct machine support, but strings are basic values even though strings are not built into machines.

Operations for Constructing and Inspecting Values

The structuring methods in this section will be presented by specifying a set of values together with a set of operations. We concentrate on operations for constructing and inspecting the elements of the set. For example, along with lists there are operations to extend a list by adding a new first element, or to test whether a list is empty. Thus, we concentrate on operations that deal with the structure of values; the actual operations associated with a structuring method depend on the language.

Basic Types

basic values are atomic

A type is *basic* if its values are atomic—that is, if the values are treated as whole elements, with no internal structure.

For example, the *boolean* values in the set {**true**, **false**} are basic values.

Operations on Basic Values

Basic values have no internal structure, so the only operation defined for all basic types is a comparison for equality; for example, the equality $2=2$ is true, and the inequality $2 \neq 2$ is false.[1]

Products of Types

pairs are of product type

The *product* $A * B$ of two types A and B consists of *ordered pairs* written as (a, b), where a is a value of type A and b is a value of type B.

Thus, $(1, "one")$ is a pair consisting of the integer 1 and the string "*one*".

A product of n types $A_1 * A_2 * \cdots * A_n$ consists of *tuples* written as $(a_1, a_2, \ldots, a_n)$, where a_i is a value of type A_i, for $1 \le i \le n$.

Operations on Pairs

A pair is constructed from a and b by writing (a, b) — that is, by enclosing them within parentheses, separated by a comma. Associated with pairs are operations called *projection functions* to extract the first and second elements from a pair. The first element of the pair (a, b) is a; the second element is b.

Projection functions can be readily defined:

---

[1] Technically, an operation is a function. Thus, the equality test on integers is a function from pairs of integers to booleans. It is an element of the type **int** * **int** → **bool**, where **int** is type integer and **bool** is type boolean.

```
fun  first(x,y) = x;
fun  second(x,y) = y;
```

Lists of Elements

in ML, all list
elements have the
same type

A *list* is a finite-length sequence of elements. The type *A* **list** consists of all lists of elements, where each element belongs to type *A*. For example,

int list

consists of all lists of integers.

List elements will be written between brackets [and], and separated by commas. The empty list is written equivalently as [ ] or as **nil**.

The list [1, 2, 3] is a list of three integers, 1, 2, and 3. The list

["red", "white", "blue"]

is a list of three strings.

Operations on Lists

List-manipulation programs must be prepared to construct and inspect lists of any length. The following operations on lists are from ML:

null(x)	True if x is the empty list and false otherwise.
hd(x)	The first or head element of list x.
tl(x)	The tail or rest of the list after the first element is removed.
$a :: x$	Construct a list with head a and tail x.

Thus, *null* returns true if it is applied to the empty list [ ] or **nil**, but not if it is applied to a list [1, 2, 3] of three integers. The head of [1, 2, 3] is 1, and its tail is [2, 3].

The role of the :: operator, pronounced "cons," can be seen from the following equalities:

[1, 2, 3] = 1::[2, 3] = 1::2::[3] = 1::2::3::[ ]

The cons operator :: is right associative; the expression 1::2::[3] is equivalent to 1::(2::[3]).

Functions from a Domain to a Range

functions can be
from any type to
any type

Associated with the type $A \rightarrow B$ is the set of all functions from A to B. For example, if Q is the set of quilts in Section 8.1, then function *turn* from quilts to quilts is an element of $Q \rightarrow Q$. Function *sew* from pairs of quilts to quilts is an element of $Q*Q \rightarrow Q$.

A function f in $A \rightarrow B$ is *total* if it is defined at each element of A—that is, if it associates an element of B with each element of A. A is called the *domain* and B is called the *range* of f. Function f is said to *map* elements of its domain to elements of its range.

A function f in $A \rightarrow B$ is *partial* if it need not be defined at each element of A; that is, it is possible for there to be no element of B associated with an element of A.

Function Application

Section 8.3 is devoted to function specification, so suppose for the moment that functions can somehow be constructed.

A key operation associated with the set $A \rightarrow B$ is *application*, which takes a function f in $A \rightarrow B$ and an element a in A, and yields an element b of B.

A function is applied in ML by writing it next to its argument; f a is the application of f to a. Parentheses do not affect the value of an expression, so f a is equivalent to $f(a)$ and to $(f$ $a)$. Since application is left associative, f a b is equivalent to $(f$ $a)$ b, the application of f a to b.

If f maps a to b, we write f a $=$ b and call b the *value* of f at a.

Types in ML

Having examined sets of values and associated operations, we now consider some types in ML.

The predeclared basic types of ML appear in Fig. 8.8, along with examples of values and operations. Strings are treated as atomic; the individual characters in a string cannot be directly extracted in ML.

define a basic type by enumerating values New basic types can be defined as needed by enumerating their elements in a **datatype** declaration. A new basic type `direction` with four elements `ne`, `se`, `sw`, and `nw` is declared by

type	name	values	operations
boolean	**bool**	`true, false`	`=, <>, ` $\cdots$
integer	**int**	$\cdots$ `, -1, 0, 1, 2, ` $\cdots$	`=, <>, <, +, *,div, mod,` $\cdots$
real	**real**	$\cdots$ `, 0.0, ` $\cdots$ `, 3.14, ` $\cdots$	`=, <>, <, +, *,/,` $\cdots$
string	**string**	`"foo", "\"quoted\""`	`=, <>, ` $\cdots$

Figure 8.8 Predeclared basic types of ML.

```
datatype direction = ne | se | sw | nw;
```

The symbol | separates the enumerated elements. The names ne, se, sw, and nw are called *value constructors*, or simply *constructors*, of type direction; they construct elements of direction out of nothing. The names of value constructors cannot be reused for other purposes. The general form of datatype declarations in ML, with parameterized value constructors, is considered in Section 9.5.

The structured types in this section are shown in the table below.

type	*constructor*	*notation*	*example*
function	->	infix	int -> bool
product	*	infix	int*int
list	list	postfix	string list

The type constructors are listed in order of decreasing precedence; that is, list has higher precedence than *, which has higher precedence than ->. Thus, a function from lists of integers to lists of pairs of strings has the type

```
int list -> (string*string) list
```

A **type** declaration gives a name to a type. For example, the declaration

```
type intpair = int*int;
```

makes intpair a synonym for int*int.

A Representation of Quilts in ML

We illustrate the types in this section by building a data representation for quilts from Section 8.1. This data representation is close to a form that can be output. Alternative representations, say closer to the abstract syntax of quilts, can be defined after the general form of **datatype** declarations in ML is considered in Section 9.5.

ML does not draw pictures, so quilts cannot be drawn directly. The following view of quilts leads to a data representation:

A quilt is a list of rows.

A row is a list of squares.

A square has a texture and a direction.

Call the textures *arcs* and *bands*.

Call the directions *ne, se, sw,* and *nw*.

Quilts are made up of the primitive pieces

Type `texture` is motivated by the arcs and bands in these pieces:

```
datatype  texture = arcs | bands;
```

Type `direction` is motivated by the four possible positions of the dot in a piece:

```
datatype  direction = ne | se | sw | nw;
```

Any operation on types `texture` and `direction`, other than a test for equality, must be defined explicitly as a function.

The following declarations complete the representation of quilts:

```
type square = texture*direction;
type row = square list;
type quilt = row list;
```

The quilt a

has one row consisting of one square with texture `arcs` and direction `ne`. It is represented as

```
[ [(arcs, ne)] ];
```

a list of one row `[(arcs,ne)]`, which is a list of one square `(arcs,ne)`, which is a pair with first element `arcs` of type `texture` and second element `ne` of type `direction` (see also Fig. 8.9).

8.3 FUNCTION DECLARATIONS

Having introduced values, the next step is to define expressions. An expression is formed by applying a function or operation to subexpressions; this section will thus consider function declarations. Once a function is declared, it can be applied as an operator within expressions.

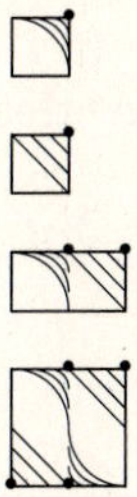

$[\ [(arcs,ne)] \ ]$

$[\ [(bands,ne)] \ ]$

$[\ [(arcs,ne), (bands,ne)] \ ]$

$[\ [(arcs,ne), (bands,ne)], [(bands,sw), (arcs,sw)] \ ]$

Figure 8.9 A representation of quilts in ML.

Functions as Algorithms

A function in a programming language comes together with an algorithm for computing the value of the function at each element of its domain. A function declaration has three parts:

1. The name of the declared function
2. The parameters of the function
3. A rule for computing a result from the parameters

Syntax of Function Declarations and Applications

The basic syntax for function declarations is

    fun $\langle name \rangle$ $\langle formal\text{-}parameter \rangle$ = $\langle body \rangle$;

Parentheses around the formal parameter are optional. An example is

    fun $successor$ $n = n + 1;$

The keyword **fun** marks the beginning of a function declaration, $\langle name \rangle$ is the function name, $\langle formal\text{-}parameter \rangle$ is a parameter name, and $\langle body \rangle$ is an expression to be evaluated. The term "formal parameter" is sometimes abbreviated to *formal*.

The formal parameter can be parenthesized. Thus, function *successor* can alternatively be declared by

    fun $successor(n) = n + 1;$

The use of a function within an expression is called an *application* of the function. Prefix notation is the rule for the application of declared functions:

⟨*name*⟩ ⟨*actual-parameter*⟩

Again, ⟨*name*⟩ is the function name and ⟨*actual-parameter*⟩ is an expression corresponding to the parameter name in the declaration of the function. Thus,

successor(2+3)

is the application of function *successor* to the actual parameter (2+3). The parentheses belong to the parameter (2+3) and are not part of the syntax of function application. The term "actual parameter" is sometimes abbreviated to *actual*.

In informal usage, we use "parameter" for formal parameter and "argument" for actual parameter.

A function that computes the absolute value of a number is defined by

fun *abs*(n) = **if** $n \geq 0$ **then** n **else** $0 - n$

Recursive Functions

A function f is *recursive* if its body contains an application of f. More generally, a function f is recursive if f can activate itself, possibly indirectly through other functions.

Example 8.1 Function *len* counts the number of elements in a list:

fun *len*(x) =
  if *null*(x) **then** 0 **else** 1 + *len*(*tl*(x))

This function is recursive because the body

if *null*(x) **then** 0 **else** 1 + *len*(*tl*(x))

contains an application of *len*; it is *len*(*tl*(x)).

When *len* is applied to the empty list [ ], the condition *null* [ ] is true, and the result is 0.

The length of a nonempty list is defined recursively to be one greater than the length of its tail. Thus,

len ["*hello*", "*world*"] = 1 + *len* ["*world*"]   □

Example 8.2 Elements of the Fibonacci sequence 1, 1, 2, 3, 5, 8, ⋯ are computed by the function

fun *fib*(*n*) =
  if *n* = 0 **orelse** *n* = 1 **then** 1 **else** *fib*(*n* − 1) + *fib*(*n* − 2)

This function is recursive because its body contains the two applications *fib*(*n* − 1) and *fib*(*n* − 2). Function *fib* satisfies the following equalities:

fib(0) = 1
fib(1) = 1
fib(2) = 2
fib(3) = 3
fib(4) = 5
fib(5) = 8
fib(6) = · · · □

8.4 APPROACHES TO EXPRESSION EVALUATION

The rules for expression evaluation in this section are based on the structure of expressions. For example, one approach to evaluating an expression of the form

$$E_1 + E_2$$

is to evaluate the subexpressions E_1 and E_2 and add the values of the subexpressions.

The various forms of evaluation differ in the order in which subexpressions are evaluated. In some cases, subexpressions are evaluated only if they are needed.

The rules for expression evaluation in this section emphasize clarity over efficiency. They show what result a language implementation must compute, not how the result ought to be computed. The interpretation of names like x in an expression can be tricky; so to build the reader's intuition, the rules describe evaluation by substituting arguments for formal parameters. Argument values are usually kept in machine registers and not actually substituted into the function body.

Innermost Evaluation

Under the *innermost-evaluation* rule, a function application

⟨*name*⟩ ⟨*actual-parameter*⟩

is computed as follows:

Evaluate the expression represented by ⟨*actual-parameter*⟩.
Substitute the result for the formal in the function body.
Evaluate the body.
Return its value as the answer.

After the declaration

fun   *successor n = n* + 1;

innermost evaluation of the application *successor*(2+3) proceeds as follows:

Evaluate the argument (2+3).
Substitute its value 5 for formal *n* in the body *n*+1.
Evaluate the resulting expression 5+1.
Return the answer 6.

Each evaluation of a function body is called an activation of the function. If we rewrite *successor*(2+3) as *successor*(*plus*(2, 3)), then its computation can be described as:

Activate *plus* to evaluate *plus*(2, 3).
Return the result 5 from *plus*.
Activate *successor* 5.
Return the answer 6.

*innermost
evaluation is
inside-out
evaluation of
expressions, as in
call-by-value*

The approach of evaluating arguments before the function body is also referred to as *call-by-value* evaluation. The term "innermost" describes the inside-out activation of nested functions in expressions like *successor*(*plus*(2, 3)).

Call-by-value can be implemented efficiently, so it is widely used. Under call-by-value, all arguments are evaluated, whether their values are needed or not. Occasionally, call-by-value may result in unnecessary evaluation of arguments that will never be used.

Selective Evaluation

*selective
evaluation occurs
in conditionals and
booleans*

The ability to evaluate selectively some parts of an expression and ignore others is provided by the construct

if ⟨*condition*⟩ **then** ⟨*expression*₁⟩ **else** ⟨*expression*₂⟩

Here, ⟨*condition*⟩ is an expression that evaluates to either **true** or **false**. If ⟨*condition*⟩ evaluates to **true**, then the value of ⟨*expression*₁⟩ becomes the value of the entire construct; otherwise, the value of ⟨*expression*₂⟩ becomes the value of the entire construct. Either ⟨*expression*₁⟩ or ⟨*expression*₂⟩ is evaluated, not both.

Evaluation of Recursive Functions

No new ideas are needed to evaluate applications of recursive functions. As usual, the actual parameters are evaluated and substituted into the function body.

The application *len* ["*hello*","*world*"] in Example 8.1 is evaluated by substituting the list for *x* in the body of *len*, yielding

if *null* ["*hello*","*world*"] **then** 0 **else** 1 + *len*(*tl*(["*hello*","*world*"]))

Since the list is not empty, this expression simplifies to

1 + *len*(*tl*(["*hello*","*world*"]))

Innermost evaluation activates *tl*; the result of this activation is the list ["*world*"].

The following equalities summarize the computation:

$$
\begin{aligned}
len\ ["hello","world"] &= 1 + len(\ tl(["hello","world"])\ ) \\
&= 1 + 1 + len(\ tl(["world"])\ ) \\
&= 1 + 1 + len(\ [\ ]\ ) \\
&= 1 + 1 + 0 \\
&= 2 \qquad\qquad\qquad\qquad \square
\end{aligned}
$$

Outermost Evaluation from Left to Right

parameters are evaluated as they are needed in outermost evaluation

Under the *outermost-evaluation rule*, a function application is computed as follows:

Substitute the actual for the formal in the function body.
Evaluate the body.
Return its value as the answer.

Innermost and outermost evaluation produce the same result if both terminate with a result. The distinguishing difference between the evaluation methods is that actual parameters are evaluated as they are needed in outermost evaluation; they are not evaluated before substitution. The difference between innermost and outermost evaluation will be illustrated by considering two examples. In the first, outermost evaluation appears to do redundant work, because it reevaluates an actual parameter. Clever implementations avoid the redundant work. In the second example, outermost evaluation succeeds, where innermost evaluation loops forever.

Standard ML uses call-by-value or innermost evaluation. Other languages, including some variants of ML, use a form of outermost evaluation.

Example 8.3 The "91-function," attributed to John McCarthy, is defined by

> **fun** $f(x)$ =
>   **if** $x > 100$ **then** $x - 10$ **else** $f(f(x+11))$

Innermost and outermost evaluation of $f(100)$ are compared in Fig. 8.10. In either case, evaluation begins with the substitution of 100 for the formal x in the function body:

> **if** $100 > 100$ **then** $100 - 10$ **else** $f(f(100+11))$

Since $100 > 100$ is false, this expression simplifies to

> $f(f(100+11))$

The expression $f(f(100+11))$ has an outer occurrence of f with argument $f(100+11)$ and an inner occurrence of f with argument $100+11$. Under outermost evaluation, the argument $f(100+11)$ is substituted into the function body:

> **if** $f(100+11) > 100$ **then** $f(100+11) - 10$ **else** $f(f(f(100+11)+11))$

Note the three occurrences of $f(100+11)$ in the function body after substitution.

The first occurrence of $f(100+11)$ is in the test for the conditional. Its evaluation proceeds as follows:

> $f(100+11)$
> $= $ **if** $100+11 > 100$ **then** $100+11 - 10$ **else** $f(f(100+11+11))$
> $= $ **if** $111 > 100$ **then** $100+11 - 10$ **else** $f(f(100+11+11))$
> $= 100+11 - 10$
> $= 111 - 10$
> $= 101$

Innermost Evaluation

$$f(100) = \textbf{if } 100 > 100 \textbf{ then } 100 - 10 \textbf{ else } f(f(100+11))$$
$$= f(f(100+11))$$
$$= f(f(111))$$
$$= f(\textbf{ if } 111 > 100 \textbf{ then } 111 - 10 \textbf{ else } f(f(111+11)) \ )$$
$$= f(\ 111-10\ )$$
$$= f(\ 101\ )$$
$$= \textbf{if } 101 > 100 \textbf{ then } 101 - 10 \textbf{ else } f(f(101+11))$$
$$= 101 - 10$$
$$= 91$$

Outermost Evaluation

$$f(100) = \textbf{if } 100 > 100 \textbf{ then } 100 - 10 \textbf{ else } f(f(100+11))$$
$$= f(f(100+11))$$
$$= \textbf{if } f(100+11) > 100 \textbf{ then } f(100+11) - 10 \textbf{ else } f(f(f(100+11)+11))$$

For simplicity, the next few lines show only the evaluation of $f(100+11)$:

$$f(100+11) = \textbf{if } 100+11 > 100 \textbf{ then } 100+11 - 10 \textbf{ else } f(f(100+11+11))$$
$$= \textbf{if } 111 > 100 \textbf{ then } 100+11 - 10 \textbf{ else } f(f(100+11+11))$$
$$= 100+11 - 10$$
$$= 111 - 10$$
$$= 101$$

Returning to the evaluation of $f(100)$:

$$f(100) = \textbf{if } 101 > 100 \textbf{ then } f(100+11) - 10 \textbf{ else } f(f(f(100+11)+11))$$
$$= f(100+11) - 10$$
$$\cdots$$
$$= 91$$

Figure 8.10 Innermost and outermost evaluation of $f(100)$, where f is the 91-function.

The conditional therefore becomes

$$\textbf{if } 101 > 100 \textbf{ then } f(100+11) - 10 \textbf{ else } f(f(f(100+11)+11))$$

Since $101 > 100$ is true, we get

$$f(100+11) - 10$$

"outermost"
appears to do more
work than
"innermost"

A clever implementation of outermost evaluation would have kept track of the substituted copies of the actual parameter $f(100+11)$ and would immediately recognize that its value has already been computed to be 101. An implementation that does not recognize that $f(100+11)$ is a copy would do extra work because it would reevaluate the actual parameter.   □

A second example comparing innermost and outermost evaluation is included in the discussion of short-circuit evaluation.

Short-Circuit Evaluation

The operators **andalso** and **orelse** in ML perform *short-circuit evaluation* of boolean expressions, in which the right operand is evaluated only if it has to be. Expression E **andalso** F is false if E is false; it is true if both E and F are true. The evaluation of E **andalso** F proceeds from left to right, with F being evaluated only if E is true.

Similarly, using short-circuit evaluation, the value of the expression

E **orelse** F

is **true** if E evaluates to **true**. F is skipped; it is not evaluated. Evaluation of the expression

true orelse F

terminates even if F leads to a nonterminating computation.

Example 8.4   The only difference between **orelse** and the following function *or* is that call-by-value results in the evaluation of both arguments of *or*:

```
fun  or(x, y) =
    if x = true then true
    else if y = true then true
    else false
```

Since y denotes one of the two boolean values, **true** and **false**, function *or* can be declared more succinctly as

```
fun  or(x, y) =
    if x then true else y
```

"outermost" can
terminate where
"innermost" fails

Under the innermost-evaluation rule, both subexpressions E and F in $or(E, F)$ are evaluated before they are substituted into the function body. Thus, *or*(**true**, *F*)

results in a nonterminating computation if the evaluation of *F* does not terminate.

Under the outermost-evaluation rule, actuals are substituted for formals without being evaluated, so

or(**true**, *F*) =
  if true then true else *F*

The right side immediately simplifies to **true** and the nonterminating computation *F* is never reached. ☐

Since ML uses innermost evaluation, the operator **orelse** has to be provided by the language. It cannot be user-defined as part of a program.

8.5 LEXICAL SCOPE

if local variables can be renamed, the result is lexical scope

It seems reasonable to suppose that consistent renaming of variables has no effect on the value of an expression. Renaming is made precise by introducing a notion of local or "bound" variables; bound occurrences of variables can be renamed without changing the meaning of a program. This renaming principle is the basis for the *lexical scope rule* for determining the meanings of names in programs.

Changing the formal parameter from *x* to *n* in the declaration of the successor function

fun *successor*(*x*) = *x* + 1;
fun *successor*(*n*) = *n* + 1;

should have no effect on the meaning of a program. The value of the expression *successor*(5) is 6 with either declaration.

Subtleties arise when a function declaration can refer to names that are not formal parameters. For example, the result returned by the function *addy* depends on the value of *y*:

fun *addy*(*x*) = *x* + *y*;

Since *y* is not a parameter, some context determines its value. The question is, which context?

Lexical scope rules use the program text surrounding a function declaration to determine the context in which nonlocal names are evaluated. The program text is static in contrast to run-time execution, so such rules are also called static scope rules.

Lexical scope rules are studied in this section using two forms of let-expressions:

$$\textbf{let val} \quad x = E_1 \ \textbf{in} \ E_2 \ \textbf{end}$$
$$\textbf{let fun} \ f(x) = E_1 \ \textbf{in} \ E_2 \ \textbf{end}$$

In either case, the value of the let-expression is the value of E_2.

Val Bindings

The occurrence of x to the right of keyword **val** in

$$\textbf{let val} \ x = E_1 \ \textbf{in} \ E_2 \ \textbf{end}$$

is called a *binding occurrence* or simply *binding* of x. All occurrences of x in E_2 are said to be within the *scope* of this binding; the scope of a binding includes itself. The occurrences of x within the scope of a binding are said to be *bound*. A binding of a name is said to be *visible* to all occurrences of the name in the scope of the binding.

Occurrences of x in E_1 are not in the scope of this binding of x.

The lines in the following diagram go from a binding to bound occurrences of x:

$$\textbf{let val} \ x \ = \ 2 \ \textbf{in} \ x \ + \ x \ \textbf{end}$$

A precise counterpart of "Variables can be renamed" is: The value of an expression is left undisturbed if we replace all occurrences of a variable x within the scope of a binding of x by a fresh variable. The following two expressions therefore have the same value:

$$\textbf{let val} \ x = 2 \ \textbf{in} \ x + x \ \textbf{end}$$
$$\textbf{let val} \ z = 2 \ \textbf{in} \ z + z \ \textbf{end}$$

The preceding definitions carry over directly to bindings of distinct variables. The scope of the binding of x in

$$\textbf{let val} \ x = 3 \ \textbf{in} \ \textbf{let val} \ y = 4 \ \textbf{in} \ x * x + y * y \ \textbf{end end}$$

includes the two occurrences of x in $x*x$. The scope of the binding of y includes the two occurrences of y in $y*y$.

When faced with nested bindings of the same variable, as in

$$\text{let val } x \;=\; 2 \;\text{ in } \text{let val } x \;=\; x \;+\; 1 \;\text{ in } x \;*\; x \;\text{ end end}$$

first apply renaming to the inner binding. Replacing x by y in the inner binding yields

$$\text{let val } x \;=\; 2 \;\text{ in } \text{let val } y \;=\; x \;+\; 1 \;\text{ in } y \;*\; y \;\text{ end end}$$

Here, the scope of the outer binding of x includes the x in $x+1$, and the scope of the inner binding of y includes the two occurrences of y in $y*y$. Again, lines go from binding occurrences to bound occurrences within their scope.

Fun Bindings

The occurrences of f and x to the right of keyword **fun** in

$$\text{let fun } f(x) \;=\; E_1 \;\text{ in } E_2 \;\text{ end}$$

are *bindings* of f and x.

This binding of the formal parameter x is visible only to the occurrences of x in E_1.

fun-bound functions can be recursive

This binding of the function name f is visible to all occurrences of f in both E_1 and E_2. Occurrences of f in E_1 correspond to recursive calls. For example, consider

$$\begin{aligned}
&\textbf{fun} \quad even(x) \;= \\
&\qquad\qquad x \;=\; 0 \;\textbf{orelse } even(x-2) \\
&\textbf{in} \quad even(8) \\
&\textbf{end}
\end{aligned}$$

The binding of *even* in this expression is visible within the function body

$$x \;=\; 0 \;\textbf{orelse } even(x-2)$$

and within the expression $even(8)$.[2] The arrows in the following diagram go from the binding to the bound occurrences:

---

[2] *Warning*: This declaration of function *even* leads to a nonterminating computation if *even* is applied to an odd number or to a negative number.

let fun *even* (*x*) = *x* = 0 **orelse** *even* (*x* − 2) **in** *even* (8) **end**

The treatment of formal parameters is more evident in the following expression, since there are two bindings of *x*:

let val *x* = 2 **in let fun** *f* (*x*) = *x* + 1 **in** *f* (*x*) **end end**

This expression evaluates to 3.

Nested Bindings

Sequences of **val** and **fun** bindings are treated as nested bindings. Thus,

> **let val** $x_1 = E_1$
> **val** $x_2 = E_2$
> **in** E
> **end**

is treated as if the individual bindings were nested:

> **let val** $x_1 = E_1$ **in let val** $x_2 = E_2$ **in** E **end**

This approach generalizes to any sequence of **val** and **fun** bindings.

Simultaneous Bindings

Mutually recursive functions require the simultaneous binding of more than one function name. In

> **let   fun** $f_1(x_1) = E_1$
> **and fun** $f_2(x_2) = E_2$
> **in** E

the scope of both f_1 and f_2 includes E_1, E_2, and E. The scopes of the formal parameters x_1 and x_2 are, as usual, limited to the respective function bodies. For example, consider functions *even* and *odd* satisfying the equalities:

$even(x) =$
    if $x = 0$ **then** **true** **else** **if** $x = 1$ **then** **false** **else** $odd(x-1)$
$odd(x) =$
    if $x = 0$ **then** **false** **else** **if** $x = 1$ **then** **true** **else** $even(x-1)$

In words, the number x is even if it is 0 or if $x-1$ is odd, and x is odd if it is 1 or if $x-1$ is even. (Never mind that these definitions lead to nonterminating computations for negative values of x.)

Functions *even* and *odd* are defined in terms of each other, so they have to be bound simultaneously. The keyword **and** between the bindings of *even* and *odd* leads to them being bound together:

let fun $even(x) =$
    if $x = 0$ **then** **true** **else** **if** $x = 1$ **then** **false** **else** $odd(x-1)$
and $odd(x) =$
    if $x = 0$ **then** **false** **else** **if** $x = 1$ **then** **true** **else** $even(x-1)$
in $(even(24), odd(24))$ **end**

This expression evaluates to the pair (**true**, **false**).

8.6 TYPE CHECKING

This section on type checking in ML overlaps Section 4.9 on type checking in imperative languages. The overlap allows this chapter to be read independently of Chapter 4.

Type distinctions between values carry over to expressions. Since 2 and 2 are integers, $2+2$ must also denote an integer.

A *type system* for a language is a set of rules for associating a type with expressions in the language. A type system *rejects* an expression if it does not associate a type with the expression. The rules of a type system specify the proper usage of each operator in the language.

Type Inference

Where possible, ML infers the type of an expression. The inferred type **int** for integer is included in the ML interpreter's response to the expression

```
2+2;
    val it = 4 : int
```

An error is reported if the type of the expression cannot be inferred.

Input to the interpreter is in a typewriter-like font; responses from the interpreter are in italics. A semicolon marks the end of an expression to be evaluated. Keyword **val** marks a value declaration, so this response declares the variable `it` and gives it the value of the evaluated expression. The notation

$$\langle expression \rangle : \langle type\text{-}expression \rangle$$

associates the type described by $\langle type\text{-}expression \rangle$ with $\langle expression \rangle$.

Associated with each operator **op** is a rule that specifies the type of an expression E **op** F in terms of the types of E and F. An example is the following:

> If E and F have type **int**,
>
> then $E + F$ also has type **int**.

This type inference rule is an instance of a more general rule.

At the heart of all type systems is the following rule for function applications. The symbol $\rightarrow$ is a function constructor, so $A \rightarrow B$ is the type of a function from type A to type B:

the basis for type checking

> If f is a function of type $A \rightarrow B$, and a has type A, \hfill (8.1)
>
> then $f(a)$ has type B.

The rule for + can be made to look more like the general rule (8.1) by using prefix rather than infix notation, and rewriting the expression as $+(E, F)$, with + applied to the pair (E, F):

> If + is a function of type **int** $*$ **int** $\rightarrow$ **int**, and
>
>   the pair (E, F) has type **int** $*$ **int**,
>
> then $+(E, F)$ has type **int**.

Type Names and Type Equivalence

What does it mean for two types to be equal? The question of type equivalence arises when rule (8.1) is applied, because the type of the argument a must equal the domain type of f.

Two type expressions are *structurally equivalent* if and only if they are equivalent under the following rules:

> SE1. A type name is structurally equivalent to itself.
>
> SE2. Two type expressions are structurally equivalent if they are formed by applying the same type constructor to structurally equivalent types.

SE3. After a type declaration, **type** $n = T$, the type name n is structurally equivalent to T.

By these rules, the type expressions **int** and **int** are structurally equivalent, and so are the following:

int $*$ **int** $\rightarrow$ **bool**
int $*$ **int** $\rightarrow$ **bool**

More limited notions of type equivalence are obtained if we restrict rules SE1–SE3; see Section 4.9.

ML uses structural equivalence for types.

Example 8.5 This example uses the following basic types:

```
datatype texture = arcs | bands;
datatype direction = ne | se | sw | nw;
```

The type of an expression

```
[[(arcs,ne)]];
    val it = [[(arcs,ne)]] : (texture * direction) list list
```

can be inferred from its syntax. Since lists are enclosed between [and], this expression denotes a list containing a list containing a pair.

The type of this expression is structurally equivalent to the type name *quilt*, where *quilt* is declared as follows:

```
type square = texture*direction;
type row = square list;
type quilt = row list;
```
□

Overloading: Multiple Meanings

A symbol is *overloaded* if it has different meanings in different contexts. Familiar operator symbols like + and $*$ are overloaded. For example, 2 has type **int**, so + denotes integer addition 2+2; however, 2.0 has type **real**, so + denotes real addition in 2.0 + 2.0:

```
2+2;
    val it = 4 : int
2.0+2.0;
    val it = 4.0 : real
```

The treatment of + in ML can therefore be restated using the following pair of rules:

If E has type **int** and F has type **int**,
then $E + F$ has type **int**.

If E has type **real** and F has type **real**,
then $E + F$ has type **real**.

These rules can also be made to look like the general rule (8.1) by using prefix notation.

When ML cannot resolve overloading, it complains, as in

```
fun add(x,y) = x+y;
    Error: overloaded variable "+" cannot be resolved
```

Explicit types can then be given to resolve overloading. Any hint, in the form of a type for a parameter or a result is enough for ML to infer the type of this function:

```
fun add(x,y):int = x+y;            (*  result is an integer  *)
    val add = fn : int * int -> int
fun add(x,y) = x + (y:int);        (*  y  is an integer  *)
    val add = fn : int * int -> int
```

Comments appear between (* and *).

Coercion: Implicit Type Conversion

A *coercion* is a conversion from one type to another, inserted automatically by a programming language.

ML rejects 2*3.142 because 2 is an integer and 3.142 is a real, and * expects both its operands to have the same type:

```
2*3.142;
    Error: operator and operand don't agree (tycon mismatch)
    operator domain: int * int
    operand:         int * real
```

Most programming languages treat the expression 2*3.142 as if it were 2.0*3.142; that is, they automatically convert the integer 2 into the real 2.0.

Type conversions must be specified explicitly in ML because the language does not coerce types. The integer 2 is coerced to a real in

```
real(2);
    val it = 2.0 : real
```

Polymorphism: Parameterized Types

For all lists, the function *hd* returns the head or first element of a list:

```
hd [1,2,3];
    val it = 1 : int
hd ["a","b","c"];
    val it = "a" : string
```

Thus, when applied to a list of integers, *hd* returns an integer; when applied to a list of strings, *hd* returns a string.

What is the type of *hd*?

```
hd;
    val it = fn : 'a list -> 'a
```

ML uses a leading quote, as in 'a, to identify a type parameter. The type of hd can therefore be read as, "function from a list of any type 'a to type 'a."

ML is known for its support for *polymorphic* functions, which can be applied to parameters of more than one type. Since Chapter 9 concentrates on ML, the discussion of polymorphic functions continues in Section 9.4.

Exercises

8.1 Specify each of the quilts in Fig. 8.11 in Little Quilt.

8.2 In each of the following cases, what are the activations of the defined function that occur when the function is applied to argument 3, and what is the result of the application to argument 3?

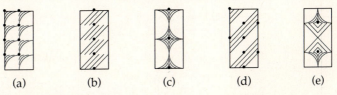

   (a)   (b)   (c)   (d)   (e)

Figure 8.11 Quilts for Exercise 8.1.

> **a. fun** *fact*(*n*) =
> > **if** *n* = 0 **then** 1 **else** *n* ∗ *fact*(*n* − 1);
>
> **b. fun** *square*(*n*) =
> > **if** *n* = 0 **then** 0 **else** *square*(*n* − 1) +2∗*n* − 1;
>
> **c. fun** *even*(*n*) =
> > **if** *n* = 0 **then true**
> > **else if** *n* = 1 **then false**
> > **else** *even*(*n* − 2);
>
> **d. fun** *g*(*n*) =
> > **if** *n* = 1 **then** 1
> > **else** *g*(**if** *even*(*n*) **then** *n* / 2 **else** 3 ∗ *n* + 1);

8.3 In each of the cases in Exercise 8.2, what happens when the defined function is applied to the argument − 1? Give the result if the computation terminates; otherwise, explain why the computation does not terminate.

8.4 The "91-function" is defined on page 324 by

> **fun** *f*(*x*) =
> > **if** *x* > 100 **then** *x* − 10 **else** *f*(*f*(*x* + 11))

Sketch the innermost evaluation of
a. *f*(102).
b. *f*(101).
c. *f*(91).
d. *f*(90).
e. *f*(89).

8.5 Expression evaluation corresponds to tree rewriting. When 7∗7 is evaluated to yield 49, the subtree for 7∗7 is replaced by a subtree for 49. The sequence of trees in Fig. 8.12 corresponds to the innermost evaluation of the expression 7∗7 − 4∗2∗3. Give a sequence of trees corresponding to the innermost evaluation of the following expressions:
a. 2 ∗ 10 + 8 ∗ 3
b. 3 = 0 **orelse** 3 = 1
c. 3 = 3 **orelse** 3 = 1
d. 1 :: 2 :: 3 :: [ ]
e. (7 + *sqrt*(25 − 2∗8))/2

8.6 Function *fib* computes Fibonacci numbers:

> **fun** *fib*(*n*) =
> > **if** *n* = 0 **orelse** *n* = 1 **then** 1 **else** *fib*(*n* − 1) + *fib*(*n* − 2)

Conditional expressions can be represented in an abstract syntax tree by a node labeled **if** with three children: from left to right, the first

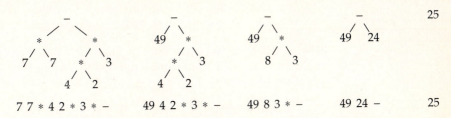

$$77 * 42 * 3 * - \qquad 49\ 42 * 3 * - \qquad 49\ 83 * - \qquad 49\ 24 - \qquad 25$$

Figure 8.12 A sequence of trees and corresponding postfix expressions. In each of these trees, the subtree to be rewritten corresponds to the leftmost operator in the postfix representation.

child represents the condition, the second child represents the then-part, and the third child represents the else-part.

a. Draw an abstract syntax tree corresponding to the function body.

b. Draw a sequence of trees corresponding to the activations of *fib* during the innermost evaluation of *fib*(3). In each tree, underline the occurrence of *fib* that is just about to be rewritten.

c. Why is function *fib* an inefficient way of computing Fibonacci numbers?

8.7 An integer is a prime if it is not a multiple of any smaller integer. More precisely, n is a *prime* if for all i, $2 \le i \le n-1$, the expression n **mod** $i \ne 0$. The **mod** operator returns the remainder after integer division.

a. Declare a function $f(n, m)$ that returns **true** if for all i, $2 \le i \le m$, the expression n **mod** $i \ne 0$.

b. Use function f from (a) to declare a function *prime*(n) that returns **true** if n is a prime and returns **false** otherwise.

8.8 An alternative to the Fibonacci function *fib*(n) in Exercise 8.6 is *fast*(n), declared as follows:

fun $g(i, j, k, n) =$
   if $k = n$ **then** j
   else $g(j, i+j, k+1, n)$;

fun *fast*(n) $= g(0, 1, 0, n)$;

a. Explain why *fib*(n) $=$ *fast*(n) for all $n \ge 0$.

b. Explain why the computation of *fast*(n) is much more efficient than the computation of *fib*(n).

8.9 A linear-recursive function with one argument can be put into the following form

$$\textbf{fun } f(x) \;=\; \textbf{if } a(x) \textbf{ then } b(x) \textbf{ else } c(x, f(d(x))) \qquad (8.2)$$

by appropriate choice of functions a, b, c, and d. What do functions a, b, c, and d correspond to in each of the cases in Exercise 8.2?

8.10 Generalize the form (8.2) in Exercise 8.9 to functions with more than one argument, and put each of the following functions into your generalized form:

    a. fun $rem(m, n) =$
               if $m < n$ **then** m **else** $rem(m - n, n)$

    b. fun $g(n, i, j) =$
               if $n = 0$ **then** i **else** $g(n - 1, j, i + j)$

    c. fun $count(x, a) =$
               if $null(x)$ **then** a **else** $count(tl(x), 1 + a)$

8.11 Declare a function f satisfying the following specification. Use additional functions as needed.

    For $x \geq 0$, $f(x)$ is the largest integer $n \geq 0$
    such that $n^2 \leq x$.

What does your function do for negative values of x?

8.12 Identify the binding and bound occurrences in the following expressions:

    a. let val $x = 3$
        in let val $y = x + 1$
           in $x + y * y$
           end
        end

    b. let val $x = 3$
        in let val $x = x + 1$
           in $x + x * x$
           end
        end

    c. let val $x = 3$
           val $y = x + 1$
        in $x + y * y$
        end

    d. let val $x =$ **let val** $x = 3$
                    in $x + 1$
                    end
       in $x + x$
       end

e.   **let fun** $sq(x)$: **int** $= x*x$
       val $x = 3$
   in $sq(x)$
   end

f. **let val** $x = 3$
       fun $sq(x)$: **int** $= x*x$
   in $sq(x)$
   end

g. **let fun** $f(x) = g(1,x)$
      and $g(a,x) = x+a$
      val $x = 3$
   in $f(x)$
   end

8.13   Evaluate the expressions in Exercise 8.12.

8.14   Extend the quilt language in Section 8.1 so functions like *copy*, suggested by the following equalities, can be declared.

$$copy(1, \square) = \square$$

$$copy(3, \square) = \square\square\square$$

Bibliographic Notes

The precise definition of functional programming, especially pure functional programming, is subject to debate. Since Scheme (Lisp) and ML do allow side effects, they are impure; although there is little difference between programs written in the pure part of these languages and programs written in pure languages like Haskell and Miranda.

Lisp's primitives for manipulating lists were inspired by those of an extension of Fortran called FLPL, for Fortran List Processing Language. Lisp was designed in part because FLPL did not have recursion and conditionals within expressions. Mathematical elegance came later. The name Lisp is a contraction of "List Processor." Chapter 10 deals with the Scheme dialect of Lisp.

ML is a functional language in the tradition of Landin's [1966] ISWIM, an acronym for "If You See What I Mean." ISWIM itself was based on Lisp, considered in Chapter 10, and the lambda calculus, considered in Chapter 14. Since ML was first created by Robin Milner in the 1970s, a number of dialects have emerged. Standard ML, the dialect used in this book, is the result of a standardization effort begun in 1983. Chapter 9 presents more information on ML.

Turner [1979, 1982, 1985] also began with ISWIM. In a sequence of language SASL, KRC, and Miranda, he won people over to nonstrict or lazy evaluation, recursion equations, and higher-order functions.

Hudak's [1989] survey of functional programming language uses examples from Haskell, a language intended to be a "culmination and consolidation of many years of research on functional languages—the design was influenced by languages as old as ISWIM and as new as Miranda."

Backus's [1978] impassioned critique of "conventional von Neumann languages" drew popular attention to functional programming. The style of programming advocated by Backus has come to be called FP; see the paper by John Williams in Darlington, Henderson, and Turner [1982]. This collection consists of lecture material compiled for a course on various aspects of functional programming.

9

Functional Programming in a Typed Language

The proposed ML is not meant to be *the* functional language. There are too many degrees of freedom for such a thing to exist: lazy or eager evaluation, presence or absence of references and assignment, whether and how to handle exceptions, types-as-parameters or polymorphic type-checking, and so on. Nor is the language or its implementation meant to be a commercial product. It aims to be a means for propagating the craft of functional programming and a vehicle for further research into the design of functional languages.

— Milner [1984], in a proposal leading up to Standard ML.

The simplicity and power of functional languages is due to properties like pure values, first-class functions, and implicit storage management, properties that are shared by all functional languages. Other properties, such as how types are treated or how expressions are evaluated, vary from language to language. All along, functional programming has been a proving ground for programming concepts and language designs. New languages continue to be designed.

The working language of this chapter is Standard ML, a general-purpose functional language. The name ML is an acronym for Meta Language—the language was initially designed for computer-assisted reasoning.

ML is typed, Scheme is not

The fundamental difference between Standard ML, the working language of this chapter, and Scheme, the working language of Chapter 10 is that ML is typed and Scheme is not. The influence of types pervades ML. Types are the reason that ML and Scheme are treated in separate chapters.

Syntax is another reason for treating the two languages in separate chapters. The Lisp family has a unique syntax, with lots of parentheses. The expression $3*4$ is written as (* 3 4) with parentheses surrounding the operator and its operands. The expression $2+3*4$ is written as

```
(+ 2 (* 3 4))              ; 2+3*4  in Scheme
    14
```

The value *14* on the line after the expression is the response from the Scheme interpreter.

ML uses familiar syntax for expressions. $2+3*4$ is written as is:

```
2+3*4;                    (* 2+3*4  in ML *)
   ··· 14 : int
```

Included in the ML interpreter's response is the value *14* and its type *int* for **integer**.

This chapter deals only with the "core" of ML, which does not include the module system.

9.1 EXPLORING A LIST

append and reverse recursively wind down a list and unwind back

Lists are the original data structure of functional programming, just as arrays are the original data structure of imperative programming.[1] Most functions on lists explore the structure of a list. For practice with such functions, this section examines two related functions, *append* and *reverse*.

Operations on Lists

A list in ML is a sequence of zero or more elements of the same type. Lists are written between brackets [and]. Commas separate the elements of a list. Thus, [1,2,3] is a list of integers.

The structure of lists is as follows:

A list is either empty, written equivalently as [ ] or as **nil**,
or it has the form $a :: y$, where
element a is the head of the list, and
the sublist y is the tail of the list.

For example, 7 is an integer, but [7] is a list containing one element, the integer 7. This list [7] has integer 7 as its head, and the empty list [ ] as its tail; that is, [7] is equivalent to 7::[ ].

The basic functions for list manipulation appear in Fig. 9.1.

[1] Lisp is either famous or notorious for encoding both programs and data as lists; the language even takes its name from lists. ML has a wider range of data types, with lists having to do less.

	function	*description*
null	*null*	Test for emptiness.
head	*hd*	Return first element.
tail	*tl*	Return all except the first element.
cons	::	Infix list constructor.

Figure 9.1 Basic functions for list manipulation.

Linear Functions on Lists

Most functions on lists consider the elements of a list one by one. They behave as follows:

> **fun** $f(x)$ = **if** list x is empty **then** $\cdots$
> **else** something involving $hd(x)$, $tl(x)$, and f

This function is recursive because f appears on the right side in the else part; control flow in functional programming is via recursion. A list is a linear sequence of elements, so functions on lists are typically linear recursive; that is, a function like f appears just once on the right side of the = sign.

An example is a function to compute the length of a list:

> **fun** $length(x)$ = **if** $null(x)$ **then** 0
> **else** 1 + $length(tl(x))$

An empty list has length 0. The length of a nonempty list x is 1 greater than the length of the tail of x.

Two Functions on Lists: Append and Reverse

Functions *append* and *reverse* are representative of functions on lists. Function *append* implements the built in operator @, which concatenates or appends two lists. Thus,

$$append(\ [1,2],\ [3,4,5]) \equiv [1,2]\ @\ [3,4,5] \equiv [1,2,3,4,5]$$

The following equalities characterize *append*:

$$append([\ ],\ z) \equiv z$$
$$append(a::y,\ z) \equiv a\ ::\ append(y,\ z)$$

In words, the result of appending the empty list onto z is the list z itself. The result of appending list $a::y$ onto z is the same as the result of first appending y and z, and then using a cons operation to make a the head element.

ML actually has convenient notation for defining functions based on such equalities. In the interests of discussing one thing at a time, this section concentrates on lists, deferring the notation to Section 9.2. Meanwhile, definitions of *append* and *reverse* appear in Fig. 9.2.

Function *reverse* can be used to reverse a list, as in

$$reverse(\,[1,2,3],\,[\,]\,) \equiv [3,2,1]$$

The equalities characterizing *reverse* are

$$reverse([\,],\,z) \equiv z$$
$$reverse(a{::}y,\,z) \equiv reverse(y,\,a{::}z)$$

The difference between *reverse* and *append* is summarized by the following equations:

$$reverse(\,a{::}y,\,z) \equiv reverse(\,y,\,a{::}z)$$
$$append(\,a{::}y,\,z) \equiv a :: append(\,y,\,z)$$

Function *reverse* is related to the ML function *rev*, which reverses the order of elements in a list:

$$rev(x) \equiv reverse(x,\,[\,])$$

Winding Down and Unwinding Back

Linear recursive functions like *reverse* and *append* have two phases:

1. a winding phase in which the function examines the tail of the list, and
2. an unwinding phase in which control unwinds back to the beginning of the list.

With function *reverse*, the cons operation occurs as we wind down the list. For example,

$$reverse(\,[2,3,4],\,[1]\,) \equiv reverse(\,[3,4],\,2{::}[1]\,) \equiv reverse(\,[3,4],\,[2,1]\,)$$

---

fun $append(x,\,z) = $ **if** $null(x)$ **then** z
$\qquad\qquad\qquad\quad$ **else** $hd(x) :: append(tl(x),\,z)$

fun $reverse(x,\,z) = $ **if** $null(x)$ **then** z
$\qquad\qquad\qquad\quad$ **else** $reverse(tl(x),\,hd(x){::}z)$

Figure 9.2   Definitions of the functions *append* and *reverse*.

The following equalities illustrate the winding phase (see also the sequence of abstract syntax trees in Fig. 9.3):

$$reverse(\,[2,3,4],\,[1]\,) \equiv reverse(\,[3,4],\,[2,1]\,)$$

$$\equiv reverse(\,[4],\,[3,2,1]\,)$$

$$\equiv reverse(\,[\,],\,[4,3,2,1]\,)$$

$$\equiv [4,3,2,1]$$

The resulting list is built up as the second argument of the successive calls of *reverse*.

On the same arguments, the winding phase of *append* consists of the successive calls

$$append(\,[2,3,4],\,[1]\,) \quad \text{calls} \quad append(\,[3,4],\,[1]\,)$$

$$append(\,[3,4],\,[1]\,) \quad \text{calls} \quad append(\,[4],\,[1]\,)$$

$$append(\,[4],\,[1]\,) \quad \text{calls} \quad append(\,[\,],\,[1]\,)$$

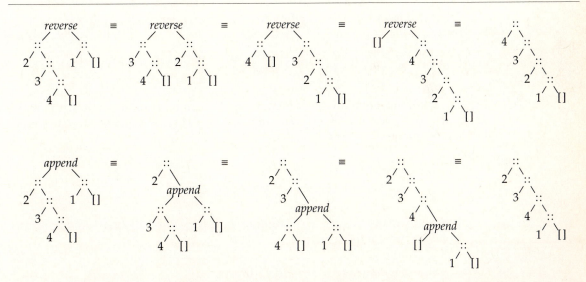

Figure 9.3 Two sequences of abstract syntax trees illustrating the evaluation of *reverse*([2,3,4], [1]) and *append*([2,3,4], [1]). A node in an abstract syntax tree is labeled with an operator; its children are labeled with the operands of the operator. The functions *reverse* and *append* are treated as operators to illustrate the computation.

The resulting list is built up as we unwind back out of these calls:

$$append([\,], [1]) \equiv [1]$$

$$append([4], [1]) \equiv [4,1]$$

$$append([3,4], [1]) \equiv [3,4,1]$$

$$append([2,3,4], [1]) \equiv [2,3,4,1]$$

9.2   FUNCTION DECLARATION BY CASES

This section introduces some convenient notation for declaring functions that manipulate structured data such as lists. Functions on lists often have two cases, one for the empty list and one for nonempty lists. A nonempty list has at least one element, so it has the form $a::y$, for some head element a and some tail y. The cases in the definition of a function *length* for computing the length of a list are described by the following equalities:

$$length([\,]) \equiv 0$$
$$length(a::y) \equiv 1 + length(y)$$

ML allows function *length* to be equivalently declared as follows:

fun $length([\,]) = 0$
| $length(a::y) = 1 + length(y)$

With this notation, the structure of a list can be examined implicitly, without the explicit use of *null*, *hd*, and *tl*. Here is an alternative declaration of function *append* from Section 9.1:

fun $append([\,], z) = z$
| $append(a::y, z) = a :: append(y, z)$

For comparison, the original definition of *append* in Fig. 9.2 has explicit operations to examine the structure of a list x:

fun $append(x, z) = $ **if** $null(x)$ **then** z
                     else $hd(x) :: append(tl(x), z)$

These two definitions of *append* work the same way. The only difference between them is that by testing whether x is the empty list, the conditional explicitly specifies the order in which the cases are examined.

Function Application

The basic syntax for function declarations is

$$\textbf{fun} \; \langle \textit{name} \rangle \; \langle \textit{formal-parameter} \rangle = \langle \textit{body} \rangle \tag{9.1}$$

An example is the function *succ*, named after "successor:"

$$\textbf{fun} \quad succ \; n \;=\; n+1$$

The application of a function f to an argument x can be written either with parentheses, $f(x)$, or without, $f \; x$. An expression of the form $f \; g \; x$ is equivalent to each of $(f \; g) \; x$, the application of f to g and then the application of the result to x; that is, function application associates to the left.

function application has higher precedence than operators
Function application has higher precedence than the following operators, listed in order of increasing precedence:

```
< <= = <> >= >
:: @
+ - ^
* / div mod
```

The symbol $\leq$ is the publication notation for <=, symbol $\neq$ for <>, and $\geq$ for >=.

Example 9.1 Function application takes precedence over multiplication. In the following expression, the successor of 4 is computed before 3 is multiplied with the result 5 to get 15:

```
3 * succ 4;
    val it = 15 : int
```

Function application and multiplication have higher precedence than the cons operator : :, so the left argument of cons in the following expression is 15 and the result is the list [15]:

```
3 * succ 4 :: [];
    val it = [15] : int list
```

Relational operators have lower precedence than the arithmetic operators. The equality is tested after the subexpression to the right of the = sign evaluates to a list:

```
[15] = 3 * succ 4 :: [];
    val it = true : bool
```

□

Example 9.2 The cons operator :: has weaker precedence than the arithmetic operators. Thus, `3+4::[]` is equivalent to `7::[]` and the parentheses in `length(7::[])` are necessary. Without the parentheses, we get an error:

```
length 7::[];
    Error: operator and operand don't agree (tycon mismatch)
    ...
    in expression:
      length 7
```

ML interprets the expression as if it were parenthesized

```
(length 7) :: []
```

with function `length` applied to the integer 7. An error occurs because `length` expects a list as an operand. The desired behavior is obtained by using parentheses to group the argument of `length`:

```
length(7::[]);
    val it = 1 : int
```
□

Patterns

a pattern is made up of variables and value constructors

Functions with more than one argument can be declared using the syntax

> **fun** ⟨*name*⟩ ⟨*pattern*⟩ = ⟨*body*⟩   (9.2)

A ⟨*pattern*⟩ has the form of an expression made up of variables, constants, pairs or tuples, and list constructors. Value constructors for datatypes, considered in Section 9.5, can also appear in patterns.

Examples of patterns are [ ] or **nil**, which match the empty list; $a :: y$, which matches a nonempty list; and (x,y), which matches a pair. The names in the pattern are formal parameters. The pattern (x, y) consists of the formals x and y and the syntax

> (,)

for constructing pairs. Except in tuples, where they are required, parentheses are used only for grouping and can be ignored.

The pattern (x,y) appears in the following declarations of the functions *first* and *second*:

> **fun**   *first*$(x, y) = x$;
> **fun**   *second*$(x, y) = y$;

Now, *second*(1, "*a*") equals "*a*". The argument (1, "*a*") matches the pattern (*x*,*y*) in the function declaration, with 1 matching *x* and "*a*" matching *y*.

An underscore _ is a "don't-care" pattern that matches any value. Thus, function *first* can be redeclared as

> **fun** *first*(*x*, _) = *x*;

Patterns and Case Analysis

cases are tested in order

Patterns together with case analysis give ML a compact and readable notation for function declarations, as in the declaration of *length* (repeated here):

> **fun** *length*([ ]) = 0
> | *length*(*a* :: *y*) = 1 + *length*(*y*)

The parentheses in the patterns ([ ]) and (*a* :: *y*) identify what *length* is applied to; they are not part of the patterns. Without the parentheses, the pattern [ ] matches the empty list of length 0. The formals in the pattern *a* :: *y* are *a* and *y*.

The declaration of a function *f* in ML can have the form

> **fun** *f* ⟨*pattern*₁⟩ = ⟨*expression*₁⟩
> | *f* ⟨*pattern*₂⟩ = ⟨*expression*₂⟩
>   . . .
> | *f* ⟨*pattern*ₙ⟩ = ⟨*expression*ₙ⟩;   (9.3)

The cases in the declaration of *f* are separated by a vertical bar |, and are tested in order. When *n* = 1, there is only one case and ⟨*expression*₁⟩ corresponds to ⟨*body*⟩ in the syntax (9.2).

The following examples explore function definition by cases. Specifically, the ML implementation issues a warning if the cases in a function declaration are not exhaustive, or if a case is redundant because of earlier cases.

cases are expected to cover all possibilities

Example 9.3   The ML interpreter complains if the cases in a function declaration are not exhaustive. The following declaration of head does not have a case for empty lists:

```
fun head(a::y) = a;
    Warning: match not exhaustive
          a :: y => ...
    val head = fn : 'a list -> 'a
```

Function head now works for nonempty lists

```
head [7];
    val it = 7 : int
```

but fails on empty lists

```
head [];
    uncaught exception Match
```

Exceptions are discussed in Section 9.6.   □

beware of misspellings in patterns

Example 9.4 In a pattern, if **nil** or the name of some other data type is misspelt, then ML cannot distinguish the misspelling from a parameter. The name nil is misspelt as nul in the following declaration:

```
fun f(nul) = 0
|    f(a::y) = 1+f(y);
    Warning: redundant patterns in match
              nul => ...
    -->    a :: y => ...
    val f = fn : 'a list -> int
```

The pattern nul is a variable that matches any list. The second pattern a::y is therefore redundant and is never reached.   □

formals must not be repeated in a pattern

Example 9.5 It is tempting but illegal to use a formal parameter more than once in a pattern. Consider a function $strip(a, x)$ that removes leading a's from list x. For example,

$$strip(1, [1,1,2,3,1,1]) \equiv [2,3,1,1]$$

Some equalities involving $strip$ are

$$strip(a, [\,]) \equiv [\,]$$
$$strip(a, a :: y) \equiv strip(a, y)$$
$$strip(a, b :: y) \equiv y \qquad \text{if } b \neq a$$

The pair $(a, a::y)$ cannot be used as a pattern:

```
fun f(a, []) = []
|    f(a, a::y) = f(a, y);
    Error: duplicate variable in pattern(s): a
```

The pair $(a, b::y)$ is a valid pattern:

```
fun g(a, []) = []
|   g(a, b::y) = if a=b then g(a,y) else b::y;
    val g = fn : ''a * ''a list -> ''a list
```

Function g passes the test for *strip*:

```
g(1, [1,1,2,3,1,1]);
    val it = [2,3,1,1] : int list
```

Function h is an alternative to g, using conditionals alone:

```
fun h(a,x) = if null(x) then nil
             else if a=hd(x) then h(a,tl(x))
             else x;
    val h = fn : ''a * ''a list -> ''a list
```

It too passes the test for *strip*:

```
h(1, [1,1,2,3,1,1]);
    val it = [2,3,1,1] : int list
```

Which is more readable, g or h? Most of the time, function declaration by cases leads to more readable code.   □

9.3 FUNCTIONS AS FIRST-CLASS VALUES

On one level, this section develops some useful functions for list manipulation. The small library in Fig. 9.4 includes functions *map*, *remove_if*, and *reduce*, defined in this section. The library consists of tools that either solve common problems or can be adapted to do so.

Several of the tools take functions as arguments. A function is called *higher order* if either its arguments or its results are themselves functions.

On another level, this section illustrates the utility and flexibility of functions as first-class values. Functions like *map* and *reduce* play a role similar to control structures in imperative programming. As we shall see, the idea behind *map* is similar to:

> **for** each element *a* of a list
> > **do** something with *a* and
> **return** a list of the results

With functions as first-class values, such control structures can be defined as needed; they need not be built into the language.

```
fun length(nil) = 0
|   length(a::y) = 1 + length(y);
```

```
fun reverse(nil, z) = z
|   reverse(a::y, z) = reverse(y, a::z);
```

```
fun append(nil, z) = z
|   append(a::y, z) = a :: append(y, z);
```

```
fun map f nil = nil
|   map f (a::y) = (f a) :: (map f y);
```

```
fun remove_if f nil = nil
|   remove_if f (a::y) =
              if f(a) then remove_if f y
              else a :: (remove_if f y);
```

```
fun reduce f nil v = v
|   reduce f (a::y) v = f(a, reduce f y v);
```

Figure 9.4   Useful functions for list manipulation.

Mapping Functions Across List Elements

A *filter* is a function that copies a list, making useful changes to the elements as they are copied. The simplest filter is *copy*, which simply copies list elements without change:

$$\textbf{fun } copy([\ ]) \ = \ [\ ]$$
$$|\quad copy(a :: y) \ = \ a :: copy(y) \tag{9.4}$$

Suppose function *square* multiplies its argument by itself—for example, $square(3)=9$. Filter *copysq* squares list elements as it copies them:

$$\textbf{fun } copysq([\ ]) \ = \ [\ ]$$
$$|\quad copysq(a :: y) \ = \ square(a) :: copysq(y) \tag{9.5}$$

For example,

$$copysq\ [1,2,3,4,5] \ \equiv \ [1,4,9,16,25]$$

Here, think of *square* as a "change function" because it makes changes to list elements as they are copied.

ML provides a function *map* to apply a function *f* to each element of a list *x*. Thus, *map* is a tool for building a filter out of *f*. For example,

map square [1,2,3,4,5] ≡ [1,4,9,16,25]

The difference between the following definition of *map* and the definitions (9.4) and (9.5) is that *map* takes a change function as an argument:

fun *map f* [ ] = [ ]
| *map f* (*a* :: *y*) = (*f a*) :: (*map f y*)   (9.6)

The Utility of Map

map is like a control structure on lists

The power and simplicity of functional programming lies in the ability to combine functions in interesting ways. It is not the individual functions but how they work together that is interesting. Before defining new functions, we therefore consider a sequence of short examples involving the *map*, which is a variant of *mapcar* in Lisp. The examples use the following functions:

square	Multiply an integer argument by itself
first	Return the first element of a pair.
second	Return the second element of a pair.

Example 9.6 Function `map` was introduced by using it to square each element of a list of integers:

```
map square [1,2,3];
    val it = [1,4,9] : int list
```

In the following example, the list consists of pairs, and `map` is used to extract the first component of the pairs:

```
map first [(1,"a"), (2,"b"), (3,"c")];
    val it = [1,2,3] : int list
```

Putting the above examples together, the following expression uses `map` once to extract the first element of a pair, and again to square the extracted elements:

```
map square (map first [(1,"a"), (2,"b"), (3,"c")]);
    val it = [1,4,9] : int list
```
□

Lists are used extensively in functional programming, and *map* is very helpful for list manipulation.

Example 9.7 Suppose matrices are represented as lists of lists, as in

```
[ [11,  12,  13,  14],
  [21,  22,  23,  24],
  [31,  32,  33,  34] ]
```

The hd operation on lists extracts the first row of such a matrix:

```
hd [ [11,12,13,14],
     [21,22,23,24],
     [31,32,33,34] ];
   val it = [11,12,13,14] : int list
```

Similarly, tl can be used to get the remaining rows after the first.

But, what if we want to extract the first column, made up of the first elements of each row. A combination of map and hd can be used for this purpose:

```
map hd [ [11,12,13,14],
         [21,22,23,24],
         [31,32,33,34] ];
     val it = [11,21,31] : int list
```

Here, hd is applied to each of the three lists corresponding to the three rows of the matrix. From each "row," hd extracts the first element, so the overall effect is to extract the first column.

Similarly, the remaining columns after the first can be extracted using a combination of map and tl:

```
map tl [ [11,12,13,14],
         [21,22,23,24],
         [31,32,33,34] ];
     val it = [[12,13,14],[22,23,24],[32,33,34]] : int list list     □
```

Anonymous Functions

In ML, an *anonymous function*, a function without a name, has the form

$$\textbf{fn } \langle formal\text{-}parameter \rangle \implies \langle body \rangle \tag{9.7}$$

An example is a function that multiplies its parameter x by 2:

$$\textbf{fn } x \implies x * 2$$

This construct is an expression. Its value is an anonymous doubling function that takes an argument *x* and applies ∗ to *x* and 2.

Anonymous functions are helpful for adapting existing functions so they can be used together with tools like *map*.

Example 9.8 Function *map* expects a change function to be unary; that is, to take one argument. This example uses anonymous functions to adapt the binary operator ∗.

Suppose that we want to multiply each element by 2. A unary function that multiplies its argument by 2 can be created from ∗, as follows:

```
fn x => x*2;
    val it = fn : int -> int
```

The doubling function is the first argument of *map* in

```
map (fn x => x*2) [1,2,3,4,5];
    val it = [2,4,6,8,10] : int list
```
□

Selective Copying

remove_if
selectively copies
list elements

Like *map*, the higher order function *remove_if* is a variant of *copy*; it removes elements from a list if some condition holds. More precisely, *remove_if* copies list element *a*, unless predicate *f* is true on *a*:

> **fun** *remove_if f* [ ] =
>   [ ]
>
> | *remove_if f* (*a* :: *y*) =
>   **if** *f*(*a*) **then** *remove_if f y*
>   **else** *a* :: (*remove_if f y*)   (9.8)

Example 9.9 We can now remove odd numbers from a list by defining a function odd

```
fun odd = (x mod 2) = 1
```

and using it together with *remove_if* to remove odd numbers from a list:

```
remove_if odd [0,1,2,3,4,5];
    val it = [0,2,4] : int list
```

The anonymous function

```
fn x => x = 0
```

tests whether an element equals 0. It is used to remove 0s in

```
remove_if (fn x => x = 0) [0,7,0,4,0];
   val it = [7,4] : int list                                    □
```

Accumulate a Result

reduce
accumulates a
result from a list

We begin with two special cases that motivate the function *reduce*. The special cases compute the sum and product, respectively, of a list of integers.

The sum of an empty list x is 0, and the sum of a nonempty list x is computed by adding the first element to the sum of the remaining elements:

fun *sum_all* [ ] = 0
| *sum_all* (a :: y) = a + *sum_all*(y)

Similarly, the product of an empty list x is 1, and the product of a nonempty list x is computed by multiplying the first element with the product of the remaining elements:

fun *product_all* [ ] = 1
| *product_all* (a :: y) = a * *product_all*(y)

Function *reduce* is a generalization of *sum_all*, *product_all*, and a host of related functions. The three parameters of *reduce* are a binary operator f, a list, and an initial value v. If the list is empty, the initial value v is returned. Otherwise, f is applied to the first element and the result obtained from the rest of the list:

fun *reduce* f [ ] v = v
| *reduce* f (a :: y) v = f(a, *reduce* f y v)   (9.9)

Example 9.10 Functions *sum_all* and *product_all* can be simulated by applying *reduce* to functions corresponding to + and *:

```
fun add(x,y)  : int = x+y;
fun multiply(x,y) : int = x*y;
```

The simulation of *sum_all* is

```
reduce add [1,2,3,4,5] 0;
   val it = 15 : int
```

Similarly, *product_all* can be simulated:

```
reduce multiply [1,2,3,4,5] 1;
    val it = 120 : int
```

Example 9.11   The operators + and ∗ can be treated as the named functions
op + and **op** ∗. That is,

$$\mathbf{op} +(3, 4) \ \equiv \ 3 + 4 \ \equiv \ 7$$

Thus, **op** + and **op** ∗ can be passed as arguments to *reduce*, instead of *add* and
multiply, respectively, in Example 9.10. For example,

```
reduce op + [1,2,3,4,5] 0;
    val it = 15 : int
```

An unexpected lexical confusion can arise with `op *`, since comments in ML
open with `(*` and close with `*)`:

```
reduce (op *) [1,2,3,4,5] 1;
    Error: unmatched close comment
```

A space between `*` and `)` solves this problem:

```
reduce (op * ) [1,2,3,4,5] 1;
    val it = 120 : int                                           □
```

9.4   ML: IMPLICIT TYPES

For a language that strictly checks types at "compile time," ML expressions
are surprisingly free of type declarations. This section considers two aspects
of types in ML, inference and polymorphism, which underlie the ease of use of
types in ML.

Type Inference

*ML cleverly infers
types*

Where possible, ML infers types without help from the user. The inferred
type *int* for integer is included in the response to the expression

```
3*4;
    val it = 12 : int
```

The interpreter evaluates the expression `3*4` and saves its value in the variable `it`. Since `3` and `4` are integers, their product must also be an integer.
This type appears to the right of *12* in the interpreter's response.

The type of an expression can be specified by writing

⟨*expression*⟩ : ⟨*type*⟩

Returning to type inference, consider the response to the following function declaration:

```
fun succ n = n+1;
    val succ = fn : int -> int
```

Here, the keyword **fn** (not to be confused with **fun**) is a placeholder for a function value.

The interpreter's response can be read as follows: The name `succ` denotes a function value of type **int → int**. With sets, the set of all functions from set A to set B is written as $A \to B$. With types, $s \to t$ denotes the type function from type s to type t.

The algorithm for type inference is beyond the scope of this book. In the expression n+1, variable n must have type integer because 1 is an integer and the built-in operator + can be applied either to a pair of integers or to a pair of reals.

Explicit types are needed sometimes to resolve overloading, as in

```
fun add(x,y) = x + y;
    Error: overloaded variable "+" cannot be resolved
```

Any hint about the type of x, y, or x+y is enough for ML to infer the type of this function:

```
fun add(x,y):int = x + y;          (*  result is an integer  *)
    val add = fn : int * int -> int
fun add(x,y) = x + (y:int);        (*  y  is an integer  *)
    val add = fn : int * int -> int
```

Parametric Polymorphism

polymorphic functions have parameterized types

What is the type of an identity function I, which maps its argument to itself?

```
fun I(x) = x;
    val I = fn : 'a -> 'a
```

The leading quote in 'a identifies it as a type parameter. Type parameters 'a, 'b, ⋯ are written as the Greek letters α, β, ⋯ in publication notation. The type of I can be read as, "function from any type α to α." Indeed, I can be applied to integers, strings, and functions, and even to itself.

A *polymorphic* function can be applied to arguments of more than one type. We concentrate on *parametric polymorphism*, a special kind of polymorphism, in which type expressions are parameterized. An example is the type expression

$$\alpha \rightarrow \alpha$$

with parameter α. (Overloading, another kind of polymorphism, is sometimes referred to as *ad-hoc polymorphism*.)

Polymorphic functions arise naturally when lists are manipulated. All elements of a list must have the same type. If this type is 'a, then the type of the list itself is 'a list. A list of integers has type int list:

```
[0,1,2];
    val it = [0,1,2] : int list
```

A list of strings has type string list:

```
["zero", "one", "two"];
    val it = ["zero","one","two"] : string list
```

An example of a polymorphic function is

```
fun length(nil) = 0
|   length(a::y) = 1 + length(y);
      val length = fn : ('a list -> int)
```

Function length is defined by cases that are checked in sequence. If the argument is nil, then the length is 0. Otherwise, if the argument has the form a::y with head a and tail y, then its length is one greater than the length of y.

Now length can be applied to a list of strings:

```
length(["hello", "world"]);
    val it = 2 : int
```

or it can be applied to a list of elements of any other type

```
length([true, true]);
    val it = 2 : int
```

ML was one of the earliest languages to allow user-defined functions to be polymorphic. Templates in C++, Section 6.7, support polymorphism. The C++

standard library uses templates extensively to provide polymorphic library functions.

9.5 DATA TYPES

Datatype declarations in ML are useful for defining types corresponding to data structures. These types can then be used as readily and flexibly as built-in types.

For example, the list data structure explored in Sections 9.1 and 9.4 can be defined as a datatype. In this section, we consider datatypes corresponding to binary trees and arithmetic expressions.

The language provides ways for constructing values of new datatypes and for examing their structure. All other operations on datatypes have to be defined explicity, using functions.

Value Constructors

constants are value constructors

In its simplest form, a datatype declaration in ML introduces a basic type as a set of values. The declaration

$$\textbf{datatype} \quad direction \ = \ north \ | \ south \ | \ east \ | \ west$$

specifies a type *direction*. The set of values associated with this basic type is

$$\{\ north,\ south,\ east,\ west\ \}$$

These values are atomic; they are constants with no components. That is, the names *north, south, east, west* are constants that cannot be reused for other purposes, so they can belong only to the set of values associated with type *direction*.

Constants like *north* and *south* in a datatype declaration are special cases of "value constructors," considered next.

Value Constructors with Parameters

datatypes can be recursive

A datatype declaration introduces

1. A type name
2. A set of *value constructors* for creating values of that type

The value constructors can have parameters, as in the following declaration of datatype *bitree*:

$$\textbf{datatype} \quad bitree \ = \ leaf \ | \ nonleaf \ \textbf{of} \ bitree * bitree$$

To the right of the = sign in this declaration are two value constructors, *leaf* and *nonleaf*, separated by the | symbol. The constructor *leaf* is parameterless. The constructor *nonleaf* has a parameter, marked by keyword **of**. The parameter is

　　bitree ∗ bitree

Value constructors without parameters are also called constants.

In words, a value of type *bitree* is either the constant *leaf* or it is constructed by applying *nonleaf* to a pair of values of type *bitree*. This recursive definition specifies a set of values corresponding to binary trees like the following:

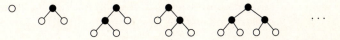

Open circles denote leaves, and filled circles denote nonleaf nodes with two subtrees.

Once the type *bitree* is declared, how do we refer to an element of its set of values? Value constructors can appear within expressions as constants if they are parameterless and as functions if they take parameters. Some trees and their corresponding expressions appear in Fig. 9.5.

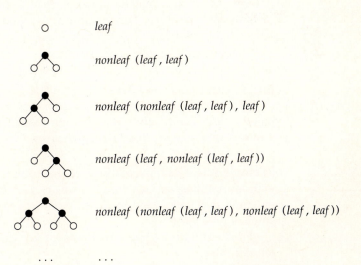

Figure 9.5　Some binary trees and their corresponding expressions.

Since the abstract syntax of expressions can be represented by trees, datatypes similar to *bitree* can be defined for abstract syntax. For example, expressions representing quilts in Section 8.1 either are *a*, *b*, or are formed by applying the operators *turn* and *sew* to subexpressions. The abstract syntax of such expressions is given by datatype *quiltsyntax*:

> **datatype** *quiltsyntax* = *a*
> | *b*
> | *turn* **of** *quiltsyntax*
> | *sew* **of** *quiltsyntax* ∗ *quiltsyntax*

Operations on Constructed Values

Patterns, introduced in Section 9.2 can be used to examine the structure of a constructed value. The patterns in the following function definition are *leaf* and *nonleaf*(*s*, *t*):

> **fun** *leafcount*(*leaf*) = 1
> | *leafcount*(*nonleaf*(*s*, *t*)) = *leafcount*(*s*) + *leafcount*(*t*);

The result of applying *leafcount* to *leaf* is 1. If *leafcount* is applied to a value constructed by *nonleaf* from trees represented by *s* and *t*, then the result is the sum of *leafcount*(*s*) and *leafcount*(*t*).

In more detail, the pattern *leaf* matches the constant *leaf* of type *bitree*. The pattern *nonleaf*(*s*, *t*) matches a value constructed by applying *nonleaf* to a pair of values of type *bitree*. For example, if function *leafcount* is applied to

> *nonleaf* (*leaf*, *nonleaf* (*leaf*, *leaf*))

then *s* matches *leaf* and *t* matches *nonleaf*(*leaf*, *leaf*).

A pattern has the form of an expression made up of variables, constants, pairs or tuples, and value constructors. List constructors considered in Section 9.1 are a special case of value constructors.

Example 9.12 Patterns allow us to manipulate the components of a datatype without defining explicit functions to extract the components. This example redefines *leafcount*, using explicit operations to examine the components of a value of type *bitree*.

Function *isleaf* returns **true** if a tree *t* is a leaf; otherwise, if *t* is a nonleaf, it returns **false**.

> **fun** *isleaf*(*leaf*) = **true**
> | *isleaf*(*nonleaf*(_)) = **false**;

Now, consider a nonleaf with two subtrees. Functions *left* and *right* extract the left and right subtrees of the tree:[2]

> **fun** *left*(*nonleaf*(*s*, *t*)) = *s*;
> **fun** *right*(*nonleaf*(*s*, *t*)) = *t*;

Operations *isleaf*, *left*, and *right* on binary trees are used to redeclare *leafcount*:

> **fun** *leafcount*(*x*) =
>   **if** *isleaf*(*x*) **then** 1
>   **else** *leafcount*(*left*(*x*)) + *leafcount*(*right*(*x*));

Whenever structured values are constructed, operations similar to *isleaf* are needed to classify values and operations similar to *left* and *right* are needed to extract components from the constructed values. Such operations can be defined explicitly, as in this example, or they can be applied implicitly, using patterns.   □

Differentiation: A Traditional Example

Symbolic differentiation of expressions like $x*(x+y)$ is a standard example for illustrating functional programming. We now consider a simple version to illustrate a datatype for representing expressions. Differentiation itself will be explored in Section 10.4, because it was one of the examples that shaped Lisp.

An expression is either a constant like 0, a variable like x, a sum like $x+y$, or a product like $x*y$. Datatype expr can be used to represent expressions:

```
datatype expr = constant of int
              | variable of string
              | sum of expr * expr
              | product of expr * expr;
```

The value constructor constant creates an expr out of an integer argument; note the type in the following value declarations of zero and one:

```
val zero = constant(0);
    val zero = constant 0 : expr
val one = constant(1);
    val one = constant 1 : expr
```

Similarly, the value constructor variable constructs an expr out of a string:

---

[2] The functions *left* and *right* are defined only for nonleaves. Evaluation of the expressions *left*(*leaf*) and *right*(*leaf*) raises an exception at run time.

```
val u = variable("u")
val v = variable("v")
val w = variable("v");
    val u = variable "u" : expr
    val v = variable "v" : expr
    val w = variable "v" : expr
```

A counterpart of the expression $v + (u*v)$ is

```
product (v, sum (u,v))
```

Let $d\ x\ E$ represent the derivative of expression E with respect to the variable x. The rules for differentiating an expression can be summarized as follows:

> **fun** $d\ x\ E =$
>   **if** E is a constant **then** 0
>   **else if** E is the variable x **then** 1
>   **else if** E is another variable **then** 0
>   **else if** E is the sum $E_1 + E_2$ **then** $d\ x\ E_1 + d\ x\ E_2$
>   **else if** E is the product $E_1 * E_2$ **then** $(d\ x\ E_1)*E_2 + E_1*(d\ x\ E_2)$

These rules motivate the definition by cases of function d in Fig. 9.6.

```
datatype expr = constant of int
              | variable of string
              | sum of expr * expr
              | product of expr * expr;

val zero = constant 0;
val one = constant 1;

fun d x (constant _) = zero
  | d (variable s) (variable t) = if s = t then one else zero
  | d x (sum (e1, e2)) = sum( d x e1, d x e2)
  | d x (product (e1, e2)) =
      let val term1 = product (d x e1, e2)
          val term2 = product (e1, d x e2)
      in sum (term1, term2)
      end;
```

Figure 9.6 A differentiation function in ML.

Value constructors are used in two ways by the differentiation function d in Fig. 9.6: for analyzing the structure of an expression and for constructing an expression. In words, the derivative of a constant is zero:

```
fun d x (constant _) = zero
```

The symbol _ stands for "don't care," and zero was just defined to be constant(0).

An instructive case in the definition of d is

```
|    d x (sum (e1, e2)) = sum( d x e1, d x e2)
```

In words, the subexpressions e1 and e2 are differentiated and their sum is returned. In more detail, On the left side of the = sign, the pattern sum(e1,e2) is used to extract subexpressions e1 and e2. On the right side, constructor sum converts the differentiated subexpressions d x e1 and d x e2 into the resulting expression that is returned.

Polymorphic Datatypes

datatypes can be recursive and polymorphic

Lists are polymorphic — that is, there can be lists of integers; lists of strings; lists of type α, for any type α. Such lists can be declared using type variables. Type variables are written using Greek letters like α and β in publication notation. Type variable α appears as a parameter in the following datatype declaration:

datatype α *List* = *Nil* | *Cons* **of** $\alpha * (\alpha \ List)$

Let us approach this declaration by exploring the desired behavior of constructors *Nil* and *Cons*, corresponding to [ ] and :: provided by ML.

The value constructor *Nil* must denote an empty list, independent of whether the list is of integers, reals, or strings, or of values of type α. Hence, the type of *Nil* can be described by

Nil : α *List*

Here, *List* is a type operator, because it is applied to a type parameter. Any type can be substituted for α. For example, in a list of integers, *Nil* has type **int** *List*.

The value constructor *Cons* must add an element to a list. For example, in *Cons*(1, *Nil*), *Cons* must construct a list with a single integer element 1. Here, *Cons* constructs an integer list of type **int** *List* from 1 of type **int** and *Nil*, which here has type **int** *List*. Hence, the parameters of *Cons* are a pair of type

> **int** ∗ (**int** *List*)

More generally, any type α can appear instead of **int**.

The following example revisits the declaration of the polymorphic datatype α *List*.

Example 9.13   In programs, type variables are written using a leading quote, as in ′a and ′b.

The following datatype declaration introduces List, Cons, and Nil, evident in the response from the ML:

```
datatype ′a List = Nil | Cons of ′a * (′a List);
    datatype ′a  List
    con Cons : ′a * ′a List -> ′a List
    con Nil : ′a List
```

The type operator List takes one parameter ′a.

The value constructor Cons takes a product of type

```
′a * ′a List
```

to the left of the -> symbol, and constructs an ′a List.

The value constructor Nil is a constant of type ′a List.

In the following expression, Cons constructs an integer list:

```
Cons(1, Nil);
    val it = Cons (1,Nil) : int List
```                                                                  □

Discussion

In their simplest form datatype declarations in ML correspond to enumerated types in a language like Pascal. An example from this section is

> **datatype** *direction = north | south | east | west*

In addition, datatypes are convenient for defining data structures like trees and expressions. This convenience results from the ability to define data types recursively. In the following declaration, the value constructor *nonleaf* recursively builds a binary tree from two binary trees. The constant *leaf* stops the recursion. The declaration is

> **datatype** *bitree = leaf | nonleaf* **of** *bitree* ∗ *bitree*

Finally, datatypes can be polymorphic. The following declaration introduces the type operator *List*, a variant of the list types in Sections 9.1–9.4:

datatype   α *List* = *Nil* | *Cons* **of** α * (α*List*)

9.6 EXCEPTION HANDLING IN ML

exceptions can be defined and raised

Exceptions are a mechanism for handling special cases or failures that occur during the execution of a program. For example, an empty list has no elements, so what is the head of an empty list?

```
hd [];
    uncaught exception Hd
```

Lisp programs often return the empty list to signal such cases; C programs often return 0.

The exception mechanism in ML allows failures to be made explicit. The simplest form of an exception declaration consists of the keyword **exception** followed by the name of an exception:

```
exception Nomatch;
    exception Nomatch : exn
```

An exception is *raised* by writing

raise ⟨*exception-name*⟩

Example 9.14 The following function `member` looks for an element `a` in a list `x` and raises exception `Nomatch` if the list is empty:

```
fun member(a, x) =
  if null(x) then raise Nomatch
  else if a = hd(x) then x
  else member(a, tl(x));
```

The normal behavior of `member` is to return the portion of a list from the first occurrence of `a` to the end:

```
member(3, [1,2,3,1,2,3]);
    val it = [3,1,2,3] : int list
```

The special case occurs in

```
member(4, []);
```
> *uncaught exception Nomatch*   □

Exceptions can be caught or handled by using the following syntax:

⟨*expression*⟩₁ **handle** ⟨*exception-name*⟩ ⟹ ⟨*expression*⟩₂

This construct behaves like ⟨*expression*⟩₁ except if ⟨*exception-name*⟩ is raised during the evaluation of ⟨*expression*⟩₁; control then passes to ⟨*expression*⟩₂ and its value is returned.

Example 9.15 Suppose that Oops and Other are exceptions:

```
exception Oops; exception Other;
```
> *exception Oops : exn*
> *exception Other : exn*

Since 2+3 evaluates to 5, the handler in the following construct is ignored and the construct behaves like 2+3:

```
2+3 handle Oops => 0;
```
> *val it = 5 : int*

Control flows to the exception handler in the following construct, so the result is 0:

```
(raise Oops) handle Oops => 0;
```
> *val it = 0 : int*

Finally, an exception handler for Oops has no effect on other exceptions:

```
(raise Other) handle Oops => 0;
```
> *uncaught exception Other*   □

Finding Handlers by Unwinding Function Calls

an exception handler is sought along the call chain

Exceptions are handled dynamically. If f calls g, g calls h, and h raises an exception, then we look for handlers along the call chain, h, g, f. The first handler along the chain catches the exception.

Example 9.16 Exception handling will be illustrated by writing an integer subtraction function that returns $m - n$ if $m \geq n$ and returns 0 otherwise.
    One of the building blocks is a function s that raises exception Neg instead of returning a negative result:

```
exception Neg;
    exception Neg : exn
fun s(m,n) : int =
  if m >= n then m-n else raise Neg;
    val s = fn : ((int * int) -> int)
s(5,3);
    val it = 2 : int
s(5,15);
    uncaught exception Neg
```

Function `subtract` provides a handler for exception `Neg`. If the exception is raised during the evaluation of `s(m,n)`, the handler returns 0 instead:

```
fun subtract(m,n) =
  s(m,n) handle Neg => 0;
    val subtract = fn : ((int * int) -> int)
subtract(5,3);
    val it = 2 : int
subtract(5,15);
    val it = 0 : int                                      □
```

Example 9.17 For a more realistic example of exceptions, consider a pattern-matching program that checks its first argument against a list of patterns in a database. Suppose that a function `match` checks a against an individual pattern and returns the pattern if they match; otherwise, the function raises exception `Nomatch`.

Function `fetch` tries the patterns in the database one by one:

```
fun fetch(a, nil) =
      raise Notfound
  | fetch(a, pat::rest) =
      match(a, pat) handle Nomatch => fetch(a, rest)
```

If the list of patterns is empty, then `fetch` raises exception `Notfound`. Otherwise, let the list of patterns be `pat::rest`. If `match(a,pat)` raises exception `Nomatch`, then `fetch` catches this exception and calls itself recursively to try the next pattern on the list.   □

9.7 LITTLE QUILT IN STANDARD ML

Since the syntax of Little Quilt is borrowed from ML, all we need to do to implement Little Quilt in ML is to define the four constants *a*, *b*, *sew*, and *turn*.

Thus, the ML interpreter can be taught Little Quilt by starting a session as follows:

```
(* definitions for a, b, sew, turn *)
val  a = ...;
val  b = ...;
fun  sew...;
fun  turn...;
(* any Little Quilt expression can be typed here *)
```

Such definitions appear in Fig. 9.7. These definitions pull together many of the concepts that have appeared in earlier sections. Here, we see how they work together.

```
datatype texture = arcs | bands;
datatype direction = ne | se | sw | nw;

type square = texture * direction;
type row = square list;
type quilt = row list;

fun clockwise ne = se
|    clockwise se = sw
|    clockwise sw = nw
|    clockwise nw = ne;

fun turnsq (tex, dir) = (tex, clockwise dir) : square;

fun emptyquilt ([]) = true
|    emptyquilt ([]::x) = emptyquilt (x:quilt)
|    emptyquilt (_) = false;

exception fail;

val a = [[ (arcs, ne) ]];
val b = [[ (bands, ne) ]];

fun sew([], []) : quilt = []
|    sew(r::x, s::y) = (r@s) :: sew(x,y)
|    sew(_) = raise fail;

fun turn x =
    if emptyquilt x then nil
    else rev (map (turnsq o hd) x) :: turn(map tl x);
```

Figure 9.7 Implementation of Little Quilt in Standard ML.

Some Auxiliary Functions

The helpful functions in Fig. 9.8 are used in the implementation of quilts. Although the three functions on lists — @, *rev*, and *map* — can be written using *null, hd, tl,* and *::*, ML provides them because they are useful building blocks for list manipulation.

The @ operator, pronounced "append," builds a list consisting of the elements of two lists:

$$[1, 2, 3] = [] @ [1, 2, 3] = [1] @ [2, 3] = [1, 2] @ [3] = [1, 2, 3] @ []$$

The expression *map f x* evaluates to a list formed by applying *f* to each element of the list *x*. For example,

$$map \ successor \ [1, 2, 3] \ = \ [2, 3, 4]$$

Function *rev* reverses the elements in a list:

$$rev \ [1, 2, 3] \ = \ [3, 2, 1]$$

The composition *g o f* of functions *g* and *f* is a function that satisfies the equality

$$(g \ o \ f) \ x \ = \ g(f(x))$$

In words, the result of applying *g o f* to *x* is equivalent to first applying *f* to *x* and then applying *g* to *f x*.

The concatenation function combines two strings into one:

$$"abc" \char94 "def" = "abcdef"$$

	symbol	usage	remark
append	@	*x @ y*	Append the elements of lists *x* and *y*.
reverse	*rev*	*rev x*	Reverse the order of the elements of list *x*.
map	*map*	*map f x*	Apply *f* to each element of list *x*.
compose	*o*	*g o f*	Compose functions *g* and *f*.
concatenate	^	*s ^ t*	Concatenate the strings *s* and *t*.

Figure 9.8 Some helpful ML functions.

Representation of Quilts

define a type quilt   Using the representation in Section 8.2, quilts are made up of individual square pieces with a texture described by the basic type

```
datatype texture = arcs | bands;
    datatype  texture
    con arcs : texture
    con bands : texture
```

The keyword **con** in the response stands for value constructor, or simply constructor.

The position of the dot in each square is described by the basic type

```
datatype direction = ne | se | sw | nw;
```

A quilt is represented as a list of rows, where a row is a list of squares, and a square has a texture and a direction.

```
type square = texture * direction;
type row = square list;
type quilt = row list;
```

The primitive quilts are called *a* and *b*:

```
val a = [[ (arcs, ne) ]];
    val a = [[(arcs,ne)]] : (texture * direction) list list
val b = [[ (bands, ne) ]];
    val b = [[(bands,ne)]] : (texture * direction) list list
```

Operation Sew

append the lists for corresponding rows   The effect of the *sew* operation on quilts is illustrated in Fig. 9.9. A quilt is represented as a list of rows, so *sew* can be implemented by appending the lists for the corresponding rows in the two operands of *sew*. The constraint that the two operands must have the same height translates into their representations having the same number of rows.

If r and s are two lists of the same type, then $r@s$ is the result of appending r and s; it is a list consisting of the elements of r followed by the elements of s. Suppose the first quilt has the form $r::x$, where r is the first row and x denotes the remaining rows, and the second quilt has the form $s::y$. Then, $r@s$ must be the first row of the sewn quilt:

$$sew(r::x, s::y) = (r@s) :: sew(x,y)$$

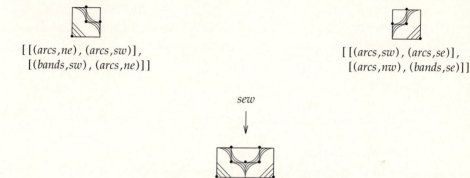

$[[(arcs,ne),(arcs,sw)],$
$\quad[(bands,sw),(arcs,ne)]]$

$[[(arcs,sw),(arcs,se)],$
$\quad[(arcs,nw),(bands,se)]]$

sew

$[[(arcs,ne),(arcs,sw),(arcs,sw),(arcs,se)],$
$\quad[(bands,sw),(arcs,ne),(arcs,nw),(bands,se)]]$

Figure 9.9   The *sew* operation on quilts can be implemented by appending the lists for their corresponding rows.

This equality is one of the cases in the implementation of *sew*. A function based on this equality recursively strips off the head or first rows. After all the rows have been considered, the remaining lists will both be empty, if the two quilts have the same height. Otherwise, an error is reported.

The implementation of *sew* reports an error if it is applied to two quilts of different heights. Exceptions will be used to stop execution; exception *fail* is declared by

```
exception fail;
    exception fail
```

Execution can be stopped by evaluating the expression **raise** *fail*.

Function *sew* is declared as follows:

```
fun sew([], []) = [] : quilt
  |   sew(r::x, s::y) = (r@s) :: sew(x,y)
  |   sew(_) = raise fail;
    val sew = fn : square list list * square list list -> square list list
```

Operation Turn

Since the *turn* operation does a lot of work on the representation, its implementation is surprisingly compact. We build up to its implementation by considering individual squares and individual rows before considering complete quilts.

Since a quilt is a list of rows, and a row is a list of squares, function *map* will be used again and again. Function *map* extends the processing of a single element to a list of elements. The expression

$$map\ f\ x$$

evaluates to a list formed by applying *f* to each element of the list *x*.

Turning a Square

turn a square by changing its direction

The turn operation affects each individual square in a quilt. The change in direction of a square is given by

```
fun clockwise ne = se
  |   clockwise se = sw
  |   clockwise sw = nw
  |   clockwise nw = ne;
    val clockwise = fn : direction -> direction
```

Individual squares can be turned by using the function *turnsq*:

```
fun turnsq (tex, dir) = (tex, clockwise dir) : square;
    val turnsq = fn : texture * direction -> square
```

Forming a Turned Row

Function *turn* builds the turned quilt a row at a time, as illustrated in Fig. 9.10.

The first column of a quilt, consisting of the head square in every row can be extracted by applying *hd* to each row — operation *hd* returns the head element of a list. Given quilt *x*, the expression *map hd x* denotes a list consisting of the first square in each row in *x*; see again Fig. 9.10.

Once the head squares are extracted, they can be turned by using *map* to apply *turnsq* to each element of the list. Thus, the expression

$$map\ turnsq\ (map\ hd\ x)$$

applies *hd* to extract the first square of each row and then applies *turnsq* to each square in the resulting list.

An alternative approach is to combine extraction and turning, using composition of functions. The composition of *turnsq* and *hd* can be used to extract the first square from a row and turn it.

$x =$
$$[\,[\,(arcs,ne)\,,\,(arcs,ne)\,,\,(bands,ne)\,,\,(bands,ne)\,]\,,$$
$$[\,(bands,ne)\,,\,(arcs,ne)\,,\,(arcs,ne)\,,\,(bands,ne)\,]\,,$$
$$[\,(bands,ne)\,,\,(bands,ne)\,,\,(arcs,ne)\,,\,(arcs,ne)\,]\,]$$

extract first square in every row

$map\ hd\ x =$
$$[\,(arcs,ne)\,,$$
$$(bands,ne)\,,$$
$$(bands,ne)\,]$$

turn the individual squares

$map\ (turnsq\ o\ hd)\ x =$
$$[\,(arcs,se)\,,$$
$$(bands,se)\,,$$
$$(bands,se)\,]$$

assemble row

$rev(map\ (turnsq\ o\ hd)\ x) =$
$$[\,(bands,se)\,,\,(bands,se)\,,\,(arcs,se)\,]$$

Figure 9.10   The leftmost column of a quilt turns into the top row.

$$(turnsq\ o\ hd)\ [\,(bands,ne)\,,\,(arcs,ne)\,,\,(bands,sw)\,]$$
$$=\ turnsq(\ hd\ [\,(bands,ne)\,,\,(arcs,ne)\,,\,(bands,sw)\,]\ )$$
$$=\ turnsq(\ (bands,ne)\ )$$
$$=\ (bands,se)$$

This operation on a single row can be extended to all rows in a quilt using *map*.

Turning a Quilt

The columns of a quilt turn into rows

Function *turn* is based on the following equality:

$$turn\ x = rev\ (map\ (turnsq\ o\ hd)\ x)\ ::\ turn\ (map\ tl\ x)$$

In words, a quilt x is turned by using

$$rev\ (map\ (turnsq\ o\ hd)\ x)$$

to build the first row of *turn x*. This expression extracts and turns the first element of each row of *x*; the resulting list of squares is then reversed using *rev*. The need for reversal can be seen from Fig. 9.10. Since the bottom-left corner of *x* corresponds to the top-left corner of *turn x*, the square extracted last from *x* becomes the first square in the top row of *turn x*.

The remaining rows of *turn x* are built by applying *turn* to what is left of quilt *x* after the head squares are extracted. This remaining quilt is *map tl x*, formed by applying *tl* to each row.

Repeated application of *tl* to a row results eventually in an empty list. Taking all the rows together, we eventually get a list of empty lists, as in

```
map tl [[(arcs,ne)], [(bands,ne)]];
    val it = [[],[]] : (texture * direction) list list
```

Thus, the recursive definition of *turn* must stop when it reaches such a list of empty lists. Function *emptyquilt* checks whether a quilt is empty:

```
fun emptyquilt ([]) = true
|   emptyquilt ([]::x) = emptyquilt (x:quilt)
|   emptyquilt (_) = false;
    val emptyquilt = fn : quilt -> bool
```

definition of turn

```
fun turn x =
    if emptyquilt x then nil
    else rev (map (turnsq o hd) x) :: turn(map tl x);
    val turn = fn : square list list -> square list list
```

Displaying a Quilt

use characters to encode squares

Now that quilts can be represented and manipulated, all that remains is to devise a way of displaying them. ML has a text-based interface, so quilts can be drawn by encoding squares using characters. One such encoding is illustrated in Fig. 9.11. Each square is displayed as a pair of strings spanning two lines.

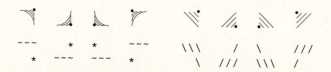

Figure 9.11   Squares encoded as pairs of strings on successive lines.

Function *encode* maps squares to pairs of strings:

```
fun encode (arcs, ne) = ("~~~", "  *")
 |  encode (arcs, se) = ("  *", "~~~")
 |  encode (arcs, sw) = ("*  ", "~~~")
 |  encode (arcs, nw) = ("~~~", "*  ")

 |  encode (bands, ne) = ("\\\\\\", "  \\")
 |  encode (bands, se) = ("  /", "///")
 |  encode (bands, sw) = ("\\  ", "\\\\\\")
 |  encode (bands, nw) = ("///", "/  ");
```
*val encode = fn : texture * direction -> string * string*

Rows will be output by concatenating the strings for the squares in the row. A pair of strings can be concatenated using the infix ^ operator. Concatenation can be extended to lists of strings, using function *reduce* from Section 9.3:

```
fun cat x = reduce op^ x "";
```

The notation op^ allows an infix operator to be treated as a prefix operator. That is, $s\char94 t$ is equivalent to **op**^(s, t).

The encoding of each square is a pair of strings. The following auxiliary functions extract the elements of a pair:

```
fun first (x,y) = x;
```
*val first = fn : 'a * 'b -> 'a*
```
fun second (x,y) = y;
```
*val second = fn : 'a * 'b -> 'b*

a row prints on two lines

Function *showrow* displays row *r* on two successive lines:

```
fun showrow(r) =
    let val encodings = map encode r
    in
      output (std_out, (cat (map first encodings)));
      output (std_out, "\n");
      output (std_out, (cat (map second encodings)));
      output (std_out, "\n")
    end;
```
*val showrow = fn : (texture * direction) list -> unit*

The list *encodings* in the body is built by applying *encode* to each square in row *r*. Each element of *encodings* is a pair of strings. With the help of *map*, function *first* extracts the first string in each pair; this list of strings is then concatenated and output. The name *std_out* denotes the standard output file. The string "\n" denotes an end-of-line. Similarly, the second line is output.

Function *show* applies *showrow* to each row in a quilt:

```
fun show (x:quilt) = map showrow x;
    val show = fn : quilt -> (unit) list
```

Expressions in Little Quilt

We are finally ready for the Little Quilt expressions from Section 8.1. The first expression describes the quilt:

The code is as follows:

```
fun unturn (x) = turn (turn (turn x))
fun pile (x, y) = unturn (sew (turn y, turn x))

val slice =
    let val aa = pile (a, turn (turn a))
        and bb = pile (unturn b, turn b)
    in let val p = sew (bb, aa)
            and q = sew (aa, bb)
       in pile (p, q)
       end
    end

val quilt1 =
        let val q = sew (slice, slice)
    in sew (q, slice)
    end;
```

The interpreter's response to this sequence of declarations is omitted. The effect of applying *show* to constructed quilt, however, is as follows:

```
show quilt1;
```

```
///~~~///~~~///~~~
/     */     */     *
   /*     /*     /*
///~~~///~~~///~~~
~~~///~~~///~~~///
  */     */     */
*     /*     /*     /
~~~///~~~///~~~///
val it = [(),(),(),()] : (unit) list
```

Here is the other quilt from Section 8.1:

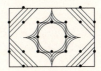

The code is as follows:

```
val quilt2 =
      let val bb = pile (turn b, unturn b)
          and ba = pile (unturn b, turn a)
   in let val c_nw = sew (bb, ba)
   in let val c_ne = turn c_nw
          and c_se = turn (turn c_nw)
          and c_sw = unturn c_nw
          and p = pile (turn a, unturn a)
          and q = pile (turn (turn a), a)
   in let val top = sew (sew (c_nw, p), sew (q, c_ne))
          and bot = sew (sew (c_sw, q), sew (p, c_se))
   in pile (top, bot)
   end end end end;
```

When *show* is applied to the constructed quilt, it produces:

```
show quilt2;
    ////   **   \\\\
   ////  ~~~~~~  \\\\
   ///  *~~~~~~*  \\\
  /   ~~~*    *~~~   \
  \   ~~~*    *~~~   /
   \\\  *~~~~~~*  ///
   \\\\  ~~~~~~  ////
    \\\\   **   ////
```

```
val it = [(),(),(),()] : (unit) list
```

Exercises

9.1 Using additional functions as needed, define the following functions:
   a. *member*(k, x) to determine whether k is in list x
   b. *least*(k, x) to return the smallest integer less than k in list x
   c. *less*(k, x) to create a list consisting of all integers in x that are less than k
   d. *adjacent*(x) to determine whether there are two adjacent occurrences of an element in list x

9.2 Write ML functions that compare adjacent list elements and respond with a list, as described in each case. The sample responses are all with the input list ["a", "b", "a", "a", "a", "c", "c"].
   a. Remove the second and succeeding adjacent duplicates, yielding ["a", "b", "a", "c"].
   b. Leave only the elements that are not repeated, yielding ["a", "b"].
   c. Leave only one copy of the repeated elements, yielding ["a", "c"].
   d. Count the number of repeated occurrences, yielding [(1, "a"), (1, "b"), (3, "a"), (2, "c")].

9.3 The following tail-recursive or iterative version of the *length* function uses an extra parameter in which it accumulates the result:

> **fun** *len*([ ], *res*) = *res*
> | *len*(a :: y, *res*) = *length*(y, 1+*res*)

For any list x, *length*(x) is equivalent to *len*(x,0). Use this technique to construct tail-recursive versions of the following functions:
   a. A function that adds together all the elements in a list
   b. A function that multiplies together all the elements in a list
   c. The factorial function

9.4 Implement a variant of Quicksort for lists. That is, sort a list as follows. Pick an element and call it the pivot. Partition the list into two sublists of elements smaller than and larger than the pivot. Recursively sort the sublists. Combine the sorted sublists and the pivot together into a sorted list.
   a. Define a function that sorts lists of integers.
   b. Define a function that takes two arguments: a predicate p for comparing elements and a list of elements to be sorted.

9.5 Suppose that sets are implemented as lists, where each element of a set appears exactly once in its list. Define functions that implement the following operations:
   a. Test whether an element is a member of a set.

   b. Construct the union of two sets.
   c. Construct the intersection of two sets.
   d. Construct the difference of two sets — that is, the set of elements
   that are in the first set but not in the second.
   e. How would your implementations change if sets were implemented
   by sorted lists without repeated elements?

9.6 Suppose that sets are implemented as lists and that the union of two
   sets is implemented by simply appending their lists. Note that the
   same element can appear more than once in the list for a set. Implement the member, intersection, and difference operations on sets.

9.7 With functions *append* and *reverse* defined in Fig. 9.4 on page 352, how
   are the following expressions evaluated:
   a. *append*([5, 6, 7], [8, 9])
   b. *append*([1, 2, 3], [])
   c. *reverse*([1, 2, 3], [])
   d. *reverse*([5, 6, 7], [8, 9])

9.8 With function *reduce* defined in Fig. 9.4, what is the value of the following expressions? Explain.
   a. *reduce add* [1, 2, 3, 4] 0, where *add*(x,y) adds integers x and y.
   b. *reduce multiply* [1, 2, 3, 4] 1, where *multiply*(x,y) multiplies integers x and y.

9.9 Suppose matrices are represented as lists of lists, as in Example 9.7 on
   page 354. Use the representation to implement the following operations on matrices:
   a. Add corresponding elements of two matrices.
   b. Transpose a matrix, so element i,j of the original becomes element
   j,i of the result matrix.
   c. Multiply two matrics.

9.10 Fill in the blanks in the following equivalences (see Section 9.3 for
   properties of the functions):
   a. *reduce* ___ x ___ ≡ *length*(x)
   b. *reduce* ___ x ___ ≡ *append*(x, z)
   c. *reduce* ___ x ___ ≡ *remove* – *if* f x
   d. *reduce* ___ x ___ ≡ *map* f x

9.11 Pattern matching and transformation rules occur frequently in symbolic computation. "Conversations" like the one in Fig. 9.12 (responses
   are in italics) can be generated using the patterns and corresponding
   response templates of Fig. 9.13. The blank spaces in a pattern, denoted
   by subscripted dashes, can be filled in with any sequence of words. A
   single word is filled in for *single*. Write a program that uses patterns

```
well my friend made me come here
     tell me about your friend

he says i am depressed
     i am sorry to hear you are depressed

i think i need help
     in what way

oh am i making sense so far
     do you believe you are making sense so far

you are making fun of me
     why do you think i are making fun of you
```

Figure 9.12   Responses generated using pattern matching.

and response templates to simulate a conversation.

9.12   Define a function to print values of datatype `expr` in Fig. 9.6 on page 364 in infix notation.

9.13   Describe how function *show* on page 378 displays the quilt corresponding to *sew(a, sew(b,a))*.

9.14   Suppose that function *explode* maps a string into a list of its characters and that function *implode* maps a list of characters into a corresponding string. Use *explode* and *implode* to implement string concatenation.

pattern	*response template*
── $_1$ my *single* ── $_2$ me ── $_3$	*tell me about your single*
── $_1$ i am ── $_2$	*i am sorry to hear you are* ── $_2$
── $_1$ am i ── $_2$	*do you believe you are* ── $_2$
── $_1$ you ── $_2$ me	*why do you think i* ── $_2$ *you*
── $_1$	*in what way*

Figure 9.13   Patterns and response templates for Exercise 9.11.

Bibliographic Notes

Textbooks on ML include Ullman [1994] and Paulson [1991].

ML began as the programming language for a machine-assisted system for formal proofs. The application to proofs motivated the emphasis on type checking. Milner, Tofte, and Harper [1990] is the defining document for Standard ML, the language used in this book. The composite report by Harper, MacQueen, and Milner [1986] includes a tutorial on the language and a preliminary description of the module facility. Modules in ML are much more general than the modules considered in Chapter 6.

As part of the early history of Lisp, McCarthy [1981] recalls the role of differentiation in motivating the following: recursive functions defined using conditional expressions, a version of *map*, the use of the lambda notation of Church [1941] to write anonymous functions, and garbage collection. "No solution [for erasure of abandoned list structure] was apparent at the time, but the idea of complicating the elegant definition of differentiation with explicit erasure was unattractive."

Exercise 9.11 is based on a program called Eliza by Weizenbaum [1966]. Eliza conversed by simply rearranging the sentences that were presented to it. Weizenbaum [1976], "was startled to see how quickly and how deeply people conversing with [Eliza] became emotionally involved" in the interchange. They talked to Eliza as if it were a person, even when they knew it to be a program.

10

Functional Programming with Lists

We shall first define a class of symbolic expressions in terms of ordered pairs and lists. Then we shall define five elementary functions and predicates, and build from them by composition, conditional expressions and recursive definitions an extensive class of functions of which we shall give a number of examples. We shall then show how these functions can themselves be expressed as symbolic expressions, and we shall give a universal function *apply* that allows us to compute from the expression for a given function its value for given arguments. Finally, we shall define some functions with functions as arguments and give some useful examples.

  – McCarthy [1960], introducing Lisp. The five elementary functions and predicates are atom, eq, car, cdr, *and* cons.

The basic concepts of functional programming originated with Lisp, designed in 1958 by John McCarthy, and probably the second oldest major language after Fortran. It is surely the first to provide recursion, first-class functions, garbage collection, and a formal language definition (in Lisp itself). Lisp implementations also led the way in integrated programming environments, which combine editors, interpreters, and debuggers.

Lisp began as a niche language because its initial implementations were inefficient. In the early 1960s, Lisp was "ultraslow" for numerical computations. Good implementations are now available.

Functional languages in general, and Lisp in particular, have played a special role in language definition. A language definition must itself be written in some notation, called a *metalanguage* or *defining language*, and defining languages tend to be functional. In fact, the first implementation of Lisp arose, almost by accident, when Lisp was used to define itself.

Language definition is the subject of Chapter 13. This chapter introduces the Lisp family of languages, using Scheme, a dialect of Lisp.

A fundamental difference between Standard ML and Scheme is that ML is strongly typed and Scheme is untyped. Otherwise, both are lexically scoped, treat functions as first-class values, rely on implicit storage management, and can be used to solve the same problems. All of the Scheme examples in this chapter can be restated in ML without changing their spirit.

10.1   SCHEME, A DIALECT OF LISP

This section introduces a functional subset of Scheme; we stay away from assignments. The list data structure is explored in Section 10.2, and functions are considered further in Section 10.3. We get started with the following:

How to interact with a Scheme interpreter

How to write an expression

How to define a function

We then cover

Conditionals

The let construct

Quoting, which allows expressions to be treated as data

Fig. 10.1 summarizes some of the constructs used in this chapter. ML counterparts of the constructs are included as comments.

Why Scheme?

Scheme is a relatively small language that provides constructs at the core of Lisp. It has two characteristics that make it especially suited for this chapter: true first-class functions and lexical scope. Earlier Lisps did not fully support first-class functions, and they used dynamic scope rules, which leave a program sensitive to the choice of local names within functions.

How to Interact with a Scheme Interpreter

A good way to learn Scheme is to interact with an interpreter and study its responses. We consider two kinds of interactions with Scheme:

1. Supply an expression to be evaluated.
2. Bind a name to a value.

Note that a value can be a function.

A transcript of an interactive session with an interpreter winds through this section. Responses from the interpreter will consistently be indented and shown in italics. When we type

```
(define pi 3.14159)                 ; give name pi to 3.14159

(define (sq x) (* x x))             ; fun sq(x) = x * x

(define sq (lambda (x) (* x x)))    ; fun sq(x) = x * x

(lambda (x) (* x x))                ; anonymous function value
                                    ;     parameter x, body x * x

(* E₁ E₂)                           ; E₁ * E₂

(E₁ E₂ E₃)                          ; apply the value of E₁ as a
                                    ;     function to arguments E₂ and E₃

(if P E₁ E₂)                        ; if P then E₁ else E₂

(cond (P₁ E₁) (P₂ E₂) (else E₃))    ; if P₁ then E₁
                                    ; else if P₂ then E₂
                                    ; else E₃

(let ((x₁ E₁) (x₂ E₂)) E₃)          ; evaluate E₁ and E₂; then
                                    ;     evaluate E₃ with x₁ and x₂
                                    ;     bound to their values

(let* ((x₁ E₁) (x₂ E₂)) E₃)         ; let val x₁ = E₁
                                    ;     val x₂ = E₂
                                    ; in E₃
                                    ; end

(quote blue)                        ; symbol blue

(quote (blue green red))            ; list (blue green red)

(list E₁ E₂ E₃)                     ; list of the values of E₁, E₂, E₃
```

Figure 10.1   Some Scheme constructs.

```
3.14159                             ; a number evaluates to itself
```

the interpreter responds with

```
3.14159
```

Comments begin with a semicolon and continue to the end of the line.
Name pi is bound to 3.14159 by

```
(define pi 3.14159)     ; bind a variable to a value
    pi
```

Now pi evaluates to 3.14159:

```
pi                                      ;  a variable evaluates to its value
    3.14159
```

*pi, Pi, pI, PI
are all the same
name*

Within names, Scheme ignores the distinction between uppercase and lower-case letters, so `pi`, `Pi`, `pI`, and `PI` are all the same name:

```
pI                                      ;  respond with value bound to pi
    3.14159
```

Names in Scheme can contain special characters but not parentheses, as in `long-name`, `research!emlin`, and `back-at-5:00pm`. In general, a name can begin with any character that cannot begin a number.

How to Write an Expression

*an expression is a
list formed by an
operator and its
operands*

Dialects of Lisp, including Scheme, use a form of prefix notation for expressions in which parentheses surround an operator and its operands. The arithmetic expression 5 * 7 is written as

```
(* 5 7)
    35
```

The general form of an expression in Scheme is

$$(E_1 \ E_2 \ \cdots \ E_k)$$

Here, expression E_1 represents an operator to be applied to the values of $E_2, \ldots, E_k$. The order of evaluation of the subexpressions $E_1, E_2, \ldots, E_k$ is unspecified; however, all the subexpressions are evaluated before the value of E_1 is applied to its operands. In other words, Scheme uses innermost or call-by-value evaluation.

Arithmetic expressions with several operators can be translated into Scheme by following their subexpression structure. The expression 4 + 5 * 7 is the sum of 4 and 5 * 7:

```
(+ 4 (* 5 7))
    39
```

The uniform use of parenthesized prefix notation gives Lisp its unique syntax, leading to irreverent remarks such as "LISP stands for Lots of Silly Parentheses." The parentheses, however, do have a silver lining: The uniformity of Lisp syntax makes it easy to manipulate programs as data.

How to Define a Function

define supports recursive functions

The following syntax is used to define recursive and nonrecursive functions:

    (define (⟨function-name⟩ ⟨formal-parameters⟩) ⟨expression⟩)

An example is

    (define (square x) (* x x))   ; **fun** *square*(*x*) = *x* * *x*
        square
    (square 5)   ; *apply function square to 5*
        25

This definition associates a function value with name `square`. The function takes a parameter and multiplies the parameter by itself.

Anonymous Function Values

lambda notation supports function values

Scheme provides the notation

    (lambda (⟨formal-parameters⟩) ⟨expression⟩)

for an unnamed function value. Thus, a function with formal parameter x and body (* x x) is written as

    (lambda (x) (* x x))

The tradition of using `lambda` to write functions goes back to Church's lambda calculus, discussed in Chapter 14.

Now `square` can be defined by

    (define square (lambda (x) (* x x)))
        square

Scheme allows an unnamed function to appear in the operator position in an expression:

    (square 5)
        25
    ((lambda (x) (* x x)) 5)   ; *unnamed function applied to 5*
        25

Further examples of the use of `lambda` appear in Section 10.4.

The benefit of lambda notation is that a function value can appear within expressions, either as an operator or as an argument. The lack of a function name, however, means that recursion is not supported directly, since there is no name that can be used to call the function recursively from the function body.

Conditionals

conditionals have two forms: if and cond

The boolean values **true** and **false** are written as #t and #f, respectively. Within conditional expressions, only #f is treated as false; all other values are treated as true.[1]

Predicates are expressions that evaluate to true or false. By convention, the names of Scheme predicates end in "?," as in

number?   Test whether argument is a number.
symbol?   Test whether argument is a symbol.
equal?   Test whether arguments are structurally equal.

Conditional expressions come in two forms. One form is

(if P E_1 E_2)   ; if P then E_1 else E_2

The other form corresponds to a sequential choice:

(cond (P_1 E_1)   ; if P_1 then E_1
      ...   ; ...
      (P_k E_k)   ; else if P_k then E_k
      (else E_{k+1}))   ; else E_{k+1}

Conditionals are needed for recursive functions, such as the following definition of the factorial function:

(define (fact n)   ; **fun** *fact*(n) =
   (if (= n 0)   ;   **if** $n = 0$
       1   ;   **then** 1
       (* n (fact (- n 1)))))   ;   **else** $n * fact(n - 1)$

The Let Construct

let* is the sequential variant

The syntax of the let construct is

(let ((x_1 E_1) (x_2 E_2) ... (x_k E_k)) F)

Its value is determined as follows. The expressions $E_1, E_2, ..., E_k$ are all evaluated. Then expression F is evaluated, with x_i representing the value of E_i. The result is the value of F.

The let construct allows subexpressions to be named. The expression

[1] Following Lisp tradition, some Scheme implementations treat () as being equivalent to #f.

```
(+ (square 3) (square 4))
   25
```

can be rewritten as follows, with name `three-sq` for `(square 3)` and `four-sq` for `(square 4)`:

```
(let ((three-sq (square 3))
      (four-sq (square 4)) )
  (+ three-sq four-sq) )
   25
```

The `let` construct can also be used to factor out common subexpressions. The recomputation of the common subexpression `(square 3)` in

```
(+ (square 3) (square 3))
   18
```

can be avoided by rewriting the expression as

```
(let ((three-sq (square 3)))
  (+ three-sq three-sq) )
   18
```

A sequential variant of the `let` construct is written with keyword `let*`. Unlike `let`, which evaluates all the expressions $E_1, E_2, \ldots, E_k$ before binding any of the variables, `let*` binds x_i to the value of E_i before E_{i+1} is evaluated. The syntax is

$$(\texttt{let*}\ ((x_1\ E_1)\ (x_2\ E_2)\ \cdots\ (x_k\ E_k))\ F)$$

The distinction between `let` and `let*` can be seen from the responses in

```
(define x 0)
   x
(let ((x 2) (y x)) y)      ; bind y before redefining x
   0
(let* ((x 2) (y x)) y)     ; bind y after redefining x
   2
```

Quoting

a quoted item evaluates to itself   Quoting is needed to treat expressions as data. A quoted item evaluates to itself. Quoting syntax will be introduced by considering symbols.

A *symbol* is an object with a spelling. Quoting is used to choose whether a spelling is treated as a symbol or as a variable name.

An item can be quoted in one of two equivalent ways:

```
(quote ⟨item⟩)
'⟨item⟩
```

Unquoted, `pi` is a variable name, bound to a value:

```
pi
    3.14159
```

We can treat `pi` as the spelling of a symbol by quoting it:

```
(quote pi)
    pi
'pi
    pi
```

Unquoted, `*` represents the multiplication function:

```
(define f *)                          ;  defines f to be a function
    f
(f 2 3)
    6
```

Quoted, `'*` represents the symbol with spelling `*`:

```
(define f '*)                         ;  defines f to be a symbol
    f
(f 2 3)
    ERROR: Bad procedure *
```

Scheme refers to functions as procedures.

10.2 THE STRUCTURE OF LISTS

Programs and data look alike in Lisp dialects. Both are represented as lists.

List Elements

parentheses enclose list elements

A *list* is a sequence of zero or more values. Any value can be a list element. Among potential list elements in Scheme are booleans, numbers, symbols, other lists, and functions (also permitted, although not considered in this chapter, are characters, strings, and vectors).

A list is written by enclosing its elements within parentheses. The *empty* or *null* list, with zero elements, is written as ().[2] The list

```
(it seems that)
```

has the symbols it, seems, and that as its three elements. The list

```
((it seems that) you (like) me)
```

has four elements, the first and third of which are lists.

Parentheses are important: like is a symbol, but (like) is a list with one element.

The structure of a list can be seen more easily from a tree representation, such as the one in Fig. 10.2 for the following lists:

```
(it seems that you like me)
((it seems that) you (like) me)
```

The relationship between lists and trees is made precise later in this section.

Note that the list

```
(a ())
```

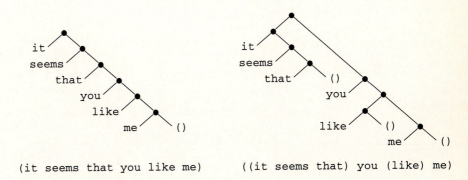

(it seems that you like me)   ((it seems that) you (like) me)

Figure 10.2   Examples of lists.

[2] Other Lisp dialects treat nil as a synonym for (), but Scheme treats nil as a name that can be bound to something else, if desired.

has two elements, the first, a, being a symbol, and the second, (), being the empty list. Thus, (a) with just one element a differs from (a ()).

Is (+ 2 3) an expression or a list? The answer is both. The Scheme interpreter treats

```
(+ 2  3)
    5
```

as an expression and responds with its value. Quoting tells the interpreter to treat (+ 2 3) as a list:

```
'(+ 2  3)
   (+ 2  3)
```

A leading single quote is sufficient to say that the construct immediately following the quote stands for itself:

```
'(no quotes at (nested levels))
   (no quotes at (nested levels))
```

The matching closing parenthesis delimits the construct affected by a leading single quote.

Operations on Lists

car extracts the head, cdr the tail

With any grouping of elements, operations are needed to inspect the elements and to construct a new grouping. So it is with lists. The basic operations on lists are summarized in Fig. 10.3.

Lists in Scheme are written between parentheses (and), with white space separating list elements. The empty list is written as (). The operations on lists are

(null? x)   True if x is the empty list and false otherwise.

(car x)   The first element of a nonempty list x.

(cdr x)   The rest of the list x after the first element is removed.

(cons a x)   A value with car a and cdr x; that is,

$$
\begin{array}{l}
\text{(car (cons a x)) = a} \\
\text{(cdr (cons a x)) = x}
\end{array}
$$

Figure 10.3   Lists in Scheme.

The predicate `null?` returns true if it is applied to the empty list, and false otherwise:

```
(null? ())
    #t
```

Note that `nil` need not be a synonym for `()`. The Scheme interpreter used for this book does not recognize it as the empty list:

```
(null? nil)
    #f
```

The operations for extracting the components of a nonempty list are `car` and `cdr` (pronounced "could-er"); these names are part of the Lisp tradition. Car extracts the head, or first element, of a nonempty list. Cdr extracts the tail, consisting of all but the first element. These operations are applied in Fig. 10.4 to a list `x` defined by

```
(define x '((it seems that) you (like) me))
    x
```

The first line of Fig. 10.4 shows list `x`. The remaining lines use `car` and `cdr` to take `x` apart. For ease of comparison, the expressions in the figure are written so that their `x`s line up.

Lisp provides a shorthand for expressions like

```
(car (cdr x))
```

consisting of successive applications of `car` and `cdr`. This expression can be abbreviated and written as `(cadr x)` using a single operator `cadr` formed by

expression	shorthand	value
x	x	((it seems that) you (like) me)
(car x)	(car x)	(it seems that)
(car (car x))	(caar x)	it
(cdr (car x))	(cdar x)	(seems that)
(cdr x)	(cdr x)	(you (like) me)
(car (cdr x))	(cadr x)	you
(cdr (cdr x))	(cddr x)	((like) me)

Figure 10.4 Use of `car` and `cdr` to take list `x` apart.

writing an opening c, a sequence of as and ds corresponding, from left to right, to the original `car` and `cdr` operators, and a trailing r.

The `cons` operation builds lists; (`cons a x`) creates a value with head a and tail x. An alternative "dotted" notation for (`cons a x`) is (`a . x`).

The dots in the tree representation

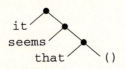

of list (`it seems that`) correspond to `cons` operations. These operations appear explicitly as dots in

```
'(it . (seems . (that . ())))
    (it seems that)
```

More precisely, a `cons` operation builds a *pair*, sometimes called a *dotted pair*, from its operands. The name *list* is reserved for a chain of pairs ending in an empty list; that is, x is a list if repeated application of `cdr` eventually results in the empty list ().

A list with several elements can alternatively be built by applying the `list` operator to the elements. Thus,

```
(list 'it 'seems 'that)
    (it seems that)
```

is equivalent to

```
(cons 'it (cons 'seems (cons 'that '())))
    (it seems that)
```

10.3   LIST MANIPULATION

The list data structure in Lisp is accompanied by a number of useful functions that are part of the lore and are often provided as library functions. These functions are in addition to basic functions like `car`, `cdr`, and `cons` for dealing with the structure of lists. Some useful functions appear in Fig. 10.5. All have short definitions, so they can be readily added or adapted, as needed. Although ML counterparts of these functions appear in Section 9.3, the examples and the notation in this section are different enough that it is worth considering the functions again.

List manipulation will be illustrated in this section by applying functions like the ones in Fig. 10.5 to list representations of expressions and dictionaries.

```
(define (length x)
  (cond ((null? x) 0)
        (else (+ 1 (length (cdr x)))) ))

(define (rev x z)
  (cond ((null? x) z)
        (else (rev (cdr x) (cons (car x) z))) ))

(define (append x z)
  (cond ((null? x) z)
        (else (cons (car x) (append (cdr x) z))) ))

(define (map f x)
  (cond ((null? x) '())
        (else (cons (f (car x)) (map f (cdr x)))) ))

(define (remove-if f x)
  (cond ((null? x) '())
        ((f (car x)) (remove-if f (cdr x)))
        (else (cons (car x) (remove-if f (cdr x)))) ))

(define (reduce f x v)
  (cond ((null? x) v)
        (else (f (car x) (reduce f (cdr x) v))) ))
```

Figure 10.5 Functions for list manipulation. ML counterparts of these functions appear in Fig. 9.4 on page 352.

A Useful Function

For practice with functions on lists, let us begin with length.

The length of an empty list is 0. The length of a nonempty list (cons a y) is 1 greater than the length of y. These observations can be restated as the equations

```
(length '())          ≡ 0
(length (cons a y)) ≡ (+ 1 (length y))
```

The equation for the nonempty list can alternatively be written as

```
(length x) ≡ (+ 1 (length (cdr x)))
```

where x is the list (cons a y) and (cdr x) is y.

These equations motivate the following definition:

```
(define (length x)
  (cond ((null? x) 0)
        (else (+ 1 (length (cdr x)))) ))
```

Appending Two Lists

The append function creates a new list consisting of the elements of its two arguments, as in the following examples:

```
(append '() '(a b c d))
   (a b c d)
(append '(a b c) '(d))
   (a b c d)
```

Function append can be implemented by considering the elements of the first list, one at a time. In the following expression, element a is pulled out of the first list (a b c) and becomes the head element of the result:

```
(cons 'a (append '(b c) '(d)))
   (a b c d)
```

This idea can be stated using equalities, as follows:

```
(append '() z)            ≡ z
(append (cons a y) z) ≡ (cons a (append y z))
```

Again, the second equality can be rewritten as

```
(append x z) ≡ (cons (car x) (append (cdr x) z))
```

These equalities motivate the code for append from Fig. 10.5:

```
(define (append x z)
  (cond ((null? x) z)
        (else (cons (car x) (append (cdr x) z))) ))
```

Example 10.1 We get a *flattened* form of a list if we ignore all but the initial opening and final closing parenthesis in the written representation of a list. The flattened form of

```
((a) ((b b)) (((c c c))))
```

is

```
(a b b c c c)
```

Alternatively, the flattened form can be thought of as the list read off the leaves of a tree representation of a list.

Function `flatten` constructs a flattened list by flattening the car and flattening the cdr of a list and appending the resulting sublists:

```
(define (flatten x)
    (cond ((null? x) x)
          ((not (pair? x)) (list x))
          (else (append (flatten (car x))
                        (flatten (cdr x)) ))))
```

The empty list is returned as itself. The Scheme function `pair?` tests whether its argument is a lis — specifically, whether it is a cons pair. If argument `x` is not a pair, then `flatten` constructs a list consisting of `x`. The remaining case is the one in which two sublists are flattened and appended.

□

Mappping a Function Across List Elements

map extends functions from elements to lists

A function `f` that can be applied to a single list element can be extended using map and applied to all elements of a list. A simple example is a function `square` that multiplies an integer by itself:

```
(define (square n) (* n n))
```

Now, `square` can be applied to each element of a list of integers:

```
(map square '(1 2 3 4 5))
    (1 4 9 16 25)
```

In the following example, map is used to extend car from lists to lists of lists. Let a *pair* be a list of two elements, such as `(a 1)`. When car is applied to this pair, the result is `a`. With the help of map, we can use car to extract the first element from each pair:

```
(map car '((a 1) (b 2) (c 3) (d 4)))
    (a b c d)
```

The behavior of map is described by the following equations:

$$(\text{map } f \ '()) \equiv '()$$
$$(\text{map } f \ (\text{cons } a \ y)) \equiv (\text{cons } (f \ a) \ (\text{map } f \ y))$$

Here is a corresponding definition of map:

```
(define (map f x)
  (cond ((null? x) '())
        (else (cons (f (car x)) (map f (cdr x)))) ))
```

map can handle more than one list   A standard Scheme extension is to allow map to apply a function to corresponding elements of $k \geq 1$ lists. In

```
(map f x y z)
```

the three-argument function f is applied to the corresponding elements of the lists x, y, and z.

For example, the expression (map list x y) applies list to the corresponding elements of x and y. In

```
(map list '(a b c) '(1 2 3))
   ((a 1) (b 2) (c 3))
```

the function list is applied to a and 1, yielding the list (a 1), to b and 2, yielding the list (b 2), and to c and 3, yielding the list (c 3).

Association Lists

an association list holds key-value pairs   An *association list*, or simply *a-list*, is a list of pairs. Association lists are a traditional implementation of dictionaries and environments, which map a key to an associated value. They can be used to map a variable to an associated value. Each element of an a-list is an association or binding, consisting of a key and a value. The association list

```
((a 1) (b 2) (c 3) ··· )
```

implements an environment that binds a to 1, binds b to 2, and so on.

It is convenient to have three operations on association lists:

1. bind returns an association list with a new binding for a key.
2. bind-all binds keys in a list keys to values in a corresponding list values.
3. assoc returns the most recent binding for a key.

As in Fig. 10.6, bind places a binding at the head of an association list.

```
(define (bind key value env)
  (cons (list key value) env))
```

The code for bind-all is illustrated in Fig. 10.7.

```
(bind 'a 1 env)      =
```

Figure 10.6 Function `bind` adds a single binding to an association list.

```
(define (bind-all keys values env)
   (append (map list keys values) env) )
```

In words, `map` applies `list` to corresponding elements of the two lists `keys` and `values`. If `keys` is `(a b c)` and `values` is `(1 2 3)`, then

```
(map list keys values)
```

yields

```
((a 1) (b 2) (c 3))
```

This list is then appended onto `env`.

Operation `assoc` is supported directly by Scheme; it extracts the first binding for a variable from an a-list, as in

```
(assoc 'a '((a 1) (b 2) (a 3)))
   (a 1)
```

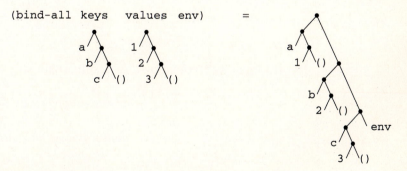

Figure 10.7 Function `bind-all` extends an association list.

```
(assoc 'b '((a 1) (b 2) (a 3)))
   (b 2)
```

If no binding is found, `assoc` returns false.

Lists of Subexpressions

(+) evaluates to 0, and (*) evaluates to 1

Lisp dialects, including Scheme, allow + and * to take a list of arguments. An expression is represented as a list in which the first element is the operator, as in

```
(+ 2 3)              ; 2+3 = 5
   5
```

The list representation also allows

```
(+ 2 3 5)            ; 2+3+5 = 10
   10
```

The function `map` was motivated by the need to manipulate lists of subexpressions in sums and products in a 1958 program, similar to the differentiation program in Section 10.4. McCarthy [1981] recalls that `map` "was obviously wanted for differentiating sums of arbitrarily many subterms, and with a slight modification, it could be applied to differentiating products."

What happens if a sum or product has just one subterm, or no subterm? Any representation must do something sensible in such cases. A sum or a product consisting of just one subexpression is equivalent to that subexpression itself:

```
(+ 2)                ; 2 = 2
   2
(* 2)                ; 2 = 2
   2
```

If there are no subexpressions, the result is 0 for sums and 1 for products:

```
(+)                  ; adding nothing yields  0
   0

(*)                  ; multiplying nothing yields  1
   1
```

Example 10.2   When applied to a list of two or more subexpressions, function `proper-sum` builds a sum by consing a + onto the list, as in

```
(proper-sum '(a b c))
   (+ a b c)
```

When applied to the empty list, it returns 0, and when applied to a list with one element, it returns the element itself:

```
(define (proper-sum x)   ;; x is a list
  (cond ((null? x) 0)
        ((null? (cdr x)) (car x))
        (else (cons '+ x)) ))
```

A similar function can be defined for products.

A Parameterized Function

Statements like "a similar function . . ." are a hint that a single parameterized function might do the job. With sums and products, the default case is to cons an operator onto a list of subexpressions, as in

```
(define (make-sum x) (cons '+ x))
(define (make-product x) (cons '* x) )
```

Now a single function `proper` with suitable parameters can be used to build a sum

```
(proper make-sum 0 '(a b c))
   (+ a b c)
```

or a product

```
(proper make-product 1 '(a b c))
   (* a b c)
```

The empty list and the list of one subexpression are handled properly:

```
(proper make-sum 0 '())
   0
(proper make-product 1 '(a))
   a
```

The definition for function `proper` is as follows:

```
(define (proper make-kind id x)
  (cond ((null? x) id)
```

```
        ((null? (cdr x)) (car x))
        (else (make-kind x)) ))
```
                                                              □

10.4   A MOTIVATING EXAMPLE: DIFFERENTIATION

Several of Lisp's, and hence Scheme's, characteristic features were motivated by the problem of differentiating expressions like $x * (x + y + z)$. The differentiation program in this section illustrates the following:

- Syntax-directed translation
- The representation of expressions as data
- The use of higher-order functions

The expressions produced by the differentiation program will be simplified by applying rules of the following form:

$$x + 0 = x$$
$$x * 1 = x$$
                                                              (10.1)

This section concludes with a small expression simplifier; in general, simplification is a difficult problem.

Syntax-Directed Differentiation

pairs of functions,
one to check
syntax, one to do
the work

What might a differentiation program look like? The following pseudocode uses the syntax of expression E to compute the derivative of E with respect to variable x.

> **fun** $d(x, E) =$
>   **if** E is a constant **then** $\cdots$
>   **else if** E is a variable **then** $\cdots$
>   **else if** E is the sum $E_1 + E_2 + \cdots + E_k$ **then** $\cdots$
>   **else if** E is the product $E_1 * E_2 * \cdots * E_k$ **then** $\cdots$ (10.2)

This pseudocode (10.2) motivates the function

```
(define (d x E)
  (cond ((constant? E) (diff-constant x E))
        ((variable? E) (diff-variable x E))
        ((sum? E) (diff-sum x E))
        ((product? E) (diff-product x E))
        (else (error "d: cannot parse" E)) ))
```

The predicates `constant?`, `variable?`, `sum?`, and `product?` determine whether expression `E` is a constant, a variable, a sum, or a product. In each case, the actual work of computing the derivative is delegated to a function devoted to that case.

The differentiation routine d manipulates expression E only through pairs of functions like sum? and diff-sum, so it is independent of the representation of expression E.

Constants

the derivative of a constant is 0

Let constants be represented as numbers. Predicate constant? is then the same as the Scheme predicate number?:

```
(define constant? number?)
```

The derivative of a number is zero. Since diff-constant is called only when expression E is a constant, it always returns 0:

```
(define (diff-constant x E) 0)
```

Variables

(d 'v 'v) is 1

Let variables be represented as symbols. Predicate variable? is then the same as the Scheme predicate symbol?:

```
(define variable? symbol?)
```

The derivative of a variable x with respect to x itself is 1. Function diff-variable therefore returns 1 if expression E equals the variable x; otherwise, diff-variable returns 0 because it expects E to be some other variable.

```
(define (diff-variable x E)
   (if (equal? x E) 1 0) )
```

Differentiation Rules for Sums and Products

Informally, the derivative of sum $E_1 + E_2$ is the sum of the derivatives of the subexpressions E_1 and E_2.

The following equalities are for binary sums and products:

$$d(x, E_1 + E_2) = d(x, E_1) + d(x, E_2) \tag{10.3}$$

$$d(x, E_1 * E_2) = d(x, E_1) * E_2 + E_1 * d(x, E_2) \tag{10.4}$$

A generalization to sums with k subexpressions is

$$d(x, E_1 + E_2 + \cdots + E_k) =$$
$$d(x, E_1) + d(x, E_2) + \cdots + d(x, E_k) \tag{10.5}$$

For ease of programming, the equality for products with k subexpressions is adapted from the binary case. It is

$$d(x, E_1 * E') = d(x, E_1) * E' + E_1 * d(x, E')$$
$$\textbf{where } E' = E_2 * \cdots * E_k \tag{10.6}$$

Differentiation of Sums

use map to handle the sum of a list

Let a sum be represented as a list consisting of the operator + and $k \geq 0$ subexpressions. Scheme has an essential predicate `pair?` that tests whether its operand is a pair created by a `cons` operation. Predicate `sum?` returns true if its argument E is a pair with car +:

```
(define (sum? E)
  (and (pair? E)
       (equal? '+ (car E)) ))
```

The body of `sum?` relies on short-circuit evaluation of boolean expressions from left to right. That is, the subexpression

```
(equal? '+ (car E))
```

is evaluated only if `(pair? E)` is true.

Function `diff-sum` does not manipulate sums directly; it uses the two complementary functions `args` and `make-sum`. Given a sum

```
(+ E₁ E₂ ··· Eₖ)
```

args extracts the list of subexpressions

```
(E₁ E₂ ··· Eₖ)
```

and `make-sum` does the converse:

```
(define (args E) (cdr E))
(define (make-sum x) (cons '+ x))
```

From equality (10.5), the derivative of $E_1 + E_2 + \cdots + E_k$ is the sum of the derivatives of the subexpressions. Function `diff-sum` uses Scheme's essential function map to differentiate each subexpression:

```
(define (diff-sum x E)
  (make-sum
   (map (lambda (expr) (d x expr))
        (args E) )))
```

For a review of lambda notation, consider the following definition of a squaring function from Section 10.1:

```
(lambda (n) (* n n))
```

This expression is an anonymous function, with formal parameter n and body (* n n), which multiplies n with itself.

The anonymous function

```
(lambda (expr) (d x expr))
```

is a unary function for differentiating an expression expr with respect to a fixed x.[3]

Example 10.3 Suppose that s is the sum of u, v, and w:

```
(define s (make-sum '(u v w)))
   s
```

The explanation of the interaction

```
(d 'v s)
   (+ 0 1 0)
```

is as follows. Since s is a sum, the differentiation function d calls diff-sum with symbol v and expression s. The body of diff-sum creates an anonymous function equivalent to

```
(lambda (expr) (d 'v expr))
```

and uses map to apply this function to each element of (args s) — that is, to (u v w), resulting in the list (0 1 0). Finally, make-sum converts this list into a sum.   □

---

[3] Variable x is free in this anonymous function because it is not bound within the anonymous function. Under the lexical scope rules of Scheme, x refers to the parameter x of diff-sum, no matter where the anonymous function is applied. The treatment of free variables is faced in Chapter 13, where an interpreter for a subset of Scheme is developed.

Differentiation of Products

Predicate `product?` is similar to `sum?`:

```
(define (product? E)
  (and (pair? E)
       (equal? '* (car E)) ))
```

Function `diff-product` will now be defined to return 0 if it is applied to the trivial expression `(*)` with zero subexpressions; to return the derivative of E_1 if it is applied to `(* `E_1`)` with one subexpression; and to call `diff-product-args` to differentiate all other expressions. The number of subexpressions of E is computed by using `args` to extract the list of subexpressions of E, and then taking the length of the list.

```
(define (diff-product x E)
  (let* ((arg-list (args E))
         (nargs (length arg-list)) )
    (cond ((equal? 0 nargs) 0)
          ((equal? 1 nargs) (d x (car arg-list)))
          (else (diff-product-args x arg-list)) )))
```

The sequential `let*` construct is needed because `nargs` is defined in terms of `arg-list`.

For convenience, equality (10.6) is repeated here:

$$d(x, E_1 * E') \;=\; d(x, E_1) * E' \;+\; E_1 * d(x, E')$$
$$\textbf{where} \;\; E' = E_2 * \cdots * E_k \tag{10.6}$$

Function `diff-product-args` implements this equality, using the following names:

E1	for	E_1
EP	for	E'
DE1	for	$d(x, E_1)$
DEP	for	$d(x, E')$
term1	for	$d(x, E_1) * E'$
term2	for	$E_1 * d(x, E')$

The code for `diff-product-args` is

```
(define (diff-product-args x arg-list)
  (let* ((E1 (car arg-list))
         (EP (make-product (cdr arg-list)))
         (DE1 (d x E1))
```

```
            (DEP (d x EP))
            (term1 (make-product (list DE1 EP)))
            (term2 (make-product (list E1 DEP))) )
     (make-sum (list term1 term2)) ))
```

Summary of the Differentiation Program

The differentiation program of this section consists of function d and its auxiliary routines to manipulate the various kinds of expressions. Function d sets up a syntax-directed translation because it uses the syntax of an expression E to translate E into the differentiated result.

The following examples use d to differentiate expressions with respect to a variable v.

```
(d 'v 'v)
    1
(d 'v 'w)
    0
(d 'v '(+ u v w))
    (+ 0 1 0)
(d 'v '(* v (+ u v w)))
    (+ (* 1 (* (+ u v w))) (* v (+ 0 1 0)))
```

10.5 SIMPLIFICATION OF EXPRESSIONS

*general
simplification is a
hard problem*

The results of the differentiation program can be made more readable by removing occurrences of 0 from sums, occurrences of 1 from products, and "flattening" sums and products. The sum

```
(+ a (+ b c) d)
```

can be rewritten as

```
(+ a b c d)
```

Further simplifications arise from the representation of expressions as lists. For example, (+) simplifies to 0 and (*) to 1.

The rest of this section implements a function `simplify` that is capable of simplifying

```
(+ (* 1 (* (+ u v w))) (* v (+ 0 1 0)))
```

into

```
(+ u v w v)
```

Function `simplify` delegates the work of simplifying sums and products; other expressions are left unchanged:

```
(define (simplify E)
  (cond ((sum? E) (simplify-sum E))
        ((product? E) (simplify-product E))
        (else E) ))
```

The rules for simplifying sums and products are symmetric; 0 is for sums what 1 is for products. Thus, `simplify-sum` and `simplify-product` call a common routine `simpl` with suitable parameters:

```
(define (simplify-sum E)
  (simpl sum? make-sum 0 E))

(define (simplify-product E)
  (simpl product? make-product 1 E))
```

The actions of function `simpl` on the product

```
(* 1 (* a (+ 0 b 0)))
```

are illustrated in Fig. 10.8. Call this product E. The figure illustrates the evaluation of

```
(simpl product? make-product 1 E)
```

The evaluation proceeds in six parts:

1. The subexpressions of E are extracted, using

   ```
   (args E)
   ```

2. Let the result of part 1 be a list u. Each subexpression in u is simplified, using

   ```
   (map simplify u)
   ```

   In Fig. 10.8, 1 simplifies to itself, and `(* a (+ 0 b 0))` simplifies to `(* a b)`.

3. Let the result of part 2 be a list v. An auxiliary function `flat` is called to flatten the list of subexpressions, using

   ```
   (flat op? v)
   ```

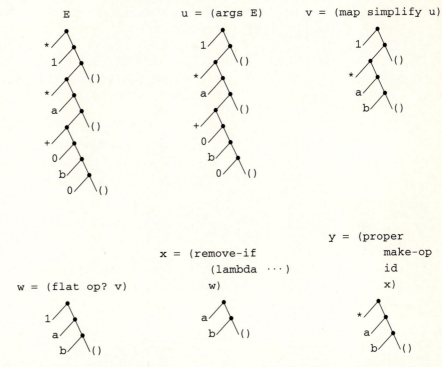

Figure 10.8   Simplification of (* 1 (* a (+ 0 b 0))) into (* a b).

In Fig. 10.8, op? is product? and (1 (* a b)) flattens to
(1 a b).

4. Let the result of part 3 be a list w. All occurrences of id are removed
   from w, using

   (remove-if (lambda (z) (equal? id z)) w)

   In Fig. 10.8, id is 1, and the result of removing 1 from (1 a b) is
   (a b). See page 355 for such uses of the ML variant of remove_if.

5. Let the result of part 4 be x. An auxiliary function proper is called to
   convert x into an expression. Function proper ensures that 0 is
   returned instead of (+) and that expr is returned instead of
   (+ expr); similarly, 1 is returned instead of (*) and expr is
   returned instead of (* expr). In Fig. 10.8, proper converts (a b)
   into (* a b).

6. Let the result of part 5 be y. Finally, y is returned.

These parts are put together in the following code:

```
(define (simpl op? make-op id E)
  (let* ((u (args E))
          (v (map simplify u))
          (w (flat op? v))
          (x (remove-if (lambda (z) (equal? id z)) w))
          (y (proper make-op id x)) )
     y))
```

The behavior of the auxiliary function `flat` can be seen from

```
(flat sum? '())
    ()

(flat sum? '(2 (+ 3 4) 5 (* 6 7)))
    (2 3 4 5 (* 6 7))
```

The sum `(+ 3 4)` is flattened; all other list elements are copied.
The code for `flat` is as follows:

```
(define (flat f x)
  (cond ((null? x) '())
        ((not (pair? x)) (list x))
        ((f (car x)) (append (flat f (args (car x)))
                             (flat f (cdr x)) ))
        (else (cons (car x) (flat f (cdr x)))) ))
```

Function `remove-if` removes elements from a list if some condition holds. More precisely, `remove-if` copies list elements, unless predicate `f` is true on a:

```
(define (remove-if f x)
  (cond ((null? x) nil)
        ((f (car x)) (remove-if f (cdr x)))
        (else (cons (car x) (remove-if f (cdr x)))) ))
```

Finally, function `proper` is as defined in Section 10.3:

```
(define (proper make-kind id x)
  (cond ((null? x) id)
        ((null? (cdr x)) (car x))
        (else (make-kind x)) ))
```

10.6 STORAGE ALLOCATION FOR LISTS

By design, programs in functional languages like Scheme and ML can be understood independently of the underlying allocation and deallocation of storage. Nevertheless, some familiarity with storage management is helpful for assessing the cost of storage management.

a list is made up of cells

Is it expensive to pass lists as parameters to functions? We see in this section that it is not; in fact, a pointer is all that is passed. This section considers the traditional implementation of lists in Lisp dialects, using cells as in Fig. 10.9. The operation to examine closely is the list constructor `cons`.

Cons Allocates Cells

cons allocates a single cell

Lists are built out of cells capable of holding pointers to the head and tail, or car and cdr, respectively, of a list. The `car` operation is named after "Contents of the Address part of Register" and `cdr` is named after "Contents of the Decrement part of Register." Words on the IBM 704, a machine long gone, could hold two pointers in fields called the *address* part and the *decrement* part. When Lisp was first implemented on the IBM 704, the `cons` operation allocated a word and stuffed pointers to the head and tail in the address and decrement parts, respectively.

The empty list `()` is a special pointer; Lisp tradition is to use 0, but any address can be reserved as the value of `()`. Think of `()` as a special address that is not used for anything else.

Each execution of `cons` returns a pointer to a newly allocated cell. The list in Fig. 10.10(a) is built by applying `cons` three times:

```
(cons 'it (cons 'seems (cons 'that '())))
```

Reading inside out, `cons` is first applied to a pointer to the symbol `that` and the empty list. The second application is for the symbol `seems` and the pointer returned from the first application.

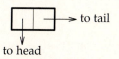

to head

to tail

Figure 10.9 A cells with pointers to the head and tail of a list.

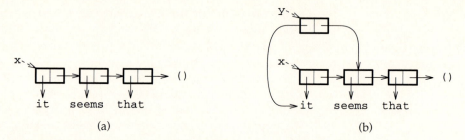

Figure 10.10   A list x and a list y created by executing `(cons (car x) (cdr x))`.

As for the remaining operations on lists, `null?` simply compares its argument for equality with `()`, `car` returns the pointer in the first field, and `cdr` returns the pointer in the second field.

Notions of Equality

The distinction between the standard Scheme functions `equal?` and `eq?` reveals the underlying representation of lists as pointers to cells. The `eq?` function checks whether its two arguments are identical pointers, so it is fussier than `equal?`, which recursively checks whether its two arguments are lists with "equal" elements.

On symbols, the two predicates `equal?` and `eq?` agree:

```
(equal? 'hello 'hello)
    #t
(eq? 'hello 'hello)
    #t
```

As might be expected, `equal?` returns `#t`, for **true**, with the following arguments:

```
(equal? '(hello world) '(hello world))
    #t
```

The implementation of quoted lists has to be studied to explain why the following expression is false in some Scheme implementations:

```
(eq? '(hello world) '(hello world))
    #f
```

This expression may be easier to understand after working out a simpler example.

Example 10.4 The list pointed to by x in Fig. 10.10 prints out as

```
(it seems that)
```

So does the list pointed to by y in part (b) of the figure. Yet x and y point to different cells.

The three cells in Fig. 10.10(a) are set up by the following definition of x:

```
(define x '(it seems that))
    x
```

Each execution of cons allocates a cell, so the following definition sets up the situation in Fig. 10.10(b):

```
(define y (cons (car x) (cdr x)))
    y
```

Now (car x) and (car y) are identical pointers and (cdr x) and (cdr y) are identical pointers. But y is bound to a different cell from x, a cell created by applying cons to the head and tail of x. Hence, equal? returns true and eq? returns false in the following:

```
(equal? x y)
    #t
(eq? x y)
    #f
```
                                                                                    □

Returning to the list

```
'(hello world)
```

each occurrence of this list is an abbreviation for

```
(cons 'hello (cons 'world '()))
```

As in Fig. 10.11, four cells are allocated to hold the arguments of eq? in

```
(eq? '(hello world) '(hello world))
```

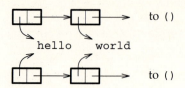

Figure 10.11   Two lists with the same elements.

The two separate occurrences of (hello world) are therefore equivalent under equal? but not under eq?.

Allocation and Deallocation

garbage collection reclaims cells

Cells that are no longer in use have to be recovered or deallocated; otherwise, we eventually run out of memory. A cell is no longer in use if nothing points to it.

A standard technique for allocating and deallocating cells is to link them on a list called a *free list*. The free list acts as a stack of cells; a pop operation on the stack returns a freshly allocated cell and a push operation returns a cell back onto the stack. A language implementation performs *garbage collection* when it returns cells to the free list automatically, without explicit instructions from a program.

What happens to the lists created during the following interactions:

```
(cons 'short-lived '())
    (short-lived)
(let ((x '(short-lived))) x)
    (short-lived)
```

In each case, a cell, (short-lived), with head short-lived and tail () is allocated. After the response, the cell is no longer reachable and can therefore be deallocated. By contrast, the cell created by cons in

```
(define x (cons 'saved '()))
    x
```

can subsequently be accessed through x:

```
x
    (saved)
```

Two of the numerous approaches to deallocation of cells are as follows:

1. *Lazy approach*. Wait until memory runs out and only then collect dead cells. If enough memory is available, the need for collecting cells may never arise. Since it takes time to examine a cell or manipulate a pointer, a disadvantage of this approach is that all other work comes to a halt when the garbage collector has control of the machine.

2. *Eager approach*. Each time a cell is reached, check whether the cell will be needed after the operation; if not, deallocate the cell by placing it on the free list. A standard technique is to set aside some space with each cell for holding a *reference count* of the number of pointers to the cell. If the reference count ever drops to zero, the cell can be deallocated.

Having looked at when garbage collection occurs, we now turn to how it can be implemented.

A simple approach to garbage collection, called the *mark-sweep approach*, is as follows:

1. *Mark phase*. Mark all the cells that can be reached by following pointers. Think of pouring colored ink through all the pointers into the cell area. The ink follows pointers from cell to cell, eventually coloring all reachable cells.

2. *Sweep phase*. Sweep through memory, looking for unmarked cells. Unlike the mark phase, which hops through memory along pointers, the sweep phase starts at one end of memory and looks at every cell. Unmarked cells are returned to the free list.

A *copying collector* avoids the expense of the sweep phase, which looks at every cell, by dividing memory into two halves, the *working* half and the *free* half. Cells are allocated from the working half. When the working half fills up, the reachable cells are copied into consecutive locations in the free half. The roles of the free and working halves are then switched. A copying collector looks only at the reachable cells, the cells that would be marked by a mark-sweep collector. Copying collectors are particularly effective in a virtual memory system.

Exercises

10.1 Consider function `member?` defined as follows:

```
define (member? k x)
   (cond ((null? x) #f)
         ((eq? k (car x)) #t)
         (else (member? k (cdr x))) ))
```

In each of the following cases, give the value of the expression and explain how it is computed.

   a. (member? 'a '())
   b. (member? 'a '(a b c))
   c. (member? 'a '(c b a))
   d. (member? 'a '(b))
   e. (member? 'a '(b c d))

10.2 Consider function least defined as follows:

```
(define (least k x)
  (cond ((null? x) k)
        ((< (car x) k) (least (car x) (cdr x)))
        (else (least k (cdr x))) ))
```

In each of the following cases, give the value of the expression and explain how it is computed.

   a. (least 5 '())
   b. (least 5 '(5 4 3))
   c. (least 5 '(4 5 6))
   d. (least 5 '(7 3 6 2))

10.3 Consider function less defined as follows:

```
(define (less k x)
  (cond ((null? x) '())
        ((< (car x) k) (cons (car x) (less k (cdr x)))
        (else (less k (cdr x))) ))
```

In each of the following cases, give the value of the expression and explain how it is computed.

   a. (less 5 '())
   b. (less 5 '(5 4 3))
   c. (less 5 '(4 5 6))
   d. (less 5 '(7 3 6 2))

10.4 Write Scheme functions that compare adjacent list elements and respond with a list, as described in each case. The sample responses are all with the input list

   (a b a a a c c)

   a. Remove the second and succeeding adjacent duplicates, yielding

     (a b a c)

   b. Leave only the elements that are not repeated, yielding

     (a b)

   c. Leave only one copy of the repeated elements, yielding

     (a c)

   d. Count the number of repeated occurrences, yielding

     ((1 a) (1 b) (3 a) (2 c))

10.5 The following tail-recursive or iterative version of the `length` function uses an extra parameter in which it accumulates the result:

$$
\begin{array}{rcl}
(\text{len nil res}) & \equiv & \text{res} \\
(\text{len (cons a y) res}) & \equiv & (\text{len y (+ 1 res)})
\end{array}
$$

For any list `x`, `(length x)` is equivalent to `(len x 0)`. Use this technique to construct tail-recursive versions of the following functions:

a. A function that adds together all the elements in a list
b. A function that multiplies together all the elements in a list
c. The factorial function

10.6 Implement a variant of Quicksort for lists. That is, sort a list as follows. Pick an element and call it the pivot. Partition the list into two sublists of elements smaller than and larger than the pivot. Recursively sort the sublists. Combine the sorted sublists and the pivot together into a sorted list.

a. Define a function that sorts lists of integers.
b. Define a function that takes two arguments: a predicate p for comparing elements and a list of elements to be sorted.

10.7 Suppose that sets are implemented as lists, where each element of a set appears exactly once in its list. Define functions that implement the following operations:

a. Test whether an element is a member of a set.
b. Construct the union of two sets.
c. Construct the intersection of two sets.
d. Construct the difference of two sets; that is, the set of elements that are in the first set, but not in the second set.
e. How would your implementations change if sets were implemented by sorted lists without repeated elements?

10.8 Suppose that sets are implemented as lists, and that the union of two sets is implemented by simply appending their lists. Note that the same element can appear more than once in the list for a set. Implement the member, intersection, and difference operations on sets.

10.9 Implement the following functions based on the Scheme report:

a. (`append` $list_1$ $list_2$ $list_3$), which appends the elements of the three lists.
b. (`list-tail` $list$ n), which returns the remaining sublist after the first n elements of a list are removed.
c. (`list-ref` $list$ n), which returns the nth element of a list.
d. (`map` f $list_1$ $list_2$ $list_3$), which applies function f to corresponding elements of three lists of the same length.

10.10   Example 10.1 deals with flattening of lists.
  a. Implement a function `same-leaves` to test whether two lists have the same flattened form.
  b. Give an efficient implementation of `same-leaves` that avoids flattening two huge lists, only to discover that their flattened forms differ in some prefix.

10.11   Fill in the blanks in the following equivalences (the function definitions appear on page 397):
  a. `(reduce ___ x ___ )`   ≡   `(length x)`
  b. `(reduce ___ x ___ )`   ≡   `(append x z)`
  c. `(reduce ___ x ___ )`   ≡   `(remove-if f x)`
  d. `(reduce ___ x ___ )`   ≡   `(map f x)`

10.12   The list-manipulation function in this exercise is motivated by a rule for differentiating products. Let E' represent the derivative with respect to x of an expression E. The rule is

$$
\begin{aligned}
(E_1 * E_2 * \cdots * E_k)' \equiv \quad & E_1' * E_2 * \cdots * E_k \\
+ \; & E_1 * E_2' * \cdots * E_k \\
& \cdots \\
+ \; & E_1 * E_2 * \cdots * E_k'
\end{aligned}
$$

  a. Define a function `foo` that applies a function `f` to each element of a list `x` and returns a list of sublists. The ith element of the ith sublist is formed by applying `f` to the ith element of `x`; the remaining elements of the ith sublist are as in `x`.
  b. Modify the differentiation program in Section 10.4 so that it differentiates products using the rule in this exercise.

10.13   In the following interaction, `d` is the differentiation program of Section 10.4:

```
(d 'v '(* u v))
    (+ (* 0 (* v)) (* u 1))
```

  a. Why does the response contain subexpression `(* 0 (* v))`? Why not `(* 0 v)` instead?
  b. Modify the differentiation program so that `d` calls `diff-sum` and `diff-product` with the variable `x` and the arguments of expression `E`, rather than `E` itself. At the same time, ensure that the simpler subexpression from (a) is produced when `(* u v)` is differentiated with respect to `v`.

Bibliographic Notes

Scheme is a lexically scoped dialect of Lisp with first-class functions, created by Steele and Sussman [1975]. As Scheme spread, dialects emerged, until a single standard version was defined (Rees and Clinger [1986]). Subsequent revisions resulted in a Revised^4 report in 1991.

Textbooks that use Scheme to cover programming concepts include Friedman, Wand, and Haynes [1992] and Abelson and Sussman [1985].

See also the bibliographic notes for Chapters 8 and 9 in this book.

V

OTHER
PARADIGMS

The two unrelated chapters in this part deal with logic programming (Chapter 11) and concurrent programming (Chapter 12).

Logic programming refers loosely to

- The use of facts and rules to represent information
- The use of deduction to answer queries

An example of a rule is

```
overlap(X, Y) :- member(M, X), member(M, Y).
```

In words, lists X and Y overlap if there is some M that is a member of both X and Y.

From such rules, a language like Prolog uses deduction to compute answers to queries.

Chapter 12 scratches the surface of a large subject, with many models of computation. The fundamental concept is that of a process or task. Interaction between processes takes two forms:

- Communication involving the exchange of data

- Synchronization involving control

Correctness of concurrent programs refers not only to getting the "right" answer but also to the rate of progress of processes. Processes can deadlock, each waiting for the other to proceed.

Chapter 12 deals with basic concepts, illustrated using the Ada programming language.

11

Logic Programming

The programming language, Prolog, was born of a project aimed not at producing a programming language but at processing natural languages; in this case French. · · · It can be said that Prolog was the offspring of a successful marriage between natural language processing and automated theorem proving.

– *Colmerauer and Roussel [1993], on "The Birth of Prolog."*

The concept of logic programming is linked historically to a language called Prolog, developed in 1972 and still the only widely available language of its kind. Prolog was first applied to natural language processing. It has since been used for specifying algorithms, searching databases, writing compilers, building expert systems—in short, for all the kinds of applications for which a language like Lisp might be used. Prolog is especially suited to applications involving pattern matching, backtrack searching, or incomplete information.

logic programs consist of facts and rules

Kowalski [1979b] illustrates the division of labor in logic programming by writing the informal equation

computation is deduction

algorithm = logic + control

Here logic refers to the facts and rules specifying what the algorithm does, and control refers to how the algorithm can be implemented by applying the rules in a particular order. This equation reflects a division of labor between us as programmers and a language for logic programming. We supply the logic part, and the programming language supplies the control.

Prolog has spawned numerous dialects, some with their own notions of control. The language in this chapter is Edinburgh Prolog, a de facto standard dialect. Nonsyntactic differences between dialects can be illustrated by writing a family of equations

$$\text{algorithm}_D \; = \; \text{logic} + \text{control}_D$$

where D is a dialect and control_D represents its notion of control.

Control in Edinburgh Prolog proceeds from left to right; see Section 11.5 for details. The rule

$$P \; \textbf{if} \; Q_1 \; \textbf{and} \; Q_2 \; \textbf{and} \; \cdots \; \textbf{and} \; Q_k.$$

$k \geq 0$, can be read as

> to deduce P,
>> deduce Q_1;
>> deduce Q_2;
>> $\cdots$
>> deduce Q_k;

This simple strategy is surprisingly versatile and flexible. Unfortunately, it sometimes gets stuck in infinite loops, and it can produce anomalies involving negation.

Prolog is a practical tool. It reduces logic programming to practice. However, it introduces a few impurities that are put into perspective if we distinguish between Prolog, the language, and logic programming, the concept. This chapter therefore begins with an informal discussion of the concept of logic programming.

11.1 COMPUTING WITH RELATIONS

relations treat arguments and results uniformly

Logic programming deals with relations rather than functions. It is based on the premise that programming with relations is more flexible than programming with functions, because relations treat arguments and results uniformly. Informally, relations have no sense of direction, no prejudice about who is computed from whom.

The running example in this section is a relation *append* on lists. Although Prolog itself is not introduced until Section 11.2, we anticipate its notation for lists. Lists are written between brackets [and], so [ ] is the empty list and $[b, c]$ is a list of two symbols b and c. If H is a symbol and T is a list, then $[H \mid T]$ is a list with head H and tail T. Hence

$$[a, b, c] \; = \; [a \mid [b, c] \,]$$

Relations

A concrete view of a *relation* is as a table with $n \geq 0$ columns and a possibly infinite set of rows. A tuple $(a_1, a_2, \ldots, a_n)$ is *in* a relation if a_i appears in column i, $1 \leq i \leq n$, of some row in the table for the relation.

Relation *append* is a set of tuples of the form (X, Y, Z), where Z consists of the elements of X followed by the elements of Y. A few of the tuples in *append* are as follows:

append		
X	Y	Z
[ ]	[ ]	[ ]
[a]	[ ]	[a]
...	...	...
[a, b]	[c, d]	[a, b, c, d]
...	...	...

Relations are also called *predicates* because a relation name *rel* can be thought of as a test of the form

Is a given tuple in relation *rel*?

For example, $([a], [b], [a, b])$ is in relation *append*, but $([a], [b], [ ])$ is not.

The rest of this section uses pseudo-English to talk informally about relation *append*. A summary of this section appears in Fig. 11.1; it is keyed to an interactive Prolog session that will be discussed in Section 11.3.

Rules and Facts

Horn clauses lead to efficient implementations

Relations will be specified by *rules*, written in pseudocode as

P **if** Q_1 **and** Q_2 **and** $\cdots$ **and** Q_k.

for $k \geq 0$.[1] Such rules are called *Horn clauses*, after Horn [1951], who studied them. Languages have tended to work with Horn clauses because Horn clauses lead to efficient implementations.

A *fact* is a special case of a rule, in which $k = 0$ and P holds without any conditions, written simply as

P.

---

[1] Looking ahead to Section 11.2, $P, Q_1, Q_2, \ldots, Q_k$ are terms. A *term* is either a constant or a variable or has the form $rel(T_1, T_2, \ldots, T_n)$, for $n \geq 0$, where *rel* is the name of a relation and $T_1, T_2, \ldots, T_n$ are terms. By convention, variable names begin with uppercase letters; constant and relation names begin with lowercase letters.

Rules

```
append([], Y, Y).                        append [ ] and Y to get Y.
append([H|X], Y, [H|Z]) :- append(X, Y, Z).   append [H | X] and Y to get [H | Z]
                                              if append X and Y to get Z
```

Queries

```
?- append([a,b], [c,d], [a,b,c,d]).      append [a, b] and [c, d] to get [a, b, c, d]?
   yes                                       Answer: yes

?- append([a,b], [c,d], Z).              append [a, b] and [c, d] to get Z?
   Z = [a,b,c,d]                             Answer: yes, when Z = [a, b, c, d]

?- append([a,b], Y, [a,b,c,d]).          append [a, b] and Y to get [a, b, c, d]?
   Y = [c,d]                                 Answer: yes, when Y = [c, d]

?- append(X, [c,d], [a,b,c,d]).          append X and [c, d] to get [a, b, c, d]?
   X = [a,b]                                 Answer: yes, when X = [a, b]

?- append(X, [d,c], [a,b,c,d]).
   no
```

Figure 11.1   A Prolog session with comments in pseudo-English.

The *append* relation is specified by two rules. The first is a fact stating that triples of the form ([ ], Y, Y) are in relation *append*. A pseudo-English statement of this fact is

append [ ] and Y to get Y.

The second rule for *append* is shown for completeness. It uses the notation $[H \mid T]$ for a list with head H and tail T:

append $[H \mid X]$ and Y to get $[H \mid Z]$
        if append X and Y to get Z

It follows from this rule that

append $[a, b]$ and $[c, d]$ to get $[a, b, c, d]$
        if append $[b]$ and $[c, d]$ to get $[b, c, d]$

Here $H = a$, $X = [b]$, $Y = [c, d]$, and $Z = [b, c, d]$. Note that $[a \mid [b]]$ is the same list as $[a, b]$ and that $[a \mid [b, c, d]]$ is the same list as $[a, b, c, d]$.

Queries

*queries are yes/fail
rather than yes/no*

Logic programming is driven by queries about relations. The simplest queries ask whether a particular tuple belongs to a relation. The query

> append $[a, b]$ and $[c, d]$ to get $[a, b, c, d]$?
>   *Answer*: yes   (11.1)

asks whether the triple $([a, b], [c, d], [a, b, c, d])$ belongs to relation *append*.

Horn clauses cannot represent negative information; that is, we cannot directly ask whether a tuple is not in a relation. Queries in this chapter will therefore have yes/fail answers rather than yes/no answers. The response "fail" indicates a failure to deduce a yes answer. Section 11.6 considers a limited form of negation based on failure.

Queries containing variables are much more interesting:

> Is there a Z such that
>   append $[a, b]$ and $[c, d]$ to get Z?
>   *Answer*: yes, when $Z = [a, b, c, d]$ (11.2)

What seems like a yes/fail query is really a request for suitable values for the variables in it. The query (11.2) is a request for a Z such that $([a\ b], [c, d], Z)$ is in the relation *append*.

A benefit of working with relations is that if we append X and Y to get Z, then any one of X, Y, and Z can be computed from the other two. This property motivates the earlier remark that relations are flexible because they have no prejudice about who is computed from whom. X can be computed from Y and Z:

> Is there an X such that
>   append X and $[c, d]$ to get $[a, b, c, d]$?
>   *Answer*: yes, when $X = [a, b]$ (11.3)

Or Y can be computed from X and Z:

> Is there a Y such that
>   append $[a, b]$ and Y to get $[a, b, c, d]$?
>   *Answer*: yes, when $Y = [c, d]$ (11.4)

Queries (11.1)–(11.4) illustrate several different ways of using the same relation *append*.

*prefix and suffix
can be defined in
terms of append*

New relations can be defined from old. In the following three rules for *prefix*, *suffix*, and *sublist*, the variables S, X, Y, and Z refer to portions of a list (see Fig. 11.2):

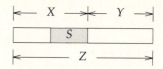

Figure 11.2   Variable names referring to portions of a list.

prefix X of Z
>**if** for some Y, append X and Y to get Z.

suffix Y of Z
>**if** for some X, append X and Y to get Z.

sublist S of Z
>**if** for some X, prefix X of Z **and** suffix S of X.

11.2   INTRODUCTION TO PROLOG

This section introduces Prolog by considering relations on atomic objects. Data structures are considered in the next section; programs that benefit from Prolog's unique abilities appear in Section 11.4.

The examples in this section are motivated by the arrows or *links* in Fig. 11.3.

Terms

Facts, rules, and queries are specified using terms; see Fig. 11.4 for the basic syntax of Edinburgh Prolog.

A *simple term* is a *number*, a *variable* starting with an uppercase letter, or an *atom* standing for itself. Examples of simple terms are

```
0   1972   X   Source   lisp   algol60
```

Here 0 and 1972 are numbers, X and Source are variables, and lisp and algol60 are atoms.

A *compound term* consists of an atom followed by a parenthesized sequence of subterms. The atom is called a *functor* and the subterms are called *arguments*. In

```
link(bcpl, c)
```

the functor is link, and the arguments are bcpl and c.

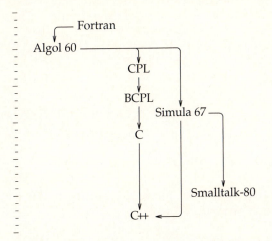

Figure 11.3 Links between languages.

A few extensions to the syntax of compound terms will be introduced as needed. Some operators can be written in infix as well as prefix notation; for example, the prefix notation = (X, Y) can equivalently be rewritten as X = Y.

The special variable "_" is a placeholder for an unnamed term. All occurrences of _ are independent of each other.

Interacting with Prolog

A snapshot of an interactive session winds its way through the rest of this section. As in earlier chapters, system responses appear in italic letters. When started, the system responds with the "prompt" characters

> *?-*

$$\begin{array}{lll} \langle \textit{fact} \rangle & ::= & \langle \textit{term} \rangle \ . \\ \langle \textit{rule} \rangle & ::= & \langle \textit{term} \rangle \ \text{:-} \ \langle \textit{terms} \rangle \ . \\ \langle \textit{query} \rangle & ::= & \langle \textit{terms} \rangle \ . \\[6pt] \langle \textit{term} \rangle & ::= & \langle \textit{number} \rangle \ | \ \langle \textit{atom} \rangle \ | \ \langle \textit{variable} \rangle \ | \ \langle \textit{atom} \rangle \ (\ \langle \textit{terms} \rangle \ ) \\[6pt] \langle \textit{terms} \rangle & ::= & \langle \textit{term} \rangle \quad | \quad \langle \textit{term} \rangle \ , \ \langle \textit{terms} \rangle \end{array}$$

Figure 11.4 Basic syntax of facts, rules, and queries in Edinburgh Prolog.

Prolog maintains a current database of rules

to indicate that a query is expected.

The *consult* construct reads in a file containing facts and rules, and adds its contents at the end of the current database of rules.[2] Thus,

```
?- consult(links).
    links consulted  ...
    yes
```

reads file `links`; its contents are shown in Fig. 11.5. A sequence of facts starting with

```
link(fortran, algol60).
```

specifies a relation `link` on atoms. According to this fact, relation `link` contains the pair (`fortran, algol60`).

Existential Queries

queries are answered with solutions

A query

$$\langle term \rangle_1 \ , \ \langle term \rangle_2 \ , \ \cdots \ , \ \langle term \rangle_k \ .$$

for $k \geq 1$, corresponds to the following pseudocode:

$$\langle term \rangle_1 \ \textbf{and} \ \langle term \rangle_2 \ \textbf{and} \ \cdots \ \textbf{and} \ \langle term \rangle_k \ ?$$

```
link(fortran,   algol60).
link(algol60,   cpl).
link(cpl,       bcpl).
link(bcpl,      c).
link(c,         cplusplus).
link(algol60,   simula67).
link(simula67,  cplusplus).
link(simula67,  smalltalk80).

path(L, L).
path(L, M) :- link(L, X), path(X, M).
```

Figure 11.5   Facts and rules in file `links`.

---

[2] Use *reconsult* to override rules in the database. Some implementations allow rules to be entered directly by consulting the special file name *user*.

Queries are also called *goals*. It is sometimes convenient to refer to the individual terms in a query as "subgoals." There is no formal distinction between a goal and a subgoal, however, just as there is no formal distinction between a term and a subterm.

Since there are no variables in the query

```
?- link(cpl,bcpl), link(bcpl,c).
    yes
```

the response is simply *yes*.

A variable in a query refers to the existence of some appropriate object. The query

```
?- link(algol60,L), link(L,M).
```

can therefore be read as

Are there *L* and *M* such that
        link(*algol*60, *L*) **and** *link*(*L*, *M*)?

A *solution* to a query is a binding of variables to values that makes the query true.[3] A query with solutions is said to be *satisfiable*. The system responds with a solution to a satisfiable query:

```
?- link(algol60,L), link(L,M).
    L = cpl
    M = bcpl
```

We now have two choices:

- Type a carriage return. Prolog responds with *yes* to indicate that there might be more solutions. It then immediately prompts for the next query.
- Type a semicolon and a carriage return. Prolog responds with another solution, or with *no* to indicate that no further solutions can be found.

The semicolons in the following interaction keep asking for further solutions:

```
?- link(algol60,L), link(L,M).
    L = cpl
    M = bcpl ;
```

---

[3] Technically, all variables in a query are implicitly existentially quantified. With the quantifiers in place, this query becomes

∃*L*, *M*. *link*(*algol*60, *L*) **and** *link*(*L*, *M*)?

```
L = simula67
M = cplusplus ;

L = simula67
M = smalltalk80 ;

no
```

Variables can appear anywhere within a query. The query

```
?- link(L, bcpl).
```

asks for an object with a link to `bcpl`, and the query

```
?- link(bcpl, M).
```

asks for an object to which `bcpl` has a link.

Universal Facts and Rules

rules are Horn clauses

A rule

$$\langle term \rangle \quad :- \quad \langle term \rangle_1 \; , \; \langle term \rangle_2 \; , \; \cdots \; , \; \langle term \rangle_k \; .$$

for $k \geq 1$, corresponds to the following pseudocode:

$$\langle term \rangle \quad \textbf{if} \quad \langle term \rangle_1 \quad \textbf{and} \quad \langle term \rangle_2 \quad \textbf{and} \quad \cdots \quad \textbf{and} \quad \langle term \rangle_k.$$

The term to the left of the `:-` is called the *head* and the terms to the right of the `:-` are called *conditions*.

A fact is a special case of a rule. A fact has a head and no conditions. The following fact and rule specify a relation `path`:

```
path(L, L).                                    (11.5)
path(L, M) :- link(L, X), path(X, M).          (11.6)
```

The idea is that a path consists of zero or more links. We take a path of zero links to be from `L` to itself. A path from `L` to `M` begins with a link to some `X` and continues along the path from `X` to `M`.

Any object can be substituted for a variable in the head of a rule. Fact (11.5) can therefore be read as

For all *L*,
   path(*L*, *L*).

Rule (11.6) has a variable X that appears in the conditions but not in the head. Such variables stand for some object satisfying the conditions.[4] Rule (11.6) can therefore be read as

> For all L and M,
>> $path(L, M)$ **if**
>>> there exists X such that
>>>> $link(L, X)$ **and** $path(X, M)$.

Negation as Failure

no means "I can't prove it"

Prolog answers *no* to a query if it fails to satisfy the query. The *negation as failure* assumption is tantamount to saying, "If I can't prove it, it must be false."

The facts in Fig. 11.5 say nothing about a link from `lisp` to `scheme`, hence the *no* answer in the following:

```
?- link(lisp,scheme).
   no
```

Similarly, the `not` operator represents negation as failure rather than true logical negation. A query `not`(P) is treated as true if the system fails to deduce P. Negation as failure works for simple cases; more complex cases are dealt with in Section 11.6. The following example contains an application for `not`.

Example 11.1 Are there two languages L and M in Fig. 11.3 with links to the same language N? A first attempt at this query is

```
?- link(L,N), link(M,N).
   L = fortran
   N = algol60
   M = fortran
```

Let us now add the requirement that variables L and M must have different values:

```
?- link(L,N), link(M,N), not(L=M).
   L = c
   N = cplusplus
   M = simula67 ;
```

---

[4] Technically, all variables in facts and rules are implicitly universally quantified. With the quantifiers in place, the rule becomes
$$\forall L, M, X. \; path(L, M) \;\; \textbf{if} \;\; (link(L, X) \;\textbf{and}\; path(X, M))$$
Since X does not appear in its head, the rule is logically equivalent to
$$\forall L, M. \; path(L, M) \;\; \textbf{if} \;\; (\exists X. \; link(L, X) \;\textbf{and}\; path(X, M))$$

```
L = simula67
N = cplusplus
M = c ;

no
```

subgoal order
affects solutions

These two solutions are different because the individual variables have different values.

As a rule of thumb, not can be used to test known values or values that become known before not is applied. The reordered query

```
?- not(L=M), link(L,N), link(M,N).
    no
```

fails because the values of variables L and M are not known at the start of the query. Unknown values could be equal, so not (L=M) fails. □

Unification

How does Prolog solve equations of the following form

```
?- f(X,b) = f(a,Y).
    X = a
    Y = b
```

An *instance* of a term T is obtained by substituting subterms for one or more variables of T. The same subterm must be substituted for all occurrences of a variable.

Thus, f(a,b) is an instance of f(X,b) because it is obtained by substituting subterm a for variable X in f(X,b). Similarly, f(a,b) is an instance of f(a,Y) because it is obtained by substituting subterm b for variable Y in f(a,Y).

As another example, g(a,a) is an instance of g(X,X), and so is g(h(b),h(b)). However, g(a,b) is not an instance of g(X,X) because we cannot substitute a for one occurrence of X and a different subterm b for the other occurrence of X.

computation is
based on
unification

Deduction in Prolog is based on the concept of unification; the two terms T_1 and T_2 *unify* if they have a common instance U. If a variable occurs in both T_1 and T_2, then the same subterm must be substituted for all occurrences of the variable in both T_1 and T_2.

Terms f(X,b) and f(a,Y) unify because they have a common instance f(a,b).

Unification occurs implicitly when a rule is applied. Suppose that the relation identity is defined by the fact

```
identity(Z,Z).
```

Now unification is used to compute the response to the query

```
?- identity( f(X,b), f(a,Y) ).
   X = a
   Y = b
```

The response is computed by unifying `identity(Z,Z)` with

```
identity( f(X,b), f(a,Y) )
```

which leads to the unification of `Z` with `f(X,b)` and with `f(a,Y)`. In effect, `f(X,b)` is unified with `f(a,Y)`.

Arithmetic

The = operator stands for unification in Prolog, so

```
?- X = 2+3.
   X = 2+3
```

simply binds variable `X` to the term `2+3`.
    The infix `is` operator evaluates an expression:

```
?- X is 2+3.
   X = 5
```

Since the `is` operator binds `X` to 5, the query

```
?- X is 2+3, X = 5.
   X = 5
```

is satisfied. However,

```
?- X is 2+3, X = 2+3.
   no
```

fails because `2+3` does not unify with 5. Term `2+3` is the application of operator `+` to arguments `2` and `3`, whereas 5 is simply the integer 5. Hence, `2+3` does not unify with 5.

11.3   DATA STRUCTURES IN PROLOG

Prolog supports several notations for writing Lisp-like lists. After reviewing the notations, we see that they are just syntactic sugar for ordinary terms; that is, they sweeten the syntax without adding any new capabilities.

The view of terms as data carries over from lists to other data structures, particularly trees.

Lists in Prolog

list notation is a way of writing terms

The simplest way of writing a list is to enumerate its elements. The list consisting of the three atoms a, b, and c can be written as

```
[a, b, c]
```

The empty list is written as [].

We can also specify an initial sequence of elements and a trailing list, separated by |. The list [a,b,c] can also be written as

```
[a, b, c | []]
[a, b | [c]]
[a | [b, c]]
```

A special case of this notation is a list with head H and tail T, written as [H|T]. The head is the first element of a list, and the tail is the list consisting of the remaining elements.

Unification can be used to extract the components of a list, so explicit operators for extracting the head and tail are not needed. The solution of the query

```
?- [H|T] = [a,b,c].
   H = a
   T = [b,c]
```

binds variable H to the head and variable T to the tail of list [a,b,c]. The query

```
?- [a|T] = [H, b, c].
   T = [b,c]
   H = a
```

illustrates Prolog's ability to deal with partially specified terms. The term [a|T] is a partial specification of a list with head a and unknown tail denoted by variable T. Similarly, [H,b,c] is a partial specification of a list with unknown head `H` and tail `[b,c]`. In order for these two specifications to unify, `H` must denote `a` and `T` must denote `[b,c]`.

Example 11.2 The append relation on lists is defined by the following rules:

```
append([], Y, Y).
append([H|X], Y, [H|Z]) :- append(X, Y, Z).
```

These rules are Prolog counterparts of the pseudo-English rules in Fig. 11.1. In words, the result of appending the empty list `[]` and a list `Y` is `Y`. If the result of appending `X` and `Y` is `Z`, then the result of appending `[H|X]` and `Y` is `[H|Z]`.

The responses to the following queries show that the rules for append can be used to compute any one of the arguments from the other two:

```
?- append([a,b], [c,d], Z).
   Z = [a,b,c,d]

?- append([a,b], Y, [a,b,c,d]).
   Y = [c,d]

?- append(X, [c,d], [a,b,c,d]).
   X = [a,b]
```

The following query shows that inconsistent arguments are rejected

```
?- append(X, [d,c], [a,b,c,d]).
   no
```

Difference lists, to be discussed in Section 11.4, lead to a faster implementation of append. □

Terms as Data

The connection between lists and terms is as follows. `[H|T]` is syntactic sugar for the term `.(H,T)`:

```
?- .(H, T) = [a,b,c].
   H = a
   T = [b,c]
```

Thus, the dot operator or functor "`.`" corresponds to cons in Lisp, and lists are terms. The term for the list `[a,b,c]` is

```
.(a, .(b, .(c, [])))
```

There is a one-to-one correspondence between trees and terms. That is, any tree can be written as a term and any term can be drawn as a tree. Any data structure that can be simulated using trees can therefore be simulated using terms. Using an example from Section 9.5, binary trees can be written as terms, using an atom `leaf` for a leaf and a functor `nonleaf` with two arguments for a nonleaf node, as in Fig. 11.6.

Example 11.3 A *binary search tree* is either empty, or it consists of a node with two binary search trees as subtrees. Each node holds an integer (see Fig. 11.7). The elements in a binary search tree are arranged so that smaller elements appear in the left subtree of a node and larger elements appear in the right subtree.

Let atom `empty` represent an empty binary search tree and let a term `node(K,S,T)` represent a tree

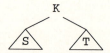

with an integer value K at the root, left subtree S, and right subtree T.

The rules in Fig. 11.8 define a relation `member` to test whether an integer appears at some node in a tree. The two arguments of `member` are an integer and a tree. The fact

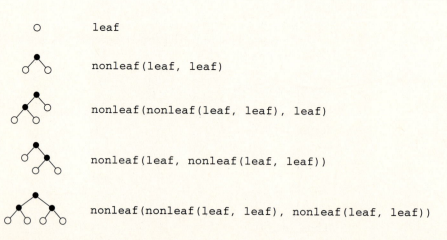

Figure 11.6   Terms for representing binary trees.

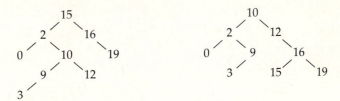

Figure 11.7   Two binary search trees.

```
member(K, node(K,_,_)).
```

can be interpreted as saying that K appears in a tree if it appears at the root. Each occurrence of the special variable _ is a placeholder for a distinct unnamed term, so node(K,_,_) represents a binary search tree with K at the root and some unnamed left and right subtrees. We can emphasize that member is a relation on pairs consisting of an integer K and a tree U by restating the preceding rule as

```
member(K, U)  :- U = node(N,S,T), K = N.
```

The rule

```
member(K, node(N,S,_))  :- K < N, member(K, S).
```

can be interpreted as

> K is in a tree $node(N, S, \_)$ **if**
> $\quad K < N$ **and** K is in the left subtree S.

It is left as an exercise to define a relation insert corresponding to

> insert K into S to get T.

```
member(K, node(K,_,_)).
member(K, node(N,S,_))  :- K < N, member(K, S).
member(K, node(N,_,T))  :- K > N, member(K, T).
```

Figure 11.8   Relation member on binary search trees.

and a relation `delete` to remove an integer from a tree.   □

The atom `empty` and the functor `node` in Example 11.3 simulate the value constructors *empty* and *node* in the following ML datatype declaration:

datatype *searchtree* = *empty* | *node* **of int** * *searchtree* * *searchtree*;

Other ML datatypes can be simulated similarly.

Beyond trees, variables in Prolog allow terms to represent data structures with sharing. The term `node(K,S,S)` represents a graph

Although this chapter does not explore the possibility, terms can also represent graphs with cycles.

11.4   PROGRAMMING TECHNIQUES

The programming techniques in this section exploit the strengths of Prolog— namely, backtracking and unification. Backtracking allows a solution to be found if one exists. Unification allows variables to be used as placeholders for data to be filled in later.

Careful use of the techniques in this section can lead to efficient programs. The programs in this section rely on the left-to-right evaluation of subgoals in Prolog. Therefore, variants of the programs may not work, for reasons that will become clear when control in Prolog is discussed in Section 11.5.

Guess and Verify

the guess subgoal generates solutions, the verify subgoal chooses satisfiable ones

A *guess-and-verify* query has the form

Is there an *S* such that
  guess(*S*) **and** *verify*(*S*)?

where *guess*(*S*) and *verify*(*S*) are subgoals. Prolog responds to such a query by generating solutions to *guess*(*S*) until a solution satisfying *verify*(*S*) is found. Such queries are also called *generate-and-test* queries.

Similarly, a *guess-and-verify* rule has the following form:

conclusion(· · ·) **if** *guess*(· · · , *S*, · · ·) **and** *verify*(· · · , *S*, · · ·)

Example 11.4   The guess-and-verify rule in this example is as follows:

```
overlap(X, Y) :- member(M, X), member(M, Y).
```

In words, two lists X and Y overlap if there is some M that is a member of both X and Y. The first goal member(M,X) guesses an M from list X, and the second goal member(M,Y) verifies that M also appears in list Y.

The rules for member are

```
member(M, [M |_]).
member(M, [_ |T]) :- member(M, T).
```

The first rule says that M is a member of a list with head M. The second rule says that M is a member of a list if M is a member of its tail T.

To see why

```
?- overlap([a,b,c,d], [1,2,c,d]).
   yes
```

produces a *yes* response, consider the query

```
?- member(M, [a,b,c,d]), member(M, [1,2,c,d]).
```

The first goal in this query generates solutions and the second goal tests to see whether they are acceptable. The solutions generated by the first goal are

```
?- member(M, [a,b,c,d]).
   M = a ;
   M = b ;
   M = c ;
   M = d ;
   no
```

The first two are not acceptable, but the third is

```
?- member(a, [1,2,c,d]).
   no

?- member(b, [1,2,c,d]).
   no

?- member(c, [1,2,c,d]).
   yes
```

□

Hint. Since computation in Prolog proceeds from left to right, the order of the subgoals in a guess-and-verify query can affect efficiency. Choose the subgoal with fewer solutions as the guess goal.

As an extreme example of the effect of goal order on efficiency, consider the following two queries:

```
?- X = [1,2,3], member(a,X).
    no

?- member(a,X), X = [1,2,3].
    [ infinite computation ]
```

Relation member is as in Example 11.4. In

```
?- X = [1,2,3], member(a,X).
    no
```

the guess goal X=[1,2,3] has just one solution, and this solution does not satisfy member(a,X) because a is not in the list [1,2,3]. On the other hand, in

```
?- member(a,X), X = [1,2,3].
    [ infinite computation ]
```

the guess goal member(a,X) has an infinite number of solutions:

```
X = [a|_] ;              a  can be the first element of  X
X = [_,a,|_] ;           a  can be the second element of  X
X = [_,_,a,|_] ;         a  can be the third element of  X
   . . .
```

none of which binds X to the list [1,2,3]. Hence, an infinite computation ensues as Prolog tries the solutions in turn, looking for one that satisfies X=[1,2,3].

Variables as Placeholders in Terms

So far in this chapter, variables have been used in rules and queries but not in terms representing objects. Terms containing variables can be used to simulate modifiable data structures; the variables serve as placeholders for subterms to be filled in later. Such terms will be used in Example 11.5 to implement queues efficiently.

Recall the use of terms to represent binary trees in Section 11.3:

○   `leaf`

           `nonleaf(leaf, leaf)`

The terms `leaf` and `nonleaf(leaf,leaf)` are completely specified. By contrast, the list `[a,b|X]` containing a variable `X` is partially specified because we do not yet know what `X` represents. This list `[a,b|X]` has `a` as its first element and `b` as its second, and it has a variable `X` representing the rest of the list. If `X` is subsequently unified with `[]`, then `[a,b|X]` will represent `[a,b]`, but if `X` is unified with `[c]`, then `[a,b|X]` will represent `[a,b,c]`, and so on, for other possible values for `X`.

an open list can be extended through its end marker

An *open list* is a list ending in a variable, referred to as the *end marker variable* of the list. An empty open list consists of just an end-marker variable. A list is *closed* if it is not open.

Internally, Prolog uses machine-generated variables, written with a leading underscore `_` followed by an integer. In the following interaction, the machine-generated variable `_1` corresponds to the end marker `X`:

```
?- L = [a,b|X].
   L = [a,b|_1]
   X = _1
```

Prolog generates fresh variables each time it responds to a query or applies a rule.

An open list can be modified by unifying its end marker. The following query extends `L` into a new open list with end marker `Y` (see Fig. 11.9):

```
?- L = [a,b|X], X = [c,Y].
   L = [a,b,c|_2]
   X = [c|_2]
   Y = _2
```

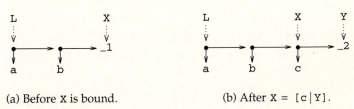

(a) Before `X` is bound.   (b) After `X = [c|Y]`.

Figure 11.9 Extending an open list by unifying its end marker.

Unification of an end-marker variable is akin to an assignment to that variable. In Fig. 11.9, list L changes from [a,b|_1] to [a,b,c|_2] when _1 unifies with [c|_2].

An advantage of working with open lists is that the end of a list can be accessed quickly, in constant time, through its end marker. The following example uses open lists to implement queues.

Example 11.5 This example discusses the rules in Fig. 11.10 for manipulating queues. The relation enter(a,Q,R) is described informally by

When element a enters queue Q, we get queue R.

Similarly, leave(a,Q,R) is described by

When element a leaves queue Q, we get queue R.

When a queue is created, it is represented by a term of the form q(L,E), where L is an open list with end marker E. Subsequent operations will, in general, extend the list L, as in the following diagram:

Therefore, L in q(L,E) represents an open list, E represents some suffix of L, and the contents of the queue q(L,E) are the elements of L that are not in E.

The implementation of queues is illustrated in Fig. 11.11, which shows the effect of the query

```
?- setup(Q), enter(a,Q,R), enter(b,R,S),
       leave(X,S,T), leave(Y,T,U), wrapup(U).
```

```
setup(q(X,X)).
enter(A, q(X,Y), q(X,Z)) :- Y = [A|Z].
leave(A, q(X,Z), q(Y,Z)) :- X = [A|Y].
wrapup(q([],[])).
```

Figure 11.10   Rules for manipulating queues.

The first goal `setup(Q)` creates an empty queue:

```
?- setup(Q).
   Q = q(_1,_1)
```

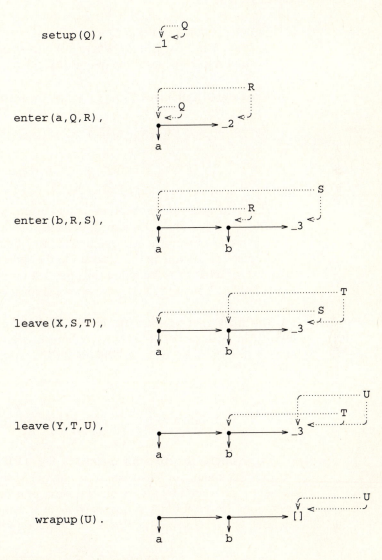

setup(Q),

enter(a,Q,R),

enter(b,R,S),

leave(X,S,T),

leave(Y,T,U),

wrapup(U).

Figure 11.11   Operations on a queue.

In Fig. 11.11, a queue q(L,E) is marked by dotted arrows to L and E. The arrows from Q therefore go to the empty open list _1 with end marker _1.

Now consider the second goal enter(a,Q,R). The rule

```
enter(A, q(X,Y), q(X,Z)) :- Y = [A|Z].
```

can be read as

> To enter A into a queue $q(X, Y)$,
>   bind Y to a list $[A \mid Z]$, where Z is a fresh end marker,
>   and return the resulting queue $q(X, Z)$.

After setup(Q) initializes Q to q(_1,_1), the second goal in

```
?- setup(Q), enter(a,Q,R).
   Q = ···
   R = q([a|_2],_2)
```

unifies _1 with [a|_2], where _2 is a fresh end marker.

The third goal enter(b,R,S) enters b into q([a|_2],_2) by unifying _2 with [b|_3], where _3 is a fresh variable.

When an element leaves a queue q(L,E), the resulting queue has the tail of L in place of L. Note in the diagram to the right of leave(X,S,T) that the open list for queue T is the tail of the open list for S. Similarly, in the diagram to the right of leave(Y,T,U), the open list for U is the tail of the open list for T.

The final goal wrapup(U) checks that the enter and leave operations leave U in an initial state q(L,E), where L is an empty open list with end marker E. Otherwise, q(L,E) will not unify with q([],[]) in the fact

```
wrapup(q([],[])).
```

In Fig. 11.11, U refers to q(_3,_3) and wrapup(q(_3,_3)) unifies _3 with []. □

Surprisingly, the rules for queues in Fig. 11.10 support "deficit" queues, which an element can leave before it enters. More precisely, an unspecified element represented by a variable can leave and be later filled in by an enter operation. In the following query, element X leaves the initial queue before we learn from the goal enter(a,R,S) that X represents a:

```
?- setup(Q), leave(X, Q, R), enter(a, R, S), wrapup(S).
   Q = q([a],[a])
   X = a
```

```
R = q([],[a])
S = q([],[])
```

Difference Lists

a difference list consists of a list and its suffix

Applications that use lists can be adapted to use open lists instead. Open-list versions require more care, but they can be more efficient. Care is needed because an open list changes when its end marker is unified (see again Fig. 11.9). Difference lists are a technique for coping with such changes.

A *difference list* is made up of two lists L and E, where E unifies with a suffix of L. The contents of the difference list consist of the elements that are in L but not in E. We write this difference list as dl(L,E). The lists L and E can be either open or closed. They are typically open.

Examples of difference lists with contents [a,b] are

```
dl([a,b], []).
dl([a,b,c], [c]).
dl([a,b|E], E).
dl([a,b,c|F], [c|F]).
```

In effect, the variables in dl(L,E) allow us to refer directly to the endpoints of its contents. The append operation on difference lists can be implemented in constant time using a nonrecursive rule. An informal reading of the following rule is that if X extends from L up to M and Y extends from M to N, then Z, the result of appending X and Y, extends from L to N:

```
append_dl(X, Y, Z) :-
    X = dl(L,M), Y = dl(M,N), Z = dl(L,N).
```

We close this section with an example that leads into the discussion of control in Prolog in Section 11.5. It is tempting to define a rule

```
contents(X, dl(L,E)) :- append(X, E, L).
```

to formalize the notion that the contents of dl(L,E) are the elements that are in L but not in E. The following queries confirm that each of the following difference lists has contents [a,b]:

```
?- contents([a,b], dl([a,b,c], [c])).
    yes

?- contents([a,b], dl([a,b,c|F], [c|F])).
    F = _1
    yes
```

An attempt to ask for the contents of dl([a,b|E],E) leads to a response that will be explained in Section 11.5:

```
?- contents(X, dl([a,b|E], E)).
    X = []
    E = [a,b,a,b,a,b,a,b,a,b,a,b,a,b,a,b,a,b, ...
```

11.5   CONTROL IN PROLOG

goal order and rule order are significant

In the informal equation

algorithm = logic + control

"logic" refers to the rules and queries in a logic program and "control" refers to how a language computes a response to a query. The pseudocode in Fig. 11.12 is an overview of control in Prolog.

Control in Prolog is characterized by two decisions in Fig. 11.12:

1. *Goal order.* Choose the leftmost subgoal.
2. *Rule order.* Select the first applicable rule.

The response to a query is affected both by goal order within the query and by rule order within the database of facts and rules.

Example 11.6   The examples in this section use the rules in Fig. 11.13. A sublist *S* of *Z*

```
start with a query as the current goal;
while the current goal is nonempty do
    choose the leftmost subgoal;
    if a rule applies to the subgoal then
        select the first applicable rule;
        form a new current goal
    else
        backtrack
    end if
end while;
succeed
```

Figure 11.12   Control in Prolog.

```
append([], Y, Y).
append([H|X], Y, [H|Z]) :- append(X,Y,Z).
prefix(X,Z) :- append(X,Y,Z).
suffix(Y,Z) :- append(X,Y,Z).
appen2([H|X], Y, [H|Z]) :- appen2(X,Y,Z).
appen2([], Y, Y).
```

Figure 11.13   Database of rules for examples in Section 11.5.

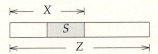

can be specified in the following seemingly equivalent ways:

> prefix X of Z **and** suffix S of X.
> suffix S of X **and** prefix X of Z.

The corresponding Prolog queries usually produce the same responses. Their responses differ, however, if S is not a sublist of Z:

```
?- prefix(X,[a,b,c]), suffix([e],X).
   no

?- suffix([e],X), prefix(X,[a,b,c]).
   [ infinite computation ]
```

We look closely at the suffix-prefix goal order in this section.

Rule order can also make a difference. New solutions are produced on demand for

```
?- append(X, [c], Z).
   X = []
   Z = [c] ;

   X = [_1]
   Z = [_1,c] ;

   X = [_1,_2]
   Z = [_1,_2,c]

   yes
```

(Recall that the `yes` means there might be more solutions.)

Relation `appen2` in Fig. 11.13 has the same rules as `append`, but they are written in the opposite order. The response

```
?- appen2(X, [c], Z).
    [ infinite computation ]
```

is also explained in this section.   □

Unification and Substitutions

definition of unification Since unification is central to control in Prolog, we now define it more formally than we did on page 436.

A *substitution* is a function from variables to terms. Let us write a substitution as a set of elements of the form $X \rightarrow T$, where variable X is mapped to term T. Unless stated otherwise, if a substitution maps X to T, then variable X does not occur in term T. The following is an example of a substitution: $\{V \rightarrow [b,c], Y \rightarrow [a,b,c]\}$.

$T\sigma$ is a standard notation for the result of applying substitution σ to term T. The result of applying a substitution to a term is given by

$$X\sigma = U \qquad \text{if } X \rightarrow U \text{ is in } \sigma$$
$$X\sigma = X \qquad \text{otherwise, for variable } X$$
$$(f(T_1, T_2))\sigma = f(U_1, U_2) \qquad \text{if } T_1\sigma = U_1, \; T_2\sigma = U_2$$

This definition generalizes to functors f with $k \geq 0$ arguments. In words, if σ contains $X \rightarrow U$, then the result of applying σ to variable X is U; otherwise $X\sigma$ is simply X. The result of applying σ to a term $f(T_1, \ldots, T_k)$, for $k \geq 0$ is obtained by applying σ to each subterm. For example,

$$Y \{V \rightarrow [b,c], Y \rightarrow [a,b,c]\} = [a,b,c]$$
$$Z \{V \rightarrow [b,c], Y \rightarrow [a,b,c]\} = Z$$
$$(append([\,],Y,Y)) \{V \rightarrow [b,c], Y \rightarrow [a,b,c]\} = append([\,],[a,b,c],[a,b,c])$$

A term U is an *instance* of T, if $U = T\sigma$, for some substitution σ. Terms T_1 and T_2 unify if $T_1\sigma$ and $T_2\sigma$ are identical for some substitution σ; we call σ a *unifier* of T_1 and T_2. Substitution σ is the *most general unifier* of T_1 and T_2, if for all other unifiers σ', $T_1\sigma'$ is an instance of $T_1\sigma$.[5]

---

[5] In the definition of most general unifier, it is enough to say that $T_1\sigma'$ is an instance of $T_1\sigma$. Since σ and σ' are both unifiers, $T_2\sigma'$ is automatically an instance of $T_2\sigma$, because $T_1\sigma = T_2\sigma$ and $T_1\sigma' = T_2\sigma'$.

The terms *append*([ ], *Y*, *Y*) and *append*([ ], [*a*|*V*], [*a*,*b*,*c*]) unify because they have a common instance *append*([ ], [*a*,*b*,*c*], [*a*,*b*,*c*]). Their most general unifier is the substitution {*V* → [*b*,*c*], *Y* → [*a*,*b*,*c*]}.

Applying a Rule to a Goal

if a rule applies, then unification refines the current goal

The pseudocode in Fig. 11.14 restates control in Prolog in terms of substitutions and unifiers. We explore it by first considering an example that succeeds without backtracking. Backtracking is then described in terms of a tree representation of a computation.

In Fig. 11.14, a rule $A :- B_1, \ldots, B_n$ *applies* to a subgoal G if its head A unifies with G. Variables in the rule are renamed before unification to keep them distinct from variables in the subgoal.

Example 11.7 The response to the query

```
?- suffix([a],L), prefix(L,[a,b,c]).
   L = [a]
```

is computed without backtracking, as in Fig. 11.15. Initially, the current goal consists of the two subgoals in this query:

$$\text{suffix([a],L), prefix(L,[a,b,c])} \tag{11.7}$$

Choose the leftmost subgoal `suffix([a],L)`. Select the only rule that applies to this subgoal. Rename the variables in the rule to keep them distinct

---

start with a query as the current goal;
while the current goal is nonempty **do**
    let the current goal be $G_1, \ldots, G_k$, where $k \geq 1$;
    choose the leftmost subgoal G_1;
    if a rule applies to G_1 **then**
        select the first such rule $A :- B_1, \ldots, B_j$, where $j \geq 0$;
        let σ be the most general unifier of G_1 and A;
        the current goal becomes $B_1\sigma, \ldots, B_j\sigma, G_2\sigma, \ldots, G_k\sigma$
    else
        backtrack
    end if
end while;
succeed

Figure 11.14 Control in Prolog: A restatement of Fig. 11.12.

G̲O̲A̲L̲

```
suffix([a],L), prefix(L,[a,b,c])
```

$$suffix([a], L) \quad \textbf{if} \quad append(\_1, [a], L).$$

```
append(_1,[a],L), prefix(L,[a,b,c])
```

$\{\_1 \rightarrow [\,], L \rightarrow [a]\} \quad append([\,], [a], [a]).$

```
prefix([a],[a,b,c])
```

$$prefix([a], [a,b,c]) \quad \textbf{if} \quad append([a], \_2, [a,b,c]).$$

```
append([a],_2,[a,b,c])
```

$$append([a], \_2, [a,b,c]) \quad \textbf{if} \quad append([\,], \_2, [b,c]).$$

```
append([],_2,[b,c])
```

$\{\_2 \rightarrow [b,c]\} \qquad append([\,], [b,c], [b,c]).$

yes

Figure 11.15 A computation that succeeds without backtracking.

---

from any variables in the goal. With X′, Y′, and Z′ as the renamed variables, the rule for suffix becomes

```
suffix(Y′, Z′) :- append(X′, Y′, Z′).
```

The substitution {Y′ → [a], Z′ → L} unifies the rule head with the chosen subgoal. The rule as it applies to the subgoal suffix([a],L) is given by the pseudocode:

$$suffix([a], L) \quad \textbf{if} \quad append(\_1, [a], L)$$

Here, [a] takes the place of Y′, L takes the place of Z′, and a Prolog-like name _1 takes the place of X′.

Replace the subgoal suffix([a],L) in (11.7) by the condition append(_1,[a],L) to get the new current goal:

```
append(_1,[a],L), prefix(L,[a,b,c])
```
                                                                    (11.8)

The fact `append([],Y'',Y'')` applies to the new leftmost subgoal `append(_1,[a],L)` because `[]` unifies `_1` and `Y''` unifies with both `[a]` and `L`. Since a fact consists of a head and no conditions, the new current goal is

$$prefix([a],[a,b,c]) \tag{11.9}$$

Note that `[a]` has been substituted for variable `L`.

The rest of the computation can be seen from Fig. 11.15.   □

Prolog Search Trees

if no rule applies, backtrack

The chain of goals in Fig. 11.15 generalizes into *Prolog search trees*, which depict computations that explore all possible solutions to a goal. Nodes in a Prolog search tree represent goals. A node has a child for each rule that applies to the leftmost subgoal at the node. The order of the children is the same as the rule order in the database of rules.[6]

A Prolog computation explores a Prolog search tree in a "depth-first" manner. It starts at the root and explores the subtrees at the children of each node from left to right. The computation produces a *yes* response each time it reaches a node in the subtree with an empty goal.

Example 11.8   A portion of the Prolog search tree for the query

```
?- suffix([b], L), prefix(L, [a,b,c]).
   L = [a,b]
```

appears in Fig. 11.16.

There is only one rule for `suffix`, so the root has only one child. The approach of Example 11.7 yields the following goal at the child of the root:

$$append(_1,[b],L), \; prefix(L,[a,b,c]) \tag{11.10}$$

Both of the rules for `append` apply to the leftmost subgoal in (11.10). The node for (11.10) therefore has two children. Prolog tries rules in the order they appear in the database of rules. It therefore unifies `append(_1,[b],L)` with `append([],Y',Y')` to get the substitution

$$\{_1 \rightarrow [], \; L \rightarrow [b]\}$$

---

[6] The definition of Prolog search trees presupposes that rules are applied to the leftmost subgoal. A more general definition of search trees would allow any subgoal to be chosen as the subgoal to which rules are applied. Furthermore, a more general definition would allow rules to be selected in any order.

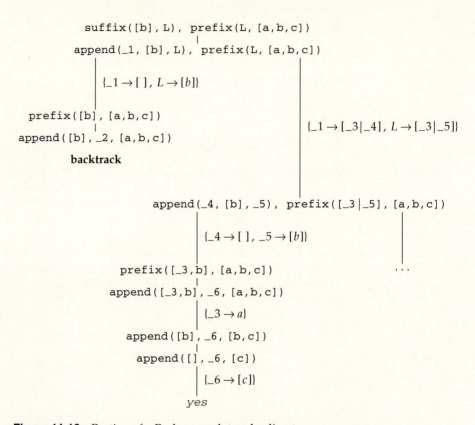

Figure 11.16 Portion of a Prolog search tree leading to a *yes* response.

Since the first rule for `append` is a fact, it has no conditions, so the new goal formed from (11.10) is

$$\texttt{prefix([b],[a,b,c])} \tag{11.11}$$

There is only one rule for `prefix`, and it leads to a new goal,

$$\texttt{append([b],\_2,[a,b,c])} \tag{11.12}$$

Now we have a problem. This subgoal does not unify with either of the rules for `append`. Prolog therefore backtracks to the nearest goal with an untried rule. Such a goal is (11.10), presented again here:

$$append(\_1,[b],L), \; prefix(L,[a,b,c]) \hspace{3cm} (11.10)$$

The first rule for append did not lead to success, so Prolog tries the second one. A suitable instance of the second rule is

$$append([\_3|\_4], \; [b], \; [\_3|\_5]) \; :- \; append(\_4,[b],\_5).$$

A new goal is formed from (11.10) using the substitution

$$\{\_1 \rightarrow [\_3|\_4], \; L \rightarrow [\_3|\_5]\}$$

The new goal is

$$append(\_4,[b],\_5), \; prefix([\_3|\_5],[a,b,c]) \hspace{2cm} (11.13)$$

The computation now proceeds without backtracking to a *yes* response in Fig. 11.16. □

Figure 11.17 presents a final restatement of control in Prolog. Procedure *visit* calls itself recursively to try new subgoals. In terms of search trees, a recursive call corresponds to visiting one of the children of a node. The recursion can stop in one of two ways:

1. The goal *G* is empty and **succeed** is reached.
2. No rule applies to the leftmost subgoal of *G* and the activation ends.

Backtracking corresponds to the latter case, in which no rule applies to *G* and control returns to the caller.

Goal Order Changes Solutions

rules are applied to the leftmost subgoal

The order of subgoals within a query affects the Prolog search tree for a query. The reason is that rules are always applied to the leftmost subgoal.

From Example 11.7 or from Fig. 11.15, the solution *L=[a]* to the following query is produced without backtracking. Note, however, that an infinite computation ensues if we ask for another solution.

```
?- suffix([a],L), prefix(L,[a,b,c]).
  L = [a] ;
  [ infinite computation ]
```

The leftmost subgoal

```
?- suffix([a],L).
  L = [a] ;
```

```
procedure visit(G);
begin
    if the current goal G is nonempty then
        let G be G₁, ..., Gₖ, where k ≥ 1;
        choose the leftmost subgoal G₁;
        for i := 1 to the number of rules do
            let rule i be A :- B₁, ..., Bⱼ, where j ≥ 0;
            if rule i applies to G₁ then
                let σ be the most general unifier of G₁ and A;
                let G' be B₁σ, ..., Bⱼσ, G₂σ, ..., Gₖσ;
                visit(G');
            end if
        end for
    else
        succeed
    end if
    { backtrack by returning to caller }
end visit
```

Figure 11.17   Control in Prolog as a recursive procedure.

```
L = [_1,a] ;
L = [_1,_2,a] ;
   ...
```

has an infinite number of solutions, only the first of which satisfies `prefix(L,[a,b,c])`.

In other words, the Prolog search tree for the goal

```
suffix([a],L), prefix(L,[a,b,c])
```

has exactly one *yes* node that is reached without backtracking as in Fig. 11.15. A futile search through the rest of the infinite tree ensues if we ask for a further solution.

By contrast, the reordered query

```
?- prefix(X,[a,b,c]), suffix([a],X).
   L = [a] ;
   no
```

has a finite Prolog search tree. The portion leading up to the only *yes* node appears in Fig. 11.18. The same solution L=[a] is reached without backtrack-

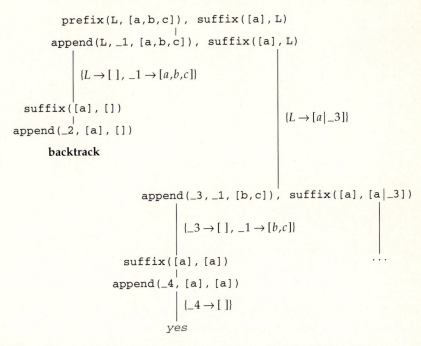

Figure 11.18   The effect of changing goal order; compare with Fig. 11.15.

ing in Fig. 11.15 and with backtracking in Fig. 11.18. Hence, a change in goal order leads to a change in the Prolog search tree.

Rule Order Affects the Search for Solutions

rules are applied in order

The rule order in the database of rules determines the order of the children of a node in a Prolog search tree. Rule order therefore changes the order in which solutions are reached by a Prolog computation.

The Prolog search trees in Fig. 11.19 are based on the following rule order:

```
append([], Y, Y).
append([H|X], Y, [H|Z]) :- append(X,Y,Z).

appen2([H|X], Y, [H|Z]) :- appen2(X,Y,Z).
appen2([], Y, Y).
```

The search tree for appen2(X,[c],Z) is a mirror image of the search tree for append(X,[c],Z). Unfortunately, the Prolog computation for

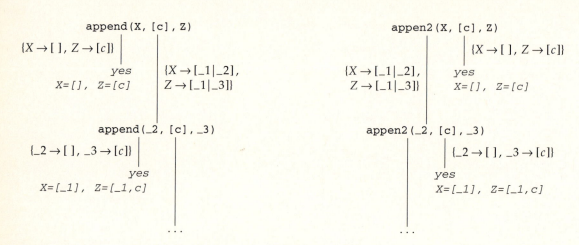

Figure 11.19 Rule order determines the order of the children of a node.

appen2(X, [c], Z) never reaches a solution because it keeps going deeper and deeper down an infinite path:

```
?- appen2(X, [c], Z).
   [ infinite computation ]
```

The computation for append(X, [c], Z), on the other hand, goes from one solution to the next:

```
?- append(X, [c], Z).
   X = []
   Z = [c] ;

   X = [_1]
   Z = [_1,c] ;
      . . .
```

The Occurs-Check Problem

occurs checks
prevent cycles
In the name of efficiency, Prolog neglects to check whether a variable X occurs in a term T before it unifies X with T; such checks are called *occurs checks*. When X does indeed occur in T, then unification of X and T can lead to a non-terminating computation. For example, consider

```
?- append([], E, [a,b|E]).
    E = [a,b,a,b,a,b,a,b,a,b,a,b,a,b,a,b,a,b, ···
```

For `append([],E,[a,b|E])` to unify with `append([],Y,Y)`, variable `Y` must unify with both E and with the term `[a,b|E]` containing E.

Prolog neglects to check whether E occurs within `[a,b|E]`. When we attempt to substitute `[a,b|E]` for E, we get

$$E = [a,b|E] = [a,b,a,b|E] = [a,b,a,b,a,b|E] = \cdots$$

Some variants of Prolog construct cyclic terms like the following if a variable is unified with a term containing it:

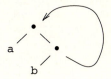

11.6 CUTS

cuts are procedural

Informally, a cut prunes or "cuts out" an unexplored part of a Prolog search tree. Cuts can therefore be used to make a computation more efficient by eliminating futile searching and backtracking. Cuts can also be used to implement a form of negation, something Horn clauses cannot do.

Cuts are controversial because they are impure. As we saw in Section 11.5, control in Prolog sometimes sends it into an infinite loop that could be avoided by choosing a different order of evaluation. Pure logic is order independent, so Prolog is an approximation of pure logic. Cuts make Prolog depart further from pure logic, to the point where a Prolog program must be read procedurally; that is, it must be read in terms of its computation.

A *cut*, written as !, appears as a condition within a rule. When a rule

$$B :- C_1, \ldots, C_{j-1}, !, C_{j+1}, \ldots, C_k$$

is applied during a computation, the cut tells control to backtrack past $C_{j-1}, \ldots, C_1, B$, without considering any remaining rules for them. We explore the implications of this remark before considering programming applications of cuts.

A Cut as the First Condition

Consider rules of the form $B :- !,C$, in which a cut appears as the first condition. If the goal C fails, then control backtracks past B without considering any remaining rules for B. Thus, the cut has the effect of making B fail if C fails.

To see the effect of a cut on a Prolog search tree, consider the following rules for b:

```
b :- c.
b :- d.
b :- e.
```

Since there are three rules for b, any node with b as the first subgoal has three children, one for each rule. Suppose that the condition at a node is b, G, where G represents some additional subgoals. Then the subtree rooted at the node has the following form:

Now, suppose a cut is inserted in the second rule, changing it to

```
b :- !, d.
```

This cut eliminates the rule b:-e from ever being considered. The new Prolog search tree is as follows. (The dotted part is shown only for comparison; it is not part of the new search tree.)

In more detail, a cut as the first subgoal in !, d, G is satisfied immediately, leaving d, G as the new goal. During backtracking, however, the cut has the side effect of eliminating the third rule b:-e from consideration.

Example 11.9   The following database of rules is designed specifically for the Prolog search tree in Fig. 11.20(a):

```
a(1) :- b.
a(2) :- e.
b :- c.
b :- d.
```

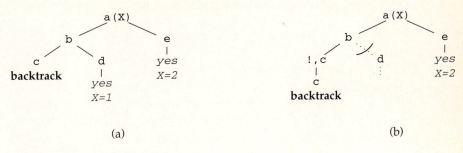

Figure 11.20   The effect of a cut.

```
d.
e.
```

The query a(X) has two solutions:

```
?- a(X).
    X = 1 ;
    X = 2 ;
    no
```

If the rule b:-c is changed to b:-!, c by inserting a cut as the first condition, the Prolog search tree changes to the one in Fig. 11.20(b). The query a(X) then has just one solution:

```
?- a(X).
    X = 2 ;
    no
```
□

The Effect of a Cut

cuts restrict backtracking

As mentioned earlier, when a rule

$$B :- C_1, \ldots, C_{j-1}, !, C_{j+1}, \ldots, C_k$$

is applied during a computation, the cut tells control to backtrack past $C_{j-1}, \ldots, C_1$, B, without considering any remaining rules for them.

The following example considers the effect of inserting a cut in the middle of a guess-and-verify rule. As discussed in Section 11.4, the right side of a guess-and-verify rule has the form *guess(S)*, *verify(S)*, where *guess(S)* generates potential solutions until one satisfying *verify*(S) is found. The effect of inserting a cut between them, as in

$$conclusion(S) \;:\!-\; guess(S), \,!, \, verify(S)$$

is to eliminate all but the first guess.

Example 11.10 The search trees in Fig. 11.21 are based on the rules in Fig. 11.22. The computation depicted by Fig. 11.21(a) begins with the succession of goals:

```
a(Z)              starting goal
b(Z)              from  a(X) :- b(X).
g(Z),v(Z)         from  b(X) :- g(X), v(X).
```

The subgoal `g(Z)` generates values 1, 2, and 3 for `Z`. Each of these values leads to a solution of the original goal `a(Z)`.

The fourth solution `Z=4` in Fig. 11.21(a) is obtained by backtracking and trying the alternative rule for b:

```
b(X)  :- X=4, v(X).
```

We get to the final solution `Z=5` by backtracking all the way back to the original goal `a(Z)` and trying the rule

```
a(X)  :- f(X).
```

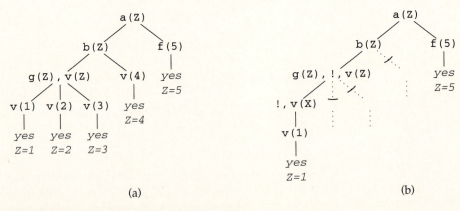

(a)   (b)

Figure 11.21   Solutions eliminated by a cut.

```
a(X)  :- b(X).              a(X)  :- b(X).
a(X)  :- f(X).              a(X)  :- f(X).
b(X)  :- g(X), v(X).        b(X)  :- g(X), !, v(X).
b(X)  :- X = 4, v(X).       b(X)  :- X = 4, v(X).
g(1).                       g(1).
g(2).                       g(2).
g(3).                       g(3).
v(X).                       v(X).
f(5).                       f(5).

        (a)                          (b)
```

Figure 11.22   Insertion of a cut in the third rule.

Now, consider the database of Fig. 11.22(b), where a cut appears in the first rule for b:

```
b(X)  :- g(X), !, v(X).
```

The insertion of this cut changes the Prolog search tree in Fig. 11.21(a) into the tree in Fig. 11.21(b). This cut tells control to backtrack past g(X) and b(X) without considering any remaining rules for g and b, as in Fig. 11.21(b). The goal a(Z) now has just two solutions.   □

Cuts in Prolog are frequently misunderstood, perhaps with good reason. From the search tree in Fig. 11.21(b), the query a(Z) has two solutions:

```
?- a(Z).
   Z = 1 ;
   Z = 5 ;
   no
```

We might expect from these responses that a(2), a(3), and a(4) are unsatisfiable. In fact, the search trees in Fig. 11.23 reach a *yes* response for each of a(2), a(3), and a(4).

The queries a(2) and a(3) lead to a *yes* response without backtracking, as in Fig. 11.23(a-b). Since no backtracking is needed, the cut does not prevent the computation from reaching a *yes*.

Finally consider the query a(4). The computation in Fig. 11.23(c) never reaches the cut, because g(4) is unsatisfiable. The cut therefore has no effect, and the computation reaches a *yes*.

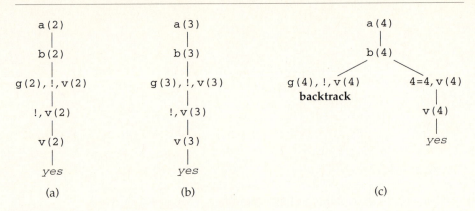

Figure 11.23   Prolog search trees based on the rules in Fig. 11.22(b).

Programming Applications of Cuts

green cuts skip fruitless searches

A relatively benign use of cuts is to prune parts of a Prolog search tree that cannot possibly reach a solution. Such cuts have been called *green* cuts; they make a program efficient without changing its solutions. Cuts that are not green are called *red*.

By restricting backtracking, cuts reduce the memory requirements of a program. Without cuts, every single rule application and unification has to be recorded until the overall computation succeeds or backtracking occurs.

Example 11.11   For an example of green cuts, consider the following rules for binary search trees, from Fig. 11.8:

```
member(K, node(K,_,_)).
member(K, node(N,S,_)) :- K < N, member(K, S).
member(K, node(N,_,T)) :- K > N, member(K, T).
```

These three rules are mutually exclusive because only one of K=N, K<N, and K>N can be true at a time. The cut in the second rule,

```
member(K, node(K,_,_)).
member(K, node(N,S,_)) :- K < N, !, member(K, S).
member(K, node(N,_,T)) :- K > N, member(K, T).
```

is therefore a green cut. It is reached only if K<N, so the third rule cannot possibly apply if the cut is reached. The cut makes the program more efficient in the following case: K < N but member(K, S) fails because K is not in the tree.

Without the cut, Prolog will backtrack and try the third rule, only to fail on the test K > N — there could be many such futile tests during a single unsuccessful search.   □

Variants of the lookup relation in the following example have been used in compilers written in Prolog. The compilers use binary search trees. For simplicity, however, the example uses linear search to look for a key in a list of key-value pairs.[7]

Example 11.12 The only difference between the rules for lookup and install is a cut in the first rule for lookup:

```
lookup(K,V, [(K,W)|_]) :- !, V = W.
lookup(K,V, [_|Z]) :- lookup(K,V,Z).

install(K,V, [(K,W)|_]) :- V = W.
install(K,V, [_|Z]) :- install(K,V,Z).
```

The lookup relation can be used to enter information into a table of key-value pairs. The table is maintained as an open list, ending in a variable.

```
?- lookup(p,72,D).
    D = [(p,72)|_1] ;
    no
```

(Recall that we type a semicolon to ask for more solutions. The *no* response means that there are no more solutions.) An attempt to enter two different values for the same key ends in failure:

```
?- lookup(p,72,D), lookup(p,73,D).
    no
```

The following query uses relation lookup both to enter pairs and to look up a value:

```
?- lookup(1,58,D), lookup(p,72,D), lookup(p,Y,D).
    D = [(1,58),(p,72)|_1]
    Y = 72 ;

    no
```

Lacking the cut, relation install behaves quite differently. The following query has an infinite number of solutions:

[7] The simplified syntax of terms in Section 11.2 does not allow terms of the form (K,V), but Prolog does. The term (K,V) is a pair with first component K and second component V.

```
?- install(p,72,D).
  [(p,72)|_1] ;
  [_2,(p,72)|_3] ;
  [_2,_4,(p,72)|_5]

  yes
```

Relation `install` also allows two different values to be entered for the same key:

```
?- install(p,72,D), install(p,73,D).
  [(p,72),(p,73)|_1] ;
```

The role of the cut can be seen more clearly from the following equivalent version of the above rules for `lookup`:

```
lookup(K,V,L) :- L = [(K,W)|_], !, V = W.
lookup(K,V,L) :- L = [_|Z], lookup(K,V,Z).
```

If D is a fresh variable, we get the following succession of goals:

`lookup(p,72,D)`	*starting goal*
`D=[(p,_1)|_2], !, 72=_1`	*apply first rule*
`!, 72=_1`	*D unifies*
`72=_1`	
`yes`	*72 unifies with _1*

The cut prevents further solutions by eliminating consideration of the second rule for `lookup`.

Now consider the query

```
?- lookup(p,72,D), lookup(p,73,D).
  no
```

As we just saw, the subgoal `lookup(p,72,D)` leaves D bound to a list `[(p,72)|_2]`. We therefore get the following succession of goals:

`lookup(p,73,[(p,72)|_2])`	
`[(p,72)|_2]=[(p,_3)|_4], !, 73=_3`	*apply first rule*
`!, 73=72`	*the lists unify*
`73=72`	

The cut forces failure by preventing consideration of the second rule for `lookup`.   □

Negation as Failure

The not operator in Prolog is implemented by the rules

```
not(X)  :- X, !, fail.
not(_).
```

Informally, the first rule attempts to satisfy the argument X of not. If the goal
X succeeds, then the cut and fail are reached. The construct fail forces failure and the cut prevents consideration of the second rule. On the other hand,
if the goal X fails, then the second rule succeeds, because _ unifies with any
term.

These rules for not explain the difference between the responses to

```
?- X = 2, not(X = 1).
   X = 2
```

and

```
?- not(X = 1), X = 2.
   no
```

In the first of these two queries, the subgoal X=2 unifies X with 2, as
shown in Fig. 11.24(a), leaving not(2=1) as the current goal. The first rule
for not yields the new goal

```
2=1, !, fail
```

Since 2=1 fails, the cut is not reached; hence, the cut is not shown in Fig.
11.24(a). Then, the second rule for not is tried and the goal not(2=1) succeeds.

The search tree for the second query appears in Fig. 11.24(b). The first rule
for not yields the current goal

```
X=1, !, fail, X=2.
```

The subgoal X=1 succeeds, the cut is satisfied, and fail is reached. The cut
eliminates consideration of the other rule for not so the entire computation
fails. Note that the subgoal X=2 is never reached.

In general, it is safe to apply not to a term without variables because such
terms have no variables to be changed by unification.

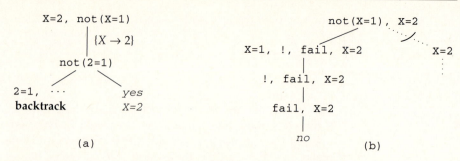

Figure 11.24 Prolog search trees illustrating negation as failure.

Exercises

11.1 Given the relations

father(X,Y)	X is the father of Y
mother(X,Y)	X is the mother of Y
female(X)	X is female
male(X)	X is male

define relations for the following:
a. Sibling
b. Sister
c. Grandson
d. First cousin
e. Descendant

11.2 Using only the append relation, formulate queries to determine the following:
a. The third element of a list
b. The last element of a list
c. All but the last element of a list
d. Whether a list is a concatenation of three copies of the same sublist
e. Whether a list Y is formed by inserting an element A somewhere in a list X

11.3 Define relations to determine the following:
a. Is a list a permutation of another list?
b. Does a list have an even number of elements?
c. Is a list formed by merging two lists?
d. Is a list a palindrome; that is, does it read the same from left to right as it does from right to left?

11.4   Define relations corresponding to the following operations on lists:

   a. Remove the second and succeeding adjacent duplicates.

   b. Leave only the elements that do not have an adjacent duplicate.

   c. Leave only one copy of the elements that have adjacent duplicates.

11.5   Complete Example 11.3 by defining relations `insert` and `delete` on binary search trees.

11.6   Arithmetic can be performed in Prolog by using subgoals of the form

⟨*variable*⟩ is ⟨*expression*⟩

This subgoal succeeds if the result of evaluating the expression unifies with the variable, as in

```
?- X is 2, Y is X+1.
   X = 2
   Y = 3
```

An error occurs if the expression after `is` contains any unbound variables, as in

```
?- Y is X+1, X is 2.
   Error
```

   a. Define a relation corresponding to the factorial function.

   b. Define a relation corresponding to a tail-recursive version of the factorial function.

11.7   Draw Prolog search trees for the query

```
?- reverse([a,b,c,d],W).
```

where `reverse` is defined by the rules:

   a.
```
reverse([],[]).
reverse([A|X],Z) :- reverse(X,Y), append(Y,[A],Z).
```

   b.
```
reverse(X,Z) :- rev(X,[],Z).
rev([],Y,Y).
rev([A|X],Y,Z) :- rev(X,[A|Y],Z).
```

11.8   Consider a relation `member` defined by the rules

```
member(M, [M|_]).
member(M, [_|T]) :- member(M, T).
```

Draw the portion of the Prolog search tree that corresponds to the responses in the following:

   a.
```
?- member(b, [a,b,c]).
     yes
```

   b.
```
?- member(d, [a,b,c]).
     no
```

    c. *?- member(b, X).*

        X = [b|_] ;

        X = [_,b|_] ;

        X = [_,_,b|_]

        yes

11.9   With the relation `member` as in Exercise 11.8, draw Prolog search trees for the following queries:

    a. `X = [1,2,3], member(a,X).`

    b. `member(a,X), X = [1,2,3].`

11.10 Except for the cut in the first rule, the following rules are the same as those in Section 11.5:

```
append([], Y, Y) :- !.
append([H|X],Y,[H|Z]) :- append(X,Y,Z).
prefix(X,Z) :- append(X,Y,Z).
suffix(Y,Z) :- append(X,Y,Z).
```

Compare the Prolog search trees for the following queries with the trees in Fig. 11.15 and 11.16:

    a. `suffix([a],L), prefix(L,[a,b,c]).`

    b. `suffix([b],L), prefix(L,[a,b,c]).`

Bibliographic Notes

Prolog, from *programmation en logique*, is the name of a programming language developed by Alain Colmerauer and Phillipe Roussel in 1972. Companion articles by Kowalski [1988] and Cohen [1988] provide a glimpse of its early history. The development of the language was influenced by W-grammars (van Wijngaarden et al. [1975]), the description language for Algol 68, and by Robinson's [1965] resolution principle for mechanical theorem proving.

    Kowalski notes, "Looking back on our early discoveries, I value most the discovery that computation could be subsumed by deduction." His early examples included "computationally efficient axioms for such recursive predicates as addition and factorial." He continues, "For [Colmerauer], the Horn clause definition of appending lists was much more characteristic of the importance of logic programming."

    Cohen offers reasons why Prolog developed slowly, relative to Lisp: (1) the lack of interesting examples illustrating the expressive power of the language, (2) the lack of adequate implementations, and (3) the availability of Lisp. He adds, "It is fair to say that the subsequent interpreters and compilers developed by Warren played a major role in the acceptance of Prolog." Warren [1980] describes how Prolog itself can be used for compiler writing.

More information on Prolog programming techniques can be found in textbooks such as Sterling and Shapiro [1994] and Clocksin and Mellish [1987]. Example 11.5 and Exercise 11.7 are motivated by examples in Sterling and Shapiro [1994]. Cohen [1988] cites difference lists as Colmerauer's valuable contribution to Roussel's original Prolog interpreter; Clark and Tärnlund [1977] is a published reference for difference lists.

Cuts were introduced by Colmerauer to conserve memory space. See Clark [1978] for a treatment of negation-as-failure.

For a discussion of logic programming in general, see Kowalski [1979a] or Hogger [1984].

12

An Introduction to
Concurrent Programming

I don't think we have found the right programming concepts for parallel computers yet. When we do, they will almost certainly be very
different from anything we know today.

> – *Brinch Hansen [1993], concluding his history of the monitor concept and moni-
tors in Concurrent Pascal.*

My only serious debate with your account is with the very last sentence. I do not believe there is any "right" collection of programming
concepts for parallel (or even sequential) computers. The design of a
language is always a compromise, in which the designer must take
into account the desired level of abstraction, the target machine architecture, and the proposed range of applications.

> – *Hoare [1993], commenting on Brinch Hansen [1993].*

Concurrency in a programming language and parallelism in the underlying
hardware are independent concepts. Hardware operations occur in *parallel* if
they overlap in time. Operations in the source text are *concurrent* if they could
be, but need not be, executed in parallel. Operations that occur one after the
other, ordered in time, are said to be *sequential*. We can have concurrency in a
language without parallel hardware, and we can have parallel execution without concurrency in the language. In short, concurrency refers to the potential
for parallelism.

study
communication
and
synchronization
between processes

  The fundamental concept of concurrent programming is the notion of a
process. In this chapter, a *process* corresponds to a sequential computation,
with its own thread of control. The *thread* of a sequential computation is the
sequence of program points that are reached as control flows through the
source text of the program. Sequential processes have traditionally been used

to study concurrency. Ada, the working language of this chapter, deals with sequential processes.

Interactions between processes take two forms:

1. *Communication* involves the exchange of data between processes, either by an explicit message or through the values of shared variables. A variable is *shared* between processes if it is visible to the code for the processes.

2. *Synchronization* relates the thread of one process with that of another. If p is a point in the thread of a process P, and q is a point in the thread of a process Q, then synchronization can be used to constrain the order in which P reaches p and Q reaches q. In other words, synchronization involves the exchange of control information between processes.

The need for communication and synchronization can be visualized in terms of competition and cooperation between processes. Competition occurs when processes require exclusive use of a resource — for example, when two processes compete to use the same printer, or to reserve a seat on a flight. Here, synchronization is needed to grant a process exclusive use of a resource. Cooperation occurs when two processes work on parts of the same problem, and typically involves both communication and synchronization.

12.1 PARALLELISM IN HARDWARE

Since hardware developments have long provided the impetus for studying and controlling concurrency, this section takes a brief look at machine organization.

Input/Output in Parallel with Execution

synchronization was needed to keep two channels from writing to the same printer

Parallelism in hardware dates back to the late 1950s, when the speed disparities between instruction execution and input/output led to the introduction of special-purpose processors called *data channels* for controlling input/output devices. A hundred thousand instructions could be executed in the time it took to read a single card or print a single line. By attending to input/output, channels allowed the central processor to concentrate on instruction execution.

Conceptually, the hardware organization changed from that in Fig. 12.1(a), with a single processor and a single memory, to that in Fig. 12.1(b), with several processors accessing a shared memory. The IBM 709, circa 1958, could have seven processors: a central general-purpose processor, and up to six data channels. The machine could therefore simultaneously perform arithmetic operations and read from tapes or cards and write to tapes or printers.

The casual programmer was insulated from this complexity in the hardware by precursors of operating systems. Mock and Swift [1959] describe an

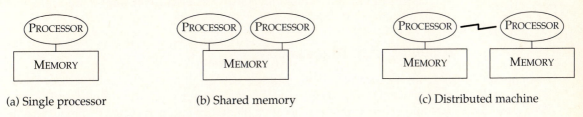

Figure 12.1 Three machine organizations.

elaborate buffering system for managing input/output so "programmers need not be particularly aware of the fact that parallel operations are occurring."

Parallelism raised the problem of synchronized access to shared resources such as memory locations and input/output devices. How could a data channel be prevented from obliterating a precious value in a shared memory location, just before an instruction used it? Or, how could two data channels be prevented from writing to the same printer and mixing up its output?

An unattractive solution, called *busy waiting* or *polling*, consisted of having a processor continually check a condition, such as the completion of input/output by a data channel. The following pseudocode for busy waiting emphasizes that no useful work is done until the condition becomes true:

> **repeat** (∗ nothing ∗) **until** ⟨*condition*⟩;

Interrupts and Time Sharing

time-shared programs appear to run in parallel

Hardware signals called *interrupts* allowed the activities of a central processor to be synchronized with those of the data channels. If a program P needed to read a card, the processor could initiate the read action on a data channel and start executing another program Q. Once the card had been read, the channel sent an interrupt to the central processor, which could then resume execution of P.

Interrupts, together with a hardware clock, also made it possible to do *time sharing* or *time slicing*, whereby a processor divides its time between several programs. Every so often, the clock sends an interrupt to the processor, which then suspends one program and restarts another. Programs can of course be suspended for input/output as well.

A time-sharing system makes it appear as if several programs are running in parallel, although only one of them is making progress at any time. The rate at which the programs run is unpredictable because it depends on outside factors such as the number of programs that happen to be sharing the machine.

Time slicing can be used as an implementation technique for a concurrent language running on sequential hardware because it allows multiple processes to share a processor.

Multiprocessor Organization

communication can be synchronous or asynchronous

True multiprocessors, with multiple central processors, were developed soon after channels. The Burroughs B5000, circa 1960, allowed two central processors and four channels to access a shared memory. A shared memory facilitates communication through shared variables that are visible to the communicating processes. Communication can then be *synchronous*; that is, a value is sent and received simultaneously, without communication delays.

The third organization in Fig. 12.1(c) is a distributed machine in which each processor has its own exclusive memory. Distributed processors communicate by message passing. If the processors are geographically separated, then communication delays cannot be ignored. With *asynchronous* communication, an unspecified amount of time can elapse between the time a message is sent and the time it is received.

Variants of the organizations in Fig. 12.1 can be created by using combinations of exclusive and shared memory or by imposing constraints on the processors. For example, SIMD (single-instruction multiple-data) machines have arrays of processors that all execute the same instruction at the same time on data local to each processor.

Reactive Systems

use separate processes for keyboard, mouse, and windows

On a different scale, the potential for parallelism occurs in systems that interact with their environment. Examples of such *reactive systems* are user interfaces, process controllers, communication networks, and games.

Consider a user interface with a keyboard, a mouse, and a display supporting multiple windows. The keyboard and mouse are independent input devices, so the user interface must deal concurrently with characters typed at the keyboard and with the movements of the mouse. At the same time, it must display information in one or more windows. In a language that supports concurrency, separate processes can be used to manage the keyboard, the mouse, each window, and the display as a whole.

12.2   STREAMS: IMPLICIT SYNCHRONIZATION

Each process in this section is a traditional sequential program. Communication between processes is through their inputs and outputs, with the output of one process becoming the input of another. The sequence of values that flow from one process to another is called a *stream*. Processes connected by streams are called *coroutines*. Coroutines have zero or more input streams and zero or more output streams.

Support for coroutines and streams can be found in both imperative and functional languages, especially those with lazy evaluation. The examples in this short section use the pipe construct of the UNIX operating system because of its simplicity.

Synchronization is conspicuous by its absence in this section. If we measure the complexity of a concurrent program by the amount of explicit synchronization, then this section considers one of the simplest settings for concurrency — the individual processes are written in isolation, without thinking of how they will be put together to form a concurrent program. A process waits for its input to arrive, as a C program waits when it calls the standard function

```
getchar()
```

to get a character. Such waiting is the only form of synchronization between processes.

Process Networks

The *pipe* construct, written as " | ," allows traditional sequential programs to be combined into a concurrent program. A UNIX command of the form

$$P_1 \mid P_2 \mid \cdots \mid P_k$$

specifies concurrent execution of the processes $P_1, P_2, \ldots, P_k$, with the the output of process P_i becoming the input of process P_{i+1}, for $1 \le i < k$. Such commands are referred to as *pipelines*. Each process in a pipeline is typically a program in a sequential language such as C.

coroutines in a process network are connected by streams

A *process network* is a generalization of a pipeline. It consists of a set of processes together with edges of the form $P \to Q$, representing a stream flowing from process P to process Q. Each process runs concurrently with the others, at its own pace, as long as it has input. An edge $P \to Q$ therefore represents an unbounded buffer into which P puts values and from which Q gets values. Thus, P and Q are a producer-consumer pair.

Examples of Pipelines

The pipeline

```
bc | number
```

is illustrated in Fig. 12.2. Process bc transforms a stream of expressions into a stream of integers, which process number transforms into a stream of English words for the integers. A variant of this pipeline

```
bc | number | speak
```

where speak converts English words into sounds, was used by blind programmers around Bell Laboratories.

The power of pipes as a programming construct is based on two things:

- A standard input/output interface, consisting of a stream of characters
- A suitable collection of primitive processes

Each primitive process does a simple job, perhaps even a trivial job, but short pipelines of processes can do what would otherwise be done by substantial programs. Time and again, combinations of tools have been used for applications that their authors had not anticipated.

Since UNIX tools transform character streams into character streams, a number of tools deal with character manipulation. Each tool treats a character stream as a sequence of lines.

Example 12.1   How frequently do names like i and n appear in a collection of programs? Do they appear more or less frequently than keywords like while and if? A name is any sequence of letters and digits beginning with a letter. Such information is helpful in designing the lexical analyzer in a compiler to ensure that it recognizes frequently occurring words quickly.

One possible solution to this word-frequency problem is given by the following pseudocode:

```
extract each string of letters and digits and place it on a separate line
|keep only the strings that begin with a letter
|sort lines so that all occurrences of a name are adjacent
```

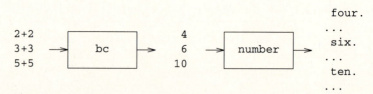

Figure 12.2   Processes as stream transformers.

|count occurrences and attach the count to each name
|sort the lines by order of decreasing count

Each line in this solution corresponds to a coroutine.[1] Figure 12.3 illustrates the effect of these coroutines on a small C program:

```
#include <stdio.h>
main(void) {
    char c;
    while( (c=getchar()) != EOF )
        putchar(c);
    return 0;
}
```

The output of the first coroutine consists of the strings of letters and digits extracted from this program, with each string appearing on a separate line. Names must begin with a letter, so the string 0 is eliminated by the second

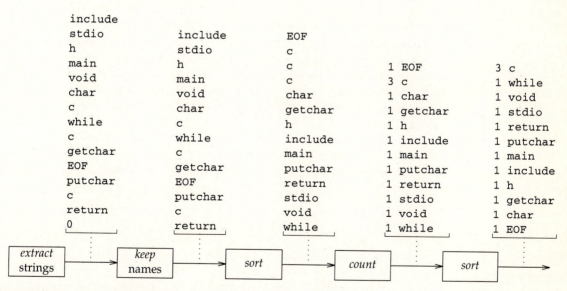

Figure 12.3   Finding the frequently occurring words in a program.

---

[1] For readers familiar with UNIX, the solution is based on the following program:

```
tr -cs A-Za-z0-9 '\012'|grep "^[A-Za-z]"|sort|uniq -c|sort -rn
```

The symbol \012 is the ASCII code for a newline.

coroutine. After the lines are sorted, all occurrences of a word appear on adjacent lines, with EOF as the first line. The number of occurrences of each word is then counted and attached at the beginning of the line. The final output is obtained by sorting the lines a second time, this time to put them in order of decreasing frequency of occurrence. Lines with the same count appear in reverse dictionary order in Fig. 12.3. ☐

12.3 CONCURRENCY AS INTERLEAVING

Concurrent computations will be described in terms of events, where an *event* is an uninterruptible action. An event might be the execution of an assignment statement, a procedure call, the evaluation of an expression — in short, anything the language in question chooses to treat as atomic. The thread of a process corresponds to a sequence of events.

Interleaving of Threads

interleavings show the relative order of atomic events

Interleaving of threads is a convenient technical device for studying the concurrent execution of processes. An interleaving of two sequences s and t is any sequence u formed from the events of s and t, subject to the following constraint: The events of s retain their order in u and so do the events of t.

Interleaving is based on the assumption that concurrent programs can be characterized by the relative order of events. If a and z are concurrent events, then we consider the case in which a occurs before z and the case in which z occurs before a, but ignore the case in which a and z occur at the same time. As the number of events on a thread increases, the number of possible interleavings grows rapidly.

If an execution of a process A consists of two events a b and an execution of a process Z consists of three events x y z, then concurrent execution of A and Z can be studied by considering the possible interleavings:

$$
\begin{array}{ccccc}
a & b & x & y & z \\
a & x & b & y & z \\
  & \cdots & & & \\
x & y & z & a & b \\
\end{array}
$$

Interleaving preserves the relative order of events in a thread, so a must occur before b, but x, y, and z, being on a separate concurrent thread, can occur in any order relative to a and b. Similarly, x must occur before y and y must occur before z, but a and b, being on a separate thread, can occur in any order relative to x, y, and z.

The 10 possible interleavings of the threads of A and Z are illustrated geometrically by the 10 diagrams in Fig. 12.4. The solid lines in each diagram

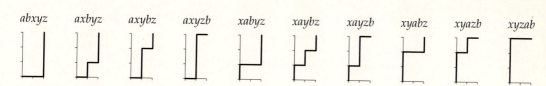

Figure 12.4   Interleavings of the threads *a b* and *x y z*.

have a horizontal step for an event in the thread of *A* and a vertical step for a thread in the event of *B*. Thus, the interleaving *a b x y z* is represented by two horizontal steps followed by three vertical steps. Although interleaving generalizes to any number of tasks, two-dimensional diagrams can be drawn only for interleavings of two processes.

Concurrent Tasks in Ada

The rest of this section illustrates interleaving by considering processes in Ada.

The sequential aspects of Ada are similar enough to Pascal that they will be mentioned as needed. We concentrate on programs consisting of a single procedure, with the following structure:

```
procedure ⟨name⟩ is
   ⟨declarations⟩
begin
   ⟨statements⟩
end ⟨name⟩;
```

The complete sequential program in Fig. 12.5 prints the string

```
hello world
```

The first line of the program,

```
with text_io; use text_io;
```

imports procedure put_line from a module text_io.

Modules are called *packages* in Ada. Except in strings, Ada does not distinguish between uppercase and lowercase letters. Comments begin with -- and continue to the end of the line.

Processes, called *tasks* in Ada, correspond to modules with their own thread of control. A task is declared in two parts, called a *specification* and a

```
with text_io; use text_io;     -- import character input/output procedures
procedure hello is
begin
    put_line("hello world");
end hello;
```

Figure 12.5 A complete Ada program.

body. A self-contained task that does not synchronize or communicate with other processes is specified simply by

task ⟨*name*⟩;

The body of a task consists of optional declarations and a sequence of statements between **begin** and **end**. The body can be thought of as the implementation of a task.

Procedure identify in Fig. 12.6 contains the specifications and bodies of two tasks p and q. When a procedure is activated, the tasks declared within it are activated as well. The procedure activation is called the *parent* of the tasks activated within it. The tasks execute concurrently with their parent, so p, q, and the procedure body execute concurrently.

```
with text_io; use text_io;
procedure identify is
    task p;                 -- task specification for  p
    task body p is
    begin
        put_line("p");
    end p;

    task q;                 -- task specification for  q
    task body q is
    begin
        put_line("q");
    end q;
begin                       -- procedure body sets up parent of  p  and  q
    put_line("r");
end identify;
```

Figure 12.6 A procedure with two tasks declared within it.

The calls to `put_line` in the procedure body and the two tasks can be interleaved in six possible ways. The procedure and tasks identify themselves by writing a character on a line. The six possible outcomes appear in the following columns:

p	p	q	q	r	r
q	r	p	r	p	q
r	q	r	p	q	p

12.4 LIVENESS PROPERTIES

liveness deals with fairness, deadlock, and livelock

The concurrent execution of processes raises two kinds of correctness issues: safety and liveness. *Safety* deals with getting the "right" answer. *Liveness* deals with the rate of progress of a process — that is, with the rate at which its computation proceeds.

This section introduces the concepts of deadlock, livelock, and fairness. Relevant to any set of processes, these liveness properties are illustrated by an abstract problem in which processes called philosophers compete for resources called forks.

Resource Sharing Constrains Concurrency

Competition for resources imposes constraints on the interleaving of threads. Consider two processes A and Z that compete for a resource. Suppose that the thread of process A is the sequence of events

$$a \quad lock_A(R) \quad b \quad c \quad unlock_A(R) \quad d$$

and the thread of process Z is

$$w \quad lock_Z(R) \quad x \quad y \quad unlock_Z(R) \quad z$$

Between events $lock_A(R)$ and $unlock_A(R)$, the resource R is unavailable to process Z; that is, event $lock_Z(R)$ cannot occur while process A maintains a lock on R. Similarly, $lock_A(R)$ cannot occur between $lock_Z(R)$ and $unlock_Z(R)$. Competition for the resource therefore constrains the possible interleavings of the threads for A and Z.

The competition between A and Z for resource R is illustrated geometrically in Fig. 12.7. The line stepping to the right and up from the origin corresponds to the interleaving

$$a \quad w \quad lock_A(R) \quad b \quad c \quad unlock_A(R) \quad lock_Z(R) \quad x \quad d \quad y \quad unlock_Z(R) \quad z$$

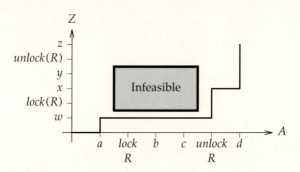

Figure 12.7 Competition for a resource constrains interleaving.

The region marked "infeasible" corresponds to situations that cannot occur because both processes cannot simultaneously hold the same resource.

The Dining Philosophers

Five philosophers sit at a table, alternating between eating spaghetti and thinking. In order to eat, a philosopher must have two forks (or chopsticks, as in Fig. 12.8). The problem is that there is a single fork between each pair of philosophers, so if one of them is eating, a neighboring one cannot be eating. A philosopher puts down both forks in their place before thinking.

Deadlock: The Inability to Proceed

A concurrent program is in *deadlock* if all processes are waiting, unable to proceed. For an example of deadlock, suppose that each philosopher executes the following pseudocode:

Figure 12.8 Place settings for the dining philosophers.

```
loop
      pick up the fork to the left;
      pick up the fork to the right;
      eat;
      release the forks;
      think;
end;
```

The concurrent system consisting of two or more such philosophers deadlocks if each philosopher picks up the fork to the left and then waits for the fork to the right.

a chain of dependencies can lead to deadlock

Forks correspond to resources, and picking up a fork corresponds to locking the resource. Deadlock often involves a chain of dependencies in which one process depends on a resource held by the next. With the system of five philosophers, the first philosopher's left fork is the fifth philosopher's right fork.

Livelock: No Process Makes Progress

Another situation illustrated by the dining-philosophers problem is *livelock*, in which the system is not in deadlock but no process makes any progress. Suppose that a philosopher's program is changed so that the left fork is released if the right fork is not available. Livelock occurs if all philosophers go into the infinite loop:

```
pick up left fork;
release left fork;
pick up left fork
release left fork;
· · ·
```

Fairness

This chapter makes the *finite-progress* assumption; that is, any process that wants to run will be able to do so within a finite amount of time. In other words, a process that wants to run cannot be blocked indefinitely.

The fairness assumption implies that any philosopher who wants to will eventually be able to eat. An unfair solution is to let just one philosopher eat all the time, with the other processes perpetually waiting. Fairness is a delicate issue, because processes may run at different rates. Thus, strict alternation between processes P and Q

$$P, Q, P, Q, P, Q, \cdots$$

may be unfair if P is 10 times as fast as Q and is needlessly delayed until Q takes its turn.

Deadlock Prevention

ordered resource usage prevents deadlock

The deadlocked philosophers can be illustrated geometrically when the system consists of only two philosophers A and Z seated facing each other. Let R and S be the forks between them. Deadlock can occur if one philosopher picks up the forks in the order RS and the other picks up the forks in the opposite order SR. This ordering can leave both philosophers holding one fork and waiting for the other.

The geometric diagrams in Fig. 12.9 show the order in which philosophers A and Z pick up and release forks. In (a), the region marked "deadlock" corresponds to the case in which A holds fork R and Z holds fork S. Neither can now proceed. The infeasible region corresponds to situations that cannot occur because both philosophers cannot simultaneously hold the same fork.

Deadlock can be prevented by *ordered resource usage*, whereby all processes request resources in the same order. When philosophers A and Z both pick up forks in the same order RS, then deadlock cannot occur. If R is unavailable, then S is left untouched, so the philosopher who gets R will be able to pick up S as well. The corresponding diagram in Fig. 12.9(b) has an infeasible region but no region marked deadlock. Ordered resource usage works for any number of resources.

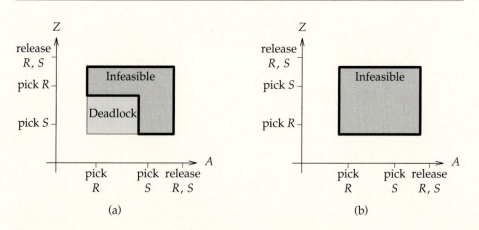

Figure 12.9   Geometric interpretation of resource locking.

12.5 SAFE ACCESS TO SHARED DATA

This section explores a notion of safety for concurrent programs with shared variables.

"Nondeterministic" Processes

A program is *deterministic* if every execution of the program on the same data sets up the same computation. Programs that are not deterministic are said to be *nondeterministic*.[2]

    With concurrent programs, it seems natural to allow arbitrary choices to be made during a computation, thereby giving up determinism. An element of choice enters into both of the following examples. Suppose that two processes P and Q send their output to a printer. As long as their output is not interleaved, it usually does not matter whether P's output appears first or Q's output appears first. As another example, suppose that two travel agents P and Q concurrently attempt to reserve the sole remaining seat on a flight. Only one of them can get the seat, and from the point of view of the reservation system, it does not matter which one gets it.

Critical Sections and Mutual Exclusion

We now formulate a notion of safety that imposes constraints on interleaving without insisting on a unique deterministic result.

critical sections are not interleaved

    A *critical section* in a process is a portion or section of code that must be treated as an atomic event. Two critical sections are said to be *mutually exclusive* because their executions must not overlap.

    A concurrent program with critical sections is *safe* if it executes the critical sections contiguously, without interleaving. The two cyclic processes in Fig 12.10 are allowed to execute their critical sections in any order, even if P executes more often than Q.

Example 12.2 For a technical example of the need for critical sections, consider the following two assignments:

$$x := x+1; \ x := x+2;$$

In a sequential language, these assignments increment the value of x by 3. This behavior remains the same if the order of the assignments is reversed:

$$x := x+2; \ x := x+1;$$

---

[2] The use of the term "nondeterministic" for "not deterministic" conflicts with the technical use of "nondeterministic" in automata theory. Since mathematical studies of concurrency use automata theory as a point of departure, care is needed in using the term "nondeterministic."

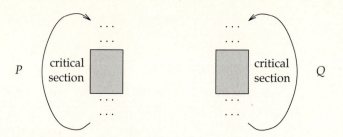

Figure 12.10 Two cyclic processes with critical sections.

A concurrent language, however, might not treat an assignment as an atomic event. Suppose that these assignments are split and implemented as two concurrent processes P and Q:

PROCESS P	PROCESS Q
$t := x;$	$u := x;$
$x := t + 1;$	$x := u + 2;$

If the assignments of Q are interleaved between those of P,

```
t := x;
    u := x;
        x := u + 2;
x := t + 1;
```

then x is incremented by 1 instead of 3. Such interleaving can be prevented by treating the assignments as critical sections.   □

More realistic examples of the use of critical sections arise in connection with objects that support operations on private data. Interleaved execution of the operations can produce undesirable results. Using the concept of data invariants from Section 6.2, sequential execution of the operations is expected to preserve the data invariants for the object, but interleaved execution could leave the private data in a state that does not satisfy the data invariants.

Safety as Serializability

allow interleavings that are equivalent to serial execution   In database systems, a set of processes is said to execute *serially* if one process executes completely before another process begins. Under the *serializability criterion*, any serial execution is said to produce a safe result. Furthermore, any interleaved execution of P and Q is said to be safe if it is equivalent to a serial execution. In other words, safety is taken to be synonymous with serializability. Serializability generalizes the requirement that critical sections be uninterruptible because it allows critical sections to be interleaved as long as the result of the interleaving is the same as that produced by some serial execution.

Example 12.3 As a technical example, consider two processes P and Q:

Process P	Process Q
$t := x;$	$u := x;$
$x := t + 1;$	$y := u * 2;$

The serial order $P\ Q$ corresponds to the following computation:

$t := x;$	x is initially 0
$x := t + 1;$	x is now 1
$\quad u := x;$	
$\quad y := u * 2;$	$x = 1$ and $y = 2$

The opposite order $Q\ P$ corresponds to

$\quad u := x;$	x is initially 0
$\quad y := u * 2;$	y is now 0
$t := x;$	
$x := t + 1;$	$x = 1$ and $y = 0$

The following interleaved execution is safe because it is equivalent to the serial order $Q\ P$:

$\quad u := x;$	x is initially 0
$t := x;$	
$\quad y := u * 2;$	y is now 0
$x := t + 1;$	$x = 1$ and $y = 0$

As a quick exercise, explain why the interleaving in Example 12.2 is not serializable. □

12.6 CONCURRENCY IN ADA

This section uses a sequence of small complete programs to introduce the concurrency constructs of Ada. The aim is to develop a reading knowledge of the language. The programs set up processes that simply identify themselves; more realistic applications appear in Section 12.7.

Synchronization by Rendezvous

client and server threads come together in a rendezvous

Synchronization in Ada is achieved by a form of procedure call known as a *rendezvous*. We refer to the caller in the rendezvous as a *client* and to the callee as the *server*. A rendezvous combines two events (see Fig. 12.11):

1. A call within a client process P
2. Acceptance of the call by the server process Q

Conceptually, the threads of the two processes come together during the rendezvous and then separate to let the two processes run independently. Alternatively, we can think of the client as being suspended during the rendezvous.

Since the client and the server have their own threads, they must both reach corresponding program points before a rendezvous can take place. The program point in the client is a call of the following form:

⟨*server-name*⟩ . ⟨*entry-name*⟩

In Fig. 12.11, the server name is Q, the entry name is *synch*, and the call is $Q.synch$.

The corresponding program point within the server is an **accept** statement for that entry name, of the following form:

accept ⟨*entry-name*⟩ **do**
   . . .
end ⟨*entry-name*⟩

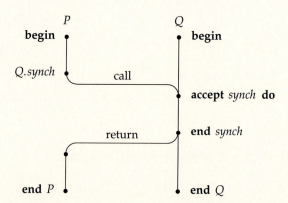

Figure 12.11   A rendezvous.

We do not care about the order in which the client and server reach these corresponding program points. For the moment, suppose that there is a single client and a single server.

- If the client calls before the server is ready to accept, then the client waits until the rendezvous can occur.
- If the server reaches an **accept** statement before the client calls, then the server waits until the rendezvous can occur.

a server can have several clients

In general, a single server can have several clients. This asymmetric relationship arises because a client explicitly names a server. Since several clients can name the same server, there can be several waiting clients when control reaches an **accept** statement. The server accepts the call from one of these clients, executes the statements between the keyword **accept** and the corresponding **end**, and continues with the rest of the body. The remaining clients wait until the server is ready to accept again.

Synchronized Communication

Ada combines synchronization and communication during a rendezvous. As with a procedure call, a call from the client can carry actual parameters along with it, and the server can return a result to its caller.

For an example of communication from caller to callee, we shall redo the earlier example in which three tasks printed out an identifying character. Specifically, we want to set up two similar tasks p and q that accept a character as a parameter and print it.

Tasks in Ada

example has two tasks of the same type

Similar tasks can be declared by specifying a *task type*. The program in Fig. 12.12 specifies a task type `emitter` and then declares p and q as follows:

```
p, q : emitter;
```

If there is only one task of a given task type, then the task can be declared directly. The following declaration of an independent task p

```
task p;
```

is an abbreviation of

```
task type p_type;
p : p_type;
```

The threads of the three processes in the program of Fig. 12.12 are shown in Fig. 12.13; we treat the procedure body as a process, with a thread separate

```
with text_io; use text_io;
procedure task_init is
    task type emitter is
        entry init(c : character);
    end emitter;

    p, q : emitter;

    task body emitter is
        me : character;
    begin
        accept init(c : character) do
            me := c;
        end init;
        put(me); new_line;
    end emitter;
begin
    p.init('p');
    q.init('q');
    put('r'); new_line;
end task_init;
```

Figure 12.12   Rendezvous init initializes tasks of type emitter.

from that of the two tasks, p and q. For clarity, the thread for the procedure body is drawn between the threads for p and q.

calls can carry parameters into a rendezvous

The procedure body begins with a call p.init('p'). The corresponding accept statement is

```
accept init(c : character) do
    me := c;
end init;
```

When the rendezvous occurs, the actual parameter 'p' corresponds to the formal c in the accept statement. This character is assigned to variable me and the rendezvous ends.

A similar rendezvous occurs when the procedure body executes the call q.init('q').

The output from the three processes in Fig. 12.12 is not synchronized because

```
put(me); new_line;
```

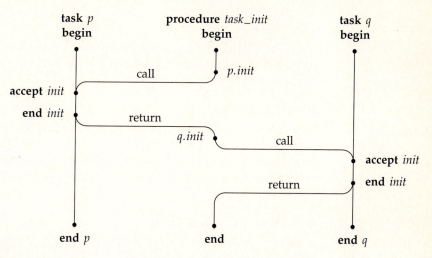

Figure 12.13 Threads for the tasks set up by the program in Fig. 12.12.

in the body of task type `emitter` occur after the accept statement, and the statements in the procedure body

```
put('r'); new_line;
```

occur after the calls. Hence, these statements can be interleaved in any order.

Concurrency is maximized by putting as little as possible between an **accept** and its **end**. Often, such intervening statements are used just to pass parameters. For example, consider the effect of changing the body of task `emitter` to produce output during the rendezvous:

> **task body** *emitter* **is**
>   *me* : **character**;
> **begin**
>   **accept** *init*(*c* : **character**) **do**
>   *me* := *c*;
>   *put*(*me*); *new_line*;
>   **end** *init*;
> **end** *emitter*;

Now the only possible output of the program is

```
p
q
r
```

From Fig. 12.13, 'p' is printed during the first rendezvous with task p, 'q' is printed during the second rendezvous with task q, and then 'r' is printed by the procedure body.

Task Initialization

initialization may need a rendezvous

Any communication between tasks in Ada must occur through a rendezvous. Upon activation, if a task needs any values to initialize itself, then an initial rendezvous is needed to pass these values. In this chapter, *init* will be the entry name for such an initial rendezvous. The first thing the parent of a task will do is to call *init*.

Dynamically Created Tasks

redo example using pointer types

A pointer type is known as an *access type* in Ada. Tasks can be created dynamically through access types to tasks.

The program in Fig. 12.14 was formed by modifying the program in Fig. 12.12 to dynamically create tasks that print 'p' and 'q'.

The type emitter_ptr is declared to be a pointer to a task type emitter by

```
type emitter_ptr is access emitter;
```

Two tasks of type emitter are created dynamically when the following statements are executed:

```
p := new emitter;
q := new emitter;
```

Pointers to the newly created tasks are assigned to p and q. Pointers are dereferenced automatically in entry calls, so p.init('p') is a call to entry init of the task accessed through p.

Selective Acceptance

a server can selectively offer services

Until now, tasks have had at most one entry, so the question of choosing between entries has not arisen. The **select** construct in Ada allows a server to offer a selection of services to its clients. For example, a buffer process might offer two services, corresponding to information entering and leaving the buffer.

The code for a vending machine might use a select statement like the following to offer a choice between delivering milk and juice:

```
with text_io; use text_io;
procedure pointers is

    task type emitter is
        entry init(c : character);
    end emitter;

    type emitter_ptr is access emitter;
    p, q : emitter_ptr;

    task body emitter is
        me : character;
    begin
        accept init(c : character) do
            me := c;
        end init;
        put(me); new_line;
    end emitter;

begin
    p := new emitter;
    q := new emitter;
    p.init('p');
    q.init('q');
    put('r'); new_line;
end pointers;
```

Figure 12.14   Dynamic creation of tasks through access types.

```
select
    accept deliver_milk do
        . . .
    end deliver_milk;
or
    accept deliver_juice do
        . . .
    end deliver_juice;
end select;
```

A more general form of the **select** construct allows the alternatives to be "guarded." A construct is *guarded* by a boolean expression if the boolean expression is tested to determine whether control should flow to the construct. The boolean expression is called a *guard*.

The accept statements in the following pseudocode are guarded by *notfull* and *notempty*:

select
    when *notfull* ⇒ **accept** *enter*(*c* : **in character**) **do**
        . . .
    end *enter*;
or
    when *notempty* ⇒ **accept** *leave*(*c* : **out character**) **do**
        . . .
    end *leave*;
end select;

This pseudocode is for a buffer process — guard *notfull* must be true for information to enter the buffer, and guard *notempty* must be true for information to leave the buffer.

The guards in a **select** statement in Ada are evaluated once when control reaches the select statement. An exception is raised if all guards are false.

12.7 SYNCHRONIZED ACCESS TO SHARED VARIABLES

Techniques for providing synchronized access to shared variables are illustrated in this section by considering the producer-consumer problem.

A producer process and a consumer process communicate through a bounded buffer. The producer puts values into the buffer at some rate, and the consumer gets values out of the buffer at some possibly different rate. The problem is to synchronize the processes so that the buffer acts as a first-in/first-out queue. In particular, correctness can be compromised if the producer attempts to put values into a full buffer or if the consumer attempts to get values out of an empty buffer.

The diagrams in Fig. 12.15 illustrate the historical progression of constructs for synchronization. In (a), both processes have unsynchronized access to a circular buffer. Semaphores, introduced in this section, can be used to synchronize the processes so that the data invariants for the buffer are preserved. This section also briefly considers monitors, which encapsulate all the code for the buffer in one place. The final diagram (d) treats the buffer as a separate process, an approach that can be implemented directly in Ada.

Direct Access to the Buffer

direct access is unsafe   If the producer and the consumer manipulate the buffer without synchronization, then a proof of correctness must take into account all possible interleavings of their actions.

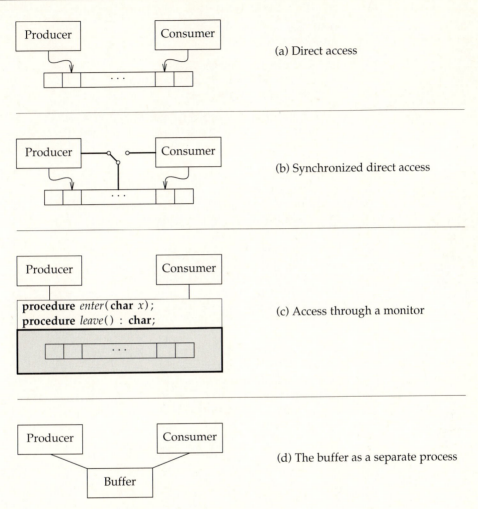

Producer   Consumer

(a) Direct access

Producer   Consumer

(b) Synchronized direct access

Producer   Consumer

procedure *enter*(**char** *x*);
procedure *leave*() : **char**;

(c) Access through a monitor

Producer   Consumer

Buffer

(d) The buffer as a separate process

Figure 12.15   Solutions to the producer-consumer problem.

The pseudocode in Fig. 12.16 illustrates potential problems and is not rec-
ommended for programming.[3] It contains the bodies of two tasks, *producer*
and *consumer*, which manipulate the buffer. As in earlier chapters, the buffer
consists of an array *buf*, an index *rear* telling the producer where to put the
next value, and an index *front* telling the consumer from where to get the next

[3] The pseudocode in Fig. 12.16 happens to work because of the guards *notfull* and *notempty*. In
general, however, direct access can lead to incorrect results. Errors can occur if there is more than
one producer, or if there is more than one consumer.

```
with text_io; use text_io;
procedure direct is

    size : constant integer := 5;
    buf : array(0..size−1) of character;
    front, rear : integer := 0;

    function notfull return boolean is ··· end notfull;
    function notempty return boolean is ··· end notempty;

    task producer;
    task body producer is
        c : character;
    begin
        while not end_of_file loop
            if notfull then
                get(c);
                buf(rear) := c;
                rear := (rear+1) mod size;
            end if;
        end loop;
    end producer;

    task consumer;
    task body consumer is
        c : character;
    begin
        loop
            if notempty then
                c := buf(front);
                front := (front+1) mod size;
                put(c);
            end if;
        end loop;
    end consumer;

begin
    null;
end direct;
```

Figure 12.16 Pseudocode for unsynchronized access to the buffer.

value. We can see from the highlighted code that the producer and the consumer manipulate the buffer directly.

An array index is enclosed between parentheses in Ada, so the ith element of array a is written as $a(i)$. The procedures *get* and *put* are library procedures for character input and output, respectively.

Since the two tasks are not synchronized, their buffer-manipulation code can be interleaved. One possible interleaving is as follows:

producer	*consumer*
notfull returns **true**;	
get(c);	
buf(rear) := c;	
	notempty returns **true**;
	c := buf(front);
	front := (front + 1) **mod** *size*;
rear := (rear + 1) **mod** *size*;	
	put(c);

Note that the consumer touches the buffer between the time the producer assigns a value to *buf(rear)* and the time it updates the index *rear*.

Semaphores: Mutual Exclusion

A *semaphore* is a construct that has an integer variable *value* and supports two operations:

1. If *value* ≥ 1, then a process can perform a p operation to decrement the value by 1. Otherwise, a process attempting a p operation waits until the value becomes greater than or equal to 1.

2. A process can perform a v operation to increment variable *value* by 1.[4]

semaphores ensure
mutual exclusion

A *binary semaphore* is a semaphore whose value is constrained to be either 0 or 1. If the value of a binary semaphore is 1, then a process attempting a v operation on it is suspended until its value becomes 0. In other words, the p and v operations on a semaphore must be performed alternately.

Ada does not provide semaphores directly; however, they can be implemented using tasks. Binary semaphores can be implemented by

```
task type binary_semaphore is
    entry p;
    entry v;
end binary_semaphore;
```

---

[4] Semaphores were introduced by Dijkstra [1968b]. Andrews and Schneider [1983] note that Dijkstra named the p operation after the Dutch word *passeren*, meaning "to pass," and the v operation after *vrygeven*, the Dutch word for "to release."

```
task body binary_semaphore is
begin
    loop
        accept p;
        accept v;
    end loop;
end binary_semaphore;
```

A binary-semaphore task has two entries p and v that are accepted one after the other. Since the accept statements are used purely for synchronization, the syntax

```
accept ⟨entry-name⟩;
```

can be used instead of the verbose

```
accept ⟨entry-name⟩ do
    null;
end ⟨entry-name⟩;
```

Mutual exclusion can be implemented by enclosing each critical section between the operations $s.p$ and $s.v$, where s is a binary semaphore:

```
process Q                        process R

    . . .                            . . .

s.p;                             s.p;
critical section for Q;          critical section for R;
s.v                              s.v

    . . .                            . . .
```

Mutual exclusion of the critical sections is guaranteed by the constraint that the p and v operations on a semaphore must be performed alternately. If process Q is the first to execute $s.p$, then it enters its critical section immediately. Process R must wait to execute $s.p$ until after Q executes $s.v$.

Busy Waiting

Although the producer and consumer can indeed be synchronized by treating the highlighted code segments in Fig. 12.17 as critical sections, the code in the figure has another failing—namely, busy waiting. If the buffer is full, the producer busily loops and tests until the buffer is not full. Similarly, if the buffer is empty, the consumer busily loops and tests until the buffer is not empty.[5] Busy waiting will be avoided in the solutions discussed next.

[5] Busy waiting also occurs in the program in Fig. 12.16, where the producer and consumer access the buffer directly. In one execution of the program, the guards *notfull* and *notempty* were false over 99 percent of the time; in other words, less than 1 percent of the loop iterations led to characters moving in or out of the buffer.

producer   *consumer*

```
    ...                                                 ...
if notfull then                                    if notempty then
   get(c);                                             c := buf(front);
   buf(rear) := c;                                     update front;
   update rear;                                        put(c);
end if;                                             end if;
    ...                                                 ...
```

Figure 12.17   The producer and consumer as cyclic processes with critical sections.

Semaphores and a Bounded Buffer

Generalized semaphores can take on integer values greater than 0 and 1. After a brief look at how semaphores might be implemented in Ada, we return to the producer-consumer problem.

The body of task *semaphore* in Fig. 12.18 has three entries: *init*, *p*, and *v*. When a task of type *semaphore* is created, its parent should immediately call *init* to initialize variable *value* in the semaphore. After initialization, the task enters a loop around a select statement with alternatives for *p* and *v*. The *p* alternative has a guard *value* ≥ 1, so any task attempting a rendezvous when *value* = 0 will wait until some other task calls *v* to increment the value. The *v* alternative is unguarded, so the task is always ready to accept a rendezvous for *v*.

The solution of the producer-consumer problem in Fig. 12.19 uses three semaphores. The bodies of tasks *producer* and *consumer* appear side by side in Fig. 12.19 for ease of comparison. Calls to a binary semaphore *critical* enclose their critical sections. A process waits to perform *critical.p* before it enters its critical section. On exit from the section, it performs *critical.v* to release the semaphore. This semaphore ensures mutual exclusion of the critical sections.

Suitable initial values for the semaphores *filling* and *emptying* prevent the producer from entering a value into a full buffer and also prevent the consumer from taking a value from an empty buffer. If the buffer can hold *n* elements, then the initial values are given by

$$filling.value := n; \quad emptying.value := 0;$$

The initial value *n* allows the producer to immediately execute *filling.p*, enter its critical section, and then execute *emptying.v*. On each pass through its criti-

```
task body semaphore is
    value : integer;
begin
    accept init(n : integer) do              -- initialization
        value := n;
    end init;
    loop
        select
            when value ≥ 1 ⇒                  -- p operation
                accept p do
                    value := value - 1;
                end p;
        or  accept v do                      -- v operation
                value := value + 1;
            end v;
        end select;
    end loop;
end semaphore;
```

Figure 12.18   A semaphore as a task in Ada.

cal section, the producer decrements semaphore *filling* and increments semaphore *emptying*.

The initial value 0 forces the consumer to initially wait at its *emptying.p* operation until the producer has passed through its critical section. A little

```
task body producer is                task body consumer is
    c : character;                       c : character;
begin                                begin
    while not end_of_file loop           loop
        get(c);                              emptying.p;
        filling.p;                           critical.p;
            critical.p;                          c := buf(front);
            buf(rear) := c;                      front := (front+1) mod size;
            rear := (rear+1) mod size;       critical.v;
        critical.v;                          filling.v;
        emptying.v;                          put(c);
    end loop;                            end loop;
end producer;                        end consumer;
```

Figure 12.19   Use of the semaphores *filling, emptying,* and *critical.*

thought shows that the semaphores correctly implement a bounded buffer of size n.

semaphore solution is dispersed, not encapsulated

With its symmetric use of semaphores, the solution of Fig. 12.19 has a certain elegance, but it is also delicate because its correctness relies on the cooperation of the producer and the consumer. One misplaced p or v operation brings the solution to its knees. Furthermore, these operations appear in the code for the cooperating processes, so the correctness of the solution depends on calls dispersed in different places in the code.

A Brief Look at Monitors

Critical sections and semaphores represent an early approach to providing exclusive access to shared data. Another approach is to encapsulate the shared data in a construct called a monitor, which is a generalization of the class construct of Chapters 6 and 7. A *monitor object* is a collection of shared variables and procedures with the constraint that only one process is allowed to execute a monitor procedure at a time. In other words, the thread of at most one process can be within a monitor at a time.

The pseudocode for a monitor, *buffer*, in Fig. 12.20 shows two procedures, *enter* and *leave*, for entering and extracting characters from the buffer, respectively. The pseudocode does not show the private data and any private operations of the monitor.

If the producer process is executing procedure *enter*, then the consumer process is not allowed to execute procedure *leave*, and vice versa. Monitors allow a language to check and enforce synchronized access to shared data.

The main problem with monitors is that a process may block within a monitor. For example, suppose that a producer grabs a buffer monitor and starts to execute the *enter* procedure. What if the buffer is full? We face a problem because the producer has exclusive use of the monitor and finds it cannot complete execution of the procedure it has started.

Processes that block inside a monitor can be handled by maintaining queues of blocked processes. Execution by a process P of

$wait(q);$

blocks P on the queue q. Subsequently, if a process R executes

$signal(q);$

then a blocked process, if any, is taken off the queue q and restarted.

Procedure *enter* uses a queue *filling* to hold a producer that blocks when the buffer is full. Symmetrically, procedure *leave* uses a queue *emptying* to hold a consumer that blocks when the buffer is empty.

```
monitor buffer is
   buf : ...;

      procedure enter(c : in character);
      begin
         if buffer full then wait(filling);          -- block producer
         enter c into buffer;
             . . .
         signal(emptying);                           -- unblock consumer
      end enter;

      procedure leave(c : out character);
      begin
         if buffer empty then wait(emptying);        -- block consumer
         c := next character;
             . . .
         signal(filling);                            -- unblock producer
      end leave;

begin
   initialize private data;
end buffer;
```

Figure 12.20   A monitor for a bounded buffer.

To see how queues are used, suppose that the buffer is not empty, and that a producer executes *enter*. After character *c* is entered into the buffer, the procedure body executes

$$signal(emptying)$$

This signal has no effect if there is no blocked process in queue *emptying*; otherwise, a blocked process is taken off the queue and restarted.

Similarly, just before control exits from procedure *leave*,

$$signal(filling)$$

allows a blocked producer, if any, to resume execution.

The advantage of monitors is that all the code for the buffer appears together. Queues of blocked processes have to be handled with care, however.

The Buffer as a Process

We conclude this section with a solution to the producer-consumer problem that is appropriate for a language like Ada, where processes can be used to synchronize access to shared data.

The time to test for a full buffer is before a producer starts to enter an element into the buffer, and the time to test for an empty buffer is before a consumer starts to take an element out. In Ada these tests can be implemented as guards on an **accept** statement. An outline of a task *buffer* is as follows:

```
task body buffer is
   ⟨data-declarations⟩
begin
   loop
      select
         when notfull ⇒
            accept enter(x : in integer) do
               . . .
            end  enter;
      or  when notempty ⇒
            accept leave(x : out integer) do
               . . .
            end  leave;
      end select;
   end loop;
end buffer;
```

Exercises

12.1 Give geometric interpretations of all possible interleavings of the following:

  a. The threads *a b* and *y z*

  b. The threads *a b c* and *x y z*

12.2 In each of the following cases, give a geometric interpretation of the interactions between the two processes. Plot the thread of one process along the horizontal axis, and the thread of the other process along the vertical axis. Clearly mark the infeasible regions.

  a. A system of two philosophers executing the following pseudocode:

```
pick up left fork;
pick up right fork;
eat;
release right fork;
release left fork;
```

    b. Two philosophers as in (c), but with the forks released in the opposite order.

    c. A rendezvous between two tasks in Ada.

    d. Two cyclic processes with critical sections.

12.3 Show how process networks can be implemented in Ada by inserting a buffer between two processes connected by an edge $P \to Q$. What are the interactions between the processes in your answer?

12.4 Consider a data type *stream* consisting of a possibly infinite sequence of values with three operations:

head(s)	Return the first element of a stream *s*.
tail(s)	Return the rest of *s* after the first element.
qcons(a, s)	Return a new stream with head *a* and tail *s*.

The difference between the operation *qcons* and `cons` in Scheme is that *qcons* performs *lazy evaluation*, where arguments are evaluated only as they are needed. Thus,

    head(*qcons*(a, s))

evaluates to *a* without attempting to evaluate *s*. For example, the following function *integers* returns a stream of integers starting with *n*:

    fun *integers*(n) = *qcons*(n, *integers*(n + 1))

    a. Define a function *nonmultiples*(n, s) to return a stream consisting of the elements of *s* that are not multiples of *n*. An integer *m* is a multiple of *n* if *m* **mod** *n* is 0.

    b. Define a function *sieve* to compute a stream of prime numbers. The sieve method for computing primes is discussed in Section 7.5.

    c. Scheme provides an operator `delay` to defer evaluation of an expression, and an operator `force` to evaluate a delayed expression. Implement function *sieve* from (b) in Scheme.

12.5 Consider the stream, *hamming*, consisting of integers of the form $2^i 3^j 5^k$, for $i \geq 0$, $j \geq 0$, $k \geq 0$, in increasing order. A variant *ham23* of *hamming*, consisting of integers of the form $2^i 3^j$ is characterized by

    ham23 = *qcons*(1, *merge*(*times*(2, *ham23*), *times*(3, *ham23*)))

where *qcons* is as in Exercise 12.4, *times*(n, s) returns the stream formed by multiplying each element of *s* by *n*, and *merge*(s, t) throws away duplicates as it merges the streams *s* and *t* of integers in increasing order.

    a. Define a function to compute the stream *hamming*.

    b. What are the first dozen elements of *hamming*? Explain how you computed these elements.

12.6 Show that the pseudocode in Fig. 12.16, page 500, for unsynchronized access to a buffer, becomes unsafe under the following circumstances:
a. There is more than one producer.
b. There is more than one consumer.

12.7 Write an Ada program to compute prime numbers using the sieve method described in Section 7.5. The program must create processes corresponding to the components for computing primes in Fig. 7.12, page 275.

12.8 Given $n > 0$ processes with critical sections, use semaphores to allow any k of them, $0 < k \leq n$, to simultaneously execute their critical sections.
a. Use generalized semaphores.
b. Use binary semaphores.

*12.9 Show that generalized semaphores can be simulated by binary semaphores; that is, show that any program using generalized semaphores can be transformed to use binary semaphores instead.

12.10 The *readers-and-writers problem* is as follows. A reader reads a resource without changing it. A writer changes the resource. Ensure that multiple readers can simultaneously read a resource but that each writer has exclusive access to the resource at any time.
a. Give a solution in Ada for the readers-and-writers problem.
b. Use semaphores to solve the problem.

12.11 Dijkstra's [1975] *guarded commands* are sequential statements of the form

$$\langle guard \rangle \rightarrow \langle statement\text{-}list \rangle$$

where $\langle guard \rangle$ is a boolean expression. The statement list in a guarded command is said to be *open* if its guard is true.
    A *guarded alternative construct* has the form:

if $\langle guard \rangle_1 \rightarrow \langle statement\text{-}list \rangle_1$
[] $\langle guard \rangle_2 \rightarrow \langle statement\text{-}list \rangle_2$
[] $\cdots$
[] $\langle guard \rangle_k \rightarrow \langle statement\text{-}list \rangle_k$
fi

An alternative construct is executed by choosing any one of the open statement lists and executing it. This choice makes programs using guarded commands nondeterministic. An error occurs if none of the guards is true.
    A *guarded repetitive construct* has the form:

do $\langle guard \rangle_1 \rightarrow \langle statement\text{-}list \rangle_1$
[] $\langle guard \rangle_2 \rightarrow \langle statement\text{-}list \rangle_2$

$$[] \quad \cdots$$
$$[] \quad \langle guard \rangle_k \rightarrow \langle statement\text{-}list \rangle_k$$
od

A repetitive construct is executed by repeatedly evaluating guards and executing one of the open statement lists. Control leaves a repetitive construct only when all the guards are false.

a. Use guarded commands to compute the minimum of x and y. Treat x and y symmetrically.

b. What are the possible threads through the following program fragment:

$$\text{initialize } x, y, \text{ and } z;$$
$$max := 0;$$
$$\textbf{do } max < x \rightarrow max := x$$
$$[] \quad max < y \rightarrow max := y$$
$$[] \quad max < z \rightarrow max := z$$
$$\textbf{od}$$

12.12 Compare and contrast the rules for the guarded alternative construct in Exercise 12.11 with the rules for select statements in Ada.

Bibliographic Notes

The groundwork for the concepts in this chapter was laid by Dijkstra [1968b]. Written in 1965, this paper discusses mutual exclusion, a producer and consumer interacting through a bounded buffer, semaphores, and generalized semaphores. The dining-philosophers problem is from Dijkstra [1971]. Monitors, developed by Hoare [1974] and Brinch Hansen [1975] were influenced by classes in Simula.

Brinch Hansen [1975, 1978, 1981] has introduced a succession of languages for concurrent programming, including Concurrent Pascal, Distributed Processes, and Edison, The concepts of classes, monitors, and processes in Concurrent Pascal are subsumed into processes in Distributed Pascal. Holt et al. [1978] describe a system CSP/k that uses monitors.

Among the books and surveys that explore concepts from concurrent programming are the survey by Andrews and Schneider [1983] and the book by Ben-Ari [1990]. A detailed review of the literature appears in Filman and Friedman [1984].

Ada is the result of language-design competition run by the U. S. Department of Defense. A series of increasingly detailed specifications—Strawman, Woodenman, Tinman, Ironman, Steelman—laid the basis for the winning design, named in honor of Augusta Ada Byron, who was Charles Babbage's programmer.

Ichbiah et al. [1979] note that the design of Ada was influenced by the communication primitives in CSP (CSP stands for communicating sequential processes; see Hoare [1978]) and by Distributed Processes (Brinch Hansen [1978]). Burns [1985] and Gehani [1984] discuss concurrent programming in Ada. Concurrency in Ada is compared with other proposals by Wegner and Smolka [1983] and Welsh and Lister [1981].

The historical surveys by Rosin [1969] and Rosen [1969] describe early hardware and operating systems.

Conway [1963] introduced the term coroutine, and applied the concept to organize a compiler. Simula 67 had a "resume" statement, which could be used to send control explicitly from one coroutine to another (Dahl and Hoare [1972]). The novelty of pipes, discussed in Section 12.2, is that independently written programs can be combined into a linear network. Ritchie [1984] notes, "Pipes appeared in UNIX® in 1972 . . . at the suggestion (or perhaps insistence) of M. D. McIlroy." Pipes have encouraged the development of collections of programs that can be used as primitives in a pipeline. Kernighan and Plauger [1976, 1981] describe such collections. The word-frequency problem of Example 12.1 is explored by Bentley, Knuth, and McIlroy [1986] — Bentley posed the problem, Knuth solved it, and then McIlroy reviewed the solution. The pipeline in Fig. 12.3 is based on McIlroy's review. Hanson [1987] begins with the same problem.

The sieve method for computing prime numbers, discussed in Section 7.5, appeared in an unpublished yet influential manuscript by McIlroy [1968]. Kahn and MacQueen [1977] use the sieve method and the sequence *hamming* of Exercise 12.5 to illustrate process networks; the exercise is based on their work. Dijkstra [1976] attributes the sequence of Exercise 12.5 to R. W. Hamming, and gives a sequential solution using guarded commands.

Landin [1965] describes streams in connection with functional programming. Several examples of the use of the stream operations in Exercise 12.4 can be found in Burge [1975]. The concept of lazy evaluation appears in the work of Vuillemin [1974] and Wadsworth [1971], and was applied to Lisp-like programs by Henderson and Morris [1976] and Friedman and Wise [1976].

The observation that ordered resource usage prevents deadlock appears in Coffman, Elphick, and Shoshani [1971]. The book by Francez [1986] is a comprehensive treatment of fairness. The concept of serializability is due to Eswaran et al. [1976]; see also Papadimitriou [1986].

Theoretical studies of concurrency often build on Milner's [1980] Calculus of Communicating Systems (CCS). The theoretical version of CSP in Hoare [1985] is influenced by CCS.

Exercise 12.9 is based on Kessels and Martin [1979]. The readers-and-writers problem in Exercise 12.10 was introduced by Courtois, Heymans, and Parnas [1971].

VI

LANGUAGE DESCRIPTION

Semantics is usually defined informally in English, by attaching explanations and examples to syntax rules in a grammar for the language. This combination of informal semantics and formal syntax is the norm for reference manuals.

A formal definition is a precise description of a language, aimed at specialists. Formal definitions are also organized around syntax rules.

Several methods of formal definition have been developed to meet different needs, ranging from language implementation to language design. Tools such as compilers and type checkers must efficiently process the complete language. *Definitional interpreters*, used for experiments in language design, must be readable and flexible and may only apply to language fragments.

Chapter 13 introduces semantic methods, ranging from attributes used for language translation, to logical rules for used type inference, to interpreters used for clarifying subtle language questions. The techiques in Chapter 13 apply to both static and dynamic semantics. *Static* semantics, deals with "compile-time" properties such as type correctness or translation, properties that can be determined from the static text of a program, without running the program on actual data. *Dynamic* semantics deals with "run-time" properties, such as the value of an expression or the effect of a statement, properties that can only be determined by actually doing a computation.

Chapter 14 introduces the lambda calculus, which has just three constructs: variables, function application, and function creation. It has proven to be a convenient vehicle for studying languages, especially types in programming languages.

13

Semantic Methods

An important and frequently used method of defining a programming language is to give an interpreter for the language which is written in a second, hopefully, better understood language. ··· (Of course, interpretation can provide an implementation as well as a definition, but there are large practical differences between these usages. Definitional interpreters often achieve clarity by sacrificing all semblance of efficiency.)

> — *Reynolds [1972], introducing a classification of definitional interpreters based on whether the interpreter contains higher-order functions, and on whether parameter evaluation in the defined language depends on parameter evaluation in the defining language.*

Any property of a construct can be defined to be its semantics or meaning. In an expression evaluator, the semantics of an expression $2+3$ can be its value. In a type checker, the semantics of $2+3$ can be the type **int** for integer. In an infix-to-postfix translator, the semantics of $2+3$ can be the string + 2 3.

a formal definition attaches semantic rules to the syntax

Several methods for defining semantics are summarized in Fig. 13.1, by applying them to let-expressions with the syntax:

$$E ::= \text{ let } x = E_1 \text{ in } E_2$$

Let-expressions are a good test case because they contain variables. The values of variables a and b in an expression $a + b$ depend on the environment — an environment consisting of bindings from variables to values. By contrast, the value of an expression like $7*7 - 4*2*3$ is 25, independent of where the expression appears. This value, 25, can be built up or synthesized from the values of the subexpressions $7*7$ and $4*2*3$.

Syntax

The following production is from a grammar for expressions:

$$E ::= \text{let } x = E_1 \text{ in } E_2$$

Informal Semantics

Occurrences of x in E_2 denote the value E_1. The value of E_2 is the value of the whole expression E.

Attribute Grammar

Attribute *val* of E denotes a value. Attribute *env* for environment binds variables to values. The operation $bind(x, v, env)$ creates a new environment with x bound to v; the bindings for all other variables are as in *env*.

$E.val$	$:= E_2.val$	The value of E is the value of E_2.
$E_1.env$	$:= E.env$	Variable bindings in E_1 are the same as in E.
$E_2.env$	$:= bind(x, E_1.val, env)$	In E_2, x is bound to the value of E_1.

Operational Semantics

The interpreter *eval* takes two parameters: an expression to be evaluated and an environment with variable bindings.

$$eval(E, env) = eval(E_2, bind(x, eval(E_1, env), env))$$

Denotational Semantics

The meaning of expression E, written as $[\![E]\!]$ is a function from environments to values. Thus, $[\![E]\!]\, env$, the application of $[\![E]\!]$ to environment *env* is a value.

$$[\![\text{ let } x = E_1 \text{ in } E_2]\!]\, env = [\![E_2]\!]\, bind(x, [\![E_1]\!]\, env, env)$$

Natural Semantics

Read the logical formula $env \vdash E : v$ as, "In environment *env*, expression E has value v." The rule for let-expressions is

$$\frac{env \vdash E_1 : v_1 \qquad bind(x, v_1, env) \vdash E_2 : v_2}{env \vdash \text{let } x = E_1 \text{ in } E_2 : v_2} \qquad \text{(let)}$$

Figure 13.1   Methods for specifying the semantics of let-expressions.

Figure 13.1 perhaps overstates the similarity of the methods because it uniformly applies them to a single construct. In practice, the approaches are used for different purposes by different communities:

- Synthesized attributes, the topic in Section 13.1, build up the meaning of a construct from its components. They are used extensively in compilers and programming environments. They work well with grammars and concrete syntax, complete with precedence rules for operators. Synthesized attributes are typically used for static semantics.

- Attribute grammars, Section 13.2, are a generalization of synthesized attributes. They allow the meaning at a node in a parse tree to depend not only on its subtree but on information from the rest of the tree. Information from the rest of the tree is said to be inherited. Attribute grammars are also geared to static semantics.

- Natural semantics, Section 13.3, is a logical notation. It is typically based on abstract syntax so key semantic properties can be compactly summarized and highlighted. Natural semantic rules will be used in Chapter 14 for type deduction.

- Denotational semantics, Section 13.4, provides a firm mathematical foundation. Denotational semantics will be presented briefly because the mathematical underpinnings are beyond the scope of this book.

- Operational semantics, Sections 13.5–13.8, describes meaning in terms of *definitional interpreters*, so called because they are used primarily to define the dynamic semantics of the interpreted language. They are meant to be readable; efficiency is not a concern.

Sections 13.5–13.7 lead up to a definitional interpreter for a small subset of Scheme. Such interpreters have long been used in the Lisp and functional programming language community to explore language designs.

A definitional interpreter deals with two languages: a *defined* language that is interpreted and a *defining* language, in which the interpreter itself is written. The interpreter for the Scheme subset is itself written in Scheme, making Scheme both the defined and the defining language.

13.1 SYNTHESIZED ATTRIBUTES

synthesize the meaning of a construct from that of its components

The semantics of a construct can be any quantity or set of quantities associated with the construct. For example, the semantics of an expression $2+3$ can be the integer value 5, the type **int**, or the string + 2 3.

A quantity associated with a construct is called an *attribute*. We write $X.a$ for attribute a of X, where X is either a nonterminal or a terminal. $E.val$ refers to attribute *val* of expression E. All the grammar symbols in Fig. 13.2 have one

attach attributes to
grammar symbols

attach semantic
rules to
productions

attribute, *val*. In general, a grammar symbol can have any number of attributes.

Attributes have values. More precisely, each occurrence of an attribute in a parse tree has a value. Attribute $E.val$ at the root of the parse tree in Fig. 13.2 has value 11. Attribute **num**.*val* at the bottom-left of the figure has value 7.

Attributes for terminal symbols are assumed to come with the symbol. When a lexical analyzer recognizes token **num** in the input, it also determines the value of the token — this value is assumed to come with **num** as attribute **nul**.*val*.

Attribute values for nonterminals are defined by *semantic rules* attached to productions in a grammar. This section deals with synthesized attributes. Attribute $N.a$ is *synthesized* if the rules defining $N.a$ are attached to productions with N on the left side. A semantic rule defining $N.a$ will be written as an assignment to $N.a$.

The use of synthesized attributes is also known as a *syntax-directed* approach to defining semantics. Together, a syntax specification and its associated semantic rules are called a *syntax-directed definition*. Although syntax-directed definitions can be based on either concrete or abstract syntax, it is more natural to base them on abstract syntax.

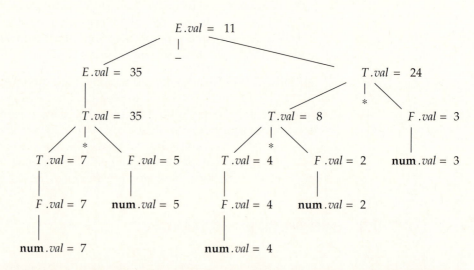

Figure 13.2   The grammar symbols at the nodes in this parse tree have an attribute *val* attached to them. The notation $E.val = 11$ at the root means that attribute *val* of symbol E has value 11. Attribute $E.val$ can have a different value at other nodes in the parse tree.

Example 13.1　The syntax-directed definition in Fig. 13.3 is based on a grammar for expressions. Each grammar symbol has a synthesized attribute *val*. Each production has one semantic rule associated with it; the rule appears on the same line.

A *decorated* parse tree has attributes attached to the nodes. The decorated parse tree in Fig. 13.2 was created by applying the productions and semantic rules in Fig. 13.3.

The leaves of a parse tree are labeled with terminals. Terminals can and do have attributes; however, there are no semantic rules for defining the values of terminals. Working bottom-up from the left of the parse tree in Fig. 13.2, the rule

$$F.val := \mathbf{num}.val$$

defines attribute *val* of the leftmost node for F to be 7. The rule

$$T.val := F.val$$

associated with $T ::= F$ copies this value, so $T.val$ is also 7.

The value at a node generated by

$$T ::= T_1 * F$$

---

production	semantic rules
$E ::= E_1 + T$	$E.val := E_1.val + T.val$
$E ::= E_1 - T$	$E.val := E_1.val - T.val$
$E ::= T$	$E.val := T.val$
$T ::= T_1 * F$	$T.val := T_1.val * F.val$
$T ::= T_1 \ \mathbf{div} \ F$	$T.val := T_1.val \ \mathbf{div} \ F.val$
$T ::= F$	$T.val := F.val$
$F ::= (E)$	$F.val := E.val$
$F ::= \mathbf{num}$	$F.val := \mathbf{num}.val$

Figure 13.3　Rules for evaluating arithmetic expressions. Each grammar symbol has a synthesized attribute *val*. Since **num** is a terminal in the grammar, attribute **num**.*val* is assumed to come with the terminal, presumably from the lexical analyzer.

is the product of the values of T_1 and F. Hence, the left child of the root has value 35. The semantic rule associated with the production at the root defines the value of E to be the difference of the values at its children. □

Evaluation Order

With synthesized attributes, information flows bottom-up in a parse tree. An attribute value at a node is defined in terms of attributes at the children of the node. Thus, the attribute values in Fig. 13.2 can be computed by working from the leaves toward the root.

Summary

Synthesized attributes are used as follows to define the meaning of a construct:

1. *Attributes*: Attach attributes to grammar symbols.
2. *Semantic rules*: Attach semantic rules to productions. Synthesized attribute $N.a$ is defined by semantic rules attached to productions with N on the left side.

The rest of this chapter sidesteps syntactic issues involving operator precedence by considering prefix expressions with operators `plus` and `times`. Let nonterminal E and terminal **num** have an attribute *val*. Associated with each production for E in Fig. 13.4 is a semantic rule that defines $E.val$.

13.2 ATTRIBUTE GRAMMARS

Attribute grammars are a generalization of synthesized attributes. They allow the meaning of a construct to depend on the surrounding context, by allowing attribute values to flow up and down a parse tree. The meaning at a node in a parse tree can depend not only on its subtree but on information from the rest of the tree.

Attribute grammars are used as follows to define the meaning of a construct:

production	semantic rules
$E ::= $ plus $E_1 E_2$	$E.val := E_1.val + E_2.val$
$E ::= $ times $E_1 E_2$	$E.val := E_1.val * E_2.val$
$E ::= $ **num**	$E.val := $ **num**.val

Figure 13.4   Productions and semantic rules for evaluating prefix expressions.

rules define synthesized attributes on the left side, and inherited attributes on the right side of a production

1. *Attributes*: Attach attributes to grammar symbols. For each attribute, designate whether it is synthesized or inherited.

2. *Semantic rules*: Attach semantic rules to productions. If nonterminal *N* appears on the left side of a production, then attach semantic rules defining the synthesized attributes of *N*. If nonterminal *A* appears on the right side of a production, then attach semantic rules defining the inherited attributes of *A*.

Example 13.2 Consider the problem of translating decimal numbers between 0 and 99 into their English phrases:

number	phrase
0	zero
1	one
10	ten
19	nineteen
20	twenty
29	twenty nine
30	thirty
31	thirty one

The translation `thirty one` of 31 is built up from `thirty`, the translation of 3 on the left, and `one`, the translation of 1 on the right. But, there are exceptions. The translation of 30 is `thirty`, not `thirty zero`. The translation of 19 is `nineteen`, not `ten nine`.

Inherited attributes will be illustrated by translating numbers between 0 and 99, generated by the following grammar:

$N ::= D \mid D\,P$

$P ::= D$

$D ::= 0 \mid 1 \mid 2 \mid 3 \mid 4 \mid 5 \mid 6 \mid 7 \mid 8 \mid 9$

A parse tree for 68 appears in Fig. 13.5(a).

Nonterminal *D* has a synthesized attribute *val*, which represents the value of the digit generated by *D*. Nonterminal *N* has a synthesized attribute *trans*, which gives the translation of the number generated by *N*. Nonterminal *P* has an inherited attribute *in* and a synthesized attribute *trans*.

The arrows in Fig. 13.5(b) illustrate how the translation of a number is synthesized at the node for *P* as attribute *P.trans*. The values of both digits are used to build *P.trans*. Associated with the production $P ::= D$ is a semantic rule that defines *P.trans* in terms of *P.in* (the value of the digit to the left) and *D.val*. In Fig. 13.5, *P.in* = 6 and *D.val* = 8, and *P.trans* is the phrase for $68 = 10 * P.in + D.val$.

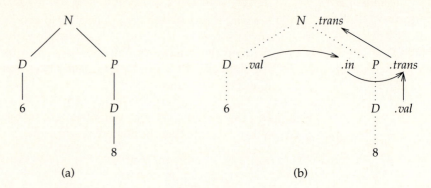

Figure 13.5   The parse tree for the number 68.

The complete attribute grammar appears in Fig. 13.6. The production $N ::= D\ P$ has two semantic rules associated with it:

$P.in \qquad := D.val$

$N.trans := P.trans$

In words, $P.in$ inherits the value $D.val$ of the digit to its left, and $P.trans$ becomes the translation $N.trans$.

Attached to the production $P ::= D$ is the semantic rule that defines $P.trans$. This rule is based on the following pseudocode for the translation of a number n:

production	semantic rules
$N ::= D$	$N.trans := spell(D.val)$
$N ::= D\ P$	$P.in := D.val$
	$N.trans := P.trans$
$P ::= D$	$P.trans :=$ **if** $D.val = 0$ **then** $decade(P.in)$
	$\qquad\qquad$ **else if** $P.in \leq 1$ **then** $spell(10*P.in + D.val)$
	$\qquad\qquad$ **else** $decade(P.in)\ \|\ spell(D.val)$
$D ::= 0$	$D.val := 0$
$D ::= 1$	$D.val := 1$
$\cdots$	
$D ::= 9$	$D.val := 9$

Figure 13.6   Semantic rules illustrating the use of the inherited attribute $P.in$.

> **if** n is a multiple of 10 **then** $decade(n$ **div** 10$)$
>
> **else if** $n < 20$ **then** $spell(n)$
>
> **else** $decade(n$ **div** 10$)$ $\|$ $spell(n$ **mod** 10$)$

Functions *spell* and *decade* satisfy the equalities:

$$spell(1) = \texttt{one}, \; spell(2) = \texttt{two}, \cdots, \; spell(19) = \texttt{nineteen}$$
$$decade(0) = \texttt{zero}, \; decade(1) = \texttt{ten}, \cdots, \; decade(9) = \texttt{ninety}$$

The rule associated with the production $P := D$ is as follows:

> $P.trans$:= **if** $D.val = 0$ **then** $decade(P.in)$
>
> **else if** $P.in \leq 1$ **then** $spell(10*P.in + D.val)$
>
> **else** $decade(P.in) \| spell(D.val)$

The synthesized attribute $P.trans$ is defined in terms of the inherited attribute $P.in$ and the synthesized attribute $D.val$.   □

Inherited attributes make the flow of information explicit. They are not necessary, however, since anything that can be defined using inherited and synthesized attributes can be defined using synthesized attributes alone. The attribute grammar in Fig. 13.6 can be modified into an equivalent grammar using synthesized attributes alone. The reason for considering it is that it illustrates how inherited attributes can be used.

13.3 NATURAL SEMANTICS

natural semantics has logical rules for deducing meaning

Natural semantics associates logical rules with the syntax of a language. The logical rules can be used to deduce the meaning of a construct. The rules translate directly into Prolog, so they can be run. Scheme implementations based on such rules appear in later sections. Natural semantics sidesteps issues of parsing and evaluation order, so it allows the semantics of a language to be captured in a small set of rules.

A Calculator

We begin with a preliminary version of natural semantics that can be thought of as associating synthesized attributes with constructs in a language. In order to keep the semantics self-contained, we use the abstract syntax **num**(*val*) for numbers, where **num** is a token, and *val* is its associated value. Expressions therefore have the form

$$E ::= \mathbf{num}(val)$$
$$\quad | \;\; \texttt{plus} \; E_1 \; E_2$$
$$\quad | \;\; \texttt{times} \; E_1 \; E_2$$

The preliminary version of natural semantics can handle these expressions, but it needs to be extended to handle variables, whose values depend on the context.

The value of $\texttt{plus} \; E_1 \; E_2$ is the sum of the values of E_1 and E_2. This rule can be written as

$$\frac{E_1 \; : \; v_1 \qquad E_2 \; : \; v_2}{\texttt{plus} \; E_1 \; E_2 \; : \; v_1 + v_2} \qquad \text{(sum)}$$

In words, if E_1 has value v_1 and E_2 has value v_2, then $\texttt{plus} \; E_1 \; E_2$ has value $v_1 + v_2$. To the left of the colon in the formula

$$E : v$$

is an expression E. Its value v appears to the right of the colon. Thus, in the formula

$$\texttt{plus} \; E_1 \; E_2 \; : \; v_1 + v_2$$

the expression $\texttt{plus} \; E_1 \; E_2$ belongs to the defined language, and $v_1 + v_2$ belongs to the defining language.

The rules for numbers, sums, and products are collected in Fig. 13.7. Each rule has a name, in parentheses to its right. As usual in logical rules, conditions appear above a line and the conclusion appears below the line. If there are no conditions, as in the rule for numbers, then the conclusion appears by itself, without a line. Rules without conditions are called *axioms*. The axiom for numbers says that the value of a number $\mathbf{num}(val)$ is simply its associated attribute, *val*.

Environments Bind Names to Values

The value of an expression $\texttt{plus} \; \texttt{a} \; \texttt{b}$ depends on the values of the variables $\texttt{a}$ and $\texttt{b}$. To handle variables, we introduce environments, which bind a variable to a value.

Environments will be treated as objects with two operations:

1. *bind*(x, v, env) is a new environment that binds variable x to value v; the bindings of all other variables are as in the environment *env*.
2. *lookup*(x, env) is the value bound to variable x in environment *env*.

The empty environment *nil* binds no variables.

logical rules are based on sequents

Environments are shown explicitly in natural semantics by writing formulas called *sequents*, of the form

$$env \vdash E : v$$

This formula says, "In environment *env*, expression *E* has value *v*." The rule for sums is now written as

$$\frac{env \vdash E_1 : v_1 \qquad env \vdash E_2 : v_2}{env \vdash \texttt{plus } E_1\, E_2 : v_1 + v_2} \qquad \text{(sum)}$$

Let Bindings

The defined language in Fig. 13.8 contains numbers, variables, sums, products, and let expressions. The rules for numbers, sums, and products are obtained by adding environments to the rules in Fig. 13.7.

Read the following axiom as, "in environment *env*, variable *x* has value *lookup*(*x*, *env*):"

$$env \vdash x : lookup(x, env) \qquad \text{(variable)}$$

Read the following rule for let expressions backwards, from the conclusion to the conditions:

$$\frac{env \vdash E_1 : v_1 \qquad bind(x, v_1, env) \vdash E_2 : v_2}{env \vdash \texttt{let } x = E_1 \texttt{ in } E_2 : v_2} \qquad \text{(let)}$$

The value of the expression $\texttt{let } x = E_1$ in E_2 is v_2 in environment *env*, if

1. E_1 evaluates to v_1 in environment *env*, and
2. E_2 evaluates to v_2 in the environment with *x* bound to v_1.

$$\mathbf{num}(val) : val \qquad \text{(number)}$$

$$\frac{E_1 : v_1 \qquad E_2 : v_2}{\texttt{plus } E_1\, E_2 : v_1 + v_2} \qquad \text{(sum)}$$

$$\frac{E_1 : v_1 \qquad E_2 : v_2}{\texttt{times } E_1\, E_2 : v_1 * v_2} \qquad \text{(product)}$$

Figure 13.7　A preliminary example of natural semantics.

$$env \ \vdash \ \mathbf{num}(val) \ : \ val \qquad \qquad \text{(number)}$$

$$\frac{env \ \vdash \ E_1 \ : \ v_1 \qquad env \ \vdash \ E_2 \ : \ v_2}{env \ \vdash \ \mathtt{plus} \ E_1 \ E_2 \ : \ v_1 + v_2} \qquad \text{(sum)}$$

$$\frac{env \ \vdash \ E_1 \ : \ v_1 \qquad env \ \vdash \ E_2 \ : \ v_2}{env \ \vdash \ \mathtt{times} \ E_1 \ E_2 \ : \ v_1 * v_2} \qquad \text{(product)}$$

$$env \ \vdash \ x \ : \ lookup(x, env) \qquad \qquad \text{(variable)}$$

$$\frac{env \ \vdash \ E_1 \ : \ v_1 \qquad bind(x, v_1, env) \ \vdash \ E_2 \ : \ v_2}{env \ \vdash \ \mathtt{let} \ x = E_1 \ \mathtt{in} \ E_2 \ : \ v_2} \qquad \text{(let)}$$

Figure 13.8   Environments are used in the rules (variable) and (let).

Example 13.3   It follows from the rules in Fig. 13.8 that 4 is the value of

```
let y = num(2) in plus y y
```

The axiom for numbers yields value 2 for **num**(2):

$$nil \ \vdash \ \mathbf{num}(2) \ : \ 2 \qquad \qquad (13.1)$$

The environment $bind(\mathtt{y}, 2, nil)$ binds y to 2 and has no bindings for other variables. This value 2 is extracted by function $lookup$:

$$lookup(\mathtt{y}, bind(\mathtt{y}, 2, nil)) \ = \ 2 \qquad \qquad (13.2)$$

Hence, the axiom for variables yields value 2 for y:

$$bind(\mathtt{y}, 2, nil) \ \vdash \ \mathtt{y} \ : \ 2 \qquad \qquad (13.3)$$

From (13.3) and the rule for sums, (plus y y) has value 4:

$$\frac{bind(\mathtt{y}, 2, nil) \ \vdash \ \mathtt{y} \ : \ 2 \qquad bind(\mathtt{y}, 2, nil) \ \vdash \ \mathtt{y} \ : \ 2}{bind(\mathtt{y}, 2, nil) \ \vdash \ \mathtt{plus} \ \mathtt{y} \ \mathtt{y} \ : \ 4} \qquad (13.4)$$

Finally, from (13.1) and (13.4), the value of the expression is 4:

$$\frac{nil \ \vdash \ \mathbf{num}(2) \ : \ 2 \qquad bind(\mathtt{y}, 2, nil) \ \vdash \ \mathtt{plus} \ \mathtt{y} \ \mathtt{y} \ : \ 4}{nil \ \vdash \ \mathtt{let} \ \mathtt{y} = \mathbf{num}(2) \ \mathtt{in} \ \mathtt{plus} \ \mathtt{y} \ \mathtt{y} \ : \ 4} \qquad \square$$

A Prolog Implementation

natural semantics can be implemented readily in Prolog

The rules in the natural semantics of a language can be encoded directly in Prolog. Expressions in the defined language are encoded as terms, axioms are encoded as facts, and semantic rules are encoded as Prolog rules. The semantics in Fig. 13.8 leads to the Prolog rules in Fig. 13.9.

The defined language in Fig. 13.9 consists of terms of the form

$$
\begin{aligned}
E ::= &\ \texttt{num(}\ \textit{val}\ \texttt{)} \\
| &\ \texttt{var(}\ \textit{atom}\ \texttt{)} \\
| &\ \texttt{plus(}\ E_1\ \texttt{,}\ E_2\ \texttt{)} \\
| &\ \texttt{times(}\ E_1\ \texttt{,}\ E_2\ \texttt{)} \\
| &\ \texttt{let(}\ \texttt{var(}\ \textit{atom}\ \texttt{)}\ \texttt{,}\ E_1\ \texttt{,}\ E_2\ \texttt{)}
\end{aligned}
$$

A little "syntactic sugar"—a minor change in syntax—converts these terms into expressions in the defined language of Fig. 13.8.

A sequent $env \vdash E : v$ is encoded as `seq(Env, E, V)`. Variables in Prolog begin with uppercase letters, so env is encoded as `Env` and v is encoded as `V`.

The axiom

$$env\ \vdash\ \mathbf{num}(\textit{val})\ :\ \textit{val} \qquad\qquad\qquad \text{(number)}$$

in Fig. 13.8 leads to the following fact in Fig. 13.9:

```
seq(Env, num(Val), Val).                                   (number)

seq(Env, plus(E1, E2), V) :-
    seq(Env, E1, V1), seq(Env, E2, V2), V is V1 + V2.        (sum)

seq(Env, times(E1, E2), V) :-
    seq(Env, E1, V1), seq(Env, E2, V2), V is V1 * V2.    (product)

seq(Env, var(X), V) :-
    lookup(X, Env, V).                                    (variable)

seq(Env, let(var(X), E1, E2), V2) :-
    seq(Env, E1, V1), seq(bind(X, V1, Env), E2, V2).         (let)

lookup(X, bind(X, V, _), V).

lookup(X, bind(Y, _, Env), V) :-
    lookup(X, Env, V).
```

Figure 13.9   A Prolog version of the natural semantics in Fig. 13.8.

```
seq(Env, num(Val), Val).
```

The following rule in the natural semantics

$$\frac{env \;\vdash\; E_1 \;:\; v_1 \qquad env \;\vdash\; E_2 \;:\; v_2}{env \;\vdash\; (\texttt{plus}\; E_1\; E_2) \;:\; v_1 + v_2} \qquad \text{(sum)}$$

leads to the Prolog rule

```
seq(Env, plus(E1, E2), V) :-
    seq(Env, E1, V1), seq(Env, E2, V2), V is V1 + V2.
```

The conclusion appears before the conditions in Prolog, with `:-` appearing between them. The goal

```
V is V1 + V2
```

evaluates the expression V1 + V2 and associates its value with V.

Example 13.4 Environments are represented simply as terms in Fig. 13.9. The environment

```
bind(y, 2, nil)
```

binds variable var(y) to the value 2.
   The following query uses the rules in Fig. 13.9:

```
?- E = let(var(y), num(2), var(y)),  seq(nil, E, V).
    E = let(var(y),num(2),var(y))
    V = 2
```

For convenience, this query uses variable E to refer to the expression to be evaluated; the actual evaluation is done in response to the query seq(nil, E, V). The result, 2, is the value computed by Prolog for V.
   Another example is

```
?- Y = var(y), E = let(Y, num(2), plus(Y, Y)),
    seq(nil, E, V).
    Y = var(y)
    E = let(var(y),num(2),plus(var(y),var(y)))
    V = 4
```

13.4 DENOTATIONAL SEMANTICS

*denotational
semantics
synthesizes the
meaning of a
construct*

The term "denotational" comes from the verb "denote." In the *denotational* approach, constructs in a language denote or represent meanings, which are usually functions. The meaning of an expression $a+b$ will be a function from environments to values.

A denotational semantics is in two parts:

1. *Domains* are like types; they identify the syntactic and semantic objects relevant to a language. For the language of prefix expressions, the semantic objects are values and environments; the syntactic objects are expressions, variables, constants, and operators.

2. *Semantic rules* synthesize the meaning of a construct in terms of that of its components.

A fundamental contribution of the work on denotational semantics is a firm mathematical foundation for domains and semantic rules. These mathematical aspects are beyond the scope of this book.

Since let-expressions and environments have already been introduced in Section 13.3, we are ready to write the rules for let-expressions.

The meaning of an expression E, written as $[\![E]\!]$, is a function from environments to values.[1] A function is applied by writing it next to its argument, as in Chapters 8 and 9, and *fab* is equivalent to $(fa)b$, the application of $f\ a$ to b. The value of E with environment *env* is therefore given by

$$[\![\ E\ ]\!]\ env$$

With this notation, the value of a variable x with environment *env* is

$$[\![\ x\ ]\!]\ env\ =\ lookup(x, env)$$

Read this rule as, "when the meaning of x as an expression is applied to environment *env*, we get the value $lookup(x, env)$."

The rules for sums and products are

$$[\![\ \texttt{plus}\ E_1\ E_2\ ]\!]\ env\ =\ [\![\ E_1\ ]\!]\ env\ +\ [\![\ E_2\ ]\!]\ env$$
$$[\![\ \texttt{times}\ E_1\ E_2\ ]\!]\ env\ =\ [\![\ E_1\ ]\!]\ env\ *\ [\![\ E_2\ ]\!]\ env$$

In either case, the same environment *env* is used for an expression and its subexpressions.

---

[1] In general, there can be several kinds of meaning associated with a construct; for example, expressions can have types as well as values. The kind of meaning can be identified by attaching a tags like **val** and **type** to the special brackets, as in **val**$[\![E]\!]$ or **type**$[\![E]\!]$.

In the rule for let-expressions, note that environment *env* is used for E_1 and that a modified environment is used for E_2:

$$[\![\; \texttt{let} \; x \; = \; E_1 \; \texttt{in} \; E_2 \;]\!] \; env \; = \; [\![E_2]\!] \; bind(x, \; [\![E_1]\!] \; env, \; env)$$

The value of the let-expression is the value of the subexpression E_2 in an environment with x bound to $[\![E_1]\!] \; env$, the value of E_1.

13.5 A CALCULATOR IN SCHEME

Sections 13.5–13.8 lead up to an interpreter for a small subset of Scheme. This section introduces notation, by redoing expression evaluation. Section 13.6 explores lexical scope. The interpreter itself appears in Sections 13.7 and 13.8.

Expressions consisting of numbers, sums, and products are simple enough that their interpreter can be shown in its entirety in Fig. 13.10. Its main routine `calc` uses predicates `constant?`, `sum?`, and `product?` to analyze the syntax of expression `E`. Once the syntax of `E` is recognized, a corresponding function is called to evaluate `E`.

```
(define (calc E)                        ; the main routine
  (cond ((constant? E) (calc-constant E))
        ((sum? E)      (calc-sum E))
        ((product? E)  (calc-product E))
        (else (error "calc: cannot parse" E)) ))


(define constant? number?)             ; constants are numbers
(define (calc-constant E) E)           ; evaluating to themselves


(define (sum? E)                       ; a sum is a list with head plus
  (and (pair? E) (equal? 'plus (car E))) )
(define (calc-sum E)                   ; evaluate subexpressions and apply +
  (apply + (map calc (cdr E))))


(define (product? E)                   ; a product is a list with head times
  (and (pair? E) (equal? 'times (car E))) )
(define (calc-product E)               ; evaluate subexpressions and apply *
  (apply * (map calc (cdr E))))
```

Figure 13.10 An interpreter for numbers, sums, and products.

constants are numbers evaluating to themselves

Constants in the defined language are numbers. Predicate `constant?` is therefore implemented by `number?`:

```
(define constant? number?)
```

Scheme interprets a number by returning its value, so `calc-constant` simply returns its argument:

```
(define (calc-constant E) E)
```

Scheme has a built-in lexical analyzer that converts the character representation of a number into an internal form, so we can think of numbers as numbers, not as tokens with associated values.

a sum has a list of subexpressions that are evaluated and added

A sum has the form

$$(\text{plus } E_1 \ E_2 \ \cdots \ E_k)$$

Predicate `sum?` returns true if it is applied to a list, and the head of the list is the symbol `plus`:

```
(define (sum? E)
  (and (pair? E) (equal? 'plus (car E))) )
```

The interpreter evaluates a sum by evaluating each of the subexpressions and then using the Scheme function + to compute their sum. The subexpressions of E are given by `(cdr E)`. A list consisting of their values is computed by

```
(map calc (cdr E))
```

which applies `calc` to each element of the list of subexpressions `(cdr E)`.

The function `apply` in Scheme satisfies the equality

$$(\text{apply } + \ (\text{list } E_1 \ E_2 \ \cdots \ E_k)) \ = \ (+ \ E_1 \ E_2 \ \cdots \ E_k)$$

Function `apply` is used by `calc-sum` to add the values of the subexpressions of E:

```
(define (calc-sum E)
  (apply + (map calc (cdr E))) )
```

Since `calc-sum` is called only on sums, it does not check whether its argument E is indeed a sum.

Products are handled similarly.

13.6 LEXICALLY SCOPED LAMBDA EXPRESSIONS

under lexical scope, free variables are bound in the definition environment

With all functions, including those denoted by lambda expressions, there is a distinction between the environment in which the function is defined and the environment in which the function is applied. Call these the *definition* and *activation* environments, respectively.

For the lambda expression `(lambda (y) (* y z)` in

```
    ...
    (let ((f (lambda (y) (* y z))))   ; definition environment
      ...
      (f 2) )))                       ; activation environment
```

the definition environment is the one in which the lambda expression is bound to `f`, and the activation environment is the one in which function `f` is applied during the evaluation of `(f 2)`.

A difficulty arises if a lambda expression contains free variables, as in

```
(lambda (y) (* y z))
```

where `z` is free. The value of the formal parameter `y` will become available when this lambda expression is applied, but what is the value of the free variable `z`?

Under the lexical scope rules of Scheme, the value of a free variable is taken from the definition environment. Under the dynamic scope rules of other Lisp dialects, the value of a free variable is taken from the activation environment. The following example explores the distinction between these scope rules.

Example 13.5 Most expressions have the same values under both the lexical and dynamic scope rules. This example develops an expression that has different values under the two scope rules.

The essential building block is a lambda expression containing a free variable `z`:

```
(lambda (y) (* y z))
```

The following fragment binds `f` to this function and later applies it to the actual parameter 2:

```
    ...
    (let ((f (lambda (y) (* y z))))   ; definition environment
```

```
    . . .
        (f 2) )))                              ; activation environment
```

The two pieces missing from this fragment are bindings for z. We will choose them to ensure that the value of z in the definition environment is different from its value in the activation environment.

The definition environment binds z to 0:

```
(let ((z 0))
  (let ((f (lambda (y) (* y z))))
    . . .
      (f 2) )))
```

Already, we can say that Scheme will evaluate (f 2) to 0, independent of the missing piece. The complete expression is

```
(let ((z 0))
  (let ((f (lambda (y) (* y z))))
    (let ((z 1))
      (f 2) )))
      0
```

Lisp dialects that use dynamic scope evaluate this expression to 2 instead of to 0.   □

Natural Semantics of Lambda Expressions

In the natural semantics in Fig. 13.11, the definition and activation environments are denoted by the variables *def-env* and *act-env*.

Before studying the rules, let us reexamine the example

```
    . . .
    (let ((f (lambda (y) (* y z))))    ; definition environment
      . . .
        (f 2) )))                      ; activation environment
```

The treatment of the lambda expression in this example can be explained as follows:

1. When the lambda expression is bound to f, the value of the free variable z is frozen.
2. The body (* y z) is evaluated when the value of the formal parameter y becomes known. That is, a multiplication occurs during the evaluation of (f 2).

a closure consists of an expression and its environment

The two rules in Fig. 13.11 correspond to these two steps. Rule (lambda) simply saves a lambda expression and its definition environment into a data structure called a *closure*. A closure formalizes the notion of freezing the values of the free variables in the lambda expression; whenever the value of a free variable is needed, it will be taken from the saved environment.

An explanation of rule (apply-lambda) is as follows. (Evaluation takes place in the activation environment, unless specified otherwise.) The expression $(F\ A)$, the application of F to A, has value v if three conditions hold:

1. F evaluates to a closure. The lambda expression in the closure has formal parameter x and body B. The environment saved in the closure is *def-env*.

2. A evaluates to a.

3. The body B of the lambda expression evaluates to v in an environment $bind(x, a, def\text{-}env)$. In this environment, the formal parameter x is bound to the value a of the actual parameter. The definition environment *def-env*, saved in the closure, is used for the free variables in B.

Example 13.6 An application of the rule (apply-lambda) yields the value 0 for the subexpression (f 2) in the expression from Example 13.5:

```
(let ((z 0))
  (let ((f (lambda (y) (* y z))))
    (let ((z 1))
      (f 2) )))
```

Rule (lambda)

$$def\text{-}env \ \vdash \ (\text{lambda } (x)\ E) \ : \ \textbf{closure}((\text{lambda } (x)\ E), def\text{-}env)$$

Rule (apply-lambda)

$$
\begin{array}{c}
act\text{-}env \ \vdash \ F \ : \ \textbf{closure}((\text{lambda } (x)\ B), def\text{-}env) \\[4pt]
act\text{-}env \ \vdash \ A \ : \ a \\[4pt]
bind(x, a, def\text{-}env) \ \vdash \ B \ : \ v \\
\hline
act\text{-}env \ \vdash \ (F\ A) \ : \ v
\end{array}
$$

Figure 13.11 Call-by-value evaluation of lexically scoped lambda expressions.

Suppose that evaluation starts in the empty environment *nil*. The definition environment for the lambda expression is therefore *bind*(z, 0, *nil*). The details of the activation environment *act-env* are not shown. All we need to know is that *act-env* binds f to the closure shown in the following:[2]

$$act\text{-}env \vdash \texttt{f} \;:\; \textbf{closure}((\texttt{lambda (y) (* y z)}),\, bind(\texttt{z}, 0, nil))$$

$$act\text{-}env \vdash \texttt{2} \;:\; 2$$

$$bind(\texttt{y}, 2, bind(\texttt{z}, 0, nil)) \vdash (\texttt{* y z}) \;:\; 0$$

$$act\text{-}env \vdash (\texttt{f 2}) \;:\; 0 \hspace{4cm} \square$$

An Implementation of Environments

Environments can be implemented in Scheme using key-value pairs called association lists or a-lists. The association list

```
((a 1) (b 2) (c 3) ··· )
```

implements an environment that binds a to 1, binds b to 2, and so on.

Association lists and the following operations on them were introduced in Section 10.3:

1. bind returns an association list with a new binding for a key.
2. bind-all binds keys in a list keys to values in a corresponding list values.
3. assoc returns the most recent binding for a key.

The code for bind and bind-all is repeated here; see Section 10.3 for details:

```
(define (bind key value env)
  (cons (list key value) env))
(define (bind-all keys values env)
  (append (map list keys values) env) )
```

13.7 AN INTERPRETER

This section develops an interpreter val that takes two parameters: an expression E to be evaluated and an environment env holding values for the variables. Function val has a case for each of the following constructs: numbers, quoted items, variables, conditionals, let expressions, lambda expressions, and function applications. Function applications are kept to the end because any

---

[2] Technically, we should use the abstract syntax **num**(2) instead of 2 in the rules.

list that does not match one of the earlier forms is by default treated as a function application.

```
(define (val E env)
   (cond ((constant? E)      (val-constant E env))
         ((quote? E)         (val-quote E env))
         ((variable? E)      (val-variable E env))
         ((if? E)            (val-if E env))
         ((let? E)           (val-let E env))
         ((lambda? E)        (val-lambda E env))
         ((application? E)   (val-application E env))
         (else (error "val: cannot parse" E)) ))
```

Now we examine the constructs one by one. The representation of a construct is examined only by its predicate, its evaluation function, and any supporting functions. For example, the representation of a let expression is examined only by the predicate `let?` and the evaluation function `val-let`. Supporting functions will be defined only for lambda expressions.

Constants

constants are numbers that evaluate to themselves

Constants are numbers.

```
(define constant? number?)
```

Constants evaluate to themselves:

```
(define (val-constant E env) E)
```

Quoted Items

the quote is stripped off a quoted item

The syntax of a quoted item is

```
(quote Item )
```

Hence, `quote?` checks whether its argument is a pair with `quote` as its first element:

```
(define (quote? E) (starts-with? E 'quote))

(define (starts-with? E symbol)
   (and (pair? E) (equal? symbol (car E))) )
```

A quoted item is evaluated by stripping the quote and returning the item:

```
(define (val-quote E env) (cadr E))
```

Variables

variables are symbols, looked up in the environment

A variable is represented as a symbol:

```
(define variable? symbol?)
```

A variable is looked up in the environment. If operation `assoc` finds a binding, the value from it is returned; otherwise, an error is reported.

```
(define (val-variable E env)
  (let ((found (assoc E env)))
    (if found (cadr found) (error "val: unbound" E)) ))
```

Conditionals

a conditional corresponds to if-then-else

A conditional has the form

```
(if E₁ E₂ E₃)
```

For simplicity, predicate `if?` simply tests whether its argument is a list with `if` as its head. Further checking and error messages are left as an exercise.

```
(define (if? E) (starts-with? E 'if))
```

Function `val-if` uses `cadr`, `caddr`, and `cadddr` to pick out the subexpressions E_1, E_2, and E_3 in a conditional (see Fig. 13.12):

```
(define (val-if E env)
  (if (val (cadr E) env)
      (val (caddr E) env)
      (val (cadddr E) env) ))
```

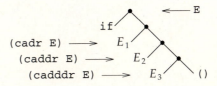

Figure 13.12   A conditional expression (if E_1 E_2 E_3).

Let Expressions

a let-expression
binds a list of
variables

A let expression has the following form (see Fig. 13.13):

$$(\text{let } ((x_1 \ E_1) \ (x_2 \ E_2) \ \cdots \ (x_k \ E_k)) \ F)$$

Predicate `let?` returns true if its argument starts with keyword `let`:

```
(define (let? E) (starts-with? E 'let))
```

Function `val-let` extracts a list `vars` of variables $(x_1 \ x_2 \ \cdots \ x_k)$. A corresponding list `exprs` consists of expressions $(E_1 \ E_2 \ \cdots \ E_k)$. The values of these expressions are collected in list `values`, and `bind-all` is called to bind the variables to the values. Expression F is evaluated in the new environment after the variables are bound.

```
(define (val-let E env)
  (let* ((vars (map car (cadr E)))
         (exprs (map cadr (cadr E)))
         (values (map (lambda (x) (val x env)) exprs))
         (new-env (bind-all vars values env)) )
    (val (caddr E) new-env) ))
```

Lambda Expressions

A lambda expression has the form

```
(lambda ( Formals ) E )
```

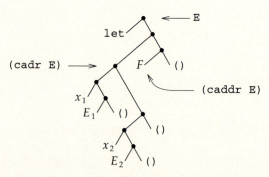

Figure 13.13 The structure of $(\text{let } ((x_1 \ E_1) \ (x_2 \ E_2)) \ F)$.

Predicate `lambda?` returns true if its argument starts with symbol `lambda`:

```
(define (lambda? E) (starts-with? E 'lambda))
```

a lambda expression evaluates to a closure

Lambda expressions are interpreted in two parts, corresponding to the two rules in the natural semantics of lambda expressions in Section 13.6. Function `val-lambda` builds a closure consisting of a lambda expression and its definition environment. The environment in the closure holds bindings for any free variables in the lambda expression. A closure will be represented as a list starting with symbol `closure`:

```
(define (val-lambda E env) (list 'closure E env) )
```

A supporting predicate `closure?` will be needed later:

```
(define (closure? x) (starts-with? x 'closure))
```

a closure carries the definition environment

Function `apply-lambda` has two parameters: `clos`, a closure containing the lambda expression to be applied, and `actuals`, a list of values for the formal parameters of the lambda expression.

```
(define (apply-lambda clos actuals)
  (let* ((lam (cadr clos))
         (def-env (caddr clos))
         (formals (cadr lam))
         (body (caddr lam))
         (new-env (bind-all formals actuals def-env)))
    (val body new-env) ))
```

Variable `lam` represents the lambda expression, `def-env` its definition-time environment, `formals` its list of formal parameters, `body` its body, and `new-env` the environment formed after binding the formals to the actuals. Function `apply-lambda` returns the result of interpreting body with respect to `new-env`; that is, it returns the value of

```
(val body new-env)
```

Function Applications

a function is either a built-in procedure or a closure

If an expression `E` is not recognized as one of the earlier constructs, the interpreter `val` uses predicate `application?` to check whether `E` has the form

$$(E_1 \ E_2 \ \cdots \ E_k)$$

If so, E_1 evaluates to a function to be applied to the values of $E_2, \ldots, E_k$. Since E_1 can be any expression, predicate `application?` returns true if E is a list:

```
(define (application? E) (pair? E))
```

In the following code for `val-application`, variable op represents the value of E_1 in

$$(E_1 \ E_2 \ \cdots \ E_k)$$

and `actuals` represents the list of values of $E_2, \ldots, E_k$. If op denotes a Scheme procedure, then the procedure is applied directly to the list of values. Otherwise, if op denotes a closure formed from a lambda expression, then `apply-lambda` is called:

```
(define (val-application E env)
  (let ((op (val (car E) env))
        (actuals (map (lambda (x) (val x env))
                      (cdr E) )))
    (cond ((procedure? op) (apply op actuals))
          ((closure? op) (apply-lambda op actuals))
          (else (error "val-application: on" E)) )))
```

An Initial Environment

In Section 13.5, the desk calculator `calc` evaluated expressions of the form

```
(plus 2 3)
```

by using the addition procedure of Scheme to add the values of subexpressions 2 and 3.

Interpreter `val` in this section also allows Scheme's built-in procedures to be used, indirectly, through an initial environment. The following program fragment shows some of the bindings in `initial-env`:

```
(define initial-env
  (list (list '+ +)
        (list 'please-add +)
        (list 'null? null?)
        (list 'cons cons)
        ··· ))
```

Within this environment, the symbol + evaluates to the Scheme procedure +. To distinguish between these two uses of +, `initial-env` includes a symbol `please-add`, also bound to the Scheme procedure +.

Using the Interpreter

Finally, here are some examples of the use of the interpreter.

- A number evaluates to itself in any environment, even the empty environment `()`:

```
(val 3.14 '())
    3.14
```

- The expression in

```
(val '(please-add 2 3) initial-env)
    5
```

is recognized as a function application. Symbol `please-add` evaluates to the Scheme addition procedure and 2 and 3 evaluate to themselves. The response 5 is the result of applying the addition procedure to the list of values of 2 and 3.

- A lambda expression by itself evaluates to a closure:

```
(val '(lambda (x) x) '())
    (closure (lambda (x) x) ())
```

The closure is a list consisting of the symbol `closure`, the original lambda expression, and its empty definition-time environment.

- A similar example involving nested lambda expressions is

```
(val '(lambda (x) (lambda (y) x)) '())
    (closure (lambda (x) (lambda (y) x)) ())
```

- The response remains the same if we give name K to this lambda expression and ask for K.

```
(val '(let ((K (lambda (x) (lambda (y) x))))
          K )
     '())
    (closure (lambda (x) (lambda (y) x)) ())
```

- Now, apply K to 5:

```
(val '(let ((K (lambda (x) (lambda (y) x))))
          (K 5) )                            ; changed line
     '())
    (closure (lambda (y) x) ((x 5)))
```

This time, the closure contains a lambda expression with a free variable x, and an environment binding x to 5.

- We get the desired response *0* for the running example of Section 13.6:

```
(val '(let ((z 0))
        (let ((f (lambda (y) (* y z))))
          (let ((z 1))
            (f 2) )))
      initial-env )
  0
```

13.8   AN EXTENSION: RECURSIVE FUNCTIONS

Interpreters like the one in Section 13.7 can be readily extended, making them useful for experiments with language design. This section extends the interpreter to support recursive functions.

Recursive functions will be implemented by modifying the implementation of lambda expressions. The notation for recursive functions is therefore a variant of lambda notation; it is not supported by Scheme.

A function that multiplies its parameter x by itself can be written using lambda notation:

```
(lambda (x) (* x x))
```

This expression has the form

```
(lambda ( formals ) body )
```

A variant of this notation includes a name *f* that can appear recursively within the *body*:

```
(rec f (lambda ( formals ) body ))
```

Using this syntax, the factorial function is defined by

```
(rec fact (lambda (x)
            (if (eq? x 0)
                1
                (* x (fact (- x 1))) )))          (13.5)
```

Recursive Functions as Values

From Section 13.6, lambda expressions can be implemented as follows:

1. A lambda expression evaluates to a closure consisting of the lambda expression and its definition environment. The definition environment is saved in the closure because it provides values for the free variables in the body of the lambda expression.

2. A closure is applied as a function by evaluating the body of the lambda expression with formal parameters bound to actuals (see Section 13.6 for details).

The key difference with recursive functions is the treatment of the function name:

1. An expression (`rec` *f lambda-expression*) will evaluate to a data structure called a *label closure*, consisting of the function name in addition to the lambda expression and the definition environment. Occurrences of the name *f* in the body of the lambda expression correspond to recursive calls of *f*.

2. A label closure is applied like a closure, with one key difference, a special binding for the function name. The body of the lambda expression is evaluated with *f* bound to the label closure itself.

Example 13.7 The expression (13.5) for the recursive factorial function has the form

```
(rec fact lam)
```

where *lam* represents the lambda expression in (13.5). This expression evaluates to the label closure

```
(label fact lam def-env)
```

With argument 4, the application

```
((rec fact lam) 4)
```

is implemented by evaluating

```
(lam 4)
```

using an environment with a binding for `fact`:

```
(bind fact (label fact lam def-env) def-env)
```

Since *lam* represents the lambda expression in (13.5) and 4 is not equal to 0, the evaluation of (*lam* 4) yields

```
(* 4 (fact 3))
```

The environment binds `fact` to the label closure, so the application `(fact 3)` will be implemented as a recursive call of `fact`.   □

Modifying the Interpreter

Interpreter `val` in Section 13.7 has an added line to allow an expression to be a recursive-function definition:

```
(define (val E env)
  (cond ((constant? E)      (val-constant E env))
        ((quote? E)         (val-quote E env))
        ((variable? E)      (val-variable E env))
        ((if? E)            (val-if E env))
        ((let? E)           (val-let E env))
        ((lambda? E)        (val-lambda E env))
        ((rec? E)           (val-rec E env)) ; addedline
        ((application? E)   (val-application E env))
        (else (error "val: cannot parse" E)) ))
```

Recursive Function Definitions

A recursive function definition starts with `rec`:

```
(define (rec? E) (starts-with? E 'rec))
```

It is evaluated by building a label data structure:

```
(define (val-rec E env)
  (list 'label (cadr E) (caddr E) env))

(define (label? x) (starts-with? x 'label))
```

Application of Recursive Functions

The following code from Section 13.7 has an added line to allow a label data structure to be applied like a function:

```
(define (val-application E env)
  (let ((op (val (car E) env))
        (actuals (map (lambda (x) (val x env))
                      (cdr E) )))
    (cond ((procedure? op) (apply op actuals))
          ((closure? op) (apply-lambda op actuals))
          ((label? op) (apply-rec op actuals)) ; added line
          (else (error "val-application: on" E env)) )))
```

A recursive function is applied by building a suitable lambda expression and an environment:

```
(define (apply-rec lab actuals)
  (let* ((fn (cadr lab))
         (lam (caddr lab))
         (def-env (cadddr lab))
         (new-env (bind fn lab def-env)))
    (val (cons lam (map (lambda (x) (list 'quote x)) actuals) )
         new-env) ))
```

Exercises

13.1 The natural semantics in Fig. 13.8, page 526, allows an expression in the defined language to be a number, a variable, a sum, a product, or a let expression.

  a. Extend the defined language to allow subtraction and division operations within expressions.

  b. Extend the defined language to allow a list of expressions to appear wherever a single expression is now allowed. The value of an expression list is the value of the last expression. A special variable `previous` refers to the value of the previous expression in a list.

13.2 Implement the semantic rules from Exercise 13.1 in Prolog.

13.3 Write an evaluator in Scheme corresponding to the Prolog rules in Fig. 13.9. Use syntactic sugar, as needed, to make the defined language easier to manipulate in Scheme.

13.4 Under dynamic scope rules, the value of a free variable is taken from the activation environment. Give semantic rules similar to those of Fig. 13.11 for call-by-value evaluation of dynamically scoped lambda expressions.

13.5 Suppose that a list `built-ins` consists alternately of symbols and their associated procedures, as follows:

```
('+ + 'please-add + '* * 'car car ···)
```

Using the Scheme predicates `procedure?` and `symbol?` define a function to build the initial environment `initial-env` of Section 13.5, from `built-ins`.

13.6 Add the following constructs to the defined language of the interpreter `val` in Section 13.7:

  a. The `cond` construct of Scheme.

  b. The construct

$$(F \text{ where } (x_1 \; E_1) \; (x_2 \; E_2) \; \cdots \; (x_k \; E_k))$$

with the same value as

$$(\text{let } ((x_1 \; E_1) \; (x_2 \; E_2) \; \cdots \; (x_k \; E_k)) \; F)$$

13.7 How would you extend the interpreter `val` in Section 13.7 to allow it to interpret itself?

Bibliographic Notes

McCarthy's original paper on Lisp contains a description of a Lisp function *eval*[*e*, *a*] that computes the value of a Lisp expression *e* in an environment *a*. McCarthy [1981] recalls, "S. R. Russell noticed that *eval* could serve as in interpreter for LISP, promptly hand coded it, and we now had a programming language with an interpreter." The interpreter used dynamic scope, which McCarthy viewed "as just a bug."

Interpreters for Lisp and Scheme are closely related to interpreters for the lambda calculus, which is discussed in Chapter 12. Landin [1964] describes an evaluator, called the SECD machine, for the lambda calculus. A definitional interpreter is easier to write if constructs in the defined language can be interpreted directly by constructs in the defining language. Reynolds [1972] presents several interpreters, including one in which a language with higher-order functions and call-by-name evaluation is defined using first-order functions and call-by-value evaluation; call-by-name evaluation is considered in Section 14.3.

Natural semantics grows out of the work of Plotkin [1981], and has been vigorously pursued by Kahn [1987] and Clément et al. [1985], who have automated the translation of natural semantics into Prolog.

14

Static Types
and the Lambda Calculus

Church was struck by certain similarities between his new concept and that used in Whitehead and Russell [1925] for the class of all x's such that $f(x)$; to wit, $\hat{x}f(x)$. Because the new concept differed quite appreciably from class membership, Church moved the caret down from over the x to the line just to the left of x; specifically, $\wedge xf(x)$. Later, for reasons of typography, an appendage was added to the caret to produce a lambda; the result was $\lambda xf(x)$.

> – *Rosser [1984], from an after-dinner talk on the history of the lambda calculus in which he presented "a still shorter and more perspicuous" proof of the Church-Rosser theorem.*

Static or compile-time type checking anticipates run-time behavior, so it is reasonable to study types at the end of this book, after the dynamic semantics of expressions is understood. Only then can we hope to make sense out of claims like "strong typing prevents run-time errors." It is easier to study error prevention if we know what an error is.

Claims about error prevention have to be worded carefully because static types prevent only certain kinds of run-time errors. At compile time, we can detect an attempt to add procedures instead of numbers or an attempt to use a pointer instead of a record, but we cannot always detect an attempt to divide by zero or an attempt to use an out-of-bounds array index.

The notion of the dynamic state of a computation, central to imperative programming, has little to do with static types, which are a property of the program text. Type checking of an assignment

$$i := i + 1$$

deals only with the types of the left and right sides and not with the values of variables. Types can therefore be studied by concentrating on expressions and functional languages. Statements can be checked by giving them a special type **void**. For example, the type-checking rule for conditional statements

$$S \; ::= \; \textbf{if } E \textbf{ then } S_1 \textbf{ else } S_2$$

can be expressed as follows:

> The **if-then-else** construct is built up of an expression E of type **bool** for boolean, and statements S_1 and S_2 of type **void**; the result S has type **void**.

This rule treats the **if-then-else** constructor as if it were an operator in an expression.

Functional languages can themselves be reduced to smaller core languages that are more convenient for the study of types.

The Lambda Calculus

the lambda calculus is a vehicle for studying languages

The small syntax of the lambda calculus makes it a convenient vehicle for studying types in programming languages. The pure lambda calculus has just three constructs: variables, function application, and function creation. Nevertheless, it has had a profound influence on the design and analysis of programming languages. Its surprising richness comes from the freedom to create and apply functions, especially higher-order functions of functions.

The lambda calculus gets its name from the Greek letter lambda, λ. The notation $\lambda x. M$ is used for a function with parameter x and body M. Thus, $\lambda x. x * x$ is a function that maps 5 to $5 * 5$. Functions are written next to their arguments, so $f \, a$ is the application of function f to argument a, as in $\sin \theta$ or $\log n$. In

$$(\lambda x. \; x * x) \; 5$$

function $\lambda x. x*x$ is applied to 5. Formulas like $(\lambda x. x*x) \, 5$ are called terms.

Church [1941] introduced the pure lambda calculus in the 1930s to study computation with functions. He was interested in the general properties of functions, independently of any particular problem area. The integer 5 and the multiplication operator $*$ belong to arithmetic and are not part of the pure calculus.

A grammar for *terms* in the *pure lambda calculus* is:

$$M \; ::= \; x \mid (M_1 \; M_2) \mid (\lambda x. M)$$

We use letters f, x, y, z for variables and M, N, P, Q for terms. A term is either a *variable* x, an *application* $(M\,N)$ of function M to N, or an *abstraction* $(\lambda x.\,M)$. A constant c can represent values like integers and operations on data structures like lists. That is, c can stand for basic constants like **true** and **nil** as well as constant functions like $+$ and *head*.

The lambda calculi are therefore a family of languages for computation with functions. Members of the family are obtained by choosing a set of constants. In informal usage, "the lambda calculus" refers to any member of this family.

The progression in this chapter is as follows:

- The pure lambda calculus is untyped. Functions can be applied freely; it even makes sense to write $(x\,x)$, where x is applied to itself. In formulating a notion of computation for the pure calculus, we look at scope, parameter passing, and evaluation strategies.

- A functional programming language is essentially a lambda calculus with appropriate constants. This view will be supported by relating a fragment of ML to a lambda calculus.

- The typed lambda calculus associates a type with each term.

- Finally, we consider a lambda calculus with polymorphic types that has been used to study types in ML.

14.1 EQUALITY OF PURE LAMBDA TERMS

beta-equality provides a notion of value

This chapter opened with an informal description of the pure lambda calculus: x is a variable, $(M\,N)$ represents the application of function M to N, and the abstraction $(\lambda x.\,M)$ represents a function with parameter x and body M. Now it is time to be more precise about the roles of abstraction and application.

This section develops an equality relation on terms, called *beta-equality* for historical reasons. We write $M =_\beta N$ if M and N are beta-equal. Informally, if $M =_\beta N$, then M and N must have the "same value."

Beta-equality deals with the result of applying an abstraction $(\lambda x.\,M)$ to an argument N. In other words, beta-equality deals with the notions of function call and parameter passing in programming languages. An abstraction corresponds to a function definition, and an application to a function call. Suppose that function *square* is defined by

fun *square*$(x) = x * x$;

The function call *square*(5) is evaluated by substituting 5 for x in the body $x * x$. In the terminology of this section, *square*$(5) =_\beta 5 * 5$.

Syntactic Conventions

The following abbreviations make terms more readable:

- Parentheses may be dropped from $(M\ N)$ and $(\lambda x.\ M)$. In the absence of parentheses, function application groups from left to right. Thus, $x\ y\ z$ abbreviates $((x\ y)\ z)$, and the parentheses in $x\ (y\ z)$ are necessary to ensure that x is applied to $(y\ z)$. Function application has higher precedence than abstraction, so $\lambda x.\ x\ z$ abbreviates $(\lambda x.\ (x\ z))$.

- A sequence of consecutive abstractions, as in $\lambda x.\ \lambda y.\ \lambda z.\ M$, can be written with a single lambda, as in $\lambda xyz.\ M$. Thus, $\lambda xy.\ x$ abbreviates $\lambda x.\ \lambda y.\ x$.

The following terms will be used within the examples in this chapter:

$$I = \lambda x.\ x$$
$$K = \lambda xy.\ x$$
$$S = \lambda xyz.\ (x\ z)\ (y\ z)$$

Here, S could have been written with fewer parentheses as $\lambda xyz.\ x\ z\ (y\ z)$. Its full form is

$$S\ =\ (\lambda x.\ (\lambda y.\ (\lambda z.\ ((x\ z)\ (y\ z)))))$$

A pure lambda term without free variables is called a *closed term*, or *combinator*.

Free and Bound Variables

care is needed with free and bound variables

Abstractions of the form $\lambda x.\ M$ are also referred to as bindings because they constrain the role of x in $\lambda x.\ M$. Variable x is said to be *bound* in $\lambda x.\ M$. The set *free*(M) of *free variables* of M, the variables that appear unbound in M, is given by the following syntax-directed rules:

$$free(x)\ =\ \{x\}$$
$$free(M\ N)\ =\ free(M)\ \cup\ free(N)$$
$$free(\lambda x.\ M)\ =\ free(M)\ -\ \{x\}$$

In words, variable x is free in the term x. A variable is free in $M\ N$ if it is either free in M or free in N. With the exception of x, all other free variables of M are free in $\lambda x.\ M$.

Free variables have been a trouble spot in both programming languages and the lambda calculus, so we take a closer look at them. For example, z is a free variable of the following term because it is free in the subterm $\lambda y.\ z$:

$$(\lambda y.\ z)\ (\lambda z.\ z)$$

We now introduce a way of distinguishing between this first occurrence of z and the other ones in the subterm $(\lambda z.\ z)$.

The occurrence of x to the right of the λ in $\lambda x.\ M$ is called a *binding occurrence* or simply a *binding* of x. All occurrences of x in $\lambda x.\ M$ are *bound* within the *scope* of this binding. All unbound occurrences of a variable in a term are *free*. Each occurrence of a variable is either free or bound; it cannot be both.

The only occurrence of x in $\lambda x.\ y$ is bound within its own scope. The lines in the following diagram go from a binding to a bound occurrence of y, and from a binding to bound occurrences of z.

$$\lambda\ y.\ \lambda\ z.\ x\ z\ (\ y\ z\ )$$

In this diagram, the occurrence of x is free because it is not within the scope of any binding within the term.

Substitution

a name clash occurs if a free variable in N is bound in M

The result of applying an abstraction $(\lambda x.\ M)$ to an argument N will be formalized by "substituting" N for x in M. Informally, N replaces all free occurrences of x in M. A definition of substitution is rather tricky, as evidenced by a long history of inadequate definitions. The following definition first tackles the easy case, which suffices for most examples. A more precise syntax-directed definition appears in Section 14.2.

The *substitution* of a term N for a variable x in M is written as $\{N/x\}\ M$ and is defined as follows:

1. Suppose that the free variables of N have no bound occurrences in M. Then, the term $\{N/x\}\ M$ is formed by replacing all free occurrences of x in M by N.

2. Otherwise, suppose that variable y is free in N and bound in M. Consistently replace the binding and corresponding bound occurrences of y in M by some fresh variable z.[1] Repeat the renaming of bound variables in M until case 1 applies, then proceed as in case 1.

Example 14.1 In each of the following cases, M has no bound occurrences, so N replaces all occurrences of x in M to form $\{N/x\}\ M$:

---

[1] The syntax of λ-terms can be made independent of the spellings of variables by using positional indexes, as in de Bruijn [1972]. Positional indexes eliminate the need for renaming.

$$\{u/x\}\ x\ =\ u$$
$$\{u/x\}\ (x\ x)\ =\ (u\ u)$$
$$\{u/x\}\ (x\ y)\ =\ (u\ y)$$
$$\{u/x\}\ (x\ u)\ =\ (u\ u)$$
$$\{(\lambda x.\ x)/x\}\ x\ =\ (\lambda x.\ x)$$

In the following cases, M has no free occurrences of x, so $\{N/x\}\ M$ is M itself:

$$\{u/x\}\ y\ =\ y$$
$$\{u/x\}\ (y\ z)\ =\ (y\ z)$$
$$\{u/x\}\ (\lambda y.\ y)\ =\ (\lambda y.\ y)$$
$$\{u/x\}\ (\lambda x.\ x)\ =\ (\lambda x.\ x)$$
$$\{(\lambda x.\ x)/x\}\ y\ =\ y$$

In the following cases, free variable u in N has bound occurrences in M, so $\{N/x\}\ M$ is formed by first renaming the bound occurrences of u in M:

$$\{u/x\}\ (\lambda u.\ x)\ =\ \{u/x\}\ (\lambda z.\ x)\ =\ (\lambda z.\ u)$$
$$\{u/x\}\ (\lambda u.\ u)\ =\ \{u/x\}\ (\lambda z.\ z)\ =\ (\lambda z.\ z) \qquad \square$$

Beta-Equality

beta-equality is a congruence: equals can be replaced by equals

The key axiom of beta-equality is as follows:

$$(\lambda x.\ M)\ N\ =_\beta\ \{N/x\}\ M \qquad\qquad (\beta\ \text{axiom})$$

Thus, $(\lambda x.\ x)\ u\ =_\beta\ u$ and $(\lambda x.\ y)\ u\ =_\beta\ y$.

The following axiom allows bound variables to be systematically renamed:

$$(\lambda x.\ M)\ =_\beta\ \lambda z.\ \{z/x\}\ M \quad \text{provided that } z \text{ is not free in } M \quad (\alpha\ \text{axiom})$$

Thus, $\lambda x.\ x\ =_\beta\ \lambda y.\ y$ and $\lambda xy.\ x\ =_\beta\ \lambda uv.\ u$.

The remaining rules for beta-equality formalize general properties of equalities (see Fig. 14.1). Each of the following must be true with any notion of equality on terms:

Idempotence. A term M equals itself.

Commutativity. If M equals N, then, conversely, N must equal M.

Transitivity. If M equals N and N equals P, then M equals P.[2]

---

[2] An *equivalence* relation on a set S is any binary relation that has the idempotence, commutativity, and transitivity properties.

$$(\lambda x.\ M)\ =_\beta\ \lambda z.\ \{z/x\}\ M \qquad \text{provided that } z \text{ is not free in } M \qquad (\alpha \text{ axiom})$$

$$(\lambda x.\ M)\ N\ =_\beta\ \{N/x\}\ M \qquad\qquad\qquad (\beta \text{ axiom})$$

$$M\ =_\beta\ M \qquad\qquad\qquad (\text{idempotence axiom})$$

$$\frac{M\ =_\beta\ N}{N\ =_\beta\ M} \qquad\qquad\qquad (\text{commutativity rule})$$

$$\frac{M\ =_\beta\ N \qquad N\ =_\beta\ P}{M\ =_\beta\ P} \qquad\qquad\qquad (\text{transitivity rule})$$

$$\frac{M\ =_\beta\ M' \qquad N\ =_\beta\ N'}{M\ N\ =_\beta\ M'\ N'} \qquad\qquad\qquad (\text{congruence rule})$$

$$\frac{M\ =_\beta\ M'}{\lambda x.\ M\ =_\beta\ \lambda x.\ M'} \qquad\qquad\qquad (\text{congruence rule})$$

Figure 14.1 Axioms and rules for beta-equality.

The replacement of equals for equals is formalized by the two *congruence* rules in Fig. 14.1. The first rule can be read as follows:

If $M =_\beta M'$ and $N =_\beta N'$, then $M\ N =_\beta M'\ N'$.

Furthermore,

If $M =_\beta M'$, then $\lambda x.\ M =_\beta \lambda x.\ M'$.

Example 14.2 The axioms and rules for beta-equality will be applied to show that

$$SII\ =_\beta\ \lambda z.\ z\ z$$

Application groups from left to right, so SII is written for $(SI)I$. S is reserved for $\lambda xyz.\ xz\ (yz)$ and I is reserved for $\lambda x.\ x$, so SII is

$$(\lambda xyz.\ xz(yz))\ (\lambda x.\ x)\ (\lambda x.\ x)$$

This example concentrates on the α and β axioms; subterms to which these axioms apply will be highlighted by underlining them. We begin by using the α axiom to rename bound variables, for clarity.

$$(\lambda xyz.\ xz(yz))\ \underline{(\lambda x.\ x)}\ (\lambda x.\ x) \quad =_\beta \quad (\lambda xyz.\ xz(yz))\ (\lambda u.\ u)\ (\lambda x.\ x)$$

The second copy of $\lambda x.\ x$ is now renamed into $\lambda v.\ v$:

$$(\lambda xyz.\ xz(yz))\ (\lambda u.\ u)\ \underline{(\lambda x.\ x)} \quad =_\beta \quad (\lambda xyz.\ xz(yz))\ (\lambda u.\ u)\ (\lambda v.\ v)$$

The resulting term on the right side of this equality has only one binding for each variable.

The first change in the structure of the term is due to the β axiom:

$$\underline{(\lambda xyz.\ xz(yz))\ (\lambda u.\ u)}\ (\lambda v.\ v) \quad =_\beta \quad (\lambda yz.\ (\lambda u.\ u)\ z\ (yz))\ (\lambda v.\ v)$$

The right side is formed by substituting $(\lambda u.\ u)$ for x in $(\lambda yz.\ xz(yz))$. Three more applications of the β axiom are needed to complete the proof of $SII =_\beta \lambda z.\ zz$:

$$
\begin{aligned}
SII \quad &=_\beta \quad (\lambda yz.\ \underline{(\lambda u.\ u)\ z}\ (yz))\ (\lambda v.\ v) \\
&=_\beta \quad \underline{(\lambda yz.\ z\ (yz))\ (\lambda v.\ v)} \\
&=_\beta \quad \lambda z.\ z\ (\ \underline{(\lambda v.\ v)\ z}\ ) \\
&=_\beta \quad \lambda z.\ zz \qquad\qquad\qquad \square
\end{aligned}
$$

14.2   SUBSTITUTION REVISITED

The description of substitution on page 551 can be summarized as follows. If the free variables of N have no bound occurrences in M, then $\{N/x\}\,M$ is formed by replacing all free occurrences of x in M by N; otherwise, bound variables in M are renamed until this rule applies. This section contains a syntax-directed definition of substitution.

The next example motivates the renaming of bound variables during substitution.

Example 14.3   Consider the term $\lambda xy.\ minus\ x\ y$. Formally, *minus* is just a variable; intuitively, *minus* $x\ y$ stands for the subtraction $x - y$. This example studies the term

$$(\lambda uv.\ minus\ u\ v)\ v\ u$$

Since bound variables can be renamed, we can rewrite this term as

$(\lambda xy.\ minus\ x\ y)\ v\ u$

Two applications of the β axiom from Fig. 14.1 yield

$$(\lambda xy.\ minus\ x\ y)\ v\ u \quad =_\beta \quad (\lambda y.\ minus\ v\ y)\ u$$
$$=_\beta \quad minus\ v\ u$$

The original term therefore satisfies the equality

$$(\lambda uv.\ minus\ u\ v)\ v\ u \quad =_\beta \quad minus\ v\ u$$

The naive approach of implementing $\{N/x\}\ M$ by putting N in place of the free occurrences of x in M incorrectly suggests the following equality:

$$\{v/u\}(\lambda v.\ minus\ u\ v) \quad ?= \quad \lambda v.\ minus\ v\ v$$

The correct result is obtained if the bound variable v is renamed:

$$\{v/u\}(\lambda z.\ minus\ u\ z) \quad = \quad \lambda z.\ minus\ v\ z \qquad \qquad \square$$

The *substitution* of N for x in M, written $\{N/x\}M$, is defined by the syntax-directed rules in Fig. 14.2. We use P and Q to refer to subterms of M.

In words, the substitution of N for x in x yields N. If y is a variable different from x, then y is left unchanged by the substitution of N for x in y.

The substitution of N for x distributes across an application $(P\ Q)$; that is, we substitute N for x in both P and Q.

The tricky case occurs when N is substituted for x in an abstraction:

$$\{N/x\}\ x = N$$
$$\{N/x\}\ y = y \qquad\qquad\qquad\qquad y \neq x$$
$$\{N/x\}\ (P\ Q) = \{N/x\}\ P\ \{N/x\}\ Q$$
$$\{N/x\}\ (\lambda x.\ P) = \lambda x.\ P$$
$$\{N/x\}\ (\lambda y.\ P) = \lambda y.\ \{N/x\}\ P \qquad\qquad y \neq x, y \notin free(N)$$
$$\{N/x\}(\lambda y.\ P) = \lambda z.\ \{N/x\}\{z/y\}P \qquad y \neq x, z \notin free(N), z \notin free(P)$$

Figure 14.2   Rules for substitution.

---

1. Since x is not free in $\lambda x.\ P$, the term $\lambda x.\ P$ itself is the result of substituting N for the free occurrences of x in it.

2. Consider the substitution of N for x in $\lambda y.\ P$, with y different from x. If y is not free in N, then the result is $\lambda y.\ \{N/x\}P$.

3. Finally, suppose that y is free in N. Bound variables can be renamed, so we rename y in $\lambda y.\ P$ by a fresh variable z. Of course, z must be a variable that is not free in N and not free in P. The renaming of y in $\lambda y.\ P$ yields $\lambda z.\ \{z/y\}P$. The substitution of N for x in $\lambda z.\ \{z/y\}P$ yields $\lambda z.\ \{N/x\}\{z/y\}\ P$.

Example 14.4   The reader is urged to verify the following equalities:

$$\{u/x\}\ (\lambda u.\ x) = (\lambda z.\ u)$$
$$\{u/x\}\ (\lambda u.\ u) = (\lambda z.\ z)$$
$$\{u/x\}\ (\lambda y.\ x) = (\lambda y.\ u)$$
$$\{u/x\}\ (\lambda y.\ u) = (\lambda y.\ u)$$

The first equality deals with the substitution of u for x in $(\lambda u.\ x)$. Blind substitution of u for x leads to the wrong answer $(\lambda u.\ u)$.   □

14.3   COMPUTATION WITH PURE LAMBDA TERMS

reductions can be applied in any order

Computation in the lambda calculus is symbolic. A term is "reduced" into as simple a form as possible. Among the two beta-equal terms

$$(\lambda x.\ M)\ N \ =_\beta\ \{N/x\}\ M$$

the right side $\{N/x\}\ M$ is considered to be simpler than $(\lambda x.\ M)\ N$. Among

$$(\lambda xy.\ x)\ u\ v \ =_\beta\ (\lambda y.\ u)\ v \ =_\beta\ u$$

u is simpler than $(\lambda y.\ u)\ v$, which in turn is simpler than $(\lambda xy.\ x)\ u\ v$.

These observations motivate a rewriting rule called β-*reduction*. An additional rule, called α-*conversion*, renames bound variables.

$$(\lambda x.\ M)\ N \ \underset{\beta}{\Rightarrow}\ \{N/x\}\ M \qquad\qquad\qquad (\beta\text{-reduction})$$
$$\lambda x.\ M \ \underset{\alpha}{\Rightarrow}\ \lambda y.\ \{y/x\}\ M \quad y \text{ not free in } M \qquad (\alpha\text{-conversion})$$

Now $(\lambda xy.\ x)\ u \underset{\beta}{\Rightarrow} (\lambda y.\ u)$ and $(\lambda y.\ u)\ v \underset{\beta}{\Rightarrow}\ u$.

This section examines β-reduction. A fundamental result of the lambda calculus implies that the result of a computation is independent of the order in which β-reductions are applied.

Reductions

We write $P \underset{\beta}{\Rightarrow} Q$ if a subterm of P is β-reduced to create Q. A subterm of the form $(\lambda x.\ M)\ N$ is called a *redex*, for "reduction expression." Thus, if $P \underset{\beta}{\Rightarrow} Q$ then P has a redex $(\lambda x.\ M)\ N$ that is replaced by $\{N/x\}\ M$ to create Q. Similarly, we write $P \underset{\alpha}{\Rightarrow} Q$ if α-conversion of a subterm of P yields Q.

a term is in normal form if it cannot be reduced

A *reduction* is any sequence of β-reductions and α-conversions. A term that cannot be β-reduced is said to be in β-*normal form*, or simply in *normal form*. The term $\lambda z.\ zz$ is in normal form because none of its subterms is a redex of the form $(\lambda x.\ M)\ N$.

The following example considers alternative reductions that start with SII and end with the normal form $\lambda z.\ zz$.

Example 14.5   In Fig. 14.3, redexes are underlined and arrows represent β-reductions. Some of the lines are dashed for clarity.

The starting term at the top of the figure is SII. Again, S is $\lambda xyz.\ xz\ (yz)$ and I is $\lambda x.\ x$, so the starting term is

$$(\lambda xyz.\ xz\ (yz))\ (\lambda x.\ x)\ (\lambda x.\ x)$$

Upon β-reduction of the only redex in this term, we get

$$(\lambda yz.\ (\lambda x.\ x)\ z\ (yz))\ (\lambda x.\ x)$$

This term has two redexes. The entire term is a redex, and so is the subterm $(\lambda x.\ x)\ z$. The following reduction begins by reducing the inner redex:

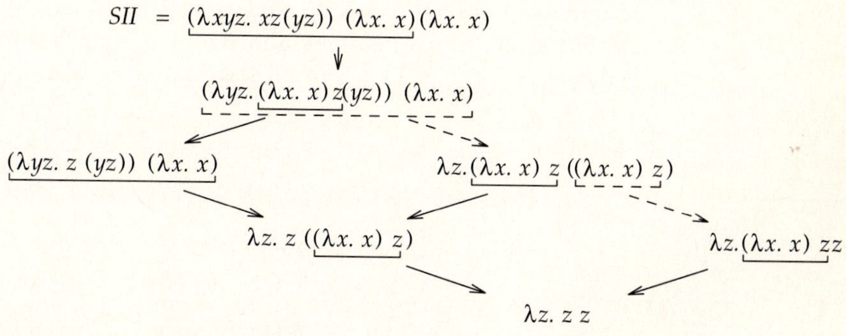

Figure 14.3   Alternative reductions from SII to $\lambda z.\ zz$.

$$(\lambda yz.\ \underline{(\lambda x.\ x)\ z}\ (yz))\ (\lambda x.\ x) \underset{\beta}{\Rightarrow} \underline{(\lambda yz.\ z\ (yz))\ (\lambda x.\ x)}$$
$$\underset{\beta}{\Rightarrow} \lambda z.\ z\ (\ \underline{(\lambda x.\ x)\ z}\ )$$
$$\underset{\beta}{\Rightarrow} \lambda z.\ z\ z$$

Each path in Fig. 14.3 represents a reduction from *SII* to $\lambda z.\ zz$. □

Nonterminating Reductions

It is possible for a reduction to continue forever, without reaching a normal form. Reductions starting with

$$(\lambda x.\ xx)(\lambda x.\ xx)$$

do not terminate. For clarity, let us α-convert the first $(\lambda x.\ xx)$ into $(\lambda y.\ yy)$. Then

$$(\lambda y.\ yy)(\lambda x.\ xx) \underset{\beta}{\Rightarrow} (\lambda x.\ xx)(\lambda x.\ xx)$$

and we are back where we started.

The first few steps of a more "useful" nonterminating computation appear in Fig. 14.4. The computation begins with *Yf*, where *Y* is a special term such that *Yf* reduces to $f(Yf)$. *Y* is an example of a "fixed-point combinator."

A combinator is a pure lambda term without free variables. A combinator *M* is called a *fixed-point combinator* if $Mf =_\beta f\ (Mf)$. The significance of fixed-point combinators is explored in Section 14.4, where fixed-point combinators will be used to set up recursions.

The Church-Rosser Theorem

The result "normal forms are unique, if they exist," applies to reductions that terminate in normal forms. A stronger result, called the *Church-Rosser theorem*, applies to all reductions, even nonterminating ones. One form of this theorem is illustrated in Fig. 14.5. For all starting terms *M*, suppose that one sequence

---

$$Yf = (\lambda f.\ (\lambda x.\ f(xx))\ (\lambda x.\ f(xx)))\ f$$
$$\underset{\beta}{\Rightarrow} (\lambda x.\ f(xx))\ (\lambda x.\ f(xx))$$
$$\underset{\beta}{\Rightarrow} f\ ((\lambda x.\ f(xx))\ (\lambda x.\ f(xx)))$$
$$= f\ (Yf)$$

Figure 14.4 The term *Yf* β-reduces to $f\ (Yf)$.

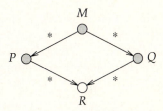

Figure 14.5 If M reduces to P and to Q, then both can reach some common R.

of reductions takes M to P and that another sequence takes M to Q. Then we can always find some common term R, such that P can reduce to R and Q can also reduce to R. The filled circles next to M, P, and Q emphasize that the result holds for all such M, P, and Q. The open circle at R emphasizes that only some terms R are reachable from both P and Q.

The following statement of the Church-Rosser theorem uses the notation $\overset{*}{\Rightarrow}$ for a sequence of zero or more α-conversions and β-reductions. We write $P \Rightarrow Q$ if $P \underset{\alpha}{\Rightarrow} Q$ or if $P \underset{\beta}{\Rightarrow} Q$. Thus, $P \overset{*}{\Rightarrow} Q$ means that for some terms $P_0, P_1, \ldots, P_k$, where $k \geq 0$,

$$P = P_0 \Rightarrow P_1 \Rightarrow \cdots \Rightarrow P_k = Q$$

Note that $P \overset{*}{\Rightarrow} P$ holds; this case corresponds to $k = 0$.

Church-Rosser Theorem. For all pure λ-terms M, P, and Q, if $M \overset{*}{\Rightarrow} P$ and $M \overset{*}{\Rightarrow} Q$, then there must exist a term R such that $P \overset{*}{\Rightarrow} R$ and $Q \overset{*}{\Rightarrow} R$. □

The Church-Rosser theorem says that the result of a computation does not depend on the order in which reductions are applied. All possible reduction sequences progress toward the same end result. The end result is a normal form, if one exists.

The Church-Rosser theorem extends to any two beta-equal terms: If $P =_\beta Q$, then there must exist a term R such that $P \overset{*}{\Rightarrow} R$ and $Q \overset{*}{\Rightarrow} R$.

Computation Rules

Function applications $M\,N$ in programming languages are often implemented as follows: evaluate both M and N, then pass the value of the argument N to the function obtained from M. With this approach, functions are said to be called by value. A similar computation rule can be defined for β-reductions in the lambda calculus.

leftmost-outermost
reaches a normal
form if there is one

A *reduction strategy* for the lambda calculus is a rule for choosing redexes; formally, a reduction strategy maps each term P that is not in normal form into a term Q such that $P \underset{\beta}{\Rightarrow} Q$.

The *call-by-value reduction strategy* chooses the leftmost-innermost redex in a term. By contrast, the *call-by-name reduction strategy* chooses the leftmost-outermost redex. Here, inner and outer refer to nesting of terms. For example, the entire term is the outermost redex in

$$\underline{(\lambda yz.\ (\lambda x.\ x)\ z\ (yz))\ (\lambda x.\ x)}$$

The innermost redex is the subterm $(\lambda x.\ x)\ z$:

$$(\lambda yz.\ \underline{(\lambda x.\ x)\ z}\ (yz))\ (\lambda x.\ x)$$

The call-by-name strategy is also referred to as *normal-order reduction*; it is guaranteed to reach a normal form, if one exists. Call-by-value, on the other hand, can get stuck, forever evaluating an argument that will never be used. An example can be constructed using $K = \lambda xy.\ x$:

$$(\lambda xy.\ x)\ z\ N \underset{\beta}{\Rightarrow} (\lambda y.\ z)\ N \underset{\beta}{\Rightarrow} z \qquad\qquad \text{(call-by-name)}$$

Call-by-value, however, will reduce the innermost redex in the subterm N rather than the entire term $(\lambda y.\ z)\ N$. If reductions starting from N do not terminate, then call-by-value will fail to reach the normal form z. Such an N is $(\lambda x.\ xx)(\lambda x.\ xx)$, which reduces to itself:

$$(\lambda y.\ z)\ ((\lambda x.\ xx)(\lambda x.\ xx)) \underset{\beta}{\Rightarrow} (\lambda y.\ z)\ ((\lambda x.\ xx)(\lambda x.\ xx))$$

$$\underset{\beta}{\Rightarrow} (\lambda y.\ z)\ ((\lambda x.\ xx)(\lambda x.\ xx))$$

$$\underset{\beta}{\Rightarrow} \quad \cdots \qquad\qquad \text{(call-by-value)}$$

Despite the possibility of an avoidable runaway evaluation, functional languages have used call-by-value because it can be implemented efficiently and it reaches the normal form sufficiently often.

Example 14.6 Call-by-value can reach a normal form faster than call-by-name, where faster means using fewer β-reductions. The term in this example has the form $(\lambda x.\ xx)\ N$. Since the body xx of $\lambda x.\ xx$ has two copies of x, call-by-value will win by first reducing N to a normal form.

The call-by-value reduction takes three steps:

$$(\lambda x.\ xx)\ (\ \underline{(\lambda y.\ y)\ (\lambda z.\ z)}\ )\ \underset{\beta}{\Rightarrow}\ (\lambda x.\ xx)\ (\lambda z.\ z)$$
$$\underset{\beta}{\Rightarrow}\ (\lambda z.\ z)\ (\lambda z.\ z)$$
$$\underset{\beta}{\Rightarrow}\ (\lambda z.\ z)$$

The call-by-name reduction takes four steps:

$$\underline{(\lambda x.\ xx)\ ((\lambda y.\ y)\ (\lambda z.\ z))}\ \underset{\beta}{\Rightarrow}\ ((\lambda y.\ y)\ (\lambda z.\ z))\ ((\lambda y.\ y)\ (\lambda z.\ z))$$
$$\underset{\beta}{\Rightarrow}\ (\lambda z.\ z)\ ((\lambda y.\ y)\ (\lambda z.\ z))$$
$$\underset{\beta}{\Rightarrow}\ (\lambda y.\ y)\ (\lambda z.\ z)$$
$$\underset{\beta}{\Rightarrow}\ (\lambda z.\ z)\qquad\qquad \square$$

14.4 PROGRAMMING CONSTRUCTS AS LAMBDA-TERMS

Constants and a little syntactic sugar will be added to the pure lambda calculus in this section to build a tiny functional programming language, called ML0 . The purpose is not to build a real language but to support the claim that a functional language is essentially a lambda calculus. Certain properties of programming languages can therefore be studied in terms of the lambda calculus.

An Applied Lambda Calculus

add constants to get an applied lambda calculus

Terms in an *applied lambda calculus* have the following syntax:

$$M\ ::=\ c\ |\ x\ |\ (M_1\ M_2)\ |\ (\lambda x.\ M)$$

Constants, represented by c, correspond to the built-in constants and operators in a programming language. Each applied lambda calculus has its own set of constants. The constants in this section are

> **true**, **false**
> **if**
> **0**, **iszero**, **pred**, **succ**
> **fix**

The definitions of free and bound variables, substitution, α-conversion, and β-reduction carry over from the pure calculus to an applied calculus. As usual, parentheses can be dropped, so

> **if** $x\ y$ **false**

is a way of writing

$$(((\textbf{if} \ x) \ y) \ \textbf{false})$$

Currying

Functions of several variables are simulated in the lambda calculus by using a technique called "currying," after the logician Haskell B. Curry, who used it extensively.

Function g is said to be a *curried* form of a function f if f and g satisfy the equality

$$f(x_1, x_2, \ldots, x_k) \ = \ g \, x_1 \, x_2 \cdots \, x_k$$

Function f has $k \geq 0$ arguments, which g takes one at a time. A curried form of the binary operator $*$ is

$$\lambda xy. \ x * y$$

The arithmetic expression $2 * 3$ corresponds to $(\lambda xy. \ x * y) \ 2 \ 3$:

$$(\lambda xy. \ x * y) \ 2 \ 3 \ \underset{\beta}{\Rightarrow} \ (\lambda y. \ 2 * y) \ 3 \ \underset{\beta}{\Rightarrow} \ 2 * 3$$

Currying is useful for partial evaluation, where the arguments of a function are not all available at once. With only the first argument 2 available,

$$(\lambda xy. \ x * y) \ 2 \ \underset{\beta}{\Rightarrow} \ \lambda y. \ 2 * y$$

is a function that multiplies its argument y by 2.

Reduction Rules for Constants

The intended use of a constant is formalized by defining reduction rules called δ-rules. The following are two of the δ-rules from Fig. 14.6:

$$\textbf{if true} \ M \ N \ \underset{\delta}{\Rightarrow} \ M$$
$$\textbf{if false} \ M \ N \ \underset{\delta}{\Rightarrow} \ N$$

The constant **if** is a curried conditional. These δ-rules capture the property that a conditional with first argument **true** reduces to its second argument and a conditional with first argument **false** reduces to its third argument.

For an example of the use of these rules, consider a combinator *or*, defined by

$$or \ = \ \lambda xy. \ \textbf{if} \ x \ \textbf{true} \ y$$

$$\textbf{if true}\ M\ N\ \underset{\delta}{\Rrightarrow}\ M$$

$$\textbf{if false}\ M\ N\ \underset{\delta}{\Rrightarrow}\ N$$

$$\textbf{fix}\ M\ \underset{\delta}{\Rrightarrow}\ M(\textbf{fix}\ M)$$

$$\textbf{iszero}\ 0\ \underset{\delta}{\Rrightarrow}\ \textbf{true}$$

$$\textbf{iszero}\ (\textbf{succ}^k\ 0)\ \underset{\delta}{\Rrightarrow}\ \textbf{false}\qquad \text{where } k \geq 1$$

$$\textbf{iszero}\ (\textbf{pred}^k\ 0)\ \underset{\delta}{\Rrightarrow}\ \textbf{false}\qquad \text{where } k \geq 1$$

$$\textbf{succ}\ (\textbf{pred}\ M)\ \underset{\delta}{\Rrightarrow}\ M$$

$$\textbf{pred}\ (\textbf{succ}\ M)\ \underset{\delta}{\Rrightarrow}\ M$$

Figure 14.6   Reduction rules for some constants.

Now *or x y* reduces to **true** if x is **true** and to y if x is **false**. Only the first argument x is supplied in the following reductions:

$$(\lambda xy.\ \textbf{if}\ x\ \textbf{true}\ y)\ \textbf{true}\ \underset{\beta}{\Rrightarrow}\ \lambda y.\ \textbf{if true true}\ y$$
$$\underset{\delta}{\Rrightarrow}\ \lambda y.\ \textbf{true}$$

$$(\lambda xy.\ \textbf{if}\ x\ \textbf{true}\ y)\ \textbf{false}\ \underset{\beta}{\Rrightarrow}\ \lambda y.\ \textbf{if false true}\ y$$
$$\underset{\delta}{\Rrightarrow}\ \lambda y.\ y$$

The δ-rule for the constant **fix** is

$$\textbf{fix}\ M\ \underset{\delta}{\Rrightarrow}\ M(\textbf{fix}\ M)$$

Technically, **fix** is not needed in an untyped lambda calculus because the fixed point combinator Y plays a similar role:

$$Y\ M\ =_\beta\ M\ (Y\ M)$$

The need for **fix** will become evident when types are added. Also, there are alternative fixed-point combinators, such as ZZ, defined as follows:

$$ZZ\quad \text{where}\quad Z = \lambda z.\ \lambda x.\ x(z\ z\ x)$$

By using **fix** we avoid commitment to any particular choice of fixed-point combinator.

The notation $M^k\ N$, for $k \geq 0$ stands for k successive applications of M to N. More precisely, $M^0\ N = N$ and $M^k\ N = M^{k-1}\ (M\ N)$, for $k > 0$.

The remaining δ-rules in Fig. 14.6 simulate integer arithmetic. The constants **succ** and **pred** correspond to the successor and predecessor functions, respectively. Thus, $\textbf{succ}^k\ 0$ corresponds to the integer k and $\textbf{pred}^k\ 0$ corresponds to the integer $-k$. We return to integer arithmetic after introducing some syntactic sugar.

The Language ML0

a functional language is essentially a lambda calculus

ML0 is a syntactically sugared version of an applied lambda calculus. Its constructs appear in Fig. 14.7. Variables, constants, and functional application have the same syntax in the two languages. Following the Standard ML programming language, $\lambda x.\ M$ is written as **fn** $x \Rightarrow M$ in ML0. As mentioned earlier, $\textbf{succ}^k\ 0$ is written as k, so $\textbf{succ}^1\ 0$ is written as 1 and $\textbf{succ}^2\ 0$ as 2. Similarly, $\textbf{pred}^1\ 0$ is written as -1 and $\textbf{pred}^2\ 0$ as -2.

The keywords **then** and **else** make conditionals more readable. Thus, **if** $P\ M\ N$ is written as

   if P **then** M **else** N

The relationship between x, N, and M in the redex $(\lambda x.\ M)\ N$ motivates the notation

   let val $x = N$ **in** M **end**

This **let-val** construct can be written for $(\lambda x.\ M)\ N$. For example,

construct	lambda calculus	ML0
variable	x	x
constant	c	c
application	$M\ N$	$M\ N$
abstraction	$\lambda x.\ M$	**fn** $x \Rightarrow M$
integer	$\textbf{succ}^k\ 0$, for $k > 0$	k
integer	$\textbf{pred}^k\ 0$, for $k > 0$	$-k$
conditional	**if** $P\ M\ N$	**if** P **then** M **else** N
let	$(\lambda x.\ M)\ N$	**let val** $x = N$ **in** M **end**
recursive function	$(\lambda f.\ M)\ (\textbf{fix}\ (\lambda f.\ \lambda x.\ N))$	**let fun** $f(x) = N$ **in** M **end**

Figure 14.7   Syntactic sugar for an applied lambda calculus.

let **val** x = **false**
in **if** x **then** **true**
      else y
end

is a sugared form of the term

$(\lambda x.\ \textbf{if}\ x\ \textbf{true}\ y)\ \textbf{false}$

The Fixed-Point Operator

How does the constant **fix** give us the ability to define recursive functions? The relevant δ-rule is

$$\textbf{fix}\ M\ \underset{\delta}{\Rrightarrow}\ M(\textbf{fix}\ M)$$

In dealing with **fix** it is convenient to have a notion of equality that takes δ-rules into account. The relation $=_{\beta\delta}$ is an extension of beta-equality that treats terms P and Q as equal if $P \underset{\delta}{\Rrightarrow} Q$. A formal definition of $=_{\beta\delta}$ can be given by adding a δ axiom to the axioms and rules for beta-equality in Section 14.1.

Example 14.7 We explore the relationship between **fix** and recursive functions by developing a term *plus* motivated by the arithmetic operator +. Just as + satisfies the equality

$$x + y = \begin{cases} y & \text{if } x = 0 \\ (x-1) + (y+1) & \text{otherwise} \end{cases}$$

plus satisfies the equality

$$plus\ x\ y =_{\beta\delta} \begin{cases} y & \text{if } \textbf{iszero}\ x \\ plus\ (\textbf{pred}\ x)\ (\textbf{succ}\ y) & \text{otherwise} \end{cases}$$

The term *plus* must therefore satisfy the following equality:

$$plus =_{\beta\delta} \lambda xy.\ \textbf{if}\ (\textbf{iszero}\ x)\ y\ (plus\ (\textbf{pred}\ x)\ (\textbf{succ}\ y)) \tag{14.1}$$

We claim that a suitable term for *plus* is **fix** M, where M is

$$M = \lambda f.\ \lambda xy.\ \textbf{if}\ (\textbf{iszero}\ x)\ y\ (f\ (\textbf{pred}\ x)\ (\textbf{succ}\ y))$$

The claim that *plus* = **fix** M satisfies the equality (14.1) can be verified as follows. Begin with the following equality based on the δ-rule for **fix**:

$$\textbf{fix}\ M \quad =_{\beta\delta} \quad M(\textbf{fix}\ M)$$

Since *plus* is **fix** M, the term $M(\textbf{fix}\ M)$ is simply $M(plus)$. From the definition of M,

$$
\begin{aligned}
plus \quad &=_{\beta\delta} \quad M(plus)\\
&= \quad (\lambda f.\ \lambda xy.\ \textbf{if}\ (\textbf{iszero}\ x)\ y\ (f\ (\textbf{pred}\ x)\ (\textbf{succ}\ y)))\ plus\\
&=_{\beta\delta} \quad \lambda xy.\ \textbf{if}\ (\textbf{iszero}\ x)\ y\ (plus\ (\textbf{pred}\ x)\ (\textbf{succ}\ y))
\end{aligned}
$$

and we have verified the equation (14.1).   □

Another example of the use of **fix** are

$$
\begin{aligned}
times\ =\ &\textbf{fix}\ \lambda f.\ \lambda xy.\ \textbf{if iszero}\ x\ \textbf{then}\ 0\\
&\qquad\qquad\qquad\quad \textbf{else}\ plus\ y\ (f\ (\textbf{pred}\ x)\ y)
\end{aligned}
$$

The right side is based on the equality $x * y = y + (x - 1) * y$.

Finally, the ubiquitous factorial function can be defined as

$$
\begin{aligned}
factorial\ =\ &\textbf{fix}\ \lambda f.\ \lambda x.\ \textbf{if iszero}\ x\ \textbf{then}\ (\textbf{succ}\ 0)\\
&\qquad\qquad\qquad\quad \textbf{else}\ times\ x\ (f\ (\textbf{pred}\ x))
\end{aligned}
$$

14.5   THE TYPED LAMBDA CALCULUS

Constants brings the lambda calculus closer to programming languages because constants can play the role of built-in data values and operations. Constants can represent values like 0 and operations like +.

Constants raise a problem, however, because they permit "erroneous" terms like $(0\ x)$, where 0 is applied to x, and **if** $(\lambda x.x)\ y\ z$, where a function $\lambda x.x$ appears instead of **true** or **false**.[3]

Restrictions on the use of constants will be studied in this section by introducing types into the lambda calculus. Consider type expressions with the following syntax:

---

[3] Errors can be formalized by partitioning terms in normal form into those that are in error and those that are not. For example, normal forms include undesirable terms like $(0\ x)$ and desirable terms like **succ** 0, which corresponds to 1. This approach is predicated on the existence of unique normal forms. As the following contrived example shows, ill-chosen δ-rules need not lead to unique normal forms. The example consists of three constants **a**, **b** and **c** and the rules $\textbf{a} \underset{\delta}{\Rightarrow} \textbf{b}$ and $\textbf{a} \underset{\delta}{\Rightarrow} \textbf{c}$. The term **a** can lead to two different normal forms **b** and **c**.

$$\tau ::= b \mid \tau \to \tau$$

Letters a and b will be used for basic types like **int**, and the Greek letters σ and τ will be used for type expressions. As usual, the type expression $\sigma \to \tau$ represents a function from type σ to type τ. Examples of type expressions are

> **int**
>
> **int** $\to$ (**int** $\to$ **bool**)
>
> $(a \to b) \to (a \to b)$

The $\to$ type constructor associates to the right, so $(a \to b) \to (a \to b)$ can be written equivalently as $(a \to b) \to a \to b$. This type is not the same as $a \to b \to a \to b$, which is equivalent to $a \to (b \to (a \to b))$.

if free variables can be handled, then so can constants

Since types are motivated by constants, it may seem surprising that the following syntax for the *typed lambda calculus* does not include constants:

$$M ::= x \mid (M\ N) \mid (\lambda x : \tau.\ M)$$

According to this syntax, a term is either a variable x, an application $(M\ N)$, or a typed abstraction $(\lambda x : \tau.\ M)$, where the bound variable x is declared to have type τ. The typed calculus inherits from the pure calculus the conventions for dropping parentheses, the definition of substitution, and the notion of reductions.

An identity function from integers to integers is written as

> $\lambda\ x :$ **int**. x

The type of a term in the typed lambda calculus can be deduced from the types of its free variables. It is this provision for free variables that allows us to drop constants from the syntax, because the type checking rules for constants are similar to those for free variables. In a term

> **if** $x\ y\ z$

if, x, y, and z are all treated as free variables, whose type is given by an environment. There is no need to single out the "constant" **if** for special treatment as far as type checking is concerned.

Another reason for dropping constants is that "nonsensical" expressions can now be constructed using variables alone. Since the bound variable x is declared to have type **int**, the subterm $x\ y$ makes as much, or as little, sense as $(0\ y)$:

> $\lambda\ x :$ **int**. $x\ y$

Natural Semantics for Type Deduction

A term in the typed lambda calculus will be said to be *type correct* if the natural semantics in Fig. 14.8 associates a type with the term; otherwise, the term is *type incorrect*. (See Section 13.3 for an introduction to natural semantics.)

The rules in Fig. 14.8 are written in terms of sequents of the form

$$env \vdash M : \tau$$

where *env* is an environment mapping variables to types, *M* is a term, and τ is a type. The axiom for variables says that the type of a variable is looked up in the environment:

$$env \vdash x : lookup(x, env) \qquad \text{(variable)}$$

The rule for function application ensures that the type of an argument is the same as the type expected by a function. In the following rule, the argument *N* has type σ, the function *M* has type $\sigma \rightarrow \tau$, and the type of (*M N*) is τ:

$$\frac{env \vdash M : \sigma \rightarrow \tau \qquad env \vdash N : \sigma}{env \vdash (M\ N) : \tau} \qquad \text{(application)}$$

The rule for abstractions deduces a result type from the type of the bound variable. If with *x* bound to type σ, the type of *M* is τ, then $\lambda x : \sigma.\ M$, where *x* is declared to have type σ, must be a term of type $\sigma \rightarrow \tau$:

$$\frac{bind(x, \sigma, env) \vdash M : \tau}{env \vdash (\lambda x : \sigma.\ M) : \sigma \rightarrow \tau} \qquad \text{(abstraction)}$$

Example 14.8 This example applies the rules in Fig. 14.8 to deduce the type $a \rightarrow (b \rightarrow a)$ for $\lambda x : a.\lambda y : b.\ x$ in the empty environment *nil*.

With *x* bound to *a* and *y* bound to *b*, the type of the variable *x* is *a*:

$$env \vdash x : lookup(x, env) \qquad \text{(variable)}$$

$$\frac{env \vdash M : \sigma \rightarrow \tau \qquad env \vdash N : \sigma}{env \vdash (M\ N) : \tau} \qquad \text{(application)}$$

$$\frac{bind(x, \sigma, env) \vdash M : \tau}{env \vdash (\lambda x : \sigma.\ M) : \sigma \rightarrow \tau} \qquad \text{(abstraction)}$$

Figure 14.8 Type-deduction rules for the typed lambda calculus.

$$bind(y, b, bind(x, a, nil)) \;\vdash\; x \;:\; a$$

The rule for abstractions now yields

$$bind(x, a, nil) \;\vdash\; (\lambda y{:}\, b.\; x) \;:\; b \to a$$

A second application of rule (abstraction) yields the desired type:

$$nil \;\vdash\; (\lambda x{:}\, a.\; \lambda y{:}\, b.\; x) \;:\; a \to (b \to a) \qquad\qquad \square$$

The type-deduction rules in Fig. 14.8 are similar to those for languages like Modula-2 and C, in which each name has a unique type that can be determined at compile time.

14.6 POLYMORPHIC TYPES

polymorphic types will be treated as parameterized types

The Standard ML programming language motivates the study in this section of a lambda calculus with polymorphic types. Before introducing the lambda calculus, we consider some ML examples.

Examples from Standard ML

The ML function *hd* determines the head or first element of a list, and the function *tl* determines the tail or rest of the list. This description of *hd* and *tl* is independent of the types of the elements of a list; that is, *hd* and *tl* can be applied to integer lists, string lists, lists of integer lists, or any other type of list.

The notion of polymorphic types in this section formalizes the types of functions like *hd* and *tl*. Meanwhile a polymorphic type can be thought of as a parameterized type.

ML was one of the earliest programming languages to allow user-defined polymorphic functions. Realistic examples of polymorphic functions deal with lists, a prototypical example being *map*, which takes as arguments a function f and a list x, and applies f to each element of list x. The only constraint on the types of f and x is that f be applicable to the elements of x. If x is a list of elements of type s, then f must have type $s \to t$, for some t. Here s and t are type variables.

The running example in this section is a toy function *twice* based on the untyped lambda term

$$\lambda f.\; \lambda x.\; f\,(f\,x)$$

The name *twice* comes from the two applications of f to x in $f\,(f\,x)$.

We will use an ML version of *twice* to compute 2 by applying an integer successor function twice to 0. The successor function `succ` is defined by

```
fun succ(n) = n+1;
    val succ = fn : int -> int
```

The response says that `succ` is a function value of type integer to integer.
The ML syntax

```
fn f => M
```

corresponds to $\lambda f.\, M$. The following let-expression therefore defines `twice` as the ML counterpart of $\lambda f.\, \lambda x.\, f(f\; x)$ and applies it to the function `succ` and the constant 0:

```
let val twice =
    fn f => fn x => f(f x)
in
    twice succ 0
end;
    val it = 2 : int
```

The subterm `twice succ 0` is equivalent to

```
succ(succ(0));
    val it = 2 : int
```

The polymorphic nature of `twice` will become evident when we examine the subexpression

```
twice twice succ 0
```

in the following program fragment:

```
let val twice =
    fn f => fn x => f(f x)
in
    twice twice succ 0
end;
    val it = 4 : int
```

The result 4 seems deceptively reasonable. The reader is encouraged to reduce

```
twice twice succ 0
```

to a β-normal form to see how `twice` is used in this subexpression.
How does ML determine a type for the following application?

```
twice twice
```

Answers to such questions require a more general notion of types than in the typed lambda calculus of Section 14.5, which does not permit self-applications of the form $x\ x$.

Explicit Polymorphism

The name *Core-XML* for the language in this section stands for "core of an explicitly typed variant of ML." Core-XML allows types to be supplied as parameters. A variant of *twice* in Core-XML is based on the following idea:

> Given a type t,
> a function f of type $t \rightarrow t$,
> and a term x of type t,
> the result is $f\ (f\ x)$.

Type t is an explicit parameter. It must be bound just as f and x are bound. For clarity, we use an uppercase lambda, Λ, to denote a type binding. Lower-case lambda, λ, will continue to be used for variable bindings. The variant of *twice* is written as

$$\Lambda t.\ \lambda f : t \rightarrow t.\ \lambda x : t.\ f\ (f\ x)$$

A term that is a Λ-abstraction will be called an *explicitly polymorphic function*, abbreviated for convenience to *polymorphic function*. A polymorphic function expects to be applied to a type.

The polymorphic variant of *twice* expects to be applied to a type t and then to a function f of type $t \rightarrow t$. In the following term, it is applied to **int** and then to **succ**:

$$(\Lambda t.\ \lambda f : t \rightarrow t.\ \lambda x : t.\ f\ (f\ x))\ \textbf{int}\ \textbf{succ}$$

Monotypes and Polytypes

The typed lambda calculus of Section 14.5 deals with terms that have a *monotype* or single type. This section introduces *polytypes*, which are quantified types of the form for all types t, ⟨some expression involving t⟩

Their syntax is as follows:

$$Polytype \quad ::= \quad \tau \quad | \quad \forall\, t\,.\; Polytype$$
$$\tau \quad ::= \quad b \quad | \quad t \quad | \quad \tau \to \tau$$

As in Section 14.5, the letters a and b represent basic types, and the Greek letters σ and τ represent type expressions. The letters s and t will be used for type variables.

A monotype suffices for the term

$$\lambda f : \textbf{int} \to \textbf{int}.\; \lambda x : \textbf{int}.\; f\,(f\,x)$$

which has type $(\textbf{int} \to \textbf{int}) \to \textbf{int} \to \textbf{int}$. A polytype is needed, however, for the polymorphic function

$$\Lambda t.\; \lambda f : t \to t.\; \lambda x : t.\; f\,(f\,x)$$

This term has type $\forall t.\, (t \to t) \to (t \to t)$. Since $\to$ associates to the right, the type can be rewritten with fewer parentheses as $\forall t.\, (t \to t) \to t \to t$.

Another example is the polymorphic identity function

$$\Lambda t.\; \lambda x : t.\; x$$

which has polytype $\forall t.\, t \to t$.

The syntax of Core-XML is given by

$M ::= x$		variable
$\mid\ (M\ M)$		application
$\mid\ (\lambda\,x : \tau\,.\,M\,)$		abstraction
$\mid\ (M\ \tau)$		type application
$\mid\ (\Lambda\,t\ .\,M\,)$		type abstraction
$\mid\ \textbf{let}\ x : Polytype = M\ \textbf{in}\ M$		let-expression

The key difference between a lambda binding in an abstraction and a let-binding in a let-expression is that a lambda-bound variable has a monotype, but a let-bound variable can have a polytype. This distinction is motivated by a similar distinction in ML.

The following Core-XML program computes 2 by applying **succ** twice to the constant 0:

let *twice* : $\forall t.\ (t \to t) \to t \to t$ =
   $\Lambda t.\ \lambda f : t \to t.\ \lambda x : t.\ f\ (f\ x)$
in
   twice **int succ** 0

Note the two uses of *twice* in the following program for computing 4:

let *twice* : $\forall t.\ (t \to t) \to t \to t$ =
   $\Lambda t.\ \lambda f : t \to t.\ \lambda x : t.\ f\ (f\ x)$
in
   twice (**int** $\to$ **int**) (*twice* **int**) **succ** 0

This program makes the polymorphic nature of *twice* explicit because *twice* is applied to the type **int** $\to$ **int** and separately to the type **int**.

Type Rules for Core-XML

The rules for variables, application, and abstraction in Fig. 14.9 are essentially the same as the corresponding rules for the typed lambda calculus. The only difference is that a type expression τ in Core-XML can be a type variable.

The rule for let-expressions is in terms of the polytype $poly_M$ of M and $poly_N$ of N:

$$env \ \vdash \ x \ : \ lookup(x, env) \qquad\qquad\qquad \text{(variable)}$$

$$\frac{env \ \vdash \ M \ : \ \sigma \to \tau \qquad env \ \vdash \ N \ : \ \sigma}{env \ \vdash \ (M\ N) \ : \ \tau} \qquad \text{(application)}$$

$$\frac{bind(x, \sigma, env) \ \vdash \ M \ : \ \tau}{env \ \vdash \ (\lambda x : \sigma.\ M) \ : \ \sigma \to \tau} \qquad \text{(abstraction)}$$

$$\frac{env \ \vdash \ M \ : \ poly_M \qquad bind(x, poly_M, env) \ \vdash \ N \ : \ poly_N}{env \ \vdash \ \textbf{let}\ x : poly_M = M\ \textbf{in}\ N \ : \ poly_N} \qquad \text{(let)}$$

$$\frac{env \ \vdash \ M \ : \ \forall t.\ poly}{env \ \vdash \ (M\ \tau) \ : \ \{\tau/t\}poly} \qquad \text{(type application)}$$

$$\frac{env \ \vdash \ M \ : \ poly}{env \ \vdash \ (\Lambda t.\ M) \ : \ \forall t.\ poly} \qquad t \text{ not free in } env \qquad \text{(type abstraction)}$$

Figure 14.9   Type rules for Core-XML.

$$\frac{env \;\vdash\; M \;:\; poly_M \qquad bind(x, poly_M, env) \;\vdash\; N \;:\; poly_N}{env \;\vdash\; \textbf{let } x : poly_M = M \textbf{ in } N \;:\; poly_N} \qquad \text{(let)}$$

If with x bound to polytype $poly_M$, the type of N is $poly_N$, then the type of the let-expression is $poly_N$.

The rule for type application is a form of β-reduction for types. If M has a polytype $\forall t.\ poly$, then the type of term $M\ \tau$ is obtained by substituting τ for the free occurrences of t in $poly$:

$$\frac{env \;\vdash\; M \;:\; \forall t.\ poly}{env \;\vdash\; (M\ \tau) \;:\; \{\tau/t\}poly} \qquad \text{(type application)}$$

The notion of free occurrences of t is with respect to the binder $\forall$. Note also that the type substituted for t is a monotype.

The final rule is for type abstraction. When a Λ binds type t in a term M, a corresponding $\forall$ binds t in the type $poly$ of M:

$$\frac{env \;\vdash\; M \;:\; poly}{env \;\vdash\; (\Lambda t.\ M) \;:\; \forall t.\ poly} \qquad t \text{ not free in } env \qquad \text{(type abstraction)}$$

The caveat that t not be free in env prevents the newly introduced variable t from clashing with any free variables in the type expressions in env.

The derivation in Fig. 14.10 determines the polytype

$$\forall t.\ (t \to t) \to t \to t$$

for the expression

$$\Lambda t.\ \lambda f : t \to t.\ \lambda x : t.\ f\ (f\ x)$$

To fit sequents on a line, the environment

$$bind(x, t, bind(f, t \to t, env))$$

is written as

$$x : t,\ f : t{\to}t,\ env$$

Similarly, $bind(f, t \to t, env)$ is written as $f : t{\to}t,\ env$.

The last line of the derivation

$$env \;\vdash\; \Lambda t.\ \lambda f : t \to t.\ \lambda x : t.\ f\ (f\ x) \;:\; \forall t.\ (t \to t) \to t \to t$$

$x : t, f : t{\rightarrow}t, env \;\vdash\; x \;:\; t$		variable
$x : t, f : t{\rightarrow}t, env \;\vdash\; f \;:\; t \rightarrow t$		variable
$x : t, f : t{\rightarrow}t, env \;\vdash\; f\,x \;:\; t$		application
$x : t, f : t{\rightarrow}t, env \;\vdash\; f\,(f\,x) \;:\; t$		application
$f : t{\rightarrow}t, env \;\vdash\; \lambda x : t.\; f\,(f\,x) \;:\; t \rightarrow t$		abstraction
$env \;\vdash\; \lambda f : t \rightarrow t.\; \lambda x : t.\; f\,(f\,x) \;:\; (t \rightarrow t) \rightarrow t \rightarrow t$		abstraction
$env \;\vdash\; \Lambda t.\; \lambda f : t \rightarrow t.\; \lambda x : t.\; f\,(f\,x) \;:\; \forall t.\, (t \rightarrow t) \rightarrow t \rightarrow t$		type abstr.

Figure 14.10   Derivation of a polytype for a Core-XML term.

is obtained by the rule for type abstraction. We assume that t is not free in the environment *env*. Note how t is simultaneously bound by Λ in the term and by $\forall$ in the type.

The usage of *twice* in

$$twice\; (\textbf{int} \rightarrow \textbf{int})\; (twice\; \textbf{int})\; \textbf{succ}\; 0$$

can be explored by starting with

$$twice : \forall t.\, (t \rightarrow t) \rightarrow t \rightarrow t,\; env \;\vdash\; twice \;:\; \forall t.\, (t \rightarrow t) \rightarrow t \rightarrow t$$

Let $\sigma = \textbf{int} \rightarrow \textbf{int}$. The mnemonic significance of σ is that it is the type of the successor function. The type application *twice* σ yields

$$twice : \forall t.\, (t \rightarrow t) \rightarrow t \rightarrow t,\; env \;\vdash\; twice\; \sigma \;:\; (\sigma \rightarrow \sigma) \rightarrow \sigma \rightarrow \sigma$$

Similar reasoning yields the type $\sigma \rightarrow \sigma$ for *twice* **int**:

$$twice : \forall t.\, (t \rightarrow t) \rightarrow t \rightarrow t,\; env \;\vdash\; twice\; \textbf{int} \;:\; \sigma \rightarrow \sigma$$

The rule for applications now yields

$$\cdots \;\vdash\; (twice\; \sigma)\; (twice\; \textbf{int}) \;:\; \sigma \rightarrow \sigma$$

This function is now ready to be applied to **succ**.

It follows from the discussion of explicit types that the ML subexpression

```
twice twice succ 0
```

does not apply twice to itself. Instead, the two occurrences of twice represent functions of different monotypes, obtained from the same polymorphic function.

Exercises

14.1   Use the syntax-directed definition of substitution in Section 14.2 to verify the following equalities:

   a. $\{u/x\} (\lambda u.\ x) = (\lambda z.\ u)$

   b. $\{u/x\} (\lambda u.\ u) = (\lambda z.\ z)$

   c. $\{u/x\} (\lambda y.\ x) = (\lambda y.\ u)$

   d. $\{u/x\} (\lambda y.\ u) = (\lambda y.\ u)$

14.2   Verify the following equalities:

   a. $SIII =_\beta I$, where S is $\lambda xyz.\ (xz)(yz)$ and I is $\lambda x.\ x$.

   b. $twice(twice) f\ x =_\beta f(f(f(f\ x)))$, where $twice$ is $\lambda f\ x.\ f(f\ x))$.

14.3   Draw a diagram showing all possible reductions from $twice(twice) f\ x$ to the normal form $f(f(f(f\ x)))$.

14.4   The term ZZ, where Z is $\lambda z.\ \lambda x.\ x(z\ z\ x)$, satisfies the requirement of fixed-point combinators that $ZZM =_\beta M(ZZM)$. Show that it satisfies the stronger requirement $ZZM \overset{*}{\Rightarrow} M(ZZM)$.

14.5   Using the applied lambda calculus of Section 14.4, define a function to compute elements of the Fibonacci sequence.

14.6   Construct terms in the typed lambda calculus of Section 14.5 by adding types to each of the following pure λ-terms:

   a. $\lambda x.\ x$
   b. $\lambda xy.\ x$
   c. $\lambda xyz.\ (x\ z)\ (y\ z)$
   d. $(\lambda x.\ x)\ (\lambda x.\ x)$
   e. $(\lambda xyz.\ (x\ z)\ (y\ z))\ (\lambda x.\ x)\ (\lambda x.\ x)$

14.7   Consider the term

   let $I = \lambda x.\ x$ **in** $I(I)$

   a. Add types to this term to obtain a program in the language Core-XML of Section 14.6.
   b. Use the type rules for Core-XML to verify that your answer to (a) is well typed.

14.8   Instead of the type rule (let) in Fig. 14.9,

$$\frac{env \ \vdash \ M \ : \ poly_M \qquad bind(x, poly_M, env) \ \vdash \ N \ : \ poly_N}{env \ \vdash \ \textbf{let} \ x : poly_M \ = \ M \ \textbf{in} \ N \ : \ poly_N}$$

Mitchell and Harper [1988] use the rule

$$\frac{env \ \vdash \ M \ : \ poly_M \qquad bind(x, poly_M, env) \ \vdash \ N \ : \ \tau_N}{env \ \vdash \ \textbf{let} \ x : poly_M \ = \ M \ \textbf{in} \ N \ : \ \tau_N}$$

Note that the type of N is restricted to be a monotype in their rule. Does the replacement of rule (let) by this restricted rule change the types that can be derived using the type rules in Fig. 14.9? Justify your answer.

Bibliographic Notes

Rosser [1984] is a brief history of the lambda calculus of Church [1941]. Combinators predate the lambda calculus, despite the definition of combinators as closed lambda terms in Section 14.1. Combinatory logic, the use of combinators to study functions, complements the lambda calculus. Combinators were introduced independently by Schönfinkel [1924] and by Curry in the 1930s; see Curry and Feys [1958]. The two fundamental combinators are K and S, characterized by the following equations:

$$Kxy = x$$
$$Sxyz = xz(yz)$$

All pure lambda terms without free variables correspond to terms built up entirely out of K and S.

It was not until 1969 that a mathematical semantics was given for the lambda calculus by Scott; see Scott [1977] for a retrospective view.

Hindley and Seldin [1986] give an introductory treatment of the lambda calculus and combinators. Barendregt [1984] is a comprehensive account. The essays collected by Hindley and Seldin [1980] are representative of research topics that were being pursued at the time the collection appeared.

Applied lambda calculi, or functional languages, have long been used as defining languages for specifying the semantics of programming languages. The definitional interpreters in Chapter 11 have a functional defining language. Landin [1965] used a modified lambda calculus to define Algol 60. The denotational semantics approach of Scott and Strachey [1971] uses an applied lambda calculus, without modifications. For more on denotational semantics, see the books by Gordon [1979], Schmidt [1986], and Stoy [1977].

The survey by Cardelli and Wegner [1985] is a good starting point for studying static types. The papers in Kahn, MacQueen, and Plotkin [1984] are a more advanced starting point.

Lambda calculi with polymorphic types were introduced independently by Girard [1972] and Reynolds [1974]. The language Core-XML is from Mitchell and Harper [1988].

Types do not have to be declared explicitly in the ML programming language because the implementation uses a clever algorithm based on unification to infer types. Extending Curry's work on type inference (see Curry and Feys [1958]), Hindley [1969] observed that unification could be used for type inference. A similar independent observation by Milner led to the type checking algorithm for ML (Milner [1978]). Type rules for ML are given by Damas and Milner [1982]; see also Clément et al. [1986]. The interaction between types and modules in ML can be seen from MacQueen's description of the module facility in the composite report by Harper, MacQueen, and Milner [1986].

15

A Look at
Some Languages

This committee had nearly completed its detailed work in the autumn of 1957, when its members, aware of the many algorithmic languages already in existence, concluded that, rather than present still another such language, they should make an effort towards worldwide unification.

> *– Rutishauser [1967], on the European effort that resulted in Algol.*

The years 1958–1959 were years in which many new computers were introduced. The time was ripe for experimentation in new languages. As mentioned earlier there are many elements in common in all Algebraic languages, and everyone who introduced a new language in those years called it Algol, or a dialect of Algol. The initial result of this first attempt at standardization of Algebraic languages was the proliferation of such languages in great variety.

> *– Rosen [1964], looking back over a decade during which computers went from being quite rare to being part of a multibillion dollar industry.*

This chapter collects reference material about the main languages in this book. Each section contains notes on the origins of a language, a program in the language, and an overview of program structure.

15.1 PASCAL: A TEACHING LANGUAGE

Pascal is one of a series of languages developed by Wirth [1971]. It was designed for teaching programming, especially systems programming. The language spread rapidly, after the first compiler became available in 1970. It is widely available and has served as a base for numerous language extensions.

579

Jensen and Wirth [1974] is an original reference for Pascal. See Fig. 15.1 for the origins of the language.

The design of an expression evaluator in Section 6.3 includes a discussion of program structure in Pascal. For statements in Pascal, see Section 3.2; for declarations, begin with Section 4.1; and for procedures, see Section 5.1.

Program Structure in Pascal

A Pascal program has three parts: a heading, optional declarations, and a body consisting of executable statements:

$$\langle program \rangle \quad ::= \quad \langle heading \rangle \ \langle declarations \rangle \ \langle body \rangle$$

The heading of the program in Fig. 15.2 is

```
program trap(input, output);
```

It gives the name `trap` to the program and specifies that the program does input/output.

The declarations consist of optional sections for labels, constants, types, variables, and procedures. Keywords `label`, `const`, `type`, and `var` open the sections for labels, constants, types, and variables, respectively. The

---

Language design in the 1960s was dominated by attempts to improve upon Algol 60. "Here was a language so far ahead of its time that it was not only an improvement on its predecessors, but also on nearly all its successors," writes Hoare [1973].

In 1964, Wirth joined IFIP Working Group 2.1, chartered with defining a successor to Algol 60 that would be suitable for both scientific and commercial applications. Wirth's 1965 proposal for a successor reflected the views of a pragmatic faction. But, a majority favored a competing proposal that eventually turned into Algol 68.

Wirth's implementation of his own proposal came to be known as Algol W. It supported dynamically allocated data using records and pointers, as suggested by Hoare. Algol W "failed to be an adequate tool for systems programming, partly because it was burdened with features unnecessary for systems programming tasks, partly because it lacked adequately flexible data structuring facilities," so Wirth started anew.

The goals for Pascal in 1968 were twofold: "The language was to be suitable for expressing the fundamental constructs known at the time in a concise and logical way, and its implementation was to be efficient and competitive with existing Fortran compilers."

Figure 15.1   The origins and design goals for Pascal, based on Wirth [1993].

```
program trap(input, output);
   var result: real;

   function square(x : real) : real;
   begin
       square := x * x;
   end;

   function area(a, b : real; function f(x:real) : real) : real;
   begin
       area := (b-a)*(f(a)+f(b))/2
   end;
begin
   result := area(2, 5, square);
   writeln(2, 5, result)
end.
```

Figure 15.2 A complete Pascal program containing two procedures, from page 153.

nonempty sections in Fig. 15.2 are the ones for variables and procedure declarations.

The body consists of a compound (begin-end) statement followed by a period, ".".

Declarations

The variable declaration in Fig. 15.2

```
var result: real;
```

specifies that the name result is a variable that can be assigned real values.

The structure of a procedure is similar to that of the overall program:

⟨*procedure-declaration*⟩   ::=   ⟨*heading*⟩ ⟨*declarations*⟩ ⟨*body*⟩ ;

The procedure heading begins with keyword function for a function procedure and with keyword procedure for a proper procedure. The heading contains the procedure name, parameters, and a result type, in the case of functions. The declarations in a procedure have sections for labels, constants, types, variables, and nested procedures.

The heading for function square is

```
function square(x : real) : real;
```

Enclosed within parentheses is the formal parameter `x` of type `real`. The result type, after the closing parenthesis and colon, is also `real`. Result types are restricted to type names. The parentheses surrounding the formal parameters are dropped if there are no parameters.

The default parameter-passing method is call-by-value. Parameters are passed by reference if keyword `var` appears before a formal parameter.

The value returned from a function is determined by assignments to the function name within the procedure body.

Types

Pascal accepts types specified by the following grammar (from page 104):

$$
\begin{array}{lcl}
\langle simple \rangle & ::= & \langle name \rangle \\
 & | & \langle enumeration \rangle \\
 & | & \langle subrange \rangle \\
\langle type \rangle & ::= & \langle simple \rangle \\
 & | & \texttt{array [} \langle simple \rangle \texttt{] of } \langle type \rangle \\
 & | & \texttt{record } \langle field\text{-}list \rangle \texttt{ end)} \\
 & | & \texttt{set of } \langle simple \rangle \\
 & | & \texttt{\^{} } \langle name \rangle \\
\langle enumeration \rangle & ::= & \texttt{(} \langle name\text{-}list \rangle \texttt{)} \\
\langle subrange \rangle & ::= & \langle constant \rangle \texttt{ .. } \langle constant \rangle \\
\langle field \rangle & ::= & \langle name\text{-}list \rangle \texttt{ : } \langle type \rangle
\end{array}
$$

Expressions

The operators of Pascal are (from page 108):

```
<  <=  =  <>  >=  >  in     in tests set membership
+  -  or
*  /  div mod and
not
```

The inequality relation is typed as `<>`. The operators all associate to the left. All operators on a line have the same precedence; the lines are in order of increasing precedence.

Statements

Pascal accepts statements with the following syntax (from page 65):

$$\langle statement \rangle ::= \langle expression \rangle := \langle expression \rangle$$
$$| \quad \langle name \rangle \ (\ \langle expression\text{-}list \rangle \ )$$
$$| \quad \text{begin} \ \langle statement\text{-}list \rangle \ \text{end}$$
$$| \quad \text{if} \ \langle expression \rangle \ \text{then} \ \langle statement \rangle$$
$$| \quad \text{if} \ \langle expression \rangle \ \text{then} \ \langle statement \rangle \ \text{else} \ \langle statement \rangle$$
$$| \quad \text{while} \ \langle expression \rangle \ \text{do} \ \langle statement \rangle$$
$$| \quad \text{repeat} \ \langle statement\text{-}list \rangle \ \text{until} \ \langle expression \rangle$$
$$| \quad \text{for} \ \langle name \rangle := \langle expression \rangle \ \text{to} \ \langle expression \rangle \ \text{do} \ \langle statement \rangle$$
$$| \quad \text{for} \ \langle name \rangle := \langle expression \rangle \ \text{downto} \ \langle expression \rangle \ \text{do} \ \langle statement \rangle$$
$$| \quad \text{case} \ \langle expression \rangle \ \text{of} \ \langle cases \rangle \ \text{end}$$

$$\langle statement\text{-}list \rangle ::= \langle empty \rangle$$
$$| \quad \langle statement \rangle \ ; \ \langle statement\text{-}list \rangle$$

$$\langle cases \rangle \qquad ::= \langle constant \rangle \ : \ \langle statement \rangle$$
$$| \quad \langle constant \rangle \ : \ \langle statement \rangle \ : \ \langle cases \rangle$$

15.2   C: SYSTEMS PROGRAMMING

C was created in 1972 by Dennis Ritchie as an implementation language for software associated with the UNIX operating system. In 1973, the UNIX system itself was rewritten in C. C continues to be a popular implementation language. Kernighan and Ritchie [1988] is the primary reference for C. See Fig. 15.3 for the origins of the language.

Program Structure in C

A C program consists of a sequence of global declarations of function procedures, types, and variables. Types and variables can also be declared local to a function; however, a function cannot be declared local to another.

A complete C program appears in Fig. 15.4. Lines beginning with # are instructions to a macro preprocessor. The line

```
#include <stdio.h>
```

provides access to a standard input/output library. The line

```
#define N 7
```

C came after B. The two were influenced by BCPL, the implementation language for CPL.

CPL (Combined Programming Language) remained a laboratory for studying concepts; it was never fully implemented. In a collection of working papers, Strachey [1966] notes, "One of the principal aims in designing CPL was to make it a practical application of a logically coherent theory of programming languages." Strachey was later to play a pivotal role in the development of the denotational approach to describing the semantics of programming languages.

BCPL (Basic CPL) was developed by Richards [1969] as a compiler-writing tool. "BCPL adopted much of the syntactic richness of CPL and strived for the same high standard of linguistic excellence; however, to achieve the efficiency necessary for systems programming its scale and complexity are far less than that of CPL."

B, written by Ken Thompson in 1970, was very close to BCPL semantically, but had a syntax that permitted a tiny compiler. The pointer and array constructs of C come from BCPL and B.

"The major advance of C [over B] is its typing structure. . . . The typeless nature of B and BCPL had seemed to promise a great simplification in the implementation, understanding, and use of these languages . . . [but] seemed inappropriate, for purely technological reasons, to the available hardware," write Ritchie et al. [1978]. The C type system was extended in 1977 to improve the portability of C programs, after a project to move UNIX from one machine to another revealed widespread type-checking violations in programs that worked on one machine, but not on another, primarily due to confusion between pointers and integers.

Figure 15.3   The origins of C, based on Ritchie et al. [1978]; see also Ritchie [1993].

instructs the preprocessor to replace instances of the name N by the constant 7. The preprocessor is also used to partition a program into files, as discussed later in this section.

The rest of the program in Fig. 15.4 consists of the declarations of the variables yes and no; the array X; the variable T; and the functions search and main.

Functions in C

C is geared to function procedures, declared by

⟨*result-type*⟩ ⟨*name*⟩ (⟨*formal-parameter-declarations*⟩) {
    ⟨*declaration-list*⟩
    ⟨*statement-list*⟩
}

All of the nonterminals in this syntax, except ⟨*name*⟩, are optional.

```
#include <stdio.h>
#define N 7
int yes = 1, no = 0;
int X[] = { 0, 11, 22, 33, 44, 55, 66, 77 };
int T;
int search(int lo, int hi) {
    int k;
    if( lo > hi ) return no;
    k = (lo + hi) /2;
    if( T == X[k] ) return yes;
    else if( T < X[k] ) return search(lo, k-1);
    else if( T > X[k] ) return search(k+1, hi);
}
int main(void) {
    scanf("%d", &T);
    if( search(1,N) )
        printf("found\n");
    else
        printf("notfound\n");
    return 0;
}
```

Figure 15.4   A complete C program, from page 187.

Execution of a C program begins in a function `main`. The smallest complete C program is

```
main() {}
```

A missing result type is taken by default to be `int`. A special type name `void` indicates the absence of a value. A result type `void` indicates that a "function" is a proper procedure with no result.

A more fully specified variant of the smallest program is

```
int  main(void)   { return 0; }
```

Function `main` returns an integer termination status. A zero status conventionally indicates normal termination.

Variable Declarations in C

The basic types of C include

```
char              characters
int               integers
unsigned int      integers, with arithmetic modulo 2^n
float             real
double            double-precision real
```

but they do not include booleans. In tests, a nonzero value is treated as **true** and 0 is treated as **false**.

Declarations in C begin with a type name and declare a sequence of names. For example,

```
int i, j;
```

declares i and j to be integer variables. An array is declared by writing its size after the name, as in

```
int A[3], B[5][7];
```

A is an array of three integers and B is an array of five arrays of seven integers. Zero is the lower bound of all arrays, so the three elements of A are A[0], A[1], and A[2].

A pointer to an integer is declared by writing * before the variable name, as in the following declaration of p, a pointer to an integer:

```
int *p;
```

Variable declaration and initialization can be combined, as in the following excerpts from Fig. 15.4:

```
int yes = 1, no = 0;
int X[] = { 0, 11, 22, 33, 44, 55, 66, 77 };
```

An array can be initialized by enclosing a sequence of values between braces { and }. The lower bound 0 and upper bound 7 of array X are filled in from the array initializer.

Expressions

C allows assignments to appear within expressions. The assignment operator = is right associative. A sequence of assignments can be combined into one expression, using the comma operator. A sequence of expressions separated by commas

$$E \; , \; F$$

is evaluated from left to right; the value of the sequence is the value of the last expression.

The following partial table of binary operators in C is formed by adding the comma operator to the table on page 45:

sequence	,
assignment	=
logical or	||
logical and	&&
inclusive or	|
exclusive or	^
and	&
equality	== !=
relational	< <= >= >
shift	<< >>
additive	+ -
multiplicative	* / %

The operators are in order of increasing precedence; that is, the comma operator has the lowest precedence and the multiplicative operators *, /, and % have the highest precedence. All operators on the same line have the same precedence and associativity. The assignment operator is right associative; all other operators are left associative.

The unary operators include ! for logical negation, & for creating a pointer, and * for dereferencing a pointer. These unary operators have higher precedence than the binary operators.

C provides a special increment operator, ++, and a special decrement operator, --. When applied to integer variables, these operators change the value of the variable by 1.

C uses short-circuit evaluation for the boolean operators && and \|\|, corresponding to **and** and **or**, respectively. Both operands are evaluated by & and \|, the bit-wise "and" and "or" operators.

Control Flow in C

Control flow in C is discussed in Section 3.7. C accepts statements with the syntax (from page 91):

⟨*statement*⟩ ::= ;

     | ⟨*expression*⟩ ;

     | { ⟨*stmt-list*⟩ }

     | if (⟨*expression*⟩) ⟨*statement*⟩

     | if (⟨*expression*⟩) ⟨*statement*⟩ else ⟨*statement*⟩

     | while (⟨*expression*⟩) ⟨*statement*⟩

     | do ⟨*statement*⟩ while (⟨*expression*⟩) ;

     | for (⟨*opt-expr*⟩ ; ⟨*opt-expr*⟩ ; ⟨*opt-expr*⟩ ;) ⟨*statement*⟩

     | switch (⟨*expression*⟩) ⟨*statement*⟩

     | case ⟨*constant-expression*⟩ : ⟨*statement*⟩

     | default : ⟨*statement*⟩

     | break ;

     | continue ;

     | return ;

     | return ⟨*expression*⟩ ;

     | goto ⟨*label-name*⟩ ;

     | ⟨*label-name*⟩ : ⟨*statement*⟩

⟨*stmt-list*⟩ ::= ⟨*empty*⟩

     | ⟨*stmt-list*⟩ ⟨*statement*⟩

⟨*opt-expr*⟩ ::= ⟨*empty*⟩

     | ⟨*expression*⟩

Pointers and Arrays

An array name A is simply a pointer to the zeroth element A[0]. See Section 4.8 for the use of arrays and pointers to maintain a table of variable-length strings.

As another example, the following linear search through a table

```
a[0] = x; i = n;
while( a[i] != x )
    --i;
return i;
```

can therefore be rewritten, using pointers, as

```
a[0] = x; p = a+n;
while( *p != x )
    --p;
return p-a;
```

Instead of using i as the index of element a[i], the rewritten fragment maintains p as a pointer to a[i]. Instead of initializing i to n, the rewritten fragment initializes p to be a pointer to a[n]. Subsequently, instead of decrementing i, the rewritten fragment decrements p, since p-1 points to a[i-1] if p points to a[i]. Finally,

```
return i;
```

changes into

```
return p-a;
```

If p is a pointer to a[i], then p must equal a+i, so

```
i == p-a
```

Header Files

C and C++ programmers conventionally partition a program into files corresponding loosely to modules. The conventions are not a part of C or C++, yet their use is so prevalent that they deserve mention. A *header* file, with a .h suffix, corresponds to a definition module; it is a collection of declarations. A corresponding implementation file, with a .c suffix, contains additional declarations and code needed for the names declared in the header file.

For example, the program in Fig. 15.5 is partitioned into three files, called buf.h, buf.c, and buftest.c.

The implementation file buf.c begins with

```
#include "buf.h"
```

which a preprocessor replaces by the contents of the file buf.h.

File buftest.c "includes" the contents of three files, buf.h, an input/output library stdio.h, and a library of mathematical functions math.h. The difference between the quotes in "buf.h" and the enclosing brackets, < >, in <stdio.h> lies in where the operating system looks for the files.

Standard Input/Output

The standard input/output library provides the functions printf and scanf for output and input, respectively. The first argument of printf is a string that specifies the format of the output. In the call

```
printf("->f: n = %d; count = %d\n", n, count);
```

File buf.h:

```
const int MAXBUF = 4;
interface declarations
```

File buf.c:

```
#include "buf.h"
implementation of the interface
```

File buftest.c:

```
#include "buf.h"
#include <stdio.h>
#include <math.h>
main() {
    ...
}
```

Figure 15.5   The static subdivision of a program into files.

---

the format string is

```
"->f: n = %d; count = %d\n"
```

The symbol \n represents a newline character.

The occurrences of the substring %d are replaced by the integer values of n and count.

The specifier %g instructs C to choose a suitable output representation, based on the type of the value being output. The specifier %d is for an integer decimal, %c for a character, %s for a string, and %f for a floating point representation.

Character input/output is done using getchar and putchar, as in

```
while( (c=getchar()) != EOF )
    putchar(c);
```

The name EOF denotes the end of the input file.

Formatted input is done using scanf, which takes as arguments a format string and a sequence of addresses. Note the use of & in

```
scanf("%d", &T);
```

to create the address of T. This call of scanf reads an integer value from the input and assigns it to T.

15.3   C++: A RANGE OF PROGRAMMING STYLES

"I built C++ as a bridge over which people would pass from traditional programming to styles relying on data abstraction and object-oriented programming," writes Stroustrup [1994]. The groundwork for C++ was laid around 1980. C programs are accepted essentially as is by C++; all of the constructs of C in Section 15.2 carry over unchanged into C++. Stroustrup [1991] is the primary source for C++. See Fig. 15.6 for the origins of the language.

Classes in C++

The members of a class in C++ are variables and functions. The complete C++ program in Fig. 15.7 consists largely of the declaration of class Stack and its member functions; these declarations appear above the line

```
#include <stdio.h>
```

Stroustrup [1991] writes, "Clearly C++ owes most to C. C is retained as a subset, and so is C's emphasis on facilities that are low-level enough to cope with the most demanding systems programming tasks. The other major source of inspiration was Simula67; the class concept (with derived classes and virtual functions) was borrowed from it. C++'s facility for overloading operators and the freedom to place a declaration wherever a statement can occur resembles Algol68."

A snapshot of C++ around 1980 would show a fledgling named "C with Classes," formed by grafting the class construct of Simula onto C++. The name C++ itself was given in 1983, by combining "C" and the increment operator "++".

Templates and exception handling are useful for building libraries. These facilities and multiple inheritance were added after the publication of the 1986 edition of Stroustrup [1991].

A standardization effort began in 1990 to round out the language and its definition, to address compatibility between C and C++, and to agree on libraries that ought to be required for every implementation. Stroustrup [1994] underscores the importance of libraries by noting that the first release of C++ "should have been delayed until a larger library including some fundamental classes such as singly and doubly linked lists, an associative array class, a range-checked array class, and a simple string class could have been included."

Figure 15.6   The origins of C++, based on Stroustrup [1991]. For a detailed history, see Stroustrup [1994].

```
class Stack {
public:
        Stack() { top = 0; }
    char pop();
    void push(char);
private:
    int  top;
    char elements[101];
};
char Stack::pop() {
    top = top - 1;
    return elements[top+1];
}

void Stack::push(char c) {
    top = top + 1;
    elements[top] = c;
}


#include <stdio.h>

main() {
    Stack s;
    s.push('!'); s.push('@'); s.push('#');
    printf("%c %c %c\n", s.pop(), s.pop(), s.pop());
}
```

Figure 15.7   A complete C++ program, adapted from Fig. 6.11 on page 234.

which provides access to an input/output library. Below this line is the function main, where Stack is used as a type to declare variable s.

Keywords public, private, and protected control the accessibility of members in a class declaration.

A special member function, with the same name as the class, is called a constructor. It is called automatically when an object of the class is created.

The full name of a member is formed by prefixing the class name and the name resolution operator ::. Thus, Stack::pop is the full name of member pop of class Stack.

For more information on classes, dynamic allocation, and templates, see Sections 6.5–6.7.

Inheritance in C++

In C++ terminology, the extension of a base class is called a derived class. Class D in Fig. 15.8 is derived from class B. The complete C++ program in Fig. 15.8 is from Section 7.4.

The declaration of class D begins with the line

```
class D : public B {
```

Keyword public identifies B as a public base class; that is, members of B retain their accessibility in the derived class.

Function f in the base class is virtual, marked by keyword virtual. Thus, when testF calls the virtual function f, the body in the derived class is used. Hence, the output of the program is

```
B  B
D  B
```

For more information on class derivation and virtual functions, see Section 7.4.

```
class B {
public:
virtual char    f()       { return 'B'; }
        char    g()       { return 'B'; }
        char    testF()   { return f(); }
        char    testG()   { return g(); }
};
class D : public B {
public:
        char    f()       { return 'D'; }
        char    g()       { return 'D'; }
};
#include <stdio.h>
main() {
        B b;
        D d;
        printf("%c   %c\n", b.testF(), b.testG());
        printf("%c   %c\n", d.testF(), d.testG());
}
```

Figure 15.8   A complete C++ program contrasting the virtual function f with the non-virtual function g. This program is from page 270.

15.4   SMALLTALK, THE LANGUAGE

Smalltalk, the language, is part of an overall object-oriented programming environment. Goldberg and Robson [1983] is the primary reference for the language. They note, "The Smalltalk-80 system is based on the Simula language and from the visions of Alan Kay, who first encouraged us to try to create a uniformly object-oriented system." See Fig. 15.9 for the origins of the language. The concepts in Sections 7.2 and 7.3 apply directly to Smalltalk; however, the language itself is covered in passing in Sections 7.7 and 7.8.

The five basic words of the Smalltalk vocabulary are:

object	Collection of private data and public operations.
class	Description of a set of objects.
instance	An instance of a class is an object of that class.
method	A procedure body implementing an operation.
message	A procedure call. Request to execute a method.

On the printed page, where possible, we collect all the information about a class in one place. For example, class `Diagram` in Fig. 15.10 is a Smalltalk variant of diagrams in Example 7.2 on page 259.

Alan Kay coined the name Smalltalk, "as in 'programming should be a matter of . . .' and 'children should program in . . .'." He was interested in a language for kids, to be used on a personal computer, at a time (around 1970) when computers were large, expensive, and character-oriented.

Smalltalk-72, the first real version of the language, was created on a bet to come up with "the most powerful language in the world" in "a page of code." Alan Kay's Smalltalk interpreter was inspired by John McCarthy's Lisp interpreter (see Chapter 13). Unlike the Lisp interpreter, which used conditionals to decide how to evaluate a construct, the Smalltalk interpreter put the code to evaluate an object with the object itself, and used messages to invoke the code.

The idea that everything in a system is an object, the keyword syntax, and inheritance appeared in Smalltalk-76, credited to Dan Ingalls.

Smalltalk now refers to Smalltalk-80, the language described in Goldberg and Robson [1983]. As they note, the language is part of a "big system . . . made up of many components. It includes objects that provide functions usually attributed to a computer operating system: automatic storage management, a file system, display handling, text and picture editing, keyboard and pointing device input, a debugger, a performance spy, processor scheduling, compilation and decompilation."

Figure 15.9   The origins of Smalltalk, based on Kay [1993].

---

class Diagram   **superclass** OrderedCollection

instance variables

    angle

class methods

    new
        ^ super new initialize

instance methods

    initialize
        self setangle: 0
    addShape: aShape
        self add: (aShape setalign: angle)
    setangle: degrees
        angle := (0 - degrees) degreesToRadians.
    draw: aStylus
        | newStylus |
        newStylus := aStylus deepCopy.
        self do: [:aShape | aShape draw: newStylus].
        ^ newStylus

Figure 15.10   A view of class Diagram, written in Smalltalk.

Expressions

Expressions have a unique syntax in Smalltalk (see Fig. 15.11).

A message is written to the right of its recipient. A message without arguments, called a unary message, consists simply of a name. Messages that carry arguments are built of names that end in a colon; such names are called keywords. The general form of a message in Smalltalk, called a keyword message, consists of a sequence of keyword-argument pairs.

Evaluation proceeds from left to right. All arithmetic operators have the same precedence, so the addition in the expression 2 + 3 * 5 is done before the multiplication; that is, the following equivalences hold:

$$2 + 3 * 5 \equiv (2 + 3) * 5 \equiv 25$$

The assignment operator is ← or :=, depending on the implementation. The left side of an assignment must be a variable. Data structures are objects, so changes to components of a data structure are made by sending an appropriate message to that object.

Smalltalk	*comment*
s pop	message pop to object s
s push: 10	message push: with argument 10 to object s
self isEmpty	message isEmpty from an object to itself
$a	character a
$$	character $
'string'	string 'string' of six characters
top ← 0	*top* := 0
A at: i put: x	$A[i]$:= x, where A is an array
y ← A at: i	y := $A[i]$, where A is an array
#(2 3 5)	unnamed array with elements 2, 3, 5
#(2 $3 'five')	unnamed array of number 2, character 3, and string 'five'
2 + 3 * 5	note left-to-right evaluation: (2 + 3) * 5 ≡ 25

Figure 15.11   Syntax of expressions in Smalltalk.

Arrays support both at: and at:put: messages. An at: message looks up the value of an array element, while an at:put: changes the value of an array element. Thus,

        A   at: i

corresponds to $A[i]$, the value of the element of array A at position i. On the other hand,

        A   at: i   put: x

corresponds to $A[i]$:= x; the value of x is assigned to the element of array A at position i.

By design, at: and at:put: messages are supported by all Smalltalk objects that store information in components; examples are arrays, dictionaries, and tables.

Class and Instance Methods

Most classes respond to a message new by creating an instance of the class. Class Diagram in Fig. 15.10 redefines new:

```
new
    ^ super new initialize
```

The symbol `^` returns the value of the expression to its right. Here, `super` denotes the superclass `OrderedCollection`, which creates an object in response to message new. This object receives the message `initialize`. The expression returns the initialized object.

System Classes

The Smalltalk system provides a large number of existing classes that can be adapted, through inheritance, to the needs of a particular application. The system typically comes with the code for a number of useful system classes. Properties of these classes can be studied by browsing through the code.

An example of a system class is `Collection`, which supports several messages to carry out iterations of the form (see Fig. 15.12):

> **for** each element x of a collection **do**
> something with x
> **end**

Subclasses of `Collection`, such as `OrderedCollection`, `Set`, and `Dictionary`, inherit these messages.

---

class `Collection` **superclass** `Object`
instance methods

`add: anObject`	Add `anObject` as an element to this collection.
`do: aBlock`	Evaluate `aBlock` for each element of this collection.
`select: aBlock`	Evaluate `aBlock` for each element of this collection. Return a collection consisting of the elements for which the block evaluates to `true`.
`reject: aBlock`	Evaluate `aBlock` for each element of this collection. Return a collection consisting of the elements for which the block evaluates to `false`.
`collect: aBlock`	Evaluate `aBlock` for each element of this collection. Return a collection formed from the results of the successive evaluations of the block.

Figure 15.12   Operations on elements in a collection.

The Smalltalk counterpart of "do something with *x*" is a block that takes an argument x. The notation for such a block is

[: ⟨*variable*⟩ | ⟨*expression-sequence*⟩]

The value of a block is the value of its last expression.

The following examples illustrates the use of system classes.

Example 15.1 Class Diagram in Fig. 15.10 relies on two system classes, OrderedCollection and Pen.

In Example 7.2, page 259, a diagram object uses a variable *shapelist* to hold a list of shapes. No such variable is needed by an object of class Diagram in Fig. 15.10 because Diagram is a subclass of OrderedCollection. That is, a diagram object is a collection. When a new diagram is created, it is an empty collection, with no shapes. Shapes can be added using message add:, supported by all collection classes; see again Fig. 15.12.

In response to a draw: message, a diagram object executes a method containing the expression

```
self do: [:aShape | aShape draw: newStylus]
```

The do: operation evaluates the block

```
[:aShape | aShape draw: newStylus]
```

for each element aShape held by the diagram object itself.

The system class Pen implements messages that draw on a display. A pen is initially positioned at the center of the display or screen.

Class Stylus in Fig. 15.13 is a subclass of Pen. In addition to being a pen, a stylus keeps track of a last shape, so it can position itself relative to that shape in response to message attachAt.

Classes Diagram and Stylus in this example are taken from a Smalltalk implementation of the shape example in Section 7.2.   □

15.5   STANDARD ML

This book deals with the functional part of the Standard ML Core Language; Robin Milner has played a prominent role in its development. Standard ML also has a module system, not covered in this book, initially proposed by David MacQueen. The imperative features of ML are not considered in this book.

```
class Stylus    superclass Pen
```

instance variables

> "variable lastShape remembers the last shape drawn"
> lastShape

class methods

> new
> > "initialize with a default lastShape"
> > ^ super new lastShape: (Shape new)

instance methods

> attachAt: angle
> > "position the pen relative to lastShape"
> > self place: (self destX) @ (self destY)
> > > + (lastShape offset: angle).
> lastShape: aShape
> > lastShape := aShape

Figure 15.13   The use of inheritance to customize pen objects. A stylus is a pen that remembers the last shape to be drawn and can position itself relative to that last shape.

For introductory treatments of Standard ML, see the textbooks by Paulson [1991] and by Ullman [1994]. Milner, Tofte, and Harper [1990] is the defining document for Standard ML; see Fig. 15.14 for the origins of the language.

Interacting with the ML Interpreter

In an interactive session with an ML interpreter, we type lines terminated by semicolons, as in

```
3*4;
    val it = 12 : int
```

The interpreter evaluates the expression 3*4 and declares the name it to have its value 12 of type integer. Note that the semicolon is not part of the expression; it prompts a response from the interpreter.

Negative Numbers

In ML, a negative number begins with the symbol ~, not –:

```
~2 + 2;
    val it = 0 : int
```

ML began 1974 as a language for computer-assisted reasoning.

"This demand established the character of ML. In order to be sure that, when the user and the computer claim to have together performed a rigorous argument, their claim is justified, it was seen that the language must be strongly typed. On the other hand, to be useful in a difficult application, the type system had to be rather flexible, and permit the machine to guide the user rather than impose a burden." Robin Milner's solution was to use an elegant type inference algorithm that supported polymorphic types.

Imperative features and an exception mechanism were added "for practical reasons; no-one had experience of large useful programs written in a pure functional style."

The initial design of ML was done by Robin Milner, in collaboration with the other authors of Gordon et al. [1978].

ML was redesigned and evolved between 1983 and 1986 into the Standard ML Core Language, combining polymorphic types, function definition by pattern matching, records, and generalized exceptions. Pattern matching came from HOPE, due to Burstall, MacQueen, and Sanella [1980]. Records came from a 1980 implementation by Luca Cardelli, which was efficient enough to be used by students.

The ML module system descends from parameterized specifications in CLEAR by Burstall and Goguen [1977], through the module system designed by David MacQueen for HOPE. MacQueen's module system accommodated polymorphic types.

"In designing [Standard] ML, the interplay among three activities--language design, definition, and implementation--was extremely close . . . In general, those who took part in the three activities cannot now imagine how they could have been properly done separately."

Figure 15.14   The origins of Standard ML, based on Milner, Tofte, and Harper [1990].

```
2 + ~2;
   val it = 0 : int
```

Overloaded Arithmetic Operators

The arithmetic operators + and * are used both for operations on integers and on reals. The following attempt to define a function *square* fails because it does not specify whether integers or reals are to be multiplied:

```
fun square(x) = x*x;
   Error: overloaded variable "*" cannot be resolved
```

The overloading can be resolved by specifying the type of the parameter or the type of the result. In the following, the type of the result is specified:

```
fun square(x) = x*x : int;
    val square = fn : int -> int
```

Function *real* converts integers to reals:

```
real(2);
    val it = 2.0 : real
```

Reals can be converted to integers using functions *floor* and *ceiling*, which return integers that bracket the value of a real number:

```
floor(3.14159);
    val it = 3 : int
ceiling(3.14159);
    val it = 4 : int
```

Function Declaration by Pattern Matching

Patterns together with case analysis, discussed in Section 9.2, give ML a compact and readable notation for function declarations. Patterns are especially convenient for defining functions on lists. An example is the following function to compute the length of a list:

```
fun length ([]) = 0
|   length (a::y) = 1 + length(y);
    val length = fn : ('a list -> int)
```

This declaration has two cases, separated by a vertical bar |. The two cases are tested in order. The parentheses in the patterns ([]) and (a::y) identify what length is applied to; the parentheses can be ignored.

Function length is polymorphic. The leading quote in 'a identifies it as a type parameter. All elements of a list must have the same type. If this type is 'a, then the type of the list itself is 'a list.

Datatypes

A datatype declaration introduces a type name, and a set of value constructors for creating values of that type.

The differentiation example in Fig. 15.15 uses a datatype expr corresponding to expressions made up of constants, integers, sums, and products. See Section 9.5 for further information on datatypes.

Exceptions

Exception handling in ML is discussed in Section 9.6.

```
datatype expr = constant of int
              | variable of string
              | sum of expr * expr
              | product of expr * expr;

val zero = constant 0;
val one = constant 1;

fun d x (constant _) = zero
  | d (variable s) (variable t) = if s = t then one else zero
  | d x (sum (e1, e2)) = sum( d x e1, d x e2)
  | d x (product (e1, e2)) =
        let val term1 = product (d x e1, e2)
            val term2 = product (e1, d x e2)
        in sum (term1, term2)
        end;
```

Figure 15.15   A differentiation function in ML, from page 364.

Once an exception `Nomatch` is declared,

```
exception Nomatch;
```
    exception Nomatch : exn

it can be raised and handled. From Example 9.17, suppose that a function `match(a,pat)` either returns `pat` or raises exception `Nomatch`. The second case in the following function declaration has a handler for `Nomatch`:

```
fun fetch(a, nil) =
        raise Notfound
  |   fetch(a, pat::rest) =
        match(a, pat) handle Nomatch => fetch(a, rest)
```

If its second argument is the empty list, then `fetch` raises exception `Notfound`. Otherwise, let the list be `pat::rest`. If `match(a,pat)` raises exception `Nomatch`, then `fetch` catches this exception and calls itself recursively on the tail of the list.

15.6   SCHEME, A DIALECT OF LISP

The Scheme dialect of Lisp was created by Steele and Sussman [1975]. The Scheme report, edited by Clinger and Rees [1991], is a primary reference for the language. Abelson and Sussman [1985] and Friedman, Wand, and

Haynes [1992] are textbooks that use Scheme to illustrate programming concepts. See Fig. 15.16 for the origins of the language.

Scheme is introduced in Chapter 10. One of the main examples in the chapter is differentiation, a motivating example during the creation of Lisp. Scheme is also used in Chapter 13 as a defining language for operational semantics. The calculator in Fig. 15.17 illustrates the syntax-directed organization of a definitional interpreter.

Basic Constructs

Scheme's uniform syntax means that the language has remarkably few constructs. Instead, the language relies on standard functions such as `map` to combine functions in useful ways.

A name can be bound to a value by

John McCarthy designed Lisp in 1958. His interest in artificial intelligence had led him to work with lists and experiment with FLPL, for Fortran List Processing Language. Lists were represented on the IBM 704 by putting a pair of pointers into the "address" and "decrement" parts of a machine word. The name *car* (*cdr*) comes from "Contents of the Address (Decrement) Register." Lisp was designed in part because FLPL did not have conditional expressions and recursion.

In order to demonstrate the naturalness of Lisp as a language for defining computable functions, McCarthy wrote a universal Lisp function *eval*[*e*,*a*] that computes the value of a Lisp expression *e* in an environment *a*. "S. R. Russell noticed that *eval* could serve as an interpreter for LISP, promptly hand-coded it, and we now had a programming language with an interpreter," recalls McCarthy [1981]. The interpreter used dynamic scope, which he viewed "as just a bug."

The Lisp interpreter makes it easy to experiment with language designs.

Guy Steele and Gerald Jay Sussman created Scheme in an attempt to understand Carl Hewitt's object-oriented *actors*, which were influenced by Smalltalk. They wrote a tiny Lisp interpreter in MacLisp, the dominant dialect of Lisp at MIT, and then modified the interpreted to simulate actors. They called the resulting language Schemer, but a 6-character limitation on names prompted the shorter name Scheme.

Scheme is statically scoped and has first-class functions, as in the lambda calculus. The Scheme report (Clinger and Rees [1991]) notes, "Scheme was the first major dialect of Lisp to distinguish procedures from lambda expressions and symbols, to use a single lexical environment for all variables, and to evaluate the operator position of a procedure call in the same way as an operand position." Scheme also provides "first-class escape procedures."

Some of Scheme's innovations have been adopted in Common Lisp (Steele [1984]).

Figure 15.16   The origins of the Scheme dialect of Lisp; see also the history papers, McCarthy [1981] and Steele and Gabriel [1993].

```
(define (calc E)                          ;  the main routine
  (cond ((constant? E) (calc-constant E))
        ((sum? E)       (calc-sum E))
        ((product? E)   (calc-product E))
        (else (error "calc: cannot parse" E)) ))


(define constant? number?)                ;  constants are numbers

(define (calc-constant E) E)              ;  evaluating to themselves


(define (sum? E)                          ;  a sum is a list with head plus
  (and (pair? E) (equal? 'plus (car E))) )

(define (calc-sum E)                      ;  evaluate subexpressions and apply +
  (apply + (map calc (cdr E))))


(define (product? E)                      ;  a product is a list with head times
  (and (pair? E) (equal? 'times (car E))) )

(define (calc-product E)                  ;  evaluate subexpressions and apply *
  (apply * (map calc (cdr E))))
```

Figure 15.17   An interpreter for numbers, sums, and products, from page 530.

```
(define pi 3.1415926535)
    pi
```

Scheme does not distinguish between uppercase and lowercase letters, so the name `pi` is the same as `Pi`:

```
Pi
    3.1415926535
```

The predicates for classifying the entities that Scheme deals with are

```
boolean?   number?   string?   vector?
char?      pair?     symbol?
```

For example, `pi` is a symbol:

```
(symbol? 'pi)
    #t
```

The quote in `'pi` means that the argument of symbol is `pi`, rather than the value represented by `pi`. Without the quote, `pi` has been defined to denote a number:

```
(symbol? pi)
    #f
```

A function is applied by writing a list, enclosed within parentheses, consisting of the function and its arguments, as in

```
(+ 0 1 2 3 4 5)
    15
```

Functions, recursive and nonrecursive, can be defined using `define`:

```
(define (sq x) (* x x))
    sq
(sq 5)
    25
```

Anonymous functions can be defined using lambda notation. The following expression is the application of an anonymous function to argument 5:

```
((lambda (x) (* x x)) 5)
    25
```

The use of the conditional construct `if` is illustrated by the following definition of `max`:

```
(define (max x y) (if (> x y) x y) )
    max
(max 2 3)
    3
(max (+ 2 3) 4)
    5
```

Another form of conditional `cond` is used for sequential choice, as in the definition of `calc` in 15.17. A small example is

```
(define (len x)
  (cond ((null? x) 0)
        (else (+ 1 (len (cdr x)))) ))
    len
(len '(a b c))
    3
```

The distinction between `let` and `let*` can be seen from

```
(define x 0)               ; initial value of x
    x
(let ((x 2) (y x)) y)      ; bind y before redefining x
    0
```

```
(let* ((x 2) (y x)) y)   ; bind y after redefining x
   2
```

See Section 10.1 for an explanation.

List Manipulation

Lists in Scheme are written between parentheses (and), with white space separating list elements. The empty list is written as (). The operations on lists are

(null? x)   True if x is the empty list and false otherwise.

```
(null? '())
  #t
```

(car x)   The first element of a nonempty list x.

```
(car '(+ 2 3))
  +
```

(cdr x)   The rest of the list x after the first element is removed.

```
(cdr '(+ 2 3))
  (2 3)
```

(cons a x)   A value with car a and cdr x.

```
(cons '+ '(2 3))
  (+ 2 3)
```

(list ...)   A list formed by the values of the arguments of list.

```
(list 'a 'b 'c)
  (a b c)
```

Scheme provides a number of useful functions for list manipulation, including

(length x)   The length of list x.

```
(length '(a b c))
  3
```

(append x y) A list formed from the elements of list x followed by the elements of list y.

```
(append '(a b) '(c))
  (a b c)
```

(reverse x)   A list formed by the elements of x, in reverse order.

```
(reverse '(a b c))
  (c b a)
```

(map f x)   A list formed by applying f to each element of list x.

```
(map sq '(1 2 3 4 5))
  (1 4 9 16 25)
```

An extension allows `map` to be applied to functions `f` with more than one argument.

```
(map list '(a b c) '(1 2 3))
    ((a 1)  (b 2)  (c 3))
```

15.7 PROLOG

Prolog is introduced in Section 11.2. The rules in Fig. 15.18 illustrate the use of Prolog to define the semantics of a simple expression language.

Prolog, from *programmation en logique*, is the name of a programming language developed by Alain Colmerauer and Phillipe Roussel in 1972. Prolog programming techniques can be found in textbooks such as Sterling and Shapiro [1994] and Clocksin and Mellish [1987]. Figure 15.19 summarizes the origins of the language.

Terms

Facts, rules, and queries are specified using terms. A simple term is a number like 1972, a variable starting with an uppercase letter like `Env`, or an atom standing for itself like `seq`.

A compound term `plus(E1,E2)` consists of an atom `plus` followed by a parenthesized sequence of subterms. The atom is called a functor and the sub-

---

```
seq(Env, num(Val), Val).

seq(Env, plus(E1, E2), V) :-
    seq(Env, E1, V1), seq(Env, E2, V2), V is V1 + V2.

seq(Env, times(E1, E2), V) :-
    seq(Env, E1, V1), seq(Env, E2, V2), V is V1 * V2.

seq(Env, var(X), V) :-
    lookup(X, Env, V).

seq(Env, let(var(X), E1, E2), V2) :-
    seq(Env, E1, V1), seq(bind(X, V1, Env), E2, V2).

lookup(X, bind(X, V, _), V).

lookup(X, bind(Y, _, Env), V) :-
    lookup(X, Env, V).
```

Figure 15.18   Prolog rules, from page 527.

"The programming language, Prolog, was born of a project aimed not at producing a programming language but at processing natural language; in this case, French." The definitive version, intended as a programming language, and not just as a deductive system, appeared in 1973.

"There is no question that Prolog is essentially a theorem prover 'a la Robinson'. Our contribution was to transform that theorem prover into a programming language."

in 1969, Alain Colmerauer approached machine translation between English and French by implementing sets of rewriting rules called Q-systems. Despite their "bewildering" execution times, Q-systems were successful enough that he was ready to gamble on creating a programming language like Prolog. Q-systems were influenced by W-grammars (van Wijngaarden et al. [1975]), the description language for Algol 68.

The preliminary version of Prolog in 1972 was intended to be used for knowledge representation as well as for processing text. "The success of the project hinged on the decision concerning the choice of logic system and on the basic inference method." They chose first-order logic and a variant of the resolution method of Robinson [1965]. They also introduced practical restrictions that made Prolog possible, restrictions that have been criticized because they depart from pure logical inference.

Kowalski [1988] notes, "Looking back on our early discoveries, I value most the discovery that computation could be subsumed by deduction." His early examples included "computationally efficient axioms for such recursive predicates as addition and factorial." He continues, "For [Colmerauer], the Horn clause definition of appending lists was much more characteristic of the importance of logic programming."

Cohen [1988] offers reasons why Prolog developed slowly, relative to Lisp: (1) the lack of interesting examples illustrating the expressive power of the language, (2) the lack of adequate implementations, and (3) the availability of Lisp. He adds, "It is fair to say that the subsequent interpreters and compilers developed by Warren played a major role in the acceptance of Prolog." Warren [1980] describes how Prolog itself can be used for compiler writing.

Figure 15.19   The origins of Prolog, based on Colmerauer and Roussel [1993]; see also Kowalski [1988] and Cohen [1988].

terms are called arguments. See Fig. 15.20 for the basic syntax of Edinburgh Prolog.

Some operators can be written in infix as well as prefix notation; for example, the prefix notation $= (X, Y)$ can equivalently be rewritten as $X = Y$.

The special variable "_" is a placeholder for an unnamed term. All occurrences of _ are independent of each other.

⟨*fact*⟩   ::=   ⟨*term*⟩ .

⟨*rule*⟩   ::=   ⟨*term*⟩ :- ⟨*terms*⟩ .

⟨*query*⟩ ::=   ⟨*terms*⟩ .

⟨*term*⟩   ::=   ⟨*number*⟩ | ⟨*atom*⟩ | ⟨*variable*⟩ | ⟨*atom*⟩ (⟨*terms*⟩)

⟨*terms*⟩   ::=   ⟨*term*⟩ | ⟨*term*⟩ , ⟨*terms*⟩

Figure 15.20   Basic syntax of facts, rules, and queries in Edinburgh Prolog, from page 431.

Interacting with Prolog

The consult construct reads in a file containing facts and rules, and adds its contents at the end of the current database of rules. Thus,

```
?- consult(letfile).
   letfile consulted ···
   yes
```

Use reconsult to override rules in the database.

Rules

A rule

$$⟨term⟩ \quad :- \quad ⟨term⟩_1 , ⟨term⟩_2 , \cdots , ⟨term⟩_k .$$

for $k \geq 1$, corresponds to the following pseudocode:

$$⟨term⟩ \quad \mathbf{if} \quad ⟨term⟩_1 \ \mathbf{and} \ ⟨term⟩_2 \ \mathbf{and} \ \cdots \ \mathbf{and} \ ⟨term⟩_k.$$

The term to the left of the :- is called the head and the terms to the right of the :- are called conditions.

A fact is a special case of a rule, with a head and no conditions.

Queries

A query has the form

$$⟨term⟩_1 , ⟨term⟩_2 , \cdots , ⟨term⟩_k .$$

Queries are also called goals; the individual terms in a query are called sub-goals. A query with solutions is said to be *satisfiable*. The system responds with a solution to a satisfiable query:

```
?- E = let(var(y), num(2), var(y)),  seq(nil, E, V).
     E = let(var(y),num(2),var(y))
     V = 2
```

This query uses the rules in Fig. 15.18.

When a query has multiple solutions, type a semicolon and a carriage return to get additional solutions. Prolog responds with *no* if no further solutions can be found.

Arithmetic

The = operator stands for unification in Prolog, so

```
?- X = 2+3.
     X = 2+3
```

simply binds variable X to the term 2+3.

The infix is operator evaluates an expression:

```
?- X is 2+3.
     X = 5
```

Terms as Data

The list consisting of the three atoms a, b, and c can be written in any of the following ways:

```
[a, b, c]
[a, b, c | []]
[a, b | [c]]
[a | [b, c]]
```

Unification can be used to extract the components of a list, so explicit operators for extracting the head and tail are not needed. The solution of the query

```
?- [a|T] = [H, b, c].
     T = [b,c]
     H = a
```

binds variable T to the tail and variable H to the head of the list specified by
[a|T] and [H,b,c].

The connection between lists and terms is as follows. [H|T] is syntactic
sugar for the term . (H,T):

```
?- .(H, T) = [a,b,c].
    H = a
    T = [b,c]
```

Thus, the dot operator or functor "." corresponds to cons in Lisp, and lists
are terms.

There is a one-to-one correspondence between trees and terms. That is,
any tree can be written as a term and any term can be drawn as a tree. Any
data structure that can be simulated using trees can therefore be simulated
using terms.

Bibliography

Abelson, H., and Sussman, G. J., with Sussman, J. [1985]. *Structure and Interpretation of Computer Programs*. MIT Press, Cambridge, Mass.

Abrahams, P. W. [1966]. A final solution to the dangling else of Algol 60 and related languages. *Comm. ACM* **9**, 679–682.

Aho, A. V., Kernighan, B. W., and Weinberger, P. J. [1988]. *The AWK Programming Language*. Addison-Wesley, Reading, Mass.

Aho, A. V., Sethi, R., and Ullman, J. D. [1986]. *Compilers: Principles, Techniques, and Tools*. Addison-Wesley, Reading, Mass.

Andrews, G. R., and Schneider, F. B. [1983]. Concepts and notations for concurrent programming. *ACM Computing Surveys* **15:1**, 3–43.

Apt, K. R. [1981]. Ten years of Hoare's logic: A survey — Part I. *ACM TOPLAS* **3:4**, 431–483.

Backus, J. W. [1960]. The syntax and semantics of the proposed international algebraic language of the Zurich ACM-GAMM Conference. *International Conference on Information Processing, June 1959*. Unesco, Paris, 125–132.

Backus, J. W. [1978]. Can programming be liberated from the von Neumann style? A functional style and its algebra of programs. *Comm. ACM* **21:8**, 613–641.

Backus, J. W. [1981]. The history of Fortran I, II, and III. In Wexelblat [1981], 25–74.

Backus, J. W., Beeber, R. J., Best, S., Goldberg, R., Haibt, L. M., Herrick, H. L., Nelson, R. A., Sayre, D., Sheridan, P. B., Stern, H., Ziller, I., Hughes, R. A., and Nutt, R. [1957]. The Fortran automatic coding system. *Western Joint Computer Conference*, 188–198.

Baker, B. S., and Kosaraju, S. R. [1979]. A comparison of multilevel **break** and **next** statements. *J. ACM* **26:3**, 555–566.

Barendregt, H. P. [1984]. *The Lambda Calculus: Its Syntax and Semantics*, 2nd ed. North-Holland, Amsterdam.

Bauer, F. L. [1981]. More on attention to implementation. In Wexelblat [1981], 166.

Bauer, F. L., and Wössner, H. [1972]. The "Plankalkül" of Konrad Zuse: A forerunner of today's programming languages. *Comm. ACM* **15**, 678–685.

Ben-Ari, M. [1990]. *Principles of Concurrent and Distributed Programming.* Prentice-Hall International, Englewood Cliffs, N. J.

Bentley, J. L. [1986]. *Programming Pearls.* Addison-Wesley, Reading, Mass.

Bentley, J. L., Knuth, D. E., and McIlroy, M. D. [1986]. Programming pearls: A literate program. *Comm. ACM* **29:6**, 471–483.

Böhm, C., and Jacopini, G. [1966]. Flow diagrams, Turing machines and languages with only two formation rules. *Comm. ACM* **9:5**, 366–371.

Borning, A., and Ingalls, D. [1982]. Multiple inheritance in Smalltalk-80. *AAAI-82, The National Conference on Artificial Intelligence*, American Association for Artificial Intelligence, 234–237.

Brinch Hansen, P. [1975]. The programming language Concurrent Pascal. *IEEE Trans. Software Engineering* **SE-1:2**, 199–207.

Brinch Hansen, P. [1978]. Distributed processes: A concurrent programming concept. *Comm. ACM* **21:11**, 934–941.

Brinch Hansen, P. [1981]. The design of Edison. *Software—Practice and Experience* **11**, 363–396.

Brinch Hansen, P. [1993]. Monitors and Concurrent Pascal: A personal history. *ACM SIGPLAN Notices* **28:3** (March), 1–35.

Bruno, J., and Steiglitz, K. [1972]. The expression of algorithms by charts. *J. ACM* **19:3**, 517–525.

Burge, W. H. [1975]. *Recursive Programming Techniques.* Addison-Wesley, Reading, Mass.

Burns, A. [1985]. *Concurrent Programming in Ada.* Cambridge University Press, Cambridge, England.

Burstall, R. M., and Goguen, J. A. [1977]. Putting theories together to make specifications. *Fifth Annual Intl. Joint Conf. on Artificial Intelligence*, 1045–1058.

Burstall, R. M., MacQueen, D. B., and Sanella, D. T. [1980]. HOPE: An experimental applicative language. CSR-62-80, Computer Science Dept., University of Edinburgh.

Cardelli, L., and Wegner, P. [1985]. On understanding types, data abstraction, and polymorphism. *ACM Computing Surveys* **17:4**, 471–522.

Chomsky, N. [1956]. Three models for the description of language. *IRE Trans. on Information Theory* **IT-2:3**, 113–124.

Church, A. [1941]. *The Calculi of Lambda Conversion.* Annals of Math. Studies, No. 6, Princeton University Press, Princeton, N. J.

Clark, K. L. [1978]. Negation as failure. In H. Gallaire and J. Minker (Eds.), *Logic and Databases*. Plenum Press, New York, 293–322.

Clark, K. L., and Tärnlund, S. A. [1977]. A first order theory of data and programs. *Information Processing 77*. North-Holland, Amsterdam, 939–944.

Clarke, L. A., Wileden, J. C., and Wolf, L. [1980]. Nesting in Ada is for the birds. *ACM SIGPLAN Notices* **15:11** (November), 139–145.

Clément, D., Despeyroux, J., Despeyroux, T., Hascoet, L., and Kahn, G. [1985]. Natural semantics on the computer. Rapport de Recherche No. 416, INRIA, Sophia-Antipolis, France.

Clément, D., Despeyroux, J., Despeyroux, T., and Kahn, G. [1986]. A simple applicative language: Mini-ML. *1986 ACM Conference on Lisp and Functional Programming*, 13–27.

Clinger, W., and Rees, J. (Eds.). [1991]. Revised[4] report on the algorithmic language Scheme. See also Rees and Clinger [1986].

Clocksin, W. F., and Mellish, C. S. [1987]. *Programming in Prolog*, 3rd ed. Springer-Verlag, New York.

Coffman, E. G. Jr., Elphick, M. J., and Shoshani, A. [1971]. System deadlocks. *ACM Computing Surveys* **3:2**, 67–78.

Cohen, J. [1988]. A view of the origins and development of Prolog. *Comm. ACM* **31:1**, 26–36.

Colmerauer, A., and Roussel, P. [1993]. The birth of Prolog. *ACM SIGPLAN Notices* **28:3** (March), 37–52.

Conway, M. E. [1963]. Design of a separable transition-diagram compiler. *Comm. ACM* **6:7**, 396–408.

Cook, S. A., and Reckhow, R. A. [1972]. Time-bounded random access machines. *Fourth ACM Symposium on Theory of Computing*, 73–80.

Cooper, D. C. [1967]. Böhm and Jacopini's reduction of flow charts. *Comm. ACM* **10:8**, 463,473.

Courtois, P. J., Heymans, F., and Parnas, D. L. [1971]. Concurrent control with readers and writers. *Comm. ACM* **14:10**, 667–668.

Curry, H. B., and Feys, R. [1958]. *Combinatory Logic*, Vol. 1. North-Holland, Amsterdam.

Dahl, O. J., Dijkstra, E. W., and Hoare, C. A. R. [1972]. *Structured Programming*. Academic Press, London.

Dahl, O. J., and Hoare, C. A. R. [1972]. Hierarchical program structures. In Dahl, Dijkstra, and Hoare [1972], 175–220.

Damas, L., and Milner, R. [1982]. Principal type-schemes for functional programs. *Ninth ACM Symposium on Principles of Programming Languages*, 207–212.

Darlington, J., Henderson, P., and Turner, D. A. (Eds.). [1982]. *Functional Programming and Its Applications: An Advanced Course*. Cambridge University Press. Cambridge, England.

de Bruijn, N. G. [1972]. Lambda calculus notation with nameless dummies, a tool for automatic formula manipulation. *Indag. Math.* **34**, 381–392. See Appendix C of Barendregt [1984].

Deutsch, L. P. [1984]. Efficient implementation of the Smalltalk-80 system. *Eleventh ACM Symposium on Principles of Programming Languages*, 9–16.

Dijkstra, E. W. [1960]. Recursive programming. *Numerische Math.* **2**, 312–318. Reprinted in Rosen [1967], 221–228.

Dijkstra, E. W. [1968a]. Go to statement considered harmful. *Comm. ACM* **11:3**, 147–148.

Dijkstra, E. W. [1968b]. Co-operating sequential processes. In F. Genuys (Ed.), *Programming Languages: NATO Advanced Study Institute*. Academic Press, London, 43–112.

Dijkstra, E. W. [1971]. Hierarchical ordering of sequential processes. *Acta Informatica* **1**, 115–138.

Dijkstra, E. W. [1972]. Notes on structured programming. In Dahl, Dijkstra, and Hoare [1972], 1–82.

Dijkstra, E. W. [1975]. Guarded commands. *Comm. ACM* **18:8**, 453–457.

Dijkstra, E. W. [1976]. *A Discipline of Programming*. Prentice-Hall, Englewood Cliffs, N. J.

Eswaran, K. P., Gray, J. N., Lorie, R. A., and Traiger, I. L. [1976]. The notions of consistency and predicate locks in a database system. *Comm. ACM* **19:11**, 624–633.

Filman, R. E., and Friedman, D. P. [1984]. *Coordinated Computing*. McGraw-Hill, New York.

Fleck, A. C. [1976]. The impossibility of content exchange through the by-name parameter transmission technique. *ACM SIGPLAN Notices* **11:11** (November), 38–41.

Floyd, R. W. [1967]. Assigning meanings to programs. In J. T. Schwartz (Ed.), *Mathematical Aspects of Computer Science*. Symposium on Applied Math. **19**, American Math. Society, Providence, Rhode Island, 19–32.

Francez, N. [1986]. *Fairness*. Springer-Verlag, New York.

Friedman, D. P., Wand, M., and Haynes, C. T. [1992]. *Essentials of Programming Languages*. MIT Press, Cambridge, Mass..

Friedman, D. P., and Wise, D. S. [1976]. Cons should not evaluate its arguments. In S. Michaelson and R. Milner (Eds.), *Automata, Languages and Programming*. Edinburgh University Press, 257–284.

Gannon, J. D., and Horning, J. J. [1975]. Language design for programming reliability. *IEEE Trans. Software Engineering* **SE-1:2**, 179–191.

Gehani, N. H. [1984]. *Ada: Concurrent Programming*. Prentice-Hall, Englewood Cliffs, N. J.

Geschke, C. M., Morris, J. H. Jr., and Satterthwaite, E. H. [1977]. Early experience with Mesa. *Comm. ACM* **20:8**, 540–553.

Girard, J. Y. [1972]. *Interpretation fonctionelle et elimination des coupres de l'arithmetique d'ordre superieur*. These D'Etat, Universite Paris VII.

Goguen, J. A., Thatcher, J. W., and Wagner, E. G. [1978]. An initial algebra approach to the specification, correctness, and implementation of abstract data types. In R. T. Yeh (Ed.), *Current Trends in Programming Methodology: Vol. IV Data Structuring*. Prentice-Hall, Englewood Cliffs, N. J., 80–149.

Goldberg, A., and Robson, D. [1983]. *Smalltalk-80: The Language and its Implementation*. Addison-Wesley, Reading, Mass.

Goldstine, H. H. [1972]. *The Computer: From Pascal to von Neumann*. Princeton University Press, Princeton, N. J.

Gordon, M. J. C. [1979]. *The Denotational Description of Programming Languages*. Springer-Verlag, New York.

Gordon, M., Milner, R., Morris, L., Newey, M., and Wadsworth, C. [1978]. A metalanguage for interactive proof in LCF. *Fifth ACM Symposium on Principles of Programming Languages*, 119–130.

Gries, D. [1981]. *The Science of Programming*. Springer-Verlag, New York.

Hamming, R. W. [1969]. One man's view of computer science. *J. ACM* **16:1**, 3–12.

Hanson, D. R. [1981]. Is block structure necessary?. *Software—Practice and Experience* **11**, 853–866.

Hanson, D. R. [1987]. Literate programming: Printing common words. *Comm. ACM* **30:7**, 594–599. Moderated by C. J. Van Wyk and reviewed by J. R. Gilbert.

Harper, R., MacQueen, D. B., and Milner, R. [1986]. Standard ML. ECS-LFCS-86-2, Laboratory for Foundations of Computer Science, University of Edinburgh.

Henderson, P., and Morris, J. H. Jr. [1976]. A lazy evaluator. *Third ACM Symposium on Principles of Programming Languages*, 95–103.

Hindley, J. R. [1969]. The principal type-scheme of an object in combinatory logic. *Trans. AMS* **146**, 29–60.

Hindley, J. R., and Seldin, J. P. (Eds.). [1980]. *To H. B. Curry: Essays on Combinatory Logic, Lambda Calculus and Formalism.* Academic Press. New York.

Hindley, J. R., and Seldin, J. P. [1986]. *Introduction to Combinators and λ-Calculus.* Cambridge University Press, New York.

Hoare, C. A. R. [1962]. Quicksort. *Computer J.* **5:1**, 10–15.

Hoare, C. A. R. [1969]. An axiomatic basis for computer programming. *Comm. ACM* **12:10**, 576–580,583.

Hoare, C. A. R. [1973]. Hints on programming language design. CS-73-403, Computer Science Dept., Stanford University. Reprinted in Horowitz [1987], 31–40, and in Wasserman [1980], 43–52.

Hoare, C. A. R. [1974]. Monitors: An operating system structuring concept. *Comm. ACM* **17:10**, 549–557.

Hoare, C. A. R. [1978]. Communicating sequential processes. *Comm. ACM* **21:8**, 666–677.

Hoare, C. A. R. [1981]. The emperor's old clothes. *Comm. ACM* **24:2**, 75–83.

Hoare, C. A. R. [1985]. *Communicating Sequential Processes.* Prentice-Hall International, Englewood Cliffs, N.J.

Hoare, C. A. R. [1993]. Letter to Per Brinch Hansen.. In Brinch Hansen [1993], 31.

Hogger, C. J. [1984]. *Introduction to Logic Programming.* Academic Press, Orlando, Fl.

Holt, R. C., Graham, G. S., Lazowska, E. D., and Scott, M. A. [1978]. *Structured Concurrent Programming with Operating Systems Applications.* Addison-Wesley, Reading, Mass.

Hopper, G. M. [1981]. Keynote address: ACM SIGPLAN History of Programming Languages Conference. In Wexelblat [1981], 5–24.

Horn, A. [1951]. On sentences which are true of direct unions of algebras. *J. Symbolic Logic* **16**, 14–21. Referenced in Kowalski [1979a].

Horowitz, E. (Ed.). [1987]. *Programming Languages: A Grand Tour*, 3rd ed. Computer Science Press. Rockville, Maryland.

Hudak, P. [1989]. Conception, evolution, and application of functional programming languages. *ACM Computing Surveys* **21:3**, 359–411.

Ichbiah, J. D., Barnes, J. G. P., Heliard, J. C., Krieg-Brueckner, B., Roubine, O., and Wichmann, B. A. [1979]. Rationale for the design of the Ada programming language. *ACM SIGPLAN Notices* **14:6B** (June).

Ingalls, D. H. H. [1978]. The Smalltalk-76 programming system: Design and implementation. *Fifth ACM Symposium on Principles of Programming Languages*, 9–16.

Ingerman, P. Z. [1967]. Panini-Backus form suggested. *Comm. ACM* **10:3**, 137.

Jackson, M. [1975]. *Principles of Program Design*. Academic Press, New York.

Jensen, K., and Wirth, N. [1974]. *Pascal User Manual and Report*. Springer-Verlag, New York. 3rd ed. (1985) prepared by A. B. Mickel and J. F. Miner.

Johnson, S. C. [1975]. Yacc—yet another compiler compiler. Computing Science Technical Report No. 32, Bell Labs, Murray Hill, N. J.

Johnson, S. C., and Ritchie, D. M. [1978]. Portability of C programs and the UNIX system. *Bell System Technical J.* **57:6.2**, 2021–2048.

Johnson, S. C., and Ritchie, D. M. [1981]. The C language calling sequence. Computing Science Technical Report No. 102, Bell Labs, Murray Hill, N. J.

Kahn, G. [1987]. Natural semantics. Rapport de Recherche No. 601, INRIA, Sophia-Antipolis, France.

Kahn, G., and MacQueen, D. B. [1977]. Coroutines and networks of parallel processes. *Information Processing 77*. North-Holland, Amsterdam, 993–998.

Kahn, G., MacQueen, D. B., and Plotkin, G. (Eds.). [1984]. *Semantics of Data Types*. Lecture Notes in Computer Science **173**, Springer-Verlag. Berlin.

Kay, A. C. [1993]. The early history of Smalltalk. *ACM SIGPLAN Notices* **28:3** (March), 69–95.

Kernighan, B. W., and Plauger, P. J. [1976]. *Software Tools*. Addison-Wesley, Reading, Mass.

Kernighan, B. W., and Plauger, P. J. [1978]. *The Elements of Programming Style*, 2nd ed. McGraw-Hill, New York.

Kernighan, B. W., and Plauger, P. J. [1981]. *Software Tools in Pascal*. Addison-Wesley, Reading, Mass.

Kernighan, B. W., and Ritchie, D. M. [1988]. *The C Programming Language*, 2nd ed. Prentice-Hall, Englewood Cliffs, N. J.

Kessels, J. L. W., and Martin, A. J. [1979]. Two implementations of the conditional critical region using a split binary semaphore. *Information Processing Letters* **8:2**, 67–71.

Knuth, D. E. [1974]. Structured programming with go to statements. *ACM Computing Surveys* **6:4**, 261–301.

Knuth, D. E. [1986]. *Computers and Typesetting*, Vol. 1: TEX. Addison-Wesley, Reading, Mass.

Knuth, D. E., and Trabb Pardo, L. [1977]. Early development of programming languages. *Encyclopedia of Computer Science and Technology* **7**, 419–493.

Koenig, A. [1988]. An example of dynamic binding in C++. *J. Object-Oriented Programming* **1:3** (August/September), 60–62.

Kosaraju, S. R. [1974]. Analysis of structured programs. *J. Computer and System Sciences* **9**, 232–255.

Kowalski, R. A. [1979a]. *Logic for Problem Solving*. Elsevier North Holland, New York.

Kowalski, R. A. [1979b]. Algorithm = Logic + Control. *Comm. ACM* **22:7**, 424–436.

Kowalski, R. A. [1988]. The early years of logic programming. *Comm. ACM* **31:1**, 38–43.

Landin, P. J. [1964]. The mechanical evaluation of expressions. *Computer J.* **6:4**, 308–320.

Landin, P. J. [1965]. A correspondence between Algol 60 and Church's lambda-notation. *Comm. ACM* **8:2,3**, 89–101,158–165.

Landin, P. J. [1966]. The next 700 programming languages. *Comm. ACM* **9:3**, 157–166.

Liskov, B., and Guttag, J. [1986]. *Abstraction and Specification in Program Development*. MIT Press, Cambridge, Mass.

Liskov, B., and Zilles, S. [1974]. Programming with abstract data types. *ACM SIGPLAN Notices* **9:4** (April), 50–59.

McCarthy, J. [1960]. Recursive functions of symbolic expressions and their computation by machine, Part I. *Comm. ACM* **3:4**, 184–195.

McCarthy, J. [1963]. Towards a mathematical science of computation. *Information Processing 1962*. North-Holland, Amsterdam, 21–28.

McCarthy, J. [1981]. History of Lisp. In Wexelblat [1981], 173–185.

McCarthy, J., Abrahams, P. W., Edwards, D. J., Hart, T. P., and Levin, M. I. [1965]. *Lisp 1.5 Programmer's Manual*, 2nd ed. MIT Press, Cambridge, Mass.

McIlroy, M. D. [1968]. Coroutines. manuscript, Bell Labs, Murray Hill, N. J.

McIlroy, M. D. [1980]. Development of a spelling list. *IEEE Trans. Communications* **COM-30:1**, 91–99.

Metropolis, N., Howlett, J., and Rota, G. C. (Eds.). [1980]. *A History of Computing in the Twentieth Century*. Academic Press. New York.

Miller, G. A. [1967]. *The Psychology of Communication*. Basic Books, New York.

Milner, R. [1978]. A theory of type polymorphism in programming. *J. Computer and System Sciences* **17:3**, 348–375.

Milner, R. [1980]. *A Calculus of Communicating Systems.* Lecture Notes in Computer Science **92**, Springer-Verlag, New York.

Milner, R. [1984]. A proposal for Standard ML. *ACM Symposium on Lisp and Functional Programming,* 184–197.

Milner, R., Tofte, M., and Harper, R. [1990]. *The definition of Standard ML.* MIT Press, Cambridge, Mass..

Mitchell, J. C., and Harper, R. [1988]. The essence of ML. *Fifteenth ACM Symposium on Principles of Programming Languages,* 28–46.

Mock, O., and Swift, C. J. [1959]. The Share 709 system: Programmed input-output buffering. *J. ACM* **6** (March), 145–151.

Morris, J. H. Jr. [1982]. Real programming in functional languages. In Darlington, Henderson, and Turner [1982], 129–176.

Morris, J. H. Jr., Schmidt, E., and Wadler, P. [1980]. Experience with an applicative string processing language. *Seventh ACM Symposium on Principles of Programming Languages,* 32–46.

Morrison, P., and Morrison, E. (Eds.). [1961]. *Charles Babbage and His Calculating Engines.* Dover. New York.

Naur, P. [1981]. The European side of the last phase of the development of Algol 60. In Wexelblat [1981], 92–172.

Naur, P. (Ed.). [1963a]. Revised report on the algorithmic language Algol 60. *Comm. ACM* **6:1**, 1–17.

Naur, P. [1963b]. Go to statements and good Algol style. *BIT* **3:3**, 204–208.

Nori, K. V., Ammann, U., Jensen, K., Nageli, H. H., and Jacobi, C. [1981]. Pascal-P implementation notes. In D. W. Barron (Ed.), *Pascal — The Language and its Implementation.* John Wiley, New York, 125–170.

Nygaard, K., and Dahl, O. J. [1981]. The development of the Simula languages. In Wexelblat [1981], 439–493.

Papadimitriou, C. [1986]. *The Theory of Database Concurrency Control.* Computer Science Press, Rockville, Maryland.

Parnas, D. L. [1972]. On the criteria to be used in decomposing systems into modules. *Comm. ACM* **15:12**, 1053–1058.

Paulson, L. C. [1991]. *ML for the Working Programmer.* Cambridge University Press, New York.

Perlis, A. J. [1978]. Letter to P. Naur. Quoted by Naur in Wexelblat [1981], 160.

Perlis, A. J., and Samelson, K. [1958]. Preliminary report—International Algebraic Language. *Comm. ACM* **1:12** (December), 8–22.

Plotkin, G. D. [1981]. A structural approach to operational semantics. DAIMI FN-19, Computer Science Dept., Aarhus University, Aarhus, Denmark.

Randell, B., and Russell, L. J. [1964]. *Algol 60 Implementation*. Academic Press, New York.

Rees, J., and Clinger, W. (Eds.). [1986]. Revised[3] report on the algorithmic language Scheme. *ACM SIGPLAN Notices* **21:12** (December), 37–79. See also Clinger and Rees [1991].

Reynolds, J. C. [1972]. Definitional interpreters for higher-order programming languages. *25th ACM Annual Conference*, 717–740.

Reynolds, J. C. [1974]. Towards a theory of type structure. *Colloque sur la Programmation*. Lecture Notes in Computer Science **19**, Springer-Verlag, New York, 408–425.

Richards, M. [1969]. BCPL: A tool for compiler writing and systems programming. *AFIPS Conference Proceedings*, 34, 557–566.

Ritchie, D. M. [1978]. UNIX time-sharing system: A retrospective. *Bell System Technical J.* **57:6.2**, 1947–1969.

Ritchie, D. M. [1984]. The evolution of the UNIX time-sharing system. *Bell Labs Technical J.* **63:8.2**, 1577–1593.

Ritchie, D. M. [1993]. The development of the C language. *ACM SIGPLAN Notices* **28:3** (March), 201–208.

Ritchie, D. M., Johnson, S. C., Lesk, M. E., and Kernighan, B. W. [1978]. The C programming language. *Bell System Technical J.* **57:6.2**, 1991–2019.

Robinson, J. A. [1965]. A machine-oriented logic based on the resolution principle. *J. ACM* **12:1**, 23–41.

Rosen, S. [1964]. Programming systems and languages—a historical survey. *Proc. Eastern Joint Computer Conference* **25**, 1–15. Reprinted in Rosen [1967], 3–22.

Rosen, S. (Ed.). [1967]. *Programming Systems and Languages*. McGraw-Hill. New York.

Rosen, S. [1969]. Electronic computers: A historical survey. *ACM Computing Surveys* **1:1**, 7–36.

Rosin, R. [1969]. Supervisory and monitor systems. *ACM Computing Surveys* **1:1**, 37–54.

Ross, D. T., and Rodriguez, J. E. [1963]. Theoretical foundations for the computer-aided design system. *AFIPS Spring Joint Computer Conference*, 305–322.

Rosser, J. B. [1984]. Highlights of the history of the lambda-calculus. *Annals of the History of Computing* **6:4**, 337–349.

Rutishauser, H. [1967]. *Description of Algol 60.* Springer Verlag, New York.

Schmidt, D. A. [1986]. *Denotational Semantics: A Methodology for Language Development.* Allyn and Bacon, Boston, Mass.

Schönfinkel, M. [1924]. Uber die Bausteine der mathematischen Logik. *Mathematische Annalen* **92**, 305–316. English translation, "On the building blocks of mathematical logic," in van Heijenoort [1967], 355–366.

Scott, D. S. [1977]. Logic and programming languages. *Comm. ACM* **20:9**, 634–640.

Scott, D. S., and Strachey, C. [1971]. Towards a mathematical semantics for computer languages. *Symposium on Computers and Automata.* Polytechnic Press, Brooklyn, N. Y., 19–46.

Sedgewick, R. [1978]. Implementing Quicksort programs. *Comm. ACM* **21**, 847–857.

Sethi, R. [1981]. Uniform syntax for type expressions and declarators. *Software—Practice and Experience* **11:6**, 623–628.

Shepherdson, J. C., and Sturgis, H. E. [1963]. Computability of recursive functions. *J. ACM* **10:2**, 217–255.

Steele, G. L. Jr. [1984]. *Common LISP.* Digital Press, Burlington, Mass.

Steele, G. L. Jr., and Gabriel, R. P. [1993]. The evolution of Lisp. *ACM SIGPLAN Notices* **28:3** (March), 231–270.

Steele, G. L. Jr., and Sussman, G. J. [1975]. Scheme: An interpreter for the extended lambda calculus. Memo 349, MIT Artificial Intelligence Lab., Cambridge, Mass.

Sterling, L., and Shapiro, E. [1994]. *The Art of Prolog,* 2nd ed. MIT Press, Cambridge, Mass.

Stoy, J. E. [1977]. *Denotational Semantics.* MIT Press, Cambridge, Mass.

Strachey, C. (Ed.). [1966]. *CPL working papers.* University Mathematical Laboratory, Cambridge and University of London Institute for Computer Science.

Stroustrup, B. [1991]. *The C++ Programming Language,* 2nd ed. Addison-Wesley, Reading, Mass.

Stroustrup, B. [1994]. *The Design and Evolution of C++.* Addison-Wesley, Reading, Mass.

Taylor, W., Turner, L., and Waychoff, R. [1961]. A syntactical chart for Algol 60. *Comm. ACM* **4:9**, 393.

Turner, D. A. [1979]. A new implementation technique for applicative languages. *Software—Practice and Experience* **9:1**, 31–49.

Turner, D. A. [1982]. Recursion equations as a programming language. In Darlington, Henderson, and Turner [1982], 1–28.

Turner, D. A. [1985]. Miranda: A non-strict functional language with polymorphic types. *Functional Programming Languages and Computer Architecture*. Lecture Notes in Computer Science **201**, Springer-Verlag, New York, 1–16.

Ullman, J. D. [1994]. *Elements of ML Programming*. Prentice Hall, Englewood Cliffs, N. J..

van Heijenoort, J. (Ed.). [1967]. *From Frege to Gödel*. Harvard University Press. Cambridge, Mass.

van Wijngaarden, A., Mailloux, B. J., Peck, J. E. L., Koster, C. H. A., Sintzoff, M., Lindsey, C. H., Meertens, L. G. L. T., and Fisker, R. G. [1975]. Revised report on the algorithmic language Algol 68. *Acta Informatica* **5**, 1–236.

Vuillemin, J. [1974]. Correct and optimal implementations of recursion in a simple programming language. *J. Computer and System Sciences* **9:3**, 332–354.

Wadsworth, C. [1971]. *Semantics and Pragmatics of the Lambda Calculus*. Ph. D. Thesis, Oxford University.

Warren, D. H. D. [1980]. Logic programming and compiler writing. *Software—Practice and Experience* **10:2**, 97–125.

Wasserman, A. I. (Ed.). [1980]. *Tutorial: Programming Language Design*. IEEE Computer Society Press.

Wegner, P. [1976]. Programming languages—the first 25 years. *IEEE Trans. Computers* **C-25:12**, 1207–1225.

Wegner, P., and Smolka, S. A. [1983]. Processes, tasks, and monitors: A comparative study of concurrent programming primitives. *IEEE Trans. Software Engineering* **SE-9:4**, 446–462.

Weizenbaum, J. [1966]. Eliza—a computer program for the study of natural language communication between man and machine. *Comm. ACM* **9:1**, 36–45.

Weizenbaum, J. [1976]. *Computer Power and Human Reasoning*. W. H. Freeman, San Francisco, Calif.

Welsh, J., and Lister, A. [1981]. A comparative study of task communication in Ada. *Software—Practice and Experience* **11**, 257–290.

Wexelblat, R. L. (Ed.). [1981]. *History of Programming Languages*. Academic Press. New York.

Wheeler, D. J. [1952]. Unpublished proceedings. *First ACM National Conference*. Quoted in Knuth [1974].

Whitehead, A. N., and Russell, B. [1925]. *Principia Mathematica*. Cambridge University Press, Cambridge, England.

Wilkes, M. V., Wheeler, D. J., and Gill, S. [1951]. *Preparation of Programs for an Electronic Digital Computer*. Addison-Wesley, Reading, Mass. Reprinted by Tomash Publishers, Los Angeles, 1982.

Wirth, N. [1971]. The programming language Pascal. *Acta Informatica* **1:1**, 35–63.

Wirth, N. [1979]. The module: A system structuring facility in high-level programming languages. *Language Design and Programming Methodology*. Lecture Notes in Computer Science **79**, Springer-Verlag, New York, 1–24.

Wirth, N. [1981]. Pascal-S: A subset and its implementation. In D. W. Barron (Ed.), *Pascal — The Language and its Implementation*. John Wiley, New York, 199–259.

Wirth, N. [1988]. From Modula to Oberon. *Software—Practice and Experience* **18:7**, 661–670.

Wirth, N. [1993]. Recollections on the development of Pascal. *ACM SIGPLAN Notices* **28:3** (March), 333–342.

Wirth, N., and Hoare, C. A. R. [1966]. A contribution to the development of Algol. *Comm. ACM* **9:6**, 413–431.

Wulf, W. A., and Shaw, M. [1973]. Global variables considered harmful. *ACM SIGPLAN Notices* **8:2** (February), 80–86.

Zuse, K. [1980]. Some remarks on the history of computing in Germany. In Metropolis, Howlett, and Rota [1980], 611–627.

Credits

Epigraph Credits

Chapter 1 from *The Design and Evolution of C++* by B. Stroustrup, p. 7, ©1994. Reprinted by permission of Addison-Wesley Publishing Company, Inc.

Chapter 2 from *International Conference on Information Processing*, ©1960, quote by J. W. Backus, p. 129. Reprinted by permission of Association for Computing Machinery Inc. From *History of Programming Languages*, editor Wexelblat, ©1981, quote by P. Naur, p. 99. Reprinted by permission of Academic Press.

Chapter 3 from Dahl/Dijkstra/Hoare, *Structured Programming*, ©1972. Reprinted by permission of Academic Press.

Chapter 4 from Metropolis/Howlett/Rota, *A History of Computing in the Twentieth Century*, ©1980, quote by K. Zuse, p. 623 and pp. 621–622. Reprinted by permission of Academic Press.

Chapter 5 from *History of Programming Languages*, editor Wexelblat. ©1981, quote by A. J. Perlis, p. 160, and F. L. Bauer, p. 166. Reprinted by permission of Academic Press.

Chapter 6 from *Communications Association for Computing Machinery*, ©1972, 15:12, quote by D. L. Parnus, p. 1058. Reprinted by permission of Association for Computing Machinery Inc.

Chapter 7 from *History of Programming Languages*, editor Wexelblat, ©1981, quote by K. Nygaard and O. J. Dahl, pp. 439-493. Reprinted by permission of Academic Press.

Chapter 8 from Darlington/Henderson/Turner (eds), *Functional Programming and Its Applications*, ©1982, quote by J. H. Morris, p. 173. Reprinted with the permission of Cambridge University Press.

Chapter 9 from *Association for Computing Machinery Symposium on Lisp and Functional Programming*, ©1984, quote by R. Milner, pp. 184-197. Reprinted by permission of Association for Computing Machinery Inc.

Chapter 10 from *Communications Association for Computing Machinery*, ©1960, 3:4, quote by J. McCarthy, p. 186. Reprinted by permission of Association for Computing Machinery Inc.

Chapter 11 from *Association for Computing Machinery SIGPLAN Notices*, ©1993, 28:3, quote by A. Colmerauer and P. Roussel, p. 37. Reprinted by permission of Association for Computing Machinery Inc.

Chapter 12 *Association for Computing Machinery SIGPLAN Notices*, ©1993, 28:3, quote by P. Brinch Hansen, p. 21. Reprinted by permission of Association for Computing Machinery Inc.

Chapter 13 from *25th Association for Computing Machinery Annual Conference*, ©1972, quote by J. C. Reynolds, p. 717. Reprinted by permission of Association for Computing Machinery Inc.

Chapter 14 from *Annals of the History of Computing*, ©1984, 6:4, quote by J. B. Rosser, p. 338. Reprinted by permission of Association for Computing Machinery Inc.

Chapter 15 from *Description of Algol 60* by H. Rutishauser, ©1967. Reprinted with permission of Springer-Verlag New York, Inc.

Index

A

Abelson, H., 421, 602
Abrahams, P. W., 15, 52
abstract
   specification, 217
   syntax, 31–32, 41–43, 53, 518
   syntax trees, 32, 41–43, 345
abstraction
   data, 206, 217, 252
   modular, 206
   procedure, 154, 206
access link, 176–177, 182,
      191–196
access type, Ada, 496–497
accessibility of names, *see also*
      visibility of names
accessibility of names, C++, 232,
      237–238, 241, 269, 281–284
activation
   environment, 532–535
   procedure, 147–148, 172–198
   record, 172, 175–198, 202
   recursive, 152–153, 172–176,
      186–190
   time, 172
   trees, 174–175, 177–178
actual parameters, 149–150,
      155–160, 165, 184, 195
ad-hoc polymorphism, 359
Ada, 12, 483–485, 491–498,
      510–511
   access type, 496–497

program structure, 483
task, 483–485, 493–498
Ada 95, 12
Ada Byron, Augusta, 510
address computation, array,
      113–115
Aho, A. V., 53, 202, 252
Algol, 11–13, 25, 27, 99, 577
   dynamic array, 115–117
Algol 58, 25, 27
Algol 60, *see* Algol
Algol 68, 12, 146, 591
Algol W, 146, 580
alias, 159–160
allocation, 113, 115–116, 147,
      179–198
   C++ dynamic, 238–243
   dynamic, 125–133
   heap, 126, 129, 179, 182, 191,
      239
   Lisp dynamic, 413–417
   stack, 179–198, 202
   static, 116
ambiguity
   dangling-else, 39–40, 52,
      75–76
   syntactic, 38–40
Ammann, U., 191
analysis
   lexical, 112–113, 211, 221–222
   syntax, 211
Andrews, G. R., 501, 510
anonymous function, *see also*

lambda notation
anonymous function
   ML, 354–356
   Scheme, 389–390, 407
applied lambda calculus,
      561–566, 577
Apt, K. R., 99
arithmetic
   expression, 28–31
   expression syntax, 41–48
   expression type system, 138
   Prolog, 437
arity, operator, 29
array
   address computation, 113–115
   Algol dynamic, 115–117
   and pointer, C, 134–136
   bounds, 109, 111–117
   initialization, C, 117
   layout, 105, 113–117, 120
   Pascal, 105–106, 112–113
   static, 116
   type, 105, 111–117
assembly language, 5–8
assertions, 62, 81, 87, 99–100
assignment
   pointer, 126–133
   statements, 6–7, 59–61
association list (a-list), 400–402,
      535
associativity, 30–31, 41, 43–45
   left, 30, 43–45
   right, 30, 44–45

asynchronous communication, 478
attribute
  evaluation, 520
  grammar, 516–523
  inherited, 521–523
  synthesized, 517–523
axiom, 524
axiomatic semantics, *see* proof rules

B

B, 584
Babbage, C., 23, 510
backtracking, 442, 453–469
Backus, J. W., 11, 25, 52, 99, 340
Baker, B. S., 100
Barendregt, H. P., 577
Barnes, J. G. P., 511
base class
  C++, 261, 267–284, 593
  C++ private, 281–284
  C++ public, 269, 281–284, 593
basic type, 103–105, 107–111, 314
Bauer, F. L., 146–147
BCPL (Basic CPL), 12, 584
Beeber, R. J., 11
Bell Laboratories, 480
Ben-Ari, M., 510
Bentley, J. L., 81, 100, 511
Best, S., 11
beta-equal terms, 549, 552–554, 556, 559, 565
binary operator, 28
binary search, 81, 100, 187–189
binding
  dynamic, 137
  early, 137
  late, 137
  occurrence, 166–169, 551
  static, 137
  type, 571
bit-wise operator, 124
block-structured language, 190, 202
BNF (Backus-Naur Form),

35–37, 46, 52
body, procedure, 147, 151, 161, 163–165, 186, 191
Bohm, C., 100
Borning, A., 299
bottom-up parsing, 40
bound
  occurrence, 166–169, 551, 554
  variable, 550–551, 554, 556, 572
bounded buffer, 218–219, 498–507, 510
break statements, 77–80, 93–94, 99
Brinch Hansen, P., 475, 510–511
Bruno, J., 100
bucket sort, 143
buffer, bounded, 218–219, 498–507, 510
bugs, 8–9
Burge, W. H., 511
Burns, A., 511
Burroughs, 478
Burstall, R. M., 600
busy wait, 477, 502

C

C, 11–13, 16, 133–136, 583–591
  array and pointer, 134–136, 588–589
  array initialization, 117
  declarations, 51, 168–170, 585–586
  expression, 90–92, 109, 586
  header file, 589
  input/output, 583, 589–591
  macro preprocessor, 583
  memory layout, 182–183
  operators, 587
  origins, 584
  parameter-passing, 158
  pointer, 158, 186, 587–589
  procedure, 181–190
  program structure, 583
  short-circuit evaluation, 587
  statements, 77–80, 90–94, 587–588

static data, 116, 180
  type, 133–137, 140–142, 146, 584
C++, 12, 16, 232–248, 252, 267–284, 591–593
  accessibility of names, 232, 237–238, 241, 269, 281–284
  base class, 261, 267–284, 593
  constructor, 214, 234, 239–242, 268
  constructor order, 273–274, 277–278
  derived class, 261, 268–269, 277–278, 281–284, 593
  destructor, 214, 234, 239–240, 268
  destructor order, 274
  dynamic allocation, 238–243
  friend declaration, 241–242
  inheritance, 268–284, 593
  initialization, 234, 236, 268, 273
  member names, 232–238
  name-resolution, 235
  origins, 591
  parameterized type, 244–245
  parameter-passing, 155
  private base class, 281–284
  private member, 245
  public base class, 269, 281–284, 593
  structure, 232
  virtual function, 269–271, 279–280, 593
call, procedure, 149
call-by-name, *see also* outermost evaluation
call-by-name, 155, 165, 202
call-by-reference, 155, 157–160
call-by-value, *see also* innermost evaluation
call-by-value, 155–159, 184, 322, 388, 534
call-by-value-result, 155, 159–160
car operation, Lisp, 413
Cardelli, L., 577, 600
case statements, 70–71, 99

cdr operation, Lisp, 413
chart, syntax, 53
checking
    dynamic, 142–143
    static, 142–143
    type, 103, 125, 136–143,
        331–335, 357–360, 383, 547,
        567–576, 578
chess, 101
Chomsky, N., 52
Church, A., 383, 547–548, 577
Church-Rosser theorem, 547,
    558–559
circular type, 141
Clark, K. L., 473
Clarke, L. A., 202
class, 256, 591–598
    C++ base, 261, 267–284, 593
    C++ derived, 261, 268–269,
        281–284, 593
    C++ private base, 281–284
    C++ public base, 269,
        281–284, 593
    hierarchy, 256–258, 260, 285
    instance, 258
    method, Smalltalk, 287–294
    Smalltalk system, 299,
        597–598
    variable, Smalltalk, 286
CLEAR, 600
Clément, D., 546, 578
Clinger, W., 421, 602–603
Clocksin, W. F., 473, 607
CLOS (Common Lisp Object
    System), 12, 15
closure, 534, 539
    recursive, 543
CLU, 252
Cobol, 146
code, 4, 8
code inspection, 9
coercion, type, 110–111, 139, 334
Coffman, E. G. Jr., 511
Cohen, J., 472–473, 608
collection, garbage, 101, 179,
    385, 416–417
Colmerauer, A., 16, 425,
    472–473, 607–608

column-major layout, 115
combinator, 550, 558, 562–563,
    577
    fixed-point, 558, 563
command, guarded, 511
comments, 33–34
communication, 511
    asynchronous, 478
    process, 476, 478, 493
    synchronous, 478
compile time, 18, 101, 137
compiler, 18–21
compound statements, 64
concrete
    representation, 217
    syntax, 35, 37, 42
Concurrent Pascal, 12, 475, 510
concurrent programming,
    475–511
conditional
    expression, 390
    statements, 65–66
constructor
    C++, 234, 268
    type, 317
    value, 317, 360–366
context-free grammar, 35–41
continue statements, 77–80,
    93–94
control link, 176–178, 182–183,
    188, 190–192, 194–195,
    197–198
conversion, type, 334
Conway, M. E., 511
Cook, S. A., 24
Cooper, D. C., 100
copy rule, 161
copy-in/copy-out, see call-by-
    value-result
Core-XML, 571–573, 575, 578
coroutine, 173, 478–482, 511
correctness
    partial, 86–87
    process, 485
    total, 87
Courtois, P. J., 511
CPL, 12, 584
critical section, 489–490, 501–505

CSP, 12, 510–511
Curry, H. B., 562, 577–578
currying, 562
cuts
    green, 466
    Prolog, 461–469, 473

D

Dahl, O. J., 209, 253, 299, 511
Damas, L., 578
dangling pointer, 128–129, 186
dangling-else ambiguity, 39–40,
    52, 75–76
Darlington, J., 340
data
    abstraction, 206, 217, 252
    C static, 116, 180
    global, 182–183
    invariant, 218–219, 490
    layout, 101, 104–105, 110
    representation, 102
datatype, ML, 316–318
de Bruijn, N. G., 551
deadlock, process, 486–488, 511
declaration, 103–146
    ML function, 318–321,
        346–351
    procedure, 148–154, 169–171
    type, 105, 140
    variable, 148, 166–169, 172
decorated parse tree, 519
deduction, type, 568
defined language, 515, 517, 546
defining language, 385, 515, 517,
    546
definite iteration, 69
definition environment,
    532–535, 543
definitional interpreter, 515,
    517, 546, 577, 603
    Lisp, 15
    Scheme, 535–545
denotational semantics, 516,
    529–530, 577
depth, nesting, 193, 195–198
dereferencing, pointer, 126, 135

derivation, 40
derived class, C++, 261,
    268–269, 281–284, 593
Despeyroux
    J., 546, 578
    T., 546, 578
destructor, C++, 214, 234, 268
Deutsch, L. P., 299
diagram, flow, 79, 99–100
difference list, 449–450, 473
differentiation, 363–365, 383,
    402, 404–409
Dijkstra, E. W., 9, 24, 59, 81,
    99–100, 202, 501, 510–511
dining philosophers, 486–488
display, 196–198, 202
Distributed Processes, 12
dynamic
    allocation, 125–133
    allocation, C++, 238–243
    allocation, Lisp, 413–417
    array, Algol, 115–117
    binding, 137
    checking, 142–143
    link, 177, 191
    property, 20
    scope, 161–165, 177–178, 386,
        532, 546
    semantics, 547

E

early binding, 137
EBNF (Extended BNF), 46–48,
    222
Eckert, J. P. Jr., 24
Edinburgh Prolog, 425–426, 609
EDVAC, 24
Edwards, D. J., 15
Eliza, 383
Elphick, M. J., 511
encapsulation, 217, 299
ENIAC, 24
enumerated type, 107, 109, 112
environment
    activation, 532–535
    definition, 532–535, 543
    lexical, 186, 196–197

equivalence
    name, 140
    structural, 140–141, 333
    type, 139–141, 332–333
Eratosthenes, 274
error, type, 142
Eswaran, K. P., 511
evaluation
    attribute, 520
    expression, 49
    innermost, 321–327, 336–337,
        560
    lazy, 340, 479, 511
    outermost, 323–327, 560
    partial, 562
    selective, 322
    short-circuit, 109, 406
evaluator, expression, 211–212,
    221–229, 249, 530
exception handling, 367–369
exclusion, mutual, 489–490,
    501–505, 510
expansion, in-line, 247
export
    name, 229
    type, 229–232
expression
    arithmetic, 28–31
    as data, 404
    C, 90–92, 109
    conditional, 390
    evaluation, 49
    evaluator, 211–212, 221–229,
        249, 530
    Pascal, 108
    simplification, 409–412
    syntax, arithmetic, 41–48
    syntax, Scheme, 388
    tree, 31
    type, 103, 140, 313, 332, 359
    type system, arithmetic, 138

F

failure, Prolog negation as,
    435–436, 469
fairness, process, 485–488, 511
Feys, R., 577–578

Fibonacci sequence, 337
field
    name, 106, 119
    tag, 121–122
Filman, R. E., 510
first-class function, 341, 385
Fisker, R. G., 472, 608
fixed-point combinator, 558, 563
Fleck, A. C., 202
flow diagram, 64, 79, 99–100
Floyd, R. W., 99
formal parameter, 150–151, 155
    scope, 168
Fortran, 1, 7–8, 11–12, 19, 24, 99,
    138–139
frame
    layout, 183, 191
    stack, 182–183, 192
Francez, N., 511
free
    occurrence, 551–552, 554–556
    variable, 550–552, 554, 558,
        574, 577
Friedman, D. P., 421, 510–511,
    602
function
    declaration, ML, 318–321,
        346–351
    first-class, 341, 385
    higher-order, 340, 404, 515,
        546, 548
    ML anonymous, 354–356
    procedure, 148–149, 151–152
    projection, 314
    Scheme anonymous, 389–390,
        407
functional language, *see* func-
    tional programming
functional
    language, 101–102, 305,
        339–341, 385, 413
    programming, 14–15, 301–421
    programming, pure, 339

G

Gabriel, R. P., 603
Gannon, J. D., 53, 99

garbage, 128–129
    collection, 101, 179, 385,
        416–417
Gehani, N. H., 511
general purpose language, 4
generate-and-test, 442
Geschke, C. M., 252
Gill, S., 100, 206
Girard, J. Y., 578
global data, 182–183
goal order, Prolog, 436, 444,
        450–469
Gofer, 12, 15
Goguen, J. A., 252, 600
Goldberg, A., 285–286, 299, 594
Goldberg, R., 11
Goldstine, H. H., 5, 23
Gordon, M. J. C., 577, 600
goto statements, 80, 99
Graham, G. S., 510
grammar
    attribute, 516–523
    context-free, 35–41
    symbol, 35
Gray, J. N., 511
green cuts, 466
Gries, D., 100
guarded command, 511
guess-and-verify, 442–444, 463
Guttag, J., 252

H

Haibt, L. M., 11
Hamming, R. W., 299, 511
Hanson, D. R., 202, 511
Harper, R., 383, 578, 599–600
Hart, T. P., 15
Hascoet, L., 546
Haskell, 12, 15, 339–340
Haynes, C. T., 421, 602
heap allocation, 126, 129, 179,
        182, 191, 239
Heliard, J. C., 511
Henderson, P., 340, 511
Herrick, H. L., 11
Hewitt, C. E., 603
Heymans, F., 511

hiding
    implementation, 154, 217, 220
    information, 263, 281
hierarchy, class, 285
higher-level language, 4, 7–8, 18
higher-order function, 340, 404,
        515, 546, 548
Hindley, J. R., 577–578
Hoare, C. A. R., 24, 99–100, 146,
        475, 510–511, 580
Hogger, C. J., 473
Holt, R. C., 510
HOPE, 600
Hopper, G. M., 147
Horn, A., 427
Horn clause, 427, 429, 461, 472,
        608
Horning, J. J., 53, 99
Howlett, J., 23
Hudak, P., 340
Hughes, R. A., 11

I

IBM, 1, 11, 476
Ichbiah, J. D., 511
imperative
    language, 61, 101–102, 139
    programming, 11–13, 16,
        55–299
implementation
    hiding, 154, 217, 220
    inheritance, 282
import, name, 229
indefinite iteration, 66, 92
independence, representation,
        217
index, permuted, 251–252
inference, type, 358, 569–576,
        578
infix notation, 28, 30–31, 41, 43
information hiding, 263, 281
Ingalls, D. H. H., 299
Ingerman, P. Z., 52
inheritance, 257, 260–267, 285,
        291, 299, 597, 599
    C++, 268–284, 593
    implementation, 282

multiple, 257
inherited
    attribute, 521–523
    method, 260, 292–293
initialization, 214
    C++, 234, 236, 268
    module, 218, 220, 228
    object, 218
in-line expansion, 247
innermost evaluation, 321–327,
        336–337, 560
instance, 256
    class, 258
    method, Smalltalk, 286–287,
        291–292
    variable, Smalltalk, 286–288,
        291
interleaving, 482–486, 489–491,
        501
InterLisp, 12, 15
interpreter, 18–21
    definitional, 515, 517, 546,
        577, 603
    Lisp definitional, 15
    Prolog, 473
interrupt, 477
invariant, 59, 62, 77, 80–90,
        99–100
    data, 218–219, 490
is-a relation, 281–282
ISWIM, 12, 339–340
iteration
    definite, 69
    indefinite, 66, 92

J

Jackson, M., 220
Jacobi, Ch., 191
Jacopini, G., 100
Jacquard, J. M., 23
Jensen, K., 191, 579
Johnson, S. C., 24, 112, 125, 133,
        183, 203, 584

K

Kahn, G., 511, 546, 577–578

Kay, A. C., 299, 594
Kernighan, B. W., 100, 110, 209, 252, 511, 583–584
Kessels, J. L. W., 511
keyword, 31, 33, 35
keyword-in-context, 251
Knuth, D. E., 24, 99–100, 133, 511
Koenig, A., 299
Kosaraju, S. R., 100
Koster, C. H. A., 472, 608
Kowalski, R. A., 425, 472–473, 608
KRC, 340
Krieg-Brueckner, B., 511

L

lambda
    calculus, 339, 546–578
    calculus, applied, 561–566, 577
    calculus, pure, 548
    calculus, typed, 563, 566–569
    expression, 532–535
    notation, 389, 407
    term, closed, 550
Landin, P. J., 15, 339, 511, 546, 577
language
    assembly, 5–8
    block-structured, 190, 202
    defined, 515, 517, 546
    defining, 385, 515, 517, 546
    definition, 385, 515–546
    description, 15, 25–26
    functional, 101–102, 305, 339–341, 385, 413
    general purpose, 4
    higher-level, 4, 7–8, 18
    imperative, 61, 101–102, 139
    level, 4
    machine, 4–5, 11
late binding, 137
layout
    array, 105, 113–117, 120
    C memory, 182–183
    column-major, 115

data, 101, 104–105, 110
    frame, 183, 191
    memory, 182–183
    pointer, 126
    record, 118, 120, 130
    row-major, 114–115
    static, 104, 127
    string, 134–135
    variant record, 121–122
Lazowska, E. D., 510
lazy evaluation, 340, 479, 511
leak, memory, 128–129
leap year, 66
left associativity, 30, 43–45
Lesk, M. E., 584
level, language, 4
Levin, M. I., 15
lexical
    analysis, 112–113, 211, 221–222
    environment, 186, 196–197
    scope, 161–171, 177, 181–190
    scope, ML, 327–331
    scope, Scheme, 532–535
    syntax, 27, 33–34
libraries, 154
Lindsey, C. H., 472, 608
linear search, 82–85
link
    access, 176–177, 182, 191–196
    control, 176–178, 182–183, 188, 190–192, 194–195, 197–198
    dynamic, 177, 191
    static, 177, 191
linked list, 127–128, 240–243, 273
Liskov, B., 252
Lisp, 12, 14–16, 385–421, 511, 532–533, 546, 594, 602–608
    car operation, 413
    cdr operation, 413
    Common, 12
    definitional interpreter, 15, 535–545
    dynamic allocation, 413–417
    function, universal, 385
    list, 392–404

list
    difference, 449–450, 473
    linked, 127–128, 240–243, 273
    Lisp, 392–404
    manipulation, 342–346, 351–357, 396–404
    open, 445–449, 467
    Prolog, 438–439, 445–450
Lister, A., 511
livelock, process, 487–488
liveness, process, 485–488
local
    module, 193
    variable, 176, 180, 182–184, 190–192, 194–195
    variable storage, 172, 175–176, 179
    variables, renaming, 161–163, 165
location, machine, 103–104, 126
locking, resource, 488, 511
logic programming, 16–17, 425–473
logical rule, 523–524
Lorie, R. A., 511

M

machine
    language, 4–5, 11
    location, 103–104, 126
    von Neumann, 4–5, 24
MacLisp, 12, 15, 603
MacQueen, D. B., 383, 511, 577–578, 600
macro expansion, 161, 163–165
Mailloux, B. J., 472, 608
management, storage, 341, 413
manual, reference, 26–27
Mariner, 9
Martin, A. J., 511
Mauchly, J. W., 24
McCarthy, J., 15, 53, 162, 202, 303, 324, 383, 385, 402, 546, 603
McIlroy, M. D., 24, 275, 511
Meertens, L. G. L. T., 472, 608
Mellish, C. S., 473, 607

member
  names, C++, 232–238
  private, 237, 240–241, 247
  protected, 237
  public, 232, 237
memory
  layout, 182–183
  leak, 128–129
  shared, 476–478
Mesa, 12, 252
message, 256, 258
metalanguage, 385
metasymbol, 47
method, 256, 258
  inherited, 260, 292–293
  resolution, 472
Metropolis, N., 23
Miller, G. A., 205
Milner, R., 15, 341, 383, 511, 578,
    599–600
Miranda, 12, 15, 339–340
Mitchell, J. C., 578
mixfix notation, 31
ML, 12, 15, 305–383, 569–576,
    578, 598–602
  anonymous function, 354–356
  datatype, 316–318, 360–367,
    601
  exceptions, 367–369, 601–602
  fun binding, 329
  function declaration, 318–321,
    346–351, 601
  lexical scope, 327–331
  list, 315, 342–346, 351–357
  operators, 347
  origins, 600
  output, 378
  overloading, 358, 600
  patterns, 348–351, 362,
    600–601
  type inference, 331, 357–360,
    569–576, 578
  types, 316–318, 331–335,
    357–367, 598–602
  val binding, 328
Mock, O., 476
Modula-2, 12, 51, 70, 72–77, 109,
    141, 149, 151, 193

Modula-3, 12, 179
modular abstraction, 206
module, 209, 212–214, 216,
    220–232, 248, 251–252, 600
  design, 220
  initialization, 218, 220, 228
  local, 193
  visibility, 220
monitor, 475, 505–507, 510
Morris, J. H. Jr., 252, 305, 511
Morris, L., 600
Morrison
  E., 23
  P., 23
Morrison, P., 23
most general unifier, 452
most-closely-nested rule, 169
multiple inheritance, 257
mutual exclusion, 489–490,
    501–505, 510

N

Nageli, H. H., 191
name
  equivalence, 140
  export, 229
  field, 106, 119
  import, 229
  type, 104–106, 126, 139–140
name-resolution, C++, 235
naming conflict, 164–165
natural semantics, 516, 523–528,
    533–535, 546, 568
Naur, P., 25, 52, 99, 202
negation as failure, Prolog,
    435–436, 469
Nelson, R. A., 11
nested procedures, 168–169,
    190, 193, 225
nesting depth, 193, 195–198
network, process, 511
Newey, M., 600
Newton, I., 299
nondeterministic process, 489
nonterminal, 35–38, 45, 48
  starting, 35–36, 38, 40
Nori, K. V., 191

normal form, 557–560, 566
normal-order reduction, 560
notation, lambda, 389, 407
Nutt, R., 11
Nygaard, K., 209, 253, 299

O

Oberon, 12, 179, 193
object, 102, 256
  initialization, 218
object-oriented programming,
    15–16, 253–299
occurrence
  binding, 166–169, 551
  bound, 166–169, 551, 554
  free, 551–552, 554–556
occurs-check, Prolog, 460–461
open list, 445–449, 467
operational semantics, 516
operator
  arity, 29
  binary, 28
  bit-wise, 124
  precedence, 30–31, 41, 44–45
operator/operand structure, 32
operators, C, 587
outermost
  evaluation, 323–327, 560
  reduction, 560–561
overloading, 138, 333–334, 359

P

Panini, 52
Papadimitriou, C., 511
parameter
  formal, 150–151, 155
  passing, 155, 163–165
parameterized type, 244, 335,
    358–360
parameter-passing
  C, 158
  C++, 155
parameters
  actual, 149–150, 155–160, 165,
    184, 195

parameters
  procedures as, 180, 185–186, 196–197
parametric polymorphism, 359
parenthesis-free notation, 28
Parnas, D. L., 209, 251, 511
parse
  tree, decorated, 519
  trees, 37–41, 43–44
parser, 211, 221
parsing, 38
  bottom-up, 40
  top-down, 40
partial
  correctness, 86–87
  evaluation, 562
Pascal, 11–13, 146, 579–583
  array, 105–106, 112–113
  Concurrent, 12, 475, 510
  expression, 108
  origins, 580
  parameter-passing, 155–158
  pointer, 126–133
  procedure, 148–154, 190–198
  program structure, 223–229, 580
  record, 105–106, 117–123
  set, 123–125
  statements, 64–70, 90
  syntax, 72–76
  type, 104–135, 137, 140–142
  type conversion, 111
passing, parameter, 155
patterns, ML, 348–351, 362, 600–601
Paulson, L. C., 383, 599
Peck, J. E. L., 472, 608
Perlis, A. J., 11, 147
permuted index, 251–252
philosophers, dining, 486–488
pipe, UNIX, 479–482, 511
Plankalkul, 99, 146
Plauger, P. J., 100, 252, 511
Plotkin, G. D., 546, 577
point, program, 62
pointer
  assignment, 126–133
  C, 158, 186

C array and, 134–136
  dangling, 128–129, 186
  dereferencing, 126, 135
  layout, 126
  Pascal, 126–133
  type, 104, 125–133, 142
polymorphism
  parametric, 359
  type, 139, 244, 335, 357–360, 569–576
Pope Gregory XIII, 66
portability, 7–8
postcondition, 80–90
postfix notation, 28–29, 31
precedence, operator, 30–31, 41, 44–45
precondition, 80–90
predicate, recursive, 472
prefix notation, 28–29, 31
prime-number sieve, 274, 511
privacy, 282–283, 287
private
  base class, C++, 281–284
  member, 237, 240–241, 247
problem
  producer-consumer, 498–507
  word-frequency, 480, 511
procedure, 147–203, 210–211, 216
  abstraction, 154, 206
  activation, 147–148, 172–198
  body, 147, 151, 161, 163–165, 186, 191
  C, 181–190
  call, 149
  declaration, 148–154, 169–171
  Pascal, 148–154, 190–198
  recursive, 147, 152–153, 172–173, 176, 180, 186, 202
procedures as parameters, see also higher-order functions
procedures
  as parameters, 180, 185–186, 196–197
  nested, 168–169, 190, 193, 225
process, 475
  communication, 476, 478, 493
  correctness, 485

deadlock, 486–488, 511
  fairness, 485–488, 511
  livelock, 487–488
  liveness, 485–488
  network, 479–482, 511
  nondeterministic, 489
  safety, 485, 489–491
  serializability, 490–491, 511
  synchronization, 476, 479, 491–507
producer-consumer problem, 498–507
production, 35–40, 45, 48
program
  point, 62, 80
  structure, Ada, 483
  structure, Pascal, 223–229
  testing, 9
programming
  concurrent, 475–511
  functional, 14–15, 301–421
  imperative, 11–13, 16, 55–299
  logic, 16–17, 425–473
  object-oriented, 15–16, 253–299
  pure functional, 339
  structured, 10, 24, 59, 61, 63, 81
projection function, 314
Prolog, 12, 16–17, 425–426, 430–473, 527–528, 546, 607–611
  arithmetic, 437, 610
  control, 450–469
  cuts, 461–469, 473
  Edinburgh, 425–426, 609
  functor, 607
  goal order, 436, 444, 450–469
  interpreter, 473
  list, 438–439, 445–450
  negation as failure, 435–436, 469
  occurs-check, 460–461
  origins, 608
  query, 432–437, 442–469
  rule, 434–435, 442–450
  rule order, 450–469
  search trees, 455

Prolog,
    terms, 430–431, 607–608
    terms as data, 439–442
proof rules, 86–90, 99
property
    dynamic, 20
    static, 20
protected member, 237
public
    base class, C++, 269, 281–284,
        593
    member, 232, 237
pure
    functional programming, 339
    lambda calculus, 548

Q

query, Prolog, 432–437, 442–469
quicksort, 97, 100
quilt example, 306–313, 369–380
quoting, 394

R

RAM, *see* random-access
        machine
Randell, B., 202
random-access machine, 5–7, 22,
        24
reactive system, 478
readability, 4, 8, 24
readers-and-writers, 511
Reckhow, R. A., 24
record selector, *see* field name
record
    activation, 172, 175–198, 202
    layout, 118, 120, 130
    Pascal, 105–106, 117–123
    type, 105–106, 117–123
    variant, 120–123
recursion, tail, 186, 189–190
recursive
    activation, 152–153, 172–176,
        186–190
    closure, 543
    predicate, 472

procedure, 147, 152–153,
        172–173, 176, 180, 186, 202
redex, 557, 560, 564
reduction, 556–560, 562–563
    normal-order, 560
    outermost, 560–561
Rees, J., 421, 602–603
reference parameter, *see* call-
        by-reference
reference manual, 26–27
regular expression, 27
relation, is-a, 281–282
renaming
    local variables, 161–163, 165
    principle, 327
rendezvous, 492–496
repeat statement, *see* indefinite
        iteration
representation
    concrete, 217
    data, 102
    independence, 217
reserved word, 33
resolution method, 472, 608
resource locking, 488, 511
return statements, 80
rewriting rule, 556
Reynolds, J. C., 515, 546, 578
Richards, M., 584
right associativity, 30, 44–45
Ritchie, D. M., 8, 72, 110, 125,
        183, 203, 209, 511, 583–584
Robinson, J. A., 472, 608
Robson, D., 285–286, 299, 594
Rodriguez, J. E., 251
Rosen, S., 511, 579
Rosin, R., 511
Ross, D. T., 251
Rosser, J. B., 547, 577
Rota, G. C., 23
Roubine, O., 511
Roussel, P., 16, 425, 472–473,
        607–608
row-major layout, 114–115
rule
    copy, 161
    logical, 523–524
    most-closely-nested, 169

order, Prolog, 450–469
Prolog, 434–435, 442–450
rewriting, 556
scope, 217
semantic, 518, 521, 529
run time, 19
Russel, S. R., 546
Russell, B., 547
Russell, L. J., 202
Rutishauser, H., 579

S

safe, type, 122, 142
safety, process, 485, 489–491
Samelson, K., 11
Sanella, D. T., 600
SASL, 12, 340
saved state, 176, 183–185,
        191–192, 195
Sayre, D., 11
scanner, 211, 221
Scheme, 12, 15, 386–421,
        530–546, 602–607
    anonymous function,
        389–390, 407, 605
    association list, 400–402
    constructs, 387
    definitional interpreter,
        535–545
    expression syntax, 388
    function definition, 389–390
    lexical scope, 532–535
    list manipulation, 392–404,
        606–607
    origins, 603
    quoting, 391–392
Schemer, 603
Schmidt, D. A., 577
Schmidt, E., 252
Schneider, F. B., 501, 510
Schonfinkel, M., 577
scope, 160
    dynamic, 161–165, 177–178,
        386, 532, 546
    formal parameter, 168
    lexical, 161–171, 177, 181–190
    ML lexical, 327–331

scope, rule, 217
  Scheme lexical, 532–535
Scott, D. S., 577
Scott, M. A., 510
search
  binary, 81, 100, 187–189
  linear, 82–85
section, critical, 489–490,
  501–505
Sedgewick, R., 100
Seldin, J. P., 577
selective evaluation, 322
self, Smalltalk, 285, 292–294
semantic
  methods, 515–546
  rule, 518, 521, 529
semantics, 25–27, 53
  denotational, 516, 529–530,
    577
  dynamic, 547
  natural, 516, 523–528,
    533–535, 546, 568
  operational, 516
semaphore, 501–505, 510
semicolon, 46, 53, 65, 73
sentinel, 83–86, 100
sequent, 525
serializability, process, 490–491,
  511
set type, 123–125
Sethi, R., 53, 202
shape example, 254–256,
  259–260, 270–274
Shapiro, E., 473, 607
shared memory, 476–478
Shaw, M., 202
Shepherdson, J. C., 24
Sheridan, P. B., 11
short-circuit evaluation, 109, 406
Shoshani, A., 511
sieve, prime-number, 274, 511
simple type, 104, 123
simplification, expression,
  409–412
Simula, 12, 15–16, 209, 252–253,
  256, 261, 299, 511, 591, 594
single-entry/single-exit, 64,
  79–80

single-instruction multiple-data,
  478
Sintzoff, M., 472, 608
Smalltalk, 12, 16, 261, 285–294,
  299, 594–598, 603
  class method, 287–294, 596
  class variable, 286
  collection class, 597
  conditionals, 290
  expression, 288–290, 595–596
  inheritance, 285
  instance method, 286–287,
    291–292, 596
  instance variable, 286–288,
    291
  message syntax, 288–289
  origins, 594
  return value, 290
  self, 285, 292–294
  super, 294
  system class, 285–286, 299,
    597–598
  terminology, 256
Smolka, S. A., 511
software engineering, 9
sort, bucket, 143
specification, abstract, 217
spelling checker, 17–18, 24
spelling, token, 27, 33–34
stack frame, see activation
  record
stack
  allocation, 179–198, 202
  frame, 182–183, 192
Standard ML, see ML
starting nonterminal, 35–36, 38,
  40
state, saved, 176, 183–185,
  191–192, 195
statements, 59, 64–65
  assignment, 6–7, 59–61
  break, 77–80, 93–94, 99
  C, 77–80, 90–94
  case, 70–71, 99
  compound, 64
  conditional, 65–66
  continue, 77–80, 93–94
  goto, 80, 99

return, 80
structured, 59
static scope, see lexical scope
static
  allocation, 116
  array, 116
  binding, 137
  checking, 142–143
  layout, 104, 127
  link, 177, 191
  property, 20
  variable, 180
Steele, G. L. Jr., 15, 421, 602–603
Steiglitz, K., 100
Sterling, L., 473, 607
Stern, H., 11
storage
  local variable, 172, 175–176,
    179
  management, 341, 413
storage allocation, see also layout
storage allocation, see allocation
Stoy, J. E., 577
Strachey, C., 577, 584
stream, 478–482, 511
string layout, 134–135
strong type system, 142
Stroustrup, B., 3, 209, 252, 299,
  591
structural equivalence, 140–141,
  332–333
structure, operator/operand, 32
structured
  programming, 10, 24, 59, 61,
    63, 81
  statements, 59
Sturgis, H. E., 24
subclass, 257, 261, 267, 291–294
subrange type, 109
substitution, 452–453, 551,
  554–556
  textual, 163–164
sugar, syntactic, 527, 561, 564
super, Smalltalk, 294
superclass, 257, 261, 267,
  291–294
Sussman, G. J., 15, 421, 602–603

Sussman, J., 421, 602
Swift, C. J., 476
symbol, grammar, 35
synchronization, process, 476, 479, 491–507
synchronous communication, 478
syntactic
    ambiguity, 38–40
    sugar, 527, 561, 564
syntax, 25
    abstract, 31–32, 41–43, 53, 518
    analysis, 211
    arithmetic expression, 41–48
    chart, 46, 48, 53
    concrete, 35, 37, 42
    lexical, 27, 33–34
    Scheme expression, 388
    trees, abstract, 32, 41–43, 345
syntax-directed definition, 518
synthesized attribute, 517–523
system
    class, Smalltalk, 299, 597–598
    reactive, 478
    strong type, 142
    type, 122, 137–143, 331–332
    weak type, 142

T

tag field, 121–122
tail recursion, 186, 189–190
Tarnlund, S. A., 473
task, Ada, 483–485, 493–498
Taylor, W., 53
terminal, 33, 35–38
testing, program, 9
TeX, 133–134
textual substitution, 163–164
Thatcher, J. W., 252
theorem
    Church-Rosser, 547, 558–559
    proving, 425, 472, 608
thread, 475, 482–483, 485–486
time
    activation, 172
    compile, 18, 101, 137
    run, 19

sharing, 477–478
slicing, 477
translation, 18
Tofte, M., 383, 599–600
token, 33–37, 47
    spelling, 27, 33–34
top-down parsing, 40
total correctness, 87
Trabb Pardo, L., 24, 99
Traiger, I. L., 511
translation time, 18
tree, decorated parse, 519
trees
    abstract syntax, 32, 41–43, 345
    activation, 174–175, 177–178
    parse, 37–41, 43–44
Turner, D. A., 340
Turner, L., 53
tutorial, language, 26
type
    array, 105, 111–117
    basic, 103–105, 107–111, 314
    binding, 571
    C, 133–137, 140–142, 146
    checking, 103, 125, 136–143, 331–335, 357–360, 383, 547, 567–576, 578
    circular, 141
    coercion, 110–111, 139, 334
    constructor, 317
    conversion, 334
    conversion, Pascal, 111
    declaration, 105, 140
    deduction, 568
    enumerated, 107, 109, 112
    equivalence, 139–141, 332–333
    error, 142
    export, 229–232
    expression, 103, 140, 313, 332, 359
    inference, 358, 569–576, 578
    inference, ML, 331, 578
    name, 104–106, 126, 139–140
    parameterized, 244, 335, 358–360
    Pascal, 104–135, 137, 140–142
    pointer, 104, 125–133, 142
    polymorphism, 139, 244, 335,

357–360, 569–576
    polymorphism, ad-hoc, 359
    record, 105–106, 117–123
    safe, 122, 142
    set, 123–125
    simple, 104, 123
    subrange, 109
    system, 122, 137–143, 331–332
    system, arithmetic expression, 138
    system, strong, 142
    system, weak, 142
    user-defined, 210, 213–216, 229–232, 235
typed lambda calculus, 563, 566–569
types, ML, 598–602

U

Ullman, J. D., 53, 202, 383, 599
unification, 436–438, 442, 445, 452–453
unifier, most general, 452
unit, *see* module
universal Lisp function, 385
UNIX, 8, 13, 17, 24, 584
    pipe, 479–482, 511
user-defined type, 210, 213–216, 229–232, 235

V

value parameter, *see* call-by-value
value constructor, 317, 360–366
van Wijngaarden, A., 472, 608
variable
    bound, 550–551, 554, 556, 572
    declaration, 148, 166–169, 172
    free, 550–552, 554, 558, 574, 577
    local, 176, 180, 182–184, 190–192, 194–195
    static, 180
variant record, 120–123
    layout, 121–122

virtual function, 269–271
visibility, 190–191, 193, 217, 219, 281
  module, 220
von Neumann, J., 24
von Neumann machine, 4–5, 24
Vuillemin, J., 511

W

Wadler, P., 252
Wadsworth, C., 511, 600
Wagner, E. G., 252
wait, busy, 477, 502
Wand, M., 421, 602
Warren, D. H. D., 472, 608
Waychoff, R., 53
weak type system, 142
Wegner, P., 24, 511, 577
Weinberger, P. J., 252
Weizenbaum, J., 383
Welsh, J., 511
Wexelblat, R. L., 24
W-grammars, 608
Wheeler, D. J., 100, 206
while statement, *see* indefinite
    iteration
white space, 33–34
Whitehead, A. N., 547
Wichmann, B. A., 511
Wileden, J. C., 202
Wilkes, M. V., 100, 206
Williams, J., 340
Wirth, N., 13, 112, 146, 193, 252, 579–580
Wise, D. S., 511
Wolf, L., 202
word-frequency problem, 480, 511
Wossner, H., 146
Wulf, W. A., 202

Y

Yacc, 112, 133–134
year, leap, 66

Z

ZetaLisp, 12
Ziller, I., 11
Zilles, S., 252
Zuse, K., 99, 101, 146